Worldly Wisdom

A MULTICULTURAL INTRODUCTION TO PHILOSOPHY

Daniel Bonevac

University of Texas at Austin

MAYFIELD PUBLISHING COMPANY
Mountain View, California
London • Toronto

In memory of Wilfrid Sellars

Library of Congress Cataloging-in-Publication Data

Bonevac, Daniel A.
Worldly wisdom : a multicultural introduction to philosophy / Daniel Bonevac.
p. cm.
Includes index.
ISBN 0-7674-0820-9 (alk. paper)
1. Philosophy—Introductions. I. Title.
BD21 .B56 2000
100—dc21

00-064730

Manufactured in the United States of America
10 9 8 7 6 5 4 3 2 1

Mayfield Publishing Company
1280 Villa Street
Mountain View, California 94041

Sponsoring editor, Kenneth King; production, Strawberry Field Publishing; manuscript editor, April Wells-Hayes; design manager, Susan Breitbard; text and cover designer, Joan Greenfield; cover image, Mark Rothko, *Green and Maroon,* 1953. Oil on canvas. 91¼ × 54¾ in. Acquired 1957. Photo © The Phillips Collection, Washington, DC. © 1998 Kate Rothko Prizel and Christopher Rothko/Artists Rights Society (ARS), New York; art editor, Robin Mouat; illustrator, Larry Daste; manufacturing manager, Danielle Javier. The text was set in 9/12 Stone Serif by G & S Typesetters and printed on 45# Highland Plus by Malloy Lithographing, Inc.

Text credits continue at the back of the book on pages 493–494, which constitute an extension of the copyright page.

Preface

Introducing students to philosophy is, I think, the most exciting, rewarding, and important task that a teacher can perform. The great works of Western and non-Western traditions represent the "best that has been thought and written" about subjects of intense human concern throughout the ages. Their probing questions, careful arguments, trenchant criticisms, and imaginative visions provide an inspiring model of what thinking can be and do. Correspondingly, writing this book has been one of the most exciting but also most difficult enterprises I have ever undertaken. If it succeeds in helping you to communicate the passion, wonder, and beauty of philosophy in the classroom, I will have succeeded.

Worldly Wisdom presupposes no background in philosophy. Intended as a text for a one- or two-semester introduction to philosophy, it seeks to lead students on a world tour—a tour through the greatest works of Western and non-Western philosophy. There is no need to follow the tour in the particular order I have presented it. And instructors and students alike should feel free to tag along for some parts of the tour and explore on their own at other points. I offer a comprehensive and varied itinerary from which instructors can construct a tour that suits them and their students.

I have organized this book topically around major themes in epistemology, metaphysics, and ethics. On every theme, I have integrated Western and non-Western approaches. Western philosophers develop a wide array of perspectives on basic philosophical issues; non-Western philosophers broaden that array much further, asking many of the same questions as their Western colleagues but proposing, in many cases, strikingly different answers. There are sometimes surprising parallels, sometimes dramatic contrasts. I think the presence of non-Western materials sheds light on philosophical issues themselves and on Western approaches to those issues by tracing some paths unexplored in the West. Instructors who want to focus heavily on non-Western material can do that; instructors who want to use non-Western materials in a supporting role or even omit them entirely can do that. But I think Western and non-Western thinkers have so much to say to each other that the boundary between the two—already fuzzy, as thinkers such as Avicenna, Maimonides, and Nishitani illustrate—is bound to become even less distinct. We are on our way toward a global philosophical community.

I have views on many of the issues discussed in this book, but I have refrained from pressing them. I hope to inspire students to come to their own conclusions about fundamental philosophical questions. Real philosophical work often occurs in the discussions, in class and outside it, that reading and thinking about philosophy initiate. I have structured my presentations of issues and positions to provide material for those discussions, not to anticipate or preempt them.

This book stems from twenty-five years of teaching philosophy to introductory-level students. Philosophy, I believe, is at once the most abstract and most practical of all disciplines. Nothing is more useful than living wisely, exercising good judgment, and understanding yourself and the world around you. Nothing is more helpful, however you earn a living, than being able to think clearly, argue forcefully, and write insightfully and persuasively. So philosophy has something very important to offer anyone.

But it is not easy. Philosophical works are often abstract, dense, and difficult. I have found that students even at elite institutions need help in getting anything out of them. Moreover, delving deeply into particular works can be rewarding, leading to insight into a particular philosopher's thought, but it can also obscure the philosophical issues themselves. My strategy in this book is to organize readings around issues and general approaches to them and to give students ample guidance. Many passages included here are short; longer ones are broken down into pieces and discussed paragraph by paragraph. Reading questions appear in the margins to help students focus on the right issues and to check their understanding of what they are reading. My goal is to teach students how to read philosophy by showing them. I also hope to show students how to do philosophy by showing them how some of the world's greatest minds have done it.

HOW TO USE THIS BOOK

I have written this book in a modular fashion. There are connections between chapters and sections of chapters, but I have tried to make them independently intelligible. So no chapter presupposes another; an instructor can approach them in any order he or she prefers.

My tour begins with epistemology. Chapter 1, "Truth," begins by discussing the nature of philosophy, using Socrates and Confucius as exemplars. It then turns to semantic, correspondence, coherence, and pragmatist theories of truth. It concludes with a discussion of various forms of relativism and perspectivism, including deconstruction and feminism. (There is also an appendix, "Logic in a Nutshell," which explains validity, soundness, inductive reliability, and some common fallacies.) Most instructors will want to begin their courses with the first section of this chapter, "Philosophy and Truth," no matter how they choose to organize the rest of the course. The remaining sections can be used to begin a study of epistemology, but they can also be postponed until after Chapter 3. Students at that point will have been exposed to Kant and can benefit by seeing coherence theories, pragmatism, relativism, and perspectivism against that background.

Chapter 2, "Knowledge," presents internalist and externalist perspectives on knowledge and discusses skepticism and its opponents. This is gripping material, in my experience; it is a rare student who does not worry, at least a little, that the rest of the world will not be there when he or she leaves the classroom.

Chapter 3, "Experience," centers on the debate between rationalists and empiricists over whether all knowledge comes from experience. I present the vocabulary in which this debate has often been conducted, present rationalism and empiricism as classically conceived, discuss empiricist attempts to account for necessity and universality, and present Kant's "Copernican revolution" as a purported resolution of the debate. I also consider some non-Western views falling under the heading "dogmatic empiricism," which hold that we can have knowledge of the world as it is (in Kantian language, of things-in-themselves) even if all knowledge comes from experience.

The next three chapters concern metaphysics. Chapter 4, "Mind," presents important Western and non-Western theories of the mind and self. Both in the West and beyond it, some philosophers see the self as divided; some see it as unified; and some see no self at all. Especially interesting in the last category is Zen Buddhism, which receives extensive treatment. The chapter concludes with a discussion of contemporary positions in the philosophy of mind against the backdrop of the schism between our manifest and scientific images of the world. I think it makes sense to treat these issues together, but some instructors may want to focus solely on theories of the self; others may want to focus on the mind/body problem.

Chapter 5, "World," covers many central topics in metaphysics: form, categories, the nature of substance, essential and accidental properties, natures, "quiddities," primary and secondary qualities, real and nominal essences, idealism and realism. All arise quite readily from the question, What is there? for all concern what it is to be an object. This is philosophy at its most abstract. Some instructors may want to omit it. In my view, however, and in the opinion of most of my readers, this is the best chapter in the book. Some instructors may want to focus on Plato or Aristotle; others may want to omit them, focusing instead on primary and secondary qualities or the idealism/realism debate.

Chapter 6, "God," discusses concepts of religion and God in Western and non-Western religions. It then turns to arguments for God's existence—the argument from thought, the cosmological argument, the ontological argument, Pascal's wager, and Kant's moral argument—concluding with the problem of evil. Again, the parts are modular; some instructors may devote considerable attention to contrasting concepts of religion and God, whereas others may want to jump directly to the arguments.

The book's last three chapters concern ethics and political philosophy. Chapter 7, "Virtue," considers Western and non-Western theories of virtue. In addition to Plato and Aristotle, the chapter covers Confucian, Daoist, Buddhist, and feminist conceptions of virtue. It also raises questions about the unity and compatibility of the virtues and about the contingency of virtue.

Chapter 8, "Right and Wrong," discusses ethical theories that distinguish right from wrong action. Some rest on the triumph of reason over inclination or desire; some, on happiness; some, on conscience; and some, on religion. The chapter covers Western and non-Western theories of each type and contains a great wealth of material; many instructors will want to cover only some of it. The chapter's modularity should make it easy to pick just those approaches the instructor chooses to cover.

Chapter 9, "Politics," introduces students to political philosophy. It begins with Aristotle's understanding of political virtue and progresses to Aristotelian theories of natural law. It then considers aggression and the justification of political authority. The remainder of the chapter uses Sir Isaiah Berlin's distinction between negative and positive conceptions of liberty to organize the discussion of classical liberalism and various forms of socialism.

Finally, the book includes not only a glossary of all philosophical terms introduced in the book but also an appendix on how to write a philosophy paper. An instructor's manual accompanies this book, as well as a Web site with resources for instructors and students: www.mayfieldpub.com/worldly.

Throughout, I introduce philosophers with a short biography the first time they appear. For later appearances, I provide only dates of birth and death together with a reference to other chapters in which that philosopher appears.

ACKNOWLEDGMENTS

Many people have helped me in writing this book. I am grateful especially to Stephen Phillips, who has taught me much about Indian philosophy over the years and who permitted me to use some material originally written for our jointly edited books *Beyond the Western Tradition* and *Understanding Non-Western Philosophy.* I also owe thanks to William Boon for his help in selecting passages from medieval Islamic thinkers. Nicholas Asher has helped me in thinking about issues in metaphysics, ethics, and political philosophy. In our team-taught courses I have learned a great deal from him.

I owe many people at Mayfield Publishing Company a debt of thanks for their work in making this project a reality. Above all, I must thank Ken King, my editor, whose vision, encouragement, and nagging have kept me going. I am also grateful to April Wells-Hayes for her elegant and judicious editing; to Melanie Field for her work in producing the book; and to Lynn Rabin Bauer for managing the process.

I am grateful to the reviewers of the manuscript: Robert J. Blackburn, Roger Williams University; Dr. Stanley Browne, Alabama A&M University; Marie-Louise Friquegnon, William Paterson University; Wendy Lee-Lampshire, Bloomsburg University; John McPhee, Marist College; Susan Morris, Ferris State University; Jan Pielke-Brenneke, San Bernardino Valley College; Matt Schulte, Montgomery College; Katherine Shamey, Santa Monica College; Paul Shepard, El Camino College; M. Lorain Stowe, Highline Community College; Sister Ruth Stuckel, Avila College; Richard Trussell, Pikes Peak Community College; and Barry Vaughan, Mesa Community College, who helped me greatly to retain a focus on students throughout this project.

Finally, I am grateful to my students, who, over the past twenty-five years, have taught me as much as I have taught them.

To the Student

Philosophy is in many ways the most abstract of all disciplines. The questions it addresses are very general: What is real? How do we know? What should we do? But philosophy is also the most practical of all disciplines. It aims at wisdom. Living wisely, displaying good judgment, understanding yourself and your surroundings—these offer immense benefits to all, no matter who they are or how they earn a living. Living *wisely* is a key to living *well.* For just that reason, Aristotle thought that philosophy was the highest human activity and that the contemplative life was the highest and happiest form of life possible for a human being.

Philosophy is practical in more mundane ways too. It trains people to think carefully and critically. It teaches people how to construct and evaluate arguments. It teaches them how to look for hidden assumptions and unexamined presuppositions. It teaches them to read closely and write clearly. These skills have immense value; they apply to the arts, the sciences, business, law, and personal relationships as well as to philosophy itself. It is no accident that philosophy majors, on average, score higher on the LSAT (Law School Admission Test) than students with any other major. Philosophy is an ideal pre-law course of study. But it is also excellent preparation for many other careers. On the GRE (Graduate Record Examination), only physics majors do as well as philosophy majors.

What can you do with a philosophy degree? I went to graduate school in philosophy and became a philosophy professor. But relatively few philosophy majors do that. Many become lawyers; others go to divinity school and become clergy. Many go into business, where their thinking skills give them a distinct advantage. One of the philosophy majors in my class at college has gone on to become vice-president and chief marketing officer of a major bank. He writes that our years as philosophy majors "provided us with great educations that pay dividends every day. I think about those times—studying philosophy and thinking 'out there' on a far orbit. Even now in business, people say, 'How do you think like that?' I smile—what can I tell them? It's a [philosophy] thing." Many philosophy majors end up starting their own businesses, where their creativity and critical thinking skills pay off directly.

But you do not need to major in philosophy to gain these benefits. Even one philosophy course can make you think more clearly and deeply than you have before. You will do better in your other courses and in your career than you would have without any exposure to philosophy. Most importantly, you will understand yourself and the world around you better than you would have otherwise. And that truly does pay dividends every day.

USING THIS BOOK

I have tried to introduce basic philosophical problems by examining important discussions of them in Western and non-Western philosophical traditions. Ample amounts of original texts (or their translations) appear here. But I also try to split them into digestible chunks and explain them. Be sure to read both the philosophical text and the explanation; one without the other may make little sense. Questions appear in the margins to help you check your understanding as you read along. These are also useful for reviewing the main ideas of each section.

I introduce philosophers with a short biography the first time they appear in the book. For later appearances, I provide only dates of birth and death together with a reference to other chapters in which that philosopher appears.

The book includes not only a glossary of all philosophical terms introduced but also an appendix on how to write a philosophy paper. Writing philosophy is difficult for most beginning philosophy students. I urge you to consult the appendix even for short assignments. It will help you write not only philosophy papers but other kinds of papers as well.

Contents

CHAPTER 7 *Virtue*

CHAPTER 8 *Right and Wrong*

CHAPTER 9 *Politics*

Contents of Excerpted Readings

Chapter 2 KNOWLEDGE

Chapter 3 EXPERIENCE

Chapter 4 MIND

Chapter 5 WORLD

Chapter 6 GOD

Give me truths;
For I am weary of the surfaces,
And die of inanition.

—Ralph Waldo Emerson, "Blight"

He preached upon "Breadth" till it argued him
narrow—
The Broad are too broad to define
And of "Truth" until it proclaimed him a Liar—
The Truth never flaunted a Sign—

—Emily Dickinson, 1207

CHAPTER 1

Truth

Philosophy, as many have observed, begins in wonder—wonder at the richness, order, and beauty of the world around us, wonder at the grandeur and horror of the acts we perpetrate, and, not least, wonder at the mystery and elusiveness of our own nature. In that respect, everyone is philosophical sometimes. But if philosophy begins in wonder, it does not stop there. Philosophers reflect on all these matters, trying to understand the world and themselves.

Though philosophers have discussed many topics over the centuries, they have generally taken several questions as central:

1. What is there? (And what, in particular, am I?)
2. How do I know?
3. What should I do?

The areas of philosophy that address these questions are *metaphysics, epistemology,* and *ethics,* respectively. The parts of this book correspond to those divisions. Chapters 1–3 concern epistemology, the theory of knowledge. Chapters 4–6 concern metaphysics, the study of what there is. And Chapters 7–9 concern ethics, what we ought to do.

Philosophers tend to address these questions in the light of a tradition. They consider the answers of previous philosophers and reflect on them, gaining insight but also finding difficulties and trying to resolve them. One long-standing and immensely rich tradition stretches from ancient Greece through medieval Europe to contemporary Europe and America. But other philosophical traditions are also rich in insight. Traditions in India and China are traced from ancient times to the present. Traditions in Japan and Latin America stem from others but contain distinctive elements of their own. And traditions in Africa and among Native Americans have been written down only occasionally.

These traditions have much to say to each other. Philosophers in different traditions have chosen different starting points but have addressed many of the same questions. They have proposed answers that are sometimes startlingly similar—and sometimes strikingly different. Bringing them together sheds light on philosophical questions themselves by giving us a greater appreciation of the depth of the questions and the breadth of the array of possible answers.

PHILOSOPHY AND TRUTH

Philosophy begins in wonder and progresses to reflection. Philosophers try to understand the world and themselves. So, one might think, do mythmakers, storytellers, poets, and religious prophets. But philosophers differ from mythmakers and prophets in that, as philosophers, they claim no special revelation. They use reason to understand the world. They differ from storytellers and poets in that they try to portray the world as it is. Imagination may be a component of philosophical reflection, but it is not the whole. Perhaps the most important distinguishing mark of philosophers is that they submit their reflections to critical examination. They not only outline a vision of how the world is and ought to be but seek to defend it.

To gain a better understanding of the nature of philosophy, let's consider two figures who began major philosophical traditions: Socrates and Confucius.

Socrates

Philosophical reflection in the West reached a turning point in fifth-century Athens. Socrates (470–399 B.C.E.) was a contemporary of the great Greek playwrights Sophocles, Euripides, and Aristophanes, as well as the historians Thucydides and Herodotus. He is in many ways the central figure of Western philosophy. He was not the first person to advance philosophical *ideas;* Confucius and the Buddha, for example, died about a decade before Socrates was born. He was not even the first person to do so in Greece; Thales, Heraclitus, and Parmenides all preceded him. But it is significant that we call the latter the **pre-Socratics**, defining their position in the history of ideas in terms of Socrates. For Socrates was the first person in the West to advance philosophical *arguments*. As his student Plato (427–347 B.C.E.) portrayed him, Socrates put forward no particular theories of his own—indeed, he wrote nothing—but used arguments to clarify, investigate, and, usually, refute the views of others.

This constitutes the **Socratic method** (also called **dialectic**). In Plato's dialogues, Socrates asks what piety, or courage, or friendship, or justice is. Someone answers. Socrates analyzes the proposed definition and begins asking questions, leading the parties involved in the conversation to see that the definition cannot be right. Sometimes, the definition is unclear; sometimes, it includes too much; sometimes, it does not include enough. Someone then proposes another definition, and the process continues.

To reflect the back-and-forth play of questions and answers, Plato writes dialogues rather than treatises. The early dialogues end with at least some of the participants leaving the discussion discouraged, embarrassed, or irritated at being unable to give a good definition. Socrates himself takes no position. In fact, he maintains that he knows only that he knows nothing. These dialogues evidently portray something close to the historical Socrates.

In the *Apology,* Plato recounts Socrates's trial and conviction of the charges of atheism and corrupting the youth of Athens. Socrates, in responding to his conviction and the prosecution's proposal for the death penalty, not only displays but also defines a philosophical cast of mind. Permitted to propose an alternate penalty, Socrates suggests free meals:

What qualities is Socrates ascribing to himself? Why does he deserve free meals?

> And so he [Meletus, the prosecutor] proposes the death penalty. What shall I propose, O men of Athens? Clearly that which is my due. And what should I pay or receive? What should be done to a man who has never had the wit to be idle during his whole life? I have been careless of what the many care about—wealth, family interests, military offices, speaking in the assembly, magistracies, plots, and parties.

> Reflecting that I was really too honest a man to live like this, I didn't go where I could do no good to you or to myself, but where I could do the greatest good privately to every one of you. I sought to persuade every one of you to look to himself, and seek virtue and wisdom before he looks to his private interests, and look to the state before he looks to the interests of the state; and that this should be the order which he observes in all his actions. What should be done to someone like me? Doubtless some good thing, O men of Athens, if he has what he deserves. The good thing should be suitable to him. What would be a reward suitable to a poor man who is your benefactor, who desires the leisure to instruct you? There can be no more fitting reward than free meals in the Prytaneum,[1] O men of Athens, a reward which he deserves far more than the citizen who has won the prize at Olympia in the horse or chariot race, whether the chariots were drawn by two horses or by many. For such a victor does not need free meals, but I do. He only gives you the appearance of happiness; I give you the reality. So, if I'm to estimate the penalty justly, I say that free meals in the Prytaneum are a fair punishment.[2]

Notice Socrates's self-description (and irony). He has been honest; he has sought the greatest good for all; he has sought to persuade people to look to themselves, and seek virtue and wisdom. In short, he persuades people to philosophize.

Socrates realizes that free meals will not strike the average juror as an appropriate punishment! But he contends that any real penalty would be unjust:

Why does Socrates decline to propose any lesser penalty?

> Perhaps you think that I'm mocking you in saying this, as in what I said before about the tears and prayers. But that's not so. I speak because I'm convinced that I never intentionally wronged anyone. I can't convince you of that—for we've had a short conversation only. If there were a law in Athens, as there is in other cities, that a capital case should not be decided in one day, then I believe that I could have convinced you. But now the time is too short. I can't refute great slanders in a moment. Since I'm convinced that I never wronged anyone, I will certainly not wrong myself. I will not say that I deserve any punishment, or propose any penalty. Why should I? Because I'm afraid of the penalty of death which Meletus proposes? When I don't know whether death is a good or an evil, why should I propose a penalty which would certainly be an evil? Shall I say imprisonment? And why should I live in prison, and be subject to the periodically appointed officers of the law? Or should I pay a fine, and be jailed until it is paid? There is the same objection: I would have to lie in prison, for I have no money, and can't pay. And if I say exile—and this may be a penalty you would accept—I would have to be blinded by the love of life to think that others would put up with me when you, my own fellow citizens, can't endure my discourses and words, and have found them so

[1]The Prytaneum was something like the civic center of Athens; it contained the city hearth. City leaders held meals there, inviting randomly selected citizens. Some heroes—Olympic medalists, for example—were given lifetime invitations to the meals. Socrates is thus proposing that he be treated like an Olympic medalist. The jury was not amused. It sentenced him to death by a wider margin than that by which it had convicted him.

[2]This and subsequent quotations from Plato are (unless otherwise noted) from Plato, *Apology,* translated by Benjamin Jowett, from *The Dialogues of Plato* (Oxford: Oxford University Press, 1892), 36b–37a. I have altered the translation slightly for readability.

> grievous and odious that you would want to get rid of them. No, indeed, men of Athens, that isn't very likely. And what kind of life would I lead, at my age, wandering from city to city, living in ever-changing exile, and always being driven out! For I'm quite sure that, wherever I go, the young men will come to me as they do here. If I drive them away, they will have their elders drive me out; if I let them come, their fathers and friends will drive me out for their sakes. (37a–e)

Socrates feels compelled to philosophize; he cannot refrain from it. To seek wisdom and virtue is the highest good; *the unexamined life is not worth living.*

> Someone will say: Yes, Socrates, but can't you hold your tongue? Then you could go into a foreign city and no one would interfere with you. Now I have great difficulty in making you understand my answer to this. For if I tell you that this would be a disobedience to a divine command, and therefore that I can't hold my tongue, you won't think I'm serious. If I say again that the greatest thing a man can do is to converse about virtue every day, and that the unexamined life is not worth living—you are still less likely to believe me. And yet what I say is true, though it's hard for me to persuade you of it. (37e–38a)

To philosophize, in Socrates's view, is to seek wisdom and virtue, to lead an examined life—in short, to reflect on what human life is and ought to be. It is to put one's life in perspective, to see and reflect on "the big picture." This goes beyond the bounds of any single human life.

Confucius

Kong Fuzi (K'ung Fu-Tzu)—Grand Master Kong, or, as he became known in the West, Confucius (551–479 B.C.E.)—was a contemporary of Lao Tzu, the Buddha, Aesop, Thales, and many of the Biblical prophets. Born into a poor family in Lu (now Shandong province in northeastern China), he was completely self-educated. His father died when he was three. At nineteen, he married, and had a son and two daughters. He got a government job, first managing a state granary and then managing herds of cattle and sheep. But at twenty-two he quit his job and opened a school. He taught principles of proper living and good government, eventually earning the attention of the Duke of Lu. For a while he even became Minister of Justice. Living in a time of great political and intellectual upheaval called the Warring States period, he was convinced that his teachings could restore order and prosperity. He rose from poverty and obscurity to become the most influential and revered person in the history of China. From the 13th to the 20th century, the Chinese civil service examinations were based on the texts of Confucius.

We will consider Confucius's theories in detail in Chapter 7. Here I wish only to portray his conception of philosophy. Unlike Socrates, Confucius says little about the nature of philosophy itself. But he does write extensively about the superior person (***junzi,*** literally "child of a ruler," but in Confucius, not one of noble birth but rather one of noble character). And he occasionally speaks of himself. From those comments, we can learn something of Confucius's idea of philosophy.

Why are 'partisan' and 'open-minded' opposites?

First, the philosopher tries to understand the world with an open mind. When we philosophize, we do not argue a case or press the "party line" but seek the truth wherever it leads.

2:14. The Master said, "The superior person is open-minded and not partisan. The mean person is partisan and not open-minded." [3]

Second, what we seek is in ourselves. The understanding we seek can be gained through reflection, though it also requires a thorough knowledge of things in general as well as respect for the traditional social rules that define proper behavior.

6:25. The Master said, "The superior person studies all learning extensively and restrains himself by propriety. So, he doesn't swerve from the Way."

15:20. The Master said, "What the superior person seeks is in himself. What the inferior person seeks is in others."

Third, we must seek *clarity* of perception, of thought, and of speech. We must focus on virtue—on what we ought to be and do—and remain open to higher laws, principles, and values: "the ordinances of heaven." But to put virtue and general principles into practice, we must understand the force of words and the world around us.

How do all these manifest a quest for clarity?

16:10. Confucius said, "The superior person thoughtfully considers nine things: With his eyes, he wants to see clearly. With his ears, he wants to hear distinctly. In countenance, he wants to be warm. In demeanor, he wants to be respectful. In speech, he wants to be sincere. In business, he wants to be careful. When in doubt, he wants to ask others. When angry, he thinks of difficulties that might result. When he sees opportunity for gain, he thinks of righteousness."

20:3. The Master said, "Without recognizing the ordinances of heaven, it's impossible to be a superior person. Without acquaintance with propriety, it's impossible to establish one's character. Without knowing the force of words, it's impossible to know people."

Fourth, we must "attend to the root of things," seeking true *understanding,* not merely the accumulation of facts. Only when we understand the underlying principles of things can we understand how we ourselves should act. To do the right thing, we need to think things through, understanding the situation and understanding why we are to act that way.

1:2. . . . The superior person attends to the root of things. From the root grows the Way.

7:27. The Master said, "Maybe some act without knowing why. I don't. Hearing much, selecting what is good, and following it, seeing much and remembering it, are the second style of knowledge."

Fifth, we must have self-knowledge. Socrates takes seriously the motto of the oracle of Delphi, "Know thyself," and responds that he knows only that he knows nothing. Similarly, Confucius says that true knowledge is self-aware: it is knowing what you know and what you don't.

---

[3] This and subsequent selections from Confucius are from Confucius, *Analects,* from *The Four Books,* edited and translated by James Legge; originally published in *The Chinese Classics,* Volume I (Oxford: Clarendon, 1893). I have revised the translation slightly to modernize the style and to conform to Pinyin transliteration.

2:17. The Master said, "Yu, shall I teach you what knowledge is? When you know something, to maintain that you know it; when you don't know something, to admit that you don't know it—this is knowledge."

Confucius, as these passages suggest, gives us sayings rather than dialogues or arguments. The theme of examining oneself runs throughout. Leading the examined life is clearly part of Confucius's conception of the superior person. We see few examples of the process of examination. Sometimes, however, we glimpse the flavor of what Confucius has in mind:

14:36. Someone said, "What do you say about the principle of repaying injury with kindness?" The Master said, "How then will you repay kindness? Repay kindness with kindness and injury with justice."

We will discuss the ethical implications of this in Chapter 7. For now, notice what Confucius does. Someone asks about a principle of repaying injury with kindness—"turning the other cheek," in effect. Confucius responds that this principle will erase the difference between the consequences of kindness and injury. Someone hurts you; you respond by being kind. Someone is kind to you; you respond by being kind. You draw no distinctions, and the one who injures suffers no consequences. Confucius does not spell out why he thinks this result is unacceptable. But he clearly thinks it is. This reflects a common pattern: Confucius considers a principle and draws out its consequences.

So, although Socrates and Confucius arise from different cultures, hold different philosophical views, and philosophize in different styles, they nevertheless hold much the same conception of philosophy. For both, to philosophize is to seek wisdom and virtue, to seek clarity, to lead an examined life. It is to reflect on what human life is and ought to be. It is to put one's life in perspective, to understand yourself in relation to the rest of a world much larger than you.

Fields of Philosophy

Philosophy, as we have noted, addresses the questions

1. What is there?
2. How do I know?
3. What should I do?

Metaphysics is the study of what there is and how those things relate to each other. What are the ultimate constituents of the world? Physical objects such as tables and chairs, "cabbages and kings"? Microphysical particles such as quarks? Events? Minds? **Epistemology** is the theory of knowledge: the study of what we know, how we know it, and what, if anything, lies beyond the bounds of knowledge. **Ethics** is the pursuit of good judgment about action, asking questions such as "What should I do"? "What kind of person should I be?" and "How should we as a society organize ourselves?" Within these broad divisions are more specialized endeavors, some devoted to the way in which a particular art or science fits into the overall picture of the world (hence the philosophies of art, physics, mathematics, biology), and some devoted to particular questions falling under one of the foregoing headings (for example, the philosophy of mind or political philosophy).

The philosopher, by definition, seeks wisdom. But what is wisdom? This is itself a substantive and difficult philosophical question. At the very least, wisdom is good judgment. What is good judgment? This too is not an easy question to answer. But having good judgment in a situation involves understanding that situation and knowing how to respond to it. So philosophy involves understanding and knowing how to respond—in the broadest sense, knowing how to live. So philosophy requires knowledge. Philosophers by trade seek wisdom and therefore seek the truth.

They seek, moreover, *reflective* knowledge of truth. They want not only to know truths about the world and to understand how such truths fit together but also to understand why they are true. This is part of what Socrates means in recommending the examined life. It is part of what Confucius means in insisting that we seek the root of things. Philosophers, in keeping an eye on the whole, seek to craft a large-scale understanding of the world. But philosophy differs from mythology, literature, religion, and other ways of pursuing an overall vision of the world. Philosophers want not only to sketch a big picture but also to give reasons for seeing the world that way. They want their big picture to result from examination and to stand up to the examinations of others. From this perspective, Socrates's stress on philosophical argument is no surprise. To lead an examined life is to subject one's opinions, beliefs, assumptions, and choices to rational scrutiny. It is to think hard about their justifications. So philosophers not only must construct big pictures of how things hang together but also must subject those pictures to rational scrutiny, seeking to evaluate them, to discover to what extent they are justified.

SEMANTIC THEORIES OF TRUTH

Philosophy, we have seen, is intimately concerned with truth. Philosophy is the pursuit of wisdom; it is the attempt to lead an examined life. Philosophers reflect to try to understand the world and themselves. They want to know the truth about what the world is made of, how we can gain knowledge of it, and how we ought to live.

But what is truth? Just what are philosophers seeking? What are we seeking? Pontius Pilate famously asked the question:

> Pilate said to him, "So you are a king?" Jesus answered, "You say that I am a king. For this I was born, and for this I have come into the world, to bear witness to the truth. Everyone who is of the truth hears my voice." Pilate said to him, "What is truth?" (*John* 18:37–38)

Pilate did not stay for an answer. But philosophers over the centuries have contemplated his question and have devised three main philosophical theories of truth in response. These theories are important, for they shape not only a philosopher's theory of knowledge but also his or her conception of philosophy itself.

What is a theory of truth? A **semantic theory of truth** gives an account of the meaning of the word 'true' by accounting for inferences we make involving that word. The chief task of such theories, Polish logician Alfred Tarski (1901–1983) pointed out, is to entail **target sentences** or **(T)-sentences** of the form

> 'Snow is white' is true if and only if snow is white.

Tarski, leader of a group of philosophers known as the Warsaw Circle, originally published his work in Polish in the late 1920s. Not until he published it in German and English in the 1930s did it begin to influence philosophical discussions of truth. Shortly thereafter, Tarski fled from the Nazis, escaping the fate that awaited most other members of the Warsaw Circle, and spent the remainder of his career teaching logic and mathematics at the University of California at Berkeley. He developed what he called the "semantic conception of truth," intended as a neutral conception without problematic philosophical commitments.

What is an equivalence of form (T)? When is a definition of truth adequate?

> Consider the sentence "*snow is white.*" We ask the question under what conditions this sentence is true or false. It seems clear that if we base ourselves on the classical conception of truth, we shall say that the sentence is true if snow is white, and that it is false if snow is not white. Thus, if the definition of truth is to conform to our conception, it must imply the following equivalence:
>
> *The sentence "snow is white" is true, if, and only if, snow is white.*
>
> We shall now generalize the procedure which we have applied above.
>
> *(T) X is true if, and only if, p.*
>
> We shall call any such equivalence (with "*p*" replaced by any sentence of the language to which the word "*true*" refers, and "*X*" replaced by a name of this sentence) an "*equivalence of the form (T).*"
>
> Now at last we are able to put into a precise form the conditions under which we will consider the usage and the definition of the term "*true*" as adequate from the material point of view: we wish to use the term "*true*" in such a way that all equivalences of the form (T) can be asserted, and *we shall call a definition of truth "adequate" if all these equivalences follow from it.*[4]

This is harder than it might seem, for 'true' easily leads us into *paradoxes:* contradictions following from plausible premises. The classic paradox, the liar, also merits mention in the New Testament:

> One of themselves, a prophet of their own, said, "Cretans are always liars. . . ." (*Titus* 1:12)

This is not itself paradoxical. If a Cretan says, "Cretans are always liars," we cannot deduce a contradiction. We can only deduce that he lies; Cretans are not always liars. (If what the Cretan says is true, and all Cretans always lie, then he lies, so what he says must be false.) But if someone says, "I am lying," or "This sentence is false," then we have a paradox; the sentence is true if and only if it is false. Let L (the **liar sentence**) be the sentence 'L is false'. Then the target sentence for this puzzling assertion is

> 'L is false' is true if and only if L is false.

But, since L = 'L is false', that implies

> L is true if and only if L is false.

Tarski concluded that natural languages such as English, German, and Polish are inconsistent, containing no coherent concept of truth.

[4] Alfred Tarski, "The Semantic Theory of Truth," *Philosophy and Phenomenological Research* 4 (1944).

Tarski found a way to make talk of truth respectable, but only by eliminating the self-reference involved in the above sentences. Consider a language without the predicate 'true'. (Call it the **object language.**) Now, introduce the predicate so that the target sentences follow: for each sentence S of the object language. (Call that expanded language the **metalanguage.**) The liar sentence can no longer be formulated, for no sentence can talk about its own truth. This is a radical solution, for many sentences seem to talk about their own truth without any hint of paradox:

> Everything I'm telling you is true.

So contemporary logicians try to develop other, less drastic ways of dealing with the liar paradox. But their goal is still semantic: to understand the meaning of 'true'.

CORRESPONDENCE

A **philosophical theory of truth,** in contrast, tries to go beyond accounting for inferences involving the word 'true' by explaining what makes true sentences true. What is it for a sentence or belief to be true? What are we saying about sentences when we describe them as true or false? By virtue of what are true sentences true and false sentences false? Some philosophers, Tarski included, think there are no useful answers to these questions. They are content with a logical theory of truth and see no need to raise any further philosophical issues. But many philosophers find these questions compelling. There must be something, they reason, that true sentences have in common; there must be something that explains why we call them all 'true'.

The most common, and most commonsensical, philosophical theory of truth is the **correspondence theory.** According to that theory, a sentence (or statement or belief) is true if it corresponds with reality—that is, if it corresponds to some fact. It is false if there is no corresponding fact. Aristotle first articulated the correspondence theory in his *Metaphysics:*

> To say of what is that it is not, or of what is not that it is, is false, while to say of what is that it is, and of what is not that it is not, is true; so that he who says of anything that it is, or that it is not, will say either what is true or what is false. . . .[5]

Can you restate Aristotle's definition in your own terms?

The correspondence theory accounts for the dependence of truth on the external world. What makes it true that snow is white? The fact that snow is white. By virtue of what is it true that my cat is asleep? The fact that my cat is asleep. What are we saying about 'Nineveh was the capital of the Assyrian Empire' when we call it true? We are saying that it corresponds to the fact that Nineveh *was* the Assyrian capital.

Thomas Aquinas

Aristotle says little more about the correspondence theory. But St. Thomas Aquinas (1224–1274), perhaps the greatest of all Catholic theologians and philosophers, does. He was born in Roccasecca, Italy, and studied at Naples, Paris, and Cologne. At age thirty-two he was awarded a doctorate in theology at Paris; he joined the faculty there the next year. Starting in 1259 he spent a decade teaching at various Dominican

[5] Aristotle, *Metaphysics* IV, 7 (1011b26–28), translated by W. D. Ross.

monasteries near Rome, returning to Paris to teach in 1268. In 1272, at forty-eight, he joined the faculty in Naples and died just two years later.

Aquinas's version of the correspondence theory starts from the premise that truth is the goal of our intellectual activity. When we think about something, we want to know what is true of it. Truth is what thinking aims at.

At what does desire aim? At what does the intellect aim? Where does the analogy between the two fail?

> As the appetite tends toward the good, so the intellect tends toward truth. There is a difference between the appetite and the intellect or any knowledge whatever: someone knows a thing when it is in him or her, while someone desires a thing when he or she tends toward it. Thus the goal of the appetite, namely the good, is in the desirable object; the goal of the intellect, namely truth, is in the intellect itself. Now good exists in a thing so far as it is related to the appetite. Hence goodness passes from the desirable thing to the appetite; the appetite is called good if its object is good. Similarly, truth is in the intellect in so far as the intellect is conformed to the object understood. Thus truth passes from the intellect to the object understood. The thing understood is said to be true in so far as it has some relation to the intellect.[6]

Truth is what thinking aims at, just as the good is what desire aims at. Of course, we attribute truth to our belief rather than to the thing about which we have the belief, while we attribute goodness to the thing we desire. We may call our desire good, if the thing we desire is good. Similarly, we call our belief true if it conforms to its object. We may define truth, then, as the conformity of intellect and thing.

When is a belief about an object—this book, for example—true?

> Truth resides primarily in the intellect. Now since something is true if it has the form proper to its nature, the intellect, in so far as it knows, must be true; as knowing, it has the likeness of the thing known—this being its form. Hence truth may be defined as the conformity of intellect and thing; to know this conformity is to know truth. (Q 16 A 2)

To know something, then, is to make your intellect conform to an object. Your thought must be in some way similar to the object it is about; it must agree with the way things are. Your thought and the object must in some sense have the same form. Later philosophers have sometimes interpreted this in terms of a picture theory: your thought is true if it correctly depicts reality, if it is an accurate (though of course incomplete) picture of how things are. The goal of thinking is thus to picture reality accurately, to come to have the same form as reality itself.

What is "the cause of knowledge"? What does Aquinas mean by this?

> 'True' expresses the correspondence of being to the knowing power, for all knowing is produced by an assimilation of the knower to the thing known. That assimilation is said to be the cause of knowledge. . . .
>
> The first reference of being to the intellect, therefore, consists in its agreement with the intellect. This agreement is called "the conformity of thing and intellect." This conformity is the formal part of truth. This is what truth adds to being, namely, the conformity or equation of thing and intellect. As we said, the knowledge of a thing is a consequence of this conformity; therefore, it is an effect of truth, even though the fact that the thing is a being is prior to its truth. (Q 1 A 1)

[6]This and subsequent quotations from Aquinas are from Thomas Aquinas, *Truth;* the translation is my own.

It sounds odd to say that knowledge is an effect of truth. But Aquinas means that a belief counts as knowledge, if it does, because it conforms to its object—because, that is, it is true.

Aquinas articulates the core of the correspondence theory in a particularly clear way. Beliefs are in the mind; facts are in the world. A belief is true when mind and world match up in the right way. A true belief has a form similar to what it is about. It is isomorphic to some part or aspect of the world. To use a different metaphor, a true belief maps into the world, in the sense that its content matches a portion of reality. My belief that my cat is asleep is true, for I can match it up with reality: 'my cat' refers to my cat, an animal in the world, and that animal is in fact asleep.

Bertrand Russell

Bertrand Russell (1872–1970), British philosopher, social reformer, and godson of John Stuart Mill, defended the correspondence theory of truth in the twentieth century. Born an aristocrat, Russell became an orphan at age four. He was raised and homeschooled by his grandmother. At eighteen he entered Cambridge, studying first mathematics and then philosophy. Ten years later he discovered the work of Italian mathematician Giuseppe Peano, which opened his eyes to the power of modern logic. He published a series of important and influential philosophical works, including the three volumes of *Principia Mathematica,* co-authored with Alfred North Whitehead (1861–1947). Russell's views, though they varied over the years, became known as the philosophy of **logical atomism.**

Like Aquinas, Russell stresses the dependence of truth on reality:

The truth of a belief about the death of Charles I depends on what, according to Russell?

> . . . the truth or falsehood of a belief always depends upon something which lies outside the belief itself. If I believe that Charles I died on the scaffold, I believe truly, not because of any intrinsic quality of my belief, which could be discovered by merely examining the belief, but because of an historical event which happened two and a half centuries ago. If I believe that Charles I died in his bed, I believe falsely: no degree of vividness in my belief, or of care in arriving at it, prevents it from being false, again because of what happened long ago, and not because of any intrinsic property of my belief. Hence, although truth and falsehood are properties of beliefs, they are properties dependent upon the relations of the beliefs to other things, not upon any internal qualities of the beliefs.[7]

My belief that Charles I died on the scaffold is true if and only if Charles I died on the scaffold. This is one of Tarski's target sentences, which all philosophical theorists of truth would accept. But Russell goes one step further. He interprets the target sentence as saying that my belief is true if and only if there is a fact, in this case, that Charles I died on the scaffold. And there is such a fact because there was a certain historical event, namely, Charles I's hanging.

In general, a belief is true if there is a corresponding fact:

> . . . truth consists in some form of correspondence between belief and fact. (121)
> Thus a belief is true when there is a corresponding fact, and is false when there is no corresponding fact. (129)

[7] Bertrand Russell, *The Problems of Philosophy* (London: Williams and Norgate, 1912), 121.

To develop the correspondence theory, one must have a theory of facts and also an account of the correspondence relation between beliefs or sentences and facts. Russell has detailed analyses of both. But examining them would take us far afield into his metaphysics. (See Chapter 5, World.) It is enough to say that he relies on modern logic for the structure of both accounts.

Because philosophy is at least in part the pursuit of truth, conceptions of what philosophy is and how it should be done depend heavily on conceptions of truth. The correspondence theory thus determines a certain outlook toward the nature and practice of philosophy, which is commonly known as the **analytic method.** Indeed, Russell is usually considered the founder of **analytic philosophy,** the style of philosophy that has dominated the philosophical community in Britain and the United States ever since Russell's time (specifically, since the publication of his profoundly influential paper "On Denoting" in a 1905 issue of *Mind*). But earlier correspondence theorists—including Aristotle, Aquinas, and seventeenth- and eighteenth-century philosophers such as René Descartes, Thomas Hobbes, John Locke, George Berkeley, and David Hume—also pursued the analytic method.

The correspondence theory of truth, as we have seen, holds that a sentence or belief is true if and only if there is a corresponding fact. Truth, that is, is a matter of the world's being a certain way. Whether or not a sentence is true typically depends on the world. (There may be truths of logic that are true no matter what or contradictions that are false no matter what. For more about them, see Chapter 3, Experience.) That has implications for philosophical method. Philosophers, in seeking truth, are investigating the world. They are investigating reality, just as natural scientists are; their method should be that of the natural sciences. Moreover, beliefs are made true by facts. To determine whether something is true, we need to find out whether the corresponding facts exist. We do not need to understand the world as a whole to do this. We need only investigate the particular facts at issue. Was Nineveh the capital of the Assyrian Empire? That depends on a limited set of historical circumstances, which we can in principle determine by looking at a limited set of data. In short, we can understand the world piece by piece. We can seek to understand how things hang together by looking at the things one by one, analyzing complex circumstances by breaking them down into their simpler components. And that is the method of analysis.

Philosophers using the analytic method seek to understand complex wholes by analyzing their parts. As Descartes put it,

> If we perfectly understand a problem we must abstract it from every superfluous conception, reduce it to its simplest terms and, by means of an enumeration, divide it up into the smallest possible parts.[8]

This is the method of the natural sciences, which since Galileo have sought to explain complex phenomena by breaking them into their parts. Galileo, Kepler, and Newton, for example, explained the solar system in terms of the motions of its parts and a few general laws governing them. Lavoisier and other chemists explained the properties of chemical substances by analyzing them, examining their elements; twentieth-

[8] René Descartes, *Discourse on Method,* from *The Philosophical Works of Descartes,* Volume I, translated by Elizabeth S. Haldane and G. R. T. Ross (Cambridge: Cambridge University Press, 1911).

century physicists explained the properties of those elements by appeal to atoms and then the structure within atoms.

Philosophers holding a correspondence theory of truth and hence pursuing the analytic method thus see their work as continuous with that of the natural sciences. They admit that philosophy differs from science in its level of generality and thus in its level of explanation. But they see no fundamental difference in method between them. Indeed, many analytic philosophers have done scientific work themselves. Aristotle most famously wrote treatises on physics, astronomy, and zoology that were unsurpassed for more than 1500 years. Descartes worked on physics and founded analytic geometry. Locke was a doctor who engaged in medical research. Russell was a mathematician. These philosophers saw themselves not as pursuing two different kinds of activities but as applying the same method to different areas and at different levels of generality.

COHERENCE

Philosophers have objected to the correspondence theory for various reasons. Some find its assumption of an independent reality troubling or at any rate unjustified. Others see no way to explain "facts" or "correspondence" without begging the question. Still others see no way to explain necessary or counterfactual truths such as '7 + 5 = 12' or 'The Red Sox would have won if Buckner had caught the ball.' (To what do they correspond?) And some simply reject the analytic method and its assumption that the parts into which we analyze reality behave independently enough for us to investigate them independently. So people have developed alternatives.

The **coherence theory** of truth holds that a sentence or belief is true if it coheres with a comprehensive theory of the world. Francis Herbert Bradley (1846–1924), a nineteenth-century British philosopher, articulated this theory in its classic form. A minister's son, he became Fellow of Merton College, Oxford, which he remained for fifty-four years. Bradley was an **idealist,** holding that reality is mind-dependent. This naturally gave him reason to reject the correspondence theory. The correspondence theory sees beliefs as in the mind, facts as in the world, and truth as resulting from the right kind of match between mind and world. For an idealist, however, mind and world are not distinct—and not just in the obvious sense that a person's mind is part of the world. Reality is mind-dependent: the world is a mental construction, itself a part or construction of mind.

But idealism is only part of Bradley's motivation. He decries facts as a "vicious abstraction." He advocates *holism,* a method completely opposed to that of analysis. Instead of explaining wholes in terms of parts, he explains parts in terms of wholes.

> What I maintain is that in the case of facts of perception and memory the test which we do apply, and which we must apply, is that of system. I contend that this test works satisfactorily, and that no other test will work. And I argue in consequence that there are no judgments of sense which are in principle infallible.[9]

When should you take something as a fact, according to Bradley?

[9] F. H. Bradley, *Essays on Truth and Reality* (Oxford: Clarendon Press, 1914), 202.

We cannot evaluate knowledge claims apart from an entire system—a language, but also a theory, a collection of other beliefs or assertions we advocate. A true belief is one that coheres with a maximally coherent and comprehensive system of beliefs.

> The test which I advocate is the idea of a whole of knowledge as wide and as consistent as may be. In speaking of system I mean always the union of these two aspects, and this is the sense and the only sense in which I am defending coherence. (202)

Think, for example, of the capital of the Assyrian Empire. A vast array of beliefs is somehow implicated in that concept. To know whether Nineveh was the capital of that empire, we must know what an empire is; what, specifically, the Assyrian Empire was; what a capital city is; what Nineveh was; and so on. There is no simple fact, "Nineveh was the capital of the Assyrian Empire." There is a vast complex of beliefs about empires, Assyria, and so on, with which any claim about Nineveh must fit.

Bradley is thus suspicious of the idea of mind-independent "facts" inhabiting reality. The correspondence theorist, he thinks, needs such facts to match up to beliefs. But there are no mind-independent facts in this sense. What we take as "fact" already contains our own interpretation of reality; we single out "facts" using language and a system of concepts. We cannot isolate any mind-independent "given."

> And why, I ask, for the intelligence must there be datum without interpretation any more than interpretation without datum? (204)
>
> My experience is solid, not so far as it is a superstructure [built on a foundation of facts] but so far as in short it is a system. (210)

We take something as a "fact" when it fits into a coherent and comprehensive theory of the world.

> 'Facts' are justified because and as far as, while taking them as real, I am better able to deal with the incoming new 'facts' and in general to make my world wider and more harmonious. The higher and wider my structure, and the more that any particular fact or set of facts is implied in that structure, the more certain are the structure and the facts. (211)
>
> The question throughout is as to what is better or worse for our order as a whole. (212)

As American philosopher Brand Blanshard summarized the coherence theory,

> The degree of truth of a particular proposition is to be judged in the first instance by its coherence with experience as a whole, ultimately by its coherence with that further whole, all-comprehensive and fully articulated, in which thought can come to rest.[10]

Just as the correspondence theory leads to a certain conception of philosophy and philosophical method as analytic, breaking down complex problems into their constituent parts, so the coherence theory leads to another and quite opposite conception. Truth is coherence with a coherent and comprehensive system of beliefs. To assess the truth of a belief, we must see how it fits with our best overall system. We cannot evaluate beliefs one by one; we must evaluate them in the context of a system.

---

[10] Brand Blanshard, *The Nature of Thought* (New York: Macmillan, 1941).

The coherence theory, then, leads to the following philosophical method: to understand things, see them as parts of a comprehensive whole. We cannot understand a root without understanding it as part of a plant. We cannot understand an eye without understanding it as part of an animal. We cannot understand an idea without understanding it as part of a system of ideas. This method is **contextual,** asserting that we must understand things in the contexts in which they occur. It is **functionalist,** for we must understand things in terms of the functions they play in a larger whole. And ultimately it is **holist,** for we must ultimately evaluate beliefs by evaluating their coherence with a comprehensive system of beliefs. The fundamental unit of evaluation is the whole of knowledge.

PRAGMATISM

Russell, who began his philosophical career as an idealist and follower of Bradley, became dissatisfied with the coherence theory of truth. He advances two primary arguments. First, the coherence theory says that a belief is true if it fits with a coherent and comprehensive system of beliefs. But what if there are many coherent and comprehensive systems, and a belief coheres with only some of them?

> . . . there is no reason to suppose that only *one* coherent body of beliefs is possible. . . . Thus coherence as the definition of truth fails because there is no proof that there can be only one coherent system. (122)

Second, Russell argues that truth cannot be defined in terms of coherence, because coherence presupposes truth.

> The other objection to this definition of truth is that it assumes the meaning of 'coherence' known, whereas, in fact, 'coherence' presupposes the truth of the laws of logic. (122–123)

What is it for a system of beliefs to be coherent? This is complicated; the system should, for example, be unified by explanatory relations among beliefs in the system. But at least the system should be consistent; it should not contain any contradictions. However, how do we define consistency? A set of sentences or beliefs is consistent if and only if it implies no contradiction or, equivalently, if and only if it can be true. A system of beliefs, then, is coherent only if it is consistent and consistent if and only if all the beliefs of the system could be true at the same time. So coherence must be defined in terms of truth. But that means that any attempt to define truth in terms of coherence is circular.

The third important, traditional philosophical theory of truth, the **pragmatic theory,** tries to eliminate these problems. The founder of pragmatism was an American philosopher, Charles Sanders Peirce (1839–1914). The son of a Harvard mathematician, he was born in Cambridge, Massachusetts. He attended Harvard and at twenty-four earned a degree in chemistry. He worked for thirty years for the U.S. Coast and Geodetic Survey, occasionally teaching at various universities, though he was never able to secure a permanent academic position. But he worked on philosophical and mathematical questions, developing modern logic (independently from Gottlob Frege, who developed his theory of quantification around the same time) and outlining the principles of pragmatism. In 1887 he moved to Milford, Pennsylvania, to write philosophy. Over the next twenty-seven years he earned a little money by lecturing and writing but lived most of the time in poverty and ill health.

Peirce worried that the coherence theory was not enough. In fact, he feared that philosophers had too great a tendency to rely on coherence without investigating the facts:

> Still, it will sometimes strike a scientific man that the philosophers have been less intent on finding out what the facts are, than on inquiring what belief is most in harmony with their system. It is hard to convince a follower of the a priori method by adducing facts; but show him that an opinion he is defending is inconsistent with what he has laid down elsewhere, and he will be very apt to retract it.[11]

Peirce thus seeks to combine the insights of the coherence and correspondence theories. He does so by stressing the importance of action. We can understand what we are thinking and, in general, account for meaning by understanding how our thoughts systematically relate to action:

According to Peirce, how must we explain the meaning of a thought?

> . . . the whole function of thought is to produce habits of action; and that whatever there is connected with a thought, but irrelevant to its purpose, is an accretion to it, but no part of it. If there be a unity among our sensations which has no reference to how we shall act on a given occasion, as when we listen to a piece of music, why we do not call that thinking. To develop its meaning, we have, therefore, simply to determine what habits it produces, for what a thing means is simply what habits it involves. Now, the identity of a habit depends on how it might lead us to act, not merely under such circumstances as are likely to arise, but under such as might possibly occur, no matter how improbable they may be. What the habit is depends on when and how it causes us to act. As for the when, every stimulus to action is derived from perception; as for the how, every purpose of action is to produce some sensible result. Thus, we come down to what is tangible and conceivably practical, as the root of every real distinction of thought, no matter how subtile it may be; and there is no distinction of meaning so fine as to consist in anything but a possible difference of practice.

There is no difference in meaning without a difference in practice. Meaning, in short, depends entirely on practice. So to get clear about the meanings of our terms and thoughts, we need to be clear about their practical antecedents and effects:

> It appears, then, that the rule for attaining the third grade of clearness of apprehension is as follows: Consider what effects, that might conceivably have practical bearings, we conceive the object of our conception to have. Then, our conception of these effects is the whole of our conception of the object.

This is what Peirce calls "the Principle of Pragmatism," which defines a pragmatist philosophical method:

> In order to ascertain the meaning of an intellectual conception we should consider what practical consequences might conceivably result by necessity from the truth

---

[11] Charles Sanders Peirce, "How to Make Our Ideas Clear," *Popular Science Monthly* 12 (January 1878), 286–302.

> of that conception; and the sum of these consequences will constitute the entire meaning of the conception.[12]

What about truth? Thought aims at truth. Not all practice does. Much of what we do is directed purely at practical ends—getting food, seeing friends, and so on. But inquiry—scientific activity—aims at truth. It aims in particular at stable belief, beliefs that will not have to be given up in the face of further information. The correspondence theorist thinks of this as defining scientific activity; it is that activity that aims at the truth. Peirce turns this on its head. The truth is that at which scientific activity aims.

> So with all scientific research. Different minds may set out with the most antagonistic views, but the progress of investigation carries them by a force outside of themselves to one and the same conclusion. This activity of thought by which we are carried, not where we wish, but to a fore-ordained goal, is like the operation of destiny. No modification of the point of view taken, no selection of other facts for study, no natural bent of mind even, can enable a man to escape the predestinate opinion. This great hope is embodied in the conception of truth and reality. The opinion which is fated to be ultimately agreed to by all who investigate, is what we mean by the truth, and the object represented in this opinion is the real. That is the way I would explain reality.

Under what circumstances would a belief about the death of Charles I be true in Peirce's view?

The truth, then, is "the opinion which is fated to be agreed to by all who investigate." Scientific practice is not arbitrary; the scientist collects evidence, conducts experiments, and evaluates hypotheses. Many hypotheses are proposed only to be rejected or revised as investigation proceeds. But eventually science will lead us to hypotheses that no further investigation will subvert. Those hypotheses will constitute the truth.

Peirce defines reality as that which is independent of what people think about it. But he defines the truth in terms of what the ideal limit of scientific inquiry will lead us to accept. Is there a tension between these two definitions? No, because scientific practice is not arbitrary. No matter who is inquiring, or the order in which hypotheses occur to them, they will eventually reach the same conclusions.

> But it may be said that this view is directly opposed to the abstract definition which we have given of reality, inasmuch as it makes the characters of the real depend on what is ultimately thought about them. But the answer to this is that, on the one hand, reality is independent, not necessarily of thought in general, but only of what you or I or any finite number of men may think about it; and that, on the other hand, though the object of the final opinion depends on what that opinion is, yet what that opinion is does not depend on what you or I or any man thinks. Our perversity and that of others may indefinitely postpone the settlement of opinion; it might even conceivably cause an arbitrary proposition to be universally accepted as long as the human race should last. Yet even that would not change the nature of the belief, which alone could be the result of investigation carried sufficiently far; and if, after the extinction of our race, another should arise with faculties and

Could something be true, according to Peirce, even if no one ever believes it?

[12] Peirce, "The Architectonic Construction of Pragmatism" in *The Collected Papers of Charles Sanders Peirce,* edited by Charles Hartshorne and Paul Weiss (Cambridge: Harvard University Press, 1934), 5.9.

disposition for investigation, that true opinion must be the one which they would ultimately come to. "Truth crushed to earth shall rise again," and the opinion which would finally result from investigation does not depend on how anybody may actually think. But the reality of that which is real does depend on the real fact that investigation is destined to lead, at last, if continued long enough, to a belief in it.

Truth, then, is a kind of coherence, or, as Peirce prefers to call it, **concordance,** but with the **ideal limit** of scientific inquiry:

> Truth is that concordance of an abstract statement with the ideal limit towards which endless investigation would tend to bring scientific belief, which concordance the abstract statement may possess by virtue of the confession of its inaccuracy and one-sidedness, and this confession is an essential ingredient of truth. A further explanation of what this concordance consists in will be given below. Reality is that mode of being by virtue of which the real thing is as it is, irrespectively of what any mind or any definite collection of minds may represent it to be. The truth of the proposition that Caesar crossed the Rubicon consists in the fact that the further we push our archaeological and other studies, the more strongly will that conclusion force itself on our minds forever—or would do so, if study were to go on forever.[13]

For Peirce, in short, the truth is what we all eventually are bound to agree on. Peirce's theory of truth had sweeping influence on the later course of American philosophy. One of the most important of those who seized the pragmatist banner was philosopher and psychologist William James (1842–1910), the elder brother of novelist Henry James. Born in New York City, James traveled extensively as a child, eventually earning an M.D. from Harvard, where he taught for the remainder of his career. James interpreted pragmatism quite differently from Peirce—who, as a result, changed the name of his theory to 'pragmaticism', "which is ugly enough to be safe from kidnappers" (CP 5.415).

Under what circumstances would a belief about the death of Charles I be true in James's view?

James identifies truth with verifiability in practice:

> Pragmatism, on the other hand, asks its usual question, "Grant an idea or belief to be true," it says, "what concrete difference will its being true make in any one's actual life? How will the truth be realized? What experiences will be different from those which would obtain if the belief were false? What, in short, is the truth's cash-value in experiential terms?"
>
> The moment pragmatism asks this question, it sees the answer: *True ideas are those that we can assimilate, validate, corroborate and verify. False ideas are those that we can not.* That is the practical difference it makes to us to have true ideas; that therefore, is the meaning of truth, for it is all that truth is known as.
>
> This thesis is what I have to defend. The truth of an idea is not a stagnant property inherent in it. Truth *happens* to an idea. It *becomes* true, is *made* true by events. Its verity *is* in fact an event, a process: the process namely of its verifying itself, its veri-*fication.* Its validity is the process of its valid*ation.*[14]

---

[13] Peirce, "A Survey of Pragmaticism" in *The Collected Papers of Charles Sanders Peirce,* edited by Charles Hartshorne and Paul Weiss (Cambridge: Harvard University Press, 1934), 5.464.

[14] William James, *Pragmatism: A New Name for Some Old Ways of Thinking* (New York: Longmans, Green, 1907).

James's decree that a true statement is one "*we can assimilate, validate, corroborate and verify*" is hard to understand, for these do not appear to be the same thing. "Assimilating" a belief sounds a bit like absorbing it into a system of beliefs; in short, it suggests the coherence theory. "Corroborating" a belief sounds like finding evidence for it; "verifying" it sounds like proving it. Since we can find evidence for lots of things and prove very few, these suggest very different standards for truth. Finally, in summarizing his view, James uses different terms, suggesting that truth is what works:

> Yet since almost any object may some day become temporarily important, the advantage of having a general stock of *extra* truths, of ideas that shall be true of merely possible situations, is obvious. We store such extra truths away in our memories, and with the overflow we fill our books of reference. Whenever such an extra truth becomes practically relevant to one of our emergencies, it passes from cold storage to do work in the world and our belief in it grows active. You can say of it then either that "it is useful because it is true" or that "it is true because it is useful." Both these phrases mean exactly the same thing, namely that here is an idea that gets fulfilled and can be verified. True is the name for whatever idea starts the verification-process, useful is the name for its completed function in experience.

James appears to be saying that a belief is true if and only if it is useful in the sense that it "becomes practically relevant to one of our emergencies." Truth, that is, is a kind of expediency:

> *"The true," to put it very briefly, is only the expedient in the way of our thinking, just as "the right" is only the expedient in the way of our behaving.*

This sounds very different from Peirce's view of truth as the ideal limit of scientific investigation. And indeed Peirce took it to be so. But James had a view of expediency, of usefulness, that helps to explain his apparent sloppiness in speaking indifferently of assimilation, verification, corroboration, and validation. He saw science as a process of belief revision. We adopt certain beliefs in response to our experience as a way of adapting to our experience and better fitting ourselves for future experiences. We then encounter new information and update our beliefs, keeping some, rejecting others, and adding new ones. Truth is what works in that context of belief revision. Truth, in other words, is that on which our process of belief revision stabilizes.

What rule is James suggesting for revising our beliefs in the light of new information?

> The individual has a stock of old opinions already, but he meets a new experience that puts them to a strain. Somebody contradicts them; or in a reflective moment he discovers that they contradict each other; or he hears of facts with which they are incompatible; or desires arise in him which they cease to satisfy. The result is an inward trouble to which his mind till then had been a stranger, and from which he seeks to escape by modifying his previous mass of opinions. He saves as much of it as he can, for in this matter of belief we are all extreme conservatives. So he tries to change first this opinion, and then that (for they resist change very variously), until at last some new idea comes up which he can graft upon the ancient stock with a minimum of disturbance of the latter, some idea that mediates between the stock and the new experience and runs them into one another most felicitously and expediently.
>
> This new idea is then adopted as the true one. It preserves the older stock of truths with a minimum of modification, stretching them just enough to make

> them admit the novelty, but conceiving that in ways as familiar as the case leaves possible. An outré explanation, violating all our preconceptions, would never pass for a true account of a novelty. We should scratch round industriously till we found something less eccentric. The most violent revolutions in an individual's beliefs leave most of his old order standing. Time and space, cause and effect, nature and history, and one's own biography remain untouched. New truth is always a go-between, a smoother-over of transitions.[15]

A sentence is true, on this conception, if we can assert it and keep on asserting it—in short, if assertions of it are stable. We might think of finding points of equilibrium in our search for knowledge. It is always possible that further evidence could disrupt the equilibrium, forcing us to give up our assertion. But sometimes it never does. Those points of stable equilibrium are truths.

RELATIVISM

Perhaps the oldest challenge to theories of truth is also the oldest challenge to philosophy itself: **relativism.** Relativism is the thesis that there are no universally valid truths about the world. Tarski observes, uncontroversially, that truth is relative to a language. Truth is also relative to context; "It's 90° today" may be true or false, depending on when and where it is uttered. But relativism goes far beyond these commonplace observations. Can we speak of sentences, assertions, or beliefs—in a given language and given context—as true or false? The **absolutist** or **objectivist** says yes. As seventeenth-century Ethiopian philosopher Zera Yacob (1599–1692; see Chapter 8) insists, "Truth is one." [16] The relativist says no. We can speak of sentences, assertions, or beliefs as true or false only relative to something else—to a society, culture, historical epoch, "interpretative community," or individual person. The relativist, that is, holds that something might be true for you but false for me, or true for us but false for residents of other times and places.

The first relativist of whom we have any record was the Greek Sophist Protagoras (490–420 B.C.E.). He traveled about Greece teaching young people rhetoric, philosophy, and self-improvement for a fee. He visited Athens frequently and became a friend of Pericles, who asked him to draw up a legal code for the colony of Thurii. Eventually, however, according to tradition—in a striking foreshadowing of the fate of Socrates—he was tried for impiety, convicted, and sentenced to exile, dying in a shipwreck on his journey. Protagoras began his work "Truth" with his most famous words:

> Man is the measure of all things—of things that are, that they are; of things that are not, that they are not.[17]

He argued not that truth is relative to humanity in general, as the quotation in isolation might suggest, but that there is no objective truth at all. The world is as it appears;

---

[15] William James, "Pluralism, Pragmatism, and Instrumental Truth" from *A Pluralistic Universe* (New York: Longmans, Green, 1909).

[16] Zera Yacob, "The Treatise of Zera Yacob" in Claude Sumner, *The Source of African Philosophy: The Ethiopian Philosophy of Man* (Stuttgart: Franz Steiner Verlag Wiesbaden GmbH, 1986).

[17] Protagoras, "Truth," in Guthrie, W. K. C. (William Keith Chambers), *The Sophists* (Cambridge: Cambridge University Press, 1971).

there is no difference between how things seem and how they are. Truth is in the eye of the beholder. As Socrates explains it, Protagoras holds

> that things are to you such as they appear to you, and to me such as they appear to me.[18]

Clearly something can look red to you but orange to me or taste sweet to you but bitter to me. In short, appearances *are* relative to individual perceivers. If reality is nothing but appearance, however, then reality too is relative to individuals. Something may *be* red for you and orange for me, or sweet for you and bitter for me.

Plato saw relativism as a threat to philosophy, for, according to Protagoras, there is no such thing as wisdom; there is no such thing as reaching an understanding of the world. There is only appearance. Aristotle put Plato's concern eloquently:

> And it is in this direction that the consequences are most difficult. For if those who have seen most of such truth as is possible for us (and these are those who seek and love it most)—if these have such opinions and express these [relativist] views about the truth, is it not natural that beginners in philosophy should lose heart? For to seek the truth would be to follow flying game.[19]

Why does relativism threaten the possibility of philosophy?

Plato advances a series of complex arguments against relativism. The first and most fundamental, however, is straightforward. It is called **the argument from error (or illusion):**

> SOCRATES. Let us not leave the argument unfinished, then; for there still remains to be considered an objection which may be raised about dreams and diseases, in particular about madness, and the various illusions of hearing and sight, or of other senses. For you know that in all these cases the *esse-percipi* [to be is to be perceived] theory appears to be unmistakably refuted, since in dreams and illusions we certainly have false perceptions; and far from saying that everything is which appears, we should rather say that nothing is which appears.
>
> THEAETETUS. Very true, Socrates.
>
> SOCRATES. But then, my boy, how can any one contend that knowledge is perception, or that to every man what appears is?

In other words, people make mistakes. We sometimes dream things we know not to be real, misperceive things, misjudge situations, draw the wrong conclusions. Some people are mad and do these things routinely. But what does this mean? People are wrong when things are not as they appear to them. It seems that Protagoras's thesis implies that this cannot happen; things are as they appear. But that implies that error, illusion, madness, and so on, are impossible.

In fact, we do not need to establish error to make the point; it is enough to have the possibility of error. Plato raises a classic skeptical argument, usually intended to undermine knowledge (see Chapter 2):

> SOCRATES. Do you see another question which can be raised about these phenomena, notably about dreaming and waking?

---

[18] Plato, *Thaetetus,* translated by Benjamin Jowett, from *The Dialogues of Plato* (Oxford: Oxford University Press, 1892), 152a.

[19] Aristotle, *Metaphysics* IV, 5, 1009b33–39, translated by W. D. Ross.

> THEAETETUS. What question?
>
> SOCRATES. A question which I think that you must often have heard persons ask:— How can you determine whether at this moment we are sleeping, and all our thoughts are a dream; or whether we are awake, and talking to one another in the waking state?
>
> THEAETETUS. Indeed, Socrates, I do not know how to prove the one any more than the other, for in both cases the facts precisely correspond;—and there is no difficulty in supposing that during all this discussion we have been talking to one another in a dream; and when in a dream we seem to be narrating dreams, the resemblance of the two states is quite astonishing.
>
> SOCRATES. You see, then, that a doubt about the reality of sense is easily raised, since there may even be a doubt whether we are awake or in a dream. And as our time is equally divided between sleeping and waking, in either sphere of existence the soul contends that the thoughts which are present to our minds at the time are true; and during one half of our lives we affirm the truth of the one, and, during the other half, of the other; and are equally confident of both.

On Protagoras's view, the skeptical worry makes no sense, for things are as they appear. In fact, however, we worry about whether or not things are as they seem to be. That worry shows that there is a difference between appearance and reality.

Can a relativist distinguish error from success, illusion from perception, appearance from reality? If we equate appearance and reality, then evidently not. But a relativist does not need to do that. Protagoras, in making man the measure of all things, need not make each one of us, at a given moment, the measure of all things. I can come to realize, for example, that I was only dreaming or that I was mistaken. Borrowing ideas from Peirce and James, we might say that what is true for me is what I will believe in the long run; it is that around which my beliefs will stabilize—or would stabilize, if I were to live long enough and face favorable conditions for inquiry. We would then have a basis for distinguishing appearance from reality, truth from error, and so on. Moreover, we might avoid a second Socratic argument, that, on Protagoras's account, there is no difference between wisdom and foolishness: "He assumed all to be equal and sufficient in wisdom." Some might be closer than others to what they will or would believe in the long run. We might have a basis for criticizing views from their own perspectives on their own criteria.

This, in effect, is the strategy of such contemporary philosophers as Hilary Putnam and Richard Rorty. They pursue the idea differently, but the basic idea is the same. Return for a moment to the pragmatist theory of truth. We might define truth, as Peirce does, as that on which the community will eventually agree. But the relativist can object that there is more than one community of inquirers, and there is no guarantee that they will converge to agree on the same thing. Perhaps one community will converge to one set of beliefs and another community to another. Perhaps different individuals will stabilize on different sets of beliefs, even under ideal circumstances. If so, then we can still define the truth *for X* as the set of beliefs *X* will accept in the long run. But we have no way of defining truth, period.

This strategy would deal with another objection Plato raises against Protagoras:

> Protagoras . . . says that man is the measure of all things, and that things are to me as they appear to me, and that they are to you as they appear to you. . . . But if Pro-

> tagoras is right, and the truth is that things are as they appear to anyone, how can some of us be wise and some of us foolish?[20]

This tells against Protagoras's claim that things are as they appear. Against our more sophisticated version of relativism, however, things are not so clear. Some of us might stabilize on a set of beliefs very slowly. Some might stabilize on a set of beliefs that can be criticized by their own standards; they might stabilize, that is, where they shouldn't stabilize, even by their own lights. They might stabilize on an incoherent set of beliefs. Others might stabilize on a set of beliefs they have no means of criticizing, but the wiser person does. Some perspectives, in other words, might include but go beyond others. Much would have to be said to make these ideas precise, and explain how these things are possible. But the sophisticated relativist may be able to allow that some people are wiser than others.

Socrates also advances another fairly straightforward argument against Protagoras, charging him with arbitrariness and ultimately incoherence. If truth is relative, then the truth of relativism is at most relative. So we can say to Protagoras, "Who cares what is true for you? We have no reason to think that relativism is true for us."

> SOCRATES. I am charmed with his doctrine, that what appears is to each one, but I wonder that he did not begin his book on Truth with a declaration that a pig or a dog-faced baboon, or some other yet stranger monster which has sensation, is the measure of all things; then he might have shown a magnificent contempt for our opinion of him by informing us at the outset that while we were reverencing him like a God for his wisdom he was no better than a tadpole, not to speak of his fellow-men—would not this have produced an over-powering effect? For if truth is only sensation, and no man can discern another's feelings better than he, or has any superior right to determine whether his opinion is true or false, but each, as we have several times repeated, is to himself the sole judge, and everything that he judges is true and right, why, my friend, should Protagoras be preferred to the place of wisdom and instruction, and deserve to be well paid, and we poor ignoramuses have to go to him, if each one is the measure of his own wisdom? Must he not be talking *ad captandum* [to a captive audience] in all this? I say nothing of the ridiculous predicament in which my own midwifery and the whole art of dialectic is placed; for the attempt to supervise or refute the notions or opinions of others would be a tedious and enormous piece of folly, if to each man his own are right; and this must be the case if Protagoras' Truth is the real truth, and the philosopher is not merely amusing himself by giving oracles out of the shrine of his book.

Socrates is claiming that a relativist cannot make sense of education or inquiry. Why?

In fact, not only is Protagoras's relativism arbitrary and perhaps incoherent, it also leaves us with a puzzle about its own truth. Protagoras thinks man is the measure of all things, so evidently that, on his own view, is true for him. But most people disagree. So, it must be false for them. But then isn't his position self-undermining?

> SOCRATES. And the best of the joke is, that he acknowledges the truth of their opinion who believe his own opinion to be false; for he admits that the opinions of all men are true.

[20] Plato, *Cratylus* 386a, c, translated by Benjamin Jowett, from *The Dialogues of Plato* (Oxford: Oxford University Press, 1892).

But Socrates's arguments hardly lay the question of relativism to rest. Let us turn to some defenders of relativism or a related doctrine, perspectivism.

Maybeism: Jainism

The Indian religious leader Mahavira (599–527 B.C.E.), the founder of Jainism, was roughly contemporary with Confucius, Laozi, and the Buddha. Mahavira is also known as the *Jina,* "the Victor" (over passion). There is some evidence that his followers merged with another group to establish the religion of the Jina, Jainism.

Like other Indian philosophies of the early period, Jainism proclaims a mystical, personal highest good achieved by austere living and contemplation. But of all the mystically oriented early Indian views, the Jain is the most renowned for its ethical commitment to the value of life. Jains are vegetarians; Jain monks have been known to wear masks so that their breathing will not cause injury to microscopic insects. Regarding even vegetable life as sentient, some Jain monks have starved themselves to death to prevent injury to others. Noninjury, ***ahimsa***—an ideal popularized in modern times by Mahatma Gandhi—was propagated in ancient and classical India foremost by Jains.

Jains argue that injuring any sentient life is morally wrong because all souls are equally valuable. I recognize that injury to me is bad for me. I must conclude that injury to others is similarly bad for them. Their souls are as valuable as my own. Therefore, I must refrain from injuring them.

Later Jain thinkers such as Vadi Devasuri (c. 1150), a contemporary of Maimonides and Averröes, propagate two engaging metaphilosophical positions, **nonabsolutism** and **maybeism.** The two extend the noninjury ethic into the area of philosophical dialectic. Just as all souls are valuable, all views are valuable.

Some have held that, just as all souls are equally valuable, all views are equally valuable. Most, however, do not go so far. Jains argue for nonabsolutism, the view that no metaphysical claim should be taken as absolutely true. Every view represents only one perspective (***naya***) among infinitely many. They also argue for maybeism: every view should be regarded as right *maybe* ('***syat***', 'in some respects'). There is at least a grain of truth in every position, and the 'maybe' directs us to find and appreciate what is correct in what an opponent is saying.

Maybeism implies nonabsolutism, for, if every view is right in some respects, the opposite of any view is also right in some respects. That means that every view is wrong in some respects as well. So nothing can be true absolutely, that is, in every respect or from every standpoint.

Many scholars see Jainist nonabsolutism as a form of relativism. There are three ways of interpreting maybeism and nonabsolutism, however, depending on how one reads *syat:* 'maybe', 'in some respects', or 'from some perspective'.

1. *The epistemic reading:* If we read *syat* as 'maybe', then maybeism is the thesis that any view might be right, for all we know, and nonabsolutism is correspondingly the thesis that no view is absolutely certain—a position known as **fallibilism.** No matter how secure we think our knowledge is, we could turn out to be wrong. Are you reading this book? You think you are; maybe you even *know* you are. But you could be

mistaken. Perhaps you are only dreaming about reading this book. Perhaps this is not a book but an alien creature disguised as a book.

On this reading, then, nonabsolutism is a mild form of skepticism, maintaining that absolute certainty is impossible. It is not a form of relativism.

2. *The aspects reading.* If we read *syat* as 'in some respects', then maybeism is the thesis that every view is right in some respects. Nonabsolutism, then, is the thesis that no view is right in every respect. Every view requires qualification; every yes–no question must be answered, "Well, in some respects, yes; in other respects, no." Are you reading this book? In some respects, yes, of course; how else would you be coming into contact with these words? In some respects, however, the answer is no. Your mind is doing many things—including thinking about the question whether you are reading this book!—only some of which could be called reading. Similarly, if we ask whether a historical figure—Franklin Delano Roosevelt, say—is admirable or successful, a natural answer is, "In some ways, yes; in other ways, no." Roosevelt was an outstanding leader during most of World War II, for example, but much less successful in the war's later stages, when his own debilitating illness allowed Stalin to take advantage of him. He gave inspiration to many during the Great Depression but allowed the Federal Reserve to follow a contractionary monetary policy throughout that period. And so on. The same is true of anyone. We are all admirable in some ways and not so admirable in others. We succeed in some respects and not others.

On this reading, nonabsolutism maintains that things are complicated, having many aspects; our ordinary statements about things fail to single out a single aspect. We can evaluate them only by singling out a particular aspect. This is not a form of relativism, for the aspects may be completely objective. It is one thing to say that we cannot judge someone as successful, say, except in some particular respect, and quite another to say that we cannot judge them as successful except relative to a community, a person, or a set of subjective standards.

3. *The relativist reading.* We might read *syat* as 'from some perspective' or 'from some standpoint'. Then maybeism says that every view is right from some perspective. Nonabsolutism becomes the thesis that no view is right from every perspective. Every view, then, is right from some points of view and wrong from others. One can say whether something is right or wrong only relative to a perspective, a standpoint, a point of view. This is a form of relativism known as **perspectivism.** (Its foremost Western proponent is Friedrich Nietzsche.)

A key premise underlying the Jainist view, however it should be interpreted, is that things have many (indeed, infinitely many) aspects (*nayas*). You, for example, are a person. You are you; you are human; you have eyes; you are literate; you are reading this book. Some of these characteristics are permanent, but others are transitory. You will remain you for as long as you exist, but you have not always been literate, and you will not be reading this book forever. (You may not even be human forever; Jains believe in reincarnation.) In some respects, therefore, you are permanent; in others, you change. 'You are permanent' is thus true in some respects but false in others. Similarly, in some respects you and I are alike; in some, we differ. So, 'we are alike' is true in some respects and false in others. Things are many-sided: descriptions of them are true in some respects and false in others.

Perspectivism: Ortega y Gasset

Philosophers have sometimes felt unhappy about choosing between Platonic truth and Protagorean relativism. Spanish philosopher José Ortega y Gasset (1883–1955) tries to develop a third way, *perspectivism.* Born in Madrid, he studied there and in Germany, returning to Madrid at age twenty-seven to become professor of metaphysics. He taught there for twenty-six years until the Spanish Civil War, when his vocal support for the Spanish Republic forced him to flee. He returned to his homeland after World War II and remained until his death ten years later. A brilliant writer, Ortega avoided philosophical jargon and wrote frequently for newspapers and magazines. His work was immensely influential, especially in Spain and Latin America.

Ortega summarized his views in four theses:

What does Ortega mean by "the circumstantiality of life"?

1. That human life in the proper and original sense is each individual's life seen from itself, hence that it is always *mine*—that it is personal.
2. That it consists in man's finding himself, without knowing how or why, obliged, on pain of succumbing, always to be doing something in a particular circumstance—which we shall call the circumstantiality of life, or the fact that man's life is lived in view of circumstances.
3. That circumstance always offers us different possibilities for acting, hence for being. This obliges us, like it or not, to exercise our freedom. We are forced to be free. Because of this, life is a permanent crossroads and constant perplexity. At every instant we have to choose whether in the next instant or at some other future time we shall be he who does this or he who does that. Hence each of us is incessantly choosing his "doing," hence his being.
4. Life is untransferable. No one can take my place in the task of deciding what I am to do, and this includes what I am to suffer, for I have to accept the suffering that comes to me from without. My life, then, is constant and unescapable responsibility to myself. What I do—hence, what I think, feel, want—must *make sense,* and *good sense,* to me.[21]

Ortega, speaking of "vital reason," stressed that things are real only insofar as they affect life—specifically, *my* life. This implies what he terms his perspectivism. If what is real for me is what affects my life, then something may be real for me but unreal for you. What matters to me in my circumstances may differ from what matters for you in your circumstances. This seems to be a kind of relativism.

Ortega, however, sees his perspectivism not as a form of relativism but as a way of overcoming the long-standing debate between objectivists (or, in Ortega's terms, *rationalists*) and relativists. He offers metaphors to illustrate the differences. Individual knowers, cultures, or historical epochs act not to shape reality but to select from it:

> When a sieve or a net is placed in a current of liquid it allows certain things to permeate it and keeps others out; it might be said to make a choice, but assuredly not

[21] José Ortega y Gasset, *Man and People,* translated by William R. Trask (New York: W. W. Norton and Co., Inc., 1957).

> to alter the forms of things. This is the function of the knower, of the living being face to face with the cosmic reality of his environment. He does not allow himself, without more ado, to be permeated by reality, as would the imaginary rational entity created by rationalist definitions. Nor does he invent an illusory reality. His function is clearly selective. From the infinite number of elements which integrate reality the individual or receiving apparatus admits a certain proportion, whose form and substance coincide with the meshes of his sensitized net. The rest, whether phenomena, facts, or truths, remain beyond him. He knows nothing of them and does not perceive them. (88)[22]

As the name 'perspectivism' suggests, people, cultures, and historical epochs have different perspectives on reality, just as people viewing a scene do so from different perspectives.

What is a "perspective"?

> Two men may look, from different view-points, at the same landscape. Yet they do not see the same thing. Their different situations make the landscape assume two distinct types of organic structure in their eyes. The part which, in the one case, occupies the foreground, and is thrown into high relief in all its details, is, in the other case, the background, and remains obscure and vague in its appearance. Further, inasmuch as things which are put one behind the other are either wholly or partially concealed, each of the two spectators will perceive portions of the landscape which elude the attention of the other. (89)

So far, it appears that Ortega is mostly concerned to stress the circumstantiality of life, including knowledge: knowledge is always knowledge from some point of view.

> All knowledge is knowledge from a definite point of view. Spinoza's *species aeternitatis,* or ubiquitous and absolute point of view, has no existence on its own account: it is a fictitious and abstract point of view. . . . Every life is a point of view directed upon the universe. Strictly speaking, what one life sees no other can. (90–91)

And this does not by itself imply relativism. We might agree that everyone viewing a scene does so from a particular point of view, while insisting there is nevertheless an objective truth about the scene itself. Each eyewitness to the assassination of President Kennedy, for example, saw the event from some perspective inevitably incomplete. Still, there is an objective truth about what happened in Dealey Plaza in Dallas, Texas, on November 22, 1963. No one person has access to that objective truth, but that does not mean that it does not exist.

Ortega, however, sometimes goes beyond this. He sees the rationalists as saying that one perspective is right, while others are wrong. That is pointless; all are perspectives on the actual scene. He sees relativists, in contrast, as trying to say that all perspectives are in some way illusory and that truth is therefore impossible. But that mistakes what truth is. "Cosmic reality is such that it can only be seen in a single definite perspective" (90). Truth depends on a particular point of view.

There are two ways of taking Ortega's conception of truth. We might interpret him as a relativist, specifically a **historicist,** who maintains that truth is relative to a

[22]José Ortega y Gasset, *The Modern Theme,* translated by James Cleugh (New York: Harper and Row, 1961).

culture or historical epoch. Alternatively, we may read his perspectivism epistemically. We all have different perspectives on reality, but truth ultimately depends on that reality, not on our perspectives. Just as there really is something passing through a sieve or net, and just as there really is a landscape various observers are seeing, so there is a reality that makes what we say and believe true or false. We have access to it only through a certain perspective, but that is like saying we can see what is going on inside our neighbor's house only by looking in the window. That limits our knowledge of the goings on, but the truth of what we say and believe about them is not relative to the window—it is determined by what actually goes on inside the house.

Deconstructionism: Jacques Derrida

Jacques Derrida (b. 1930), a French philosopher, is the founder of *deconstructionism*. **Deconstruction** is a method of uncovering inconsistencies in theories, literary or philosophical works, or intellectual traditions. It focuses on binary oppositions—good/bad, right/wrong, true/false, for example—that reveal the structure of the thought being analyzed. It then proceeds to show how the theory, work, or tradition under consideration undermines those very oppositions. Deconstruction is thus an internal conceptual critique; it uses the basic distinctions, assumptions, and forms of argument of a view to show that it is self-contradictory, self-defeating, or self-undermining.

So far, this might seem to have no implications about truth. Contradictory hypotheses and incoherent theories are possible on anyone's view. But Derrida seems to imply that anything can be deconstructed. If *any* theory, work, or tradition is ultimately incoherent, then knowledge is impossible. At least, then, deconstruction implies a sweeping skepticism.

But Derrida goes even further than this, seeking to undermine language, thought, meaning, and significance themselves. He seeks to transform our ways of thinking about the relation of language to the world. And that involves transforming our idea of truth. Derrida traces the history of Western philosophy to "problematize" our concept of truth; he "calls it into question." In other words, he seeks to expose the assumptions and operations of language underlying our talk of truth. It turns out that, when we do this, we see that we cannot escape language. We try to reflect on the world, but the very act of reflection leads us to reflect on language instead. We aim at the world and hit the word.

From this point of view, deconstruction emerges as just the kind of critique in which a relativist might engage. As we saw in discussing Protagoras, relativists need not say that appearance and reality are the same. They might instead say that what is true for a person is what that person will or would eventually believe—that, in other words, on which his/her beliefs would stabilize. That makes error and criticism possible. But criticism must be criticism according to standards the target of the criticism can accept. Derrida is saying that we can criticize Western talk of truth by its own standards, finding that it undermines itself—specifically, in that it depends on an access to the world independently of language that it itself holds to be impossible.

Derrida considers the notion of structure, which, he argues, inevitably has a center. Read literally, this is absurd; there can be structures with no center. But what he has in mind is that a language, theory, or tradition draws distinctions. In his language, it is a system of differences. It relies on dichotomies, establishing a structure into which it tries to fit reality. Some of these may be peripheral, inessential to the language, theory, or tradition. But others are central; they are the basic distinctions used to organize the world. They constitute the center of the structure. They also limit the range of possibilities the structure can match; they "limit what we might call the *freeplay* of the structure" (248).[23]

So far, so good. But at some point something happens—an event Derrida calls a *rupture*—when we begin to reflect on the structure as such, and it loses its center:

> From then on it was probably necessary to begin to think that there was no center, that the center could not be thought in the form of a being-present, that the center had no natural locus, that it was not a fixed locus but a function, a sort of non-locus in which an infinite number of sign-substitutions came into play. This moment was that in which language invaded the universal problematic; that in which, in the absence of a center or origin, everything became discourse—provided we can agree on this word—that is to say, when everything became a system where the central signified, the original or transcendental signified, is never absolutely present outside a system of differences. (249)

We reflect, for example, on the correspondence theory of truth. We would like to say that 'snow is white' is true if and only if snow is white, seeing a sentence on the left being made true by a fact on the right. But, reflecting, we see that we have words on both sides of the 'if and only if'. We find no fact. Tarski relies on just this to argue that his semantic conception of truth is philosophically neutral. So let us try to make the dependence of truth on the world more explicit by saying, "'Snow is white' is true if and only if it is a fact that snow is white." Again, however, we have words on both sides of the 'if and only if'; we cannot build the fact itself into our statement. We try to talk about the relationship between language and the world, and all we get is more language! As Derrida says, everything becomes discourse. Our attempt to philosophize about the world ends in failure or, more precisely, in discourse. Everything becomes text. It is in this sense that we aim at the world and hit the word.

There are two ways to react to this problem, which Derrida calls the problem of "the absent origin"—our inability to get outside language. One is "sad, *negative,* nostalgic, guilty, Rousseauist" (see Chapter 9 for Rousseau's theory of the original state of nature); the other is "the Nietzschean *affirmation*—the joyous affirmation of the freeplay of the world and without truth, without origin, offered to an active interpretation" (264). It takes the attitude expressed by the title of a paper by contemporary American philosopher Richard Rorty: "The World Well Lost."

> *This affirmation then determines the non-center otherwise than as a loss of the center.* And it plays the game without security. For there is a *sure* freeplay; that which is limited to the *substitution* of *given and existing, present,* pieces. (264)

What is "sure freeplay"?

When we seek to understand the world and our relation to it, we face two choices. We may continue to seek reality itself, trying to break through the bonds of language to

[23]Jacques Derrida, "Structure, Sign, and Play in the Discourse of the Human Sciences," in Richard Macksey and Eugenio Donato (eds.), *The Languages of Criticism and the Sciences of Man: The Structuralist Controversy* (Baltimore: The Johns Hopkins University Press, 1970), 247–272.

encounter the world as it really is. That ineluctably leads to frustration. Or, we may recognize that we are trapped in language, and take that as a sign of our freedom. If we cannot break through to the world itself, it cannot constrain us. We may affirm our ability to talk and theorize as we like, seeing in the very concept of truth an impossible attempt to escape language and reach reality itself.

> There are thus two interpretations of interpretation, of structure, of sign, of freeplay. The one seeks to decipher, dreams of deciphering, a truth or an origin which is free from freeplay and from the order of the sign, and lives like an exile the necessity of interpretation. The other, which is no longer turned toward the origin, affirms freeplay and tries to pass beyond man and humanism, the name man being the name of that being who, throughout the history of metaphysics or of ontotheology—in other words, through the history of all of his history—has dreamed of full presence, the reassuring foundation, the origin and the end of the game. (264–265)

Derrida urges us to abandon the attempt to make sense of an absolute, objective concept of truth and to see freeplay as an alternative. The correspondence theory of truth is in a sense right: Our concept of truth *does* rely on the idea of a relation between language and the world, specifically, on the idea of a sentence being made true by the facts. So much the worse, Derrida concludes, for our concept of truth. He does not advance an alternative account of truth; he advocates abandoning the notion.

Feminism: Elizabeth Grosz

Feminists such as contemporary Australian philosopher Elizabeth Grosz tend to be inspired by the perspectivism of thinkers such as Ortega y Gasset. Grosz welcomes the idea that there are various ways of understanding the world, including some that are distinctly feminine or have been unfairly excluded by traditional philosophy. But she is troubled by the prospect of relativism. Grosz refuses to accept all perspectives as equally valid. Some perspectives, including historically important ones, unjustly exclude women and shortchange their experiences and perspectives. So she seeks a view that allows more than one point of view to be legitimate and correct without thereby making *every* point of view legitimate and correct. Grosz writes:

> Radical feminists instead aim to expand and multiply the criteria for what is considered true, rational, or valid and to reject or condemn those they perceive to be discriminatory. They insist on retaining the right to judge other positions, to criticize them, and also to supersede them. Radical feminists are not absolutists nor objectivists nor relativists nor subjectivists. They advocate a *perspectivism* which acknowledges other points of view but denies them equal value.[24]

Grosz outlines what a feminist philosophy ought to say about truth:

> Instead of a commitment to truth and objectivity, it can openly accept its own status (and that of all discourses) as context-specific. It accepts its *perspectivism,* that

[24] Elizabeth Grosz, "Philosophy," in Sneja Gunew (ed.), *Feminist Knowledge: Critique and Construct* (London: Routledge, 1990).

> fact that all discourses represent a point of view, have specific aims and objectives, often not coinciding with those of their authors. Rather than seeing itself as disinterested knowledge, it can openly avow its own political position: all texts speak from or represent particular positions within power relations.

What does Grosz mean by "perspectivism"?

Grosz, in short, stresses Ortega's circumstantiality thesis. Everyone speaks and engages in inquiry from a certain, particular set of circumstances that inevitably shapes his or her view of the world. As a feminist, Grosz stresses the political aspects of that set of circumstances. Any view is shaped in part by the power relations that constitute the political circumstances of its creation. As we have seen in examining Ortega's thought, however, that does not imply relativism. To put it crudely: that everyone is biased does not mean that there is no truth. That nobody can be fully objective does not entail that truth itself is not fully objective.

Grosz recognizes this; she does not want to draw a relativist conclusion, for she wants to be able to criticize views she finds unacceptable. But she holds that circumstances provide the key to appropriate grounds for criticism. Grosz accepts Derrida's idea that criticism should proceed by raising questions about the distinctions that form the center of the view being criticized. But she permits a wider basis for criticism. A philosophical view, she says,

> may be judged according to its *intersubjective* effects, that is, its capacity to be shared, understood, and communicated by those occupying similar positions; and also by its *intertextual* effects, that is, its capacity to affirm or undermine various prevailing or subordinated discursive systems, and the effects it has on other discourses.

In short, we may criticize a philosophical view for its political characteristics. Feminists, she insists, think strategically; they are concerned, not with truth and falsehood, but with advancing certain political goals. She advocates evaluating theories and traditions by the extent to which they advance or retard achievement of those goals.

But suppose that some philosophical theory does lead away from feminist goals. Suppose that it somehow encourages inequalities, for example, or reinforces images of the self as "a knowing subject free of personal, social, political, and moral interests." Why is that a legitimate basis for criticism? Because, she says, such a theory reflects the political circumstances that give rise to it and affects future political circumstances, criticism of both kinds of circumstances is relevant to evaluating the view. We must, in other words, see theories both as shaped by circumstances and as shaping them. We may evaluate theories by evaluating those circumstances. Admittedly, we can do so only from our own perspective. But that is why Grosz urges feminists to think strategically and make their own goals explicit.

Critics of Relativism, Perspectivism, Deconstruction, and Feminism

Relativism, perspectivism, deconstruction, and feminism have provoked criticism from a range of contemporary philosophers. Plato thought that, in defending truth against the Sophists, he was defending the possibility of philosophy itself. If there is no such thing as truth, then there is nothing for a philosopher to seek. There is moreover no point to reflection. Typically, we recommend the examined life as a way of attaining truth more reliably. But if there is no truth, there is nothing to attain, and reliability is meaningless.

Derrida, we have seen, seeks to undermine our faith in meaning by pointing out that language is a system of signs that ultimately cannot be explained except by using further signs. He advocates an attitude of freeplay, seeing the attempt to take language, meaning, and truth seriously as otherwise leading inevitably to frustration. Twenty-two hundred years earlier, Aristotle critiqued such a view:

> If, however, they [the number of possible meanings of a word] were not limited but one were to say that the word has an infinite number of meanings, obviously reasoning would be impossible; for not to have one meaning is to have no meaning, and if words have no meaning our reasoning with one another, and indeed with ourselves, has been annihilated; for it is impossible to think of anything if we do not think of one thing; but if this is possible, one name might be assigned to this thing.[25]

Contemporary American classicist Camille Paglia is one of the most flamboyant critics of deconstruction. She rejects its contention that we cannot escape language, that everything is a text. Derrida criticizes the correspondence theory of truth on the ground that we are trapped in language; we cannot link language to the world in the way the theory seems to require. Indeed, Derrida goes so far as to deny that there is such a thing as perception. We have no way to relate to the world except through the medium of language. Understanding perception as "a concept of an intuition or of a given originating from the thing itself, present itself in its meaning, independently from language," Derrida says,

> Now I don't know what perception is and I don't believe that anything like perception exists. (272)

There is no experience apart from language.

Paglia finds this assumption absurd:

How does brain science refute deconstructionism, in Paglia's view?

> Never have so many been wrong about so much. It is positively idiotic to imagine that there is no experience outside of language. I am in love with language, but never for a moment did I dream that language encompasses and determines all knowledge. It has been a truism of basic science courses for decades in America that the brain has multiple areas of function and that language belongs only to specific areas, injured by trauma and restored by surgery or speech therapy. For thousands of years, sages and mystics of both East and West have taught us about the limitations of language in seeking truth.[26]

In effect, Derrida argues that truth is correspondence with the facts; but there are no language-independent facts; therefore, there is no such thing as truth. Or, more precisely, truth is uninteresting and self-undermining; if we were ever to attain it, we would never know it. This too Paglia finds ridiculous:

---

[25] Aristotle, *Metaphysics* IV, 4, 1006b5–12, translated by W. D. Ross.

[26] Camille Paglia, "Junk Bonds and Corporate Raiders: Academe in the Hour of the Wolf," *Arion* 1991, 139–212.

> What is needed now is a return to genuine historicism, based on knowledge of and respect for the past. The fashionable French posturing—"there are no facts"—has got to stop. There are no certainties, but there are well-supported facts which we can learn and build on, always with the flexible scholarly skepticism that allows us to discard prior assumptions in the face of new evidence. If there were no facts, surgeons couldn't operate, buildings would collapse, and airplanes wouldn't get off the ground.

There is a place for freeplay in language, in other words, but it is limited. Poets may play with words, but surgeons and engineers may not. Surgeons and engineers, and the medical researchers, biologists, physicists, chemists, and other scientists whose work underwrites what they do, are not simply playing with symbolic structures. They are trying to get things right. If they succeed, patients live, buildings survive, and planes fly. If they fail, patients die, buildings fall, and planes never leave the runway or come crashing back down. Living and dying, standing and falling, flying and crashing—these are events in the world, marked, to be sure, by words, but not in any sense created by our linguistic activity. To the deconstructionists, Paglia shouts,

> Hey fellas: there's something out there that electrocutes people on beaches, collapses buildings like cardboard, and drowns ships and villages. It's called nature.

We aim at the world, that is, and, whether or not we can hit *it,* it certainly can hit *us.*

Other philosophers have criticized perspectivism and relativism. British philosopher and novelist Iris Murdoch (see Chapter 8), for example, worries about the moral consequences of relativism and deconstruction. The relativist is right to stress that particular people make assertions or hold beliefs in particular, concrete situations. We must interpret what they say and believe in those contexts. But that does not undermine the idea of truth; it merely indicates that truth is context-sensitive. Her chief complaint, however, is moral. "'Truth'," she writes, "is inseparable from individual and contextual human responsibilities."[27] We may think it is exciting to open ourselves up to a "freeplay" of language, in which traditional constraints are removed and we become the measure of all things. But ultimately this is destructive to thinking and to philosophy itself.

> If all meaning is deferred our ordinary distinctions, for instance between what is clearly true and what is dubious and what is false, are removed and we begin to lose confidence (as structuralists urge us to do) in what is made to seem the simple, old-fashioned, ordinary concept of truth and its *related morality.* If, in some 'deep sense', it cannot finally be established whether or not the cat is on the mat, then how can we have the energy to trouble ourselves about the truth or falsity of more obscure and difficult matters? (194)

Relativism, perspectivism, and deconstruction thus become licenses to play, fantasize, and, in short, become irresponsible. Play and fantasy are fine in art and literature, but not everywhere. To adapt Paglia's examples, we do not pay surgeons and engineers to play or construct linguistic fantasies. We pay them to get things right. They are responsible for getting things right, and people die if they don't. In everyday

---

[27] Iris Murdoch, *Metaphysics as a Guide to Morals* (London: Penguin, 1992), 194.

contexts, we may indulge in play and fantasy, but only up to a point. Fantasy does not put dinner on the table. In excess, it earns one admission to a mental hospital.

> Ordinary-life truth-seeking, a certain level of which is essential for survival, is a swift instinctive testing of innumerable kinds of coherence against innumerable kinds of *extra-linguistic* data. The (essential) idea of 'correspondence' is in place, not as a rival theory of truth, but as representing the fundamental fact and feel of the constant comparison and contrast of language with a non-linguistic world, with a reality not yet organised for present needs and purposes. (195–196)

Murdoch points out that correspondence theorists, coherence theorists, and pragmatists all share the idea that truth imposes constraints on us. We must, in our thinking, seek correspondence with reality, or coherence, or stability. We are responsible for meeting certain intellectual standards, however they are to be understood.

Do relativism, perspectivism, deconstruction, and feminism imply irresponsibility? Do we no longer have an obligation to seek truth? Are we free from all standards? Protagoras's relativism does seem to have that consequence. After all, if I am the measure of all things, who can measure my measuring but me? There is no obligation to seek truth, for truth is nothing over and above appearance—we already have it.

A more sophisticated relativism, as we've seen, might adopt a pragmatist strategy and define truth in a community as that on which the community would agree in the long run. But it would deny that all communities would converge to the same beliefs. That form of relativism might hold people responsible for seeking truth. It might require gathering evidence, drawing conclusions, seeking explanations, and so on—in short, seeking greater, more comprehensive coherence—while denying that the process leads to a single determinate outcome, no matter where one starts or how one pursues inquiry.

Perspectivism, too, seems to make us responsible for seeking truth. Ortega, for example, insists that we are responsible for every aspect of our lives in a uniquely personal way. Every perspective may be a legitimate perspective, but some are surely more comprehensive, more revealing, more sophisticated, than others. There is no progression to one unified perspective, or even to a set of stable perspectives, any more than there is an all-revealing perspective we might have on a country scene. But there is still a sense in which I am responsible for my own perspective and have an obligation to be aware that it is only one limited perspective among many.

Murdoch directs her attack at Derrida. Does deconstruction free us of the obligation to seek the truth? Insofar as it undermines the very concept of truth, the answer is evidently yes. But although Derrida stresses the freedom that gives us, he and those inspired by him do not think it frees us from all obligations and standards. Grosz, for example, thinks we have political obligations that imply certain epistemic obligations—that is, obligations to accept or reject assertions depending on their political effects. We should judge assertions by their capacities "to be shared, understood, and communicated by those occupying similar positions." So, we should believe what we can communicate to our peers, and reject what we cannot communicate. We should also judge assertions by their capacities "to affirm or undermine various prevailing or subordinated discursive systems." In other words, we should believe what undermines the status quo, and reject what reinforces it.

From Murdoch's perspective, of course, this is in some ways worse than having no obligations or standards at all. Someone alleges that a politician has been involved in a scandal; Grosz tells us, in effect, to look at his or her voting record. If the politician is progressive, reject the allegation; it would "undermine a subordinated discursive system," that is, hurt somebody helping the powerless. If the politician is conservative, believe the allegation; it would "undermine a prevailing discursive system," that is, hurt somebody helping those in power. The fact—whether the politician actually did what is being alleged—is utterly irrelevant. This is political correctness run amok. Our obligation to seek the truth is important precisely because it *counters* our tendency to believe and assert what favors us and reject what puts us in a bad light. Grosz substitutes obligations that reinforce that tendency. This is the moral hazard posed by deconstruction and Grosz's brand of feminism.

Contemporary British/American philosopher Susan Haack responds to relativism in another way. She defends a commonsense realism as an adequate basis for the correspondence theory of truth:

> The world—the one, real, world—is largely independent of us. Only "largely," not "completely," independent of us, because human beings intervene in the world in various ways, and because human beings and their physical and mental activities are themselves part of the world.
>
> We humans describe the world, sometimes truly, sometimes falsely. Whether a (synthetic) description of the world is true depends on what it says, and on whether the world is as it says. What a description says depends on our linguistic conventions; but, given what it says, whether it is true or it is false depends on how the world is.[28]

Haack defends the commonsense claims that there is one real world; that the world is largely independent of us, our linguistic activity, and our mental states; and that we say true things when we describe the world correctly. What we say depends on language, but whether what we say is true or false depends on the world. This is common sense, but it is also philosophically important. Anyone who wants to deny it not only flies in the face of common sense but uses terms such as 'true', 'false', 'fact', and 'corresponds' in something other than the usual way.

SUMMARY

To philosophize is to try to live an examined life—to submit your ideas and beliefs to critical reflection. That requires you to do many things. One of the most important is to seek the truth, wherever it may lead. But what is truth? The correspondence theory says that a sentence or belief is true if it corresponds with the facts. The coherence theory says that a sentence or belief is true if it fits with a coherent and comprehensive body of beliefs. The pragmatist theory says that a sentence or belief is true if an ideal community would agree to it in the long run. The relativist, finally, says that a

[28] Susan Haack, *Manifesto of a Passionate Moderate* (Chicago: University of Chicago Press, 1998), 156.

sentence or belief is true for a person if it seems true to them (Protagoras), or if he or she (or his or her community) would agree to it in the long run.

It might seem that a debate about truth is purely academic, having no impact on how people actually do anything. But theories of truth dictate styles of philosophy. A correspondence theory of truth naturally motivates an analytic philosophical method. A coherence theory naturally motivates a contextual, holistic, functional method. A pragmatist theory motivates a method focused on practical results. Varieties of relativism motivate still other approaches, some of which suggest that the search for truth is unnecessary, unimportant, or subservient to politics. How we think about and conduct the search for truth has tremendous consequences outside a philosophy classroom. As American pragmatist John Dewey (1859–1952) writes, a philosophical conception of truth "is far more than an academic deduction; it is a fighting proposition."[29]

APPENDIX: LOGIC IN A NUTSHELL

Philosophy is intimately concerned with truth. Anyone concerned with truth should also be concerned with reasoning, for successful reasoning leads us to truth. Some ways of reasoning are reliable, leading from truths to truths; others are unreliable, leading frequently from truth to falsehood. Anyone seeking to live an examined life needs to know the difference. Socrates finds that even the wisest citizens of Athens cannot defend their opinions. But he remains convinced that it is possible to think through philosophical issues carefully and systematically. To do that, it is necessary to understand some basic elements of logic, the science of reasoning.

Arguments are bits of reasoning in language. Frequently, we think of arguments as conflicts. But philosophers and logicians primarily use 'argument' in a different sense, in which one argues for a conclusion. An argument starts with some assertions and tries to justify a thesis.

Arguments

Aristotle (384–322 B.C.E.) is the founder of Western logic. Born in Stagira, he was the son of Nicomachus, the court physician to Amyntas II, the king of Macedon. Nicomachus died when Aristotle was a boy. After studying medicine, Aristotle entered Plato's Academy in Athens. He stayed twenty years until Plato's death. At forty-two, he became tutor to Alexander the Great, Amyntas's grandson, who was just thirteen. Aristotle stayed in the Macedonian court as Alexander's teacher for three years until Alexander was appointed regent. He then returned to Athens to establish his own school, the Lyceum. When Alexander died in 322 B.C.E., Athenians suspected Aristotle for his links to Macedonia. Fearing that he might be put to death as Socrates had

[29] John Dewey, Boyd H. Bode, and William Heard Kilpatrick, "An Active, Flexible Personality," National Education Association, Implications of Social-Economic Goals for Education: A Report of the Committee on Social-Economic Goals of America (Washington, D.C.: National Education Association, 1937), pp. 57–66.

been, he fled "lest the Athenians sin twice against philosophy." He died a year later in Chalcis of chronic indigestion brought about by overwork.

A contemporary of Demosthenes, the famous orator, and Euclid, who axiomatized geometry in his *Elements,* Aristotle developed an account of argument that was unsurpassed for two thousand years. This is only one of his many intellectual achievements. His treatises on astronomy, biology, physics, psychology, poetry, rhetoric, ethics, politics, and metaphysics have also been enormously influential. In the Middle Ages, in Europe, North Africa, and West Asia, Aristotle was known simply as "the Philosopher."

Aristotle defines a good argument (or, in his terms, a **syllogism**) as a

> discourse in which, certain things being stated, something other than what is stated follows of necessity from their being so. I mean by the last phrase that they produce the consequence, and by this, that no further term is required from without in order to make the consequence necessary.[30]

Today, logicians distinguish the question of what an argument *is* from the question of what makes an argument *good.*

As stated earlier, an argument starts with some assertions and tries to justify a thesis. The initial assertions of an argument are its **premises;** the thesis the argument tries to justify is its **conclusion.**

Arguments consist of **statements,** sentences that can be true or false. This is Aristotle's definition:

> Every sentence is significant . . . but not every sentence is a statement-making sentence, but only those in which there is truth and falsity.[31]

Almost every sentence in this book falls into this category. Statements are declarative, in the indicative mood; they say something about the way the world is, correctly or incorrectly.

How can we recognize arguments? The premises of an argument are *meant* to support the conclusion. We can recognize arguments, then, by recognizing when some statements are offered in support of others. We can do this most easily, in turn, if we can distinguish premises from conclusions. But how can we pick out the conclusion of an argument? In English, various words and phrases can signal the premises or the conclusion of an argument.

Conclusion Indicators

therefore	thus	hence
consequently	it follows that	in conclusion
as a result	then	must
accordingly	this implies that	this entails that
we may infer that		

Premise Indicators

because	as	for
since	given that	for the reason that

[30] Aristotle, *Prior Analytics* 24b18–22, translated by A. J. Jenkinson.

[31] Aristotle, *De Interpretatione* 4, 17a1–3, translated by E. M. Edghill.

To take an example: This is a simple argument from English philosopher Thomas Hobbes (1588–1679; see Chapter 9):

> Whatsoever we imagine is finite. Therefore there is no idea or conception of anything we call infinite.[32]

The premise is "Whatsoever we imagine is finite." The conclusion, signaled by the word 'therefore': "Therefore there is no idea or conception of anything we call infinite."

Hobbes plainly believes his premise to be true. Aristotle calls such premises advanced as truths **demonstrative.** But premises may also be advanced as hypotheses or even as assumptions that are about to be reduced to absurdity. That is, someone may draw conclusions from premises to make their consequences explicit and even to refute them. Aristotle calls such premises **dialectical.** Here, for example, is a dialectical argument from contemporary African philosopher Kwasi Wiredu:

> If all ideas are determined; and to be determined is to be false; then it follows that truth is impossible.[33]

Wiredu does not believe that all ideas are determined and that to be determined is to be false; indeed, he is trying to show that such a combination of ideas is absurd.

Questions, commands, and other kinds of sentences can appear in arguments in rhetorical fashion, making statements in a covert way. Consider this argument from ancient Chinese philosopher Mencius (372?–289 B.C.E.?; see Chapter 8):

> Is the arrow-maker less benevolent than the maker of armour of defense? And yet the arrow-maker's only fear is lest men should not be hurt, and the armour-maker's only fear is lest men should be hurt. So it is with the priest and the coffin maker. The choice of profession, therefore, is a thing in which great caution is required.[34]

The first premise seems merely to ask a question. But Mencius means to affirm that, personally, the arrow-maker is no less virtuous than the armour-maker. Yet one profession seeks to protect people, while the other seeks to injure them. Mencius concludes (signaled by 'therefore') that the choice of profession requires great caution. It does so, notice, not only because some professions require one to seek or hope for injury to others, but also because choosing or practicing such a profession requires no personal vice. One can be perfectly nice to individuals and still commit atrocities by choosing the wrong profession. The conclusion thus rests on the statement covertly expressed by Mencius's question.

Validity

The premises of an argument are meant to support the conclusion. That defines what an argument is. We must now ask, What distinguishes good from bad arguments? What makes a good argument good? In a successful argument, the premises really *do*

---

[32] Thomas Hobbes, *Leviathan* (London: Printed for Andrew Crooke, 1651).

[33] Kwasi Wiredu, *Philosophy and an African Culture* (Cambridge: Cambridge University Press, 1980).

[34] Mencius, *The Works of Mencius,* translated by James Legge, from *The Chinese Classics, Volume II* (Oxford: Clarendon, 1895), 2A7.

support the conclusion. A good argument links its premises to its conclusion in the right way.

Good arguments fall into two groups: those that are **deductively valid** and those that are **inductively reliable.** In a *deductively valid* argument, the truth of the premises *guarantees* the truth of the conclusion. If the premises are all true, then the conclusion *has* to be true. As Aristotle puts it, the conclusion "follows of necessity from" the premises. Or, as Charles Sanders Peirce explains,

> The object of reasoning is to find out, from the consideration of what we already know, something else which we do not know. Consequently, reasoning is good if it be such as to give a true conclusion from true premises, and not otherwise. Thus, the question of validity is purely one of fact and not of thinking.[35]

If the conclusion of a valid argument is false, at least one premise must also be false.

Consider, for example, the argument:

Every event has a cause.
World War II was an event.
Therefore World War II had a cause.

In any circumstance in which the premises of this argument are true, the conclusion must be true as well. It is impossible to conceive of a state of affairs in which, although every event has a cause, and World War II is an event, it nevertheless had no cause. If World War II had no cause, then either it wasn't an event, or there is at least one event that had no cause.

Here are some valid philosophical arguments, together with their *forms* and their traditional names:

	Modus ponens
If I am thinking, I must exist.	If p, then q
I am thinking.	p
Therefore, I exist.	Therefore, q
	Modus tollens
If God does not exist, then everything is permitted.	If p, then q
Not everything is permitted.	Not q
Therefore, God does not fail to exist.	Therefore, not p
	Disjunctive syllogism
God is either a body or a spirit.	p or q
God is not a body.	Not p
Therefore, God is a spirit.	Therefore, q
	Syllogism
All ideas are determined.	All A are B
Everything determined is false.	All B are C
Therefore, all ideas are false.	Therefore, all A are C

[35] Charles Sanders Peirce, "The Fixation of Belief," *Popular Science Monthly* 12 (November 1877), 1–15.

Each of these arguments is valid. If the premises are true, the conclusion must be true. In fact, any arguments of these forms are valid.

This introduction is too short to develop a detailed concept of form. But Aristotle's insight is that validity is *formal* in the sense that arguments can be classified into certain general patterns, or forms, of which individual arguments are instances. Consider the forms listed above. In each case, you can substitute a statement or term for a variable in the form to derive the argument. Each argument on the left is thus an *instance* of the form on the right.

An argument form is valid if and only if *every* instance of it is valid. An argument form is invalid if and only if *some* instance of it is invalid. To show that an argument form is invalid, we may find an instance with true premises and a false conclusion.

Consider, for example, two classic *formal fallacies,* arguments with invalid forms:

	Denying the antecedent
If a fetus is a person, abortion is wrong.	If p, then q
A fetus is not a person.	Not p
So, abortion is not wrong.	Therefore, not q
	Affirming the consequent
If a fetus is a person, abortion is wrong.	If p, then q
Abortion is wrong.	q
So, a fetus is a person.	Therefore, p

The first argument is invalid; abortion might be wrong for other reasons. To show this, we might construct a **counterexample**—an argument of the same form with true premises but a false conclusion. The following, for example, is also an instance of denying the antecedent:

If John falls off the Golden Gate Bridge, he will die.
John won't fall off the Golden Gate Bridge.
So, John won't die.

It's easy to imagine the premises being true while the conclusion is false.

Consider the second argument. It too is invalid because abortion could be wrong for other reasons. Once again, we can construct a counterexample, an argument of the same form leading from truth to falsehood:

If John falls off the Golden Gate Bridge, he will die.
John will die.
So, John will fall off the Golden Gate Bridge.

Soundness

Validity isn't everything. That an argument is valid does not mean that it establishes its conclusion. It means that the conclusion must be true *if* the premises are true. The premises, however, may or may not be true. This, for example, is a valid argument:

All mice chase cats.
Aristotle is a mouse.
Therefore, Aristotle chases cats.

An argument is **sound** if it is valid and all its premises are true. All sound arguments thus have true conclusions. Ultimately, philosophers want to say true things; they want to believe them rationally, on the basis of reasons. So they want to argue for their views and thus establish them as true. To do that, philosophers need to advance valid arguments—something logic can judge—but also start from true premises, something that goes beyond the bounds of logic. So, to evaluate an argument, you must ask first, Are the premises true? and second, Is the argument valid?

Underlying Assumptions

Often arguments leave certain premises unstated. An important philosophical task, in fact, is discovering the hidden premises or assumptions that underlie various philosophical arguments. Consider, for example, Hobbes's argument above:

> Whatsoever we imagine is finite. Therefore there is no idea or conception of anything we call infinite.

This is not valid as it stands; nothing relates ideas or conceptions to imagination. But we can ask how they must relate if the argument is to be valid. To make it valid, we need to supply a premise connecting ideas and imagination, for example:

> Everything we imagine is finite.
> If we have an idea or conception of something, we thereby imagine it.
> Therefore, we have no idea or conception of anything infinite.

Now, we can ask whether the hidden premise, "If we have an idea or conception of something, we thereby imagine it," is true or false. René Descartes (1596–1650; see Chapter 2) criticizes Hobbes on just this point, observing that we can form a coherent conception of a *chiliagon,* a thousand-sided figure, without being able to imagine it. The assumption underlying Hobbes's argument, Descartes argues, is false. So, the argument is unsound; either it is invalid, or one of its premises is false.

Evaluating Validity

Logic develops precise ways of determining whether arguments are valid. But the most powerful ways of evaluating arguments are intuitive. An argument is valid if the truth of the premises guarantees the truth of the conclusion. To show that an argument is invalid, therefore, one needs to show that the premises could all be true while the conclusion is false.

There are two ways of doing this. We have already used both to demonstrate the invalidity of denying the antecedent and affirming the consequent. The first, the *direct* method, is simply to describe a possible circumstance in which the premises were all true but the conclusion false. Consider a crude argument for relativism:

> Societies differ in their fundamental beliefs.
> Therefore, truth is relative to culture.

To show that this is invalid, we might imagine a circumstance in which societies differ in fundamental beliefs because one or both are wrong, not because truth is relative.

Aristotle devised another method, as we've seen, based on the idea of *form:* the method of *counterexamples.*

> To show that an argument is invalid, produce another argument of the same form with true premises and a false conclusion.

Recall that an argument form is invalid if and only if some instance of it is invalid. To show that an argument form is invalid, then, find an instance with true premises and a false conclusion.

To show that an individual argument is invalid, the method of counterexamples requires that we find an argument with true premises and a false conclusion that shares the *specific form* of the original argument: the most explicit form we can devise, displaying the most structure.

To apply the method of counterexamples to the argument for relativism, we find an argument with the same specific form but with true premises and false conclusion:

> Societies differ in their fundamental astronomical beliefs.
> Therefore, astronomical truth is relative to culture.

Ancient Greeks believed that the sun revolves around the earth. We believe that the earth revolves around the sun. But nobody thinks that the truth of the matter is culturally relative; the earth and sun did not switch places at some point in the last two thousand years.

Even if an argument is valid, it may not be sound; one or more premises may be false. Consider another argument sometimes advanced for relativism, the argument from the lack of a neutral vantage point. This version is offered, only to be rejected, by Ethiopian philosopher Zera Yacob (1599–1692):

> "What will other men tell me other than what is in their heart?" Indeed each one says: "My faith is right. . . ." . . . Who would be the judge for such a kind of argument? No single human being can judge: for all men are plaintiffs and defendants between themselves. . . . Where could I obtain a judge that tells the truth?[36]

We might express the form of the argument as follows:

> Members of society X use X's standards in evaluating assertions.
> Their use of X's standards biases them.
> They judge X to be right.
> Therefore, they cannot neutrally judge which society is right.

If everyone judges things by the standards of his or her own society, and this creates a bias, then none can neutrally judge which society is right. So the argument appears to be valid. One can certainly raise questions about the truth of its premises, however. Members of a society often use different standards, while people from different societies use similar standards, making the first premise doubtful. A person's use of the standards of his or her own society may not create bias if there is significant overlap between those standards and those of the competing society. It may be possible to evaluate which society is right on the basis of standards that both accept. The second premise thus seems false. Finally, members of a society can judge their own society and its standards inadequate even by its own standards; the standards themselves may contain norms of self-improvement. That casts doubt on the third premise.

---

[36] Zera Yacob, "The Treatise of Zera Yacob," in Claude Sumner, *The Source of African Philosophy: The Ethiopian Philosophy of Man* (Stuttgart: Franz Steiner Verlag Wiesbaden GmbH, 1986).

To use this argument to support relativism, one would have to argue:

Nobody can neutrally judge which society's fundamental beliefs are right.
Therefore, truths are relative to a culture.

We can combine the direct method and the method of counterexamples to show that this is not valid. Say that the Steelers and the Cowboys are about to play in the Super Bowl. Pittsburgh fans are convinced that the Steelers are the better team; Dallas fans feel similarly about the Cowboys. Before the game, there may be no way to tell who is right. But that doesn't mean that which team is better is relative to a group of fans. This argument with the same form, then, seems to have true premises but a false conclusion in such a situation:

Nobody can neutrally judge which fans' beliefs are right.
Therefore, which team is better is relative to a set of fans.

An even better example is this. Say that two groups of paleontologists have competing hypotheses about how a certain species evolved in the distant past. Suppose further that no fossil or other evidence favoring one over the other will become available. The groups, moreover, appeal to rather different standards of paleontological research. Then the premise of the following argument may be true:

Nobody can neutrally judge which hypothesis is right.
Therefore, how a certain species evolved is relative to a group of paleontologists.

But this conclusion is absurd. The species evolved however it evolved, no matter what contemporary paleontologists think.

Inductive Reliability

Valid arguments are only one species of good argument. An argument is deductively valid if and only if the truth of its premises *guarantees* the truth of its conclusion. Many successful, commonly advanced arguments, however, are not deductively valid because they carry no such guarantee. Most of our general knowledge about the world rests on **induction**—reasoning "from the known to the unknown," in the words of John Stuart Mill (1806–1873). Such reasoning is reliable but not valid deductively. Deduction dominates mathematics and a few other abstract disciplines, including philosophy. Everywhere else, induction rules. For this reason, Mill called induction "the main question of the science of logic."[37]

Arguments that are not valid may nonetheless be **inductively strong (or reliable)**. The truth of the premises of such an argument does not guarantee the truth of its conclusion, but it does make the truth of the conclusion *probable.* If the premises are true, the conclusion is likely to be true. Or, to put it another way, if the premises are true, then it is reasonable to believe the conclusion. For example, consider this argument, called an **argument from enumeration:**

Every generous person I've ever known has also been kind.
Therefore, all generous people are kind.

[37] John Stuart Mill, *A System of Logic* (New York: Harper and Brothers, 1874), 283.

It is possible for the premise to be true while the conclusion is false. There may be generous but nasty people I've never met. So the argument is invalid. Nevertheless, the premise lends some support to the conclusion. The argument is inductively strong; how strong depends, among other things, on how many generous people I've known.

As we have seen, good arguments need not only to be valid or inductively strong but also to have true premises. A sound argument is a valid argument with true premises. In any valid argument, the truth of the premises guarantees the truth of the conclusion. So a sound argument always has a true conclusion. A **cogent argument** is an inductively strong argument with true premises. In a cogent argument, the truth of the conclusion is likely but not guaranteed.

Inductively strong and deductively valid arguments do differ in two important ways. First, adding a premise can make an inductively strong argument weak. In a deductively valid argument, in contrast, the truth of the premises guarantees the truth of the conclusion. So no matter what information is added to the premises, the conclusion still follows. For example, this argument is valid:

> Socrates and Plato were philosophers.
> Therefore, Socrates was a philosopher.

It remains valid, no matter what premises we add.

But adding premises to an inductively strong argument may make it weak. The premises of an inductively strong argument support the conclusion but do not establish it conclusively. So additional information may undermine the support offered by the original premises. For example, this argument is plausible:

> Socrates and Plato were philosophers.
> Therefore, many of their students were philosophers.

Socrates and Plato undoubtedly taught philosophy to their students. So the premise offers some support for the conclusion. Adding premises, however, may destroy whatever reliability the argument has:

> Socrates and Plato were philosophers.
> They taught mostly upper-class young men destined for careers in public service.
> Therefore, many of their students were philosophers.

So adding premises may make an inductively strong argument weak, although adding premises never makes a valid argument invalid.

The second major difference between inductive and deductive arguments is that deductive validity is an all-or-nothing affair, while inductive strength is a matter of degree. An argument is valid if and only if the truth of its premises guarantees the truth of its conclusion. All valid arguments are equally valid. (A guarantee is a guarantee.) It makes no sense to make comparative judgments of validity. Nor does it make sense to speak of an argument as "somewhat valid," "moderately valid," or "very valid."

Inductive strength, in contrast, comes in degrees. Given the truth of the premises of an inductively strong argument, the conclusion is probable, and probability is a matter of degree. The premises may offer more or less support for the conclusion. So some inductively strong arguments may be stronger than others. We can speak sensibly of arguments being "somewhat strong," "moderately strong," "very strong," and the like.

Evaluating Enumerations

Arguments by enumeration generalize from known instances, having the form

Argument by Enumeration

All observed Fs are Gs.
Therefore, all Fs are Gs.

They are never deductively valid. Even if we were to enumerate all instances of a certain kind, our list of premises would not by itself imply the generalized conclusion. As British philosopher Bertrand Russell (1872–1970) noted, we would also need the premise that we have listed all the instances of the relevant kind.

Even though they are not valid, some arguments by enumeration are very strong. Dogs of all known breeds, for example, have noses. It seems reasonable to conclude that dogs of all breeds, known and unknown, observed and unobserved, have noses. Other arguments by enumeration, however, are weak. A child who has seen only one dog, which happens to be gentle, might infer that all dogs are gentle. The evidence presented by observation of one dog offers weak support for any generalization about all dogs.

What distinguishes strong from weak arguments by enumeration? Several factors help to determine the reliability of these arguments. These factors relate to characteristics of the *sample,* the class of objects appealed to in the premises.

1. *Sample Size.* How many objects of the appropriate kind have been observed? What percentage of the total population is in the sample? Other things being equal, the more objects that have been observed, the more reliable the argument from them to the conclusion. Generalizations obtained from inadequate enumeration are called **hasty.**

2. *Sample Variation.* How varied are the observed instances? How homogeneous is the sample? Other things being equal, the more varied the sample, the more reliable the argument. Ideally, we want our sample to be **representative**—to mirror the total population in its relevant characteristics. (Unrepresentative samples are **biased.**)

As the Austrian philosopher Ludwig Wittgenstein (1889–1951; see Chapter 2) pointed out, looking at just one kind of example is a common source of philosophical error. The same holds in all fields. Unless a sample is varied enough, it is likely to be biased. The bias may arise from limitations of the method used to gather the sample. It may result from habits of thought that are hard to break. And it may arise from a tendency, conscious or unconscious, to ignore contrary evidence.

Analogies

Many philosophical arguments are arguments by analogy. An **analogy** is a similarity, in certain respects, between distinct things. And an **argument by analogy** is an argument inferring a similarity from other similarities. Consider, for example, three arguments for God's existence put forward by Indian philosopher Udayana (c. 1000), who united the Nyaya (logic) and Vaisesika (particularism) schools. All of these arguments rest on analogies:

1. *Argument from effects*

Things like the earth must have a cause.
Because they are effects.
Like a pot.

By having a cause I mean active production by someone possessed of the intent to produce, and a direct knowledge concerning the matter from which the production is to be.

2. *Argument from atomic combinations*

[The world, it must be remembered, is a combination of atoms, in different degrees of complexity.] Combination is an action, and hence an action occurring at the beginning of creation that brings about the bonding of two atoms, thus originating a dyad. Such a combination is always consequent on the activity of a conscious agent.

Because it is an action.
As, for instance, the action of our bodies.

3. *Argument from the suspension of the world*

The world is supported by an active being which impedes it from falling.
Because it has the character of something suspended.
Like a twig held in the air by a bird.[38]

Note the analogies: The earth must have a cause because it is like a pot. Combinations of atoms require conscious agency because they are like actions. And the world requires support because it is "like a twig held in the air by a bird." Udayana does not spell out how the earth is like a pot or a twig or how the original combination of atoms is like a human action. But his analogies support his conclusion only if there are such similarities. Arguments by analogy have the forms:

Argument by Analogy

Object *a* has certain properties in common with Bs.
All Bs are C.
Therefore, *a* is C.

As and Bs have various properties in common.
All Bs are C.
Therefore, all As are C.

Analogical arguments are, in effect, arguments by modeling. Using them, we can reason about one situation by reasoning about another, similar situation. The situation we analyze serves as a model for the situation about which we wish to draw a conclu-

[38] Udayana, "Proofs of the Existence of God," from *Udayana's Nyayakusuanjali,* translated by José Pereira, in *Hindu Theology: A Reader* (New York: Doubleday, 1976).

sion. Modeling a situation offers many advantages. The model is usually clearer, better understood, and more familiar than the circumstance being modeled. Consequently, analyzing the model—seeing how its parts relate and interact, seeing how it evolves, reacts, and causes changes in other circumstances—is easier than reasoning directly about the less familiar and less comprehensible situation we want to understand.

Evaluating Analogical Arguments

Arguments by analogy are inductive: The existence of some similarities may make probable, but does not guarantee, the existence of further similarities. So analogies may be more or less successful. Consider Mencius's criticism of an analogical argument meant to show that virtue is the result of training and effort—nurture, in short, rather than nature:

> The philosopher Kao [Kaozi (Kao Tzu), c. 400 B.C.E.] said, "Man's nature is like the willow, and righteousness is like a cup or a bowl. The fashioning of benevolence and righteousness out of man's nature is like the making of cups and bowls from the willow."
>
> Mencius replied, "Can you, leaving untouched the nature of the willow, make with it cups and bowls? You must do violence and injury to the willow, before you can make cups and bowls with it. If you must do violence and injury to the willow in order to make cups and bowls with it, on your principles you must in the same way do violence and injury to humanity in order to fashion from it benevolence and righteousness! Your words, alas! would certainly lead all men on to reckon benevolence and righteousness to be calamities." (6A1)

There is undoubtedly some similarity between making a cup or bowl and building character. But there are also dissimilarities. In particular, you must injure the willow to make the cup. But—despite the motto "no pain, no gain"—we do not want to say that you must injure people to make them good.

In general, the strength of an analogical argument depends on several factors. They include the number and relevance of the similarities, the number and relevance of dissimilarities, the variety and number of analogous objects or circumstances, and the scope of the conclusion.

1. *The number and relevance of similarities.* The more relevant similarities the premises offer, the stronger the analogical inference. Kaozi could strengthen the argument by citing additional similarities between fashioning a bowl and developing virtue.

2. *The number and relevance of dissimilarities.* Any two objects or circumstances differ in indefinitely many ways. The mere existence of differences does not undermine the strength of an analogical argument. When the differences are relevant to the issue at hand, as above, however, they do count against the argument's strength. In general, the more relevant dissimilarities there are, the weaker the argument.

3. *The variety and number of analogous objects or circumstances.* The more objects or situations we observe with similar properties, the stronger the argument. Also, the more varied these objects or situations, the more reliable the argument.

4. *The scope of the conclusion.* The greater the scope of the conclusion we try to derive—the more informative and detailed we wish it to be—the weaker the argument becomes. A more detailed conclusion requires more extensive similarities, while it opens the door more widely for relevant dissimilarities.

5. *The possibility of using other analogies or other features of the same analogy to draw an opposed conclusion.* Sometimes it is possible to point out that another model, or even the model being invoked, can lead just as well to the opposite conclusion. Mencius does this with another of Kao's analogies:

> The philosopher Kao said, "Man's nature is like water whirling round in a corner. Open a passage for it to the east, and it will flow to the east; open a passage for it to the west, and it will flow to the west. Man's nature is indifferent to good and evil, just as the water is indifferent to the east and west."
>
> Mencius replied, "Water will indeed flow indifferently to the east or west, but will it indifferently flow up or down? The tendency of man's nature to good is like the tendency of water to flow downwards. There are none but have this tendency to good, just as all water flows downwards." (6A2)

Since additional evidence can weaken inductive arguments, one can sometimes find an analogy that directly opposes another in just this way.

Fallacies

A good argument generally presents premises to provide **evidence** for a conclusion. The conclusion follows from those premises, which are *relevant* to the conclusion *in context.* The definitions of validity and soundness, however, do not mention evidence, relevance, or context. Even sound arguments can be unsuccessful in a particular context.

In general, a **fallacy** is a kind of bad argument. Arguments committing **formal fallacies,** such as denying the antecedent and affirming the consequent, have bad forms; they are invalid. Arguments committing **informal fallacies** make other kinds of mistakes. They typically violate rules of evidence, relevance, or clarity in particular contexts. The most interesting and dangerous fallacies are those that look like good arguments.

Fallacies of Evidence The premises of a good argument offer evidence for its conclusion. Aristotle spoke of some sentences as coming before others "in the order of knowledge." If we can think of some sentences as being better known or more evident than others, then we can say that the premises of a successful argument should be more evident than the conclusion. Aristotle pointed out that "demonstration is from things more creditable and prior."[39] Or, in the words of the influential seventeenth-century *Port Royal Logic* (the standard French logic tract from the seventeenth century on), "What serves as proof must be clearer and better known than what we seek to prove."[40] The premises of a good argument should be justifiable independently of the conclusion. Several fallacies can result from violating this principle.

[39] Aristotle, *Prior Analytics* II, 16, 64b32.

[40] Antoine Arnauld (1611–1694), *Logic, or, The Art of Thinking* (Indianapolis: Bobbs-Merrill, 1964; originally published in 1662), 247.

1. Begging the question (petitio principii) An argument **begs the question** if and only if the premises include or presuppose the conclusion.[41] The most interesting kind of question begging occurs when the conclusion does not appear in the premises directly but is *presupposed* by the premises—that is, when no one could assert the premises without already taking the conclusion for granted. If the premises presuppose the argument's conclusion, then the argument fails to establish its conclusion. The premises cannot provide evidence for the conclusion because they already assume it. A classic instance of an argument whose premises presuppose its conclusion is this:

The Bible says that God exists.
The Bible was inspired by God.
Any writing inspired by God is true.
Therefore God exists.

The second premise, 'The Bible was inspired by God', presupposes the conclusion. One cannot assert it without assuming that God exists. Consequently, any evidence for the second premise would automatically be evidence for the conclusion, and any evidence against the conclusion would tell against that premise. The premise cannot be any more evident than the conclusion. The argument is therefore fallacious.

2. Complex question An argument commits the fallacy of **complex question** if and only if its premises include a question that presupposes the conclusion. Some questions have presuppositions: they cannot be asked without taking certain things for granted. They cannot be answered unless what they presuppose is true. The classic case is "Have you stopped beating your wife?" You cannot answer yes or no without in effect admitting your former wife-beating. Another example of a complex question occurs at the beginning of Cicero's first and most famous oration against Cataline: "How much longer will you abuse us, O Cataline? How much longer will your unbridled boldness thrash itself about?" These questions presuppose that Cataline has been abusing us with reckless audacity.

Does Cicero commit a fallacy? Not necessarily. A question gets a reasoner into trouble only when it presupposes the conclusion of the argument. Cicero's oration avoids it by going on to present evidence of Cataline's abuses. This suggests an important way of repairing complex question or begging the question fallacies: *supply independent evidence for the conclusion.*

3. Incomplete enumeration (false dichotomy) An argument commits the fallacy of **incomplete enumeration** if and only if it presupposes a disjunction that does not include all available possibilities. Sometimes we seem to face dilemmas: your money or

[41] This definition is Bishop Richard Whately's. See his *Elements of Logic* (New York: Sheldon and Company, 1869), page 179: An argument begs the question "when one of the Premisses (whether true or false) is either plainly equivalent to the conclusion, or depends on that for its own reception." See also page 220: In a question-begging argument, "one of the Premisses either is manifestly the same in sense with the Conclusion, or is actually proved from it or is such as the persons you are addressing are not likely to know, or admit, except as an inference from the Conclusion. . . ." Compare Aristotle's definition, which relates even more directly to evidence: "Whether a person does not conclude at all, or whether he does so through things more unknown, or equally unknown, or whether he concludes what is prior through what is posterior" (*Prior Analytics* II, 16, 64b30–32).

your life, truth or consequences, trick or treat. These dilemmas may be real. At times, however, they are only apparent; there are other possibilities. Whenever an argument passes over possibilities it ought to recognize, it is guilty of the fallacy of incomplete enumeration.

Fallacies of Relevance Relevance requires that an argument be directed at the point at issue. Sometimes a person advances an irrelevant argument as an intentional bit of sophistry to avoid a tough issue. Sometimes the parties to the conversation are confused about what the issue really is; sometimes they are arguing at cross purposes. And sometimes people agree about what the issue is at the outset but change the issue during the course of the conversation.

An argument that violates relevance is called an ***ignoratio elenchi***—an argument ignorant of its own goal or purpose—and is therefore fallacious. It misses the point, in effect slipping in one conclusion in place of another.

Some fallacies result from focusing not on the issue but on the arguer. ***Ad hominem* (or *ad personam*) arguments,** arguments "to the man (or person)," attempt to refute positions by attacking those who hold or argue for them.

4. Ad hominem abusive An argument is an **abusive *ad hominem*** argument if and only if it purports to discredit a position by insulting those who hold it. Some writers have argued that the philosophy of Bishop Berkeley (1685–1753; see Chapter 5), according to which all "material" objects are really just complexes of ideas, stems from an obsessive-compulsive neurosis—in Freudian theory, bad toilet training. This psychological hypothesis is not itself a fallacy. But to use it to discredit Berkeley's philosophy, to argue that it is false, is to commit an *ad hominem* fallacy. Other writers have condemned the works of German philosopher Friedrich Nietzsche (1844–1900) as the ravings of a lunatic. Nietzsche did spend the last years of his life in a mental institution; this does not show, however, that what he wrote is false. Neurotics and even madmen may argue validly and speak truly.

5. Ad hominem circumstantial An argument is a **circumstantial *ad hominem*** argument if and only if it purports to discredit a position by appealing to the circumstances or characteristics of those who hold it. Usually, circumstantial *ad hominem* arguments charge a person or group with holding a position solely because it serves their own interests.

Evaluating the reliability of an argument is very different from evaluating the reliability of a person. We decide whether to accept what someone else says in part on the basis of how reliable we judge that person to be. However, when someone advances an argument, giving reasons for a conclusion, then reliability is no longer so important. The reliability of others bears on whether we should accept any premises they introduce but not on whether their arguments are good and deserve to convince us. In the words of Samuel Johnson,

> Nay, Sir, argument is argument. You cannot help paying regard to their arguments if they are good. If it were testimony, you might disregard it. . . . Testimony is like an arrow shot from a long bow; the force of it depends on the strength of the hand

> that draws it. Argument is like an arrow shot from a cross bow, which has equal force though shot by a child.[42]

Circumstantial *ad hominem* arguments may establish something about the reliability of an opponent but do not establish the incorrectness of that person's position.

6. Tu quoque An argument is ***tu quoque*** if and only if it purports to discredit a position by charging those who hold it with inconsistency or hypocrisy. *Tu quoque* (pronounced too-KWOH-kway) literally means "you, too." When charging someone with inconsistency, a *tu quoque* accuses an opponent of not believing his or her own argument: If the opponent does not believe it, then surely the rest of us do not need to take it seriously. When charging someone with hypocrisy, a *tu quoque* accuses an opponent of failing to practice what he or she is preaching: If the opponent does not act on the basis of his or her own argument, then the rest of us may ignore it also.

7. Red herring An argument is a **red herring** if and only if it tries to undermine an opponent's argument by introducing a point irrelevant to the issue at hand. Such a point proves nothing concerning the issue. But a red herring is usually introduced as if it were pertinent, and may succeed in convincing an audience in spite of its irrelevance. It may show something resembling the desired conclusion, or it may wield great emotional power. In either case, however, it confuses the issue.

8. Straw man An argument erects a **straw man** if and only if it tries to justify rejecting a position by attacking a different and usually weaker position. This fallacy occurs when someone attacks an opponent's position by exaggerating it to make it seem ridiculous. It is named for the practice of training soldiers by having them attack straw men. Defeating an opponent made of straw is obviously not the same as defeating a real enemy.

9. Appeal to the people (or gallery) (ad populum) An argument is an **appeal to the people (or to the gallery)** if and only if it tries to justify its conclusion by appealing to the audience's emotions. Some politicians have made reputations for using nonrational, emotional appeals to win support for their positions. Any argument based not on rational considerations but on emotional appeals counts as an appeal to the people. (Such arguments are sometimes called "appeals to the gallery" to allude to politicians' practice of directing arguments at the observers in the gallery rather than at fellow legislators.)

10. Appeal to common practice An argument **appeals to common practice** if and only if it tries to justify a kind of action by appealing to the common practice of the community. "When in Rome, do as the Romans do." The conclusion asserts that a certain kind of action is acceptable, permissible, or even obligatory. The premises indicate that the kind of action is common practice: that everyone, or most people, or at

---

[42] Samuel Johnson, quoted in David Hackett Fischer, *Historians' Fallacies* (New York: Harper and Row, 1970), 282.

least many people are doing it. The argument urges the listener to jump on the bandwagon and agree with the conclusion.

11. Appeal to force (ad baculum) An argument **appeals to force** if and only if it tries to justify a kind of action by threatening the audience. The threat may be physical: A mobster may make you an offer you cannot refuse. (As Sherlock Holmes tells Watson, "I should be very much obliged if you would slip your revolver into your pocket. An Eley's No. 2 is an excellent argument with gentlemen who can twist steel pokers into knots."[43]) Or the threat may be financial: An employer may tell workers that they will be fired if they reveal secrets; a law may penalize speeding or littering with a hefty fine. Or the threat may involve embarrassment: A lobbyist may intimidate a legislator by threatening to expose sordid details of past business dealings.

12. Appeal to pity (ad misericordiam) An argument **appeals to pity** if and only if it tries to justify a kind of action by arousing sympathy or pity in the audience over the consequences of the action. In general, an appeal to pity is an argument relying on arousing feelings of sympathy or pity among the listeners.

Inductive Fallacies Recall that some good arguments are inductively strong rather than deductively valid. If their premises are true, their conclusions are probable but not guaranteed. Some fallacies are common inductive errors.

13. Appeal to ignorance An argument **appeals to ignorance** if and only if it tries to justify its conclusion by appealing to what is not known. Most arguments try to establish a conclusion by relying on what is known. Some, however, rely on what is unknown. This is not always fallacious. A famous example of a good inference from lack of evidence is in a Sherlock Holmes story:

> "Is there any other point to which you would wish to draw my attention?"
> "To the curious incident of the dog in the night-time."
> "The dog did nothing in the night-time."
> "That is the curious incident," remarked Sherlock Holmes.[44]

Nevertheless, arguments on the basis of a lack of knowledge easily go awry. They succeed only under certain conditions. A lack of knowledge shows something only if there has been a competent, thorough, unfrustrated attempt to secure that knowledge. Otherwise, pointing toward a lack of knowledge is an unfair attempt to shift the burden of proof onto one's opponents.

14. Appeal to authority An argument **appeals to authority** if and only if it tries to justify its conclusion by citing the opinions of authorities. Appealing to authorities to establish facts or conclusions is not in itself a fallacy. Modern life is so complex that we all rely extensively on other people for information. This is fine, provided that the

---

[43] Sir Arthur Conan Doyle, "The Adventure of the Speckled Band," *The Adventures of Sherlock Holmes* (Secaucus: Castle Books, 1980; originally published in *The Strand,* 1891), 115.
[44] Sir Arthur Conan Doyle, "The Adventure of Silver Blaze," *The Adventures of Sherlock Holmes* (Secaucus: Castle Books, 1980; originally published in *The Strand,* 1891), 196–197.

people relied on are trustworthy and knowledgeable about the matter at hand. But we must be careful to assess the reliability of our sources.

When is it appropriate to base a conclusion on the opinions of authorities? This is a traditional topic in Indian epistemology. Vatsyayana (c. 400), for example, writes:

> A trustworthy person is the speaker who has the direct knowledge of an object and is motivated by the desire of communicating the object as directly known by him.[45]

This is very restrictive: a trustworthy person must have direct knowledge. There can be no chains of testimony; knowledge must be first- or second-hand. Most contemporary philosophers would loosen the requirements to something like these: (1) The subject must be one on which there can be authorities. Some philosophers have held that there are no authorities on moral questions. Very likely nobody can be an authority on whether God exists or on what the one true religion is. (2) The opinions cited in the argument must fall within the authority's area of expertise. (3) The authority must be trustworthy; there must be no additional factors which might make the expert misrepresent matters.

15. Accident Writers on logic have described the fallacy of *accident* in two quite different ways. First, and as we will use the term, the fallacy of accident has been described as making "an unqualified judgment of a thing on the basis of an accidental characteristic."[46] Philosophers have traditionally held that some attributes of a thing are essential to it in the sense that without them the thing would not be what it is, while others are accidental in the sense that the thing could retain its identity without them. (See Chapter 5.) Your having a mind, for example, is essential to you; without a mind, you would not be the person you are. But reading this book is accidental to you; you could stop reading it without ceasing to be you. An argument commits the fallacy of **accident** if and only if it tries to justify its conclusion by treating an accidental feature of something as essential.

A famous and humorous example occurs in Shakespeare's *Henry V,* where Fluellen argues that King Henry of Monmouth is the equal of Alexander the Great of Macedon:

> If you look at the maps of the 'orld, I warrant you sall find, in the comparisons between Macedon and Monmouth, that the situations, look you, is both alike. There is a river in Macedon, and there is also moreover a river at Monmouth. It is called Wye at Monmouth; but it is out of my prains what is the name of the other river. But 'tis all one; 'tis alike as my fingers is to my fingers, and there is salmons in both.

Ruling a kingdom with a river containing salmon is accidental to being a great king; Fluellen's argument mistakes it for an essential feature of greatness.

16. Misapplication The fallacy of accident has also been characterized as "applying a general rule to a particular case whose 'accidental' circumstances render the rule inapplicable."[47] To avoid confusion, we will call this fallacy *misapplication.* An argument

---

[45] Vatsyayana's Commentary on the *Nyaya-sutra* (Translated by Mrinalkanti Gangopaghyay; Calcutta: Indian Studies, 1982).

[46] Antoine Arnauld (1611–1694), *Logic, or, The Art of Thinking* (Indianapolis: Bobbs-Merrill, 1964; originally published in 1662), 259.

[47] Irving Copi, *Introduction to Logic* (New York: Macmillan, 1979), 95.

commits a fallacy of **misapplication** if and only if it tries to justify its conclusion about a particular case by appealing to a rule that is generally sound but inapplicable or outweighed by other considerations in that case. Plato discusses a classic example of misapplication in the *Republic:*

> . . . are we to say that justice or right is simply to speak the truth and to pay back any debt one may have contracted? Or are these same actions sometimes right and sometimes wrong? I mean this sort of thing, for example: everyone would surely agree that if a friend has deposited weapons with you when he was sane, and he asks for them when he is out of his mind, you should not return them. The man who returns them is not doing right, nor is one who is willing to tell the whole truth to a man in such a state.[48]

To apply the rules "Tell the truth" and "Keep your promises" in this case would be to misapply them. These rules implicitly contain an "other things being equal" clause. But sometimes other things are not equal. Your obligation to prevent harm to your friend and others outweighs your obligation to tell the truth and keep your promise.

17. Hasty generalization To draw conclusions about a kind or large class of things, we typically examine only some of them. If we choose carefully which and how many things to sample, our conclusions may be highly reliable. If we do not, however, our conclusions may be unreliable. We may sample too few objects. Or the objects we examine may be atypical or all of one particular sort. In such cases we commit the fallacy of hasty generalization.

18. False cause One form of causal fallacy has a Latin name, ***post hoc, ergo propter hoc***—"after this, therefore because of this." As the name suggests, it involves drawing a causal conclusion simply from the temporal ordering of events. So the form of the argument is

E preceded F
Therefore E caused F

Clearly, this is a poor and unreliable form of argument. The Hundred Years' War occurred before the discovery of uranium, but it would be preposterous to conclude that the Hundred Years' War caused uranium to be discovered.

Another unreliable form of causal inference concerns statistical correlation. A correlation between two kinds of events allows inferring the existence of some causal connection but yields no information about its exact form or nature. If one quantity varies with another, changes in the former may cause changes in the latter, or changes in the latter may cause changes in the former, or changes in both quantities may result from some other causal mechanism. Finally, of course, the correlation may be just a coincidence. But it can be tempting to draw a straightforward causal conclusion from a correlation:

---

[48] Plato, *Republic,* 331c, translated by G. M. A. Grube (Indianapolis: Hackett Publishing Company, 1974).

E correlates with F.
Therefore E causes F.

That also constitutes a fallacy of false cause.

Fallacies of Clarity Sometimes arguments fail by being unclear. A premise understood in one way might be true but fail to support the conclusion; read in another way, it might support the conclusion but turn out to be false. Several fallacies arise from unclarity.

19. Equivocation An argument is guilty of **equivocation** if and only if it tries to justify its conclusion by relying on an ambiguity in a word or phrase. Most words have more than one meaning. Sometimes context does not determine which is intended. If the listener attaches a meaning to a word that the speaker did not intend, then the information the listener draws from the conversation is not what the speaker meant to convey.

20. Amphiboly An argument is guilty of **amphiboly** if and only if it tries to justify its conclusion by relying on an ambiguity in sentence structure. Some sentences are ambiguous not because they contain ambiguous words or phrases but because of their grammatical construction. Such sentences are *syntactically ambiguous* or *amphibolous;* they can be read in two different ways because they have two different syntactic or grammatical structures.

The German philosopher Immanuel Kant (1724–1804; see Chapters 3, 5, and 8) entitled his greatest work *Kritik der Reinen Vernunft* (*Critique of Pure Reason*). This is ambiguous in both English and German. Is pure reason the agent or the object of the critique? That is, is the title the nominalized form of *x critiques pure reason* (as with *the defeat of the Spanish Armada*) or of *pure reason critiques x* (as with *the ride of Paul Revere*)? Probably Kant intended both.

Another serious example concerns versions of the cosmological argument for God's existence offered by Thomas Aquinas (1225–1274) and John Locke (1632–1704; see Chapters 3, 4, and 9). At a crucial point in Aquinas's third proof, for example, he argues:

> We observe in things something that can be, and can not be, for we observe them springing up and dying away, and consequently being and not being. Now not everything can be like this, for whatever can not be, once was not. If all things could not be, therefore, at one time there was nothing.

But 'All things could not be' is ambiguous. His argument for it interprets it as meaning, 'Everything is such that it is possible for it not to exist'. But his conclusion, "at one time there was nothing," interprets it as meaning 'It would be possible for everything not to exist' (all at once, that is). The proof seems to depend on an amphiboly.

As G. W. F. Leibniz (1646–1716; see Chapter 3) pointed out, something similar happens in Locke's proof. He maintains that something has existed from all eternity. In support of this, he argues that if at any time nothing had existed, nothing could exist now. He concludes from it that there is an eternal being. But this move relies on two different readings of *something has existed from all eternity.* His premises support the assertion that at any time something or other existed at that time, but not the stronger claim that some one thing—God—has existed at every point in time.

21. Accent An argument is guilty of **accent** if and only if it tries to justify its conclusion by relying on presuppositions arising from a change in stress in a premise. Emphasis on a particular word or phrase suggests that there is an important contrast between what that word or phrase conveys and some alternative. To jump to a conclusion on the basis of such a contrast in the absence of additional information is to commit the fallacy of accent.

An old joke embodies the fallacy of accent. The first mate on a sailing ship had been doing a good job but went ashore one day and got rip-roaring drunk. The captain wrote in the log, "The first mate was drunk today." The next day, when the first mate read the log, he became angry and began thinking of ways to take revenge. That evening, he came up with an idea. He wrote in the log, "The captain was sober today."

22. Composition and division The fallacy of **composition** consists in attributing something to a whole or group because it can be attributed to the parts or members. An individual pin dropping makes no perceptible sound, but it is not reasonable to conclude that dropping a boxful of pins would make no perceptible sound. Similarly, each book in a library collection may be good without the collection as a whole being good.

A classic case of the fallacy of composition occurs in a proof of the principle of utility given by British philosopher John Stuart Mill (1806–1873; see Chapters 8 and 9). The principle of utility says that each of us ought to maximize happiness—not just our own happiness but everyone's happiness ("the general happiness"). In a key passage, his argument moves from individual happiness to everyone's happiness:

> No reason can be given why the general happiness is desirable, except that each person, so far as he believes it to be attainable, desires his own happiness. This, however, being a fact, we have not only all the proof which the case admits of, but all which it is possible to require, that happiness is a good, that each person's happiness is a good to that person, and the general happiness, therefore, a good to all aggregate of all persons.[49]

Having shown that "each person's happiness is a good to that person," he concludes that "the general happiness" is "a good to the aggregate of all persons." But this does not follow. Consider Mill's premise: "Each person . . . desires his own happiness." This does not imply that everyone desires everyone's happiness, which is what his conclusion seems to require.

The fallacy of **division** is the inverse of the fallacy of composition. It involves arguing from the properties of a group or whole to the properties of members or parts. That a forest is verdant and dense does not imply that all, or even most, trees in it are verdant and dense. That a group tends toward violent behavior does not establish that the individual members tend toward violent behavior. And that our overall system of beliefs is well confirmed does not imply that each belief is well confirmed.

[49] John Stuart Mill, *Utilitarianism* (Indianapolis: Hackett, 1979; originally published, 1861), 34.

Review Questions

1. What is the Socratic method?
2. Compare Socrates's conception of philosophy to that of Confucius. How are they similar? How do they differ?
3. What is the difference between a semantic and a philosophical account of truth?
4. What is the correspondence theory of truth? Compare the versions offered by Aristole, Aquinas, and Russell. Explain the connection between the correspondence theory and the analytic method in philosophy.
5. What is the coherence theory of truth? To what conception of philosophy does it give rise?
6. What is the pragmatic theory of truth? How does it differ from the correspondence theory? The coherence theory?
7. How does Plato argue against Protagoras's relativism? Do his arguments succeed?
8. How does perspectivism differ from relativism? Do Plato's arguments apply to it?
9. What is deconstruction? How does it challenge the correspondence theory of truth?
10. Explain Murdoch's worry about the moral hazard posed by deconstruction. Is her worry justified? Do feminism and relativism engender a similar worry?

Terms for Review

absolutism (or **objectivism**) The thesis that we can speak of sentences, assertions, or beliefs—in a given language and given context—as objectively true or false without reference to a speaker, society, or interpretive community.

accent The fallacy of trying to justify a conclusion by relying on presuppositions arising from a change in stress in the premise.

accident An argument that tries to justify its conclusion by treating an accidental feature of something as essential.

ad hominem (or ***ad personam***) **argument** An argument that attempts to refute a position by attacking those who hold or argue for it. An argument is an *abusive ad hominem* argument if and only if it purports to discredit a position by insulting those who hold it. An argument is a *circumstantial ad hominem* argument if and only if it purports to discredit a position by appealing to the circumstances or characteristics of those who hold it. An argument is *tu quoque* if and only if it purports to discredit a position by charging those who hold it with inconsistency or hypocrisy.

affirming the consequent An informal fallacy having the form 'If *p*, then *q*; *q*; therefore, *p*'.

ahimsa **(noninjury)** The thesis that one should not injure or kill any sentient being, popularized in modern times by Mahatma Gandhi and propagated in ancient and classical India foremost by Jains.

amphiboly An ambiguity in sentence structure. Also, an argument relying on such an ambiguity.

analogy A similarity in certain respects between distinct things.

analytic method A philosophical method of seeking to understand complex wholes by analyzing their parts.

analytic philosophy The style of philosophy that has dominated the philosophical community in Britain and the United States throughout the twentieth century but extends back to Plato and Aristotle, centering on breaking down complex problems into simple parts.

appeal to authority An argument that tries to justify its conclusion by citing the opinions of authorities.

appeal to common practice An argument that tries to justify a kind of action by appealing to the common practice of the community.

appeal to force An argument that tries to justify a kind of action by threatening the audience.

appeal to ignorance An argument that tries to justify its conclusion by appealing to what is not known.

appeal to pity An argument that tries to justify a kind of action by arousing sympathy or pity in the audience over the consequences of the action.

appeal to the people (or **to the gallery**) An argument that tries to justify its conclusion by appealing to the audience's emotions.

argument by analogy An argument inferring a similarity from other similarities.

argument from enumeration An argument of the form 'All observed Fs are Gs; therefore, all Fs are Gs'.

argument from error (or **illusion**) The argument that people make mistakes (dream things we know not to be real, misperceive things, misjudge situations, draw the wrong conclusions, etc.). People are wrong when things are not as they appear to them. Therefore, there is a difference between appearance and reality.

argument A discourse that starts with some assertions and tries to justify a thesis.

begging the question An argument in which the premises include or presuppose the conclusion.

biased sample A sample that does not mirror the total population in its relevant characteristics.

cogent argument An inductively strong argument with true premises.

coherence theory of truth The theory holding that a sentence or belief is true if it coheres with a comprehensive theory of the world.

complex question A question that presupposes a conclusion; also, an argument relying on such a premise.

composition The fallacy of attributing something to a whole or group because it can be attributed to the parts or members.

conclusion The thesis an argument tries to justify.

concordance In Peirce, coherence; the agreement with the ideal limit of inquiry that defines truth.

contextualism A method that stresses understanding things in the contexts in which they occur.

correspondence theory The theory holding that a sentence (or statement or belief) is true if it corresponds with reality—that is, if it corresponds to some fact. It is false if there is no corresponding fact.

counterexample To an argument: an argument of the same form with true premises but a false conclusion. To a principle: a particular case in which the principle gives the wrong result.

deconstruction A method of uncovering inconsistencies in theories, literary or philosophical works, or intellectual traditions. It focuses on binary oppositions—good/bad, right/wrong, true/false, for example—that reveal the structure of the thought being analyzed. It then proceeds to show how the theory, work, or tradition under consideration undermines those very oppositions.

deductively valid argument An argument in which the truth of the premises guarantees the truth of the conclusion.

demonstrative premise A premise advanced as true.

denying the antecedent An informal fallacy having the form 'If *p*, then *q*; not *p*; therefore, not *q*.'

dialectic (also called **Socratic method**) Socrates asks what piety or courage or friendship or justice is. Someone answers. Socrates analyzes the proposed definition and begins asking questions, leading the parties to the conversation to see that the definition cannot be right. Sometimes the definition is unclear; sometimes it includes too much; sometimes it does not include enough. Someone then proposes another definition, and the process continues.

dialectical premise A premise advanced as a hypothesis or as an assumption to be reduced to absurdity.

division The fallacy of arguing from the properties of a group or whole to the properties of members or parts.

epistemology The theory of knowledge, studying what we know, how we know it, and what if anything lies beyond the bounds of knowledge.

equivocation An ambiguity in a word or phrase. Also, an argument relying on such an ambiguity.

ethics The pursuit of good judgment about action, asking questions such as, What should I do? What kind of person should I be? How should we as a society organize ourselves?

evidence Information supporting or disconfirming a statement.

fallacy A kind of bad argument.

fallibilism The thesis that no view is absolutely certain.

false cause An argument that inappropriately draws a causal conclusion.

formal fallacy An invalid argument with a bad form.

functionalism The thesis that we must understand things in terms of the functions they play in a larger whole.

hasty generalization An argument that draws a conclusion about a kind or large class of things on the basis of a small or biased sample.

historicism The thesis that truth is relative to a culture or historical epoch.

holism The thesis that we must ultimately evaluate beliefs by evaluating their coherence with a comprehensive system of beliefs.

idealism The thesis that reality is mind-dependent.

ideal limit In Peirce's thought, the state of knowledge we approach more and more closely as we engage in scientific inquiry under perfect conditions.

ignoratio elenchi An argument ignorant of its own goal or purpose. It misses the point, in effect slipping in one conclusion in place of another.

incomplete enumeration An argument presupposing a disjunction that does not include all available possibilities.

induction Reasoning from the known to the unknown, in John Stuart Mill's phrase; the truth of the premises does not guarantee the truth of the conclusion, but, if the argument is reliable, does make it probable.

inductively strong (or **reliable**) **argument** An argument in which the truth of the premises does not guarantee the truth of its conclusion but does make the truth of the conclusion probable.

informal fallacy An argument that violates rules of evidence, relevance, or clarity in particular contexts.

junzi Superior person; literally "child of a ruler." In Confucius, one of noble character.

liar sentence A sentence that asserts its own falsehood (for example, 'This sentence is false').

logical atomism The view advocated by Bertrand Russell that the world consists of items that are logically simple (that is, indefinable but capable together of defining everything else).

maybeism The Jain thesis that every view should be regarded as right *maybe* ('*syat*', 'in some respects'). There is at least a grain of truth in every position; the 'maybe' directs us to find and appreciate what is correct in what an opponent is saying.

metalanguage A language expanded to include a truth predicate for another language.

metaphysics The study of what there is and how those things relate to each other.

misapplication An argument that tries to justify its conclusion about a particular case by appealing to a rule that is generally sound but inapplicable or outweighed by other considerations in that case.

naya In Jainism, a perspective; a way of seeing and understanding the world.

nonabsolutism The Jain view that no metaphysical claim should be taken as absolutely true.

noninjury (*ahimsa*) The thesis that one should not injure or kill any sentient being, popularized in modern times by Mahatma Gandhi and propagated in ancient and classical India foremost by Jains.

object language A language without the predicate 'true'.

objectivism (or **absolutism**) The thesis that we can speak of sentences, assertions, or beliefs—in a given language and given context—as objectively true or false, period, without reference to a speaker, society, or interpretive community.

perspectivism The thesis that one can say whether something is right or wrong only relative to a perspective, standpoint, or point of view.

philosophical theory of truth A theory that tries to go beyond accounting for inferences involving the word 'true' by explaining what *makes* true sentences true.

post hoc, ergo propter hoc "After this, therefore because of this." An argument drawing a causal conclusion simply from the temporal ordering of events.

pragmatist theory of truth The theory holding that truth is "the opinion which is fated to be agreed to by all who investigate."

premise One of the initial assertions of an argument, used to justify the conclusion.

pre-Socratics Ancient Greek philosophers such as Thales, Heraclitus, and Parmenides, who preceded Socrates.

red herring An argument that tries to undermine an opponent's argument by introducing a point irrelevant to the issue at hand.

relativism The thesis that there are no universally valid truths about the world.

representative sample A sample that mirrors the total population in its relevant characteristics.

semantic theory of truth A theory that gives an account of the meaning of the word 'true' by accounting for inferences we make involving that word.

Socratic method (also called **dialectic**) Socrates asks what piety or courage or friendship or justice is. Someone answers. Socrates analyzes the proposed definition and begins asking questions, leading the parties to the conversation to see that the definition cannot be right. Sometimes the definition is unclear; sometimes it includes too much; sometimes it does not include enough. Someone then proposes another definition, and the process continues.

sound argument A valid argument with true premises.

statement A sentence that can be true or false.

straw man An argument that tries to justify rejecting a position by attacking a different and usually weaker position.

superior person (*junzi*, literally "child of a ruler") In Confucius, one of noble character.

syat 'Maybe', 'in some respects', 'from some perspective'.

syllogism In Aristotle's original usage, a valid argument; now, usually, an argument consisting of two premises and a conclusion, together containing three general terms.

target sentences (or **(T)-sentences**) Sentences of the form "'Snow is white' is true if and only if snow is white."

tu quoque An argument that purports to discredit a position by charging those who hold it with inconsistency or hypocrisy.

For Further Reading

Socrates is a key figure in most of Plato's dialogues. The *Euthyphro, Apology, Crito,* and *Phaedo* tell the story of the trial and death of Socrates. Other accessible early dialogues giving insight into the Socratic method are the *Laches* (on courage), the *Charmides* (on self-control), and the *Lysis* (on friendship). Good secondary works on Socrates include A. E. Taylor, *Socrates* (London: Methuen, 1933) and Gregory Vlastos, *Socrates: Ironist and Moral Philosopher* (Ithaca: Cornell University Press, 1991).

Confucius's *Analects* are highly readable. Translations of selections from it and other key texts of Chinese philosophy appear in Wing-tsit Chan (ed.), *A Source Book in Chinese Philosophy* (Princeton: Princeton University Press, 1963). Good secondary works on Confucius include A. C. Graham, *Disputers of the Tao* (LaSalle: Open Court, 1989) and David L. Hall and Roger T. Ames, *Thinking Through Confucius* (Albany: State University of New York Press, 1987).

There are helpful discussions of Tarski's semantic conception of truth in W. V. O. Quine, *Philosophy of Logic* (Englewood Cliffs: Prentice-Hall, 1970) and R. M. Sainsbury, *Paradoxes* (Cambridge: Cambridge University Press, 1988). An important scholarly paper on Tarski's work is Hartry Field, "Tarski's Theory of Truth," *Journal of Philosophy,* 1972. Important but difficult recent work on the semantic theory of truth includes

Saul Kripke, "Outline of a Theory of Truth," *Journal of Philosophy,* 1975; Jon Barwise and John Etchemendy, *The Liar: An Essay on Truth and Circularity* (New York: Oxford University Press, 1987); Vann McGee, *Truth, Vagueness, and Paradox* (Indianapolis: Hackett, 1991); Dorothy Grover, *A Prosentential Theory of Truth* (Princeton: Princeton University Press, 1992); Robert Koons, *Paradoxes of Belief and Strategic Rationality* (Cambridge: Cambridge University Press, 1992); Anil Gupta and Nuel Belnap, *The Revision Theory of Truth* (Cambridge: MIT Press, 1993); and Scott Soames, *Understanding Truth* (New York: Oxford University Press, 1999).

Russell's discussions of truth occur in *The Problems of Philosophy* (London: Williams and Norgate, 1912) and in *An Inquiry into Meaning and Truth* (New York: W. W. Norton, 1940). An excellent secondary work on Russell is R. M. Sainsbury, *Russell* (London: Routledge and Kegan Paul, 1979).

For more on the pragmatist theory of truth, see William James, *The Meaning of Truth* (New York: Greenwood Press, 1909; reprinted by Cambridge: Harvard University Press, 1975); George Santayana, *The Realm of Truth* (New York: C. Scribner's Sons, 1938); and Cheryl J. Misak, *Truth and the End of Inquiry: A Peircean Account of Truth* (Oxford: Oxford University Press, 1991). A good scholarly work on Peirce is Manley H. Thompson, *The Pragmatic Philosophy of C. S. Peirce* (Chicago: University of Chicago Press, 1953).

For general reading on pragmatism, see Amelie Rorty (ed.), *Pragmatic Philosophy: An Anthology* (Garden City: Anchor, 1966); H. S. Thayer (ed.), *Pragmatism: The Classic Writings* (New York: New American Library, 1970); Charles Morris, *The Pragmatic Movement in American Philosophy* (New York: G. Braziller, 1970); John E. Smith, *Purpose and Thought: The Meaning of Pragmatism* (New Haven: Yale University Press, 1978); Bruce Kuklick, *The Rise of American Philosophy* (New Haven: Yale University Press, 1977); and H. S. Thayer, *Meaning and Action: A Critical History of Pragmatism* (Indianapolis: Hackett, 1981).

Important contemporary pragmatists include Hilary Putnam, author of *Meaning and the Moral Sciences* (London: Routledge and Kegan Paul, 1978), *Reason, Truth, and History* (Cambridge: Cambridge University Press, 1981), *Representation and Reality* (Cambridge: MIT Press, 1988), and *Pragmatism: An Open Question* (Oxford: Blackwell, 1995); and Richard Rorty, author of *Contingency, Irony, and Solidarity* (Cambridge: Cambridge University Press, 1989), *Objectivity, Relativism, and Truth* (Cambridge: Cambridge University Press, 1991), and *Truth and Progress* (Cambridge: Cambridge University Press, 1998).

Two collections with helpful essays on relativism are Martin Hollis and Steven Lukes (eds.), *Rationality and Relativism* (Cambridge: MIT Press, 1982), and Jack Meiland and Michael Krausz (eds.), *Relativism, Cognitive and Moral* (Notre Dame: University of Notre Dame Press, 1982). Discussions of the issue include Richard Bernstein, *Beyond Objectivism and Relativism* (Philadelphia: University of Pennsylvania Press, 1983); Peter Unger, *Philosophical Relativity* (Minneapolis: University of Minnesota Press, 1984); and Christopher Norris, *Reclaiming Truth* (Durham: Duke University Press, 1996).

Derrida's writings are notoriously difficult. But helpful discussions of deconstruction are Jonathan Culler, *On Deconstruction* (Ithaca: Cornell University Press, 1982); Sharon Crowley, *A Teacher's Introduction to Deconstruction* (Urbana: National Council of Teachers of English, 1989); Kathleen Wheeler, *Romanticism, Pragmatism, and De-*

construction (Oxford: Blackwell, 1993); and John D. Caputo (ed.), *Deconstruction in a Nutshell: A Conversation with Jacques Derrida* (New York: Fordham University Press, 1997). A clear exposition and criticism is John M. Ellis, *Against Deconstruction* (Princeton: Princeton University Press, 1989).

Good discussions of feminism and truth are Genevieve Lloyd, *The Man of Reason* (Minneapolis: University of Minnesota Press, 1984), and Penelope Deutscher, *Yielding Gender: Feminism, Deconstruction, and the History of Philosophy* (London: Routledge, 1997).

There are many good introductions to logic, including Irving Copi, *Introduction to Logic* (New York: Macmillan, 1989), and my own *Simple Logic* (Fort Worth: Harcourt Brace, 1999). For a more symbolic treatment, see my *Deduction* (Palo Alto: Mayfield, 1987; Oxford: Blackwell, 2002).

Was it a vision, or a waking dream?
Fled is that music:—Do I wake or sleep?

—John Keats, "Ode to a Nightingale"

CHAPTER 2

Knowledge

I know that I was born on an icy January morning in Pittsburgh, Pennsylvania, less than a mile from Forbes Field—where, just a few years later, the Pittsburgh Pirates would win a World Championship with a bottom-of-the-ninth-inning home run off the bat of Bill Mazeroski. I think Mazeroski was the greatest defensive second baseman ever to play the game—although I don't think I can claim to *know* it. I predict that the Pirates will play at least .500 ball next season, although I'm not really confident enough to affirm that I *believe* it. And I might guess—for purposes of entering a contest, for example—that the team will hit 172 home runs next season, although I would hardly call that a *prediction.*

In everyday circumstances, as this illustrates, we distinguish what we know from what we believe, predict, or guess. We think that there is something special about knowledge. We admire people who know a lot but not necessarily those who believe a lot, make a lot of predictions, or do a lot of guessing. We rely on what we know when we make decisions but are careful about relying too much on what we merely believe, predict, or guess. When people disagree, we often want to know who is right; we want to know who knows something and who doesn't.

It might seem that the chief difference between knowledge, belief, prediction, and guessing is our degree of confidence: We are firmly confident of what we know, reasonably confident of what we believe, wavering about what we predict, and diffident about what we guess to be true. But that is not the only difference, and it is certainly not the most important one. We cannot turn a guess into knowledge simply by acquiring greater confidence. We ought to have more confidence in what we know than in what we guess, because we know it. In short, the issue of knowledge is primary, and the issue of confidence is secondary.

What is the difference between knowledge and other mental states? What is knowledge? The question has real practical significance. It is also central to philosophy. Philosophy is the pursuit of wisdom or good judgment, and good judgment about anything requires knowledge—at the very least, knowledge about how to judge it. To evaluate things that other people say or that we ourselves think and to try to decide how much confidence we ought to have in them, we must be good judges of knowledge itself. To do that, we need to know something about knowledge. The branch of philosophy that studies knowledge—what it is, how we attain it, when we have it and when we don't, and what its limits are—is *epistemology,* or the *theory of knowledge.* Since the seventeenth century, Western philosophers have considered epistemological questions to be central to the project of philosophy as a whole.

INTERNALISM

What is knowledge? Answers fall into two groups. Everyone agrees that what we know must be true. For example, I can know that Mazeroski's home run won the 1960 World Series for Pittsburgh only if Mazeroski's home run did win the 1960 World Series for Pittsburgh. To that extent, everyone agrees that knowledge involves some kind of connection between a mental state and the world. Beyond that, however, **internalists** distinguish knowledge from other mental states in terms of the characteristics of that state and its relations to other mental states, including sensations. Roughly, for an internalist, knowledge is justified true belief, where beliefs are justified either intrinsically (in which case they are self-justifying or **self-evident**) or by following from other justified beliefs. In either case, the justification is fully transparent to the knower. If you have justification, you know (or at least can know) that you have justification. **Externalists** distinguish knowledge from other mental states by invoking relations between mental states and the world. Those relations are not necessarily transparent to the knower; you may know something because your belief is true and has arisen through a reliable process of belief formation—such as perception—without being able to give any justification yourself.

Plato formulates the classic internalist definition of knowledge in the *Theaetetus.* After rejecting a definition of knowledge as perception because it leads to relativism (see Chapter 1), he considers a definition of knowledge as true belief and rejects it as well.

Why does persuading a judge of the truth not necessarily give him or her knowledge?

THEAETETUS. Knowledge was said by us to be true opinion; and true opinion is surely unerring, and the results which follow from it are all noble and good.

SOCRATES. He who led the way into the river, Theaetetus, said "The experiment will show"; and perhaps if we go forward in the search, we may stumble upon the thing which we are looking for; but if we stay where we are, nothing will come to light.

THEAETETUS. Very true; let us go forward and try.

SOCRATES. The trail soon comes to an end, for a whole profession is against us.

THEAETETUS. How is that, and what profession do you mean?

SOCRATES. The profession of the great wise ones who are called orators and lawyers; for these persuade men by their art and make them think whatever they like, but they do not teach them. Do you imagine that there are any teachers in the world so clever as to be able to convince others of the truth about acts of robbery or violence, of which they were not eyewitnesses, while a little water is flowing in the clepsydra [water clock—that is, in a very short time]?

THEAETETUS. Certainly not, they can only persuade them.

SOCRATES. And would you not say that persuading them is making them have an opinion?

THEAETETUS. To be sure.

SOCRATES. When, therefore, judges are justly persuaded about matters which you can know only by seeing them, and not in any other way, and when thus judging of them from report they attain a true opinion about them, they judge without knowledge and yet are rightly persuaded, if they have judged well.

THEAETETUS. Certainly.

> SOCRATES. And yet, O my friend, if true opinion in law courts and knowledge are the same, the perfect judge could not have judged rightly without knowledge; and therefore I must infer that they are not the same.[1]

Presented with evidence in court, a jury may conclude that the defendant is guilty. Suppose that the defendant really is guilty. The jurors have a belief, and it is true. But do the jurors really *know* that the defendant is guilty? Knowledge of this kind seems to require perception. If the jury actually saw the defendant commit the crime, in person or on film, say, then perhaps they can be said to have knowledge. Otherwise, they form a correct opinion but do not really know.

Socrates might have presented a simpler case. Suppose that Jones believes that there is life on distant planets. And suppose there really *is* life on distant planets. It does not follow that Jones *knows* that there is. Or, to take an example considered earlier, suppose I am right that Mazeroski is the greatest defensive second baseman in the history of baseball. It doesn't follow that I *know* that.

Bertrand Russell presents a different sort of case, in which a true conclusion is deduced from a false premise:

> If a man believes that the late Prime Minister's name began with a B, he believes what is true, since the late Prime Minister was Sir Henry Campbell Bannerman. But if he believes that Mr. Balfour was the late Prime Minister, he will still believe that the late Prime Minister's name began with a B, yet this belief, though true, would not be thought to constitute knowledge.[2]

Socrates considers the most common internalist definition of knowledge: knowledge is justified true belief, true belief "with an account." Jones does not know that there is life on distant planets because he has no justification; he cannot explain why it must be so. I do not know that Mazeroski is the greatest defensive second baseman because, although I can give some arguments to that effect, I admit that they are inconclusive and based on limited evidence. I can explain why it is plausible to think so, but not why it must be so.

> THEAETETUS. That is a distinction, Socrates, which I have heard made by someone else, but I had forgotten it. He said that true opinion, combined with reason, was knowledge, but that the opinion which had no reason was out of the sphere of knowledge; and that things of which there is no rational account are not knowable—such was the singular expression which he used—and that things which have a reason or explanation are knowable. (201c–d)

Socrates proceeds to develop this account. It results, he contends, in what has come to be known as a **foundationalist** theory of knowledge. Jones can know something only if he can justify his belief, that is, explain why it must be true. That explanation

---

[1] Plato, *Thaetetus,* translated by Benjamin Jowett, in *The Dialogues of Plato* (Oxford: Oxford University Press, 1892), 200e–201c.

[2] Bertrand Russell, *The Problems of Philosophy* (London: Williams and Norgate, 1912), 131–132.

relies on other facts and principles that Jones must also know. So he must in turn have explanations of why those must be true in terms of still other, prior items of knowledge. Ultimately, knowledge must rest on a foundation consisting of basic items that are perceived directly. Socrates uses the analogy of words and syllables as depending on letters, which are basic.

> SOCRATES. Excellent; but then, how did he distinguish between things which are and are not "knowable"? I wish that you would repeat to me what he said, and then I shall know whether you and I have heard the same tale.
>
> THEAETETUS. I do not know whether I can recall it; but if another person would tell me, I think that I could follow him.
>
> SOCRATES. Let me give you, then, a dream in return for a dream:—Methought that I too had a dream, and I heard in my dream that the primeval letters or elements out of which you and I and all other things are compounded, have no reason or explanation; you can only name them, but no predicate can be either affirmed or denied of them, for in the one case existence, in the other non-existence is already implied, neither of which must be added, if you mean to speak of this or that thing by itself alone. It should not be called itself, or that, or each, or alone, or this, or the like; for these go about everywhere and are applied to all things, but are distinct from them; whereas, if the first elements could be described, and had a definition of their own, they would be spoken of apart from all else. But none of these primeval elements can be defined; they can only be named, for they have nothing but a name, and the things which are compounded of them, as they are complex, are expressed by a combination of names, for the combination of names is the essence of a definition. Thus, then, the elements or letters are only objects of perception, and cannot be defined or known; but the syllables or combinations of them are known and expressed, and are apprehended by true opinion. When, therefore, any one forms the true opinion of anything without rational explanation, you may say that his mind is truly exercised, but has no knowledge; for he who cannot give and receive a reason for a thing, has no knowledge of that thing; but when he adds rational explanation, then, he is perfected in knowledge and may be all that I have been denying of him. Was that the form in which the dream appeared to you?
>
> THEAETETUS. Precisely.
>
> SOCRATES. And you allow and maintain that true opinion, combined with definition or rational explanation, is knowledge?
>
> THEAETETUS. Exactly.
>
> SOCRATES. Then may we assume, Theaetetus, that today, and in this casual manner, we have found a truth which in former times many wise men have grown old and have not found?
>
> THEAETETUS. At any rate, Socrates, I am satisfied with the present statement. (201d–202d)

So far, Socrates accepts this definition of knowledge. But he quickly becomes dissatisfied. Suppose all knowledge rests on some foundation of basic items that are perceived directly and themselves receive no account, explanation, or justification. Do we know them? If knowledge is justified true belief, and they have no justification, the answer seems to be no. But how can knowledge rest on a foundation that is not itself known?

What is Socrates's analogy? Toward what conclusion is he driving?

SOCRATES. Which is probably correct—for how can there be knowledge apart from definition and true opinion? And yet there is one point in what has been said which does not quite satisfy me.

THEAETETUS. What was it?

SOCRATES. What might seem to be the most ingenious notion of all:—That the elements or letters are unknown, but the combination or syllables known.

THEAETETUS. And was that wrong?

SOCRATES. We shall soon know; for we have as hostages the instances which the author of the argument himself used.

THEAETETUS. What hostages?

SOCRATES. The letters, which are the elements; and the syllables, which are the combinations;—he reasoned, did he not, from the letters of the alphabet?

THEAETETUS. Yes; he did.

SOCRATES. Let us take them and put them to the test, or rather, test ourselves:—What was the way in which we learned letters? and, first of all, are we right in saying that syllables have a definition, but that letters have no definition?

THEAETETUS. I think so.

SOCRATES. I think so too; for, suppose that some one asks you to spell the first syllable of my name:—Theaetetus, he says, what is SO?

THEAETETUS. I should reply S and O.

SOCRATES. That is the definition which you would give of the syllable?

THEAETETUS. I should.

SOCRATES. I wish that you would give me a similar definition of the S.

THEAETETUS. But how can any one, Socrates, tell the elements of an element? I can only reply, that S is a consonant, a mere noise, as of the tongue hissing; B, and most other letters, again, are neither vowel-sounds nor noises. Thus letters may be most truly said to be undefined; for even the most distinct of them, which are the seven vowels, have a sound only, but no definition at all.

SOCRATES. Then, I suppose, my friend, that we have been so far right in our idea about knowledge?

THEAETETUS. Yes; I think that we have.

SOCRATES. Well, but have we been right in maintaining that the syllables can be known, but not the letters?

THEAETETUS. I think so.

SOCRATES. And do we mean by a syllable two letters, or if there are more, all of them, or a single idea which arises out of the combination of them?

THEAETETUS. I should say that we mean all the letters.

SOCRATES. Take the case of the two letters S and O, which form the first syllable of my own name; must not he who knows the syllable, know both of them?

THEAETETUS. Certainly.

SOCRATES. He knows, that is, the S and O?

THEAETETUS. Yes.

SOCRATES. But can he be ignorant of either singly and yet know both together?

THEAETETUS. Such a supposition, Socrates, is monstrous and unmeaning.

SOCRATES. But if he cannot know both without knowing each, then if he is ever to know the syllable, he must know the letters first; and thus the fine theory has again taken wings and departed.

THEAETETUS. Yes, with wonderful celerity. (202d–203e)

Socrates's objection is simply that knowledge cannot be justified except by other things that are known. We can justify what we know only in terms of what else we know. But this cannot go on forever. Eventually we must reach basic items (like the letters) that we cannot justify by appealing to anything else. Since we have no justification of basic items, but nevertheless know them, the definition of knowledge as justified true belief cannot be right.

Not only must the basic items that form the foundation of knowledge themselves be known, they are known much more clearly and directly than anything else:

SOCRATES. Well, but will you not be equally inclined to disagree with him, when you remember your own experience in learning to read?

THEAETETUS. What experience?

SOCRATES. Why, that in learning you were kept trying to distinguish the separate letters both by the eye and by the ear, in order that, when you heard them spoken or saw them written, you might not be confused by their position.

THEAETETUS. Very true.

SOCRATES. And is the education of the harp-player complete unless he can tell what string answers to a particular note; the notes, as every one would allow, are the elements or letters of music?

THEAETETUS. Exactly.

SOCRATES. Then, if we argue from the letters and syllables which we know to other simples and compounds, we shall say that the letters or simple elements as a class are much more certainly known than the syllables, and much more indispensable to a perfect knowledge of any subject; and if some one says that the syllable is known and the letter unknown, we shall consider that either intentionally or unintentionally he is talking nonsense?

THEAETETUS. Exactly. (206a–c)

We may put Socrates's argument in a simple form:

1. If knowledge is justified true belief, there is a foundation of knowledge that justifies everything else.
2. Items in the foundation cannot themselves be justified.
3. Items in the foundation are known—in fact, known more clearly and directly than anything else.
4. Therefore, knowledge is not justified true belief.

This suggests that there are three ways an internalist can defend the conception of knowledge as justified true belief. **Antifoundationalists**—also known as **coherentists**—deny the first premise, insisting that justification does not require a foundation, a level of ultimate justifiers. Just as words in a dictionary are defined in terms of other words in the dictionary without a collection of indefinable words, so our knowledge might be justified in terms of other things we know without any ultimate items that cannot themselves be justified. Aristotle, contemplating this possibility, objects that, if everything is to be defined, there must be an infinite regress (*a* is justified by *b*, which is justified by *c*, and so on infinitely) or a circle (for example, *a* is justified by *b*, which is justified by *c*, which is justified by *d*, which is justified by *a*). Dictionaries, which are finite, are circular, although the circles are wide enough that we still consider them informative. The coherentist argues that knowledge is similar. Ultimately, justification proceeds in circles, but as long as the circles are large enough, justification still takes place.

Many internalists pursue another option, denying the second premise. That is, they argue that items in the foundation are justified by themselves. These foundationalists maintain that basic items of knowledge are self-explanatory or, in traditional terms, self-evident. They provide evidence for themselves. Certain kinds of perceptual knowledge—"That is green," for example, or, in more cautious accounts, "That looks green to me"—are self-evident, as are certain truths of logic ("If *p*, then *p*," for example, or "$a = a$"). The *Declaration of Independence* famously cites the claim that all men are created equal and that the rights to life, liberty, and the pursuit of happiness are self-evident. As we shall see shortly, René Descartes offers the most influential version of a theory of knowledge as resting on a self-evident foundation.

Finally, an internalist may deny the third premise, maintaining that things other than beliefs or items of knowledge can justify knowledge. The most common version of this approach, sometimes called **direct realism,** holds that sensations can justify knowledge without themselves constituting knowledge. I may justify my claim that the sky is brown tonight by taking you outside and showing you. What justifies my belief in this case is not another belief but a perception—seeing how the sky looks. In the next chapter we shall examine a theory of this kind from the Indian Buddhist philosopher Dharmakirti.

EXTERNALISM

Plato's account of knowledge is internalist; it defines knowledge in terms of the state of the knower's mind. Other accounts are externalist; they define knowledge in terms of operations outside the mind. Arguably the earliest externalist theory of knowledge appears in the *Nyaya-sutra.*

Two long-running schools of Indian philosophy with a realist attitude toward the objects of experience are the ***Vaisesika*** (vie-SHAY-shi-kuh: particularism) and the *Nyaya* (NYIE-uh: logic). For centuries Indian philosophers considered the two distinct, and each could claim its own self-defining literature. But with Udayana (oo-DIE-uh-nuh), who lived around 1000 A.D., the schools merged, and proponents afterwards are called simply *Nyayayikas,* that is, adherents of Nyaya.

In pre-Udayana works, Vaisesika tends to focus more on the metaphysical question "What is there?" The Nyaya, in contrast, is more concerned with the epistemological questions "How do we know what we know?" and "What are the right methods of inquiry and debate?" The earliest Nyaya work, the *Nyaya-sutra,* by the Indian philosopher Gautama (c. 200), is concerned mainly with the means of right cognition: perception, inference, analogical acquisition of vocabulary, and reliable testimony.

The *Nyaya-sutra* and a commentary by Vatsyayana (vuht-SYIE-uh-nuh; c. 400) present characterizations of four ***pramanas,*** or means of knowledge: perception, inference, analogical acquisition of vocabulary, and reliable testimony. Knowledge, according to the *Nyaya-sutra,* is belief produced by a reliable means of knowledge.

> *Sutra 4:* Perception is the cognition[3] resulting from sense-object contact [and which is] 'not due to words', 'invariably related' [to the object] and is 'of a definite character'.
>
> *Bhasya:* The cognition which results from the contact of the sense with the object is called perception. . . .
>
> [Take a mirage, for example:] During the summer the flickering rays of the sun intermingled with the heat radiating from the surface of the earth come in contact with the eyes of a person at a distance. Due to this sense-object contact, there arises, in the rays of the sun, the cognition: this is water. Even such a knowledge may be taken for valid perceptual knowledge. Hence Gautama says, 'invariably connected with the object'. An erroneous perception is the perception of an object as something which it is not. A right perception is the perception of an object as it actually is.[4]

Perception, then, is a kind of knowledge. It results from the contact of sense organs with objects, and it involves no justification beyond the general reliability of our means of perception. The *Sutra* places three conditions on perceptual knowledge:

1. *It is not due to words.* To sketch a distinction that will play a large role in the next chapter, **analytic statements** are true or false by virtue of the meanings of their words. **Synthetic statements** are not. 'Bachelors are bachelors' and 'Bachelors are unmarried', for example, are analytic. The former is a truth of logic; one can know it to be true without having any experience of bachelors or even knowing what a bachelor is. The latter is true by definition; one can know it to be true simply by knowing the definition of 'bachelor'. 'Bachelors are unhappy', in contrast, is synthetic. Knowing the meaning of 'bachelor' and 'unhappy' does not suffice to determine whether it is true or false. To put the *Sutra*'s condition in different terms, then: Perceptual knowledge is synthetic. 'The grass is green' and 'The grass is swaying' are good candidates for perceptual knowledge, but 'Grass is grass' is not.

2. *It is invariably related to the object.* This is the *Sutra*'s way of saying that perceptual knowledge is accurate or veridical: We can know that p only if p is true. Suppose some liquid looks like water to you. You know that it is water—but only if it really is water.

3. *It is definite.* The *Sutra* gives an example of how perception can fail to yield knowledge by being indefinite:

---

[3] The Sanskrit term here is *jnana,* which is translated as 'knowledge' by Gangopadhyay but which I have replaced with 'cognition', since, according to English usage, there can be no false knowledge.

[4] From the *Nyaya-sutra,* translated by Mrinalkanti Gangopadhyay (Calcutta: Indian Studies, 1982).

> Perceiving with eyes an object at a distance, a person cannot decide whether it is smoke or dust. (Commentary to *Sutra 4*)

Our sense organs may, in short, produce in us a mental state that fails to be knowledge because it is too indefinite; we may not be sure whether we are seeing smoke or dust, water or 7-Up, grass or artificial turf. In such cases our mental state falls short of knowledge.

Not all knowledge is perceptual, of course. Some knowledge, as we have seen, results just from knowing the meanings of words. Some knowledge arises from analogy:

> *Sutra 6:* Comparison is the instrument of the valid knowledge of an object derived through its similarity with another well-known object.

We get much knowledge from the testimony of others:

> *Sutra 7:* Verbal testimony is the communication from a 'trustworthy person'.
>
> *Bhasya:* A trustworthy person is the speaker who has the direct knowledge of an object and is motivated by the desire of communicating the object as directly known by him.

Who would count as a trustworthy witness to a murder?

Note the restricted view of testimony advanced here: Testimony transmits knowledge only from someone who possesses it—directly—and wishes to transmit it. If Smith honestly tells Jones that she is hungry, then Jones knows that Smith is hungry.

It is easy to understand the basis for the restrictions. Suppose Smith tells Jones that last night's party lasted until 3:00 A.M., and suppose that's true. Does Jones now know that last night's party lasted until 3:00 A.M., on the basis of Smith's testimony? According to the *Nyaya-sutra,* the answer is yes if three conditions are fulfilled:

1. *Knowledge:* Smith must know that last night's party lasted until 3:00 A.M. to be able to pass this knowledge along to Jones. If Smith doesn't know it but is just guessing from her roommate's bedraggled appearance, then Jones doesn't know it either.

2. *Directness:* Smith's knowledge must be firsthand. If Smith was at the party, fine. If not, then Smith's knowledge is at best indirect, and Jones cannot obtain knowledge on the basis of Smith's testimony. If there are intermediaries, in other words, what Smith says counts as gossip rather than testimony. Jones may still get knowledge from it, but it will have to be based on inference, not on testimony alone. (This criterion corresponds to courtroom restrictions against hearsay.)

3. *Honesty:* Smith must intend to communicate the truth. If Smith is lying, for example, or merely reciting a line in a play, then what she says cannot give Jones testimonial knowledge, even if what she says happens to be true.

These conditions may seem too restrictive. If Smith tells Jones that the capital of the Assyrian Empire was Nineveh, then unless Smith somehow has direct knowledge of this—by a time machine, perhaps—Jones cannot be said to know that Nineveh was the capital of Assyria on the basis of Smith's testimony. But Jones may still have that knowledge inferentially.

That brings us to the final means of knowledge. We get much knowledge by inferring it from other things we know:

> *Sutra 5:* Next [is discussed] inference, which is preceded by it [that is, by perception], and is of three kinds, namely, inferring the effect . . . , inferring the cause . . . , and inferring the rule (*i.e.* where the general law[5] is ascertained by general observation).

The *Sutra* here distinguishes three kinds of inference:

1. *Inferring the effect from the cause.* We see the dark, threatening clouds and infer that it will rain. We see the lightning and brace ourselves for the thunder.

2. *Inferring the cause from the effect.* We see the wet ground and the swollen creek and infer that it rained. Or we hear thunder and infer that there was lightning.

3. *Inferring a general rule from its instances.* We see dark clouds and then rain; we see lightning and then hear thunder. We infer that, in general, dark clouds cause rain and lightning causes thunder. Or we hear Smith say things that turn out to be true. We infer that Smith's word is reliable.

Inference is very important, for it allows us to have knowledge of things that are not immediately present to us.

> Perception has for its object things present. Inference has for its object things both present and absent. Why? Because of its capacity for knowing objects belonging to the three times (*i.e.* past, present, and future). By inference one knows objects belonging to the three times. We infer: it will be, it is, and it was. (Commentary to *Sutra 5*)

Inference is what allows us to have knowledge of the world beyond the present moment.

Our quick sketch of internalism and externalism about knowledge suggests several ways of distinguishing them. First, internalists determine whether a mental state counts as knowing by examining that mental state itself and its relation to other mental states. Externalists do so by examining the method (in Sanskrit, *pramana*) producing that mental state.

Second, internalists require that the knower be able to justify a knowledge claim, while externalists do not. If a mental state results from a reliable means of knowing and characterizes the world accurately, it counts as knowledge from an externalist point of view. So, one might say that such a mental state has a justification: It was produced by a reliable means of knowing. In that sense, the externalist might agree that knowledge is justified true belief (although the externalist need not talk about belief at all). But the externalist will count Jones's true belief as justified if Jones obtained it from a reliable method.

---

[5] For example, fire causes smoke, or thunder follows lightning.

To put this another way, the externalist counts Jones's true belief as justified if *the externalist* can justify it; Jones himself need not be able to justify it or indeed have any idea what his means of knowing was. The internalist requires that *Jones* be able to justify the belief.

Third, internalists tend to hold, at least for a significant class of things, that knowledge implies knowing that one knows. Suppose that Smith knows that Albuquerque is in New Mexico. According to internalism, she has a justified true belief that Albuquerque is in New Mexico. For that justification to serve as a justification for her, she must recognize it as such. She must realize that it justifies her belief that Albuquerque is in New Mexico. But then Smith must know that she has a justified true belief that Albuquerque is in New Mexico. That is, Smith must *know* that she knows that Albuquerque is in New Mexico.

For the externalist, this doesn't follow at all. Smith's knowledge that Albuquerque is in New Mexico may result from a reliable cognitive process without her being aware of it.

SKEPTICISM

Internalists define knowledge as true belief for which the knower can provide a justification. Externalists define knowledge as true belief resulting from a reliable means of knowing. **Skeptics** hold that beliefs of certain kinds are unreliable or unjustified. For example, one might be skeptical of people's claims to have been abducted by aliens or to have psychic powers. One might be skeptical of religious claims that go beyond the realm of possible human experience or of scientific claims about the origins of the universe. In its most extreme form, skepticism maintains that all beliefs are unreliable or unjustified—in other words, that knowledge is impossible.

Skeptical philosophical schools flourished throughout the ancient world in Greece, Egypt, China, and India. They differed in the extent of their skepticism and in the conclusions they drew from it. But all attack the claims of those they call **dogmatists** to know something about the nature of the world. Because they advance no position themselves but simply critique the claims of others, Erasmus (1465–1536) called the skeptics "the least surly of the philosophers."

China: Zhuangzi

Zhuangzi (Chuang Tzu, c. 350 B.C.E.), roughly a contemporary of Plato and early Greek skeptics such as Pyrrho, and one of the great thinkers of **Daoism,** gives skepticism a mystical turn. Laozi wrote of the One, which is indescribable but nevertheless underlies the entire universe. The One, for Zhuangzi, is a universal process of spontaneous, perpetual change. Wisdom consists in seeking unity with the One. To do this, one needs to abandon thoughts of self and adapt to the ceaseless flow of nature. Zhuangzi thus agrees with Laozi in recommending a policy of passive noninterference. But Zhuangzi stresses the importance of self-development, since transformation is the essence of Nature. Also, Zhuangzi is even fonder of paradox than Laozi, suggesting that true understanding requires overcoming the distinctions and divisions inherent in intellectual activity.

Zhuangzi is explicitly skeptical: Intellectual distinctions correspond to no distinctions in reality. We cannot trust our thinking or even the experience of our senses. In consequence, there is no point to trying to accomplish anything. Zhu Xi summarizes the difference between Laozi and Zhuangzi: "Laozi still wanted to do something, but Zhuangzi did not want to do anything at all."

Zhuangzi offers four basic arguments for his conclusion that knowledge is impossible.

1. *The identity of contraries.* We can frame the question of the possibility of knowledge in terms of objectivity: Is it possible to become completely objective? Zhuangzi answers no—because subjectivity and objectivity are inevitably intertwined.

Why does the objective emanate from the subjective? Why is the subjective consequent on the objective?

> There is nothing which is not objective: there is nothing which is not subjective. But it is impossible to start from the objective. Only from subjective knowledge is it possible to proceed to objective knowledge. Hence it has been said, 'The objective emanates from the subjective; the subjective is consequent upon the objective. This is the *Alternation Theory.*' Nevertheless, when one is born, the other dies. When one is possible, the other is impossible. When one is affirmative the other is negative. Which being the case, the true sage rejects all distinctions of this and that. He takes his refuge in God [most translations have 'Nature'], and places himself in subjective relation with all things.
>
> And inasmuch as the subjective is also objective, and the objective also subjective, and as the contraries under each are indistinguishably blended, does it not become impossible for us to say whether subjective and objective really exist at all?
>
> When subjective and objective are both without their correlates, that is the very axis of Dao. And when that axis passes through the centre at which all infinities converge, positive and negative alike blend into an infinite One.[6]

The idea is that the objective (things as they are, quite apart from how we perceive or think about them) and subjective (things that depend on our states of mind) depend on each other. You can attain objective knowledge, if at all, only by beginning with your own subjective mental states and making them match reality. But if you are in a certain subjective mental state, then (a) it is objectively true that you are in that state, and (b) you are in it by virtue of certain objective truths about you. So, objectivity and subjectivity go together. They depend on each other. But they are supposed to be contraries; the subjective is that which is not objective. Zhuangzi concludes that the distinction between the subjective and the objective is incoherent.

How good is this argument? It seems to turn on an equivocation on 'subjective'. We might call something subjective if it is or relates essentially to a mental state and objective if it reflects reality. In this sense of 'subjective', 'subjective' and 'objective' are not contraries at all. Smith's feeling of heat on touching a radiator is subjective and

[6]This and subsequent quotations from Zhuangzi are from *Chung Tzu, Taoist Philosopher and Chinese Mystic,* translated by Herbert A. Giles (London: Allen and Unwin, 1926).

objective at the same time if the radiator really is hot. Alternatively, we might call something subjective if it merely relates to a mental state, that is, relates to a mental state without reflecting reality. Then, 'subjective' and 'objective' are indeed contraries, but there is no reason to expect them to go together; in particular, there is no longer any reason to think that we must get to objectivity by way of subjectivity. So, Zhuangzi's argument fails.

Zhuangzi not only argues that knowledge is impossible but also advises us about how to live. As Gisela Striker observes, this is a pattern common to skeptics: There is both a *thesis* (for example, that knowledge of certain kinds is impossible) and a *recommendation* (for example, that you ought to suspend judgment). Zhuangzi's recommendation:

> . . . the true sage rejects all distinctions of this and that. He takes his refuge in God [or Nature], and places himself in subjective relation with all things.

This recommendation is threefold: reject distinctions, take refuge in God or Nature, and place yourself in subjective relations to things—that is, give up claims to objectivity. The advice to reject distinctions and surrender pretense to objectivity is common among skeptics, for obvious reasons. If knowledge is impossible, they advise, stop pretending to know. Religious skeptics have generally gone on to recommend faith in knowledge's place. Yet the connection between the thesis and the recommendation, easy as it is to understand, is not easy for the skeptic to defend. Does the thesis (knowledge is impossible) justify the recommendation? If so, do we *know* it? Wouldn't that undermine the claim that knowledge is impossible? But if the recommendation is unreliable or unjustified, why should we accept it?

2. *The identity of all things.* Distinctions should be rejected, Zhuangzi insists, because all things are at root identical. Oddly, his argument begins with what makes individual objects distinct. Each thing has its own nature (in Laozi's language, its *de*) which determines what it is, what it can be, and what it tends to be.

> Dao operates, and given results follow. Things receive names and are what they are. They achieve this by their natural affinity for what they are and their natural antagonism to what they are not. For all things have their own particular constitutions and potentialities. Nothing can exist without these.

Strangely, he concludes that individual objects are not distinct after all.

> Therefore it is that, viewed from the standpoint of Dao, a beam and a pillar are identical. So are ugliness and beauty, greatness, wickedness, perverseness, and strangeness. Separation is the same as construction: construction is the same as destruction. Nothing is subject to either construction or destruction, for these conditions are brought together into One.

We think of things as distinct, having distinct natures. But this is only apparent, as we see when we surrender claims to objectivity:

What is the principle of the identity of all things?

> Only the truly intelligent understand this principle of the identity of all things. They do not view things as apprehended by themselves, subjectively; but transfer themselves into the position of the things viewed. And viewing them thus they

> are able to comprehend them, nay, to master them;—and he who can master them is near. So it is that to place oneself in subjective relation with externals, without consciousness of their objectivity,—this is Dao.

Zhuangzi does not spell his argument out very explicitly. But he gives an important and entertaining illustration of what he has in mind:

> A keeper of monkeys said with regard to their rations of chestnuts that each monkey was to have three in the morning and four at night. But at this the monkeys were very angry, so the keeper said they might have four in the morning and three at night, with which arrangement they were all well pleased. The actual number of the chestnuts remained the same, but there was an adaptation to the likes and dislikes of those concerned. Such is the principle of putting oneself into subjective relation with externals.

The idea is this. Things seem to have their own individual natures. But at root they are one; it is we who make distinctions between them, dividing one from another by distinguishing one nature from another. Just as the monkeys distinguish the three-in-the-morning arrangement from the three-at-night arrangement, even though the number of chestnuts is the same, so we distinguish beams from pillars, beauty from ugliness, and so on, even though the underlying reality is the same. 'Beauty is in the eye of the beholder,' people sometimes say. Zhuangzi is saying that *everything* is in the eye of the beholder. Everything is merely subjective; there is no such thing as objectivity. So there is no such thing as knowledge.

3. *Variability.* Many skeptical arguments rely on the variability of how things appear, having the form:

> *Variability:* Things are perceived differently (by different beings or at different times).
> *Undecidability:* There is no way to decide which perceptions ought to be trusted.
> *Skeptical thesis:* Therefore, knowledge is impossible.

Zhuangzi puts this in terms of creatures of different species:

> If a man sleeps in a damp place, he gets lumbago and dies. But how about an eel? And living up in a tree is precarious and trying to the nerves:—but how about monkeys? Of the man, the eel, and the monkey, whose habitat is the right one, absolutely? Human beings feed on flesh, deer on grass, centipedes on snakes' brains, owls and crows on mice. Of these four, whose is the right taste, absolutely? Monkey mates with monkey, the buck with the doe; eels consort with fishes, while men admire Mao Chiang and Li Zhi, at the sight of whom fishes plunge down deep in the water, birds soar high in the air, and deer hurry away. Yet who shall say what is the correct standard of beauty? In my opinion, the standard of human virtue, and of positive and negative, is so obscured that it is impossible actually to know it as such.

4. *The problem of the criterion.* The skeptical argument based on variability requires a premise of undecidability: There is no way to decide which way of seeing things is the right way. One might try to defuse the argument by seeking a criterion

for distinguishing correct from incorrect perceptions. But where could we get such a criterion? This is the **problem of the criterion.**

> Granting that you and I argue. If you beat me, and not I you, are you necessarily right and I wrong? Or if I beat you and not you me, am I necessarily right and you wrong? Or are we both partly right and partly wrong? Or are we both wholly right and wholly wrong? You and I cannot know this, and consequently the world will be in ignorance of the truth.
>
> Who shall I employ as arbiter between us? If I employ someone who takes your view, he will side with you. How can such a one arbitrate between us? If I employ someone who takes my view, he will side with me. How can such a one arbitrate between us? And if I employ someone who either differs from, or agrees with, both of us, he will be equally unable to decide between us. Since then you, and I, and man, cannot decide, must we not depend upon another? Such dependence is as though it were not dependence. We are embraced in the obliterating unity of God [or Nature].

Why can we not find an impartial arbitrator?

It might seem, in other words, that we could find a criterion for deciding which perceptions are accurate. But the eel will have its criterion, the monkey another criterion, the owl yet another, and so on. How can we decide which criterion to choose? That too is undecidable.

5. *The possibility of dreaming.* Many of Zhuangzi's arguments concern questions of value—standards of beauty or virtue, for example, or the value of life itself:

> How do I know that love of life is not a delusion after all? How do I know but that he who dreads to die is not as a child who has lost the way and cannot find his home?
>
> The Lady Li Zhi was the daughter of Ai Feng. When the Duke of Zhin first got her, she wept until the bosom of her dress was drenched with tears. But when she came to the royal residence, and lived with the Duke, and ate rich food, she repented of having wept. How then do I know but that the dead repent of having previously clung to life?
>
> Those who dream of the banquet, wake to lamentation and sorrow. Those who dream of lamentation and sorrow wake to join the hunt. While they dream, they do not know that they dream. Some will even interpret the very dream they are dreaming: and only when they awake do they know it was a dream.

Zhuangzi argues that there is no mark by which we can determine whether a given experience is a dream. From an internalist point of view, we cannot tell whether we are justified in believing something, for we might be dreaming it. From an externalist point of view, we cannot tell whether we are acquiring our belief from a reliable means of knowing, such as perception, or from an unreliable means such as dreaming. This is the **argument from dreams.**

> Once upon a time, I, Zhuangzi, dreamt I was a butterfly, fluttering hither and thither, to all intents and purposes a butterfly. I was conscious only of following my fancies as a butterfly, and was unconscious of my individuality as a man. Suddenly, I awaked, and there I lay, myself again. Now I do not know whether I was

> then a man dreaming I was a butterfly, or whether I am now a butterfly, dreaming I am a man.

Egypt: Philo

Skepticism as a school of Greek philosophy began with Pyrrho (c. 365–270 B.C.E.)—who, intriguingly, is said to have admired the "naked philosophers" he met in India while traveling with Alexander the Great—and extended more or less continuously through the thought of many Greek, Roman, and Alexandrian philosophers for the next thousand years. We will look here at two important figures in this development: Philo and Sextus Empiricus. Like other thinkers in the Greek skeptical tradition, they employ only some of the arguments used by Zhuangzi and add several ones. In particular, they use nothing like the arguments from the identity of contraries or the identity of all things. It is not difficult to see why. Both are metaphysical arguments, depending on the idea that we construct the objects of experience ourselves out of the unified material that constitutes the true nature of the universe. But if knowledge is impossible, how could we know that we construct objects of experience, or that the universe is One? Moreover, even if these things are true, why should we infer that knowledge is impossible? City boundaries are surely artificial human creations, but it doesn't follow that it's impossible for Jones to know that his house lies within the Austin city limits.

Philo and Sextus thus try to argue for skepticism without presupposing any theory of what the world is like. Philo, often called Philo Judaeus or Philo of Alexandria (20 B.C.E.–40), was born into a wealthy Jewish family in Alexandria, Egypt. By his time, North Africa, a part of the Roman Empire, had become an important intellectual center and would remain one during the first several centuries C.E. Alexandria was the site of a Platonic school and a world-famous library. Because of the school, Plato's influence was especially strong in Alexandria, and most important philosophers of the region were platonists. They wrote in Greek and saw themselves as part of the Hellenistic tradition. Their work often concentrates on the problems of reconciling Judaism or Christianity with the intellectual framework of Greek thought. Well educated in both Judaism and Greek thought, Philo sought to reconcile Jewish religious convictions with Greek philosophy. His central strategy was to interpret the Jewish Scriptures allegorically, treating the stories of the Books of Moses as illustrating general aspects of the human condition.

Just as Adam and Eve were tempted in the Garden of Eden, Philo argues, we are tempted to think that we can know the true nature of the world. But that, Philo argues, is a vain conceit. He advances three primary arguments. First, he develops the argument from variability in several forms. There is great variation in perception among animals of different species, among different people, and even within the same person at different times or in different circumstances. We have no way of telling which perceptions accurately portray reality.

> Not only do their judgments on the same objects vary at different times, but different persons receive different impressions of pleasure or its reverse from the same things. For what is disliked by some is enjoyed by others, and contrariwise what some receive with open arms as acceptable and agreeable to their nature is utterly

scouted by others as alien and repugnant. For example, I have often when I chanced to be in the theatre noticed the effect produced by some single tune sung by the actors on the stage or played by the musicians. Some of the audience are so moved, that in their excitement they cannot help raising their voices in a chorus of acclamation. Others are so unstirred that, as far as this is concerned, you might suppose them on a level of feeling with the senseless benches on which they sit. Others, again, are so repelled that they are off and away from the performance, and indeed, as they go, block their ears with both hands for fear that some echo of the music should remain to haunt them and produce a sense of discomfort to irritate and pain their souls.

But it is needless to quote such cases as these. Every single individual in his own person is subject, extraordinary though it be, to numberless changes and variations in body and soul, and chooses at one time and rejects at another things which do not change, but retain the natural constitution which they have had throughout. The same feelings are not experienced in health as in sickness, in wakefulness as in sleep, in youth as in age. And people receive different mental impressions according as they are standing or moving, confident or affrighted, sad or joyful, loving or hating. And why tediously pursue the subject? For to put it shortly, our bodies and souls are in a state of motion, natural or unnatural, which considered as a whole produces that ceaseless change in the mental pictures presented to us which makes us the victim of conflicting and incongruous dreams.[7]

This is essentially the argument from variability, although Philo's talk of sleep and dreaming suggests the argument from dreams.

Philo concludes that we must suspend judgment.

Why should we suspend judgment?

If it were always the case that the same objects produced the same impressions on the mind without any variation, it would perhaps be necessary that the two instruments of judgment which nature has established in us, sense and mind, should be held in high esteem as veracious and incorruptible, and that we should not suspend our judgment on any point through doubt but accept a single presentation of two different objects, and on the faith of this choose one and reject the other. But since we prove to be differently affected by them at different times, we can say nothing with certainty about anything, because the picture presented to us is not constant, but subject to changes manifold and multiform.

Second, Philo advances an **argument from illusion.** We are often mistaken; how do we know that any given occasion is not one of those?

We see that fishes in the sea, when they swim with their fins stretched, always look larger than nature has made them, and oars, however straight they are, appear bent below the water. Still more—the mind is often misled by distant objects which create false impressions. Sometimes we suppose lifeless objects to be living objects or the converse. And we have similar illusions about things stationary and moving, advancing and receding, short and long, circular and multilateral. And numberless

[7] This and subsequent quotations from Philo are from "On Drunkenness," *Philo,* Volume III, XLIII, translated by F. H. Colson and G. H. Whitaker (London: William Heinemann Ltd., 1930).

> other distortions of the truths are produced even when sight is unimpeded, which no sane person would accept as trustworthy.

The argument, to formulate it more precisely, is

> We often misperceive things.
> There is no way to tell when we are misperceiving things.
> Therefore, on any given occasion, we might be misperceiving things.

Finally, Philo advances an **argument from comparison** that foreshadows Immanuel Kant's "Copernican Revolution" (discussed extensively in the following chapter). We know not things in themselves but things as they are in relation to other things—especially, to give the argument a Kantian twist, to ourselves.

> Again, everyone knows that practically nothing at all which exists is intelligible by itself and in itself, but everything is appreciated only by comparison with its opposite; as small by comparison with great, dry with wet, hot with cold, light with heavy, black with white, weak with strong, few with many. The same rule holds with all that concerns virtue and vice. We only know the profitable through the hurtful, the noble by contrast with the base, the just and the good in general by comparison with the unjust and evil. And indeed if we consider we shall see that everything else in the world is judged on the same pattern. For in itself each thing is beyond our apprehension, and it is only by bringing it into relation with something else that it seems to be known. Now that which is incapable of attesting itself and needs to be vouched for by something else, gives no sure ground for belief. And it follows that on this principle we can estimate at their true value lightly-made affirmations and negations on any subject whatever.

The crucial premise of this argument clearly is "Now that which is incapable of attesting itself and needs to be vouched for by something else, gives no sure ground for belief." Philo gives no argument for it—although in the hands of Kant it takes on real power. There is no reason why the relational character of truths should imply skepticism; 'Chicago is north of Des Moines' seems no less knowable than 'Chicago is windy'. But, if we can know things only as they relate to us, then (Kant argues) we cannot distinguish what is really in the object from what is being contributed by our own faculties of perception and knowledge.

Philo extends these arguments to morality. Different groups of people have different ways of life. Philosophy does not provide any way of deciding which is best, for philosophers disagree as much as anyone about the nature of the good life. His recommendation: to seek not knowledge but a mystical vision of God.

Greece: Sextus

Roughly contemporaneous with the writing of the *Nyaya-sutra* was a Greek physician, Sextus Empiricus (c. 200). It is perhaps fitting that we do not know where he lived or taught, although his Greek is masterful and he displays acquaintance with Athens, Rome, and Alexandria. He offers a number of arguments, called *modes,* for skeptical conclusions. The first mode is based on the differing sensory systems of different species of animals. It is thus a version of the argument from variability. But Sextus draws the conclusion more explicitly: We cannot tell what is really in the object and what is contributed by our own cognitive faculties.

> But if the things appear different owing to the variety in animals, we shall, indeed, be able to state our own impressions of the real object, but as to its essential nature we shall suspend judgment. For we cannot ourselves judge between our own impressions and those of the other animals, since we ourselves are involved in the dispute and are, therefore, rather in need of a judge than competent to pass judgment ourselves. . . . If, then, owing to the variety in animals their sense-impressions differ, and it is impossible to judge between them, we must necessarily suspend judgment regarding the external underlying objects.[8]

Sextus's thesis is that knowledge is impossible; his recommendation, that we should suspend judgment, neither affirming nor denying anything as reflecting the true nature of the world, the "external underlying objects."

Sextus considers a *dogmatist* any philosopher who makes a claim about the true nature of the world. In addition to the argument from variability and various of Philo's arguments, Sextus offers an infinite regress argument as a version of the problem of the criterion. Many people claim to know the truth; is there any criterion to distinguish those who know from those who don't?

Does Sextus hold that there is a criterion for distinguishing knowledge from error?

> Of those, then, who have treated of the criterion some have declared that a criterion exists—the Stoics, for example, and certain others—while by some its existence is denied, as by . . . Xenophanes of Colophon, who say—"Over all things opinion bears sway"; while we have adopted suspension of judgment as to whether it does or does not exist. This dispute, then, they will declare to be either capable or incapable of decision; and if they say it is incapable of decision they will be granting on the spot the propriety of suspension of judgment; while if they say it admits of decision, let them tell us whereby it is to be decided, since we have no accepted criterion, and do not even know, but are still inquiring, whether any criterion exists. Besides, in order to resolve the dispute which has arisen about the criterion, we must possess an accepted criterion by which we shall be able to judge the dispute; and in order to possess an accepted criterion, the dispute about the criterion must have been decided. And when the argument thus reduces itself to a form of circular reasoning, the discovery of the criterion becomes impracticable, since we do not allow them to adopt a criterion by assumption, while if they offer to judge the criterion we force them into a regress ad infinitum.

Is there a criterion of truth? To settle the matter, we need a criterion—but that is exactly what's at issue! The dogmatist must either argue in a circle, using a criterion to support itself, or enter into an infinite regress, supporting the first criterion by appealing to a second, supporting the second by appeal to a third, and so on.

Sextus argues that we should suspend judgment, not only because we cannot justify our claims to know, but because suspension of judgment leads to quietude and peace of mind:

---

[8]This and subsequent quotations from Sextus Empiricus are from *Outlines of Pyrrhonism* (Cambridge: Harvard University Press, 1955).

> The Skeptic, in fact, had the same experience which is said to have befallen the painter Apelles. Once, they say, when he was painting a horse and wished to represent in the painting the horse's foam, he was so unsuccessful that he gave up the attempt and flung at the picture the sponge on which he used to wipe the paints off his brush, and the mar of the sponge produced the effect of a horse's foam. So, too, the Skeptics were in hopes of gaining quietude by means of a decision regarding the disparity of the objects of sense and of thought, and being unable to effect this they suspended judgment; and they found that quietude, as if by chance, followed upon their suspense, even as a shadow follows its substance.

It is important that Sextus does not assert that suspension of judgment causes peace of mind. That would be a claim to know the nature of things and would appear unjustified by his own lights. Instead, he tells a story and observes that the skeptic lives skeptically, suspending judgment, and simply finds that peace of mind follows.

But how can the skeptic live skeptically? To stay alive, we need to make some judgments. It is said that the extreme skeptic Pyrrho, doubting all appearances, refused to believe anything; his students had to lead him around to prevent him from being run over by chariots (the appearance of which, of course, he insisted gave him no reason whatever to believe they were really there). But Sextus advocates no such policy. Indeed, he invokes a practical criterion, telling the skeptic to accept appearances and suspend judgment only on the question of whether appearances reflect the nature of reality.

> The criterion of the Skeptic School is, we say, the appearance, giving this name to what is virtually the sense presentation. For since this lies in feeling and involuntary affection, it is not open to question. . . .
>
> Adhering, then, to appearances we live in accordance with the normal rules of life, undogmatically, seeing that we cannot remain wholly inactive.

Nagarjuna

There is a strong parallel between Sextus's skepticism and that of certain Buddhist philosophers. Early in the history of Buddhism, a split occurred among its followers concerning the goal of the practices taught by the Buddha. According to the schools that came to be associated with the Southern Canon, the sacred texts of **Theravada Buddhism**, the ideal is to become an ***arhat*** (saint), who loses all individual personality in ***nirvana,*** a universal, impersonal, unconceptualizable bliss and awareness that somehow underlies appearance. According to Northern or **Mahayana Buddhism,** in contrast, the aim is to become a ***bodhisattva,*** who, unlike the *arhat,* turns back from the final bliss and extinction of personality in *nirvana* to help every conscious being attain it.

From the perspective of a Mahayanist, the Southern Canon presents, by and large, a course of spiritual discipline and a goal that are not the best and the highest, because they are personally oriented. Mahayanists, instead, focus their efforts on acquiring the six moral, intellectual, and spiritual perfections possessed by the Buddha, which enable them to promote the welfare of all. Mahayanists do not deny many of the doctrines of the Southern Canon but interpret them as only a part of the story, as the Buddha's means of aiding people unable to appreciate higher spiritual truths.

At the time of the split over the *arhat* and *bodhisattva* conceptions, there was also much dispute about how to understand the aggregate of qualities or states of consciousness (***dharma***) that the Buddha had taught make up a person. Some early Buddhist thinkers believed that the components of what appears to be the self could be identified and analyzed. These thinkers attempt to provide comprehensive lists of these components and their groupings, sometimes with considerable sophistication. But the Indian philosopher Nagarjuna (ca. 1000 C.E.), a Mahayanist and the founder of **Madhyamika Buddhism,** believes these efforts lead away from the practical message of the Buddha and his opposition to metaphysics. Nagarjuna was born in south India but taught at Nalanda, a Buddhist university in north India. Nagarjuna, like Sextus, tries to keep people from theorizing but does not try to change how people live their everyday lives:

> For we do not speak without accepting, for practical purposes, the work-a-day world.[9]

Nagarjuna's identification of impossibilities is also part of a strategy that he claims the Buddha uses: By seeing the absurdities that arise in viewing anything as having an independent existence, one realizes that everything is ***nihsvabhava,*** "without a reality of its own." Applying this to oneself, one comes to see the truth of the Buddha's teaching of ***anatman,*** "no-self." This realization is viewed as a step toward the goal of enlightenment and perfection.

Nagarjuna mounts an onslaught on the *Nyaya* notion of a justifier or source of knowledge. His argument recalls Sextus's presentation of the problem of the criterion, but, unlike Sextus, Nagarjuna focuses on refuting an externalist theory of knowledge. He identifies the problem of an infinite regress concerning justification but construes it in terms of sources of knowledge (*pramana*). If, for example, sense experience justifies Smith's belief that she is now typing on a computer keyboard—to her or to us—what justifies the belief that her sense experience plays this role? Any answer seems to invite a further question, and so on to infinity. Nagarjuna claims that analyzing the concept of the means of knowledge leads to a vicious infinite regress: How are the means of knowledge known? He thus puts Sextus's argument in a nutshell:

> And if, for you, there is a source [of knowledge] of each and every object of proof,
> Then tell how, in turn, for you there is proof of those sources.
> If by other sources [of knowledge] there would be the proof of a source—that would be an "infinite regress";
> in that case neither a beginning, middle, or an end is proved.

He also gives a version of Philo's argument from comparison or relation, but one that is focused on the relation between sources of knowledge and their objects:

[9]This and subsequent quotations from Nagarjuna are from *Averting the Arguments,* from *Emptiness: A Study in Religious Meaning* (New York: Abingdon Press, 1967, 222–227; A Translation of Vigrahavyavartani: Averting the Arguments.)

What alternatives does Nagarjuna consider? Why does he reject them?

> If, according to you, the sources [of knowledge] are proved without being related to the objects of "that which is to be proved,"
> Then these sources will not prove anything.
> Or if the sources [of knowledge] in every case are proved in relation to "what is to be proved,"
> Then "what is to be proved" is proved without relation to the sources.
> And if "what is to be proved" is proved without relation to the sources [of knowledge],
> What [purpose] is the proof of the sources for you—since that for the purpose of which those sources exist is already proved?

Nagarjuna here recognizes that there are various sources of knowledge—sensation, analogy, testimony, and inference, to take the classic four recognized in Indian epistemology—and that to gain knowledge we must acquire it from the appropriate source. Jones cannot sense that $2 + 2 = 4$ or infer that the page looks wobbly to him at the moment. In any given case, therefore, we must appeal to the appropriate *pramana,* or source of knowledge. If we don't, we prove nothing. But if we do, we need a source of knowledge for determining when we are using the appropriate source of knowledge. If we had that, however, there would be no dispute in the first place.

Nagarjuna summarizes:

> The proof of the sources [of knowledge] is not [established] by itself, nor by each other, or not by other sources,
> It does not exist by that which is to be proved and not from nothing at all.

If we are to avoid a circle or an infinite regress, there must be some sources of knowledge that are self-supporting, for which it is self-evident that they are sources of knowledge. But first, we need some explanation for why those things and those things alone have this special status. And, second, if there is more than one, as the standard account has it, how do we know which applies to which cases?

Nagarjuna is aware that skepticism can be taken to be a self-refuting doctrine. If knowledge is impossible, how can we know the truth of skepticism? If all assertions are unreliable or unjustified, isn't skepticism itself unreliable or unjustified?

> If I would make any proposition whatever, then by that I would have a logical error;
> But I do not make a proposition, therefore I am not in error.

Nagarjuna attempts to undermine any claims to knowledge; he does not advance any view of his own. He does not, in other words, put forth the doctrine that knowledge, justification, reliability, and so on, are impossible; he undercuts any attempt to establish them. It appears that this makes his position coherent but at the cost of making it unstatable. As B. K. Matilal observes,

> The upshot is that a radical scepticism of this kind is not, or does not seem to be, a statable position. For if it is statable, it becomes incoherent or paradoxical. In other words such a position could be coherent only at the risk of being unstatable! It seems to me that both radical scepticism and Nagarjunian Buddhism would wel-

> come this situation, for here we may find the significance of the doctrine of silence in Madhyamika.[10]

Nagarjuna's followers, known as *Madhyamikas,* become greatly adept in finding difficulties in the positions of others. They see the ability to knock down others' views as a manifestation of wisdom or insight, the most important of the "perfections" that are the mark of a *bodhisattva.*

RESPONSES TO SKEPTICISM

Few philosophers are willing to remain skeptics, even if they find themselves tempted by skeptical arguments from time to time. The problem is not primarily that the position cannot be coherently stated even if it can be coherently put into practice by adopting a policy of attacking the claims to knowledge of the dogmatists. The problem, instead, is that skepticism seems to erase the epistemological distinctions with which this chapter began. We seem to know some things, believe others, make predictions about others, and guess about still more. We have great confidence in some of our judgments and very little in others. But the skeptic seems to make everything a matter of belief, even of unjustified, unreliable belief, making it hard to maintain any basis for distinguishing these levels of confidence. I feel sure that I was born in Pittsburgh, less sure that Mazeroski was baseball's greatest defensive second baseman, and not at all sure that the Pirates will win at least as many games as they lose next season. I think I have strong justification for the first assertion, weaker justification for the second, and still weaker justification for the third. If justification is impossible, however, all this makes little sense. Even if the skeptic could find some way to mimic these gradations and explain these differing degrees of confidence, skepticism seems to imply that there is nothing about which I should truly feel confident. And few philosophers have been willing to embrace that conclusion.

We will consider three responses to the skeptic's challenge. The first, developed in the *Nyaya-sutra,* argues that means of knowledge and objects of knowledge justify each other; the regress cannot start, for we justify our sources of knowledge not by citing further sources or criteria but by considering the objects of knowledge they produce. This is the standard externalist answer to skepticism. We have good reasons to treat some sources of knowledge as reliable.

The second, developed by a later *Nyayayika,* Gangesa, contends that skeptical doubts need not be taken seriously, for we can sensibly doubt only when we have grounds for doubt, and the skeptic typically gives us none. In effect, Gangesa argues that the regress never starts in a general way because we never have reason to suspect that *everything* we know is wrong.

The third, developed by twentieth-century Austrian philosopher Ludwig Wittgenstein, begins with the same point but takes the argument in a very different direction. We have no reason to doubt some things, Wittgenstein says, and that is all

[10] B. K. Matilal, *Perception: An Essay on Classical Indian Theories of Knowledge* (Oxford: Oxford University Press, 1986).

it is to be certain. We know some things with certainty—but this is just to say that we take them as starting points and do not question them.

Finally, Augustine and René Descartes contend, from a specifically internalist perspective, that there is a foundation of things that cannot reasonably be doubted. They point to certain truths that are self-evident.

Nyaya

Gautama (c. 200), the author of the *Nyaya-sutra,* and Vatsyayana, his commentator (c. 400), try to disarm skepticism by drawing an analogy to a scale. A scale is a means of knowledge (*pramana*) when the weight of a piece of gold, for example, is in question. But the same scale would be the object of knowledge (***prameya***), what is to be known—and the piece of gold the means of knowledge—when the question is calibration. If we wish to judge the accuracy of scales, we do not seek some further "scale of scales"—we take something whose weight is known independently from another source and see what the scale in question says about it.

How can a source of knowledge become an object of knowledge?

> The terms *pramana* and *prameya* may coexist (*i.e.* may be interchangeable) in the same object, if there is adequate ground for using the terms (interchangeably). And the grounds for using the terms are (as follows): *pramana* is that which produces knowledge and *prameya* is that which becomes the object of knowledge. In the event of an object of knowledge becoming instrumental in producing the knowledge of something else, the same object is termed both a *pramana* and a *prameya.* To convey this implication is said the following:
>
> *Sutra 16:* Just as the 'measuring instrument' (which usually has the status of a *pramana*) can be a *prameya* as well (*i.e.* when its own accuracy is subject to investigation).
>
> [Commentary]: The measuring instrument is a *pramana* when it gives the knowledge of correct weight. The objects of knowledge, in this case, are gold etc. which have weight. If however the accuracy of another measuring instrument is determined by gold etc. then for the knowledge of the other measuring instrument, gold etc. are *pramana*-s. And the other measuring instrument is a *prameya.*

The view put forward here appears to be a form of coherentism. There is no foundation of knowledge, no level of ultimate justifiers; the same thing may be justifier or justified depending on the circumstances. Nothing is in itself a *pramana* or a *prameya;* the same thing may be a source of knowledge in one case and an object of knowledge in another. When we seek to know whether a scale is giving the correct weight, we use it to weigh objects whose weights we already know—whose weights, in other words, we have already established by using other scales. We ask, in effect, whether the results from that scale match the results from other scales.

This example illustrates both the strength and the weakness of the coherentist Nyaya response. Doubting the accuracy of a means of knowledge in a particular case—a scale, our eyes, a bit of testimony—we consider how that means applies to other cases and how well its results cohere with those from other means of knowledge. Doubting what you say, I consider the reliability of other things you say and also try to confirm your testimony with testimony from others. Doubting my eyes, I see whether they are giving me accurate information about other things of known size, shape, color, and so on, ask others what they see, try to touch the object, and so on, to confirm or disconfirm the evidence my eyes give me. The strength of coherentism, then, is that it accords well with our practices when we doubt the accuracy of a means of knowledge. But the weakness is that at best we get coherence, not correspondence with reality. Recall our discussion in Chapter 1: Some philosophers take truth to be coherence; others take it to be correspondence with reality. Someone who holds a coherence theory of truth will not mind holding a coherentist theory of knowledge, for there is nothing more than coherence anyway. But realists typically hold a correspondence theory. From that point of view, something is true if it corresponds to reality. When our knowledge is questioned, we want to confirm it by showing that it corresponds to reality, for knowledge aims at truth. The *Nyaya* response, however, cannot give us that. Even if all our sources of knowledge agree, it remains possible that none gives us knowledge of the world as it exists. Perhaps all the scales are wrong. Perhaps everyone we talk to gives false testimony. Perhaps our eyes are deceiving us and everyone else's eyes are deceiving them too.

The *Nyaya-sutra* uses another analogy to support the means of knowledge against the skeptic:

> *Sutra 19:* . . . these (*i.e.* perception etc.) are apprehended in the same way as the light of a lamp.
>
> *Bhasya:* As for example, the light of the lamp, which is an auxiliary cause of perception, is itself an instrument of knowledge in the perception of the visible objects and it is apprehended over again by another instrument of valid perceptual knowledge, viz. its contact with the eyes. (The lamp) is inferred to be a cause of visual perception, because the presence and absence of the lamp are followed by the presence and absence of visual perception.

How should we interpret this cryptic passage? We might think it is making the point that sources of knowledge are self-revealing, just as light shows itself as it shows us the objects we see. That seems to imply that the means of knowledge are self-evident. But that does not sit well with the *Nyaya-sutra*'s externalism. Nor does it cohere with the idea that the distinction between sources and objects of knowledge is context dependent. Vatsyayana's commentary provides a different interpretation. The light is a source of knowledge when it enables us to see other objects; it is an object of knowledge when we direct our attention to the light itself. The light is the source of knowledge in one context and object of knowledge in another. There is no need, then, to meet Nagarjuna's demand for a criterion by which to recognize sources of knowledge, for such sources do not make up some distinct kind of thing. To be a source of knowledge is simply to play a certain role in an epistemic context.

On this interpretation, the *Nyaya-sutra* contains an implicit externalist response to Nagarjuna's infinite regress argument. As Matilal explicates it,

> . . . it is not essential for every entity to be *known* or revealed to us first before it can play the role of a 'means'. We see with our eyes, the sense of sight, but we do not see the sense itself. We can infer that the sense of sight exists in us from the fact that we can see, but the fact of seeing does not depend on our prior knowledge of the sense of sight. In order to use the money in my pocket, I would have to know that I have money there; but in order to use my ear-organ, my faculty of hearing,

to hear a noise, I do not have to know first that this is my faculty of hearing. A prior knowledge of the 'means' is not always necessary before that means can be used for the generation of a piece of knowledge.

Gangesa

A second strategy for responding to skepticism appears in the teachings of great Indian philosopher Gangesa (c. 1350), the founder of the New Logic (*Navya-Nyaya*). Gangesa, a contemporary of Geoffrey Chaucer and such later medieval European philosophers as John Buridan and William of Ockham, solves the problem of the criterion by insisting that there is no problem. That is, there is no reason to engage in skeptical doubt; we have no reason to think that our faculties systematically mislead us. We engage in *local* doubt when we wonder whether a given scale is accurate or worry that our eyes may be deceiving us in a particular case. Those local doubts we resolve in coherentist fashion, as the *Nyaya-sutra* explicates. Admittedly, this does not assure us that our sensations or thoughts correspond to reality. But to doubt that is to entertain a global doubt that we have no reason to entertain. We doubt a scale or our eyes when something anomalous happens—when, in short, we get a result we did not expect. But there is no global equivalent. It makes no sense to say that *nothing* is what we expected. In fact, skeptics live like everyone else; they put aside their doubts outside of specifically philosophical contexts and behave as if they had no doubts at all.

Nagarjuna would not deny this. He distinguishes our everyday attitude, which is fine from a pragmatic point of view but leads to paradoxes when analyzed carefully, from an absolute perspective we gain when we reflect on our everyday attitudes or engage in meditation. We can live like everyone else outside the study, the seminar room, or the monastery. But in those contexts we recognize the incoherence of our everyday point of view.

Gangesa charges that this twofold attitude involves a kind of pragmatic inconsistency. It gives us evidence that even skeptics do not take their own doubts seriously. They try to use "indirect proof" against the dogmatist, showing that a belief in anything leads to a contradiction. But their behavior leaves them open to exactly the same sort of argument. If the beliefs of dogmatists are incoherent, so are the actions of skeptics.

Consider a causal law such as "fire causes smoke." If skeptics want to create smoke, they start fires like everyone else. How dare they try to deduce a contradiction, then, from someone's belief that fire causes smoke? There are no real grounds for doubt.

What is a "pragmatic contradiction"?

> Indirect proof is appropriately pursued as long as there is doubt. Where there would be pragmatic contradiction (i.e., speech or other behavior contradicting the negation of the thesis to be established)—and indeed no doubt occurring—one can grasp the pervasion [causal law] without resorting to indirect proof. . . .
>
> When there is doubt, there is no regular pattern of behavior (with respect to using one thing to bring about another). When there is (such) a regular pattern, doubt does not occur.[11]

[11] Gangesa, *Tattvacintamani [The Jewel of Thought about Reality]*, edited by N. S. Ramanuja Tatacharya, Volume II, Part I, *anumana-khanda* (Tirupati: Sanskrit Vidyapeetha, 1973), translated by Stephen H. Phillips.

We have no reason to doubt, that is, that fire causes smoke. Neither do the skeptics, as their own behavior illustrates. They start fires to produce smoke just as anyone else does.

In other words, skeptics rely on a highly unusual conception of doubt. They doubt in the seminar room what they accept perfectly well outside it. Their doubt is purely theoretical. In Gangesa's view, that makes it hypocritical. Their purely theoretical doubt is not doubt at all.

> Thus it has been said (by Udayana): "That is doubted concerning which as doubted there occurs no contradiction with the doubter's action."
>
> For it is not possible at once to resort regularly to fire and the like for smoke and the like and to doubt that fire causes it (it would be meaningless behavior). This is how we should understand Udayana's saying.
>
> . . . It is the doubter's own behavior that proves the lie to the doubt, i.e., that blocks it.

Even skeptics do not really doubt that their senses give them reliable knowledge of the world. If they did, they wouldn't use the evidence of their senses to get around, find something to eat, and so on. Skeptics would respond that their doubt is purely theoretical. But, Gangesa answers, what can that mean? Why should we take it seriously?

Wittgenstein

Austrian philosopher Ludwig Wittgenstein (1889–1951) was born into a well-to-do, assimilated Jewish family in Vienna as the youngest of eight children. His mother was devoted to music; Johannes Brahms was a family friend, and Ludwig's brother Paul became a famous pianist. Ludwig was raised as a Catholic and home schooled until he was fourteen, when he went to Linz and then Berlin to study mathematics, science, and engineering. At nineteen he went to England to study engineering at Manchester. After reading Bertrand Russell's *Principles of Mathematics,* however, he devoted himself to philosophy. At twenty-three he went to Cambridge to study with Russell. The next year he inherited a large fortune when his father died. He preferred a simple life, however, and gave much of his money to a fund to support Austrian artists and writers. The rest he gave to his sisters. He returned to Austria at the outbreak of World War I to enlist in the military and scribbled his thoughts in his notebooks while serving in artillery units. By the end of the war he had a manuscript, which was published as *Tractatus Logico-Philosophicus* in 1922. By then, however, he had become a schoolteacher in a remote Austrian village. At thirty-seven he quit and became a gardener and then served as architect for a mansion for one of his sisters. At forty he returned to Cambridge and submitted the *Tractatus* for his doctoral dissertation, which was approved by Russell and G. E. Moore (1873–1958). He taught at Cambridge for the next eighteen years, interrupted only by his volunteer medical service during World War II.

During the last year and a half of his life, Wittgenstein began reflecting on Moore's refutation of skepticism. Moore attempted to defend common sense against skeptical attacks, listing "truisms, every one of which (in my own opinion) I *know,* with certainty, to be true":

> There exists at present a living human body, which is *my* body. This body was born at a certain time in the past, and has existed continuously ever since, though not without undergoing changes; it was, for instance, much smaller when it was born, and for some time after, than it is now. Ever since it was born, it has been either in contact with or not far from the surface of the earth. . . .[12]

He proves the existence of external objects, for example, as follows:

> I can prove now, for instance, that two human hands exist. How? By holding up my two hands, and saying, as I make a certain gesture with the right hand, 'Here is one hand', and adding, as I make a certain gesture with the left, 'and here is another'.[13]

Now, no skeptic would feel refuted by these "proofs." Wittgenstein begins by noting this. The skeptic's doubt is not ordinary, everyday doubt, but something peculiarly philosophical:

> . . . he will say that he was not dealing with the practical doubt which is being dismissed, but there is a further doubt *behind* that one. (19)[14]

Like Gangesa, Wittgenstein thinks that the burden of proof is on the skeptic to make this special kind of doubt intelligible. He asks,

> Doesn't one need grounds for doubt? (122)

Like Gangesa, he notes that the skeptic offers us no such grounds. He also asks, Does the idea of a purely theoretical doubt make sense?

> But someone who asks such a question is overlooking the fact that a doubt about existence only works in a language-game. Hence, that we should first have to ask: what would such a doubt be like?, and don't understand this straight off. (24)

The concept of a **language-game** is fundamental to Wittgenstein's later thought. We use language in certain ways in certain contexts; we understand each other by understanding the rules for these local language-games. Language-games are forms of life, Wittgenstein says; we participate in them by conforming to their rules. We can participate in a game of doubting. But doubt makes sense only in the context of such a game. And, Wittgenstein says, any such game must take certain things as fundamental, as unquestioned within the game. Not least, it must take for granted the meanings of the words expressing the doubt:

> If you are not certain of any fact, you cannot be certain of the meaning of your words either. (114)

Ancient skeptics were aware of this. They doubted whether communication was possible, since there is no way to know what anyone means by anything. But, if

---

[12] G. E. Moore, "A Defense of Common Sense," in *Philosophical Papers* (London: George Allen and Unwin, 1959).

[13] G. E. Moore, "Proof of an External World," in *Philosophical Papers* (London: George Allen and Unwin, 1959).

[14] This and subsequent quotations from Wittgenstein are from Ludwig Wittgenstein, *On Certainty* (New York: Harper and Row, 1969).

so, how could the skeptic ever communicate that view? We cannot doubt everything, Wittgenstein says, or doubt itself becomes unintelligible.

> If you tried to doubt everything you would not get as far as doubting anything. The game of doubting itself presupposes certainty. (115)

This is not only a matter of communication. The same point holds of evidence in general.

> For whenever we test anything, we are already presupposing something that is not tested. Now am I to say that the experiment which perhaps I make in order to test the truth of a proposition presupposes the truth of the proposition that the apparatus I believe I see is really there (and the like)? (163)

Suppose I am taking my temperature. What am I presupposing that is not tested?

Someone who doubts everything—or even some fundamental things, such as those Moore calls truisms—leaves us in a puzzling position. It is not clear what would count as evidence, argument, or justification. But if it is not clear what could reassure us and remove our doubt, is there any content to the doubt in the first place?

> If someone doubted whether the earth had existed a hundred years ago, I should not understand, for *this* reason: I would not know what such a person would still allow to be counted as evidence and what not. (231)

It is thus absurd to try to doubt everything.

> Doesn't testing come to an end? (164) The reasonable man does *not have* certain doubts. (220) Doubting and non-doubting behavior. There is the first only if there is the second. (354)

Wittgenstein also alludes to a pragmatic criterion of truth: Could skeptical doubt make any difference in practice? If it is purely theoretical and has no effect on everyday life, then to any pragmatist it has no meaning.

> But if anyone were to doubt it, how would his doubt come out in practice? And couldn't we peacefully leave him to doubt it, since it makes no difference at all? (120)

Some skeptics do take their skepticism to have practical consequences. According to legend, Pyrrho refused to believe the evidence of his own senses to the extent that he was a constant danger to himself; his students had to pull him out of the way of oncoming chariots. Most skeptics, however, have treated their skepticism as something confined to the study. And that opens them to the charge that their doubt has no content.

But Wittgenstein's chief point, in the end, is not that pragmatist one. Instead, he seeks to turn the tables on the skeptic and give a skeptical solution to the skeptical problem. Recall Nagarjuna's problem: We can justify something we know by appealing to some source of knowledge—but then how can we justify that source? This assumes that knowledge needs justification and that justification is the only antidote for doubt. This is what Wittgenstein questions.

> But I did not get my picture of the world by satisfying myself of its correctness; nor do I have it because I am satisfied with its correctness. No: it is the inherited background against which I distinguish between true and false. (94)

I do not justify my picture of the world, although I can of course be challenged to justify certain parts of it. I justify parts in terms of the whole or in terms of other parts. I can question any item in the whole but not all at once. I count as certain those things that "stand fast for me," that is, that I do not give up as I go about this process.

So we take statements like "I have two hands" as certain, not because we have some special justification for them, but because we find it hard to imagine what it would be like to give them up. In other words, we should not say that we treat such beliefs as certain because they are certain; it is better to say that they are certain because we *take* them to be certain. We play language-games, and certain moves are basic to them. To be certain or to be known is simply to have a certain status in such a game. The skeptic wants to know why they should have that special status. But there is no answer. They simply do. At best we might explain why it is useful to play such games.

Augustine

The best-known answers to skepticism in Western philosophy have been internalist and specifically foundationalist. Saint Augustine (354–430), a contemporary of Vatsyayana and by far the best known of the Christian platonists, was born to a Christian family in North Africa as the Roman Empire began to crumble. He had little interest in school as a child; although he learned Latin and a little Greek, he excelled mostly on the playground. At sixteen, after his father died, Augustine went to Carthage to study rhetoric. There he acquired a mistress, had an illegitimate child, and renounced Christianity. At eighteen he read the *Hortensius*, a dialogue of Cicero that is now lost, and decided to devote his life to the search for wisdom. Augustine became a teacher of rhetoric, setting up a school in Carthage at age twenty. At twenty-nine he traveled to Rome and Milan, where he met Bishop Ambrose. At thirty-two he decided to embrace Christianity once again. He returned to Africa and established a monastery at Tagaste. At forty-one Augustine became bishop of Hippo in what is now Tunisia. He devoted himself to the Church and wrote prolifically. He died at seventy-six as the Vandals lay siege to Hippo.

Skepticism was popular in late antiquity, partly because of the influence of the Roman orator, statesman, and philosopher Cicero (106–43 B.C.E.), partly because of the influence of Sextus and his followers, partly because Plato's Academy was now under the leadership of the skeptic Carneades, and perhaps mostly because of the plethora of philosophical, religious, and political worldviews that competed for people's attention and allegiance in the declining Roman Empire. Augustine tackles skepticism head on, arguing that logical truths, for example, can be known even if skeptical arguments are granted. Suppose, for example, that the argument from variability is correct and that there is no way to know which of several views on some subject is correct. We may nevertheless know that one or the other is correct.

What does Augustine claim to know about cosmology? What do these statements have in common?

> How, for example, are we to decide the contest between Democritus and the earlier cosmologists concerning the unity or incalculable multiplicity of the world? It was impossible to get Democritus and his own heir, Epicurus, to agree. That voluptuary was glad to grasp atoms in the darkness and to make those little bodies his mistresses, but he dissipated his entire patrimony through litigation when he allowed

> them to deviate from their proper courses and to swerve capriciously into one another's paths. . . . Nevertheless, I know something about these matters of cosmology, for I am certain that either there is only one world or there are more worlds than one. I am likewise certain that if there are more worlds than one, their number is either finite or infinite. . . . Furthermore, I know for certain that this world of ours has its present arrangement either from the nature of bodies or from a foresight of some kind. I am also certain that either it always was and always will be, or it had a beginning and will never end, or it existed before time and will have an end, or it had a beginning and will not last forever. And I have the same kind of knowledge with regard to countless cosmological problems, for those disjunctions are true, and no one can confuse them with falsehoods.[15]

No skeptical argument, Augustine maintains, can lead us to doubt that we know the truths of logic and mathematics:

> My only assertion is that this entire mass and frame of bodies in which we exist is either a unit or not a unit; and that it is what it is, whether we are asleep or awake, deranged or sane. . . . No matter what, it must be true that the world is what it is. . . . If there are one world and six more worlds, clearly there are seven worlds, no matter how I may be affected. And, with all due modesty, I maintain that I know this. . . . Even if the whole human race were fast asleep, it would still be necessarily true that *three times three* are nine. . . .

What about perceptual knowledge, knowledge attained through sense perception? Augustine is not convinced by arguments from illusion, dreaming, or madness:

> In fact, I believe that the senses are not untrustworthy because deranged persons suffer illusions or because we see things wrongly when we are asleep. If the senses correctly intimate things to the vigilant and the sane, it is no affair of theirs what the mind of a sleeping or insane person may fancy for itself.

How does this respond to the arguments from illusion, dreams, and madness?

Moreover, suppose you doubt the evidence of your senses, for example, that there is a book in front of you. You nonetheless know something, namely, that it appears to you that there is a book in front of you. We may have knowledge of appearances, even if we may not have knowledge of things themselves.

> Restrict your assent to the mere fact that you are convinced that it appears that way to you. Then there is no deception. I do not see how even an Academic Skeptic can refute a man who says: "I know that this appears white to me. I know that I am delighted by what I am hearing. I know that this smells pleasant to me. I know that this tastes sweet to me. I know that this feels cold to me."

This shows that we might have knowledge even if we grant the argument from variability.

> Tell me whether the oleaster leaves—for which a goat has a persistent appetite—are bitter in themselves? Shame on you! Isn't the goat more modest? I don't know

[15] This and subsequent quotations from Augustine are my translation.

> how oleaster leaves taste to flocks and herds; to me, they taste bitter. What more do you want to know? Perhaps somebody else doesn't find them bitter. Are you trying to annoy me? Have I said that they taste bitter to everybody? I've said that they taste bitter to me, but I don't say that they will always taste that way. What if something tastes sweet at one time and bitter on some other occasion? This is what I say: when you taste something, you can in good faith swear that it is sweet to your palate or that it isn't. No Greek sophistry can trick you out of this knowledge.

Finally, there is a special kind of self-knowledge we possess that no skeptic can undermine:

Augustine has identified three kinds of things he knows with certainty. What are they?

> But, without any delusive representations of images or phantasms, I am most certain that I am, and that I know and delight in this. In this respect, I am not at all afraid of the arguments of the Academic Skeptics, who say, What if you are deceived? For if I am deceived, I am. One who does not exist cannot be deceived. If I am deceived, by that same token I am. And since I am if I am deceived, how could I be deceived in believing that I am? It is certain that I am if I am deceived. Since, therefore, I, the person deceived, should exist—even if I were deceived—certainly I am not deceived in this knowledge that I am. And, consequently, neither am I deceived in knowing that I know. For, as I know that I am, so I know that I know. And when I love these two things, I add to them a third thing, my love, which is of equal moment. For I cannot be deceived that I love, since I am not deceived about what I love. Even if these statements were false, it would still be true that I loved false things.

On this foundation, identified by Augustine, Descartes builds his entire system.

Descartes

René Descartes (1596–1650), French philosopher, scientist, and mathematician, was a contemporary of Thomas Hobbes, Galileo, John Milton, Corneille, and Rembrandt. The inventor of analytic geometry, he is often considered the father of modern philosophy. Certainly he changed the course of Western philosophy by bringing the theory of knowledge to its center. Descartes puts skeptical arguments in their strongest form and uses a new skeptical argument of his own in order to show that there is a foundation of certain beliefs upon which all other knowledge rests.

> I noticed some years ago how many falsehoods I had from my youth admitted as true, and how doubtful was everything I had afterward based on them. And so I realized that I needed once and for all to demolish everything completely and build anew from the foundations, if I wanted to establish anything firm and lasting in the sciences.[16]

Descartes thus seeks to stop the infinite regress of justification the skeptic alleges by finding foundational truths that cannot be doubted. His method is doubt itself. Descartes promises to doubt everything he can, to see whether anything emerges as an irrefutable foundation for knowledge.

---

[16] This and subsequent quotations from Descartes are from the *Meditations,* my translation.

The argument from illusion shows that we can doubt the evidence of our senses:

> To be sure, whatever I have so far admitted as most true I have learned either from the senses or through the senses. But sometimes I have caught them deceiving me, and it is prudent never to trust fully anything that has once deceived us.

Similarly, the argument from dreaming shows that we might be deceived not only about what our senses reveal to us but about the existence and forms of our own bodies.

Why does Descartes believe that he cannot be sure he is not dreaming?

> Brilliant, to be sure! As if I were not a man who is in the habit of sleeping at night! In my sleep I experience the same things as madmen do when they are awake—or sometimes even less probable things. How often have I been persuaded, in the quiet of the night, of familiar things—that I was here in my robe sitting near the fire—when in fact I was lying disrobed between the sheets! It certainly seems to me now that I am looking at this paper with waking eyes; that this head I move is not asleep; that I deliberately and knowingly extend my hand and feel it. What happens in sleep is not so distinct. No doubt! As if I do not remember being tricked while asleep by similar thoughts on other occasions! While I think about this more carefully, I see so plainly that there are no certain indications by which we may clearly distinguish being awake from being asleep that I am dumbfounded. And my astonishment almost persuades me that I am asleep.

These arguments, Descartes believes, give us reason to doubt everything we have learned from our senses, and, generalizing, all the scientific knowledge we think we have of the world. But, as Augustine argued, these arguments leave mathematics and logic untouched. Perhaps I am deceived about whether I have a body, but surely I know that I either have a body or do not have one.

> Perhaps we might conclude from this that Physics, Astronomy, Medicine and all other disciplines which depend on the consideration of composite things are dubious, but that Arithmetic, Geometry and other subjects of that kind, which only treat of the simplest and most general things, whether they exist in nature or not, contain something certain and indubitable. For whether I am awake or asleep, two and three together always make five, and the square can never have more than four sides. It does not seem possible that truths so clear should incur any suspicion of falsity.

Descartes, however, does not stop here. He adds a new argument of his own to the skeptic's repertoire that casts doubt even on logic and mathematics:

How could I be wrong in thinking that $2 + 2 = 4$?

> Nevertheless, fixed in my mind is a certain long-standing belief: that there is a God who can do anything and who created me as the kind of being I am. How do I know that He has not brought it about that there is no earth, no heaven, no extended thing, no shape, no size, no place, and that nevertheless everything seems to me to exist exactly as it does now? Also, since I sometimes judge that others make mistakes about things they think they know best, might I not also be deceived every time I add two and three, or count the sides of a square, or something even simpler, if anything simpler can be imagined? But possibly God does not want me to be

> deceived in this way, for He is said to be supremely good. If, however, it contradicts His goodness to have made me such that I am always deceived, it would also appear to contradict His goodness to permit me to be sometimes deceived; yet that cannot be said. I cannot doubt that He does allow this.

Imagine, in other words, that God has crafted us so that we are wrong not only about what we glean from our senses but also about what results from thought itself. Perhaps God has made our minds so that we go wrong every time we try to do a mathematical calculation or perform a logical operation. Now God, Descartes will eventually show, would not do that. But an evil genius might.

> I shall therefore suppose not that God who is supremely good and the fountain of truth, but some evil genius of the greatest power and cunning, who has employed all his energies to deceive me. I shall suppose that the sky, the air, the earth, colors, shapes, sounds, and all other external things are nothing but dreams he has devised to ambush my credulity. I shall consider myself as having no hands, no eyes, no flesh, no blood, no senses, but as falsely believing myself to have all these things. I shall remain obstinately attached to this idea, and if by this means it is not in my power to know any truth, I may at least do what is in my power—that is, suspend my judgment—resolutely refusing to assent to any falsehoods, so that this deceiver cannot put one over on me, however powerful and cunning he may be.

The possibility of an evil genius who deceives us with respect to the products of both our senses and our thought processes then shows that we can be certain of nothing. Or does it? Descartes finds one thing he can know even if an evil genius is out to deceive him about everything:

> Am I myself not at least something? But I have already denied that I had senses and a body. I am stuck; what follows from that? Am I so bound to body and senses that I cannot exist without them? But I was persuaded that there was nothing in all the world, that there was no sky, no earth, that there were no minds, no bodies. Does it follow that I do not exist? No! I certainly existed if I persuaded myself of something. But there is some deceiver, of the greatest power and cunning, who always devotes his energy to deceiving me. Then undoubtedly I exist also, if he deceives me. Let him deceive me as much as he can, he can never bring it about that I am nothing so long as I think that I am something. So, after reflecting on everything carefully, I finally conclude that this proposition I am, I exist, is necessarily true each time that I pronounce it or conceive it in my mind.

'I am, I exist', (in Latin, *sum*) is true every time I think it. It is not necessarily true; I could be obliterated. But it is automatically true in the sense that it is true in every context in which it is thought or asserted. The same is true of 'I think' (in Latin, ***cogito***). In another work, Descartes draws a logical connection between these in the famous *cogito, ergo sum* ("I think, therefore I am"). In the *Meditations,* however, they appear to be on a par; both are true whenever they are entertained. They cannot be doubted. If you doubt that you exist, who is doing the doubting?

Descartes thus finds a secure foundation for knowledge. He cannot doubt that he exists; no skeptical arguments make any headway against 'I think' or 'I am'. Now some critics have thought that we can go no further; nothing belongs in the Cartesian foundation for knowledge but 'I think' and 'I am', and it is not clear how we could use those to infer any other knowledge. Descartes, however, believes that we can. His way of securing our knowledge of the world outside us depends on a proof of the existence of God that we will examine in Chapter 6. In the end, that is, the story goes like this: I exist; God exists; God is good; God would not permit me to be systematically deceived; therefore what I think I know about the external world must be right in general. But he thinks we can draw three conclusions even before saying anything about God. First, what am I? I can doubt the evidence of my senses or even my thought processes; I can doubt that I have a body. What I cannot doubt is that I think.

> But what then am I? A thing that thinks. What is that? A thing that doubts, understands, affirms, denies, wants, refuses, and also imagines and feels.

I am essentially a thing that thinks. Everything else about me I can doubt. I cannot be sure that I have a body or that, if I do, it looks anything like I conceive it to look. But I cannot doubt that I doubt, understand, affirm, deny, will, feel, and so on. The properties that are essential to me, without which I would not be what I am, are mental properties, not physical properties.

Second, I can know my own mind more directly and securely than I can know anything about my surroundings. It may be that I am deceived about everything around me, but I cannot be deceived about my own thoughts. As Descartes concludes, "I see clearly that there is nothing which is easier for me to know than my mind." This surprising conclusion sets the stage for much of the philosophical drama that has transpired in Europe and the Americas over the next several centuries.

Third, Descartes concludes that anything that I perceive clearly and distinctly must be true. In other words, he finds an answer to the problem of the criterion. What allows me to distinguish the 'I think' and 'I am' from other things I can doubt? I know them clearly and distinctly. They are self-evident; they need no other justification. As we shall see in subsequent chapters, Descartes uses this criterion to prove God's existence and distinguish the aspects of our thoughts that correspond to reality from the aspects that do not.

SUMMARY

Internalists think of knowledge as justified true belief. They think of justification as a relation among mental states such as beliefs. But they recognize that chains of justification cannot go on forever. So they face three options. First, they may take certain beliefs (such as logic, mathematics, 'I think', 'I am', etc.) as self-evident, together constituting the foundation of all our knowledge. Augustine and Descartes are foundationalists of this kind. Second, they may say that beliefs can justify each other, so that no basic level of self-evident knowledge is needed. Third, they may say that something other than beliefs, such as perceptions, justifies beliefs directly.

Externalists define knowledge in terms of the relation of beliefs to the world. They think of knowledge as true belief that results from a reliable process under normal circumstances. They see no reason to declare any level of knowledge fundamental.

Skeptics challenge the possibility of knowledge. They pose arguments on the basis of illusion, variability, and infinite regress, charging that no beliefs can be justified. Perhaps we are mistaken, as we sometimes are. Perhaps we are dreaming. Perhaps our senses mislead us; perhaps bats perceive the world as it really is. Or perhaps the problem is that we can justify our beliefs only by citing their sources; how then do we justify those sources?

How do we distinguish knowledge from belief, prediction, and guesswork? The theory of knowledge often takes the form of a debate between internalists and externalists over who can do this more effectively while keeping the skeptic at bay. But, as contemporary American philosopher Ernest Sosa suggests, we might more fruitfully think of these approaches as complementary. He observes that Descartes uses two Latin words that are usually translated as 'knowledge': *cognitio* and *scientia* (from which we get 'cognition' and 'science'). The former he understands in internalist fashion, while the latter he understands externally. We might try to capture the difference in English by speaking of what someone *really* or *reflectively* knows. It seems plausible to think that I really know some things—that I exist, for example, or that I have two hands—in the internalist sense that I am in full possession of their justification or that they are self-evident and need no further justification. And it is equally plausible to think that I know some things only in an externalist sense in that I have derived my knowledge from a reliable source (my senses, say) without myself being able to justify those sources. If that is right, there may be no single answer to the skeptic's challenge.

Review Questions

1. How does internalism differ from externalism? Is the externalist in a better position to respond to the skeptic than the internalist?
2. Why not define knowledge simply as true belief?
3. What is a foundationalist theory of knowledge? How might one object to it?
4. Why does Socrates object to the definition of knowledge as justified true belief? What options does the internalist defender of that definition have?
5. What does it mean for a proposition to be self-evident? What kinds of propositions have foundationalists taken to have that property?
6. Discuss the *Nyaya-sutra*'s *pramana* theory. What sources of knowledge does it recognize?
7. How do you know you are not dreaming?
8. Philo adds two arguments to those advanced by Zhuangzi. What are they? Do they succeed?
9. Explain and evaluate Nagarjuna's infinite regress argument for skepticism and the *Nyaya-sutra*'s response.
10. Compare the responses to skepticism offered by Gangesa and Wittgenstein. What do they have in common? How do they differ?

11. How does Augustine try to refute the skeptic? To what extent does Descartes agree with Augustine? With the skeptic?

12. What does Descartes's "evil demon" argument try to accomplish? Does it succeed?

TERMS FOR REVIEW

analytic statement A statement that is true or false by virtue of the meanings of its words.

anatman No-self; the Buddhist view that there is no self or soul.

antifoundationalism (or **coherentism**) The thesis that justification does not require a foundation or level of ultimate justifiers.

argument from comparison The argument that we know, not things in themselves, but things as they are in relation to other things—especially to ourselves.

argument from dreams A skeptical argument that we cannot attain knowledge of the world because we can never exclude the possibility that we are dreaming.

argument from illusion A skeptical argument that we can never attain knowledge of the world because we can never exclude the possibility that we are misperceiving things.

arhat In Buddhism, especially Theravada Buddhism, a saint who loses all individual personality in *nirvana.*

bodhisattva A person who, unlike the *arhat,* turns back from the final bliss and extinction of personality in *nirvana* to help every conscious being attain it.

cogito 'I think'; According to Descartes, the foundation of all knowledge.

coherentism (or **antifoundationalism**) The thesis that justification does not require a foundation or level of ultimate justifiers.

Daoism One of the world's great religions, stemming from the thought of Laozi (6th century B.C.E.); stresses the underlying unity of the world and champions the virtues of noninterference and tranquility.

dharma Duty; the aggregate of qualities or states of consciousness; appearances.

direct realism The view that sensations can justify knowledge without themselves constituting knowledge.

dogmatism The view that it is possible to attain knowledge of the world as it is. (Skeptics use this rather pejorative term to deride their opponents.)

externalism The view that knowledge is true belief resulting from a reliable means of knowing. Externalism distinguishes knowledge from other mental states by invoking relations between mental states and the world. Those relations are not necessarily transparent to the knower; you may know something because your belief is true and has arisen through a reliable process of belief formation—such as perception—without being able to give any justification yourself.

foundationalism The thesis that knowledge rests on a foundation consisting of basic items that are perceived directly.

internalism The thesis that knowledge is true belief for which the knower can provide a justification. Internalism distinguishes knowledge from other mental states in terms of the characteristics of that state and its relations to other mental states, including sensations. Roughly, for an internalist, knowledge is justified true belief—where beliefs are justified either intrinsically (in which case they are self-justifying or *self-evident*) or by following from other justified beliefs.

language-game A practice or form of life that involves using language according to certain rules.

Madhyamika Buddhism A school of Buddhist idealism, founded by Nagarjuna and known for its skepticism.

Mahayana Buddhism The Northern branch of Buddhism popular in China, Korea, and Japan, taking the *bodhisattva* as its ideal.

nihsvabhava In Nagarjuna, "without a reality of its own."

nirvana A universal, impersonal, unconceptualizable bliss and awareness that somehow underlies appearance.

pramana A source of knowledge, such as perception, testimony, and so on.

prameya An object of knowledge.

problem of the criterion The skeptical argument based on variability and undecidability: There are many ways of seeing things, and no way to decide which way of seeing things is the right way. One might try to defuse the argument by seeking a criterion for distinguishing correct from incorrect perceptions. But where could we get such a criterion?

self-evident belief A belief that provides its own justification.

skepticism The view that beliefs of certain kinds are unreliable or unjustified.

synthetic statement A statement that is not true or false by virtue of the meanings of its words.

Theravada Buddhism The Southern branch of Buddhism, popular in Southeast Asia, which takes the *arhat* as its ideal.

Vaisesika Particularism; a school of Indian realism that concentrated on metaphysical questions and merged, with the work of Udayana (c. 1000), with the Nyaya (logic) school.

For Further Reading

Thousands of books have been published on the theory of knowledge in the twentieth century alone. A good survey is Roderick Chisholm, *Theory of Knowledge* (Englewood Cliffs: Prentice-Hall, 1956).

Three excellent starting points for the study of skepticism and responses to it are Myles Burnyeat (ed.), *The Skeptical Tradition* (Berkeley: University of California Press, 1983); Julia Annas and Jonathan Barnes (eds.), *Modes of Scepticism: Ancient Texts and Modern Interpretations* (Cambridge: Cambridge University Press, 1985); and Jonathan Barnes, *The Tolls of Skepticism* (Cambridge: Cambridge University Press, 1990).

For excellent treatments of skepticism in Indian thought, see B. K. Matilal, *Perception: An Essay on Classical Indian Theories of Knowledge* (Oxford: Oxford University Press, 1986), and Stephen H. Phillips, *Classical Indian Metaphysics* (La Salle: Open Court, 1999). For Zhuangzi, see *Chuang Tzu: Basic Writings,* translated by Burton Watson (New York: Columbia University Press, 1964).

Good secondary works on Augustine are Henry Chadwick, *Augustine* (Oxford: Oxford University Press, 1986), and Christopher Kirwin, *Augustine* (New York: Routledge, 1989). On Descartes, see E. M. Curley, *Descartes Against the Skeptics* (Cambridge: Harvard University Press, 1978), and George Dicker, *Descartes* (Oxford: Oxford University Press, 1992).

On Wittgenstein, see A. J. Ayer, *Wittgenstein* (Chicago: University of Chicago Press, 1986); A. C. Grayling, *Wittgenstein* (Oxford: Oxford University Press, 1988); and P. M. S. Hacker, *Wittgenstein's Position in Twentieth Century Analytic Philosophy* (Oxford: Oxford University Press, 1996). An influential work stemming from Wittgenstein's response to skepticism is Saul Kripke, *Wittgenstein on Rules and Private Language* (Cambridge: Harvard University Press, 1982).

Say first, of God above, or man below,
What can we reason, but from what we know?
Of man, what see we but his station here,
From which to reason, or to which refer?

—Alexander Pope, "An Essay on Man"

Paradise, and groves
Elysian, Fortunate Fields—like those of old
Sought in the Atlantic Main—why should they be
A history only of departed things,
Or a mere fiction of what never was?

—William Wordsworth, "The Excursion"

CHAPTER 3

Experience

German philosopher Immanuel Kant is famous for asking three basic questions: What can we know? What should we do? And what may we hope? He divides his first question, What can we know? into three parts:

1. Can we know anything about the world independently of experience? Can philosophical reflection, in other words, teach us anything about the world? Must we, as Robert Frost writes, "say nothing until we see"? Or would that make our beliefs "a history only of departed things, or a mere fiction of what never was"?

2. Can we know anything beyond the bounds of experience? Unquestionably, our knowledge has limits. From an infinite collection of truths we can know only finitely many. But where are those limits? Are God, immortality, and freedom within or beyond them? Can we know anything about Paradise or whatever else lies beyond the grave? Can we know whether this universe is "one stupendous whole, Whose body Nature is, and God the soul," in Pope's phrase, or, in the words of Wallace Stevens, "an old chaos of the sun, Or old dependency of day and night, Or island solitude, unsponsored, free, Of that wide water, inescapable"? Can we know whether we are free, spontaneous beings who craft our lives ourselves or automata that follow a script we neither write nor understand?

3. Can we know what the world is really like? Can we know things as they are? Can we know the basic laws of the universe or of ourselves?

These questions are interrelated. Someone trying to determine what he can afford must consider his income. Just so, someone assessing the limits of his knowledge must consider its sources. What are the sources of our knowledge? Classical Indian and Islamic philosophers trace knowledge back to four sources: perception, inference, analogy, and testimony. Smith sees a bird; she infers from its appearance that it is a bird; by analogy with other birds she has seen, she infers that it can fly; and she looks it up in her field guide to learn more about it. To determine the limits of knowledge, we must understand these sources and their relation to one another. In particular, we must determine to what extent reason depends on experience.

Most commonly, philosophers have seen the sources of knowledge as determining the limits of knowledge and its ability to capture the world as it really is. They have thought that an affirmative answer to question 1 leads to an affirmative answer to 2 and 3. Likewise, they have thought that a negative answer to 1 leads to a negative answer to 2 and 3. Can we know anything about the world independently of experience? If so, then we can know something that goes beyond the bounds of experience to the nature of reality itself. If not, then we cannot. But, as we shall see, some philosophers view the questions differently. Kant himself answers yes to question 1 but no to 2 and 3. Philosophers in Indian and Islamic traditions have often answered no to 1 but yes to 2 and 3.

SOME DISTINCTIONS

What can we know? What are the sources of knowledge? What are its limits? Philosophers addressing these questions fall into two camps, depending on their answers to question 1. **Empiricists** maintain that all knowledge of the world comes from experience. **Rationalists** maintain that it does not, that we can attain some knowledge independently of experience. Rationalists stress our **innate,** or inborn, capacities; empiricists treat all our concepts as acquired. To make these positions precise, however, and to understand the debates between rationalists and empiricists, we need to draw some distinctions.

Analytic and Synthetic Truths

John Locke (1632–1704), a contemporary of Boyle, Leibniz, and Newton, is the first Western philosopher to distinguish truths of meaning from truths of fact. He was born in Wrington, England, into a liberal Puritan family. He earned a B.A. and an M.A. from Oxford and joined the faculty there as censor (professor) in moral philosophy. When he was twenty-nine, his father died, and he received a small inheritance. He studied medicine and became personal physician to the Earl of Shaftesbury. His scientific achievements earned him appointment to the Royal Society. Political turmoil in England led Locke to spend several years in France and Holland, where he became an advisor to William of Orange. The Glorious Revolution of 1688 enabled him to return to England in the company of Mary, the future queen. Locke finally published the *Essay Concerning Human Understanding* and the *Two Treatises of Government,* the philosophical works that made him famous, and served as Commissioner of the Board of Trade and Plantations with great distinction until failing health forced him to retire.

Locke distinguishes what he calls "trifling propositions" from those that convey real content about the world:

> Some propositions bring no increase to our knowledge. . . . First, all purely identical propositions. These obviously and at first blush appear to contain no instruction in them; for when we affirm the said term of itself, whether it be barely verbal, or whether it contains any clear and real idea, it shows us nothing but what we must certainly know before, whether such a proposition be either made by, or proposed to us. . . .
>
> For, at this rate, any very ignorant person, who can but make a proposition, and knows what he means when he says ay or no, may make a million of propositions of whose truth he may be infallibly certain, and yet not know one thing in the world thereby; v.g. "what is a soul, is a soul,"; or, "a soul is a soul"; "a spirit is a spirit"; "a fetiche is a fetiche," &c. These all being equivalent to this proposition,

> viz. what is, is; i.e. what hath existence, hath existence; or, who hath a soul, hath a soul. What is this more than trifling with words? It is but like a monkey shifting his oyster from one hand to the other. . . .
>
> Secondly, propositions in which a part of any complex idea is predicated of the whole. Another sort of trifling propositions is, when a part of the complex idea is predicated of the name of the whole; a part of the definition of the word defined. Such are all propositions wherein the genus is predicated of the species, or more comprehensive of less comprehensive terms. For what information, what knowledge, carries this proposition in it, viz. "Lead is a metal" to a man who knows the complex idea the name lead stands for? All the simple ideas that go to the complex one signified by the term metal, being nothing but what he before comprehended and signified by the name lead. Indeed, to a man that knows the signification of the word metal, and not of the word lead, it is a shorter way to explain the signification of the word lead, by saying it is a metal, which at once expresses several of its simple ideas, than to enumerate them one by one, telling him it is a body very heavy, fusible, and malleable.[1]

A **trifling proposition,** in other words, is one in which the predicate is the same as the subject ('A soul is a soul') or part of the subject ('Lead is a metal'). Such propositions, Locke contends, give us no real knowledge of the world. The empiricist, insisting that all knowledge of the world comes from experience, sets them aside. It takes no experience of the world to know that a soul is a soul, but it gives no knowledge of the world either.

Immanuel Kant (1724–1804), a contemporary of Bentham, Blake, Goethe, and Mozart, develops Locke's distinction into one between analytic and synthetic propositions. Born in Königsberg, East Prussia, the son of a saddlemaker and grandson of a Scottish immigrant, Kant attended the University of Königsberg, from which he graduated at twenty-two. He worked as a private tutor and then a *Privatdozent,* an unpaid lecturer who collects fees from his students, until he was appointed to a chair of logic and metaphysics at the university at age forty-six. At fifty-seven, Kant published the *Critique of Pure Reason,* which earned him fame and which is still regarded as one of the greatest works of the Western philosophical tradition. Over the next ten years he wrote four more books, primarily on ethics. Though known for his wit, conversational skill, and dinner parties—"with a decanter of wine . . . at the elbow of every guest"[2]—Kant never married and never traveled more than a few miles from the place of his birth. His habits were so regular that, according to legend, neighbors would set their clocks by his afternoon walks.

Kant distinguishes analytic from synthetic propositions by focusing on those of subject-predicate form:

What concepts are contained in the concepts of 'bachelor', 'metal', and 'toy'? Give examples of analytic judgments and synthetic judgments involving each.

> In all judgments wherein the relation of a subject to the predicate is thought (I mention affirmative judgments only here; the application to negative will be very easy), this relation is possible in two different ways. Either the predicate B belongs

[1] John Locke, *Essay Concerning Human Understanding* (London: printed for Tho. Basset, 1690).

[2] Thomas De Quincey, *The Last Days of Immanuel Kant,* quoted in Iris Murdoch, *Metaphysics as a Guide to Morals* (London: Penguin, 1992), 449.

> to the subject A, as something which is contained (though covertly) in the conception A; or the predicate B lies completely out of the concept A, although it stands in connection with it. In the first instance, I term the judgment analytic, in the second, synthetic. Analytic judgments (affirmative) are therefore those in which the connection of the predicate with the subject is thought through identity; those in which this connection is thought without identity, are called synthetic judgments. The former may be called explicative, the latter augmentative judgments; because the former add in the predicate nothing to the concept of the subject, but only analyze it into its constituent concepts, which were thought already in the subject, although in a confused manner; the latter add to our concepts of the subject a predicate which was not contained in it, and which no analysis could ever have discovered therein. For example, when I say, "All bodies are extended," this is an analytic judgment. For I need not go beyond the concept of body in order to find extension connected with it, but merely analyse the concept, that is, become conscious of the manifold properties which I think in that concept, in order to discover this predicate in it: it is therefore an analytic judgment. On the other hand, when I say, "All bodies are heavy," the predicate is something totally different from that which I think in the mere concept of a body. By the addition of such a predicate, therefore, it becomes a synthetic judgment.[3]

Kant's distinction is essentially the same as Locke's. In an analytic judgment, the predicate is contained in the subject, in the sense that the concept of the predicate is included in the concept of the subject. In a synthetic judgment, this is not so; the concept of the predicate adds something to the concept of the subject.

These definitions are not fully general. Locke and Kant mean them to be exhaustive—that is, any proposition is supposed to be analytic or synthetic, trifling or nontrifling—but they apply only to propositions in subject-predicate form. If 'A soul is a soul' is trifling or analytic, then surely 'If something is a soul, it is a soul' and 'If anything is a soul, there is a soul' are too. In that respect, Avicenna was far ahead of his time; his distinction between propositions "that may be known through Intellect" and those requiring added information extends to judgments of any form. He stresses that propositions that may be known through Intellect require knowledge of the meanings of their terms as well as reasoning. So in keeping with that insight, say that a proposition is *analytic* if it is true or false solely in virtue of the meanings of its terms. In more traditional language, the truth or falsehood of an analytic proposition depends on nothing but the concepts it contains. In particular, it does not depend on what the world is like. A proposition is *synthetic* if it is not analytic—that is, if its truth value depends on something other than the meanings of its terms (or the concepts it contains). The truth value of synthetic propositions depends on what the world is like.

Thus, 'all bachelors are unhappy' is synthetic. It conveys real content about the world. Whether it is true or false depends on the world, in particular on the mental

[3] This and subsequent quotations from Kant, unless otherwise noted, are from Immanuel Kant, *Critique of Pure Reason,* translated by J. M. D. Meiklejohn (New York: Colonial Press, 1899). Throughout, any emphasis in the quotations is Kant's; the pagination is that of the original first [A] and second [B] editions. I have replaced 'analytical' and 'synthetical' with 'analytic' and 'synthetic'; 'cognize' and 'cognition' with 'know' and 'knowledge'; 'cogitated' with 'thought'; and 'conception' with 'concept' to accord with common usage and other translations.

states of bachelors. 'All bachelors are unmarried,' in contrast, is analytic. It is true just by virtue of the meanings of its terms.

The distinction between analytic and synthetic propositions matters to the debate between rationalists and empiricists, for empiricists typically grant that *some* truths can be known without experience. We do not need to do field research on bachelors to learn that bachelors are unmarried. It is true by definition, by virtue of the meaning of the term 'bachelor'. So, in saying that all knowledge comes from experience, empiricists must be careful to exclude knowledge of analytic truths. Empiricists can argue that all knowledge of synthetic propositions comes from experience, putting analytic propositions to one side.

A Priori and a Posteriori Propositions

Empiricists contend, in other words, that the distinction between analytic and synthetic propositions corresponds to a distinction between propositions that can be known independently of experience, by reason alone, and those knowable only through experience. That distinction was pioneered by a medieval Islamic philosopher, Avicenna (Abu 'Ali al-Husayn ibn 'Abd Allah ibn Sina, 980–1037). He was born in Persia near Bukhara, in present-day Uzbekistan. His father, the provincial governor, recognized hs son's talent—Avicenna memorized the entire Koran by age ten—and provided enthusiastically for his education. By eighteen, Avicenna was teaching himself, having surpassed his tutors. By twenty-one he was a physician at the court of the ruling Samanid family, which gave him access to an extensive royal library. That lasted only a few years, however. Turkish leader Mahmud of Ghazna defeated the Samanids. Avicenna spent most of the rest of his life near Tehran, Hamadan, or Ishafan (in present-day Iran) working as a physician and writing.

Avicenna distinguishes two kinds of cognitions:

> Cognition can again be analyzed into two kinds. One is the kind that may be known through Intellect; it is known necessarily by reasoning through itself. . . . The other kind of cognition is one that is known by intuition. Whatever is known by Intellect . . . should be based on something which is known prior to the thing [that is, a priori].[4]

Some things can be known simply through reasoning, Avicenna argues, while other things require "intuition," that is, additional information in the form of sensation, testimony, common opinion, and so on. He calls those we can know through reasoning alone First Principles. Everything else we know through experience: by inference from perception, testimony, or experiment (that is, causal reasoning). Avicenna holds that four kinds of premises can be used to infer knowledge of the world:

> First Principle, Perceptual, Experiential, and Testimonial premises are used in syllogistic reasoning. This kind of reasoning gives certainty and truth.

First Principle premises are independent of experience, while the others depend on experience. Avicenna's distinction lies at the heart of the theory of knowledge.

---

[4]This and subsequent quotations from Avicenna are from *Avicenna's Treatise on Logic: Part One of Danesh-Name Alai,* translated by Farhang Zabeeh (The Hague: Martinus Nijhoff, 1971).

David Hume (1711–1776), a contemporary of Voltaire, Rousseau, Handel, Bach, and fellow Scotsman Adam Smith, develops this distinction in rigorous fashion. He entered the University of Edinburgh at age twelve. After dabbling in law and business, he went to France and wrote *A Treatise of Human Nature,* his greatest philosophical work, when still in his twenties. He argued for a skeptical empiricism, maintaining that all knowledge comes from sense experience and that, therefore, we can have no knowledge of anything beyond experience.

Hume draws just such an epistemological distinction, dividing relations of ideas from matters of fact. Knowledge of the latter depends on experience; only our knowledge of relations of ideas is certain.

Is 'Lead is lead' a relation of ideas or a matter of fact? What about 'Lead is heavier than iron'?

> All the objects of human reason or enquiry may naturally be divided into two kinds, to wit, Relations of Ideas, and Matters of Fact. Of the first kind are the sciences of Geometry, Algebra, and Arithmetic; and in short, every affirmation which is either intuitively or demonstratively certain. That the square of the hypothenuse is equal to the square of the two sides, is a proposition which expresses a relation between these figures. That three times five is equal to the half of thirty, expresses a relation between these numbers. Propositions of this kind are discoverable by the mere operation of thought, without dependence on what is anywhere existent in the universe. Though there never were a circle or triangle in nature, the truths demonstrated by Euclid would for ever retain their certainty and evidence.
>
> Matters of fact, which are the second objects of human reason, are not ascertained in the same manner; nor is our evidence of their truth, however great, of a like nature with the foregoing. The contrary of every matter of fact is still possible; because it can never imply a contradiction, and is conceived by the mind with the same facility and distinctness, as if ever so conformable to reality. That the sun will not rise tomorrow is no less intelligible a proposition, and implies no more contradiction than the affirmation, that it will rise. We should in vain, therefore, attempt to demonstrate its falsehood. Were it demonstratively false, it would imply a contradiction, and could never be distinctly conceived by the mind.[5]

Relations of ideas can be known independently of experience, by "the mere operation of thought," while matters of fact cannot.

Kant draws the same distinction with different terminology. A proposition is **a priori** if its truth value can be known independently of experience and **a posteriori** if its truth value can be known only through experience. 'All bachelors are unmarried' is a priori; knowing it does not require us to have experience of bachelors. Anyone who understands what 'bachelor' means can come to know it. 'All bachelors are unhappy' is different. It is a posteriori, for knowing it requires encounters with bachelors.

Necessary and Contingent Propositions

The distinction between analytic and synthetic propositions is semantic; it pertains to meaning and in particular to what makes a proposition true. The distinction between a priori and a posteriori propositions is epistemological; it concerns what it takes

[5] David Hume, *An Enquiry Concerning Human Understanding* (London: printed for A. Millar, 1758), III, 20–21.

to know the truth value of a proposition. Gottfried Wilhelm Leibniz (1646–1716), a German diplomat and philosopher who was a contemporary of Locke and Newton, and who independently developed the calculus, draws a third and strictly metaphysical distinction between necessary and contingent propositions:

> There are also two kinds of truths, those of reasoning and those of fact. Truths of reasoning are necessary and their opposite is impossible: truths of fact are contingent and their opposite is possible.[6]

A proposition is **necessary** if it cannot be false; **impossible** or **contradictory** if it cannot be true; and **contingent** if it is neither necessary nor impossible—that is, if it could be true and could be false. 'All bachelors are unmarried' is necessary. It could not be false. 'Some bachelors are married' is contradictory. It could not be true. 'All bachelors are unhappy' is contingent; it could be either true or false, depending on what the world is like.

Most Western philosophers of the seventeenth and eighteenth centuries hold that the distinction between a priori and a posteriori propositions corresponds exactly with the distinction between necessary and contingent propositions. They maintain that a proposition is a priori if and only if it is either necessary or impossible, and a posteriori if and only if it is contingent. Kant, in fact, explicitly advocates using necessity and strict universality as indicators of a priori propositions:

> The question now is as to a criterion, by which we may securely distinguish a pure [a priori] from an empirical [a posteriori] cognition. Experience no doubt teaches us that this or that object is constituted in such and such a manner, but not that it could not possibly exist otherwise. Now, in the first place, if we have a proposition which contains the idea of necessity in its very concept, . . . it is absolutely priori. Secondly, an empirical judgment never exhibits strict and absolute, but only assumed and comparative universality (by induction); therefore, the most we can say is—so far as we have hitherto observed, there is no exception to this or that rule. If, on the other hand, a judgment carries with it strict and absolute universality, that is, admits of no possible exception, it is not derived from experience, but is valid absolutely a priori. . . .
>
> Empirical universality is, therefore, only an arbitrary extension of validity, from that which may be predicated of a proposition valid in most cases, to that which is asserted of a proposition which holds good in all; as, for example, in the affirmation, "All bodies are heavy." When, on the contrary, strict universality characterizes a judgment, it necessarily indicates another peculiar source of knowledge, namely, a faculty of cognition a priori. Necessity and strict universality, therefore, are infallible tests for distinguishing pure from empirical knowledge, and are inseparably connected with each other. But as in the use of these criteria the empirical limitation is sometimes more easily detected than the contingency of the judgment, or the unlimited universality which we attach to a judgment is often a more

Is 'Bachelors are unmarried' strictly universal? Necessary? What about 'Bachelors are unhappy'?

[6] Gottfried Wilhelm Leibniz, *Monadology,* from *The Monadology and Other Philosophical Writings,* translated by Robert Latta (Oxford: Oxford University Press, 1898), 33.

> convincing proof than its necessity, it may be advisable to use the criteria separately, each being by itself infallible.

To put this in a simple chart,

	Necessary or Impossible	*Contingent*
A priori	Yes	No
A posteriori	No	Yes

The idea is straightforward. Suppose that a proposition is a priori. Then its truth value can be known independently of experience. But experience is what gives us information about what the world is like; if we do not need experience to know whether it is true or false, its truth value must not depend on what the world is like. So, it must be true no matter what the world is like—that is, necessary—or false no matter what the world is like—that is, impossible. So, any a priori proposition must be either necessary or impossible.

Conversely, suppose that a proposition is a posteriori. Then we can know whether it is true or false only through experience. But experience is useful precisely because it tells us what the world is like. So since we can know whether the proposition is true or false only by finding out what the world is like, its truth value must depend on what the world is like. So it must be contingent.

Rationalism and Empiricism

Avicenna, as we have seen, distinguishes cognitions known by Intellect from those known by intuition. He also distinguishes the knowledge of concepts from the knowledge of judgments:

> There are two kinds of cognition: One is called intuitive or perceptive or apprehensive (*Tasawor* in Arabic). For example, if someone says, 'Man', or 'Fairy', or 'Angel', or the like, you will understand, conceive and grasp what he means by the expression. The other kind of cognition is judgment (*Tasdiq* in Arabic). As for example, when you acknowledge that angels exist or human beings are under surveillance and the like.

Rationalists and empiricists correspondingly differ on two questions: (1) whether we have any innate concepts and (2) whether we have any innate knowledge of the world. Rationalists say we do; empiricists say we don't.

More precisely, a **concept rationalist** believes in innate concepts—specifically, that we have concepts that we do not derive from experience. Leibniz, for example, is a concept rationalist:

> . . . can it be denied that there is much that is innate in our mind, since we are, so to speak, innate to ourselves, and since in ourselves there are being, unity, substance, duration, change, activity, perception, pleasure and a thousand other objects of our intellectual ideas? And as these objects are immediate objects of our understanding and are always present (although they cannot always be consciously perceived be-

> cause of our distractions and wants), why should it be surprising that we say that these ideas, along with all that depends on them, are innate in us?[7]

A **concept empiricist** denies that we have innate concepts, insisting that all concepts come from experience. Locke, for example, writes:

> *Ideas, especially those belonging to principles, not born with children.* If we will attentively consider new-born children, we shall have little reason to think that they bring many ideas into the world with them. For, bating [excepting] perhaps some faint ideas of hunger, and thirst, and warmth, and some pains, which they may have felt in the womb, there is not the least appearance of any settled ideas at all in them; especially of ideas answering the terms which make up those universal propositions that are esteemed innate principles. One may perceive how, by degrees, afterwards, ideas come into their minds; and that they get no more, nor other, than what experience, and the observation of things that come in their way, furnish them with; which might be enough to satisfy us that they are not original characters stamped on the mind. (I, III, 2)

The mind has innate higher-order abilities—abilities to manipulate concepts themselves. Empiricists, for example, hold that the mind can take the raw material of experience, abstract ideas from it, and then separate, combine, negate, and so forth, ideas it derives in this way. Abstraction, negation, combination, and so on are cognitive abilities, but they are higher-order. No one denies that the mind has such abilities. If the mind did not, learning would be impossible. The issue between rationalists and empiricists concerns concepts that apply directly to things in the world.

A **judgment rationalist** holds that some of our knowledge of the world is innate. A **judgment empiricist** denies it. 'Innate' here means knowable independently of experience, that is, a priori. Both rationalists and empiricists think we can know analytic truths just on the basis of the meanings of their terms; experience is not required. So "knowledge of the world" means "knowledge of synthetic truths."

We may reformulate the contrast, then, as follows. A judgment rationalist believes that we can know some synthetic truths a priori—that is, that we can know independently of experience some truths that are not merely linguistic or verbal, that are not automatically true or false because of the meanings of the words that constitute them. A judgment empiricist believes that there are no synthetic a priori truths. That is, a judgment empiricist holds that only analytic truths, "trifling propositions," can be known independently of experience; anything that really yields content about the world can be known only through experience. As Leibniz frames the issue,

> There is the question whether the soul, in itself, is entirely empty, like a writing tablet on which nothing has yet been written (*tabula rasa*), (which is the opinion of Aristotle and the author of the *Essay* [Locke]), and whether everything that is inscribed upon it comes solely from the senses and experience; or whether the soul originally contains the principles of several notions and doctrines, which are merely roused on certain occasions by external objects, as I hold along with Plato

[7] Leibniz, *New Essays on Human Understanding,* from *The Monadology and Other Philosophical Writings,* translated by Robert Latta (Oxford: Oxford University Press, 1898).

> and even with the Schoolmen. . . . Hence there arises another question, whether all truths are dependent on experience, that is, on induction and instances; or whether there are some which have yet another foundation.[8]

We may again explain the contrast in a chart:

	Analytic	*Synthetic*
A priori, necessary or impossible	Yes	Controversial
A posteriori, contingent	No	Yes

Empiricists and rationalists agree about three of these four groups. They agree that some propositions are analytic, a priori, and necessary (if true) or impossible (if false): 'All bachelors are bachelors', 'All bachelors are unmarried', 'If Jones is a bachelor, then he is male', 'Smith is both a bachelor and not a bachelor', and so on. They agree that others are synthetic, a posteriori, and contingent: 'All bachelors are unhappy', 'Jones is a bachelor', 'There are bachelors', and so on. They disagree about whether there are any synthetic a priori truths. To put it another way, they disagree about whether we can know any necessary truths about the world.

RATIONALISM

As we have seen, concept rationalists hold that some first-order concepts are innate. Judgment rationalists hold that some synthetic truths can be known independently of experience, by reason alone. They believe that we can know necessary truths about the world. What kinds of innate concepts or a priori truths do rationalists have in mind? And why do they believe them to be innate?

Most rationalists understand themselves as working within the Platonic tradition. Their central problems and solutions stem directly from that tradition. To understand rationalism, therefore, we must consider the framework from which it arises.

The Platonic Tradition

Consider a judgment of perception, for example, (said pointing to a figure drawn on a blackboard) 'This is a triangle.' According to Plato, in the *Republic,* at least, the mind so judging is Janus-faced. It is turned toward a perceptual object, a triangle, if it judges correctly. It is also turned toward the abstract form of a triangle.

> You are aware that students of geometry, arithmetic, and the kindred sciences assume the odd and the even and the figures and three kinds of angles and the like in their several branches of science; these are their hypotheses, which they and everybody are supposed to know, and therefore they do not deign to give any account of them either to themselves or others; but they begin with them, and go on until they arrive at last, and in a consistent manner, at their conclusion?
>
> Yes, he said, I know.

[8] Leibniz, *New Essays on Human Understanding,* from *The Monadology and Other Philosophical Writings,* translated by Robert Latta (Oxford: Oxford University Press, 1898).

> And do you not know also that although they make use of the visible forms and reason about them, they are thinking not of these, but of the ideals which they resemble; not of the figures which they draw, but of the absolute square and the absolute diameter, and so on—the forms which they draw or make, and which have shadows and reflections in water of their own, are converted by them into images, but they are really seeking to behold the things themselves, which can only be seen with the eye of the mind?
>
> That is true. (510c-511a)[9]

Both the object and the form have real causal or explanatory power. The object is causally responsible for our perception of it. But we are able to perceive it as a triangle because we apprehend the general form of triangularity. The form of a triangle is exemplified in the triangle itself, which in turn is an instance of, or, in Plato's technical language, **participates** in the form.

The **forms** constitute the most distinctive feature of Plato's philosophy of mind. They explain our ability to think general thoughts; they account for regularities as well as changes in experience; they explain how different people (or the same person at different times) can think the same thought; and they explain how thoughts can be veridical, that is, accurate in representing the world. We may think general thoughts, for example, by thinking about the forms and how they relate. Regularities in experience involve constant relations of forms; changes occur when an object of sense stops participating in one form and begins participating in another. Two different people can think the same thought by attending to the same forms. Finally, thoughts can depict reality accurately by involving the forms that are actually instantiated—in which things actually participate.

But the forms also generate a serious puzzle. By definition, the forms are not themselves objects of experience; we do not perceive triangularity as we perceive individual triangles. How, then, do we know anything about them? How is the realm of forms, which Philo of Alexandria (20 B.C.E.–40; see Chapter 2) dubbed "the **intelligible world,**" intelligible? For Aristotle and the empiricist tradition to which he gave rise, we generate our own general concepts from experience through a process of abstraction. A Platonist may borrow this account for some general concepts but cannot use it for all. It is central to Platonism that some forms are ultimately responsible for our abilities to think the corresponding thoughts. On Plato's view, we do not abstract the idea of a pure triangle from triangular objects we perceive; indeed, we never encounter a pure triangle in experience. Instead, we recognize objects as triangular because we apprehend the form of pure triangularity and recognize that the objects approximate that pure form. In this sense, the forms have causal power; we are able to think of things as triangular by apprehending the form.

Recollection

Unfortunately, Plato has no theory that explains our interaction with the forms. He relies on two metaphors. In the *Meno* and *Phaedrus,* he speaks of recollection; we apprehend the forms by recalling a time before birth when our souls were united with them.

---

[9] Plato, *Republic,* translated by Benjamin Jowett, in *The Dialogues of Plato* (Oxford: Oxford University Press, 1892).

If learning is recollection, how did the soul gain knowledge in the first place?

MENO. And how will you enquire, Socrates, into that which you do not know? What will you put forth as the subject of enquiry? And if you find what you want, how will you ever know that this is the thing which you did not know?

SOCRATES. I know, Meno, what you mean; but just see what a tiresome dispute you are introducing. You argue that man cannot enquire either about that which he knows, or about that which he does not know; for if he knows, he has no need to enquire; and if not, he cannot; for he does not know the very subject about which he is to enquire.

MENO. Well, Socrates, and is not the argument sound?

SOCRATES. I think not.

MENO. Why not?

SOCRATES. I will tell you why: I have heard from certain wise men and women who spoke of things divine that—

MENO. What did they say?

SOCRATES. They spoke of a glorious truth, as I conceive.

MENO. What was it? and who were they?

SOCRATES. Some of them were priests and priestesses, who had studied how they might be able to give a reason of their profession: there have been poets also, who spoke of these things by inspiration, like Pindar, and many others who were inspired. And they say—mark, now, and see whether their words are true—they say that the soul of man is immortal, and at one time has an end, which is termed dying, and at another time is born again, but is never destroyed. And the moral is, that a man ought to live always in perfect holiness. "For in the ninth year Persephone sends the souls of those from whom she has received the penalty of ancient crime back again from beneath into the light of the sun above, and these are they who become noble kings and mighty men and great in wisdom and are called saintly heroes in after ages." The soul, then, as being immortal, and having been born again many times, and having seen all things that exist, whether in this world or in the world below, has knowledge of them all; and it is no wonder that she should be able to call to remembrance all that she ever knew about virtue, and about everything; for as all nature is akin, and the soul has learned all things; there is no difficulty in her eliciting or as men say learning, out of a single recollection—all the rest, if a man is strenuous and does not faint; for all enquiry and all learning is but recollection. And therefore we ought not to listen to this sophistical argument about the impossibility of enquiry: for it will make us idle; and is sweet only to the sluggard; but the other saying will make us active and inquisitive. In that confiding, I will gladly enquire with you into the nature of virtue. (80d–81e)[10]

Socrates calls a slave boy over to the conversation and proceeds to go through a geometrical proof with him. The boy, uneducated and unfamiliar with the proof, nevertheless follows and understands step by step.

SOCRATES. What do you say of him, Meno? Were not all these answers given out of his own head?

[10] Plato, *Meno,* translated by Benjamin Jowett, in *The Dialogues of Plato* (Oxford: Oxford University Press, 1892).

MENO. Yes, they were all his own.

SOCRATES. And yet, as we were just now saying, he did not know?

MENO. True.

SOCRATES. But still he had in him those notions of his—had he not?

MENO. Yes.

SOCRATES. Then he who does not know may still have true notions of that which he does not know?

MENO. He has.

SOCRATES. And at present these notions have just been stirred up in him, as in a dream; but if he were frequently asked the same questions, in different forms, he would know as well as any one at last?

MENO. I dare say.

SOCRATES. Without any one teaching him he will recover his knowledge for himself, if he is only asked questions?

MENO. Yes.

SOCRATES. And this spontaneous recovery of knowledge in him is recollection?

MENO. True.

SOCRATES. And this knowledge which he now has must he not either have acquired or always possessed?

MENO. Yes.

SOCRATES. But if he always possessed this knowledge he would always have known; or if he has acquired the knowledge he could not have acquired it in this life, unless he has been taught geometry; for he may be made to do the same with all geometry and every other branch of knowledge. Now, has any one ever taught him all this? You must know about him, if, as you say, he was born and bred in your house.

MENO. And I am certain that no one ever did teach him.

SOCRATES. And yet he has the knowledge?

MENO. The fact, Socrates, is undeniable.

SOCRATES. But if he did not acquire the knowledge in this life, then he must have had and learned it at some other time?

MENO. Clearly he must.

SOCRATES. Which must have been the time when he was not a man?

MENO. Yes.

SOCRATES. And if there have been always true thoughts in him, both at the time when he was and was not a man, which only need to be awakened into knowledge by putting questions to him, his soul must have always possessed this knowledge, for he always either was or was not a man?

MENO. Obviously.

SOCRATES. And if the truth of all things always existed in the soul, then the soul is immortal. Wherefore be of good cheer, and try to recollect what you do not know, or rather what you do not remember.

MENO. I feel, somehow, that I like what you are saying. (85b–86b)

The philosopher recollects more clearly than anyone the forms encountered before birth:

> . . . every soul of man has in the way of nature beheld true being; this was the condition of her passing into the form of man. But all souls do not easily recall the

> things of the other world; they may have seen them for a short time only, or they may have been unfortunate in their earthly lot, and, having had their hearts turned to unrighteousness through some corrupting influence, they may have lost the memory of the holy things which once they saw. Few only retain an adequate remembrance of them; and they, when they behold here any image of that other world, are rapt in amazement; but they are ignorant of what this rapture means, because they do not clearly perceive. For there is no light of justice or temperance or any of the higher ideas which are precious to souls in the earthly copies of them: they are seen through a glass dimly; and there are few who, going to the images, behold in them the realities, and these only with difficulty. [250a–c] [11]

The Good and God

In the *Republic,* Plato uses a different metaphor. He speaks of the form of the Good as analogous to the sun, shedding light on the realm of forms and making possible our apprehension of them. Plato thinks of us in the ordinary world as akin to a group of people watching shadows on the walls of a cave. Philosophical reflection can lead us out of the cave to see things as they really are, illuminated by the sun:

> . . . the prison-house is the world of sight, the light of the fire is the sun, and you will not misapprehend me if you interpret the journey upwards to be the ascent of the soul into the intellectual world according to my poor belief, which, at your desire, I have expressed—whether rightly or wrongly God knows. But, whether true or false, my opinion is that in the world of knowledge the idea of good appears last of all, and is seen only with an effort; and, when seen, is also inferred to be the universal author of all things beautiful and right, parent of light and of the lord of light in this visible world, and the immediate source of reason and truth in the intellectual; and that this is the power upon which he who would act rationally, either in public or private life must have his eye fixed. (517b–c) [12]

Neither metaphor seems to explain our apprehension of forms. The *Meno* explains the causal efficacy of the forms now by appealing to their efficacy at some earlier time; the *Republic* metaphor, by appealing to the efficacy of the form of the Good. The Neoplatonic theory of emanation, according to which the entire realm of forms is ordered, with the causal efficacy of higher levels making lower levels possible and intelligible, does not help.

Saint Augustine (354–430; see Chapters 2 and 5) solves this problem by going beyond the resources of the original theory. To put it crudely, Augustine adopts the *Republic*'s solution but replaces the idea or form of the Good with God. If we do not understand how we could interact with the forms, how can we understand how we can interact with the form of the Good? Interaction with God is not a problem, however, for God can do anything. Augustine follows Philo in identifying the forms with ideas

[11] Plato, *Phaedrus,* translated by Benjamin Jowett, in *The Dialogues of Plato* (Oxford: Oxford University Press, 1892).

[12] Plato, *Republic,* translated by Benjamin Jowett, in *The Dialogues of Plato* (Oxford: Oxford University Press, 1892).

in the mind of God. He describes the process by which we apprehend the forms as **illumination,** an act of revelation. God reveals a portion of the divine mind to us. In that way God makes our minds resemble the divine mind to some degree. We have innate cognitive abilities that reflect the principles according to which God created the world.

Going beyond Experience

Augustine's solution prevailed throughout medieval debates about the reality of the forms. René Descartes (1596–1650; see Chapter 2), however, advanced a new kind of skeptical argument that forced a change in Platonism and brought the theory of knowledge to center stage in modern philosophy. He added to the traditional skeptical arguments the possibility of an evil deceiver who systematically misaligns our minds to reality. This addition extends further than traditional skeptical arguments, for it raises the possibility that not only sensible knowledge but even logic and mathematics might be mistaken. It thus challenges Augustine's solution. Why should illumination produce knowledge? Why should we believe that God reveals the portion of the divine mind relevant to the construction of the world and not some counterfeit of it? Why should our innate ideas and the a priori knowledge arising from them have anything to do with the world?

Kant sees the force of this difficulty and thinks that within the Platonic framework it cannot be solved. He divides previous philosophers into dogmatists and skeptics. Dogmatists like Descartes and Leibniz assume that human reason can comprehend ultimate reality. They answer yes to all three questions:

1. Can we know anything about the world independently of experience?
2. Can we know anything beyond the bounds of experience?
3. Can we know what the world is really like?

Their dogmatism thus involves three factors:

D1. ***Rationalism:*** Some synthetic truths are a priori.
D2. ***Transcendence:*** Knowledge is capable of extending beyond experience to the supersensible.
D3. ***Realism:*** Human thought can discover the nature of objective reality.[13]

Descartes, for example, tries to demonstrate that God guarantees the truth of our a priori judgments by arguing that God exists and is entirely good. A good God, surely, would not be a deceiver. We may see the problem generated by the possibility of the evil deceiver as precisely that of realism: Why should we believe that our thinking can discover the nature of objective reality? Descartes's solution relies on transcendence. We may take the form of thought implicit in the *cogito,* the 'I think'—namely, the method of clear and distinct ideas—and apply it beyond the realm of our own thinking to reality, indeed to reality that transcends all possible experience. Why? The answer is rationalism. There are synthetic truths—real, not merely verbal, truths about

---

[13] The analysis is from Hans Vaihinger, *Commentar zu Kant's Kritik der Reinen Vernunft,* Volume I (Stuttgart: W. Spemann, 1881), 50; Kemp Smith, 13–14.

the world—that we can know independently of experience. For Descartes, then, rationalism does more than postulate that we gain knowledge through reason alone. It implies both transcendence and realism: It implies that we can discover the true nature of objective reality.

Synthetic a Priori Truths: Examples

If there are innate concepts and a priori truths that reveal the true nature of the world, what are they? Leibniz mentions some examples of innate concepts: "being, unity, substance, duration, change, activity, perception, pleasure." Descartes argues explicitly that the concept of God is innate. But the debate centers on purported synthetic a priori truths:

1. Descartes's 'I think, therefore I am', discussed in the previous chapter, provides a classic example of a synthetic a priori truth:

Why is 'I think, therefore I am' synthetic? A priori?

> . . . we cannot in the same way conceive that we who doubt these things are not; for there is a contradiction in conceiving that what thinks does not at the same time as it thinks, exist. And hence this conclusion *I think, therefore I am,* is the first and most certain of all that occurs to one who philosophizes in an orderly way. (VII) [14]

Whether this really ought to count as synthetic a priori, however, is not entirely clear. Avicenna, as we have seen, distinguishes analytic from synthetic truths and a priori from a posteriori truths. He discusses the case of a "flying man," a grown man created suddenly with all the intellectual powers of an adult but suffering sensory deprivation—eyes covered, suspended in empty space, limbs stretched so they cannot touch any other part of the body. Such a person would have no sensory information. Could he know anything? Avicenna, following Augustine and anticipating Descartes, says yes—he could know that he exists. Even the flying man can say, "I think, therefore I am." But that does not determine an answer to question 1. Locke too thinks you can know that you exist; he chalks it up to reflection. Not all experience is sensory experience. So, we might treat the *cogito* as a posteriori.

2. Avicenna speaks of "First Principle" premises, which

What is Avicenna's criterion for recognizing First Principle premises?

> are known by the First Intellect and cannot be doubted. No one can even remember doubting them in the past. If a person imagines that he came into the world knowing nothing except the meaning of two parts of a First Principle premise and he was asked to doubt the truth of the premise he would not be able to do so. For example, if a person knows by intuition the meaning of 'whole' and 'part', 'greater' and 'lesser', then he cannot help knowing that "the whole is greater than its parts," and that "things which are equal to the same thing are equal to one another."

Avicenna's stress on knowing meanings suggests that these are analytic truths. And some surely are. But his general theory of knowledge suggests that some are synthetic.

---

[14] Descartes, *The Principles of Philosophy,* from *The Philosophical Works of Descartes,* Volume I, translated by Elizabeth S. Haldane and G. R. T. Ross (Cambridge: Cambridge University Press, 1911).

To simplify considerably, we might identify the First Intellect with the mind of God. God illumines the realm of forms for us, giving us the ability to have knowledge of them. Part of this knowledge is knowledge of First Principles; we have only to know the meanings of their terms to know that they are true.

3. Descartes lists other examples:

> When we apprehend that it is impossible that anything can be formed of nothing, the proposition *ex nihilo nihil fit* ["Nothing is made from nothing"] is not to be considered as an existing thing, or the mode of a thing, but as a certain eternal truth which has its seat in our mind, and is a common notion or axiom. Of the same nature are the following: 'It is impossible that the same thing can be and not be at the same time,' and that 'what has been done cannot be undone,' 'that he who thinks must exist while he thinks,' and very many other propositions the whole of which it would not be easy to enumerate. (XLIX)

Are these examples strictly universal and necessary?

4. Leibniz attempts to derive all analytic truths from the principle of contradiction (for any proposition *p*, not both *p* and not *p*) and all synthetic truths from that together with one fundamental synthetic a priori principle, the principle of sufficient reason.

> Our reasonings are grounded upon two great principles, that of contradiction, in virtue of which we judge false that which involves a contradiction, and true that which is opposed or contradictory to the false;
>
> And that of sufficient reason, in virtue of which we hold that there can be no fact real or existing, no statement true, unless there be a sufficient reason, why it should be so and not otherwise, although these reasons usually cannot be known by us. (31, 32)[15]

Why does Leibniz take the principle of sufficient reason to be synthetic?

5. Kant argues that 'Every event has a cause' is a synthetic a priori truth, as are the truths of arithmetic and geometry. Descartes treats mathematical truths as analytic; so do empiricists such as Locke and Hume. But Kant contends that geometry has real content, for it describes the structure of space. Arithmetic he similarly links to the structure of time.

> First of all, we ought to observe, that mathematical propositions, properly so called, are always judgments a priori, and not empirical, because they carry along with them necessity, which can never be deduced from experience. . . .
>
> At first sight one might suppose indeed that the proposition 7 + 5 = 12 is merely analytic, following, according to the principle of contradiction, from the concept of a sum of 7 and 5. But, if we look more closely, we shall find that the concept of the sum of 7 and 5 contains nothing beyond the union of both sums into one, whereby nothing is told us as to what this single number may be which combines both. We by no means arrive at a concept of Twelve, by thinking that union

Why, according to Kant, is '7 + 5 = 12' synthetic?

[15] Leibniz, *Monadology*, from *The Monadology and Other Philosophical Writings*, translated by Robert Latta (Oxford: Oxford University Press, 1898).

> of Seven and Five; and we may analyse our concept of such a possible sum as long as we will, still we shall never discover in it the concept of Twelve. We must go beyond these concepts, and call in the assistance of the intuition corresponding to one of the two, for instance, our five fingers, . . . and so by degrees add the units of the Five, given in intuition, to the concept of the Seven. . . . An arithmetical proposition is, therefore, always synthetic. . . .

6. Medieval rationalists propose additional synthetic a priori truths, including truths of metaphysics (for example, 'The world consists of substances and their attributes', 'Every substance has an essence', 'The will is free'), theology ('God exists', 'The soul is immortal', 'God rewards good deeds and punishes evil deeds in the afterlife', and so forth), and morality ('One ought to seek the good', 'Happiness is the only thing good for its own sake and never for the sake of something else', 'Courage is a virtue', and so on).

The Inadequacy of Experience

Whatever you might think about some of these examples, it is hard to see how to do philosophy without any synthetic a priori truths. Philosophy, after all, is the pursuit of wisdom; wisdom requires knowledge, and knowledge entails truth. So philosophy involves the pursuit of truth. To the extent that philosophy involves pursuing analytic truths, it consists of analyzing concepts; it studies the meanings of words. To the extent that philosophy involves pursuing a posteriori truths, it consists of doing empirical science. For empiricists, those are the only options. Rationalists, however, see philosophy as more than conceptual analysis and empirical science. They affirm that philosophical reflection can give us knowledge of the world.

What underlies that affirmation? Rationalists argue that experience is far too poor to yield the knowledge we have of the world. As Leibniz puts it,

> For if some events can be foreseen before we have made any trial of them, it is manifest that we contribute to them something of our own. The senses, although they are necessary for all our actual acquiring of knowledge, are by no means sufficient to give us the whole of our knowledge, since the senses never give anything but instances, that is to say particular or individual truths. Now all the instances which confirm a general truth, however numerous they may be, are not sufficient to establish the universal necessity of this same truth; for it does not at all follow that what has happened will happen in the same way.[16]

Throw out synthetic a priori truths, in other words, and you throw out more than metaphysics, theology, and morality; you throw out all universal or necessary knowledge that is more than merely verbal.

> Whence it seems that necessary truths, such as we find in pure mathematics and especially in arithmetic and geometry, must have principles whose proof does

[16] Leibniz, *New Essays Concerning Human Understanding, Monadology,* from *The Monadology and Other Philosophical Writings,* translated by Robert Latta (Oxford: Oxford University Press, 1898).

> not depend upon instances nor, consequently, upon the witnesses of the senses, although without the senses it would never have come into our heads to think of them. . . . Logic also, along with metaphysics and ethics, of which the one forms natural theology and the other natural jurisprudence, are full of such truths; and consequently their demonstration can come only from the inner principles which are called innate.

We may put Leibniz's argument in this form:

> Experience is always of particular instances.
> Knowledge immediately justified by experience is always of particular instances.
> Universal truths do not follow from their instances.
> Therefore, universal truths cannot be justified by experience.

Take a simple example. We know that all birds have feathers. But even in the whole history of the universe, human beings have encountered only finitely many birds. Perhaps every bird anyone has ever experienced has had feathers. Still, it does not follow that all birds have feathers. Perhaps some unperceived birds lacked feathers; perhaps some birds will lack feathers in the future. So experience does not suffice to give us the knowledge that all birds have feathers.

To take a somewhat more complex example, consider Newton's law, $F = ma$. It states that force is equal to mass times acceleration. This holds for all bodies, in all places, at all times. It is moreover necessary; we can use it to make predictions and draw conclusions not only about circumstances that do exist but also about circumstances that might exist. (In contemporary philosophical language, laws such as $F = ma$ support *counterfactual* reasoning—reasoning about what would happen if such and such were to happen—as well as reasoning about actual courses of events.) Now this law is well confirmed scientifically. Still, it has been tested only finitely many times; our experience falls far short of supporting it for all objects in all places and times.

The rationalist argument, then, is this. Much of our knowledge of the world—especially our knowledge of basic mathematical and scientific laws—we hold to be necessary and universal, applying to all objects in all places at all times. Nothing in experience can justify those claims to universality and necessity. We thus face a dilemma: admit innate concepts and synthetic a priori knowledge, or abandon mathematics and science as unjustified. One cannot be a principled, empiricist skeptic about metaphysics and theology without also being a skeptic about mathematics and science.

EMPIRICISM

Chinese philosopher Wang Chung (27–100?) articulated the central doctrine of empiricism. Wang, an orphan, read books at a bookstore, studied at the national university, and returned to his hometown to teach. He quickly earned a reputation as a genius. He advanced skeptical arguments against the Confucians. Confucianism was China's leading philosophical school, rapidly developing into a religion and attracting a set of superstitions. Wang, a thoroughgoing naturalist, argued that nature is spontaneous, acting according to its own laws without divine intervention or interference. Natural events have no religious meaning. Nature has no discernible purpose; we can understand things only by understanding their causes. And we can gain knowledge of those only through experience.

> Neither ancient nor modern history affords any instances of men knowing spontaneously without study or being enlightened without inquiry. . . . When a man of great natural intelligence and remarkable parts is confined to his own thoughts and has no experience, neither beholding signs and omens nor observing the working of various sorts of beings, he may imagine that after many generations a horse will give birth to an ox, and an ox to a donkey, or that from a peach-tree plums may grow, or cherries from a plum-tree. . . . Let us suppose that somebody standing at that east side of a wall raises his voice, and that a Sage hears him from the west side, would he know whether he was of a dark or a pale complexion, whether he was tall or short, and which was his native place, his surname, his designation, and his origin? . . . Not that a Sage is devoid of knowledge, but this cannot be known through his knowledge. Something unknowable by knowledge may only be learned by inquiry.[17]

That is the key thesis of any empiricist: a negative answer to question 1. Everything we know about the world comes from experiencing it.

Ideas and Their Origins

Concept empiricists maintain that no first-order concepts are innate; we acquire all through experience. As Locke argues:

> . . . men, barely by the use of their natural faculties, may attain to all the knowledge they have, without the help of any innate impressions; and may arrive at certainty, without any such original notions or principles. For I imagine any one will easily grant that it would be impertinent to suppose the ideas of colours innate in a creature to whom God hath given sight, and a power to receive them by the eyes from external objects: and no less unreasonable would it be to attribute several truths to the impressions of nature, and innate characters, when we may observe in ourselves faculties fit to attain as easy and certain knowledge of them as if they were originally imprinted on the mind. (I, I, 1)

Or, in Hume's words,

> . . . all our ideas are nothing but copies of our impressions, or, in other words, that it is impossible for us to think of anything, which we have not antecedently felt, either by our external or internal senses. (*Enquiry* VII, 49)

[17] Wang Chung, *Balanced Inquiries,* from *Lun-Heng: Philosophical Essays of Wang Ch'ung,* Volume I, translated by Alfred Fonke (New York: Paragon, 1907).

Locke takes concept empiricism to imply judgment empiricism, the view that there are no synthetic a priori truths. For we could hardly have innate knowledge of truths without having the concepts they contain innately.

> Had those who would persuade us that there are innate principles not taken them together in gross, but considered separately the parts out of which those propositions are made, they would not, perhaps, have been so forward to believe they were innate. Since, if the ideas which made up those truths were not, it was impossible that the propositions made up of them should be innate, or our knowledge of them be born with us. For, if the ideas be not innate, there was a time when the mind was without those principles; and then they will not be innate, but be derived from some other original. For, where the ideas themselves are not, there can be no knowledge, no assent, no mental or verbal propositions about them. (I, III, 1)

Why, according to Locke, can we not have innate knowledge without innate concepts?

For Locke, all concepts come from sensation of the world around us and reflection on our own mental states and processes.

> All ideas come from sensation or reflection. Let us then suppose the mind to be, as we say, white paper, void of all characters, without any ideas:—How comes it to be furnished? Whence comes it by that vast store which the busy and boundless fancy of man has painted on it with an almost endless variety? Whence has it all the materials of reason and knowledge? To this I answer, in one word, from EXPERIENCE. In that all our knowledge is founded; and from that it ultimately derives itself. Our observation employed either, about external sensible objects, or about the internal operations of our minds perceived and reflected on by ourselves, is that which supplies our understandings with all the materials of thinking. These two are the fountains of knowledge, from whence all the ideas we have, or can naturally have, do spring. (II, I, 2)
>
> These two, I say, viz. external material things, as the objects of SENSATION, and the operations of our own minds within, as the objects of REFLECTION, are to me the only originals from whence all our ideas take their beginnings. (II, I, 4)

What are "the two fountains of knowledge" in Locke's view?

Hume refers to basic sensations and reflections as **impressions.**

> Here therefore we may divide all the perceptions of the mind into two classes or species, which are distinguished by their different degrees of force and vivacity. The less forcible and lively are commonly denominated Thoughts or Ideas. The other species want a name in our language, and in most others; I suppose, because it was not requisite for any, but philosophical purposes, to rank them under a general term or appellation. Let us, therefore, use a little freedom, and call them Impressions; employing that word in a sense somewhat different from the usual. By the term impression, then, I mean all our more lively perceptions, when we hear, or see, or feel, or love, or hate, or desire, or will. And impressions are distinguished from ideas, which are the less lively perceptions, of which we are conscious, when we reflect on any of those sensations or movements above mentioned. (II, 12)[18]

How does Hume distinguish impressions from ideas?

[18] David Hume, *An Enquiry Concerning Human Understanding* (London: printed for A. Millar, 1758).

The Limits of Knowledge

Impressions—which Hume also views as originating in sensation and reflection—not only are the sources of knowledge but also trace the limits of knowledge. We cannot know anything we cannot perceive in one of these ways; the contents of our thoughts stem solely from these sources. As Locke puts it:

> All our ideas are of the one or the other of these. The understanding seems to me not to have the least glimmering of any ideas which it doth not receive from one of these two. External objects furnish the mind with the ideas of sensible qualities, which are all those different perceptions they produce in us; and the mind furnishes the understanding with ideas of its own operations.
>
> These, when we have taken a full survey of them, and their several modes, combinations, and relations, we shall find to contain all our whole stock of ideas; and that we have nothing in our minds which did not come in one of these two ways. Let any one examine his own thoughts, and thoroughly search into his understanding; and then let him tell me, whether all the original ideas he has there, are any other than of the objects of his senses, or of the operations of his mind, considered as objects of his reflection. And how great a mass of knowledge soever he imagines to be lodged there, he will, upon taking a strict view, see that he has not any idea in his mind but what one of these two have imprinted;—though perhaps, with infinite variety compounded and enlarged by the understanding. . . . (II, I, 5)

> In time the mind comes to reflect on its own operations about the ideas got by sensation, and thereby stores itself with a new set of ideas, which I call ideas of reflection. These are the impressions that are made on our senses by outward objects that are extrinsical to the mind; and its own operations, proceeding from powers intrinsical and proper to itself, which, when reflected on by itself, become also objects of its contemplation—are, as I have said, the original of all knowledge. Thus the first capacity of human intellect is,—that the mind is fitted to receive the impressions made on it; either through the senses by outward objects, or by its own operations when it reflects on them. This is the first step a man makes towards the discovery of anything, and the groundwork whereon to build all those notions which ever he shall have naturally in this world. All those sublime thoughts which tower above the clouds, and reach as high as heaven itself, take their rise and footing here: in all that great extent wherein the mind wanders, in those remote speculations it may seem to be elevated with, it stirs not one jot beyond those ideas which sense or reflection have offered for its contemplation. (II, I, 24)

Hume is even more explicit in pointing out the bounds of thought implied by its origins in experience:

> What never was seen, or heard of, may yet be conceived; nor is any thing beyond the power of thought, except what implies an absolute contradiction. But though our thought seems to possess this unbounded liberty, we shall find, upon a nearer examination, that it is really confined within very narrow limits, and that all this creative power of the mind amounts to no more than the faculty of compounding, transposing, augmenting, or diminishing the materials afforded us by the senses

> and experience. . . . All our ideas or more feeble perceptions are copies of our impressions or more lively ones. (II, 13, 14)

A negative answer to question 1, that is, implies a negative answer to question 2. If all knowledge comes from experience, it can extend no further than experience.

Both Locke and Hume distinguish **simple** from **complex** ideas. Some ideas are compounded from others: the concept of a unicorn, for example, combines the concept of a horse with the concept of having one horn. Complex ideas are compounds of other ideas; simple ideas are not. Locke:

How can we distinguish simple from complex ideas?

> The better to understand the nature, manner, and extent of our knowledge, one thing is carefully to be observed concerning the ideas we have; and that is, that some of them are simple and some complex.
>
> Though the qualities that affect our senses are, in the things themselves, so united and blended, that there is no separation, no distance between them; yet it is plain, the ideas they produce in the mind enter by the senses simple and unmixed. For, though the sight and touch often take in from the same object, at the same time, different ideas;—as a man sees at once motion and colour; the hand feels softness and warmth in the same piece of wax: yet the simple ideas thus united in the same subject, are as perfectly distinct as those that come in by different senses. The coldness and hardness which a man feels in a piece of ice being as distinct ideas in the mind as the smell and whiteness of a lily; or as the taste of sugar, and smell of a rose. And there is nothing can be plainer to a man than the clear and distinct perception he has of those simple ideas; which, being each in itself uncompounded, contains in it nothing but one uniform appearance, or conception in the mind, and is not distinguishable into different ideas. (II, II, 1)

Hume, as usual, is more concise:

> There is another division of our perceptions, which it will be convenient to observe, and which extends itself both to our impressions and our ideas. This division is into simple and complex. Simple perceptions or impressions and ideas are such as to admit of no distinction or separation. The complex are the contrary to these, and may be distinguished into parts. Tho' a particular colour, taste, and smell are qualities all united together in this apple, 'tis easy to perceive they are not the same, but are at least distinguishable from each other.[19]

This distinction is important, for "all our simple ideas in their first appearance are deriv'd from simple impressions, which are correspondent to them, and which they exactly represent." We can trace complex ideas to the simple ideas of which they are composed, and then find the origins of each simple idea in experience. That, Hume says, gives us a method for resolving philosophical problems:

What method is Hume recommending? How might it apply, for example, to the idea of happiness? To the idea of God?

> All ideas, especially abstract ones, are naturally faint and obscure: The mind has but a slender hold of them: They are apt to be confounded with other resembling

[19] David Hume, *A Treatise of Human Nature* (London: printed for John Noon, 1739), I, I, 1.

> ideas; and when we have often employed any term, though without a distinct meaning, we are apt to imagine it has a determinate idea, annexed to it. On the contrary, all impressions, that is, all sensations, either outward or inward, are strong and vivid: The limits between them are more exactly determined: Nor is it easy to fall into any error or mistake in regard to them. When we entertain, therefore, any suspicion, that a philosophical term is employed without any meaning or idea (as is but too frequent), we need but enquire, *from what impression is that supposed idea derived?* And if it be impossible to assign any, this will serve to confirm our suspicion. By bringing ideas into so clear a light, we may reasonably hope to remove all dispute, which may arise, concerning their nature and reality. (II, 18)

In the case of many allegedly innate ideas—the ideas of God, causation, or substance, for example—Hume finds a corresponding impression that is inward rather than outward, something deriving from reflection rather than sensation. He traces such ideas, in other words, to something inside us. But that something is not an innate concept but a sentiment, a feeling, that we experience. Consider, for example, the idea of God:

> Even those ideas, which, at first view, seem the most wide of this origin, are found, upon a nearer scrutiny, to be derived from it. The idea of God, as meaning an infinitely intelligent, wise, and good Being, arises from reflecting on the operations of our own mind, and augmenting, without limit, those qualities of goodness and wisdom. We may prosecute this enquiry to what length we please; where we shall always find, that every idea which we examine is copied from a similar impression. (II, 15)

Descartes argues at length that only God could have caused us to have the idea of God, for ideas are at best imperfect copies of their originals; an idea of something perfect must have its origin in something perfect. (See Chapter 6.) Hume denies this. We recognize wisdom, goodness, intelligence, and power in ourselves by reflecting on our own mental operations. We can augment them without limit; we have a higher-order cognitive ability to extrapolate something we encounter to its limit, or to infinity.

To view this another way, we could say that we encounter the bounds of our own intelligence, power, wisdom, and goodness when we do something bad or stupid, or find ourselves powerless. We feel frustration at those boundaries—an inward impression, again—and know that our abilities are limited. But we have a higher-order ability to negate concepts: to go from the concept of red to the concept of non-red, or, in this case, from the concepts of limited intelligence, power, and so on, to those of unlimited qualities corresponding to them. We derive the idea of perfection not from a perfect being but from our awareness of our own abilities and their limitations.

But the crucial ideas for the success of empiricism are those of universality and necessity. Kant takes them as signs of the a priori, for they, he contends, cannot be derived from experience. So can the empiricist trace our ideas of universality and necessity back to anything in experience? Or must empiricism write off all talk of causation and scientific law?

Universality

Where do we obtain the idea of universality, of 'all'? Kant treats it as one of the pure, a priori concepts of the understanding. Empiricists, denying it to be innate, must trace it to some origin in experience. Locke has the resources to do so. Taking a cue from the *cogito,* Locke says we have a clear intuitive knowledge of our own existence through reflection:

> We perceive [that we exist] so plainly and so certainly, that it neither needs nor is capable of any proof. For nothing can be more evident to us than our own existence. (IV, IX, 3)

Now one of the most important higher-order abilities of the mind is *abstraction,* the ability to distinguish components of compound ideas. So, from the concept of 'my existence', I can abstract the concept of existence. And I have the higher-order ability to negate any concept I have. But this is all I need for universality: To say that all F are G is just to say that there does not exist an F that is not a G. 'All pigs grunt', for example, is equivalent to 'It is not the case that there exist pigs that do not grunt'. 'God created everything' is equivalent to 'It is not the case that there exists something God did not create'.

The more serious question is how we might know any univeral truths on the basis of experience. For empiricism limits knowledge not only by restricting its raw materials, ideas, to those furnished by experience, but also by restricting what we can build from them to two kinds of truths. For the judgment empiricist, there are no synthetic a priori truths.

	Analytic	*Synthetic*
A priori, necessary or impossible	Yes	No
A posteriori, contingent	No	Yes

So, all truths fall into two categories: (a) analytic, a priori truths, which we can know independently of experience but which yield no real knowledge of the world; and (b) synthetic, a posteriori truths, which do yield real knowledge of the world but which can be known only through experience. In the first category are definitions, logic, and mathematics. In the second are the empirical sciences. Those are the only two legitimate kinds of knowledge; anything else is nonsense. As Hume dramatically concludes *An Enquiry Concerning Human Understanding,*

> When we run over libraries, persuaded of these principles, what havoc must we make? If we take in our hand any volume; of divinity or school metaphysics, for instance; let us ask, *Does it contain any abstract reasoning concerning quantity or number?* No. *Does it contain any experimental reasoning concerning matter of fact and existence?* No. Commit it then to the flames: For it can contain nothing but sophistry and illusion. (XII)

How, then, can we know universal truths? They must be matters of definition, giving us merely verbal knowledge, or they must be known on the basis of experience. The former, however, give us no real knowledge of the world. So natural laws such as

$F = ma$, which do not appear to be definitions and which do seem to give us real knowledge of the world, must be known on the basis of experience. But how can our finite, limited experience ever justify a universal conclusion? Must we commit scientific laws to the flames as well?

The Scandal of Induction

Hume raises an even more radical question:

> It may, therefore, be a subject worthy of curiosity, to enquire what is the nature of that evidence, which assures us of any real existence and matter of fact, beyond the present testimony of our senses, or the records of our memory. (*Enquiry*, IV, I)

This leads to a series of additional questions:

> When it is asked, *What is the nature of all our reasonings concerning matter of fact?* the proper answer seems to be, that they are founded on the relation of cause and effect. When it is again asked, *What is the foundation of all our reasonings and conclusions concerning that relation?* it may be replied in one word, experience. But if we still carry on our sifting humour and ask, *What is the foundation of all conclusions from experience?* this implies a new question, which may be of more difficult solution. (*Enquiry*, IV, II)

Hume argues for the surprising conclusion that

> . . . even after we have experience of the operations of cause and effect, our conclusions from that experience are *not* founded on reasoning, or any process of the understanding. (*Enquiry*, IV, II)

We do draw universal conclusions from finite evidence, but we have no reason to do so. We have no justification. This is Hume's celebrated scandal of induction: Inductive inferences have no rational justification.

Consider some inductive inferences from instances to universal conclusions or further instances:

> All ravens that have been observed are black.
> So, all ravens are black.
>
> Whenever I've eaten bread, I've found it nourishing.
> So, I'll find this bread nourishing.
>
> When the sun has set, it has always risen the next morning.
> So, the sun will rise tomorrow.

Hume points out that this reasoning cannot be a priori. It certainly is not necessary. The next raven I encounter might be white. The bread in front of me might be poisoned. The sun might go nova tonight. Any support these inferences have must come from experience. But how can experience justify them? The issue is precisely how experience, by its nature finite and limited, can support universal conclusions. So to appeal to experience is to beg the question.

> All reasonings may be divided into two kinds, namely, demonstrative reasoning, or that concerning relations of ideas, and moral reasoning, or that concerning matter of fact and existence. That there are no demonstrative arguments in the case, seems evident; since it implies no contradiction, that the course of nature may change, and that an object, seemingly like those which we have experienced, may be attended with different or contrary effects. May I not clearly and distinctly conceive, that a body, falling from the clouds, and which, in all other respects, resembles snow, has yet the taste of salt or the feeling of fire? Is there any more intelligible proposition than to affirm, that all the trees will flourish in December and January, and decay in May and June? Now whatever is intelligible, and can be distinctly conceived, implies no contradiction, and can never be proved false by any demonstrative argument or abstract reasoning a priori.
>
> If we be, therefore, engaged by arguments to put trust in past experience, and make it the standard of our future judgment, these arguments must be probable only, or such as regard matter of fact and real existence, according to the division above mentioned. But that there is no argument of this kind, must appear, if our explication of that species of reasoning be admitted as solid and satisfactory. We have said, that all arguments concerning existence are founded on the relation of cause and effect; that our knowledge of that relation is derived entirely from experience; and that all our experimental conclusions proceed upon the supposition, that the future will be conformable to the past. To endeavor, therefore, the proof of this last supposition by probable arguments, or arguments regarding existence, must be evidently going in a circle, and taking that for granted, which is the very point in question. (*Enquiry,* IV, II)

Why is any rational attempt to justify induction circular?

In short, there is no rational justification for applying induction and assuming that the future will resemble the past. We do so as a matter of custom or habit, not as a matter of reason.

> . . . after the constant conjunction of two objects, heat and flame, for instance, weight and solidity, we are determined by custom alone to expect the one from the appearance of the other. This hypothesis seems even the only one, which explains the difficulty, why we draw, from a thousand instances, an inference, which we are not able to draw from one instance, that is, in no respect, different from them. Reason is incapable of any such variation. The conclusions, which it draws from considering one circle, are the same which it would form upon surveying all the circles in the universe. But no man, having seen only one body move after being impelled by another, could infer, that every other body will move after a like impulse. All inferences from experience, therefore, are effects of custom, not of reasoning. (*Enquiry* V)

Hence, we do derive universal conclusions from experience. But we do so by custom, not by any process of reasoning.

Necessity

Hume tells a similar story about necessity. Locke seeks for the origins of our idea of causation and finds it in the production of certain kinds of events:

How does Locke define 'cause' and 'effect'?

> In the notice that our senses take of the constant vicissitude of things, we cannot but observe that several particular, both qualities and substances, begin to exist; and that they receive this their existence from the due application and operation of some other being. From this observation we get our ideas of cause and effect. That which produces any simple or complex idea we denote by the general name, cause, and that which is produced, effect. Thus, finding that in that substance which we call wax, fluidity, which is a simple idea that was not in it before, is constantly produced by the application of a certain degree of heat we call the simple idea of heat, in relation to fluidity in wax, the cause of it, and fluidity the effect. So also, finding that the substance, wood, which is a certain collection of simple ideas so called, by the application of fire, is turned into another substance, called ashes; i.e., another complex idea, consisting of a collection of simple ideas, quite different from that complex idea which we call wood; we consider fire, in relation to ashes, as cause, and the ashes, as effect. So that whatever is considered by us to conduce or operate to the producing any particular simple idea, or collection of simple ideas, whether substance or mode, which did not before exist, hath thereby in our minds the relation of a cause, and so is denominated by us. (II, XXVI, 1)

Hume thinks Locke begs the question. Note the phrases 'receive this their existence from', 'produces', 'is constantly produced', 'is turned into', 'conduce or operate to the producing'. We do not experience the *production* of one event by another; we experience only one event *followed by* another. The issue is precisely what in experience can justify our classification of some such progressions as productions or instances of causation.

> When we look about us towards external objects, and consider the operation of causes, we are never able, in a single instance, to discover any power or necessary connexion; any quality, which binds the effect to the cause, and renders the one an infallible consequence of the other. We only find, that the one does actually, in fact, follow the other. The impulse of one billiard-ball is attended with motion in the second. This is the whole that appears to the outward senses. The mind feels no sentiment or inward impression from this succession of objects: Consequently, there is not, in any single, particular instance of cause and effect, anything which can suggest the idea of power or necessary connexion. . . .
>
> It appears that, in single instances of the operation of bodies, we never can, by our utmost scrutiny, discover anything but one event following another, without being able to comprehend any force or power by which the cause operates, or any connexion between it and its supposed effect. The same difficulty occurs in contemplating the operations of mind on body—where we observe the motion of the latter to follow upon the volition of the former, but are not able to observe or conceive the tie which binds together the motion and volition, or the energy by which the mind produces this effect. The authority of the will over its own faculties and ideas is not a whit more comprehensible: So that, upon the whole, there ap-

> pears not, throughout all nature, any one instance of connexion which is conceivable by us. All events seem entirely loose and separate. One event follows another; but we never can observe any tie between them. They seem conjoined, but never connected. (*Enquiry,* VII, 50, 58)

So, we do not see causal connections themselves. And we cannot infer them a priori.

> When any natural object or event is presented, it is impossible for us, by any sagacity or penetration, to discover, or even conjecture, without experience, what event will result from it, or to carry our foresight beyond that object which is immediately present to the memory and senses. (*Enquiry,* VII, 59)

Indeed, the situation is exactly parallel to the problem of induction. From one instance, we can infer nothing. From many instances, however, we happily infer a causal link.

> Even after one instance or experiment where we have observed a particular event to follow upon another, we are not entitled to form a general rule, or foretell what will happen in like cases; it being justly esteemed an unpardonable temerity to judge of the whole course of nature from one single experiment, however accurate or certain. But when one particular species of event has always, in all instances, been conjoined with another, we make no longer any scruple of foretelling one upon the appearance of the other, and of employing that reasoning, which can alone assure us of any matter of fact or existence. We then call the one object, Cause; the other, Effect. We suppose that there is some connexion between them; some power in the one, by which it infallibly produces the other, and operates with the greatest certainty and strongest necessity. (*Enquiry,* VII, 59)

Just as in the case of induction, our conclusion rests not on any process of reasoning but on custom or habit. And this reveals the impression underlying our idea of cause and effect (and thus also, for Hume, of universality): the feeling of expectation we get when we see a sequence of events happen repeatedly. The constant conjunction of events leads to a feeling of expectation on our part, and that feeling is the origin of our idea of necessity.

> It appears, then, that this idea of a necessary connexion among events arises from a number of similar instances which occur of the constant conjunction of these events; nor can that idea ever be suggested by any one of these instances, surveyed in all possible lights and positions. But there is nothing in a number of instances, different from every single instance, which is supposed to be exactly similar; except only, that after a repetition of similar instances, the mind is carried by habit, upon the appearance of one event, to expect its usual attendant, and to believe that it will exist. This connexion, therefore, which we feel in the mind, this customary transition of the imagination from one object to its usual attendant, is the sentiment or impression from which we form the idea of power or necessary connexion. Nothing farther is in the case. Contemplate the subject on all sides; you will never find any other origin of that idea. This is the sole difference between one instance, from which we can never receive the idea of connexion, and a number of similar instances, by which it is suggested. The first time a man saw the communication of motion by impulse, as by the shock of two billiard balls, he could not pronounce

> that the one event was connected: but only that it was conjoined with the other. After he has observed several instances of this nature, he then pronounces them to be connected. What alteration has happened to give rise to this new idea of connexion? Nothing but that he now feels these events to be connected in his imagination, and can readily foretell the existence of one from the appearance of the other. When we say, therefore, that one object is connected with another, we mean only that they have acquired a connexion in our thought, and give rise to this inference, by which they become proofs of each other's existence: A conclusion which is somewhat extraordinary, but which seems founded on sufficient evidence. (*Enquiry,* VII, 59)

The necessity we attribute to the world and to the causal connections within it is not there in the objects themselves. We impose it on the world. Necessity is not in the things but in us.

What impression is the origin of the idea of necessity?

> Tho' the several resembling instances, which give rise to the idea of power, have no influence on each other, and can never produce any new quality in the object, which can be the model of that idea, yet the observation of this resemblance produces a new impression in the mind, which is its real model. For after we have observ'd the resemblance in a sufficient number of instances, we immediately feel a determination of the mind to pass from one object to its usual attendant, and to conceive it in a stronger light upon account of that relation. This determination is the only effect of the resemblance; and therefore must be the same with power or efficacy, whose idea is deriv'd from the resemblance. The several instances of resembling conjunctions lead us into the notion of power and necessity. These instances are in themselves totally distinct from each other, and have no union but in the mind, which observes them, and collects their ideas. Necessity, then, is the effect of this observation, and is nothing but an internal impression of the mind, or a determination to carry our thoughts from one object to another. Without considering it in this view, we can never arrive at the most distant notion of it, or be able to attribute it either to external or internal objects, to spirit or body, to causes or effects.
>
> The necessary connexion betwixt causes and effects is the foundation of our inference from one to the other. The foundation of our inference is the transition arising from the accustomed union. These are, therefore, the same.
>
> The idea of necessity arises from some impression. There is no impression convey'd by our senses, which can give rise to that idea. It must, therefore, be deriv'd from some internal impression, or impression of reflection. There is no internal impression, which has any relation to the present business, but that propensity, which custom produces, to pass from an object to the idea of its usual attendant. This therefore is the essence of necessity. Upon the whole, necessity is something, that exists in the mind, not in objects; nor is it possible for us ever to form the most distant idea of it, considered as a quality in bodies. Either we have no idea of necessity, or necessity is nothing but that determination of the thought to pass from causes to effects, and from effects to causes, according to their experienced union. (*Treatise* I, III, XIV)

Aristotle holds that the mind, in sensation, is passive, receiving impressions from the world. He moreover holds that we can think nothing that was not in the senses first. The empiricists inherit these assumptions. So, the basic image is that of the world making an impression on our minds, like a ring making an impression on soft wax. Locke's distinction between sensation of outer objects and reflection on our own ideas, which itself shows the influence of Descartes, seems at first a minor revision of this picture. In Hume's hands, however, it becomes major. For the mind in some respects is highly active. The universality and necessity we attribute to the world come from us, not from anything in the world. This leads to a negative answer to question 3: We cannot know the world as it is. Crucial features of our understanding of it come from us, not from the world.

> 'Tis a common observation, that the mind has a great propensity to spread itself on external objects, and to conjoin with them any internal impressions, which they occasion, and which always make their appearance at the same time that these objects discover themselves to the senses. (*Treatise* I, III, XIV)

But universality and necessity are not only marks of a priori knowledge, according to rationalists, but also characteristic of scientific law. The conclusion waiting in the wings is that the regularity and law-governed character of nature have their sources not in nature itself but in us.

KANT'S COPERNICAN REVOLUTION

Immanuel Kant's *Critique of Pure Reason* brought this idea to center stage. It transformed the philosophical world, at once bringing the Enlightenment to its highest intellectual development and establishing a new set of problems that would dominate philosophy in the next two centuries. As American philosopher Richard Rorty has observed, Kant turned philosophy into a profession, if for no other reason than that after 1781 one could not be called a philosopher without having mastered Kant's first *Critique*—which, in the words of Kant's famous commentator, Norman Kemp Smith, "is more obscure and difficult than even a metaphysical treatise has any right to be."[20]

The *Critique*'s central character is "human reason," which, Kant begins his first edition's preface by noting,

> is called upon to consider questions, which it cannot decline, as they are presented by its own nature, but which it cannot answer, as they transcend every faculty of the mind. [Avii]

Reason develops principles to deal with experience; within the realm of experience, those principles are well justified. Reason finds itself driven, however, to ask questions extending beyond that realm. The very principles it has developed and upon which it properly continues to rely in dealing with experience there lead it "into confusion and contradictions" [Aviii]. Metaphysics, once "Queen of the Sciences," now surveys the battlefield on which these principles clash and mourns. Kant's aim in the *Critique*

[20] Richard Rorty, *Philosophy and the Mirror of Nature* (Princeton: Princeton University Press, 1979), 149; Norman Kemp Smith, *A Commentary to Kant's Critique of Pure Reason* (Atlantic Highlands, N.J.: Humanities Press, 1962), vii.

is to rescue metaphysics, "to secure for human reason complete satisfaction" [A856/B884] by defining its proper sphere of application.

Kant's means for achieving this end is the critical method. The title of his work is ambiguous in both English and German: Pure reason may be the agent or the object of the critique.[21] In fact it is both. The critical method requires reason to critique itself, to determine its own limits, and then to devise rules for staying within them. This, Kant thinks, is the key to reason's "complete satisfaction": "There is not a single metaphysical problem that does not find its solution, or at least the key to its solution, here" [Axiii].

Understood in this way, Kant's critical method hardly seems revolutionary. Locke's *Essay Concerning Human Understanding* and Hume's *A Treatise of Human Nature* and *An Enquiry Concerning Human Understanding* already exemplified it. They tried to define the limits of human knowledge by employing reason in a reflective act of self-criticism. Kant's most important contribution is not the general idea of the critical method but the specific form that method takes, for which he often uses the adjective 'transcendental' rather than 'critical'. Kant claims that he uses the **transcendental method** and establishes the truth of **transcendental idealism.**

What, then, is the transcendental method? To understand it, we must understand what Kant called his **Copernican revolution in philosophy.** Kant finds himself capable of setting metaphysics upon the secure path of a science by advancing a hypothesis analogous to that of Copernicus.

Explain Kant's analogy. To what does the motion of the earth correspond?

> It has hitherto been assumed that our knowledge must conform to the objects; but all attempts to ascertain anything about these objects a priori, by means of concepts, and thus to extend the range of our knowledge, have been rendered abortive by this assumption. Let us then make the experiment whether we may not be more successful in metaphysics, if we assume that the objects must conform to our knowledge. This appears, at all events, to accord better with the possibility of our gaining the end we have in view, that is to say, of arriving at the knowledge of objects a priori, of determining something with respect to these objects, before they are given to us. We here propose to do just what Copernicus did in attempting to explain the celestial movements. When he found that he could make no progress by assuming that all the heavenly bodies revolved round the spectator, he reversed the process, and tried the experiment of assuming that the spectator revolved, while the stars remained at rest. We may make the same experiment with regard to the intuition of objects. If the intuition must conform to the nature of the objects, I do not see how we can know anything of them a priori. If, on the other hand, the object conforms to the nature of our faculty of intuition, I can then easily conceive the possibility of such an a priori knowledge. Now as I cannot rest in the mere intuitions, but—if they are to become knowledge—must refer them, as representations, to something, as object, and must determine the latter by means of the former, here again there are two courses open to me. Either, first, I may assume that the concepts, by which I effect this determination, conform to the ob-

[21] Hans Vaihinger, *Commentar zu Kant's Kritik der Reinen Vernunft,* Volume I (Stuttgart: W. Spemann, 1881), 117–120.

> ject—and in this case I am reduced to the same perplexity as before; or secondly, I may assume that the objects, or, which is the same thing, that experience, in which alone as given objects they are known, conform to my concepts—and then I am at no loss how to proceed. For experience itself is a mode of knowledge which requires understanding. Before objects are given to me, that is, a priori, I must presuppose in myself laws of the understanding which are expressed in concepts a priori. To these concepts, then, all the objects of experience must necessarily conform. Now there are objects which reason thinks, and that necessarily, but which cannot be given in experience, or, at least, cannot be given so as reason thinks them. The attempt to think these objects will hereafter furnish an excellent test of the new method of thought which we have adopted, and which is based on the principle that we only know in things a priori that which we ourselves place in them. [Bxvi]

Copernicus explained the motions of the heavenly bodies as resulting, not just from their own motion, but also from the motion of the observers on earth. Just as he sought "the observed movements, not in the heavenly bodies, but in the spectator" [Bxxiin], so Kant seeks the laws governing the realm of experience not in the objects themselves but in us: ". . . We can know in things a priori only what we ourselves place in them" [Bxviii].

Phenomena and Noumena

Kant is plainly a rationalist in both senses of the word. He argues that we can deduce our possession of innate concepts—in his terms, pure concepts of the understanding—a priori, independently of experience, from the mere possibility of experience. He also holds that there are synthetic a priori truths—that is, truths about the world that we can know independently of experience. Indeed, the establishment of rationalism in both senses seems to be one of his major goals. Nevertheless, he is a highly unusual rationalist.

Kant's critical philosophy distinguishes the world of **appearance,** things as they are known to us—the **phenomenal** world—from the world of **things-in-themselves**—the **noumenal** world. We can know the former by our senses. We can discover its nature. Things-in-themselves, in contrast, lie beyond our cognitive capacities. The dogmatist (for example, Descartes) is right about the possibility of knowledge of objects, even a priori knowledge of them, but the skeptic (for example, Hume) is right that knowledge is limited to the realm of experience. For Kant, then, the answer to question 1 is yes—we can know something about the world independently of experience—but the answers to 2 and 3 are nevertheless no. Our knowledge cannot extend beyond experience, and we cannot know the world as it really is.

Question	*Descartes*	*Hume*	*Kant*
1. Synthetic a priori truth	Yes	No	Yes
2. Knowledge beyond experience	Yes	No	No
3. Knowledge of the world as it is	Yes	No	No

Both Descartes and Hume misunderstand the status of objects of experience, in Kant's view. They think that the things we see, hear, and so on are in themselves as they appear to us. But we have no reason to assume that. The phenomenal world is both sensible and knowable; the noumenal world is neither. With respect to phenomena, therefore, the skeptic is vanquished; we can have a priori knowledge of objects of experience. With respect to noumena, however, the skeptic triumphs, for we can have no knowledge of things-in-themselves.

Kant's solution to the epistemological problem of Platonism goes beyond the distinction between phenomena and noumena. Kant's solution resides in two additional changes to the traditional framework. First, Kant explains the causal efficacy of the forms by transforming them into **categories,** pure concepts of the understanding. They are innate cognitive abilities of a very general kind, but they are wholly mental; the question of their correspondence to abstract, mind-independent forms cannot arise. Without such forms there remains, of course, the possibility that the categories do not correspond to objective and concrete reality.

Second, Kant reverses the traditional conception of the relation between thought and its object, or, as he puts it, between object and concept. The Platonist traditionally sees the object as causally responsible for the veridical perception or thought of it. We see a triangle because there is a triangle there. We think of some events as causing others because they do. Kant's Copernican revolution is precisely to reverse this understanding, maintaining instead that thought is causally responsible for constituting the object. There is a triangle there because we see it. Some events cause others because we think of them as doing so.

The result is not anarchy, a circumstance of "thinking making it so," for the constitution of objects proceeds according to the categories in a universal and rule-governed way. That is what makes knowledge of objects possible. More, it makes a priori knowledge of them possible, for we can understand what we put into them—we can discover the rules according to which we constitute them. In this way Kant justifies his realism with respect to the phenomenal world without any appeal to transcendence—indeed, in the face of its outright denial.

The Categories

Kant's first change to the traditional Platonistic framework is to substitute for the forms the categories, pure concepts of the understanding. These are innate ideas of the kind smiled upon by every concept rationalist. But there is no abstract realm of forms to which they must correspond. Their independence dissolves the problem faced by Plato.

All knowledge, Kant observes, involves concepts; all concepts, in turn, "depend upon functions," "arranging diverse representations under one common representation" [A68/B93]. The representations united in a concept may be "sensible intuitions"—impressions, in Hume's terminology—or other concepts. Kant here makes an important concession to Hume: the content of concepts traces ultimately to sensation. Kant makes much of this in the second half of the *Critique,* the "Transcendental Dialectic," to refute the transcendence thesis and restrict knowledge to the realm of experience. In deriving the categories, however, he focuses on the *mediate* character of concepts. Concepts of objects always relate to those objects indirectly:

> Concepts, then, are based on the spontaneity of thought, as sensuous intuitions are on the receptivity of impressions. Now, the understanding cannot make any other use of these concepts than to judge by means of them. As no representation, except an intuition, relates immediately to its object, a concept never relates immediately to an object, but only to some other representation thereof, be that an intuition or itself a concept. A judgment, therefore, is the mediate cognition of an object, consequently the representation of a representation of it. [A68/B93]

Why does Kant think that concepts never relate to objects directly? What stands between them?

The concept of a triangle does not relate directly to the triangle but only to some thought or sensation of it. This has the consequence, crucial to the Copernican revolution Kant means to effect, that both judgments and objects are products of synthesis. They are constructed by the mind from the raw materials provided by sense.

Knowledge, Kant contends, always takes the form of judgments. (This is true at least for discursive knowledge, that is, knowing *that,* as opposed to knowing *how* or knowing *to.*) Judgments are combinations of concepts, which in turn are rules for synthesis, bringing together various sensations or concepts. A simple judgment such as 'Gold is valuable' combines the concepts *gold* and *valuable.* Those concepts may bring together other concepts—in Locke's terms, they may be complex—or they may relate directly to sensations. Concepts relate to objects in the world because they are such functions of synthesis. The concept *gold* applies to gold things because we can relate it to sensations that indicate that something is gold. We learn to relate our concept of gold to the right sensations through experience.

The categories, however, are *pure* concepts of the understanding. Kant defines a pure concept of the understanding as a concept without any empirical content, that is, as one that "universally and adequately expresses . . . a formal and objective condition of experience" [A96]. To discover the categories, therefore, we must find the functions of synthesis that are not learned through experience. Those turn out to be just the ideas—universality, substance, causation, necessity—that Hume traces to feelings rather than sense impressions.

The *content* of judgments, Kant holds, always stems from experience, for the content of the concepts in them comes from sensation. To this extent he agrees with Hume, who traces all ideas back to impressions. A concept unites *intuitions*—Kant's term for impressions—or other concepts. They in turn unite intuitions or other concepts. The chain cannot go on forever; at some point it terminates in intuition. Eventually, that is, we can trace concepts to the intuitions—the impressions, the sensations and reflections—that give them content.

Consider, for example, the concept *gold.* Kant thinks we can define 'gold' as 'yellow metal'. The concept *yellow* Locke and Hume take to be simple; it unites possible sensations of yellow directly. The concept *metal* Locke defines in terms of other concepts: *heavy, fusible,* and *malleable.* We might define those in turn in terms of other concepts. Eventually, however, we reach simple concepts that directly unite sensations—in this case, sensations of resistance or weight, melting, and shaping. Today, we might quibble with these definitions. But we still think the concept *gold* relates to gold things and sensations of gold things.

That all concepts trace their content to experience may suggest that there are no pure concepts. But a judgment has both a content and a form. The content stems from experience, but the form does not. To identify the pure concepts of the understanding, then, identify the forms of judgment. There is already a science that abstracts from the content of judgments and examines only their forms—logic. The categories—the pure concepts of understanding—are thus the basic concepts of logic.

Kant lists the pure concepts of the understanding in his table of categories [A80/B106], which includes such concepts as unity, totality (universality), reality, negation, inherence (being a quality or property of something), subsistence (substance), causality, existence, possibility, and necessity.

The table of categories outlines the possible logical forms of objects. Synthesis of "the **manifold of intuition**"—the collection of sensations and reflections we experience at a given time—is essential to concepts. In other words, concepts put impressions together. I see a red fruit, vaguely spherical in shape; I feel its firmness; I hear a crunch as I bite into it; I smell a distinctive, sweet odor with a touch of bitterness; I taste its crisp acidity. I unite—in Kant's terms, synthesize—these sensations into my concept *apple.*

But that alone is not enough for knowledge. A concept of an object puts impressions together to form *one thing.* The concept of an object is special: It is the concept of a unified thing—in this case, an apple. Concepts of objects not only tell us when a certain general term ('apple') applies, but also when it is being applied to one and the same thing ('this apple'). The concept of an apple not only specifies when something is an apple but when it is the *same* apple.

The pure concepts of the understanding "apply a priori to objects" [A79/B105]; they spell out the possible forms of objects by indicating the possible kinds of unity. Kant's key assumption in deriving the categories from the logical forms of judgments is this:

> The same function which gives unity to the different representations *in a judgment,* gives also unity to the mere synthesis of different representations *in an intuition.* [A79/B105]

Why are the unifying functions in judgments and objects the same? Judgments and objects are both products of synthesis, of combination. Moreover, knowledge is always knowledge *of* objects *through* judgments. Judgments are possible only by virtue of the unifying activity of the categories. Most importantly, to apply a concept (such as *apple*) to a thing is to make a judgment ('This is an apple').

The unity of judgments and objects alike is a unity *in a concept.* This explains why the pure concepts of the understanding have a priori validity, avoiding the challenges of the skeptics such as Hume.

What are the two conditions on the possibility of knowledge of objects? Why does knowledge of objects presuppose the concept of an object in general?

> There are only two possible ways in which synthetic representation and its objects can coincide with and relate necessarily to each other, and, as it were, meet together. Either the object alone makes the representation possible, or the representation alone makes the object possible. In the former case, the relation between them is only empirical, and an a priori representation is impossible. And this is the case with phenomena, as regards that in them which is referable to mere sensation. In the latter case—although representation alone (for of its causality, by means of the will we do not here speak) does not produce the object as to its existence, it must never-

> theless be a priori determinative in regard to the object, if it is only by means of the representation that we can know anything as an object. Now there are only two conditions of the possibility of a knowledge of objects; firstly, intuition, by means of which the object, though only as phenomenon, is given; secondly, concept, by means of which the object which corresponds to this intuition is thought. . . . Now the question is whether there do not exist, a priori in the mind, concepts of understanding also, as conditions under which alone something, if not intuited, is yet thought as object. If this question be answered in the affirmative, it follows that all empirical knowledge of objects is necessarily conformable to such concepts, since, if they are not presupposed, it is impossible that anything can be an object of experience. Now all experience contains, besides the intuition of the senses through which an object is given, a concept also of an object that is given in intuition. Accordingly, concepts of objects in general must lie as a priori conditions at the foundation of all empirical knowledge; and consequently, the objective validity of the categories, as a priori concepts, will rest upon this, that experience (as far as regards the form of thought) is possible only by their means. For in that case they apply necessarily and a priori to objects of experience, because only through them can an object of experience be thought. [A93/B126].

The categories are "concepts of an object in general" [B129]; they are "a priori conditions of the possibility of experience" [A94/B126]. We are able to experience objects, that is, only because we have the concept of an object. We do not derive this concept from experience, for we could not experience anything as an object without already having the general concept of an object.

Thinking of things in terms of concepts is thus one crucial part of Kant's account. Sensation, he holds, is a manifold. It bombards us with many possible sources of information. Out of this buzzing confusion we synthesize perceptions, concepts, and judgments. A sensation of a triangle, for example, may consist of various visual and tactile impressions received over a short interval of time. We experience it as a single sensation, usually without being aware of its complex nature. In short, we organize the data of sense into discrete, unified perceptions. The awareness of the unity of various sensations, Kant says, is a concept—a "thinking together." Kant speaks of a concept as a rule: "a concept is always, as regards its form, something universal which serves as a rule" [A106]. Specifically, a concept is a rule for the synthesis of the manifold of intuition—for combining impressions into perceptions and then into objects.

> It is only when we have thus produced synthetic unity in the manifold of intuition that we are in a position to say that we know the object. But this unity is impossible if the intuition cannot be generated in accordance with a rule by means of such a function of synthesis as makes the reproduction of the manifold a priori necessary, and renders possible a concept in which it is united. This we think of a triangle as an object, in that we are conscious of the combination of three straight lines according to a rule by which such an intuition can always be represented. This *unity of rule* determines all the manifold, and limits it to conditions which make unity of apperception possible. [A105]

Essential to recognizing something as an object, then, is a consciousness of its unity—an awareness of it as *one* object. But this consciousness is possible only if the object is constructed according to a rule. We can recognize a collection of intuitions as constituting a single object only by having a rule for uniting them into that object. We take a triangle as a single object, rather than three distinct line segments that happen to intersect, because we have a rule for uniting those segments. Without such a rule, we would be left with a manifold—three separate lines.

Necessity

The rule-governed character of object construction brings with it a kind of necessity. To count as a triangle, for example, something must be a plane figure with three sides and three angles. So, it is a necessary truth that triangles have three sides and three angles. This, it might seem, is not the sort of necessity that interests Kant; 'triangles have three angles' is analytic. But when we ask what necessary truths stem not from the rule for constructing triangles or any other specific kind of object but from the rule-governed constructions of objects in general, we obtain a more interesting answer. All objects must be unified; the concept of an object is the concept of a single thing.

Necessity, that is, comes from our unifying activity. We think by unifying the raw material of sense into objects. We do this using concepts, which are rules. So the world is rule-governed, obeying necessary laws. Hume would say that necessity is not in the world but in us. Kant says, in effect, that necessity is in the world (as we experience it) *because* it is in us.

Necessary connections, Hume observes, cannot be found in experience. We are aware of a succession of things but not of the connections between the items of the sequence. (In Frank O'Malley's words, "Life is just one damned thing after another.") Our concept of necessity, Hume concludes, must come from us, not from what we experience. So far, Kant agrees. But Hume goes on to attribute the source of our concept of necessity to the passionate side of our nature, to a feeling of expectation. Kant, in contrast, finds necessity's source in the unity of objects. We experience objects, not just a whirling mass of sensations. And, as we have seen, it is a necessary truth that all objects are unified according to rules.

But where does this unity come from? Consciousness, as far as its contents are concerned, is a mixed bag. We cannot discover its unity from its contents. When we introspect, we encounter a tangled mass of sights, sounds, smells, tastes, feelings, and thoughts. We do not encounter ourselves. Nor can we determine that a given succession of mental states makes up a single consciousness by examining the contents of those states. There is nothing obvious that all my sights, sounds, smells, tastes, feelings, and thoughts have in common.

That a given sensation or thought is mine, therefore, we cannot analyze by appeal to its internal properties. We cannot analyze it by appealing to relations to other sensations and thoughts. We must instead analyze it by appealing to a relation between the sensation or thought and something else—me. Whatever is responsible for the unity of consciousness is not to be found in what we are conscious *of* but in the relation between that and something else, outside and underlying consciousness.

Something in us must unify the buzzing confusion of sensation—what Kant calls "a rhapsody of perceptions"—according to rules. When we reflect on the contents of our own consciousness, as Hume stresses, we are aware of only a succession of mental states; we do not confront a unified self. (See Chapter 4.) The contents of consciousness are always changing: "No fixed and abiding self can present itself in this flux of inner appearances" [A107]. Thus, we find no unity through introspection. But there must be some ground of unity in us. Something must unify experience.

Kant refers to this something as the *transcendental ground* of the unity of objects and of consciousness in general—the *transcendental unity,* for short—and calls it **transcendental apperception.** The transcendental unity is "that which itself contains the ground of the unity of diverse concepts in judgment, and therefore of the possibility of the understanding, even as regards its logical employment" [B131]. At one point Kant even identifies the transcendental unity with the understanding [B134n].

This brings us to Kant's key contention: The unity of objects and of experience stems from the underlying unity of our consciousness itself. The unity of apperception is "the a priori ground of all concepts" [A107], for all concepts unify the manifold of sensibility into objects. The most general concepts, relating to the form of an object in general, are the categories. The unity of apperception and the categories underlie the lawlike connections we find among objects of experience and the synthetic a priori knowledge we have of them.

The transcendental unity of apperception manifests itself in the 'I think' that we can append to all our judgments and representations.

> I am therefore, conscious of my identical self, in relation to all the variety of representations given to me in an intuition, because I call all of them *my* representations. In other words, I am conscious myself of a necessary a priori synthesis of my representations, which is called the original synthetic unity of apperception, under which rank all the representations presented to me, but that only by means of a synthesis. . . .
>
> The synthetic unity of consciousness is, therefore, an objective condition of all knowledge, which I do not merely require in order to know an object, but to which every intuition must necessarily be subject, in order to become an object for me; because in any other way, and without this synthesis, the manifold in intuition could not be united in one consciousness. [B137-138]

A sensation is part of my empirical consciousness if it relates appropriately to my understanding, my transcendental unity of apperception—in short, my mind. This, Kant insists, is a necessary truth about our kind of consciousness.

It follows that I can receive a sensation only if it stands in relation to my mind. We can know a priori that any sensation must relate to the mind: "all the manifold of intuition should be subject to conditions of the original synthetic unity of apperception" [B136]. This proposition, furthermore, is synthetic. We derive it, not by analyzing the concept of sensation or even the concept of the transcendental unity, but by connecting the two. This permits a priori knowledge, knowledge that can be derived independently of experience and that holds necessarily, because it concerns *the form of any possible experience.*

Kant is driving toward the conclusion that "appearances have *a necessary relation to the understanding*" [A119]. Appearances, he says, are "data for a possible experience"; they therefore *have* to relate to the understanding. The mind is responsible for what Kant calls the *affinity* of our representations—that is, their being *our* representations, their constituting a single consciousness—and also the rule-governed character of the synthesis of the manifold of intuition. If that synthesis were not rule-governed, the combination of the data of sense would not yield knowledge but random and "accidental collocations" [A121] such as the products of imagination in the usual sense. We may freely combine concepts to form the notion of a three-headed dragon or a golden mountain, but we gain no knowledge of what is actual from exercising that freedom. We attain knowledge of objects because the construction of objects actually presented in experience is rule-governed.

We can know objects because we construct them: "Thus the order and regularity in the appearances, which we entitle *nature,* we ourselves introduce. We could never find them in appearances, had not we ourselves, or the nature of our mind, originally set them there" [A125]. The understanding, consequently, is nothing less than "the lawgiver of nature" [A126], for it is "an objective condition of all knowledge, which I do not merely require in order to know an object, but to which every intuition must necessarily be subject, in order to become an object for me" [B138].

We can know certain necessary truths about objects—'Every event must have a cause,' for example—independently of experience, for we can uncover the pure concepts of the understanding relating to the form of an object in general. These concepts do not arise from experience; they underlie the possibility of experience. So, we can know a priori that any experience will conform to them. This establishes realism, the view that we can attain knowledge of objective reality, within the realm of objects of experience. It also establishes concept rationalism. Most importantly, it solves the traditional Platonic problem of the conformity of the world to our innate ideas without invoking God.

The Dialectic

The Transcendental Analytic and related portions of the *Critique* attempt to justify Kant's rationalism. The Transcendental Dialectic, which comprises most of the second half of the book, tries to justify Kant's thesis of immanence, limiting knowledge to the sphere of possible experience. Our thinking extends easily beyond the realm of sense experience. We may engage in metaphysical contemplation, arguing about the freedom of the will, the existence of God, and the mortality or immortality of the soul. But Kant denies that we can attain any real knowledge of these matters.

We may imagine whatever we like. We may connect concepts and intuitions freely without concern for their presence in experience. The transcendental unity, however, directs our thought toward an object and toward reality. We can know a synthetic truth only by some connection with experience: by actual experience itself, if the truth is a posteriori, or by reflecting on the necessary conditions of possible experience, if it is a priori. This is why we cannot have knowledge that transcends experience:

Why do the categories apply only within the realm of possible experience?

> *The possibility of experience* is, then, that which gives objective reality to all our a priori knowledge. Now experience depends upon the synthetic unity of phenomena, that is, upon a synthesis according to concepts of the object of phenomena in general, a synthesis without which experience never could become knowledge, but would be merely a rhapsody of perceptions, never fitting together into any connected text, according to rules of a thoroughly united (possible) consciousness,

> and therefore never subjected to the transcendental and necessary unity of apperception. Experience has therefore for a foundation, a priori principles of its form, that is to say, general rules of unity in the synthesis of phenomena, the objective reality of which rules, as necessary conditions even of the possibility of experience, can always be shown in experience. But apart from this relation, a priori synthetic propositions are absolutely impossible, because they have no third term, that is, no pure object, in which the synthetic unity can exhibit the objective reality of its conceptions.
>
> Accordingly, the supreme principle of all synthetic judgments is: "Every object is subject to the necessary conditions of the synthetic unity of the manifold of intuition in a possible experience." [A156/B195, A158/B197]

Therefore, knowledge of things-in-themselves is impossible; knowledge is limited to the sphere of experience. The limits of knowledge become clear in thinking about the role of the categories. The pure concepts of the understanding are conditions of the possibility of experience. They have a priori validity, against the claims of the skeptic, because "all empirical knowledge of objects would necessarily conform to such concepts, because only as thus presupposing them is anything possible as an *object of experience*" [A93/B126]. Objects of experience must conform to the categories in order for us to experience them and think of them as objects. Objects beyond the realm of experience, however, face no such constraint. In fact, we have no reason to believe that the categories apply to them at all. The categories conform to objects of possible experience because we synthesize those objects from the data of sensibility. What lies beyond sensibility lies beyond the categories, for we have no reason to believe that it results from such a process of synthesis.

Kant defends rationalism, therefore, only by undercutting transcendence. "No other objects, besides those of the senses, can, as a matter of fact, be given to us, and nowhere save in the context of a possible experience; and consequently nothing is an object *for us,* unless it presupposes the sum of all empirical reality as the condition of its possibility" [A582/B610]. We may be rationalists within the realm of experience, but must remain skeptics beyond it.

Humanism

Kant carefully distinguishes his view from the idealism of Bishop Berkeley (1685–1753; see Chapter 5), which assails the notion of a reality beyond the realm of ideas. Kant's solution to Platonism's problems relies on distinguishing phenomena from noumena. Kant thus insists on the need to recognize things-in-themselves, of which our appearances are appearances.

Kant nevertheless realizes that his theory is a form of idealism—transcendental idealism, he calls it—for truth, objectivity, and existence, within the theory, become fundamentally epistemic notions. All relate a judgment to the understanding. Metaphysics is inseparable from epistemology; the root notions of metaphysics all, in the end, relate to what humans can perceive and know. We cannot say that to be is to be perceived, as Berkeley does, but we can say that to be is to be perceivable—an object of possible experience.

This is why Kant identifies a priori and necessary judgments. Contemporary American philosopher Saul Kripke has attacked this identification, pointing out that being a priori is a matter of epistemology—can something be known independently of experience?—while necessity is a matter of metaphysics. Kripke has alleged, against Kant, that there can be contingent a priori and necessary a posteriori truths.[22] This seems plausible in the metaphysical view of necessity that Leibniz and Kripke share, namely, that necessity is truth in all possible worlds. But Kant rejects that view. A judgment is a priori if it can be known independently of all experience; if, that is, it holds no matter what experience might yield, or, to put it differently, if it holds no matter what the world *looks* like. A judgment is necessary, in the Leibnizian view, if it holds no matter what the world *is* like. Kant does not confuse these notions; he rejects the latter precisely because it goes beyond the realm of experience. The truth of skepticism, Kant maintains, is that we cannot know what the world is like beyond experience. The only notion of modality we can use is epistemic, in which we consider possible experiences rather than possible worlds. On this conception, of course, the a priori and the necessary are not only equivalent but obviously so.

Moreover, it becomes possible to attain knowledge of necessary truths about objects of experience. Reason gets itself into trouble when it tries to leave the realm of possible experience. Kant is able to defend our knowledge of necessary truths against skeptics such as Hume because for him the a priori and necessary extend to the immanent sphere only, not to the transcendent. They are limited to the realm of possible experience.

The epistemic character of the basic notions of metaphysics—when these notions and, correspondingly, metaphysics are properly construed and restricted to the realm of experience—is the central consequence of Kant's Copernican Revolution. In short, from Kant's point of view, philosophy is the theory of knowledge. For Kant, as for the ancient Sophist Protagoras, man is the measure of all things. Kant, of course, takes the definite article here seriously. There is one and only one measure: the categories underlie all possible experience. Not everyone would agree. The nature and especially the uniqueness of the measure would define the primary battleground for philosophers during the next two centuries.

DOGMATIC EMPIRICISM

Recall our three questions:

1. Can we know anything about the world independently of experience?
2. Can we know anything beyond the bounds of experience?
3. Can we know what the world is really like?

Classical rationalists such as Descartes answer yes to all three questions. Classical empiricists such as Hume answer no to all three. Kant, as we have seen, answers yes only to the first; we might call him a **skeptical rationalist.** Many non-Western philosophers have answered yes to the second and third questions quite independently of any answer to the first, indeed while stressing the dependence of knowledge on expe-

[22] See *Naming and Necessity* (Cambridge: Harvard University Press, 1972, 1980), 34–39.

rience. We might call them **dogmatic empiricists.** (I do not intend 'dogmatic' to be pejorative; it indicates merely that they are empiricists but not skeptics: that is, that they think it is possible to know something beyond the bounds of experience and about things as they are, despite the fact that knowledge comes from experience.) The chief dogmatic empiricist I will discuss here is the Indian philosopher Dharmakirti (c. 600), a Buddhist philosopher who criticized the Nyaya view of knowledge. But, as we shall see, that combination of views has been common in a variety of cultures, including our own. We might express the positions in a table:

Question	*Descartes*	*Hume*	*Kant*	*Dharmakirti*
1. Synthetic a priori truth	Yes	No	Yes	No
2. Knowledge beyond experience	Yes	No	No	Yes
3. Knowledge of the world as it is	Yes	No	No	Yes

At first glance, such a combination of views seems bizarre. If all knowledge depends on experience, how can we know anything beyond the bounds of experience? But Kant's answers might also seem strange at first glance. The intelligibility of his position depends on the distinction between phenomena and noumena—things as they appear and things as they really are. The same is true of Dharmakirti. Like Kant, Dharmakirti is an idealist, but of an unusual kind.

Dharmakirti

Classical Indian philosophers tend to hold that there are four sources of knowledge: perception, inference, testimony, and analogy. Dharmakirti holds that there are only two, for testimony and analogy are kinds of inference:

> Knowledge is twofold. . . . Direct and indirect (perceptive and inferential).[23]

Direct knowledge, according to Dharmottara's commentary, is "knowledge dependent upon the senses." Inferential knowledge, like perceptual knowledge, is "a source of knowledge always connected with some (real) object." Because of this connection, it leads to "successful purposive action," which is the goal of knowledge.

Dharmakirti's theory of knowledge at first glance seems to be a realist, externalist theory very much like that of the *Nyaya-sutra* (see Chapter 2). He sees successful action as the result and indicator of knowledge; we may define knowledge in terms of the causal relations between our mental states and the world. Dharmakirti thinks of perception as constituting the basis of knowledge. All knowledge is perceptual or inferred from perceptual knowledge. His account of perceptual knowledge, moreover, is highly sophisticated. Some philosophers have thought that perception, serving as the foundation for all knowledge, must be invariably correct if knowledge itself is to be reliable. But Dharmakirti recognizes the possibility of illusion.

> Direct knowledge means here neither construction (judgment) nor illusion. . . .
> Cognition exempt from such (construction), when it is not affected by an illusion

[23] This and further quotations from Dharmakirti are from *The Pith of Right Thinking (Nyayabindu)*, with a Commentary by Dharmottara, from F. T. Scherbatsky, *Buddhist Logic,* Volume II (New York: Dover, 1962).

> produced by color-blindness, rapid motion, traveling on board a ship, sickness or other causes, is perceptive knowledge.

Dharmottara, for example, imagines someone on a ship going down a river. The trees on the bank appear to be moving. They aren't, of course; the ship is moving instead. (Note the similarity to Kant's illustration of the Copernican revolution.) Likewise, someone who is colorblind may systematically misperceive certain colors. Our perceptual systems normally give us knowledge of the world, but sometimes they malfunction. Our beliefs count as knowledge only if produced by reliable means functioning normally.

Knowledge, for Dharmakirti, is therefore defeasible: we count ourselves as knowing things that we might later have to give up as incorrect. As Dharmottara puts it, "Knowledge is cognition not contradicted (by experience)." Dharmakirti's empiricism thus differs in two important ways from that of Locke or Hume. First, sensation is not always reliable. Locke treats all simple ideas as adequate, for the mind, he says, is completely passive in receiving them. Similarly, Hume takes impressions at face value. (Even the term 'impression' suggests the passivity of the mind.) But Dharmakirti realizes that this is too simple. We are not passive in receiving information from our senses. Our sense organs are complex systems that process information in various ways—ways that can go astray. Second, although knowledge comes from experience, it is not *derived* from experience. Our goal, in knowing, is to *do* something; as Dharmottara expresses it, "knowledge is cognition which points to reality, (a reality which) is capable of satisfying purposive action." Our goal is thus to organize experience well enough to be able to act, to do what we want to do, and achieve what we want to achieve. But we have freedom in doing so. We succeed in knowing when we rely on reliable methods operating normally, avoid being contradicted by experience, and succeed in accomplishing our goals.

Knowledge, then, is a mental state with the right causal links to the world, to an object's effects on us and to our own effects on the world. Smith sees a glass of water. The glass of water affects her sense organs, leading her to the belief that a glass of water is in front of her. She drinks it. It looks, feels, smells, and tastes like water. It quenches her thirst. It is water. Under these circumstances, we say she knows that there is a glass of water in front of her.

Dharmakirti, an idealist—someone who holds that everything is mind-dependent (see Chapter 5)—generalizes the point in a different direction. We say that there is a glass of water in front of Smith. What does that mean? It means that it can be put into causal relation with some knower. To be is to be potentially causally related to someone. To be, to frame a slogan, is to be a cause or effect.

Now, however, Dharmakirti does something surprising. In terms startlingly similar to Hume, he criticizes the causal relation, holding that the world of concepts is an imaginary construct; that causal relations are just "conventional signs"; and that what we call causal relations are our own contributions, not part of reality itself.

> Thus in themselves existents are unrelated; it is imagination that relates them.[24]

---

[24] Dharmakirti, *ity amisrah svayam bhavastan misrayati kalpana,* 5b, translated by Stephen H. Phillips, *Classical Indian Metaphysics* (Chicago: Open Court, 1995), 23.

But then what of his idea that to be is to be a cause or effect? What of the idea that knowledge should be defined in terms of causal relations to the world?

The everyday perspective we have on the world—which Dharmakirti has been trying to explicate—he finds ultimately paradoxical. It depends on causal relations, but cannot make any sense of them. We cannot justify knowledge of causal links in terms of experience. Indeed, careful scrutiny shows us that *we* impose a causal organization on the world.

It might seem, then, that Dharmakirti's view resembles Hume's. We find that we cannot justify key concepts we use to understand the world. We end in a kind of skepticism. But Dharmakirti's Buddhism does not allow him to stop there. Everything he has said holds of the world as conditioned by desire. If we could be free of desire, we would be free of this paradoxical perspective and see reality as it really is. There is at least the possibility of a transcendent perspective that reveals the nature of the world to us.

This, then, is how Dharmakirti can answer yes to questions 2 and 3. It is possible to know something beyond the bounds of experience and to know things as they are if it is possible to escape from the realm of desire, the "cycle of birth and death," and achieve enlightenment.

Mystical Experience

Dharmakirti thus gives us the possibility—but only the possibility—of knowledge of things as they are. A wide variety of views in various cultures and historical periods seek to go beyond the mere possibility of such knowledge. These views rest on the idea of mystical experience. If we can experience God, or a spirit world, or things as they are directly, then we can know something about them on the basis of experience. Even on empiricist grounds, then, we can say something about the transcendent realm beyond the reach of our senses. We can say something about things as they really are.

Mysticism holds that there are ways of gaining access to reality that are not mediated by sense perception or rational, conscious thought. Mystical views are many and varied. What follows are a few samples from a rich and complex genre.

Yoga One of the oldest Indian philosophies is **yoga.** All Indian mysticism, in fact, incorporates the practice of yoga. Passages in the Upanishads allude to yoga as the means to mystical awareness of ***Brahman,*** the underlying reality of the world. Yoga is a kind of psychological discipline. Its goal is mystical insight and bliss, a state called ***mukti,*** "liberation"—freedom from consciousness and desire. Philosophers of different schools interpret yoga quite differently. They nevertheless agree that it gives insight that transcends the realm of sense experience. The basic text is the *Yogasutra* (fourth century):

> 1.2 Yoga is cessation of the fluctuations of mind and awareness.
> 1.3 Then the seer (the conscious being) rests in the true self.
> 2.2 Yoga is practiced to achieve mystic trance as well as to attenuate the detrimental fluctuations or afflictions.
> 2.3 The afflictions are spiritual ignorance, egoism, passion, hatred, and attachment to life. . . .

2.11 These (detrimental) fluctuations are banished through meditation.
2.16 Future suffering is to be banished.[25]

The process must begin with an ethical commitment to follow several restraints: do not injure, do not lie, do not steal, do not fornicate, and do not covet.

2.29 (Ethical) restraints, constraints, asanas [yogic postures, stretching exercises], breath control, withdrawal of the senses (and the three stages of meditation, namely,) concentration, "meditation," and mystic trance are the eight "limbs of yoga."
2.30 Of these, the restraints are noninjury, truthfulness, refraining from stealing, celibacy, and lack of avarice.

But the key is the process of meditation that leads to mystical awareness.

What is the goal of meditation?

3.1 Concentration is binding the mind down to a single spot.
3.3 Mystic trance is this carried to the point where there is illumination only of the object as object, empty, as it were, of what it essentially is.
4.34 **Aloneness** [*kaivalya,* the goal] entails the reversal of the course of the strands or qualities of nature, now empty of meaning and value for the conscious being. Or, it may be understood as the power of consciousness returned and established in its own true self.

The goal of yoga is often said to be ineffable, indescribable. But it involves overcoming the distinction between subject and object—between you and the things around you. The person who achieves aloneness gains a perspective on the world that removes objects of their usual essences and meanings. There is no distinction between consciousness and what it is consciousness of. There is no distinction between mind and world, between self and other. There is only a blissful awareness of unity.

Indian philosopher Sarvepalli Radhakrishnan (1888–1975), who became vice-president of India in 1952 and president in 1962, writes of the importance of mystical experience of this or some other form for all religion. As he sees it, Hinduism rests on the insights of the authors of the Vedas and the Upanishads, who practiced yoga and who excelled in achieving aloneness.

> The truths of the *rsis* [seers of the Vedic period] are not evolved as the result of logical reasoning or systematic philosophy but they are the products of spiritual intuition, *drsti* or vision. The *rsis* are not so much the authors of the truths recorded in the Vedas as the seers who were able to discern the eternal truths by raising their life-spirit to the plane of the universal spirit. They are the pioneer researchers in the realm of spirit who saw more in the world than their fellows. Their utterances are based not on transitory vision but on a continuous experience of resident life and power. . . . While the experiential character of religion is emphasized in the Hindu faith, every religion at its best falls back on it.[26]

[25] This and further quotations from the *Yogasutra* are from Daniel Bonevac and Stephen Phillips, *Understanding Nonwestern Philosophy* (Mountain View: Mayfield, 1993).
[26] Sarvepalli Radhakrishnan, *An Idealist View of Life* (London: Unwin Hyman, 1988).

Judaism, for example, has Moses encountering God face to face. Christians have not only the incarnation of Christ, enabling many to perceive God, but the direct interactions between God the Father or Holy Spirit and God the Son in Jesus's baptism, transfiguration, and resurrection. Islam treats Mohammed as having mystical insight into Allah through direct revelation.

Other religious traditions thus often contain mystical elements. St. Teresa of Avila (1515–1582), for example, entered the Carmelite order at age twenty-two and practiced meditation and prayer for twenty-five years, suffering much ill health, before seeing a vision of God and then taking an active role in reforming the order. She describes a process of achieving unity with God that resembles yoga. The goal is a direct perception of God:

> If you ask how it is possible that the soul can see and understand that she has been in God, since during the union she has neither sight nor understanding, I reply that she does not see it then, but that she sees it clearly later, after she has returned to herself, not by any vision, but by a certitude which abides with her and which God alone can give her.[27]

She describes the process in great detail in several works. In *Interior Castle* she compares the soul to a castle, with God in the center.

> I began to think of the soul as if it were a castle made of a single diamond or of very clear crystal, in which there are many rooms, just as in Heaven there are many mansions. . . . It is no small pity, and should cause us no little shame, that, through our own fault, we do not understand ourselves, or know who we are. Would it not be a sign of great ignorance, my daughters, if a person were asked who he was, and could not say, and had no idea who his father or his mother was, or from what country he came? Though that is great stupidity, our own is incomparably greater if we make no attempt to discover what we are. . . . Let us now imagine that this castle, as I have said, contains many mansions, some above, others below, others at each side; and in the centre and midst of them all is the chiefest mansion where the most secret things pass between God and the soul.[28]

To enter the soul and progress toward the center—which is a state of self-knowledge as well as knowledge of God—we must pray. Spiritual discipline is required.

> As far as I can understand, the door of entry into this castle is prayer and meditation: I do not say mental prayer rather than vocal, for, if it is prayer at all, it must be accompanied by meditation.

There are six mansions surrounding the center. We may pass through the first three by humility, meditation, and good conduct. As with yoga, we must begin with the right

[27] St. Teresa of Avila, quoted in William James, *Varieties of Religious Experience* (New York: Longman's, 1906), 409.

[28] This and subsequent quotations from St. Teresa are from St. Teresa of Avila, *Interior Castle,* translated by E. Allison Peers, in *Collected Works* (New York: Sheed and Ward, 1946).

frame of mind, and we must obey ethical restraints. The fourth mansion requires us to cease making any effort. We must put aside conscious thought. Our progress comes from God. In the fifth mansion, the soul is virtually asleep, but nevertheless possessed and illumined by God.

> . . . in order to come closer to God, the soul appears to have withdrawn so far from the body that I do not know if it has still life enough to be able to breathe. I have just been thinking about this and I believe it has not; or at least, if it still breathes, it does so without realizing it. The mind would like to occupy itself wholly in understanding something of what it feels, and, as it has not the strength to do this, it becomes so dumbfounded that, even if any consciousness remains to it, neither hands nor feet can move; as we commonly say of a person who has fallen into a swoon, it might be taken for dead.

The sixth mansion Teresa compares to a couple's first sight of one another at a betrothal. The center she compares to marriage. It is a union with God, like two candles joining into one, or falling rain blending with a river. This brings an indescribable peace of mind.

> The Spiritual Betrothal is different: here the two persons are frequently separated, as is the case with union, for, although by union is meant the joining of two things into one, each of the two, as is a matter of common observation, can be separated and remain a thing by itself. This favour of the Lord passes quickly and afterwards the soul is deprived of that companionship—I mean so far as it can understand. In this other favour of the Lord it is not so: the soul remains all the time in that centre with its God. We might say that union is as if the ends of two wax candles were joined so that the light they give is one: the wicks and the wax and the light are all one, yet afterwards the one candle can be perfectly well separated from the other and the candles become two again, or the wick may be withdrawn from the wax. But here it is like rain falling from the heavens into a river or a spring; there is nothing but water there and it is impossible to divide or separate the water belonging to the river from that which fell from the heavens. Or it is as if a tiny streamlet enters the sea, from which it will find no way of separating itself, or as if in a room there were two large windows through which the light streamed in: it enters in different places but it all becomes one. . . . This, with the passage of time, becomes more evident through its effects; for the soul clearly understands, by certain secret aspirations, that it is endowed with life by God.

This experience of union with God gives knowledge—knowledge of God as well as self-knowledge. It gives us knowledge of how the world really is, by means of an experience. But the experience is not a matter of sensation or reflection but a mystical interaction with God.

Sufism The ideal of union with God is also the driving concept of **Sufism.** Sufism distills a tendency to mysticism native to Islam into a way of life. A mystic is one who believes it possible to have direct, unmediated experience of God. This is the goal of the Sufi. Sufis want to experience God immediately, not through activities such as worship and prayer. They seek union with God.

Rabi'a al-'Adawiyya (d. 801), born in Basra, in what is now Iraq, was kidnapped and sold as a slave when she was a young child. Her master freed her because of her great religious devotion. She became one of the earliest and most influential Sufi mystics. Rabi'a disdains self-interested motives for religious devotion.

> One day Rabi'a was seen carrying fire in one hand and water in the other and she was running with speed. They asked her what was the meaning of her action and where she was going. She replied: "I am going to light a fire in Paradise and pour water on to Hell, so that both veils (i.e. hindrances to the true vision of God) may completely disappear from the pilgrims, and their purpose may be sure, and the servants of God may see Him, without any object of hope or motive or fear. What if the hope of Paradise and the fear of Hell did not exist? Not one could worship his Lord or obey Him."[29]

The only acceptable motivation is the love of God, without any concern for the self.

> O my Lord, if I worship Thee from fear of Hell, burn me in Hell; and if I worship Thee from hope of Paradise, exclude me thence; but if I worship Thee for Thine own sake, then withhold not from me Thine Eternal Beauty.

Rabi'a too uses sexual imagery in describing her longing for union with God.

> The groaning and the yearning of the lover of God will not be satisfied until it is satisfied in the Beloved.
>
> I have made Thee the companion of my heart,
> But my body is available for those who desire its company.
> And my body is friendly towards its guests,
> But the Beloved of my heart is the Guest of my soul.
>
> . . . I have separated myself from all created beings: my hope is for union with Thee, for that is the goal of my quest.

Rabi'a and other Sufis believe in the possibility of such a union. Some treat it as a source of knowledge but also, more importantly, as the goal of a quest that consumes one's entire being. Some go so far as to compare the religious person to a moth drawn to a flame. The believer cannot do anything other than desire union with God. Yet that very union would destroy the believer, for the power of God is vastly greater than that of any human.

Native American Visions A completely distinct tradition of mysticism exists in various Native American tribes, who share respect for visions as means of knowledge. Black Elk (1863–1950), for example, was an Oglala Lakota (Sioux) shaman, or medicine man, the cousin of the famous war chief Crazy Horse. He adjusted to white civilization,

[29] Margaret Smith (ed.), *Readings from the Mystics of Islam* (London: Luzac and Co., 1972).

converting to Roman Catholicism and using the name Nicholas. But he also tried to transmit traditional Lakota myths, legends, and rituals to later generations. One concerned his cousin, the great chief:

> . . . he said that Crazy Horse dreamed and went into the world where there is nothing but the spirits of all things. That is the real world that is behind this one, and everything we see here is something like a shadow from that world. He was on his horse in that world, and the horse and himself on it and the trees and the grass and the stones and everything were made of spirit, and nothing was hard, and everything seemed to float. His horse was standing still there, and yet it danced around like a horse made only of shadow, and that is how he got his name, which does not mean that his horse was crazy or wild, but that in his vision it danced around in that queer way.
>
> It was this vision that gave him his great power, for when he went into a fight, he had only to think of that world to be in it again, so that he could go through anything and not be hurt.[30]

Note that Crazy Horse gains not only knowledge but also power from his vision.

Black Elk himself had such a vision.

> As I lay in the tipi I could see through the tipi the same two men whom I saw before and they were coming from the clouds. . . . I got on top of the cloud and was raised up, following the two men, and when I looked back, I saw my father and mother looking at me. When I looked back I felt sorry that I was leaving them.

After being shown the horses of the four directions and the center of the earth, the two men showed him the earth:

> They had taken me all over the world and showed me all the powers. They took me to the center of the earth and to the top of the peak they took me to review it all. . . . I was to see the bad and the good. I was to see what is good for humans and what is not good for humans.[31]

These narratives are not unique. John Lame Deer, a Lakota shaman, was born shortly after 1900 on the Rosebud Reservation in South Dakota. He talks about the importance of the vision quest and describes his own at age sixteen. Visions can teach things that cannot be known through any other route.

> Now I was all by myself, left on a hilltop for four days and nights without food or water. . . . I wanted to become a medicine man, a *yuwipi,* a healer carrying on the ancient ways of the Sioux nation. But you cannot learn to be a medicine man like a white man going to medical school. An old holy man can teach you about herbs and the right way to perform a ceremony where everything must be in its proper place, where every move, every word has its own, special meaning. These things

---

[30] John G. Neihardt, *Black Elk Speaks* (Lincoln: University of Nebraska Press, 1932).

[31] Raymond J. DeMallie (ed.), *The Sixth Grandfather: Black Elk's Teachings Given to John G. Neihardt* (Lincoln: University of Nebraska Press, 1984).

> you can learn—like spelling, like training a horse. But by themselves these things mean nothing. Without the vision and the power this learning will do no good. It would not make me a medicine man.

Lame Deer's vision, like those of Crazy Horse and Black Elk, gives him a transcendent perspective, allowing him to escape the limitations of his own sense organs, see things he could never otherwise see, and meet his ancestors.

> Suddenly I felt an overwhelming presence. Down there with me in my cramped hole was a big bird. . . . Slowly I perceived that a voice was trying to tell me something. It was a bird cry, but I tell you, I began to understand some of it. . . . I heard a human voice too, strange and high-pitched, a voice which could not come from an ordinary, living being. All at once I was way up there with the birds. The hill with the vision pit was way above everything. I could look down even on the stars, and the moon was close to my left side. It seemed as though the earth and stars were moving below me. . . . Then I saw a shape before me. It rose from the darkness and the swirling fog which penetrated my earth hole. I saw that this was my great-grandfather, Tahca Ushte, Lame Deer, old man chief of the Minneconjou. I could see the blood dripping from my great-grandfather's chest where a white soldier had shot him. I understood that my great-grandfather wished me to take his name.[32]

The mystic of any of the above varieties holds that it is possible to experience the world in ways that go beyond perception and reflection, gaining knowledge and even power in the process. The knowledge is knowledge of things as they are and often knowledge of things that go beyond the realm of possible sense experience. Yet this knowledge results not from philosophical reflection but from experience of a very special sort.

SUMMARY

We can categorize theories of knowledge in terms of their answers to three questions. Can we know anything about the world independently of experience? Rationalists say yes; we have inborn concepts that give us innate knowledge. Empiricists say no; all our concepts come from experience.

Can we know anything beyond the realm of experience? Can we know things as they really are? Most rationalists say yes. Since we have some innate knowledge, we can apply it to things whether we experience them or not. But Kant, for example, while a rationalist, holds that our innate knowledge applies only to objects of possible experience. We can know objects only as they appear to us, not as they are in themselves.

Empiricists generally say no. Our knowledge comes from experience and so cannot reach beyond it. But there are empiricists who hold that there are different kinds

[32] John (Fire) Lame Deer and Richard Erdoes, *Lame Deer Seeker of Visions* (New York: Simon and Schuster, 1972).

of experience. If mystical experience is possible, it may give us access to a realm beyond the senses, enabling us to know things as they are, not only as they appear.

Review Questions

1. What is the difference between analytic and synthetic truths? List some of each. Would Locke and Kant consider 'Everything green is extended' analytic or synthetic?
2. What issue divides concept rationalists from concept empiricists? Judgment rationalists from judgment empiricists?
3. What puzzle does Plato's theory of forms create for the theory of knowledge? Explain and evaluate his attempts to solve it.
4. Give some examples of putative synthetic a priori truths. How might an empiricist seek to show that they are not synthetic a priori after all?
5. How does Hume distinguish impressions from ideas? How does he argue that all ideas are copies of impressions?
6. Why, according to the rationalist, can't empiricists account for the universality and necessity of scientific knowledge? Do you agree?
7. What is Hume's scandal of induction? How does he account for inductive inference?
8. Explain Kant's distinction between phenomena and noumena.
9. What are Kant's categories? Do they solve the epistemological problem of Platonism?
10. How does Kant account for the universality and necessity of knowledge? Compare his account to Hume's.
11. What is dogmatic empiricism? How might one argue for it?

Terms for Review

a posteriori proposition A proposition whose truth value can be known only through experience.

a priori proposition A proposition whose truth value can be known independently of experience.

aloneness (*kaivalya*) The goal of mystical insight and bliss in yoga.

appearance A thing as it is known to us.

Brahman In Hinduism, the underlying reality of the world.

category In Aristotle, a general kind of thing to which linguistic expressions refer. In Kant, a pure concept of the understanding; an innate cognitive ability of a very general kind; a possible logical form of an object.

complex ideas Compounds of other ideas.

concept empiricism The view that all concepts come from experience.

concept rationalism The view that there are innate concepts—that we have concepts that we do not derive from experience.

contingent proposition A proposition that is neither necessary nor impossible—that is, that could be true and could be false.

contradictory (or **impossible) proposition** A proposition that cannot be true.

Copernican revolution in philosophy Kant's view that the laws governing the realm of experience are not in the objects themselves but in us: ". . . we can know in things a priori only what we ourselves place in them."

dogmatic empiricism The view that we can know something about the world as it really is, beyond the reach of the senses, even if all knowledge depends on experience.

empiricism The view that all knowledge of the world comes from experience.

forms In Plato, abstract universals that exist independently of us. They make things what they are, and they enable us to think about things as they are.

illumination In Augustine, what enables us to know the forms. God illumines the intelligible world, making it intelligible to us.

impossible (or **contradictory) proposition** A proposition that cannot be true.

impression In Hume, sensation or reflection.

innate Inborn; not acquired or derived from experience.

intelligible world The realm of Platonic forms.

intuition In Kant, sensation or reflection.

judgment empiricism The view that there are no synthetic a priori truths. That is, a judgment empiricist holds that only analytic truths, "trifling propositions," can be known independently of experience; anything that really yields content about the world can be known only through experience.

judgment rationalism The view that some of our knowledge of the world is innate. A judgment rationalist believes that we can know some synthetic truths a priori—that is, that we can know independently of experience some truths that are not merely linguistic or verbal, that are not automatically true or false because of the meanings of the words that constitute them.

manifold of intuition In Kant, the collection of sensations and reflections—sights, sounds, tastes, smells, feels, and introspections—that someone experiences at a given time.

mukti In Hinduism, "liberation"—freedom from consciousness and desire.

mysticism The view that there are ways of gaining access to reality that do not involve sense perception or rational, conscious thought.

necessary proposition A proposition that cannot be false.

noumenon A thing-in-itself; a thing as it really is, independently of our faculties of knowledge.

participation The relation between things and forms. A thing is tall, for example, if it participates in the form of tallness.

phenomenon Appearance; a thing as it is known to us.

rationalism The view that we can attain some knowledge independently of experience.

realism The thesis that human thought can discover the nature of objective reality.

simple ideas Ideas that are not compounds of other ideas.

skeptical rationalism The view that we can know something about the world independently of experience but not beyond the bounds of experience and not about things-in-themselves.

Sufism A mystical movement within Islam stressing the possibility of experiencing Allah directly.

thing-in-itself A thing as it really is, independently of our faculties of knowledge.

transcendence The thesis that knowledge is capable of extending beyond experience to the supersensible.

transcendental apperception The transcendental ground of the unity of consciousness (that is, the imperceptible "I" that ties consciousness together) in Kant.

transcendental idealism Kant's thesis that we perceive and know, not things in themselves, but things as conditioned by our cognitive faculties.

transcendental method Kant's method of examining the contributions our own cognitive faculties make to perception and knowledge.

trifling proposition In Locke, a statement in which the predicate is the same as the subject ('A soul is a soul') or part of the subject ('Lead is a metal').

yoga A kind of psychological discipline. Its goal is mystical insight and bliss, a state called *mukti,* "liberation"—freedom from consciousness and desire.

For Further Reading

There is relatively little in English on Avicenna. See S. M. Afnan, *Avicenna, His Life and Works* (London: George Allen, 1958); H. Nasr, *Three Muslim Sages: Avicenna, Suhrawardi, Ibn 'Arabi* (Cambridge: Harvard University Press, 1964); and Arthur Hyman and James J. Walsh (eds.), *Philosophy in the Middle Ages* (New York: Harper and Row, 1967).

Locke has not, in my view, won the critical attention he deserves. But two excellent secondary sources are J. L. Mackie, *Problems from Locke* (Oxford: Oxford University Press, 1971) and Michael Ayers, *Locke* (London: Routledge and Kegan Paul, 1991). An outstanding discussion of British empiricism is Jonathan Bennett, *Locke, Berkeley, and Hume: Central Themes* (Oxford: Oxford University Press, 1971).

Hume has inspired a great deal of secondary literature. See especially Barry Stroud, *Hume* (London: Routledge and Kegan Paul, 1978); A. J. Ayer, *Hume* (Oxford: Oxford University Press, 1981); and David Norton, *David Hume: Common Sense Moralist, Sceptical Metaphysician* (Princeton: Princeton University Press, 1982).

Leibniz's thought has won the attention of some of the twentieth century's most prominent philosophers. See Bertrand Russell, *A Critical Exposition of the Philosophy of Leibniz* (London: George Allen and Unwin, 1900) for an important, if idiosyncratic, account. For commentators with less of an axe to grind, see C. D. Broad, *Leibniz: An Introduction* (Cambridge: Cambridge University Press, 1975) and Nicholas Rescher, *The Philosophy of Leibniz* (Englewood Cliffs: Prentice-Hall, 1967). A brilliant but difficult recent study is Jan Cover and John Hawthorne, *Leibniz on Substance and Individuation* (Cambridge: Cambridge University Press, 1998).

There is a vast literature on Kant in both English and German. Good places to start are Kant's own precis of the *Critique, Prolegomena to Any Future Metaphysics;* A. C. Ewing, *A Short Commentary on Kant's Critique of Pure Reason* (London: Methuen, 1950); Norman Kemp Smith, *A Commentary on Kant's Critique of Pure Reason* (New York: Humanities Press, 1962); P. F. Strawson, *The Bounds of Sense* (London: Methuen, 1966);

Ralph C. S. Walker, *Kant* (London: Routledge and Kegan Paul, 1978); and Henry Allison, *Kant's Transcendental Idealism* (New Haven: Yale University Press, 1983).

On Dharmakirti and other figures in Indian epistemology, see Stephen Phillips, *Classical Indian Metaphysics* (Chicago: Open Court, 1995); Sibajiban Bhattacharyya, *Doubt, Belief and Knowledge* (New Delhi: Indian Council of Philosophical Research and Allied Publishers, 1987); Purushottama Bilimoria, *Sabdapramana: Word and Knowledge* (Dordrecht: Kluwer, 1988); Karl Potter, *Encyclopedia of Indian Philosophies* (Five volumes; Delhi: Motilal Banarsidass, 1977–1990); and Surendranath Dasgupta, *A History of Indian Philosophy* (Three volumes; Cambridge: Cambridge University Press, 1922, 1932, 1951).

The Mind is smooth — no Motion —
Contented as the Eye
Upon the Forehead of a Bust —
That knows — it cannot see —

—Emily Dickinson, 305

CHAPTER 4

Mind

Socrates took his inspiration from the inscription on the oracle at Delphi: "Know thyself." Philosophers ever since have asked what it means to be human. Who am I? What am I? What is it to be human? What makes me a person? What makes me *me*?

These questions, as we shall see, are not at all easy to answer. They require us to develop a theory of the self, and they take us to the heart of issues in what is called **philosophy of mind,** that branch of philosophy that seeks to understand the mind and its relation to reality.

THE DIVIDED SELF

Some of the oldest traditions in Indian and Greek philosophy hold that the self is divided. I think of myself as unified, as being *one* self. Yet I often feel conflict within myself. How is this possible? Plato wrestles with this question, concluding that the soul must have different parts. His theory is strikingly similar to the ancient Indian view of the self elaborated in the Upanishads and has influenced contemporary views of the self, most notably that of Sigmund Freud.

The Upanishads

The Upanishads are among the oldest texts in Sanskrit, the intellectual language of ancient and classical India. Hinduism, the primary religion of India, regards the Upanishads as sacred. They were composed in the period between 900 and 200 B.C.E. Six orthodox schools or *darshanas* of interpretation have developed within Hinduism: Vedanta ("end of Veda, or sacred knowledge"), Samkhya ("nature"), Yoga ("discipline"), Purva Mimamsa ("exegesis, interpretation"), Vaisesika ("realism"), and Nyaya ("logic"). The first three are the most relevant to issues in the philosophy of mind.

Vedanta is a school of philosophy with distinct branches. The term *vedanta* was originally an epithet for the Upanishads. The term later came to designate the philosophical schools that expressly embrace Upanishadic views. The teaching of the Upanishads centers on questions of theological metaphysics: What is the ultimate reality, what is its nature and relation to the world, and how can it be known? The ultimate reality is called *Brahman,* and all Vedanta is Brahman-centered.

Some proponents conceive Brahman—the Absolute, the One, Reality-in-itself—as God, others as an impersonal Ground of Being. In all cases, the notion of knowledge or recognition of Brahman, ***brahma-vidya,*** is prominent. However, Vedantins differ on its meaning. ***Advaitins,*** or **non-dualists** (*advaita* = non-dualism), hold that the self (*atman*) is in reality nothing other than Brahman; in the mystical knowledge of Brahman one knows only the One, the Sole True Existent, whose nature is perfect being, consciousness, and bliss. **Vedantin theists,** in contrast, hold that the individual and God are meaningfully distinct. Thus they are called **dualists.** According to the dualists, the individual cannot know the Absolute in precisely the fashion that God knows God, for an individual knower is not identical with his or her Creator and Ground.

The history of Vedanta, then, has two tracts. Advaita Vedantins stress meditation and the study of the Upanishads to attain the mystical highest good, whereas Vedantic theists stress love and devotion to God.

To understand the role and significance of meditation, it is worth considering another school of Upanishadic interpretation, Samkhya. Samkhya ideas appear in several Upanishads as early as the fifth century. ***Samkhya*** itself means "analysis of nature." This philosophical view holds that reality consists of two irreducible elements: nature (***prakrti***) and the conscious being (***purusa***). It is thus dualist, like theistic Vedanta, but the basic division differs. Like other early Indian worldviews, the system is wedded to ideas about a mystical enlightenment, a highest good, or personal supreme good. By attaining a proper understanding of what is *other* to consciousness—namely, nature—the individual conscious being finds himself and disengages from the world. Thus the individual recovers a blissful aloneness separate from nature or, in an alternative interpretation described in the *Bhagavad Gita,* achieves an ecstatic transcendence *within* the world.

Samkhya ideas find expression not only in the Upanishads but also in the *Mahabharata,* the "Great Indian Epic," a work of about the same time. The *Yogasutra* (the basic text of the Yoga system) and the *Samkhya-karika* (a book of commentaries on the Samkhya philosophy by the Indian philosopher Isvarakrsna) elaborate similar themes but conceive the goal somewhat differently: the highest good is an absolute rupture separating the conscious being from nature. These two texts belong to the period after 200, when Indian philosophy became more argument oriented and systematic.

A theme common to all these philosophies is an analysis of nature, including one's personal nature, mind, proclivities, and so on, in terms of three ***gunas,*** or "**strands.**" These are *sattva* (light, clarity, intelligence); *rajas* (passion, dynamism); and *tamas* (darkness, inertia, stupidity). Overlapping this division is a hierarchy of manifestations of nature: the body and the senses, the sensational or emotional mind (*manas*), the ego-sense (*ahamkdra*), and the rational mind or intelligence (*buddhi*). In some texts, the individual conscious being—or, alternatively, God—is placed at the top of the order. The *Katha Upanishad* expresses these distinctions in terms of a powerful image, that of the soul as riding in a chariot:

> Know thou the soul as riding in a chariot,
> The body as the chariot.
> Know thou the intellect as the chariot-driver,
> And the mind as the reins.
>
> The senses, they say, are the horses;
> The objects of sense, what they range over.
> The self combined with senses and mind
> Wise men call "the enjoyer."[1]

[1] The *Katha Upanishad,* translated by E. Hume, in *The Thirteen Principal Upanishads* (London: Oxford, 1931).

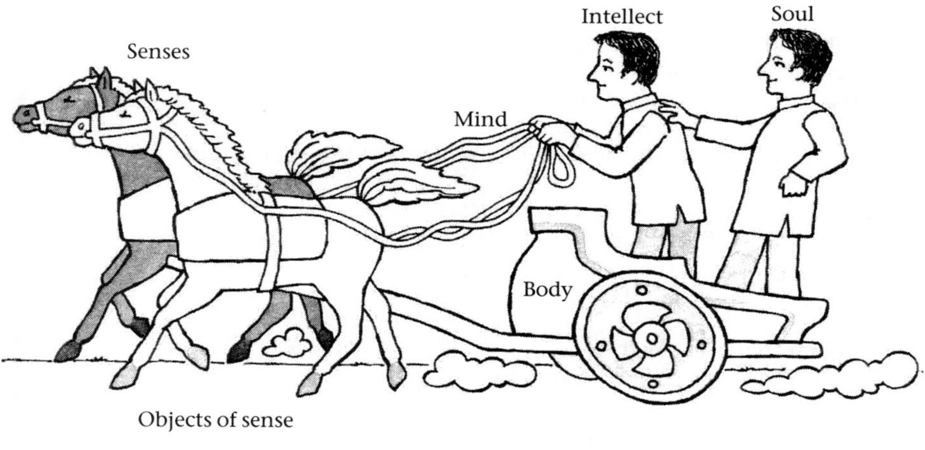

The Hindu Conception of the Self

Apparently, one attains the mystical highest good by progressively detaching oneself from each manifestation of nature. The first stage is to have the intellect control the mind firmly, keeping the senses under control.

> He who has not understanding,
> Whose mind is not constantly held firm—
> His senses are uncontrolled,
> Like the vicious horses of a chariot driver.
>
> He, however, who has understanding,
> Whose mind is constantly held firm—
> His senses are under control,
> Like the good horses of a chariot-driver.

The image suggests that the soul is separable from the body and even from the mind and intellect, just as a passenger on a chariot may embark and disembark. The soul may thus be reincarnated in a different body and mind. (Metaphorically, it may get off one chariot and climb aboard another.) Only by achieving perfect control may one avoid having to repeat this process.

What is the goal? What must one do to reach it?

> He, however, who has not understanding,
> Who is unmindful, and ever impure,
> Reaches not the goal,
> But goes on to reincarnation.
>
> He, however, who has understanding,
> Who is mindful and ever pure,
> Reaches the goal
> From which he is born no more.

He, however, who has the understanding of a chariot-driver,
A man who reins in his mind—
He reaches the end of his journey,
The highest place of Vishnu.

The distinction between the various components of the self is a hierarchy:

Higher than the senses are the objects of sense.
Higher than the objects of sense is the mind;
And higher than the mind is the intellect.
Higher than the intellect is the Great Self.

Higher than the Great is the Unmanifest.
Higher than the Unmanifest is the Person.
Higher than the Person there is nothing at all.
That is the goal. That is the highest course.

Though He is hidden in all things,
That soul shines not forth.
But he is seen by subtle seers
With superior, subtle intellect.

An intelligent man should suppress his speech and his mind.
The latter he should suppress in the Understanding-Self.
The understanding he should suppress in the Great Self.
That he should suppress in the Tranquil Self.

We gain mastery over ourselves by having higher items in this hierarchy control lower items firmly. The senses must be controlled by the objects of sense—that is, we must force ourselves to be objective, to see the world as it really is. We must pay attention. The mind must control the senses, giving them direction rather than being directed by them. We must not be swept along by every passing fad and fancy; we must keep ourselves focused on what we want to do. The intellect must control the mind; our thoughts and emotions must be subjected to the control of reason. We must be reflective, thinking hard about what we want to do and how we ought to live.

The intellect or Understanding-Self, however, is only one component of a person, and it is not the highest component. The soul, the chariot passenger, is higher, and reflects who we are more adequately. But the Upanishad draws further distinctions, between the Great Self, the Unmanifest or Tranquil Self, and the Person. This suggests that perhaps even the soul itself must go through stages of self-mastery before attaining the highest good.

How is this possible? And what is required to achieve mastery at each stage? The answer pertains to the theory of strands. Recall that the strands are, to simplify, intelligence, passion, and inertia. The senses, the mind, the intellect, and evidently even the Great Self exhibit all three strands. To gain self-mastery, intelligence must predominate over passion and inertia at each stage.

This is not the place to investigate comprehensively the portrait of reality painted by the Upanishads. But one element is crucial to understanding the Vedic theory of the self. Brahman, as we have seen, is the Absolute, the One, the ground of being, reality as it is in itself.

> [Brahman] is the sun, and the moon, and the stars.
> He is the air and the sea.
> Brahman is the Creator, Prajapati.
> He is this boy, he is that girl.
> He is this man, he is that woman,
> And he is this old man, too, tottering on his staff.
> His face is everywhere.[2]

Atman is the soul. It is the subject that thinks, feels, senses, doubts, etc.—in Kant's terms, the transcendental subject, the "I or he or it (the thing) which thinks."

> The Imperishable is the seer, though unseen;
> The hearer, though unheard;
> The thinker, though unthought;
> The knower, though unknown.
> Nothing other than the Imperishable can see, hear, think, or know.
> It is in the Imperishable that space is woven, warp and woof.[3]

> That which makes the tongue speak, but cannot be spoken by the tongue,
> Know that as the Self.
> This Self is not someone other than you.[4]

> Like two golden birds perched on the selfsame tree,
> Intimate friends, the ego and the Self, dwell in the same body.
> The former eats the sweet and sour fruits of the tree of life,
> While the latter looks on in detachment.[5]

The chief thesis of the Upanishads is the startling declaration that Brahman and *atman* are one and the same. The thesis emerges in various Upanishads:

What does it mean to say that atman *is Brahman?*

> Then Ushasta Cakrayana questioned him. "Yajnavalkhya," said he, "explain to me him who is the Brahman present and not beyond our ken, him who is the Soul in all things."

> He is your soul (*atman*), which is in all things.[6]

> He on whom the sky, the earth, and the atmosphere
> Are woven, and the mind, together with all the life-breaths,
> Him alone know as the one Soul (Atman),
> Other words dismiss. He is the bridge to immortality.[7]

---

[2] The *Shvetashvatara Upanishad,* translated by E. Eswaren, in *The Upanishads* (Petaluma: Nilgiri, 1987).
[3] The *Brhadaranyaka Upanishad,* translated by E. Eswaren, in *The Upanishads* (Petaluma: Nilgiri, 1987).
[4] The *Kena Upanishad,* translated by E. Eswaren, in *The Upanishads* (Petaluma: Nilgiri, 1987).
[5] The *Mundaka Upanishad,* translated by E. Eswaren, in *The Upanishads* (Petaluma: Nilgiri, 1987).
[6] The *Brhadaranyaka Upanishad,* translated by E. Hume, in *The Thirteen Principal Upanishads* (London: Oxford, 1931).
[7] The *Mundaka Upanishad,* translated by E. Hume, in *The Thirteen Principal Upanishads* (London: Oxford, 1931).

> In the beginning was only Being,
> One without a second,
> Out of himself he brought forth the cosmos
> And entered into everything in it.
> There is nothing that does not come from him.
> Of everything he is the inmost Self.
> Here is the truth; he is the Self supreme.
> And you are that, Shvetaketu: you are that.[8]

The non-dualists take this literally, identifying the soul with the ground of being. For both dualists and nondualists, this has sweeping implications. First, it means that we are fundamentally in harmony with the rest of the universe. We are at root identical with the ground of all being. As Huston Smith puts it, Hinduism implies that you can get what you want; the universe is attuned to our highest needs and desires, and we can realize our unity with it. Second, it means that death is unreal. Brahman cannot die; it is eternal. If *atman* is Brahman, then, it cannot die either. The soul may leave this chariot to catch another, but it cannot perish. Third, we are all One; you and I, "this boy and that girl," are all Brahman. Ethically, that entails that we all deserve consideration. Hinduism does not, however, take it to imply that we all deserve *equal* consideration. In fact, in Hinduism, one's ethical obligations depend not only upon one's social position but on one's stage of life; what it is to be a good child is not the same as what it is to be a good parent. There are different stages of life, and different sets of obligations are appropriate to them. Nevertheless, we are all one with Brahman and thus deserve respect.

Plato

Plato also divides the self into parts. In the *Republic* he distinguishes three parts of the soul: the rational part, the appetitive part, and the spirited part. The first thinks; the second desires; the third feels. Remarkably, in the *Phaedrus* Plato too uses the image of a chariot to describe their relation to one another.

> Of the nature of the soul, though her true form be ever a theme of large and more than mortal discourse, let me speak briefly, and in a figure. And let the figure be composite—a pair of winged horses and a charioteer. Now the winged horses and the charioteers of the gods are all of them noble and of noble descent, but those of other races are mixed; the human charioteer drives his in a pair; and one of them is noble and of noble breed, and the other is ignoble and of ignoble breed; and the driving of them of necessity gives a great deal of trouble to him. [246b][9]

The charioteer is the rational part of the soul. The noble horse is the spirited element, the part that feels; the ignoble horse is desire, the appetitive element, the part that craves.

What does this description imply about the parts of the soul?

> As I said at the beginning of this tale, I divided each soul into three—two horses and a charioteer; and one of the horses was good and the other bad: the division

[8] The *Chandogya Upanishad,* translated by E. Eswaren, in *The Upanishads* (Petaluma: Nilgiri, 1987).
[9] Plato, *Phaedrus,* translated by Benjamin Jowett, in *The Dialogues of Plato* (Oxford: Oxford University Press, 1892).

> may remain, but I have not yet explained in what the goodness or badness of either consists, and to that I will proceed. The right-hand horse is upright and cleanly made; he has a lofty neck and an aquiline nose; his colour is white, and his eyes dark; he is a lover of honour and modesty and temperance, and the follower of true glory; he needs no touch of the whip, but is guided by word and admonition only. The other is a crooked lumbering animal, put together anyhow; he has a short thick neck; he is flat-faced and of a dark colour, with grey eyes and blood-red complexion; the mate of insolence and pride, shag-eared and deaf, hardly yielding to whip and spur. [253d–e]

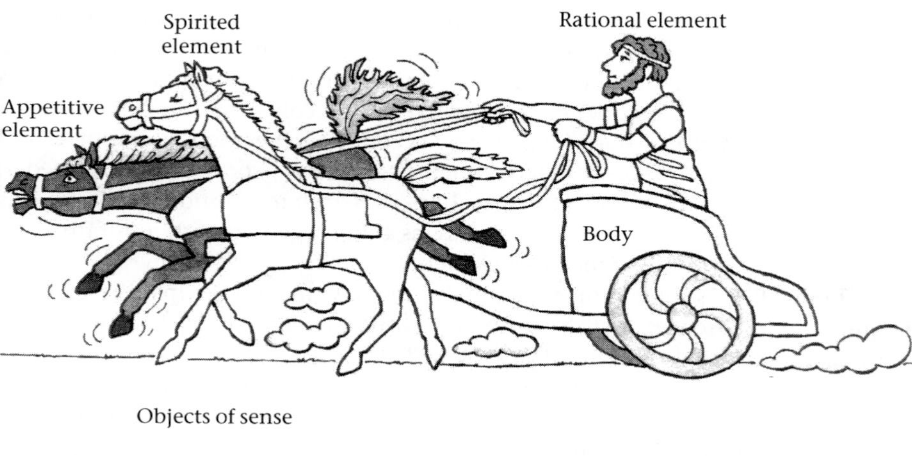

Plato's Conception of the Self

Virtue consists in subjecting the horses, especially the ignoble, rebellious horse, to the firm control of the driver:

> After this their happiness depends upon their self-control; if the better elements of the mind which lead to order and philosophy prevail, then they pass their life here in happiness and harmony—masters of themselves and orderly—enslaving the vicious and emancipating the virtuous elements of the soul; and when the end comes, they are light and winged for flight, having conquered in one of the three heavenly or truly Olympian victories; nor can human discipline or divine inspiration confer any greater blessing on man than this. [256b]

The rational element must, Plato insists, dominate the others for a person to be virtuous and happy. Plato imagines the charioteer trying to urge the horses to rise, to glimpse the forms, but having great trouble. Gods, with divinely noble horses, can rise at will. But humans have at best a tenuous hold on their desires.

> Such is the life of the gods; but of other souls, that which follows God best and is likest to him lifts the head of the charioteer into the outer world, and is carried round in the revolution, troubled indeed by the steeds, and with difficulty beholding true

> being; while another only rises and falls, and sees, and again fails to see by reason of the unruliness of the steeds. The rest of the souls are also longing after the upper world and they all follow, but not being strong enough they are carried round below the surface, plunging, treading on one another, each striving to be first; and there is confusion and perspiration and the extremity of effort; and many of them are lamed or have their wings broken through the ill-driving of the charioteers; and all of them after a fruitless toil, not having attained to the mysteries of true being, go away, and feed upon opinion. [248a–b]

Plato intends this account to explain both how psychological conflict is possible and how it ought to be resolved. Conflict occurs when parts of the soul pull in different directions. It ought to be resolved by the control of the rational part of the soul. When the charioteer has the horses well under control, the chariot rides smoothly and effectively. Just so, when the rational part of the soul dominates the others, the person is happy as well as virtuous. When the charioteer loses control of one or both of the horses, the chariot itself is out of control and becomes a danger to the charioteer and the horses as well as to others. Similarly, when a person loses control of the spirited or appetitive element, the person endangers him- or herself in addition to others. This explains why Plato sees virtue and happiness as going together; both result from the rational element's control of the other elements of the soul.

Though Plato's chariot image strikingly resembles that of the Upanishads, there are important differences. Plato's chariot has a driver, and, as in the Upanishads, it is the intellect or rational element of the self. But Plato's chariot has no passenger. In that respect, as we shall see, it resembles the Buddhist account of the self more closely than the Hindu account. Moreover, Plato's horses are desire and emotion, not the senses. In that respect, the conflict he describes is closer to the Hindu account of the strands (intelligence, passion, inertia) than to the distinction between soul, intellect, mind, and senses reflected directly in the Upanishad's chariot metaphor.

THE ABSENT SELF

We learn about ourselves partly by introspection—by what Locke calls *reflection*. We reflect on our own mental states. Looking at a flower, we can not only judge, "That's a flower," we also reflect on our own state of mind: "I'm seeing a flower," "I'm reflecting on the fact that I'm seeing a flower," and so forth. Doing this carefully, we realize that much more is going on than we can fully capture or articulate. At any given moment, we are seeing, hearing, feeling, perhaps smelling or tasting, and thinking, sometimes articulately, sometimes inchoately. There is more to our streams of consciousness than is dreamt of in even the most stream-of-consciousness writing.

When we introspect in this way, we reflect on what Kant calls *empirical consciousness*. Kant stresses the subjective unity of consciousness: we experience all those sensations and thoughts as our own. Yet the nature of that unity is mysterious. When we reflect, we reflect on seeings, hearings, smellings, thinkings, and so on; we never find *ourselves*. Our consciousness seems to be an ever-changing stream or bundle of perceptions and thoughts. Nowhere does it reveal anything that holds it together.

For that reason, some philosophers deny that there is any soul or self at all. They look inside themselves and find no self, no soul, nothing that gives consciousness any unity. So, they conclude, consciousness is nothing but a stream or bundle of perceptions, thoughts, images, feelings, desires, and so on.

Buddhism

Buddhism maintains that there is no self. The Buddha (563–483 B.C.E.), a contemporary of Confucius, Laozi, Pythagoras, and Aesop, lived in the Ganges Valley in what is now Nepal. He was born Siddhartha Gautama. According to the oldest versions of his life, he was a prince. Although he did not inherit his father's throne, as a young man he led a life of pleasure and enjoyment in the palace. He was encouraged in this by his father, who, fearing a prophecy that his son would become a religious mendicant, tried to protect him from the sight of anything unpleasant or evil. But one day the young prince journeyed some distance from the royal gardens and pleasure grounds and encountered first a diseased person, then a wrinkled and decrepit old man, and finally a corpse. Inquiring about each in turn and being told that all persons were subject to such infirmities, the prince renounced his life of enjoyments, vowing to search tirelessly for the origin and cause of these evils and the power to root them up. His experience of enlightenment, or awakening (in Sanskrit, the word *buddha* means literally "the awakened one"), did not occur right away, however; he tried out various paths of asceticism before arriving at the "Middle Way," the way of life he later proclaimed to his disciples. Finally, after a long ordeal in meditation under a Bodhi tree, he achieved enlightenment, an extinction of evil at its roots. The remainder of his life he spent traveling and preaching, helping others to reach this supreme good, which he called **nirvana.**

The Buddha, like Socrates, did not write anything. Records of his teachings and sermons were kept by his disciples, and during the reign of the Buddhist emperor Asoka about three hundred years after the Buddha was born, an enormous canon of literature sacred to Southern Buddhists was compiled. In the contemporary world, the southern branch of Buddhism, known as Theravada Buddhism, is prevalent in Sri Lanka, Burma, Thailand, and other parts of Southeast Asia. The northern branch of Buddhism, known as Mahayana Buddhism (prevalent in Nepal, Tibet, China, Korea, and Japan), recognizes a distinct literature as sacred, though it does not entirely reject the teachings of the Southern Canon. The distinct Mahayana literature was composed centuries after the oldest sections of the Southern Canon. Scholars use the term 'Early Buddhism' to refer to doctrines proclaimed in the Southern Canon, particularly teachings of the *sutta* portion, which consists of sermons ascribed to the Buddha.

The Buddha himself declined to articulate any metaphysical views; he adamantly insisted on avoiding commitments on any metaphysical issues. A disciple, Malunkyaputta, asked the Buddha whether the world was eternal, whether the world was finite, whether the soul is the same as the body, whether saints would exist after death, and so on. Meeting with silence, the disciple said in frustration, "If the Blessed One will not explain this to me, I will give up spiritual disciplines and return to the life of a layman." The Buddha responded,

"Malunkyaputta, any one who should say, 'I will not lead the religious life under The Blessed One until The Blessed One shall elucidate to me either that the world is eternal, or that the world is not eternal, . . . or that the saint neither exists nor does not exist after death';—that person would die, Malunkyaputta, before The Tathagata had ever elucidated this to him.

"It is as if, Malunkyaputta, a man had been wounded by an arrow thickly smeared with poison, and his friends and companions, his relatives and kinsfolk, were to procure for him a physician or surgeon; and the sick man were to say, 'I will not have this arrow taken out until I have learnt whether the man who wounded me belonged to the warrior caste, or to the Brahmin caste, or to the agricultural caste, or to the menial caste.'

"Or again he were to say, 'I will not have this arrow taken out until I have learnt the name of the man who wounded me, and to what clan he belongs.'

"Or again he were to say, 'I will not have this arrow taken out until I have learnt whether the man who wounded me was tall, or short, or of the middle height.'. . . That man would die, Malunkyaputta, without ever having learnt this.

"In exactly the same way, Malunkyaputta, any one who should say, 'I will not lead the religious life under The Blessed One until The Blessed One shall elucidate to me either that the world is eternal, or that the world is not eternal, . . . or that the saint neither exists nor does not exist after death';—that person would die, Malunkyaputta, before The Tathagata had ever elucidated this to him.

"The religious life, Malunkyaputta, does not depend on the dogma that the world is eternal; nor does the religious life, Malunkyaputta, depend on the dogma that the world is not eternal. Whether the dogma obtain, Malunkyaputta, that the world is eternal, or that the world is not eternal, there still remain birth, old age, death, sorrow, lamentation, misery, grief, and despair, for the extinction of which in the present life I am prescribing. . . .

"The religious life, Malunkyaputta, does not depend on the dogma that the soul and body are identical. . . .

"Accordingly, Malunkyaputta, bear always in mind what it is that I have not elucidated, and what it is that I have elucidated. And what, Malunkyaputta, have I not elucidated? I have not elucidated, Malunkyaputta, that the world is eternal; I have not elucidated that the world is not eternal; I have not elucidated that the world is finite; I have not elucidated that the world is infinite; I have not elucidated that the soul and body are identical; I have not elucidated that the soul and body are not identical; I have not elucidated that the saint exists after death; I have not elucidated that the saint does not exist after death; I have not elucidated that the saint both exists and does not exist after death; I have not elucidated that the saint neither exists nor does not exist after death. And why, Malunkyaputta, have I not elucidated this? Because, Malunkyaputta, this profits not, nor has to do with the fundamentals of religion, nor tends to aversion, absence of passion, cessation, quiescence, the supernatural faculties, supreme wisdom, and Nirvana; therefore have I not elucidated it."[10]

[10]The *Majjhima-Nikaya,* from *Buddhism in Translations,* translated by Henry Clarke Warren (Cambridge: Harvard University Press, 1896).

Nevertheless, Buddhists quickly developed characteristic philosophical approaches to such metaphysical questions. Some developed intricate theories of consciousness. Buddhaghosa (c. 400 B.C.E.), for example, elaborates an account of the self according to which there are eighty-nine kinds of consciousness! He also insists that there is no self underlying them; there is only a stream of consciousness. Nothing gives it unity. It makes no sense, therefore, to speak of a person as extended through time—existing yesterday, existing now, and existing tomorrow. At any time, there is consciousness; that is all we can say. A person, if such exists at all, exists only for a moment.

> Strictly speaking, the duration of the life of a living being is exceedingly brief, lasting only while a thought lasts. Just as a chariot-wheel in rolling rolls only at one point of the tire, and in resting rests only at one point; in exactly the same way, the life of a living being lasts only for a period of one thought. As soon as that thought has ceased the being is said to have ceased. As it has been said:—
>
> "The being of a past moment of thought has lived, but does not live, nor will it live.
>
> "The being of a future moment of thought will live, but has not lived, nor does it live.
>
> "The being of the present moment of thought does live, but has not lived, nor will it live."[11]

Not only is the self momentary, fragmented in time; it is fragmented in many other respects. I have a body, a form, thoughts, feelings, perceptions, and so on, but there is no underlying substance that unifies them into one thing. In a marvelous illustration of this view, King Milinda approaches the sage Nagasena and asks him his name. Nagasena responds:

> Your majesty, I am called Nagasena; my fellow-priests, your majesty, address me as Nagasena: but whether parents give one the name Nagasena, or Surasena, or Virasena, or Sihasena, it is, nevertheless, your majesty, but a way of counting, a term, an appellation, a convenient designation, a mere name, this Nagasena; for there is no Ego here to be found.[12]

King Milinda, astounded, replies:

> Bhante Nagasena, if there is no Ego to be found, who is it then furnishes you priests with the priestly requisites,—robes, food, bedding, and medicine, the reliance of the sick? who is it makes use of the same? Who is it keeps the precepts? who is it applies himself to meditation? who is it realizes the Paths, the Fruits, and Nirvana? . . . When you say, 'My fellow-priests, your majesty, address me as Nagasena,' what then is this Nagasena? Pray, bhante, is the hair of the head Nagasena?

Nagasena of course says no. The King asks whether the hair of the body is Nagasena. Nagasena says no. The King asks the same of nails, teeth, skin, flesh, sinews, bones, marrow, kidneys, heart, liver, spleen, lungs, intestines, stomach, feces, bile, phlegm,

---

[11] Buddhaghosa, *The Duration of Life,* from *Buddhism in Translations,* translated by Henry Clarke Warren (Cambridge: Harvard University Press, 1896).

[12] *Questions to King Milinda (Milindapanha),* from *Buddhism in Translations,* translated by Henry Clarke Warren (Cambridge: Harvard University Press, 1896).

pus, blood, sweat, tears, fat, lymph, saliva, snot, urine, and brain. Nagasena denies of each that it is Nagasena. The King then does the same for form, sensation, perception, predispositions, consciousness. Nagasena declines to identify himself with any of them. What about the combination of these? Nagasena says no to that too. He might have had different sensations, or perceptions, or thoughts, and yet still have been the same person. The King concludes:

Why does King Milinda accuse Nagasena of lying?

> Bhante, although I question you very closely, I fail to discover any Nagasena. Verily, now, bhante, Nagasena is a mere empty sound. What Nagasena is there here? Bhante, you speak a falsehood, a lie: there is no Nagasena.

Nagasena turns this strategy around. The King says that he has come in a chariot. Nagasena asks:

> Your majesty, if you came in a chariot, declare to me the chariot. Pray, your majesty, is the pole the chariot?

Of course the King says no. Nagasena asks the same question about the axle, wheels, chariot-body, banner-staff, yoke, reins, etc. What about the combination? It is not the chariot; if a wheel or the reins were replaced, for example, it would still be the same chariot. Yet there is nothing over and above these that is the chariot. Nagasena concludes:

> Your majesty, although I question you very closely, I fail to discover any chariot. Verily now, your majesty, the word chariot is a mere empty sound. What chariot is there here? Your majesty, you speak a falsehood, a lie: there is no chariot.

The King responds:

> Bhante Nagasena, I speak no lie: the word 'chariot' is but a way of counting, term, appellation, convenient designation, and name for pole, axle, wheels, chariot-body, and banner-staff.

Nagasena now draws the analogy explicitly:

What is Nagasena's analogy?

> Thoroughly well, your majesty, do you understand a chariot. In exactly the same way, your majesty, in respect of me, Nagasena is but a way of counting, term, appellation, convenient designation, mere name for the hair of my head, hair of my body, . . . brain of the head, form, sensation, perception, the predispositions, and consciousness. But in the absolute sense there is no Ego here to be found.

The **no-soul** (in Sanskrit, ***anatman;*** in Pali, *anatta*) doctrine may seem strange. Two analogies may help to make the view more intelligible. First, Nagasena's use of the chariot as an analogy to the self is surely no accident. Think back to the Upanishad's image of the self as a chariot on page 162.

The driver is the intellect; the reins are the mind. The horses are the senses, and the road the objects of sense. The passenger in the chariot is the soul, the transcendental subject, the "I or he or it (the thing that thinks)." Nagasena looks inside himself and finds no soul; indeed, he finds no chariot, except as a convenient designation for all these things put together. So we might revise the diagram to exclude the passenger, and stress in addition that it is merely a collection of parts; there is no unity to be found in it.

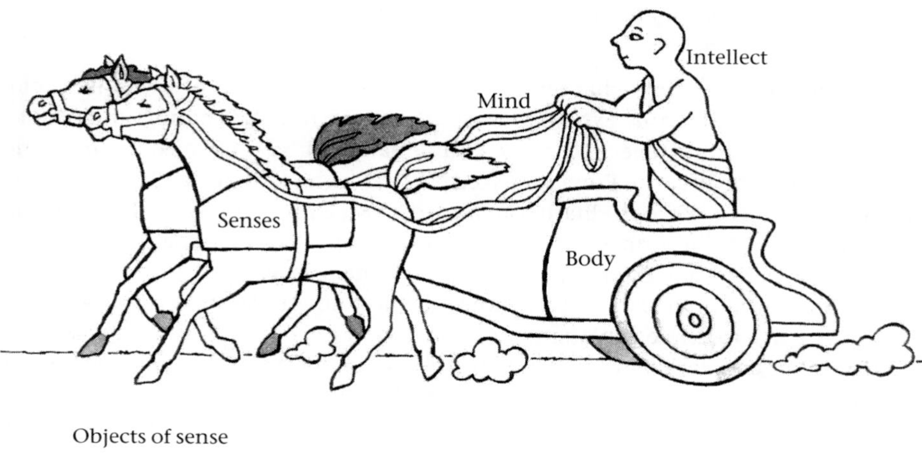

The Buddhist Conception of the Self

Second, some terms obviously have the role of being nothing more than mere appellations or convenient designations. Consider, for example, the noun 'passenger'. From one point of view, there is nothing strange about it; passengers are people who ride in a mode of conveyance—a car, ship, airplane, etc. Yet we count passengers and people differently. An airline, for instance, might announce that it carried 100,000 passengers last year. All those passengers were people. But it would not follow that the airline carried 100,000 people last year. Smith, say, may have flown to Chicago and back in January and then to Los Angeles and back in May. She is one person, but the airline would count her as four passengers (one to Chicago, one from Chicago, one to Los Angeles, one from Los Angeles). What is a passenger? There is no deep, metaphysical answer; it is just a way to carve up the world that reflects our own convenience rather than anything about the structure of reality. Buddhism holds that the same is true of 'person' (and 'chariot', and perhaps all other nouns).

Why have Buddhists advanced the no-soul doctrine? The Buddha tried to achieve self-fulfillment through self-indulgence in the palace and failed. He tried to find self-fulfillment through self-denial and ascetic discipline and failed. Enlightened, he realized that there is no path to self-fulfillment because there is no self to fulfill. The belief in an enduring, transcendental self is what leads to craving and thus to suffering. As contemporary Indian philosopher Walpola Ruhula writes,

> Buddhism stands unique in the history of human thought in denying the existence of such a Soul, Self, or *atman*. According to the teaching of Buddha, the idea of self is an imaginary, false belief which has no corresponding reality, and it produces harmful thoughts of 'me' and 'mine', selfish desire, craving, attachment, hatred, ill-will, conceit, pride, egoism, and other defilements, impurities, and problems. It is the source of all the troubles in the world from personal conflicts

> to wars between nations. In short, to this false view can be traced all the evil in the world.[13]

As we shall see in the next chapter, moreover, Buddhists and others who have embraced the no-soul doctrine extend it to all substances, not just chariots and people.

Hence, according to legend, when Bodhidharma (d. 532) traveled to China and met with Emperor Wu, the Emperor asked, "What is the first principle of this holy doctrine [Buddhism]?" Bodhidharma answered, "Vast emptiness—and there is nothing holy about it." The Emperor asked, "Then who is it who stands before me now?" "I don't know," Bodhidharma responded, and left the palace.

If Buddhists hold that there is no soul, then how is reincarnation possible? Hindus can give a simple explanation of reincarnation: The soul is like a passenger in a chariot. It can disembark and board another chariot. So, when one body wears out, the soul simply steps off and waits for another. If there is no soul, however, this explanation does not work. In short, if there is no underlying self, what could be reincarnated?

Buddhists sometimes answer metaphorically: Reincarnation is like a flame being passed from candle to candle. There is no substance being transmitted; nevertheless there is continuity of a kind. This metaphor is suggestive, but it leaves a crucial question unanswered. The link between the flames is causal. There is no obvious causal connection between a person's life and the life of that same being reincarnated in a different form. So what is the connection?

Say that Smith is reincarnated as Smythe. There need be no worldly causal connection between Smith and Smythe, and, without an otherworldly soul to play a role, it is hard to see how there could be any otherworldly causal link. In the Hindu view, Smythe is the reincarnation of Smith because these lives are being lived by the same soul, the same underlying self. In the Buddhist view, they are linked by another criterion. There must be a similarity of consciousness that is strong enough for us to count Smythe as Smith's reincarnation.

Consciousness Only

Early Buddhist texts spell out the no-soul doctrine, as we have seen. They argue that when we introspect we find no self, only particular thoughts, sensations, desires, and so on. They also argue that the self cannot be identified with any part or aspect of it or with any combination of parts or aspects. Later Buddhist philosophers develop additional arguments.

Many were advanced by the Chinese Consciousness-Only school, descending from Indian Buddhist idealism. Xuanzong (596–664) entered a Buddhist monastery at thirteen; at twenty-two, he began traveling to monasteries throughout China to study various doctrines, even leaving China against imperial order to study in India for sixteen years. At forty-nine, he returned to China with 657 Buddhist works previously unavailable there. The emperor, despite Xuanzong's disobedience, gave him a grand welcome and supported him and a large group of assistants. The emperor commissioned from them the largest translation project in Chinese history. When Xuan-

---

[13] Walpola Ruhula, *What the Buddha Taught* (New York: Grove Press, 1983), 51.

zong died at age sixty-eight, the emperor cancelled all his meetings for three days to mourn.

Most of the texts Xuanzong and his assistants translated were of the Yogacara school, or Buddhist idealism. Dharmapala (439–507) wrote commentaries on the early Indian Yogacarin Vasabandhu that exerted great influence on Xuanzong's *Treatise on the Establishment of the Doctrine of Consciousness-Only,* which, together with the notes of his student Kwei Zhi (K'uei-chi), articulate a Chinese version of what has become known as **Buddhist idealism**—combining the thesis that there is no self with the view that everything is mind-dependent.

Xuanzong analyzes the mind into eight consciousnesses: the five senses, a sense-center consciousness that coordinates the senses and forms concepts, a thought-center consciousness that wills and reasons, and storehouse consciousness. All eight are in constant flux. The storehouse consciousness receives sensations and thoughts from other consciousnesses and emits "manifestations," that is, memories, associations, and other thoughts. The thought-center consciousness interacts with storehouse consciousness, using its materials for purposes of intellectual deliberation. The sense-center consciousness combines the five senses into a coherent picture of the external world.

All these interactions occur simultaneously, according to laws of cause and effect. Objects are constructions from these eight forms of consciousness. Some *dharmas*—for example, qualities and phenomenal representations—are purely illusory or imaginary and do not exist. Some depend on other *dharmas* and so exist only temporarily. Some, finally, have their own independent natures and truly exist. Their "perfect reality" is the ultimate reality revealed in *nirvana* experience.

Xuanzong advocates the no-soul doctrine: "the self and *dharmas* are merely constructions based on false ideas and have no reality of their own."[14] How do we know? "Because neither the real self nor the real *dharma* is possible."

Xuanzong divides theories of the self into those that treat it as unified and those that treat it as an aggregate. Consider first the theories that posit a unified self. Where is this unified self? There are three possible answers. It may be universal, "as extensive as empty space," that is, existing outside the bounds of any particular body. Or it may be coextensive with the body. Finally, it may be within the body.

Suppose, as many philosophers adopting such a view have held, that the self (or soul) is transcendental, existing outside the bounds of any particular body. Then

> . . . it should not enjoy happiness or suffer sorrow along with the body. Furthermore, being eternal and universal, it should be motionless. How can it act along with the body? Again, is the self so conceived the same or different among all sentient beings?

In short, if the self is beyond the bounds of the body, its interaction with the body becomes inexplicable. And we lack any compelling way to individuate selves: Why should we count people as different selves when they have different bodies?

Suppose, then, that the self is coextensive with the body. Aristotle, who thought of the soul as the form of the body, might have held such a view. But Xuanzong finds

[14] Xuanzong, *The Treatise on the Establishment of Consciousness-Only,* from Wing Tsit-Chan (ed.), *A Source Book in Chinese Philosophy* (Princeton: Princeton University Press, 1963).

it to be "like child's play." Say Jones gains weight. Does his soul expand? Say he cuts his hair; does he lose part of his soul? Moreover, if the soul is coextensive with the body, it is divisible. But how then can it be one self?

Finally, suppose that the self is within the body. (For example, suppose one identifies the self with the brain or the nervous system or neural impulses.) Xuanzong finds it implausible that a small part of the body could cause the entire body to move. We might think that contemporary neuroanatomy puts this objection to rest. But he has another argument as well. The self, on this view, is neither one nor eternal, for there is no unity—all these options are divisible—and, being material, they perish. And if there is no unity, there is no self.

In short, if mind is separate from body, it cannot interact with the body. If mind is part or whole of the body, it lacks unity, and there is no self.

Next, consider the view that the self is an aggregate. It might be an aggregate of matter, sensation, thought, disposition, and consciousness, as Nagasena contemplates but rejects. Again, the self would be neither one nor eternal. But there is worse. The senses can be restricted (as by wearing a blindfold) or injured without changing who a person is. Thoughts and sensations are not continuous, the self is; we do not want to say that a person in a deep, dreamless sleep ceases to exist. In general, all these things depend on external causes. But the self does not. If the cat hadn't walked into the room, Smith would not have thought about feeding it. But we do not want to say that if her cat hadn't walked into the room she wouldn't have been herself.

Xuanzong raises other objections. The most powerful is based on the concept of *intentionality.* Thought is *intentional* in the sense that it is *about* things. A thought is a thought *of* something. But matter isn't *of* anything. So, thought isn't matter. The self can take things as its objects; so the self can't simply be matter. Moreover, a perception must be of something else; it cannot be a perception of itself. So the self can't perceive itself. There is thus no reason to posit a self, for there is no other evidence of its existence.

David Hume

In the West, the philosopher best known for holding a no-self doctrine is David Hume (1711–1776). Recall that Hume looks for the source of any idea in experience. But what experience (in his language, impression) could be the source for the idea of the self?

Why, according to Hume, is it impossible to find an impression from which our idea of self could be derived?

> . . . nor have we any idea of self, after the manner it is here explain'd. For from what impression cou'd this idea be deriv'd? This question 'tis impossible to answer without a manifest contradiction and absurdity; and yet 'tis a question, which must necessarily be answer'd, if we wou'd have the idea of self pass for clear and intelligible. It must be some one impression, that gives rise to every real idea. But self or person is not any one impression, but that to which our several impressions and ideas are suppos'd to have a reference. If any impression gives rise to the idea of self, that impression must continue invariably the same, thro' the whole course of our lives; since self is suppos'd to exist after that manner. But there is no impression constant and invariable. Pain and pleasure, grief and joy, passions and sensations succeed each other, and never all exist at the same time. It cannot, therefore, be

> from any of these impressions, or from any other, that the idea of self is deriv'd; and consequently there is no such idea. (I, VI, 533)[15]

Hume introspects and finds only what Kant calls *empirical consciousness,* the progression of one thought, perception, desire, etc., after another. He nowhere finds himself.

> But farther, what must become of all our particular perceptions upon this hypothesis? All these are different, and distinguishable, and separable from each other, and may be separately consider'd, and may exist separately, and have no Deed of any-thing to support their existence. After what manner, therefore, do they belong to self; and how are they connected with it? For my part, when I enter most intimately into what I call myself, I always stumble on some particular perception or other, of heat or cold, light or shade, love or hatred, pain or pleasure. I never can catch myself at any time without a perception, and never can observe any thing but the perception. When my perceptions are remov'd for any time, as by sound sleep; so long am I insensible of myself, and may truly be said not to exist. And were all my perceptions remov'd by death, and cou'd I neither think, nor feel, nor see,—nor love, nor hate after the dissolution of my body, I shou'd be entirely annihilated, nor do I conceive what is farther requisite to make me a perfect non-entity. If any one, upon serious and unprejudic'd reflection thinks he has a different notion of himself, I must confess I call reason no longer with him. All I can allow him is, that he may be in the right as well as I, and that we are essentially different in this particular. He may, perhaps, perceive something simple and continu'd, which he calls himself; tho' I am certain there is no such principle in me. (I, VI, 533–534)

Heraclitus (c. 500 B.C.E.), a pre-Socratic Greek philosopher, became famous for holding that everything is in constant flux. It is impossible, he said, to put your foot in the same river twice. By the time your foot goes in a second time, the water has moved downstream; the river is different. Hume finds the same to be true of the self. You cannot introspect the same consciousness twice. Reflection yields nothing but a flux.

> But setting aside some metaphysicians of this kind, I may venture to affirm of the rest of mankind, that they are nothing but a bundle or collection of different perceptions, which succeed each other with an inconceivable rapidity, and are in a perpetual flux and movement. Our eyes cannot turn in their sockets without varying our perceptions. Our thought is still more variable than our sight; and all our other senses and faculties contribute to this change;—nor is there any single power of the soul, which remains unalterably the same, perhaps for one moment. The mind is a kind of theatre, where several perceptions successively make their appearance; pass, re-pass, glide away, and mingle in an infinite variety of postures and situations. There is properly no simplicity in it at one time, nor identity in different; whatever natural propension we may have to imagine that simplicity and identity. The comparison of the theatre must not mislead us. They are the successive perceptions only, that constitute the mind; nor have we the most distant notion of the place, where these scenes are represented, or of the materials, of which it is compos'd. (I, VI, 534–535)

[15] David Hume, *A Treatise of Human Nature* (London: printed for John Noon, 1739).

Hume argues for this conclusion not only on the basis of the introspective evidence—we find nothing, in reflection, but particular thoughts, perceptions, and so on—but also by arguing for Heraclitus's general thesis. That is, Hume argues that *all* identity through change is imposed by the mind; physical objects are mental constructions as well.

What conclusion is Hume arguing for?

> What will suffice to prove this hypothesis to the satisfaction of every fair enquirer, is to shew from daily experience and observation, that the objects, which are variable or interrupted, and yet are suppos'd to continue the same, are such only as consist of a succession of parts, connected together by resemblance, contiguity, or causation. For as such a succession answers evidently to our notion of diversity, it can only be by mistake we ascribe to it an identity; and as the relation of parts, which leads us into this mistake, is really nothing but a quality, which produces an association of ideas, and an easy transition of the imagination from one to another, it can only be from the resemblance, which this act of the mind bears to that, by which we contemplate one continu'd object, that the error arises. Our chief business, then, must be to prove, that all objects, to which we ascribe identity, without observing their invariableness and uninterruptedness, are such as consist of a succession of related objects. (I, VI, 536–537)

A river changes, for example; but we think of ourselves as putting our foot into the *same* river, even though the water flowing past is completely different from that which flowed past a moment ago. Material objects are, less dramatically, changing all the time, losing some particles and gaining others. But we count them as persisting through time nevertheless. To be sure, a proportionately large or sudden change may make us think of the object as having changed. If a chair breaks, for example, and the back and seat are replaced, we might wonder whether the result is the same chair. But the gradual erosion of a similar mass or rock from a mountainside would never tempt us to say that it was now a different mountain. Hume takes this to show that identity is not in the world but something we impose on the world based on our own feelings of expectation.

> But supposing some very small or inconsiderable part to be added to the mass, or subtracted from it; tho' this absolutely destroys the identity of the whole, strictly speaking; yet as we seldom think so accurately, we scruple not to pronounce a mass of matter the same, where we find so trivial an alteration. The passage of the thought from the object before the change to the object after it, is so smooth and easy, that we scarce perceive the transition, and are apt to imagine, that 'tis nothing but a continu'd survey of the same object.
>
> There is a very remarkable circumstance, that attends this experiment; which is, that tho' the change of any considerable part in a mass of matter destroys the identity of the whole, let we must measure the greatness of the part, not absolutely, but by its proportion to the whole. The addition or diminution of a mountain wou'd not be sufficient to produce a diversity in a planet: tho' the change of a very few inches wou'd be able to destroy the identity of some bodies. 'Twill be impossible to account for this, but by reflecting that objects operate upon the mind, and break or interrupt the continuity of its actions not according to their real greatness, but according to their proportion to each other: And therefore, since this interrup-

> tion makes an object cease to appear the same, it must be the uninterrupted progress of the thought, which constitutes the imperfect identity.
>
> This may be confirm'd by another phenomenon. A change in any considerable part of a body destroys its identity; but 'tis remarkable, that where the change is produc'd gradually and insensibly we are less apt to ascribe to it the same effect. The reason can plainly be no other, than that the mind, in following the successive changes of the body, feels an easy passage from the surveying its condition in one moment to the viewing of it in another, and at no particular time perceives any interruption in its actions. From which continu'd perception, it ascribes a continu'd existence and identity to the object. (I, VI, 536–537)

Sometimes, moreover, we ascribe identity on the basis of a common purpose despite massive changes in parts. Ancient philosophers worried about the ship of Theseus, which has its planks replaced until no planks from the original ship remain. Is it the same ship? What if someone saves the original planks and uses the original plan to rebuild the ship? Which then counts as the ship of Theseus? The ship with the new planks, Hume tells us, for it is continuous with the original in purpose if not in matter. But this too shows that identity is a human construction, for we impose purposes on the world; they are not part of the world itself.

> There is, however, another artifice, by which we may induce the imagination to advance a step farther; and that is, by producing a reference of the parts to each other, and a combination to some common end or purpose. A ship, of which a considerable part has been chang'd by frequent reparations, is still considered as the same; nor does the difference of the materials hinder us from ascribing an identity to it. The common end, in which the parts conspire, is the same under all their variations, and affords an easy transition of the imagination from one situation of the body to another. (I, VI, 538)

Sometimes, as with animals and plants, we attribute identity on the basis of causal continuity. We say that the acorn and the oak are the same plant and the baby and the adult the same person because of their causal relations to each other. But, as we saw in the previous chapter, Hume takes causation to be something we impose in the world. All we find in experience are events following other events. Necessity and causation are our inventions. So, this kind of identity too is something we impose on the world, not something found in things themselves.

> But this is still more remarkable, when we add a sympathy of parts to their common end, and suppose that they bear to each other, the reciprocal relation of cause and effect in all their actions and operations. This is the case with all animals and vegetables; where not only the several parts have a reference to some general purpose, but also a mutual dependence on, and connexion with each other. The effect of so strong a relation is, that tho' every one must allow, that in a very few years both vegetables and animals endure a total change, yet we still attribute identity to them, while their form, size, and substance are entirely alter'd. An oak, that grows from a small plant to a large tree, is still the same oak; tho' there be not one particle of matter, or figure of its parts the same. An infant becomes a man—, and is sometimes fat, sometimes lean, without any change in his identity. (I, VI, 538)

But all these arguments apply to the mind as well as to external objects. Indeed, they apply more effectively, for the only thing that could possibly lead us to think that the mind is one thing is a causal connection among the various perceptions, thoughts, and desires we experience. But the general argument from causation now applies with a vengeance. We never experience any such a connection; we reflect and find only a sequence of impressions and ideas. Hume concludes,

> The identity, which we ascribe to the mind of man, is only a fictitious one, and of a like kind with that which we ascribe to vegetables and animal bodies. It cannot, therefore, have a different origin, but must proceed from a like operation of the imagination upon like objects. (I, VI, 540)

We began by looking for the source of the idea of mind or self-identity. Hume finds it in memory. Some of our mental states are memories of other mental states. That gives us a sense of continuity. Other mental states seem to be causes or effects of still others. We find that some states resemble others or are constantly conjoined with them. That leads us to form the idea of a self. But it is our construction and has no justification in experience itself.

Hume draws two important conclusions from this. First, the self is not a unified thing or substance; it is a complex system best compared to a commonwealth.

How is the soul analogous to a commonwealth?

> As to causation; we may observe, that the true idea of the human mind, is to consider it as a system of different perceptions or different existences, which are link'd together by the relation of cause and effect, and mutually produce, destroy, influence, and modify each other. Our impressions give rise to their correspondent ideas; said these ideas in their turn produce other impressions. One thought chases another, and draws after it a third, by which it is expell'd in its turn. In this respect, I cannot compare the soul more properly to any thing than to a republic or commonwealth, in which the several members are united by the reciprocal ties of government and subordination, and give rise to other persons, who propagate the same republic in the incessant changes of its parts. And as the same individual republic may not only change its members, but also its laws and constitutions; in like manner the same person may vary his character and disposition, as well as his impressions and ideas, without losing his identity. (I, VI, 541–542)

Second, Hume concludes that questions of identity are not questions about the world but instead questions about what we ought to impose on the world. In short, they are verbal questions about how we should use language, not real questions about things.

> The whole of this doctrine leads us to a conclusion, which is of great importance in the present affair, viz. that all the nice and subtile questions concerning personal identity can never possibly be decided, and are to be regarded rather as grammatical than as philosophical difficulties. Identity depends on the relations of ideas; and these relations produce identity, by means of that easy transition they occasion. But as the relations, and the easiness of the transition may diminish by insensible degrees, we have no just standard, by which we can decide any dispute concerning the time, when they acquire or lose a title to the name of identity. All the disputes concerning the identity of connected objects are merely verbal, except so far as the relation of parts—gives rise to some fiction or imaginary principle of union, as we have already observed. (I, VI, 543)

THE UNIFIED SELF

Views of the self as divided or even nonexistent have real power, but they seem to contradict our own sense of unity. I think of myself as one person, for example, and the things I think, want, hope, expect, feel, etc., all seem unified as part of *me.* Contrary to Hume, my experiences of the world seem not disjoint but continuous. They all have something in common—*me.* In Western philosophy, René Descartes and John Locke have elaborated into a philosophical theory that intuitive picture of the self as unified.

Dualism

René Descartes (1596–1650; see Chapter 2) begins with the method of doubt. He seeks a firm foundation for knowledge by looking for things he cannot doubt. Traditional skeptical arguments lead him to doubt the evidence of his senses; the possibility of an evil deceiver leads him to doubt even the truths of mathematics and logic. But he finds one thing he cannot doubt: that he thinks and thus that he exists. *Cogito, ergo sum,* he writes: I thing, therefore I am. That is a firm and unshakeable foundation on which he tries to construct the rest of our knowledge.

From the 'I think', Descartes draws several conclusions, as we saw in Chapter 2. First, what am I? I am a thing that thinks. I can doubt my senses or thought processes; I can doubt whether I have a body. What I cannot doubt is that I think.

> But what then am I? A thing that thinks. What is that? A thing that doubts, understands, [conceives], affirms, denies, wills, refuses, which also imagines and feels.[16]

I am essentially a thing that thinks. I cannot doubt that I doubt, understand, affirm, deny, will, feel, etc. The properties that are essential to me—without which I would not be what I am—are *mental* properties, not physical properties.

Second, therefore, I can know my own mind more directly and securely than I can know anything else. I cannot be sure that I have a body. If I do, I can wonder whether it is as it seems. Maybe I am deceived about everything around me. But I cannot be deceived about my own thoughts. As Descartes concludes, "I see clearly that there is nothing which is easier for me to know than my mind."

Nevertheless, the self is not completely unified. I have a body. How can I know that? Descartes distinguishes *imagining* from *conceiving.* Conceiving something is an act of the mind alone, but imagining requires something else. I can conceive of a thousand-sided figure, but I cannot really imagine it.

What does the example of the chiliagon show?

> And to make this plain, I examine first the difference between the imagination and pure understanding. For example, when I imagine a triangle, I not only understand it as a figure comprehended by three lines, but I also gaze at these three lines as if present to my mind's eye, and this is what I call imagining. If I want to think of a chiliagon, I understand that it is a figure composed of a thousand sides just as well as I understand that a triangle is a figure of three sides. But I cannot in this way imagine the thousand sides, nor do I gaze at them as if present.

[16] This and subsequent quotations from Descartes (unless otherwise noted) are from René Descartes, *Meditations;* the translation is my own.

This gives support to the idea that I have a body, though it does not establish it conclusively. Imagination is not essential to me, so it relies on something separate from the mind. It is plausible that this is a body.

Why does Descartes think there is likely to be something other than the mind? Why is this conclusion only probable?

> I consider that this power of imagination in me, differing as it does from the power of understanding, is not necessary to my essence, that is, the essence of my mind. For if it were absent from me I would no doubt remain the same as I am now. It seems to follow that it depends on something that differs from me. And I easily understand that if some body exists with which my mind is joined in such a way that it can apply itself to consider it whenever it pleases, it may be that by this means it can imagine corporeal things. This mode of thinking differs from pure understanding only in this respect: The mind, while it understands, in some manner turns toward itself, and looks back at some of the ideas in it. While it imagines, it turns toward the body, and there gazes at something conforming to the idea which it has either understood by itself or perceived by the senses. I can easily understand, as I say, that this is how the imagination could come about, if the body exists; and as no other convenient way of explaining it occurs to me, I conjecture that the body probably does exist. But only probably; and although I investigate everything carefully, I nevertheless do not see how, from the distinct idea of corporeal nature, which I have in my imagination, I can derive any argument on which I can base the necessary conclusion that the body exists.

Given that God exists and is not a deceiver, however, I can conclude with certainty that I have a body.

> And, really, there is no doubt that all things nature teaches me contain some truth. By nature, considered in general, I now understand nothing other than God Himself or the ordered system of created things established by God. By my nature, in particular, I understand nothing other than the combination of all the things God has given me.
>
> But there is nothing this nature teaches me more clearly than that I have a body, which is harmed when I feel pain, which needs food or drink when I feel hunger or thirst, and the like. I should not doubt that there is some truth in this.

So, I am a thing that thinks; I also have a body. But that raises a question: How does my mind relate to my body? The mind and body are closely linked, for my mind receives impressions of what my eyes see, and my mental decision to walk results in movements of my body.

> Nature also teaches me by these sensations of pain, hunger, thirst, and so on, that I am not only in my body as a sailor in a ship, but that I am so very closely joined and as it were intermingled with it that we seem to compose one unit. For otherwise, when my body is hurt, I, who am merely a thinking thing, would not feel pain, but perceive this wound by the pure understanding only, just as the sailor perceives by sight if something is broken in his ship. When my body needs food or drink, I should understand that clearly without having confused feelings of hunger and thirst. For surely all these sensations of hunger, thirst, pain, and so on are nothing other than certain confused modes of thought produced by the union and as it were intermingling of mind and body.

If mind and body are distinct, then how is their "union and as it were intermingling" possible?

The Mind/Body Problem

Princess Elizabeth of Bohemia (1619–1680), a contemporary of Descartes, Hobbes, and Galileo, wrote to Descartes to press this very question. She raises this classic objection to *dualism,* the view that mind and body exist independently. If mind and body exist and are separable, how can they interact? That is **the mind/body problem.**

What is the Princess's argument that, on Descartes's assumptions, mind and body cannot interact?

> [I ask] you to tell me how man's soul, being only a thinking substance, can determine animal spirits so as to cause voluntary actions. For every determination of movement seems to come about either by the propelling of the thing moved, by the manner in which it is propelled by that which moves it, or else by the quality and shape of the surface of the latter. Now contact is required for the first two conditions, and extension for the third. But you exclude extension entirely from the notion you have of the soul, and contact seems to me incompatible with something which is immaterial. Therefore I ask you for a more explicit definition of the soul. . . .[17]

I decide to move my legs, and they move. Descartes and common sense analyze this as a decision, a mental act, causing the motion of my legs, a physical act. But how can a mental act cause physical motion? We have a theory about what causes physical motion, and it requires contact between the cause and the thing moved, or at least that the cause be extended in space. But we have no account of mind/body contact, and the mind, according to Descartes, is not extended in space. So, how can mind and body interact?

Princess Elizabeth also objects to Descartes's identification of the soul as a thing that thinks:

> . . . that soul and thought are, like the attributes of God, inseparable, [is] a thesis difficult enough anyway to establish [for the child] in the mother's womb and in fainting spells. . . .[18]

This, of course, sets up the problem about mind/body interaction, for Descartes holds that mind and body are separate because mind is essentially a thinking thing but not essentially bodily.

Descartes responds by distinguishing two aspects of the mind: (1) its thinking, and (2) its acting and suffering with the body. Descartes says that we have the concept of the union of mind and body innately. From it we derive, a priori, concepts of mind/body interaction: of mind acting on body and body acting on mind. He takes his refutation of skepticism to show that all our a priori concepts accurately apply to the world. He concludes that mind and body do act on each other. He realizes that Elizabeth is unlikely to find this explanation satisfying. But he gives her the example of gravity, an interaction which is also puzzling, for it involves no contact. But we come

[17] Princess Elizabeth of Bohemia, letter to Descartes, May 6–16, 1643, from Margaret Wilson (ed.), *The Essential Descartes* (New York: Dutton Signet, 1969), 373.

[18] Princess Elizabeth of Bohemia, letter to Descartes, May 6–16, 1643, from Margaret Wilson (ed.), *The Essential Descartes* (New York: Dutton Signet, 1969), 373.

to accept the idea of action at a distance as unproblematic. It is just another kind of causation. So too with mind/body interaction: It is still another kind of causation.

Princess Elizabeth is indeed unsatisfied. She thinks the example of gravity works against Descartes:

> . . . our idea [of gravity] (which cannot claim the same perfection and objective reality as that of God) might have been invented out of ignorance of that which really moves these bodies toward the center (of the earth). And since no material cause is present to the senses, we would have attributed it to its opposite, the immaterial. Yet I have never been able to conceive of the immaterial except as a negation of matter with which it can have no communication.
>
> I confess that it would be easier for me to concede matter and extension to the soul, than the capacity to move a body and to be moved, to an immaterial being. . . . it is difficult also to understand how the soul, which is able to exist without the body, and has nothing in common with it, yet should be thus governed by the body. . . .[19]

Descartes's response is that we *perceive* the interaction: the union of mind and body "can be known very clearly by the senses."[20] People who do not philosophize know that the body acts on the soul and the soul acts on the body. We learn to conceive the interaction of mind and body "by means of ordinary life and conversations," not by philosophical reflection. This seems to miss the point. Princess Elizabeth is not doubting that mind and body *do* interact; she fails to see how they *could* interact if Descartes's theory were correct. The unity of the self, on his account, remains a mystery.

Personal Identity

John Locke (1632–1704; see Chapter 3), influenced by Descartes, also presents the self as unified. However, the unification he is primarily concerned with, is, in Kant's terms, not a transcendental unification but an empirical one. Descartes and Kant alike see the unity of the self in the *cogito,* the 'I think' that can accompany any thought we have. Locke sees it instead in the unity within consciousness. Our minds are not simply unstructured streams of consciousness. Its states are linked to one another in many ways, in particular by memory. Why do you think of yourself as the same person you were when you were a child? Because there is a chain of continuity linking you (now) to you (then). You may not remember being a very young child, but you can remember earlier states in which you could remember still earlier states . . . in which you could remember being a very young child.

Locke asks quite generally for criteria of identity: What makes an F the *same* F? The answer varies, he says, depending on what F is. For lumps of matter, the criterion is continuity of substance. For machines, it is continuity of structure. (I can replace the tires on my car without it becoming a different car.)

> It is not therefore unity of substance that comprehends all sorts of identity, or will determine it in every case; but to conceive and judge of it aright, we must consider

---

[19] Princess Elizabeth of Bohemia, letter to Descartes, June 10–20, 1643, from Margaret Wilson (ed.), *The Essential Descartes* (New York: Dutton Signet, 1969), 376.

[20] Descartes, letter to Princess Elizabeth, June 28, 1643, from Margaret Wilson (ed.), *The Essential Descartes* (New York: Dutton Signet, 1969), 377.

> what idea the word it is applied to stands for: it being one thing to be the same substance, another the same man, and a third the same person, if person, man, and substance, are three names standing for three different ideas. . . . (II, XXVII, 7)[21]

For animals as well as human beings, it is bodily continuity:

What is Locke's criterion for being the same man (or woman)?

> This also shows wherein the identity of the same man consists; viz. in nothing but a participation of the same continued life, by constantly fleeting particles of matter, in succession vitally united to the same organized body. He that shall place the identity of man in anything else, but, like that of other animals, in one fitly organized body, taken in any one instant, and from thence continued, under one organization of life, in several successively fleeting particles of matter united to it, will find it hard to make an embryo, one of years, mad and sober, the same man, by any supposition, that will not make it possible for Seth, Ismael, Socrates, Pilate, St. Austin, and Caesar Borgia, to be the same man. For if the identity of soul alone makes the same man; and there be nothing in the nature of matter why the same individual spirit may not be united to different bodies, it will be possible that those men, living in distant ages, and of different tempers, may have been the same man: which way of speaking must be from a very strange use of the word man, applied to an idea out of which body and shape are excluded. And that way of speaking would agree yet worse with the notions of those philosophers who allow of transmigration, and are of opinion that the souls of men may, for their miscarriages, be detruded into the bodies of beasts, as fit habitations, with organs suited to the satisfaction of their brutal inclinations. But yet I think nobody, could he be sure that the soul of Heliogabalus were in one of his hogs, would yet say that hog were a man or Heliogabalus. (II, XXVII, 6)

Locke is not arguing here against the idea of a soul or against the idea of reincarnation. He is simply pointing out that, even if we were to learn that Socrates was reincarnated as Caesar Borgia, we would still count them as different human beings. Similarly with Heliogabalus and the hog: They are different animals, even if the soul of Heliogabalus now inhabits the hog.

That is not to say that there would be some very important relation between Socrates and Borgia or Heliogabalus and the hog. But it would not be a relation of being the same animal. That is simply a matter of having the same continued life in the same organized body.

> An animal is a living organized body; and consequently the same animal, as we have observed, is the same continued life communicated to different particles of matter, as they happen successively to be united to that organized living body. And whatever is talked of other definitions, ingenious observation puts it past doubt, that the idea in our minds, of which the sound man in our mouths is the sign, is nothing else but of an animal of such a certain form. Since I think I may be confident, that, whoever should see a creature of his own shape or make, though it had no more reason all its life than a cat or a parrot, would call him still a man; or whoever should hear a cat or a parrot discourse, reason, and philosophize, would call

[21] John Locke, *An Essay Concerning Human Understanding* (London: printed for Tho. Basset, 1690).

> or think it nothing but a cat or a parrot; and say, the one was a dull irrational man, and the other a very intelligent rational parrot. (II, XXVII, 8)

If being the same human being, then, is inextricably tied to being the same life in the same body, is there another sort of identity that can express a kind of identity that is essentially related to the mind? We find it intelligible to imagine a prince being turned into a frog, for example, or Smith waking up to find herself in Jones's body, or a person being reincarnated as an ox. Whether or not these things are physically possible, they are not conceptually incoherent.

So Locke distinguishes being the same human being from being the same *person*. A human being is an animal, so being the same human being is just a matter of being the same animal. But a person is essentially rational, a "thing that thinks." So being the same person is being the same thinking being.

What is Locke's criterion for being the same person?

> This being premised, to find wherein personal identity consists, we must consider what person stands for;—which, I think, is a thinking intelligent being, that has reason and reflection, and can consider itself as itself, the same thinking thing, in different times and places; which it does only by that consciousness which is inseparable from thinking, and, as it seems to me, essential to it: it being impossible for any one to perceive without perceiving that he does perceive. When we see, hear, smell, taste, feel, meditate, or will anything, we know that we do so. Thus it is always as to our present sensations and perceptions: and by this every one is to himself that which he calls self:—it not being considered, in this case, whether the same self be continued in the same or divers substances. For, since consciousness always accompanies thinking, and it is that which makes every one to be what he calls self, and thereby distinguishes himself from all other thinking things, in this alone consists personal identity, i.e. the sameness of a rational being: and as far as this consciousness can be extended backwards to any past action or thought, so far reaches the identity of that person; it is the same self now it was then; and it is by the same self with this present one that now reflects on it, that that action was done. (II, XXVII, 9)

The identity of a person, then, consists in continuity of consciousness.

> For, it being the same consciousness that makes a man be himself to himself, personal identity depends on that only, whether it be annexed solely to one individual substance, or can be continued in a succession of several substances. For as far as any intelligent being can repeat the idea of any past action with the same consciousness it had of it at first, and with the same consciousness it has of any present action; so far it is the same personal self. For it is by the consciousness it has of its present thoughts and actions, that it is self to itself now, and so will be the same self, as far as the same consciousness can extend to actions past or to come, and would be by distance of time, or change of substance, no more two persons, than a man be two men by wearing other clothes to-day than he did yesterday, with a long or a short sleep between: the same consciousness uniting those distant actions into the same person, whatever substances contributed to their production. (II, XXVII, 10)

What makes me *me* is the network of memories, hopes, expectations, fantasies, convictions, and other thoughts that constitute my own consciousness. To ask whether

Smith and Smythe are the same person is to ask whether they share the same consciousness; whether there is a chain of memories, hopes, expectations, etc. linking them. If so, they are the same person; if not, not.

> This may show us wherein personal identity consists: not in the identity of substance, but, as I have said, in the identity of consciousness, wherein if Socrates and the present mayor of Queinborough agree, they are the same person: if the same Socrates waking and sleeping do not partake of the same consciousness, Socrates waking and sleeping is not the same person. And to punish Socrates waking for what sleeping Socrates thought, and waking Socrates was never conscious of, would be no more of right, than to punish one twin for what his brother-twin did, whereof he knew nothing, because their outsides were so like, that they could not be distinguished; for such twins have been seen. (II, XXVII, 19)

Now plainly one can be the same person or the same human being without being the same lump of matter. Every time Smith breathes, her body takes in some molecules (of oxygen, for example) and expels others. Jones might be in an accident and lose a finger and yet be the same human being and the same person. The more interesting question is whether different human beings can count as the same person, or different people count as the same human being. In other words, can one person inhabit two different bodies? Can two people inhabit the same body?

> Could we suppose two distinct incommunicable consciousnesses acting the same body, the one constantly by day, the other by night; and, on the other side, the same consciousness, acting by intervals, two distinct bodies: I ask, in the first case, whether the day and the night man would not be two as distinct persons as Socrates and Plato? And whether, in the second case, there would not be one person in two distinct bodies, as much as one man is the same in two distinct clothings? (II, XXVII, 23)

Conceptually, the answer seems to be yes:

> For the same consciousness being preserved, whether in the same or different substances, the personal identity is preserved. (II, XXVII, 13)

> So that self is not determined by identity or diversity of substance, which it cannot be sure of, but only by identity of consciousness. (II, XXVII, 23)

Locke is nevertheless highly skeptical of claims of reincarnation. For the reincarnated person has no memory of prior lives; there is no continuity of consciousness. There is no reason why there could not be such continuity, however, without a body or with a very different kind of body; so Locke has no objection to thinking that we might have a life after death. In any case, the term 'person' has great moral significance, for we may hold A responsible for what B has done only if A and B are the same person.

> Person, as I take it, is the name for this self. Wherever a man finds what he calls himself, there, I think, another may say is the same person. It is a forensic term, appropriating actions and their merit; and so belongs only to intelligent agents, capable of a law, and happiness, and misery. This personality extends itself beyond present existence to what is past, only by consciousness,—whereby it becomes concerned and accountable; owns and imputes to itself past actions, just upon the

> same ground and for the same reason as it does the present. All which is founded in a concern for happiness, the unavoidable concomitant of consciousness; that which is conscious of pleasure and pain, desiring that that self that is conscious should be happy. And therefore whatever past actions it cannot reconcile or appropriate to that present self by consciousness, it can be no more concerned in than if they had never been done: and to receive pleasure or pain, i.e. reward or punishment, on the account of any such action, is all one as to be made happy or miserable in its first being, without any demerit at all. For, supposing a man punished now for what he had done in another life, whereof he could be made to have no consciousness at all, what difference is there between that punishment and being created miserable? And therefore, conformable to this, the apostle tells us, that, at the great day, when every one shall "receive according to his doings, the secrets of all hearts shall be laid open." The sentence shall be justified by the consciousness all persons shall have, that they themselves, in what bodies soever they appear, or what substances soever that consciousness adheres to, are the same that committed those actions, and deserve that punishment for them. (II, XXVII, 26)

In all these matters, Locke speaks of what is conceptually possible. There is no contradiction in thinking of two people inhabiting the same body—indeed, men or women with multiple personalities may be an instance of this phenomenon—or of one person inhabiting different bodies. There is no contradiction in thinking of consciousness surviving death. But whether these things are *really* possible depends on the nature of the mind, something we do not know.

> I am apt enough to think I have, in treating of this subject, made some suppositions that will look strange to some readers, and possibly they are so in themselves. But yet, I think they are such as are pardonable, in this ignorance we are in of the nature of that thinking thing that is in us, and which we look on as ourselves. Did we know what it was, or how it was tied to a certain system of fleeting animal spirits; or whether it could or could not perform its operations of thinking and memory out of a body organized as ours is; and whether it has pleased God that no one such spirit shall ever be united to any but one such body, upon the right constitution of whose organs its memory should depend; we might see the absurdity of some of those suppositions I have made. But taking, as we ordinarily now do (in the dark concerning these matters), the soul of a man for an immaterial substance, independent from matter, and indifferent alike to it all; there can, from the nature of things, be no absurdity at all to suppose that the same soul may at different times be united to different bodies, and with them make up for that time one man: as well as we suppose a part of a sheep's body yesterday should be a part of a man's body to-morrow, and in that union make a vital part of Meliboeus himself, as well as it did of his ram. (II, XXVII, 27)

MIND AND ZEN

Zen Buddhism, a distinctly Chinese invention, offers a complex and hard-to-classify theory of the self. The Japanese word *zen* derives from the Chinese *chan,* which, in turn, derives from the Sanskrit *dhyana* (meditation). In China, however, the Indian idea of meditation yielded to a Taoist notion of concentration and enlightenment. Mahayana Buddhism split into five schools, one of which is Zen. The northern Chinese school stressed gradual enlightenment based on a process of eliminating error and establishing mental quietude. The southern school, which developed later but eventually won out over its northern competitor, stressed sudden enlightenment. On this conception, the mind is a unity that is simple, in the sense that it is absolutely indivisible. The Buddha is everywhere; anything can bring about its realization. The Zen practitioner seeks a state of mind in which reality becomes transparent and crystalline.

The Buddha-nature, according to both schools, is *nirvana,* which resides in everyone; everyone has the ability to become a Buddha. The northern school distinguishes true mind from false mind and seeks gradual enlightenment through the elimination of false mind. The southern school, however, treats the mind as an inseparable unity all functions of which reflect true reality or Suchness (*tathata*).

Yixuan (I-Hsüan)

The southern Zen doctrine of unity and inseparability seems to imply that all distinctions are unfounded and need to be transcended. Isn't Zen itself therefore unfounded? Perhaps, if we take the propositions advanced by Zen as describing the world. But Zen theses are means for reaching an end, ***satori*** (enlightenment), rather than literal descriptions of reality. Their point is not to give us descriptive or even normative knowledge but to lead us to undergo certain kinds of experiences.

Of course, there are many ways of undergoing the right kinds of experiences. They need not involve language; if they do, the language need not make sense in traditional terms. The goal of Zen is *satori,* enlightenment. The goal lies beyond thought and language and so cannot be described. But those who have experienced it report an experience of joy: they see the world as good and beautiful. They feel that they have a heightened sense of reality, an ability to see beyond appearance to the true nature of things. They also feel a loss of boundaries: they experience a unity of mind and world of the kind traditionally sought in Hindu meditation.

How can enlightenment be achieved? Zen training methods include meditation, ***koan***—"riddles," meant to develop insight—and various arts. ***Zazen*** is seated meditation; it borrows much from Indian meditation practices, especially raja yoga. ***Sanzen*** is consultation; this is important, for Zen can be passed on only through individual instruction and training. *Koan* are paradoxes, puzzling questions (sometimes with responses), meant to break down rational thought and force the mind to recognize its true nature. Normally, the mind thinks by discriminating. But this leads it into suffering. To escape suffering, the mind must recognize that everything is empty, that all discriminations are ultimately pointless. That can be expressed linguistically—I have just done it—but that expression itself uses discriminations and so cannot get the mind beyond them. A *koan* tries to force the mind out of its usual habits of discrimination into a direct experience of emptiness.

These are some classic *koan:*

What is the sound of one hand clapping?
What was the appearance of your face before your ancestors were born?
What direction does the twelve-face Kuan-yin face?

A cow passes by a window. The horns, the head, and the four legs pass by. Why doesn't the tail pass by?

A long time ago a man kept a goose in a bottle. It grew larger and larger until it couldn't get out of the bottle any more. He didn't want to break the bottle, and he didn't want to hurt the goose. How can he get it out?

"What is the Buddha-nature?" "Three pounds of flax."

"How do my feet resemble a donkey's feet?" "When a heron stands in the snow, its color is not the same."

"Does a dog have Buddha-nature?" "Mu!" ["nothing," "zero"]

Sometimes Zen masters use more extreme methods to clarify the mind. Yixuan (I-Hsüan, d. 867) founded the Linji (Lin-chi) school. Called ***Rinzai*** in Japanese, it is the most radical of the ninth-century Zen schools, which stresses the "lightning" method of shouting and beating to prepare the mind for enlightenment. (Yixuan himself is often called Linji or Rinzai.)

A monk asked, "What is the basic idea of the Law preached by the Buddha?" Thereupon the Master [Yixuan] shouted at him. The monk paid reverence. The Master said, "The Master and the monk can argue all right."

What is Yizuan trying to communicate by responding to this question by beating the questioner?

The Master ascended the hall. A monk asked, "What is the basic idea of the Law preached by the Buddha?" The Master lifted up his swatter. The monk shouted, and the Master beat him.

[The monk asked again,] "What is the basic idea of the Law preached by the Buddha?" The Master again lifted up his swatter. The monk shouted, and the Master shouted also. As the monk hesitated about what to say, the Master beat him.

Thereupon the Master said, "Listen, men. Those who pursue after the Law will not escape from death. I was in my late Master Huang-Po's place for twenty years. Three times I asked him about the basic idea of the Law preached by the Buddha and three times he bestowed upon me the staff. I felt I was struck only by a dried stalk. Now I wish to have a real beating. Who can do it to me?"

One monk came out of the group and said, "I can do it."

The Master picked up the staff to give him. As he was about to take it over, the Master beat him.[22]

Yixuan shocks his monks in other ways as well:

Seekers of the Way, if you want to achieve the understanding according to the Law, don't be deceived by others and turn to [your thoughts] internally or [objects] externally. Kill anything that you happen on. Kill the Buddha if you happen to meet him. Kill a patriarch or arhat if you happen to meet him. Kill your parents or relatives if you happen to meet them. Only then can you be free, not bound by material things, and absolutely free and at ease.

This sounds like an anticipation of Charles Manson! Since the first ethical precept of Buddhism is "do not kill," however, and since Chinese tradition places strong

[22]This and subsequent quotations from Yixuan are from *The Recorded Conversations of Zen Master I-Hsüan,* from Wing-tsit Chan (ed.), *A Source Book in Chinese Philosophy* (Princeton: Princeton University Press, 1963).

emphasis on respect for elders, this is startling advice not intended to be taken literally. Yixuan tries to make his students see that enlightenment cannot depend on valuing even the most valuable things.

> If you seek after the Buddha, you will be taken over by the devil of the Buddha, and if you seek after the patriarch, you will be taken over by the devil of the patriarch. If you seek after anything, you will always suffer. It is better not to do anything.

So he advises doing little. Enlightenment does not consist in accomplishing anything; it consists in experiencing life in a certain way. Seeking it actively precludes one from finding it.

> The Master told the congregation: "Seekers of the Way: In Buddhism no effort is necessary. All one has to do is to do nothing, except to move his bowels, urinate, put on his clothing, eat his meals, and lie down if he is tired. The stupid will laugh at him, but the wise one will understand. An ancient person said, 'One who makes effort externally is surely a fool.'"
>
> My views are few. I merely put on clothing and eat meals as usual, and pass my time without doing anything. You people coming from the various directions have all made up your minds to seek the Buddha, seek the Law, seek emancipation, and seek to leave the Three Worlds. Crazy people! If you want to leave the Three Worlds, where can you go? 'Buddha' and 'patriarchs' are terms of praise and also bondage. Do you want to know where the Three Worlds are? They are right in your mind which is now listening to the Law.

Although Yixuan does offer some views, he realizes the limitations of language in communicating Zen. After describing his experiences studying with Master Huang-Po, he observes, "After all, there is not much in Huang-Po's Buddhism," and he describes his own philosophical strategy in terms that make it clear he intends not to argue for or even assert philosophical theses, but to *do* something:

> I have no trick to give people. I merely cure disease and set people free. . . .

Nevertheless, there are some philosophical theses characteristic of Zen. The basic *gatha,* or motto, of Zen Buddhism is

> A special transmission outside of scriptures;
> No dependence on words or letters;
> Direct pointing at the mind of man;
> Seeing into one's nature, and the attainment of Buddhahood.[23]

Bodhidharma, who came to China in 520, met with Emperor Wu, and stayed in the Shaolinsi monastery for nine years, said that he was bringing to China a special "transmission outside the scriptures." According to tradition, the Buddha, near the end of his life, called his disciples together and gave them what is called the Flower Sermon. He said nothing; he simply took a single flower from his robe, held it up, and smiled. One disciple, Kasyapa, returned the smile, understanding the Buddha's meaning.

---

[23] Quoted in Patrick Bresnan, *Awakening: An Introduction to the History of Eastern Thought* (Upper Saddle River: Prentice-Hall, 1999), 343.

The Buddha chose him as his successor. Later, Kasyapa chose his own successor, the Buddha's favorite follower, Ananda. These handpicked successors of the Buddha are known as **patriarchs.** Bodhidharma, the twenty-eighth patriarch of India, became the first patriarch of China. (Nagarjuna, discussed in Chapter 2, was designated the fourteenth patriarch of India.) The patriarchs passed along a special message of enlightenment that cannot be written down. It lies beyond the scriptures and does not depend on words and letters because it cannot be adequately expressed in language. Instead, it seeks to transmit an experience that yields direct insight into the mind and its Buddha-nature.

Zen inherits a metaphysical perspective from earlier Buddhist schools. According to many Indian and Chinese Buddhist thinkers, all things interrelate and affect one another. Each ***dharma,*** or object, can be defined only in terms of other *dharmas.* The thesis most characteristic of Zen is that the nature of *dharmas* is empty. The ultimate truth of the world is emptiness (*sunyata*). The mind is a unity; the discriminations involved in thinking inevitably hide reality.

> *Question:* "What is meant by the mind's not being different at different times?"
>
> The Master answered, "As you deliberated to ask the question, your mind has already become different. Therefore the nature and character of dharmas have become differentiated. Seekers of the Way, do not make any mistake. All mundane and supramundane dharmas have no nature of their own. Nor have they the nature to be produced [by causes]. They have only the name Emptiness, but even the name is empty. Why do you take this useless name as real? You are greatly mistaken! . . . I know that all dharmas are devoid of characters. They exist when there is transformation [in the mind] and cease to exist when there is no transformation. The Three Worlds are but the mind, and all dharmas are consciousness only. Therefore [they are all] dreams, illusions, and flowers in the air. What is the use of grasping and seizing them?

As the *Avatamsaka Sutra* has it,

> If you wish to understand thoroughly all the Buddhas of the past, present, and future, then you should view the nature of the whole universe as being created by the mind alone.

Language

Zen may be seen as depending on a particular conception of language and reality, encapsulated in the slogan, "The dharmas are empty." The *Lankavatara Sutra* puts this elegantly:

> The ultimate truth is a state of inner experience by means of Noble Wisdom and as it is beyond the ken of words and discriminations it cannot be adequately expressed by them.[24]

---

[24] *The Lankavatara Sutra,* quoted in D. T. Suzuki, "Zen Buddhism," *Monumenta Nipponica* (1938); reprinted in D. T. Suzuki, *Studies in Zen* (New York: Dell Publishing Company, Inc., 1955).

All thought and language require discrimination. That is, every nonlogical linguistic expression plays some role in communication and does so by drawing a distinction. Consider words from various grammatical categories:

Category	*Word*	*Distinction: Extension / Anti-extension*
Noun	Pig	Pigs / Nonpigs
Verb	Fly	Fliers / Nonfliers
Adjective	Pink	Pink / Nonpink
Adverb	Quickly	Done quickly / Not done quickly
Preposition	On	x on y / x not on y

The noun 'pig' distinguishes pigs from nonpigs. The verb 'fly' distinguishes fliers from nonfliers.

But experience cannot be captured by discrimination or therefore by language. "A picture is worth a thousand words," we say; actually, no matter how many words we use, we can never give someone the experience of looking at a picture. There is a tremendous difference between reading a novel and seeing a movie or hearing a description of someone's roller coaster ride and experiencing the ride yourself. Discrimination, drawing distinctions, using language and logic—none can give us the kind of understanding of the world we get by experiencing it.

Importantly, desire too requires drawing distinctions. The *Sutra* reports the Buddha's words:

> . . . my teaching is based upon the recognition that the objective world, like a vision, is a manifestation of the mind itself; it teaches the cessation of ignorance, desire, deed and causality; it teaches the cessation of suffering that arises from the discrimination of the triple world.

Say that Jones wants an ice cream cone. He thereby distinguishes situations in which he gets an ice cream cone from those in which he does not. The former give him satisfaction, while the latter leave him frustrated. Just as a noun like 'pig' distinguishes the objects of which it is true from those of which it is false, a desire distinguishes situations in which it is satisfied from those in which it is frustrated.

> . . . the ignorant and simple-minded, not knowing that the world is only something seen of the mind itself, cling to multitudinousness of external objects, cling to the notions of being and non-being, oneness and otherness, bothness and non-bothness, existence and non-existence, eternity and non-eternity, and think that they have a self-nature of their own, all of which rises from the discriminations of the mind and is perpetuated by habit-energy, and from which they are given over to false imagination. It is all like a mirage in which springs of water are seen as if they were real. They are thus imagined by animals, who, made thirsty by the heat of the season, run after them. Animals, not knowing that the springs are an hallucination of their own minds, do not realise that there are no such springs. In the same way, Mahamati, the ignorant and simple-minded, their minds burning with the fires of greed, anger and folly, finding delight in a world of multitudinous forms, their thoughts obsessed with ideas of birth, growth and destruction, not well understanding what is meant by existent and non-existent, and being impressed by

> the erroneous discriminations and speculations since beginningless time, fall into the habit of grasping this and that and thereby becoming attached to them.

But drawing distinctions of this kind is pointless as well as harmful, for the distinctions are unreal; the dharmas are empty. The differences we postulate as being in the world are really projections of our own minds.

Why does discrimination lead to unhappiness?

> All that is seen in the world is devoid of effort and action because all things in the world are like a dream, or like an image miraculously projected. This is not comprehended by the philosophers and the ignorant, but those who thus see them truthfully. Those who see things otherwise walk in discrimination and, as they depend upon discrimination, they cling to dualism. The world as seen by discrimination is like seeing one's own image reflected in a mirror, or one's shadow, or the moon reflected in water, or an echo heard in the valley. People grasping their own shadows of discrimination become attached to this thing and that thing and failing to abandon dualism they go on forever discriminating and thus never attain tranquillity. By tranquillity is meant Oneness, and Oneness gives birth to the highest Samadhi which is gained by entering into the realm of Noble Wisdom that is realiseable only within one's inmost consciousness.

Language is the chief culprit, for it draws distinctions and leads us to see the world in a way that promotes desire.

> Why is it that the ignorant are given up to discrimination and the wise are not? The Blessed One replied: It is because the ignorant cling to names, signs and ideas; as their minds move along these channels they feed on multiplicities of objects and fall into the notion of an ego-soul and what belongs to it; they make discriminations of good and bad among appearances and cling to the agreeable. As they thus cling there is a reversion to ignorance, and karma born of greed, anger and folly, is accumulated. As the accumulation of karma goes on they become imprisoned in a cocoon of discrimination and are henceforth unable to free themselves from the round of birth and death.

In order to escape the cycle of birth and death, we must learn to see the world prelinguistically, without "becoming imprisoned in a cocoon of discrimination."

Reflective and Prereflective Experience

Zen invokes a view of language and reality. But it may also be seen as depending on a distinction between two different kinds of experience or consciousness. This is the approach of Daisetz Teitaro Suzuki (1870–1966), who was born near Kanazawa, Japan. A schoolmate of Kitaro Nishida, the founder of the Kyoto school of philosophy, he came to the Chicago World's Fair when he was twenty-three to teach Westerners about Zen Buddhism. He returned to Japan and became professor at Otani University in Kyoto, where he kept in close contact with Nishida and other members of the Kyoto school. Sometimes criticized as a popularizer, Suzuki published many works in English translations, spreading Zen throughout the Western world. He founded a journal, *The Eastern Buddhist,* committed to publishing Zen writings.

Suzuki's version of Zen, the Rinzai sect, stems from the Southern Chinese school and specifically from Yixuan's radical Linji movement. It is in many ways anti-intellectual. According to Suzuki, all distinctions are illusions. Studying the scriptures of Buddhism and other philosophical texts is, in itself, pointless. Thinking can only take us away from the truth. There is no difference between the real and the unreal, between the holy and the secular, or between the logical and the illogical.

Suzuki finds his inspiration in the *Lankavatara Sutra:*

> While Intuition does not give information that can be analysed and discriminated, it gives that which is far superior—Self-realisation through Identification.

As he explains it:

> Buddhism teaches that all is well where it is; but as soon as a man steps out to see if he is all right or not, an error is committed which leads to an infinite series of negations and affirmations, and he has to make peace within.[25]

The goal is to achieve and remain in **prereflective experience**, "clear mind": to experience without thought or self-awareness. The clear mind is like a mirror, reflecting the world just as it is. Think of driving, for example, without thinking—just driving. Or think of someone eating voraciously, thinking of nothing but the food.

> Zen upholds, as every true religion must, the direct experience of Reality. It aspires to drink from the fountain of life itself instead of merely listening to remarks about it. A Zen follower is not satisfied until he scoops with his own hands the living waters of reality, which alone, as he knows, will quench his thirst.

Reflective experience, in contrast, does involve thought and self-awareness. We can introspect upon our own mental states, moving from prereflective experience of the world to reflective awareness of what we are perceiving and thinking, from

> I am watching (driving, eating, etc.)

to

> I am thinking, "I am watching (driving, eating, etc.)"

and even

> I am thinking, "I am thinking, 'I am watching (driving, eating, etc.)'"

This process gives Descartes the *cogito,* the self-knowledge that in his view provides a secure foundation for all other knowledge. It also gives us much other self-knowledge. But from Zen's perspective it constitutes an infinite trap. We begin reflecting. How do we stop? As soon as we become aware of our own reflection, we move to yet another level of reflection. It seems that conscious thought can only get us deeper into the reflective trap. The paradox is precisely that of advice such as "Try not to try so hard," or "Don't be self-conscious." Hence the importance of the *koan,* of shouts, even of

[25] D. T. Suzuki, "Zen Buddhism," *Monumenta Nipponica* (1938); reprinted in D. T. Suzuki, *Studies in Zen* (New York: Dell Publishing Company, Inc., 1955).

beatings. They are attempts to break out of the trap and recover clear mind. As the *Lankavatara Sutra* puts it:

> The ultimate truth is Mind itself, which is free from all forms, inner and outer. No words can therefore describe Mind, no discriminations can reveal it.

To try to understand this in words or rational thought is impossible. The object is to clear thought away, not to find the correct thought. So, as Suzuki says,

> The strange situation created by Zen is that those who understand it do not understand it, and those who do not understand it understand it—a great paradox, indeed, which runs throughout the history of Zen.

This explains why Hongren (Hung-jen), the fifth Chinese patriarch, explained his choice of the humble Huineng (638?–723) as his successor: "Of my five-hundred disciples four hundred and ninety-nine possess a remarkable understanding of Zen. Only Huineng did not understand Zen. That's why I chose him."

The Zen Circle

Traditional Zen teaches that the personal element is essential: a master must pass enlightenment to a student. There is no way to teach yourself. Various writers have nevertheless tried to convey the messages of Zen to a large and predominantly Western audience. One of these writers is Seung Sahn.

Seung Sahn (b. 1927) was born in Seun Choen, North Korea, to Protestant parents. When he was seventeen, he joined the Korean resistance, fighting against the occupying Japanese army. He was captured and barely escaped execution. After his release from prison, he and two friends fled to Manchuria to join the Free Korean Army. Seung Sahn returned to Korea after World War II and studied philosophy at Dong Guk University. He then shaved his head and lived as a hermit in the mountains, studying Confucianism and Buddhism. He was ordained a Buddhist monk at the age of twenty-one. Seung Sahn had his first experience of enlightenment while spending one hundred days on Won Gak Mountain eating nothing but pine needles. At twenty-two, Seung Sahn became a Zen master; three masters certified his enlightenment. (One of them, Ko Bong, a particularly famous Zen master, never transmitted enlightenment to anyone else.) After serving in the army during the Korean War, Seung Sahn chaired a committee to reform the Chogye order of Korean Buddhism and became *abhor* (roughly equivalent to a bishop) of five temples in Seoul. For nine years, he taught in Japan; he founded temples in Hong Kong and Tokyo. At forty-five he came to the United States. He now directs Zen communities in New York, New England, and California.

Seung Sahn poses a puzzle. Smoking a cigarette, someone enters a Zen center, blows smoke in the face of the Buddha statue, and drops ashes on its lap. If you see this, what should you do? One possible answer: All distinctions are illusory. Nothing is holy; nothing is secular. Everything ultimately is one, and that is the Buddha. So there is no difference between dropping ashes on the Buddha and dropping ashes in the ashtray. Another possible answer: Everything is what it is. What is holy is holy; what is secular is secular. Ashes should he dropped on the ashtray not on the Buddha.

Zen teaches that both perspectives are in some sense right. The person dropping ashes on the Buddha, therefore, understands only partially. If you try to explain this, however, the person will simply hit you, since he or she believes that all words and all distinctions they mark are meaningless. So, what should you do? Seung Sahn's puzzle brings out forcefully a central paradox of Zen Buddhism. If all distinctions are illusions, then once we recognize this, how is discourse possible? How could the enlightened, or the even partially enlightened, communicate?

This puzzle is partly one of ethics. The immediate problem, after all, is not how communication is possible, but rather what you should do. It is a practical puzzle concerning obligations to others. The central point of Buddhism is the recognition and alleviation of suffering. The smoker dropping ashes on the Buddha suffers from an incomplete conception; you have an obligation to help. The puzzle has other serious ethical ramifications. If all distinctions are illusions, so is the distinction between good and evil. There is no difference between right and wrong. If so, how can any who understand this decide? How can they criticize, direct, or teach others—or be criticized, directed, or taught by them? We can say that Zen theses are means for achieving certain kinds of experiences or, in Wittgenstein's image, ladders to be kicked away once enlightenment is obtained. Once we see that they are mere ladders, however, how can we make further progress? Seung Sahn sees this as a primary problem for one who seeks enlightenment. He believes its solution is both possible and necessary for achieving enlightenment.

Seung Sahn's slogan is simple: "Zen is understanding yourself." He describes enlightenment as proceeding in stages, which he symbolizes in the Zen Circle:

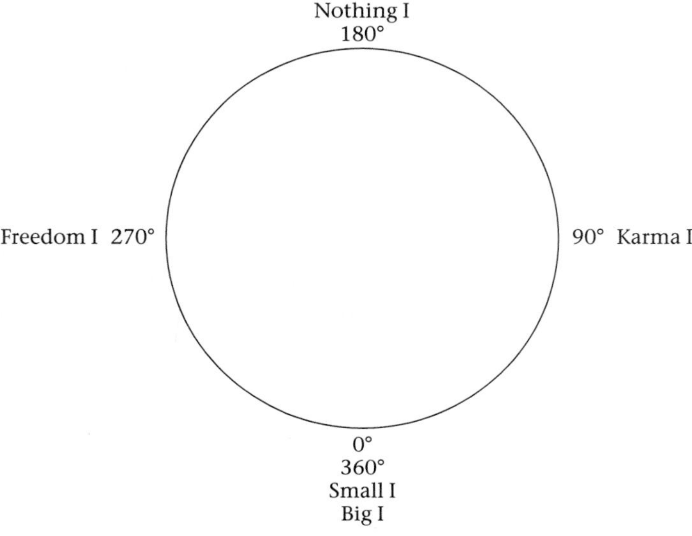

The Zen Circle

Initially, we are at the bottom of the circle, labeled 0°, as the Small I. We think about the world in the usual way, making distinctions and using language. We have an attachment to name and form. Because we think and draw distinctions, we experience desire, and we suffer. Faced with an object, we try to label and define it. We treat a book and a pencil as different objects.

> We begin from 0° to 90°. This is the area of thinking and attachment. Thinking is desire, desire is suffering. All things are separated into opposites: good and bad, beautiful and ugly, mine and yours. I like this; I don't like that. I try to get happiness and avoid suffering. So life here is suffering, and suffering is life.[26]

At the first stage to enlightenment, we move to 90°, the Karma I. This stage Seung Sahn calls Theoretical Zen. Here we are attached not to name and form but to thinking; we try to think our way out of the cycle of birth and death to enlightenment. We learn that the dharmas are empty, and we recognize that everything is a manifestation of mind. We see form as emptiness and emptiness as form. As the *Heart Sutra* declares,

What does it mean to say that form is emptiness?

> Form is emptiness; emptiness is form. Emptiness is not other than form; form is not other than emptiness. In the same way, feelings, discriminations, compositional factors, and consciousness are empty. Shariputra, in that way, all phenomena are empty, without characteristics, unproduced, unceasing, undefiled, not undefiled, not decreasing, nor increasing. Therefore, Shariputra, in emptiness there is no form, no feelings, no discriminations, no compositional factors, no consciousness, no eye, no ear, no nose, no tongue, no body, no mind, no form, no sound, no odor, no taste, no object of touch, no phenomenon.[27]

Everything, we recognize, is ultimately the same; the distinctions we draw are imposed by us, not there in the world. So, we see the book and the pencil as being the same, for all things are ultimately one.

> Past 90° is the area of the Consciousness or Karma I. Below 90° there is attachment to name and form. Here there is attachment to thinking. Before you were born, you were zero; now you are one; in the future, you will die and again become zero. So zero equals one, one equals zero. All things here are the same, because they are of the same substance.

At the second stage, we move to 180°, the Nothing I. This is the First Enlightenment; reaching it requires moving beyond Theoretical Zen to Tathagata Zen. Here, we realize that we cannot think our way to enlightenment. We move beyond thinking to true emptiness. We give up not only our attachment to name and form but also our attachment to thinking. Seeing that the dharmas are empty, we become attached to emptiness. So we cannot use words to explain anything; asked what something is, we cannot give a definition, but only a shout: "HO!" Are the book and the pencil the same or different? We can only hit the table. Everything is empty; everything is nothing.

> At 180° there is no thinking at all. This is the experience of true emptiness. Before thinking, there are no words and no speech. So there are no mountains, no rivers,

[26]This and subsequent quotations from Seung Sahn are from Seung Sahn, *Dropping Ashes on the Buddha,* compiled and edited by Stephen Mitchell (New York: Grove Press, 1976).
[27]The *Heart Sutra,* translated by John Powers, from J. Feiser and J. Powers (ed.), *Scriptures of the World's Religions* (Boston: McGraw-Hill, 1998).

> no God, no Buddha, nothing at all. There is only . . . [At this point Soen-sa hit the table.]

At the third stage on our road to full enlightenment, we reach 270°, the Freedom I. Here we become attached to freedom. We learn that even emptiness is empty. We are not bound by name, form, or thinking; we are not even bound by emptiness. The world can be anything we like. We are free. The mind need not be bound by its own dreams and visions. Realizing that they have no independent reality leads us to realize that we are masters. Are the book and pencil the same? "The book is angry, the pencil laughs."

The fourth and final stage to full enlightenment is the move to 360°, the Big I, by way of Patriarchal Zen. At this stage we see that all things are as they are. We are finally free from attachment to anything. We are free from desire and from suffering. What is this? It is what it is. Are the book and pencil the same? The book is the book; the pencil is the pencil. At last, our action is intuitive, without reflection, desire, or attachment; the mind is a clear mirror reflecting only the world as it is. "Without thinking, all things are exactly as they are. The truth is just like this." We become Bodhisattvas, who no longer harbor any desires for self but act for all. "Without thinking, just like this is Buddha."

> At 360°, all things are just as they are; the truth is just like this. 'Like this' means that there is no attachment to anything.

An important feature of the Zen Circle—the reason it is a circle—is that 0° and 360° are the same point. At final enlightenment, we get back to where we started. As the Zen Master Nam Chan says, "Everyday mind is The Way." Seung Sahn quotes the Buddha: "All beings are already enlightened."

This may make it seem that the path to enlightenment is pointless. If we end up where we started, why go? The point, however, is to achieve the recognition that experience itself is the ultimate explanation. There is nothing more; it is all here. When we reach 360°, our state of mind is stable in a way it is not at 0°.

What is intuitive action?

> The difference is that 0° is attachment thinking, while 360° is no-attachment thinking.
>
> For example, if you drive a car with attachment thinking, your mind will be somewhere else and you will go through the red light. No-attachment thinking means that your mind is clear all the time. When you drive, you aren't thinking; you are just driving. So the truth is just like this. Red light means Stop; green light means Go. It is intuitive action. Intuitive action means acting without any desire or attachment. My mind is like a clear mirror, reflecting everything just as it is.

Suppose Jones, holding an apple, asks Smith, "What is this?" As a Small I, she gives a direct answer: "It is an apple." She tries to give the essence or nature of the thing. As a Karma I, she sees that the dharmas are empty, and answers, "It is empty; it is unreal." As a Nothing I, she simply shouts. As a Freedom I, she says whatever pops into her head: "It quacks like a duck in springtime." "The grass is green, the sky is blue." Finally, as a Big I, she says nothing, but takes a bite. She shows that the experience of the thing is the best explanation of what it is, the richest understanding of it.

TWO IMAGES OF THE SELF

In the twentieth century, philosophers concerned with the nature of mind increasingly focused on the problem of reconciling two conflicting images of the mind—and thus of what it is to be human. The problem itself is not new. Descartes, prodded by Princess Elizabeth, worried about how the mind relates to the body. But the dimensions of the problem have been appreciated only more recently. We appear to ourselves to be conscious beings who act rationally, exercise freedom, and make decisions on the basis of reasons. But natural science suggests that we are complex machines, computing devices whom natural law governs as it does everything else.

Science vs. Meaning

In this section we will examine the thought of two philosophers from very different traditions: Keiji Nishitani and Wilfrid Sellars. Nishitani (b. 1900), student of Kitaro Nishida and German philosopher Martin Heidegger, joined the faculty of Kyoto University and held the chair of philosophy there for twenty-one years. He became one of the most important thinkers of the Kyoto school of philosophy. Nishitani sees the increasing reach of science as forcing the problem of **nihilism:** Is there any ultimate meaning to life? Science, as applied to human beings themselves, seems to imply that we are nothing more than particle masses driven by unyielding natural laws, tending inevitably toward death and incapable of surviving beyond it. In such a universe, how is meaning or value possible? Science seems to make nihilism intellectually compelling. Nevertheless Nishitani finds it existentially untenable. We cannot think of ourselves as science portrays us; we must invent meaning for ourselves. Zen, he contends, accomplishes this, allowing us to recognize the bottomless emptiness of life as the key to its meaning.

Wilfrid Sellars (1912–1989), son of prominent American philosopher Roy Wood Sellars, grew up in Ann Arbor, Michigan, and studied at Oxford until the outbreak of World War II, when a stint in the U.S. Navy interrupted his academic work. He taught at the University of Iowa, the University of Minnesota, and Yale before arriving at the University of Pittsburgh, where he taught for the next twenty-five years. The essays collected in his book *Science, Perception, and Reality* established him as one of the greatest American philosophers of the twentieth century. Sellars, too, concentrates on the question of human self-understanding: How is it possible to reconcile the image that science has of us with the image we have of ourselves?

Nishitani, following German philosopher Gustav Theodor Fechner (1801–1887), distinguishes between two aspects of our existence: the "**day aspect**" and the "**night aspect.**" Sellars similarly distinguishes the "**manifest image**" from the "**scientific image.**" The day aspect, the manifest image, is the world as revealed to consciousness, the world as it seems to us prereflectively. The world consists of things that have shape, color, and texture. Things have goals and purposes. We ruminate, make decisions, and act on the basis of reasons. In this consists our freedom. Life is at the center of our concerns. We see things as being meaningful; the world is full of value. There are good and evil, right and wrong, virtue and vice.

> The 'manifest' image of man in the world . . . is, first, the framework in terms of which man came to be aware of himself as man-in-the-world. It is the framework

> in terms of which, to use an existentialist turn of phrase, man first encountered himself—which is, of course, when he came to be man.[28]

The night aspect, the scientific image, is the world as portrayed by science. In this image, the world is self-sufficient, having its own laws. It is material: there is nothing but matter and energy. There is no goal or purpose for individual things or for the universe as a whole. There is no meaning, no good and evil, right and wrong, virtue and vice—the laws of nature govern even consciousness. Ordinary objects, such as tables, chairs, cats, and cabbages, are merely swarms of microparticles whose behavior determines what we perceive and ultimately what we do. Life is an accident; it develops according to the cruel evolutionary mechanisms of random mutation and natural selection. The universe, "red in tooth and claw," in Darwin's words, is a field of death rather than a home. As Nietzsche put it, we are camels in the desert.

These images are not just different: they are incompatible. As minds, we are free; what we think makes a difference not only in what we do but also in a larger sense. As bodies, however, we seem to be controlled by natural law; what we think is merely a side effect of physical processes that culminate in action. The laws of physics have no place for meaning or value. In short, on various questions the images give contradictory answers:

Free will: Are we free, or are our acts products of natural law?
Mental causation: Do our thoughts, intentions, etc., have an effect on the world, or are they merely by-products of physical processes?
Value: Is there any basis for judging acts as good or bad, right or wrong, virtuous or vicious?
Meaning: Does anything we do serve any higher purpose? Does the universe matter?

Moreover, as Sellars stresses, the scientific image claims priority and completeness. It proposes to account for not only the external world but also us as knowers. The scientific image

> . . . purports to be a *complete* image, i.e., to define a framework which could be the *whole truth* about that which belongs to the image. Thus although methodologically a development *within* the manifest image, the scientific image presents itself as a *rival* image. (20)

As Nishitani puts it,

> The world seen from a teleological outlook, the world of concrete things like mountains and rivers, animals and trees, with their various "forms" (*eidoi*), can be reduced in a mechanistic world view to material processes which can, in turn, be described in terms of mathematical formulas.[29]

But the methodological dependence of this image on the manifest image also matters; the scientific image results from the activity of people, working and making

---

[28]Wilfrid Sellars, "Philosophy and the Scientific Image of Man," in *Science, Perception, and Reality* (London: Routledge and Kegan Paul, 1963), 1–40, 6.

[29]Keiji Nishitani, "Science and Zen," in Frederick Franck (ed.), *The Buddha-Eye: An Anthology of the Kyoto School* (New York: Crossroad Publishing Company, 1982).

observations with test tubes, thermometers, pressure gauges, scales, telescopes, and so forth. So, Sellars concludes,

> . . . the scientific image cannot replace the manifest without rejecting its own foundation. (21)

Because the images conflict, we cannot simply embrace both. It seems that we must choose. But to choose the manifest image, treating science as at best a calculating device whose postulation of electrons, protons, neutrons, and so on, should not be taken seriously, is to misunderstand the nature of science. To the extent that we have evidence for scientific theories, we have evidence for the existence of the microparticles they postulate. Yet to choose the scientific image is to make unintelligible both our own existence as persons and the scientific activity of those persons who construct the scientific image itself.

Nishitani describes the puzzle similarly:

What contradiction does Nishitani discern?

> The result is that, on the one hand, scientists destroy the teleological image of the world, and with it the characteristic feature of that image as an environment for life. In its stead they present material processes without life and spirit and devoid of *telos* [a goal, purpose, or end] and meaning as the true features of the world. On the other hand, as human beings engaged in scientific research these scientists live their own personal existence within a world that constitutes an environment for life. There is a contradiction here that is difficult to describe. It is a contradiction that, rather than being the fault of individual scientists, is natural to science itself and derives from the nature of the scientific standpoint as such.

The central task of the philosophy of mind—and, frankly, of philosophy as a whole—is to find a solution to this puzzle.

The contemporary scene, East and West, is full of attempted solutions. *Dualists* such as Descartes contend that both images have a legitimate claim to reality. There really are minds, which are distinct from physical processes. Minds nevertheless interact with physical processes, making free choices and causing things in the physical world to happen when those choices are made. Neuroscience does not show that minds do not exist; it shows the detailed mechanisms according to which minds interact with bodies, receiving information from them and causing them to act. Things do have goals, purposes, and meanings, given to them by minds.

The opposite of a dualist, one who believes in two fundamental kinds of stuff, is a **monist,** one who believes that there is only one fundamental kind of stuff. Idealists such as those of the Consciousness-Only school, discussed earlier in this chapter, hold that minds are all there is; everything else is a mental construct. Though unpopular in English-speaking countries, this view attracts many adherents in Europe. It holds that the manifest image of the world has priority over the scientific image and that even the objects of the manifest image itself should be seen as constructed by mental activity. Often this view receives a social twist and takes the form of the thesis that everything is socially constructed.

The most popular view among contemporary English-speaking philosophers is **materialism** (or **physicalism**), the view that there is only one kind of stuff and it is material, that is, physical. In short, dualists hold that both mind and matter are real.

Idealists hold that everything is mind; materialists hold that everything is matter. Or, to put it another way, dualists see both the manifest and scientific images as describing ultimate reality. Idealists reduce the scientific image to the manifest image. Materialists do the opposite.

There are many kinds of materialists. If the scientific image has priority, then what status should we assign the manifest image? What can we say about our ordinary ways of speaking—our talk of ordinary macroscopic objects such as tables and chairs, our talk of goals and purposes, our talk of intentions and actions, our talk of ourselves? **Reductionists** hold that it is true because such talk is reducible to scientific language. Reductionists hold that, in principle, it would be possible to translate talk of tables and chairs and people—and of mental entities and events such as thoughts, beliefs, desires, intentions, and so on—into talk of particles and their relations to one another. Each type of mental entity or event corresponds to some type or complex of physical entities or events.

Other, **nonreductive materialists** hold that such a translation is impossible even in principle but that microparticles and their properties nevertheless determine what is true of tables, chairs, people, beliefs, desires, intentions, and so on. **Functionalists** view types of mental entities and events (for example, desires) as corresponding not to types of physical entities and events but to functions that physical entities and events play. Some use the analogy of computer programs: A step in a program does not reduce to the motions of electrons, for it might be implemented in many different ways in different kinds of computers. It nevertheless is nothing above and beyond the physical. Others, **causal-role functionalists,** think in causal terms: Types of mental entities and events correspond to causal roles that physical entities and events can play. Still other nonreductive materialists think it is a mistake to look for anything corresponding to kinds of mental entities or events. Individual mental entities or events are identical with physical entities and events, but there is no way to generalize about all entities or events of a given kind. Such philosophers are **token-identity theorists.**

Some philosophers hold that our ordinary way of speaking of macroscopic objects and persons—in short, the manifest image—is misguided. What we say about minds, goals, purposes, and so on is strictly speaking false. **Eliminativists** hold that we can and should, in principle, give up these ways of speaking. In their view, eventually the scientific image will simply displace the manifest image in the way that a better theory displaces an inadequate one. Other **error theorists** hold that we cannot and should not surrender the manifest image, for it gives a rough-and-ready description of reality that serves our purposes well and simplifies an immensely complicated underlying physical system. Nevertheless, from this point of view the manifest image oversimplifies. Our talk of hopes and dreams, goals and ends, cabbages and kings is literally false, even if we cannot do without it.

This seems like a complicated array of positions. In fact, however, it results from answering some basic questions:

Are there two kinds of basic stuff, or just one?
Two: dualism
One: monism

If there is just one, is it mental or physical?
Mental: idealism
Physical: physicalism

If the world is physical, is the manifest image true or false?
True: reductionism, functionalism
False: eliminativism, error theory

If the manifest image is true, then what are kinds of mental entities and events?
Kinds of physical entities and events: reductionism
Functions physical entities and events can fulfill: functionalism
Causal roles physical entities and events can play: causal-role functionalism
Individual mental entities and events are individual physical entities and events: token-identity theory

If the manifest image is false, can we do without it?
Yes: eliminativism
No: error theory

Nishitani's answer, interestingly, is none of these. He sees Zen as offering a distinctive solution, one beyond the duality of mental and physical, life and death. Both the mental and the physical are manifestations of the great self, the field of emptiness. Bottomless, it enables things to be what they are. The manifest and scientific images both reflect aspects of the bottomless field of emptiness. Neither should be taken as fundamental. As Nishitani sometimes paradoxically puts it, nothing has a soul, but nothing is merely material. There is a realm beyond both. What is it like? We cannot say; words are inadequate to express it. Both the mental and the physical manifest a bottomless realm beyond the intellect's reach. At best, we can suggest it: "A wooden man sings and a stone woman dances." "Iron trees come to bloom in the spring beyond the kalpas."

SUMMARY

Philosophers adopt very different views of the self. Some, such as Plato and the authors of the Upanishads, see it as divided. Others, such as Descartes and Locke, see it as unified. Still others, such as the Buddha and Hume, hold that there is no self at all. Zen Buddhism offers a highly developed account of the mind despite its insistence that the self does not exist. Contemporary philosophers continue to debate the mind/body problem, developing dualist and materialist approaches to try to reconcile our two very different commonsense conceptions of mind.

REVIEW QUESTIONS

1. Discuss the conception of the self found in the Upanishads. What does it mean to assert that *atman* is Brahman?
2. Compare Plato's conception of the self to that found in the Upanishads. How are they similar? How do they differ?

3. Compare the Buddha's conception of the self to that found in the Upanishads. How are they similar? How do they differ?
4. What is the thesis of consciousness-only? How does Xuanzong argue for it?
5. Discuss Hume's theory of identity. What does it imply about the identity of the self?
6. What is the mind/body problem? Discuss Princess Elizabeth's criticisms of Descartes. Can he be defended against her attack?
7. What is Locke's account of personal identity? From Locke's point of view, consider and critique the views of the Buddha, Descartes, or Hume.
8. According to Zen Buddhism, what is the self? What is enlightenment?
9. How does Sellars distinguish the manifest and scientific images? State the mind/body problem in those terms.
10. How does Nishitani address the mind/body problem? Compare his analysis to that of the Buddha, Xuanzong, or Yixuan.

Terms for Review

advaita **(or non-dualism)** The view that the self (*atman*) is in reality nothing other than Brahman and that in the mystical knowledge of Brahman one knows only the One, the Sole True Existent, whose nature is perfect being, consciousness, and bliss.

anatman **(no-soul)** The Buddhist view that there is no self.

brahma-vidya Knowledge or recognition of Brahman.

Buddhist idealism The thesis that there is no self but everything is mind-dependent.

causal-role functionalism The view that types of mental entities and events correspond to causal roles that physical entities and events can play.

day aspect The world as revealed to consciousness, the world as it seems to us prereflectively. The world consists of things that have shape, color, and texture. Things have goals and purposes. We ruminate, make decisions, and act on the basis of reasons. In this consists our freedom. Life is at the center of our concerns. We see things as being meaningful; the world is full of value. There are good and evil, right and wrong, virtue and vice.

dharma Duty; the aggregate of qualities or states of consciousness; appearances.

dualism The view that there are two kinds of thing: for example, form and matter, mind and body, or, in Hinduism, individual and God.

eliminativism The view that in principle we can and should give up speaking of ordinary objects and mental states and replace this talk with the language of science.

error theory The view that ordinary, commonsense views are literally false, even if we cannot do without them.

functionalism The view that types of mental entities and events (for example, desires) correspond not to types of physical entities and events but to functions that physical entities and events play.

gunas In Sankhya, "strands" of reality: *sattva* (light, clarity, intelligence); *rajas* (passion, dynamism); and *tamas* (darkness, inertia, stupidity).

koan Zen paradoxes; puzzling questions (sometimes with responses) meant to break down rational thought and force the mind to recognize its true nature.

manifest image The world as revealed to consciousness, the world as it seems to us prereflectively. The world consists of things that have shape, color, and texture. Things have goals and purposes. We ruminate, make decisions, and act on the basis of reasons. In this consists our freedom. Life is at the center of our concerns. We see things as being meaningful; the world is full of value. There are good and evil, right and wrong, virtue and vice.

materialism (or **physicalism**) The view that there is only one kind of stuff and it is material or physical.

mind/body problem If mind and body exist and are separable, how can they interact?

monist One who believes that there is ultimately only one fundamental kind of stuff.

night aspect The scientific image; the world as portrayed by science.

nihilism The view that there is no ultimate meaning to life.

nirvana A universal, impersonal, unconceptualizable bliss and awareness that somehow underlies appearance.

non-dualism (or ***advaita***) The view that the self (*atman*) is in reality nothing other than Brahman and that in the mystical knowledge of Brahman one knows only the One, the Sole True Existent, whose nature is perfect being, consciousness, and bliss.

nonreductive materialism The view that a translation of ordinary talk of objects and mental states to scientific terms is impossible, even in principle, but that microparticles and their properties nevertheless determine what is true of ordinary objects and mental states.

no-soul (in Sanskrit, *anatman;* in Pali, *anatta*) The thesis that there is no self.

patriarch A handpicked successor of the Buddha.

philosophy of mind The branch of philosophy that seeks to understand the mind and its relation to reality.

prakrti Nature; in Samkhya, one of two irreducible elements.

prereflective experience "Clear mind": experience without thought or self-awareness. The clear mind is like a mirror, reflecting the world just as it is.

purusa The conscious being; in Samkhya, one of two irreducible elements.

reductionism The view that our ordinary ways of speaking are true because such talk is reducible to scientific language. Reductionists hold that, in principle, it would be possible to translate talk of tables and chairs and people — and of mental entities and events such as thoughts, beliefs, desires, intentions, and so on — into talk of particles and their relations to one another. Each type of mental entity or event corresponds to some type or complex of physical entities or events.

reflective experience Experience that involves thought and self-awareness.

Rinzai (*Linji*) Founded by Yixuan, the most radical of the ninth-century Zen schools; stresses the "lightning" method of shouting and beating to prepare the mind for enlightenment.

Samkhya Analysis of nature; the view that reality consists of two irreducible elements: nature (*prakrti*) and the conscious being (*purusa*).

sanzen Consultation; Zen can be passed only from person to person.

satori Enlightenment; the goal of Zen.
scientific image The world as portrayed by science.
strands (*gunas*) In Samkhya, *sattva* (light, clarity, intelligence); *rajas* (passion, dynamism); and *tamas* (darkness, inertia, stupidity).
token-identity theory The view that individual mental entities or events are identical with physical entities and events but that there is no way to generalize about all entities or events of a given kind.
Vedanta A school of philosophy expressly embracing Upanishadic views.
Vedantin theism The dualist view that the individual and God are meaningfully distinct.
zazen Seated meditation.
Zen A branch of Mahayana Buddhism whose goal is *satori*, enlightenment.

For Further Reading

For readings on Plato and Descartes, see Chapter 2. For readings on Locke and Hume, see Chapter 3. Excellent and highly readable introductions to Hinduism and Buddhism may be found in Huston Smith, *The Religions of Man* (New York: Harper and Row, 1965) and in Patrick Bresnan, *Awakening: An Introduction to the History of Eastern Thought* (Upper Saddle River: Prentice-Hall, 1999). Gavin Flood, *An Introduction to Hinduism* (New York: Cambridge University Press, 1996) provides a good overview of Hinduism in theory and practice.

Good collections of Buddhist sources are Henry Clarke Warren (ed.), *Buddhism in Translation* (Cambridge: Harvard University Press, 1896) and Edward Conze (ed.), *Buddhist Scriptures* (London: Penguin, 1959). P. Harvey, *An Introduction to Buddhism: Teaching, History, and Practices* (Cambridge: Cambridge University Press, 1990), is clear and helpful. On Zen, see especially D. T. Suzuki, *Zen Buddhism* (New York: Doubleday and Company, 1956), Frederick Franck (ed.), *The Buddha-Eye: An Anthology of the Kyoto School* (New York: Crossroad Publishing Company, 1982), and Seung Sahn, *Dropping Ashes on the Buddha,* compiled and edited by Stephen Mitchell (New York: Grove Press, 1976).

For an overview of contemporary work on the philosophy of mind, see Jaegwon Kim, *Philosophy of Mind* (Boulder: Westview Press, 1996) and Samuel Guttenplan (ed.), *A Companion to the Philosophy of Mind* (Oxford: Blackwell, 1994).

You tell yourself (snapping fast your lock)
The mind is its own place, the only place.
And on the stoop, their golden heads bent down,

You see two bright-haired kids, breath held, behold
A Queen-Anne's-Lace reaching up in bloom.
Today it is a flower. Another day
They'll rip it from the ground, but for today
It is a flower. Don't say it isn't. Don't say
It's just a flower because they think it's one.

—John Burt, "Parking Downtown"

CHAPTER 5

World

Philosophy, in the words of Wilfrid Sellars, is the study of "how things in the broadest possible sense of the term hang together in the broadest possible sense of the term." [1] Nothing could be more central to this project than understanding the world: what it is, what it contains, how its basic constituents relate to each other. That quest is called *metaphysics*.

Metaphysics is one of the oldest branches of philosophy. The first Greek philosopher of whom we have any record was Thales (fl. c. 585 B.C.E., a generation before the birth of Confucius or the Buddha), famed for holding that everything is water. That may be a foolish view, but it is a thesis about the makeup of the world. Thales's theory, however implausible, was important because it introduced the idea that the world may differ systematically from how it appears. That idea was exploited by atomists such as Democritus (460?–370? B.C.E.), who held that the ordinary objects of our experience are not as they seem at all but consist of tiny, indivisible particles moving rapidly through empty space. That view has turned out to be considerably more successful.

PARTICULARS AND UNIVERSALS

Metaphysicians have debated many questions concerning the makeup and structure of the world. One traditional debate focuses on the status of **universals:** objects that may be *multiply instantiated,* that is, have instances at different times and places. Ordinary, individual objects are **particulars,** things that cannot have multiple instances. The Empire State Building, for example, is a particular. It is located at a particular place (350 Fifth Avenue at 34th Street, Manhattan, New York City) and was built at a particular time (1931). There is only one of it. If someone were to build a replica of the building in Hoboken, it would be a replica of the Empire State Building, not the Empire State Building itself. We would still say that the Empire State Building is at 350 Fifth Avenue in Manhattan—not that it was now both there and in Hoboken.

Universals, however, are different. Consider the property *tall,* or the kind *building.* They can be multiply instantiated. Many things can be tall all at the same time in different places. There can be many buildings at the same time in different places. The Empire State Building is tall; it instantiates both *tall* and *building.* But a replica of the Empire State Building would instantiate both just as well. So, for that matter,

[1] Wilfrid Sellars, "Philosophy and the Scientific Image of Man," in *Science, Perception, and Reality* (London: Routledge and Kegan Paul, 1963).

do the World Trade Center towers, the Sears Tower, the U.S. Steel Building, and Texas Commerce Plaza. The property *tall* has no specific location in space and time, although the particulars that instantiate it do. The same is true of the kind *building*.

Properties and kinds are unusual objects. Are they really parts of reality at all? There are three traditional approaches to this question. **Realists** or **platonists** (so called after the most famous advocate of this position) hold that universals are real and mind-independent. **Conceptualists** hold that they exist but are mind-dependent. And **nominalists** hold that universals do not exist at all—everything is particular.

The entire issue of the status of universals springs from Plato, who insists that there is a realm of abstract universals called **forms** (or in some translations *ideas*) that exist independently of us. They make things what they are, and they enable us to think about things as they are. (See Chapter 3.)

Plato

Plato divides reality into four parts. He distinguishes the visible from the intellectual or intelligible world—the realm of forms, which we encountered in Chapter 3—and then divides each once again:

> You have to imagine, then, that there are two ruling powers, and that one of them is set over the intellectual world, the other over the visible. . . . Now take a line which has been cut into two unequal parts, and divide each of them again in the same proportion, and suppose the two main divisions to answer, one to the visible and the other to the intelligible, and then compare the subdivisions in respect of their clearness and want of clearness, and you will find that the first section in the sphere of the visible consists of images. And by images I mean, in the first place, shadows, and in the second place, reflections in water and in solid, smooth and polished bodies and the like: Do you understand?
>
> Yes, I understand.
>
> Imagine, now, the other section, of which this is only the resemblance, to include the animals which we see, and everything that grows or is made. [509d–510a] [2]

Plato here envisions a line divided as follows:

Visible world		Intellectual world	
shadows, reflections	*objects of perception*	*mathematical forms*	*abstract forms*
perception of shadows	*opinion*	*understanding*	*reason*

Now Plato notes that shadows and reflections, while real—in the sense that there *are* shadows and reflections—are nevertheless *less* real than objects of perception. They are derivative; they are mere copies, images, of the originals.

> Would you not admit that both the sections of this division have different degrees of truth, and that the copy is to the original as the sphere of opinion is to the sphere of knowledge? [510a–b]

[2] This and subsequent quotations from Plato are from the *Republic,* translated by Benjamin Jowett, in *The Dialogues of Plato* (Oxford: Oxford University Press, 1892).

Now Plato's main move is to say that the relation of shadows to the things that cast them, and of reflections to the things reflected, is like the relation between the visible world and the intelligible world, the world of forms. A geometer, for example, trying to prove a theorem about squares and circles draws diagrams. Those diagrams are visible, concrete objects—drawings with pencil or chalk, for instance—but the geometer has an interest in them not for their own sakes but because they represent the abstract forms of squares and circles. The square drawn with chalk is to the abstract form of a square as the shadow of a pole is to the pole itself.

> And do you not know also that although they make use of the visible forms and reason about them, they are thinking not of these, but of the ideals which they resemble; not of the figures which they draw, but of the absolute square and the absolute diameter, and so on—the forms which they draw or make, and which have shadows and reflections in water of their own, are converted by them into images, but they are really seeking to behold the things themselves, which can only be seen with the eye of the mind? [510d–511a]

Just as the shadow of a pole moves although the pole remains stationary, so the objects in the visible world move and change, although the forms are eternal and immutable. The forms about which the geometer reasons are sensible forms—in particular, visual forms, the forms of things we see. We might also reason about things we hear, smell, touch, or taste. These forms are abstract—the abstract form of a circle is not in any particular place, though it may have many instances that do exist at particular times and places. Because they can be multiply instantiated, they are universals.

But there are other kinds of universals as well. Not all properties are perceptual properties; not all kinds are perceptual kinds. Philosophers seek to understand other universals with the art of dialectic. These are the most abstract universals but also, for that reason, the clearest and the most real.

How does Plato distinguish four faculties of the soul?

> And when I speak of the other division of the intelligible, you will understand me to speak of that other sort of knowledge which reason herself attains by the power of dialectic, using the hypotheses not as first principles, but only as hypotheses—that is to say, as steps and points of departure into a world which is above hypotheses, in order that she may soar beyond them to the first principle of the whole; and clinging to this and then to that which depends on this, by successive steps she descends again without the aid of any sensible object, from ideas, through ideas, and in ideas she ends.
>
> I understand you, he replied; not perfectly, for you seem to me to be describing a task which is really tremendous; but, at any rate, I understand you to say that knowledge and being, which the science of dialectic contemplates, are clearer than the notions of the arts, as they are termed, which proceed from hypotheses only: these are also contemplated by the understanding, and not by the senses: yet, because they start from hypotheses and do not ascend to a principle, those who contemplate them appear to you not to exercise the higher reason upon them, although when a first principle is added to them they are cognizable by the higher reason. And the habit which is concerned with geometry and the cognate sciences I suppose that you would term understanding and not reason, as being intermediate between opinion and reason.

> You have quite conceived my meaning, I said; and now, corresponding to these four divisions, let there be four faculties in the soul—reason answering to the highest, understanding to the second, faith (or conviction) to the third, and perception of shadows to the last—and let there be a scale of them, and let us suppose that the several faculties have clearness in the same degree that their objects have truth. [511b–e]

Plato illustrates the divided line with a famous allegory, the allegory of the cave. Socrates imagines us as inhabiting a cave, watching the play of shadows on the cave wall and thinking we are seeing the world as it really is.

> And now, I said, let me show in a figure how far our nature is enlightened or unenlightened:—Behold! human beings living in a underground den, which has a mouth open towards the light and reaching all along the den; here they have been from their childhood, and have their legs and necks chained so that they cannot move, [514b] and can only see before them, being prevented by the chains from turning round their heads. Above and behind them a fire is blazing at a distance, and between the fire and the prisoners there is a raised way; and you will see, if you look, a low wall built along the way, like the screen which marionette players have in front of them, over which they show the puppets.
>
> I see.
>
> And do you see, I said, men passing along the wall carrying [514c] all sorts of vessels, and statues and figures of animals made of wood and stone and various materials, [515a] which appear over the wall? Some of them are talking, others silent.
>
> You have shown me a strange image, and they are strange prisoners.
>
> Like ourselves, I replied; and they see only their own shadows, or the shadows of one another, which the fire throws on the opposite wall of the cave?
>
> True, he said; how could they see anything but the shadows if they were never allowed [515b] to move their heads?
>
> And of the objects which are being carried in like manner they would only see the shadows?
>
> Yes, he said.
>
> And if they were able to converse with one another, would they not suppose that they were naming what was actually before them?
>
> Very true.
>
> And suppose further that the prison had an echo which came from the other side, would they not be sure to fancy when one of the passers-by spoke that the voice which they heard came from the passing shadow?
>
> No question, he replied.
>
> To them, I said, the truth would be literally nothing but the shadows of the images. [514a–515b]

Philosophy tries to turn people away from shadows. It tries to make people see the true nature of the world—to get beyond appearances to realities. This is akin to freeing the inhabitants of the cave and showing them they have been watching mere shadows.

> And now look again, and see what will naturally follow if the prisoners are released and disabused of their error. At first, when any of them is liberated and compelled

> suddenly to stand up and turn his neck round and walk and look towards the light, he will suffer sharp pains; the glare will distress him, and he will be unable to see the realities of which in his former state he had seen the shadows; and then conceive some one saying to him, that what he saw before was an illusion, but that now, when he is approaching nearer to being and his eye is turned towards more real existence, he has a clearer vision,—what will be his reply? And you may further imagine that his instructor is pointing to the objects as they pass and requiring him to name them,—will he not be perplexed? Will he not fancy that the shadows which he formerly saw are truer than the objects which are now shown to him? [515c–d]

The first result of philosophical reflection, then, is confusion. Someone like Socrates, moreover, who forces people to engage in reflection and subject their ideas to critical examination, causes them pain.

> And if he is compelled to look straight at the light, will he not have a pain in his eyes which will make him turn away to take and take in the objects of vision which he can see, and which he will conceive to be in reality clearer than the things which are now being shown to him?
>
> True, he said.
>
> And suppose once more, that he is reluctantly dragged up a steep and rugged ascent, and held fast until he's forced into the presence of the sun himself, is he not likely to be pained and irritated? When he approaches the light his eyes will be dazzled, and he will not be able to see anything at all of what are now called realities. [515e–516a]

After a time, however, the prisoner released from the cave will be able to see—first reflections, then objects, then the moon and stars, and finally, the sun. The progression is exactly that of the philosopher moving along the divided line: from reflections to objects of perception to the mathematical forms that reflect the most abstract forms and finally to those abstract forms themselves.

> He will require to grow accustomed to the sight of the upper world. And first he will see the shadows best, next the reflections of men and other objects in the water, and then the objects themselves; then he will gaze upon the light of the moon and the stars and the spangled heaven; and he will see the sky and the stars [516b] by night better than the sun or the light of the sun by day?
>
> Certainly.
>
> Last of all he will be able to see the sun, and not mere reflections of him in the water, but he will see him in his own proper place, and not in another; and he will contemplate him as he is.
>
> Certainly.
>
> He will then proceed to argue that this is he who gives the season and the years, and is the guardian of all that is in the visible world, [516c] and in a certain way the cause of all things which he and his fellows have been accustomed to behold?
>
> Clearly, he said, he would first see the sun and then reason about him.

Socrates himself explains the significance of the allegory. The sun, which gives light to everything else, corresponds to the form of the Good.

How is the cave allegory analogous to the divided line?

This entire allegory, I said, you may now append, dear Glaucon, to the previous argument; the prison-house is the world of sight, the light of the fire is the sun, and you will not misapprehend me if you interpret the journey upwards to be the ascent of the soul into the intellectual world according to my poor belief, which, at your desire, I have expressed—whether rightly or wrongly God knows. But, whether true or false, my opinion is that in the world of knowledge the idea of good appears last of all, and is seen only with an effort; and, when seen, is also inferred to be the universal author of all things beautiful and right, parent of light and of the lord of light in this visible world, and the immediate source of reason and truth in the intellectual; and that this is the power upon which he who would act rationally, either in public or private life must have his eye fixed.

I agree, he said, as far as I am able to understand you.

Moreover, I said, you must not wonder that those who attain to this beatific vision are unwilling to descend to human affairs; for their souls are ever hastening into the upper world where they desire to dwell; which desire of theirs is very natural, if our allegory may be trusted. [517b–d]

Why should we assume that forms exist at all? Why think there is anything beyond the cave we inhabit, that is, the sensible world?

The forms, Plato contends, are necessary for knowledge. In relating to the sensible world, we can perceive and form beliefs, but we cannot *know.* We cannot *understand.* We cannot *reason.* Knowledge, understanding, and reason are all faculties dedicated to and depending on the intellectual world of forms.

Suppose there were no forms and we were restricted to the world of sense. We could experience things and perhaps even generalize about our experiences. But we could not understand why things happen as they do. We could not recognize the underlying relationships. We might describe things as round or square, for example, but we could not reflect on circles or squares as such. We could not do geometry; at best we could note some general facts about things that are round, square, and so forth. For Plato, that would not count as understanding the world at all.

Socrates, in questioning Athenians about justice, courage, piety, friendship, and other abstract forms, often receives an example rather than a definition. He asks what courage is, and gets the answer, "Staying at your post and fighting, and not running away." He then patiently points out that people can be said to display courage in many kinds of situations through many kinds of behavior and then says, "there must be something that all these instances of courage have in common—something that makes them all instances of *courage.*" In Plato's terms, there must be a *form* of courage.

The ancient Chinese philosopher Mencius (372?–298? B.C.E.; see Chapter 8) makes a similar point:

The philosopher Kao said, "Life is what we call nature."

Mencius asked him, "Do you say that by nature you mean life, just as you say that white is white?" "Yes, I do," was the reply. Mencius added, "Then is the whiteness of the white feather the same as the whiteness of snow? Or, again, is the whiteness of snow the same as the whiteness of white jade?" Kao again said, "Yes."

"Very well," pursued Mencius. "Is the nature of a dog like the nature of an ox, and the nature of an ox like the nature of a man?" (6A:3)

Mencius, like Socrates, maintains that there is something, whiteness, that white feathers and snow have in common. There is something that makes dogs dogs, and it is different from what makes oxen oxen and humans human. Since the Empire State Building, the Sears Tower, the World Trade Center, and the U.S. Steel Building are all tall, there must be something they have in common—namely, being tall. Since they are all buildings, there must be something else they have in common—being buildings. Or, to consider the example that motivates Mencius, we call virtuous people, virtuous acts, compassion, and things that benefit us good; there must be something they have in common that makes them all good.

Plato sees mathematics, science, and philosophy as reasoning not about the Empire State Building or the Sears Tower but about the abstract forms those sensible objects instantiate. Mathematicians reason about squares, circles, and other sensible forms as such, not about particular, concrete figures. Physicists reason about forces, masses, and other physical forms as such, not about particular billiard balls and their actual motions. Philosophers, similarly, reason about existence, minds, the good, and other abstractions as such, not about particular things and people. By reasoning abstractly, mathematicians, physicists, and philosophers understand general kinds of circumstances. They can then use that knowledge to draw conclusions about particular circles, objects, and people. But the process of abstraction is vital to attaining that knowledge, even just the knowledge of particular objects that follows from their general theories. Without it, nothing like mathematics, physics, or philosophy could exist.

As we saw in Chapter 3, however, Plato's theory of forms creates puzzles of its own. How do we know anything about the forms? On his view, forms have causal powers; we are able to think of the abstract form of a circle by having some mental contact with circularity. But how is this possible? In the *Meno,* Plato speaks of recollection; in the *Republic,* he takes the form of the Good as analogous to the sun, shedding the light that makes the rest of the forms visible to our mind's eye. But if it is unclear how we might have access to the realm of forms, saying that we had such access before we were born seems unhelpful: How did we gain access then? And, if it is unclear how the forms can do anything, how can the form of the Good do anything?

Modern analogues to Plato's metaphors seem more promising. Perhaps we are born with access to forms, in the sense that an ability to think about abstractions is hardwired into us, the result of God's design or of evolutionary progress. Perhaps we can account for our ability to reason abstractly in pragmatic terms by pointing out that abstract reasoning is highly successful and justified by the results it yields for concrete situations. The chief motivation for conceptualism and nominalism is the suspicion that the platonist cannot explain how we, seemingly limited to the evidence of our senses, have access to a realm of forms that by definition lie beyond the realm of sense.

Philo

Plato's theory of forms has exerted tremendous influence. His followers grappled with the theory and its problems for hundreds of years. Here I will consider just a few of the most important contributors to Plato's theory, all of whom combine Platonism with religion to find a satisfactory account of abstract thinking.

Philo of Alexandria (20 B.C.E. – 40 C.E.; see Chapter 2), a Hellenistic Jew living in Egypt, tries to harmonize Plato's philosophy with the revelations of the Hebrew Scriptures. He finds both in Plato's *Timaeus* and in *Genesis* the thesis that God is eternal. God existed before bringing the world into existence and continues to exist alongside the created world. Plato maintains that the forms are also eternal; the mind, in thinking of an object—a circle, say—is turned both toward that individual object and toward an unchanging, abstract form the object exemplifies: in this case, circularity. The forms organize reality and our thinking about reality; the fact that we think of a succession of forms explains how we can think accurately about a changing universe. Philo accepts the forms in this role but denies Plato's contention that they, like God, are eternal. Instead, he identifies them with ideas in the mind of God. Before creation, the forms existed only as ideas; afterward, they exist both as ideas and as exemplified in objects. Philo similarly alters Plato's conception of matter to accord with the scriptural doctrine that God alone is eternal. Plato holds that God created the world out of preexisting, eternal matter. Philo argues that creation occurred in two steps: a creation of matter from nothing and then a creation of the world from matter.

> We must recount as many as we can of the elements embraced in [the world]. To recount them all would be impossible. Its pre-eminent element is the intelligible world. . . . For God, being God, assumed that a beautiful copy would never be produced apart from a beautiful pattern, and that no object of perception would be faultless which was not made in the likeness of an original discerned only by the intellect. So when He willed to create this visible world He first fully formed the intelligible world, in order that He might have the use of a pattern wholly God-like and incorporeal in producing the material world, as a later creation, the very image of an earlier, to embrace in itself objects of perception of as many kinds as the other contained objects of intelligence.[3]

Just as an architect would plan out a building or a city before actually beginning construction, so God

> . . . conceived beforehand the models of its parts, and . . . out of these He constituted and brought to completion a world discernible only by the mind, and then, with that for a pattern, the world which our senses can perceive.

Philo thus labels the forms taken together "the intelligible world" and locates them in what he calls the Word.

> . . . the world discerned only by the intellect is nothing else than the Word of God when He was already engaged in the act of creation.

The power of the Word orders the "great chain of being," linking the natural world, animals, and humans to God. The Word itself is the "idea of ideas," the pattern of creation, the archetype of human reason, "the man of God" and the "second God." The Word relates God to humans and the rest of the created world, appearing to Moses in the burning bush and inspiring Moses and the prophets. This doctrine seems to have

[3] Philo, *On the Account of the World's Creation Given by Moses,* in *Philo,* volume I, translated by F. H. Colson and G. H. Whitaker (London: William Heinemann Ltd., 1929).

been Philo's own contribution, though he bases it on Scripture, for example, on *Psalm* 33: "By the word of God were the heavens made." It and related ideas had a great impact on Christian thought by way of the Gospel of John. (John's gospel begins: "In the beginning was the Word, and the Word was with God, and the Word was God.")

Philo contends that nominalism, the view that the forms do not exist and that abstract terms such as 'goodness' and 'courage' are empty names, would make the world as a whole unintelligible:

How does Philo argue that Forms must be real substances?

> Some aver that the Incorporeal Ideas or Forms are an empty name devoid of any real substance of fact, and thus they abolish in things the most essential element of their being, namely the archetypal patterns of all qualities in what exists, and on which the form and dimensions of each separate thing was modeled. These the holy tables of the law speak of as "crushed," for just as anything crushed has lost its quality and form and may be literally said to be nothing more than shapeless matter, so the creed which abolishes the Forms confuses everything and reduces it to the pre-elemental state of existence, that state devoid of shape and quality. Could anything be more preposterous than this? . . . For by abolishing the agencies which created the qualities, it abolishes the qualities also. . . .[4]

In other words, if there are no forms, there are no qualities. We lose not just circularity or tallness in general, but the circularity of this 'o' and the tallness of the Empire State Building.

Philo's chief innovation with respect to the forms is to see them as ideas in the mind of God. But how does this help explain how we can have knowledge of them? Philo says little to help. But he does recall that "we are created in God's image" (*Genesis* 1:27) and accordingly holds that our minds are images of the Word of God:

> Our great Moses likened the fashion of the reasonable soul to no created thing, but averred it to be a genuine coinage of that dread Spirit, the Divine and Invisible One, signed and impressed by the seal of God, the stamp of which is the Eternal Word. . . .[5]

What makes the intelligible world intelligible to us? Our souls have been stamped with it, as coins impressed with the image of the mind of God.

Just as importantly, however, the world has been stamped with it as well. Philo imagines God saying to Moses,

> The powers which thou seekest to know are discerned not by sight but by mind even as I, Whose they are, am discerned by mind and not by sight. . . . But while in their essence they are beyond your apprehension, they nevertheless present to your sight a sort of impress and copy of their active working. You men have for your use seals which when brought into contact with wax or similar material stamp on them any number of impressions while they themselves are not docked in any part thereby but remain as they were. Such you must conceive My powers

[4] Philo, *The Special Laws,* in *Philo,* volume VII, translated by F. H. Colson and G. H. Whitaker (London: William Heinemann Ltd., 1937).

[5] Philo, *Concerning Noah's Work as a Planter,* in *Philo,* volume III, translated by F. H. Colson and G. H. Whitaker (London: William Heinemann Ltd., 1930).

to be, supplying quality and shape to things which lack either and yet changing or lessening nothing of their eternal nature. Some among you call them not inaptly 'forms' or 'ideas', since they bring form into everything that is, giving order to the disordered, limit to the unlimited, bounds to the unbounded, shape to the shapeless, and in general changing the worse to something better. Do not, then, hope to be ever able to apprehend Me or any of My powers in Our essence. But I readily and with right goodwill will admit you to a share of what is attainable. That means that I bid you come and contemplate the universe and its contents, a spectacle apprehended not by the eye of the body but by the unsleeping eyes of the mind.[6]

Augustine

The problem Plato's theory of forms presents is quite general. Our language and our forms of reasoning seem to commit us to abstractions such as properties, kinds, numbers, relations, and so on. Yet we have no adequate account of our relation to such things. We seem to be forced into a dilemma: we must either reject the possibility of knowledge that we seem to have or invoke some special mental faculty that goes beyond sense to explain it. This is closely related to the central dilemma of Chapter 3: we must either reject the possibility of knowledge of universal truths and necessary connections or postulate a priori knowledge of the world. In both cases, the problem stems from our inability to explain certain kinds of knowledge on the basis of experience.

Plato, as we have seen, speaks of the form of the Good as illuminating the intelligible world, making us able to know the other forms. But how can the form of the Good do that? Plato has no answer and in later dialogues admits as much. The Christian philosophers Origen and Augustine solve the problem by replacing the form of the Good with God. God can do anything; certainly God can illumine the intelligible world for us, enabling us to have knowledge of the forms.

Origen (185–253), sometimes considered the first Christian theologian, was born to Christian parents in Alexandria, Egypt. He took scriptural commands very seriously. He lived in poverty with very little food or sleep. According to Eusebius, he took *Matthew* 19:12 literally and castrated himself. An intellectual prodigy, Origen became head of a Christian school in Alexandria when he was just nineteen. He taught there for twenty-seven years. He left after a disagreement with the local bishop and taught for the rest of his life at Caesarea in Palestine. He died at age sixty-nine after being tortured for alleged heresies.

Like Philo, Origen interpreted scripture allegorically. He learned Hebrew in order to read the Old Testament in the original language. Concerned to show that Christian faith can be defended by reason, Origen takes Plato's allegory of the cave and transforms it into a Christian portrait of God. In Plato's story, the philosopher leads those imprisoned in a cave up to the light of day, where they can see objects as they truly are and eventually even look at the sun, the source of light making their vision

[6] Philo, *The Special Laws,* in *Philo,* volume VII, translated by F. H. Colson and G. H. Whitaker (London: William Heinemann Ltd., 1937).

possible. Plato identifies reality with the intelligible world of the forms and takes the form of the Good as playing the role of the sun. Origen replaces that form with God, inspired by *I John* 1:5: "God is light." God makes all knowledge, including our knowledge of Him, possible.

How does God resemble the sun?

> I know that some will attempt to say that, even according to the declarations of our own Scriptures, God is a body, because in the writings of Moses they find it said, that "our God is a consuming fire;" and in the Gospel according to John, that "God is a Spirit, and they who worship Him must worship Him in spirit and in truth." Fire and spirit, according to them, are to be regarded as nothing else than a body. Now, I should like to ask these persons what they have to say respecting that passage where it is declared that God is light; as John writes in his Epistle, "God is light, and in Him there is no darkness at all." Truly He is that light which illuminates the whole understanding of those who are capable of receiving truth, as is said in the *Psalms* 36, "In Thy light we shall see light." For what other light of God can be named, "in which any one sees light," save an influence of God, by which a man, being enlightened, either thoroughly sees the truth of all things, or comes to know God Himself, who is called the truth? Such is the meaning of the expression, "In Thy light we shall see light;" i.e., in Thy word and wisdom which is Thy Son, in Himself we shall see Thee the Father. Because He is called light, shall He be supposed to have any resemblance to the light of the sun? Or how should there be the slightest ground for imagining, that from that corporeal light any one could derive the cause of knowledge, and come to the understanding of the truth?[7]

God not only illumines the realm of forms and the sensible world to us; He also allows us thereby to know something of Him.

> . . . According to strict truth, God is incomprehensible, and incapable of being measured. For whatever be the knowledge which we are able to obtain of God, either by perception or reflection, we must of necessity believe that He is by many degrees far better than what we perceive Him to be. For, as if we were to see any one unable to bear a spark of light, or the flame of a very small lamp, and were desirous to acquaint such a one, whose vision could not admit a greater degree of light than what we have stated, with the brightness and splendour of the sun, would it not be necessary to tell him that the splendour of the sun was unspeakably and incalculably better and more glorious than all this light which he saw? So our understanding, when shut in by the fetters of flesh and blood, and rendered, on account of its participation in such material substances, duller and more obtuse, although, in comparison with our bodily nature, it is esteemed to be far superior, yet, in its efforts to examine and behold incorporeal things, scarcely holds the place of a spark or lamp. But among all intelligent, that is, incorporeal beings, what is so superior to all others—so unspeakably and incalculably superior—as God, whose nature cannot be grasped or seen by the power of any human understanding, even the purest and brightest?

[7] Origen, *On Principles,* from *The Ante-Nicene Fathers,* volume IV, edited by Rev. Alexander Roberts and James Donaldson (New York: The Christian Literature Company, 1890).

Origen puts a distinctive twist on Plato's cave allegory by suggesting that we cannot look directly at the sun; we must infer its character from the light it sheds on other things.

> But it will not appear absurd if we employ another similitude to make the matter clearer. Our eyes frequently cannot look upon the nature of the light itself—that is, upon the substance of the sun; but when we behold his splendour or his rays pouring in, perhaps, through windows or some small openings to admit the light, we can reflect how great is the supply and source of the light of the body. So, in like manner, the works of Divine Providence and the plan of this whole world are a sort of rays, as it were, of the nature of God, in comparison with His real substance and being. As, therefore, our understanding is unable of itself to behold God Himself as He is, it knows the Father of the world from the beauty of His works and the comeliness of His creatures.

Saint Augustine (354–430; see Chapter 2) develops the theme further. Augustine accepts Plato's postulation of the forms, Philo's idea that the forms are ideas in the mind of God, and Origen's idea that God plays the role of the sun in Plato's allegory, shedding light on the realm of forms. The causal power that allows us to know something about the forms comes not from the forms themselves but from God, who in effect reveals a portion of His mind to us. The relation between us and the forms is thus not one of recollection but one of **illumination.** God illumines the intelligible world, making it intelligible to us.

> Concerning universals of which we can have knowledge, we do not listen to anyone speaking and making sounds outside ourselves. We listen to Truth which presides over our minds within us, though of course we may be bidden to listen by someone using words. Our real Teacher is he who is so listened to, who is said to dwell in the inner man, namely Christ, that is, the unchangeable power and eternal wisdom of God. To this wisdom every rational soul gives heed, but to each is given only so much as he is able to receive, according to his own good or evil will. If anyone is ever deceived it is not the fault of Truth, any more than it is the fault of the common light of day that the bodily eyes are often deceived. Confessedly we must pay heed to the light that it may let us discern visible things so far as we are able. . . .
>
> But when we have to do with things which we behold through the mind, that is, with intelligence and with reason, we speak of things which we look upon directly in the inner light of truth which illumines the inner man and is inwardly enjoyed. . . . He I taught not by my words but by the things themselves which inwardly God has made manifest to him.[8]

Augustine says little about God's power of illumination. Indeed, he believes there is little one can say about this or any other dimension of God's power. He does, however, speak of God's light and wisdom illumining our minds, and he identifies the light of God with Christ, the Word:

[8] Augustine, "The Teacher," from *Augustine: Earlier Writings,* translated by J. H. S. Burleigh, Vol. VI, LCC (London: Westminster Press, 1953).

What role does the Word of God play in enabling us to have knowledge, according to Augustine?

Why, then, is scarcely anything ever said in the Scriptures of wisdom, unless to show that it is begotten or created of God?—begotten in the case of that Wisdom by which all things are made; but created or made, as in men, when they are converted to that Wisdom which is not created or made but begotten, and are so enlightened; for in these men themselves there comes to be something which may be called their wisdom: even as the Scriptures foretell or narrate, that "the Word was made flesh, and dwelt among us;" for in this way Christ was made wisdom, because He was made man. Is it on this account that Wisdom does not speak in these books, nor is anything spoken of it, except to declare that it is born of God, or made by Him (although the Father is Himself wisdom), namely, because wisdom ought to be commended and imitated by us, by the imitation of which we are fashioned [rightly]? For the Father speaks it, that it may be His Word: yet not as a word producing a sound proceeds from the mouth, or is thought before it is pronounced. For this word is completed in certain spaces of time, but that is eternal, and speaks to us by enlightening us, what ought to be spoken to men, both of itself and of the Father. And therefore He says, "No man knoweth the Son, but the Father; neither knoweth any man the Father, save the Son, and he to whomsoever the Son will reveal Him:" since the Father reveals by the Son, that is, by His Word. For if that word which we utter, and which is temporal and transitory, declares both itself, and that of which we speak, how much more the Word of God, by which all things are made? . . . And therefore Christ is the power and wisdom of God, because He Himself, being also power and wisdom, is from the Father, who is power and wisdom; as He is light of the Father, who is light, and the fountain of life with God the Father, who is Himself assuredly the fountain of life. For "with Thee," He says, "is the fountain of life, and in Thy light shall we see light." Because, "as the Father hath life in Himself, so hath He given to the Son to have life in Himself:" and, "He was the true Light, which lighteth every man that cometh into the world:" and this light, "the Word," was "with God;" but "the Word also was God;" and "God is light, and in Him is no darkness at all:" but a light that is not corporeal, but spiritual; yet not in such way spiritual, that it was wrought by illumination, as it was said to the apostles, "Ye are the light of the world," but "the light which lighteth every man," that very supreme wisdom itself who is God. . . .[9]

Philosophically speaking, the important point is that we access the forms not through their power or ours but through God's power. We derive what intellectual powers we have from God.

Let us attend as much as we can, and let us invoke the everlasting light, that He may illuminate our darkness, and that we may see in ourselves, as much as we are permitted, the image of God.[10]

From one point of view this is a highly stable philosophical position. God's power solves the problem that afflicts not only platonists but also any philosopher trying to give an account that explains the world and our knowledge of it. From

[9] Augustine, *De Trinitate,* Book VII, 3, 107–108, in *The Post-Nicene Fathers of the Christian Church,* edited by Philip Schaff (Edinburgh: T & T Clark; Grand Rapids: Eerdmanns Publishing Company, 1887).
[10] Augustine, *De Trinitate,* Book IX, 2, 127, in *The Post-Nicene Fathers of the Christian Church,* edited by Philip Schaff (Edinburgh: T & T Clark; Grand Rapids: Eerdmanns Publishing Company, 1887).

another point of view, however, it can seem unsatisfying. Since we can say little about the power of God or the nature of illumination, one might suspect that Augustine has not provided any explanation of our ability to know the forms at all. Eventually, therefore, philosophers began to develop alternatives to the platonist picture.

Nominalists such as English philosopher William of Occam (also spelled *Ockham;* 1285–1347) hold that there are no universals, that abstract terms such as 'courage', 'tallness', and 'justice' are "empty noises" that stand for nothing. We have an explanation of how we can know something about concrete objects through sensation. Philosophers may disagree about the nature of this explanation—see Chapter 3—but everyone agrees that there is some such explanation. So nominalists seek to interpret sentences that seem to refer to universals as referring only to concrete particulars. We might interpret 'Socrates has courage', for instance, as 'Socrates is courageous'. We might interpret 'Courage is a virtue' as 'Courageous acts (or people) are virtuous'. Whether we can interpret *every* sentence involving abstract terms as referring only to particulars, however, is far from clear. How should we interpret 'The Empire State Building and the Sears Tower have something in common'? Or 'Orange is closer to yellow than to blue'? These questions remain subjects of contemporary debate.

Conceptualists hold that universals are mind-dependent; in effect, they replace Plato's independent realm of forms with a bank of concepts within the mind. Universals, on this view, are simply concepts. This is the Kantian strategy we examined in Chapter 3 and to which we will return later in this chapter (see "Idealism").

Perhaps the most common attitude about universals in the history of philosophy, however, is that they are real and in some cases mind-independent; but we nevertheless need no special faculty beyond sense perception to know something about them. We learn everything we can know about them from experience by encountering objects that instantiate them. We know something about what it is to be a circle, for example, by experiencing circles. We abstract from particular circles that we encounter the general features of circularity. That is the view of Aristotle, to whose theory of substance we now turn.

SUBSTANCE AND ESSENCE

So far we have been focusing on questions of the status of universals: Are there universals? If so, what are they? How do we know anything about them? But we can ask similar questions about the nature of particulars. Aristotle (384–322 B.C.E.) and the philosophical tradition arising from his thought centers on these questions by giving a theory of substance.

Ordinarily, we think of the world as made up of particular things, continuing objects such as books, tables, chairs, trees, and people. That might be doubted from a number of directions. The pre-Socratic Greek philosopher Heraclitus (fl. c. 500 B.C.E.), for example, famously held that "You cannot step twice into the same river; for fresh waters are ever flowing in upon you." The idea that there are objects that persist through time, continuing to be the same from one moment to the next, is itself a substantive assumption. As we have seen, Buddhist philosophers such as Buddhaghosa have often rejected it. In the next several sections we will consider other reasons to doubt it.

Ontology, the study of what there is, lies at the heart of metaphysics. As contemporary American philosopher W. V. O. Quine has observed, the question of ontology can be put in three Anglo-Saxon monosyllables, What is there? and has a universally agreed-upon answer: Everything. Still, as he says, there is room for disagreement over cases. Important traditions in both East and West contend that the foremost answer to the question of what there is is *substance.* A full answer requires giving a theory of **categories**—basic classifications into which things can fall—but the category of substance is primary.

Categories

Aristotle offers the paradigm of such a theory in the West. Let us begin with his theory of categories:

> Expressions which are in no way composite signify substance, quantity, quality, relation, place, time, position, state, action, or affection. To sketch my meaning roughly, examples of substance are 'man' or 'the horse', of quantity, such terms as 'two cubits long' or 'three cubits long', of quality, such attributes as 'white', 'grammatical'. 'Double', 'half', 'greater', fall under the category of relation; 'in the market place', 'in the Lyceum', under that of place; 'yesterday', 'last year', under that of time. 'Lying', 'sitting', are terms indicating position, 'shod', 'armed', state; 'to lance', 'to cauterize', action; 'to be lanced', 'to be cauterized', affection.[11]

To put this in a table, Aristotle lists ten categories (his examples are in italics):

Category	*Examples*
substance	*man, the horse,* Socrates, animal, building
quantity	*two cubits long,* six feet tall, 1 square mile
quality	*white, grammatical,* tall, angry, wise
relation	*double, half, greater than,* loves
place	*in the market place, in the Lyceum,* west of Nacogdoches
time	*yesterday, last year,* at noon, for a month
position	*lying, sitting,* standing
state	*shod, armed,* puzzled, impressed
action	*to lance, to cauterize,* to do, to make, to eat
affection	*to be lanced, to be cauterized,* to be eaten, to be thanked

An obvious question arises: What are these categories categories *of*? Aristotle considers uncombined terms—the basic building blocks from which we form sentences—and asks what they stand for. The categories are categories of the things they stand for. So the categories are *kinds of thing,* kinds of basic entity—kinds of *being.* The central task of metaphysics is to investigate how things of these kinds relate to each other.

Philosophers of other traditions have also proposed theories of categories. A long-running, realist school of Indian philosophy known as Vaisesika (particularism) focuses primarily on ontological questions, especially before the year 1000. Vaisesika

[11] Aristotle, *Categories,* 4, translated by E. M. Edghill, from *The Basic Works of Aristotle* (New York: Random House, 1941).

philosophers hammer out a system of categories (*padartha,* literally, "types of things to which words refer"). Their concerns thus parallel Aristotle's. They seek to classify into one of the categories everything we can know anything about on the basis of experience.

To the question, What is there? the early Vaisesikas (those roughly contemporary with Aristotle) answer that most generally there are three types of things that exist:

1. *Substance,* such as a pot or a cloth
2. *Quality (or attribute),* such as shapes and colors
3. *Action,* such as moving up

There are also genus and species, which Aristotle would count as kinds of substances. As the *Vaisesika-Sutra* outlines the basic categories:

> The Supreme Good (results) from the knowledge . . . of the essence of the [categories] substance, attribute, action, genus, species, and combination [inherence] by means of their resemblances and differences.
>
> Earth, water, fire, air, ether, time, space, self (or soul), and mind (are) the only substances.
>
> Attributes are color, taste, smell, and touch, numbers, measures, separateness, conjunction and disjunction, priority and posteriority, understandings, pleasure and pain, desire and aversion, and volitions.
>
> Throwing upwards, throwing downwards, contraction, expansion, and motion are actions.[12]

For Aristotle, substance and quality are also categories. The Vaisesika category of substance includes space and time, which Aristotle lists separately. The category of qualities includes relations and probably states and positions as well. And the category of actions combines, we might think, Aristotle's categories of action and affection. So the Vaisesika scheme manages to include everything in Aristotle's categories, although it divides them up differently and in some cases would require combinations of things where Aristotle finds one thing—a relation (category: quality) to a place (category: substance), for example, rather than a location.

But the Vaisesika tradition adds other categories, which allow us to make meaningful sentences and which have no parallel in Aristotle's scheme. Three occur in some texts as old as those of Aristotle, while the last is a later innovation.

4. *Inherence,* the relationship between substances and qualities. (In the case of a blue pot, inherence is the relationship between the pot and the color blue.)
5. *Universality,* such as potness and cowness
6. *Individualizer,* which differentiates ultimate particulars, such as atoms
7. *Absence,* such as of an elephant in this room (a category that is not made explicit in the *Vaisesika-sutra* but is defended in all later Vaisesika texts).

Inherence includes things like the pot's being blue or Socrates's being a man. Universality includes abstract properties and kinds such as being blue or being a man. Individualizers distinguish objects that are otherwise identical, having exactly the same

---

[12] *The Vaisesika Sutras of Kanada,* translated by Nandalal Sinha, in *The Sacred Books of the Hindus,* Volume VI (Allahabad: Panini office, 1923).

qualities. (How is one to distinguish one drop of water or one electron from another, for example?) And absences, or lacks, allow us to make sense of language that seems to refer to nothing ("the elephant in the room," "the difference between 2 and the only even prime number," etc.).

These additional categories are controversial. The original three categories spark debate, especially concerning whether some are more fundamental than others. (Can we think of substances as just bundles of qualities? As collections of events? Can we think of events as objects gaining or losing qualities?) But everyone more or less agrees that there are in some sense pots, colors, and actions. In contrast, the added categories are far more peculiar. What is inherence? Do we have to think of it as an object? That is, in addition to the pot and the color blue, do we have to recognize separately the pot's being blue? But if we do not, how do we account for sentences such as 'The pot's being blue surprised me'? Moreover, if we count inherences as objects, we seem to face an argument Plato dubbed "The Third Man." Suppose that, in addition to Socrates and the quality of being a man, we have the inherence relation between them—Socrates's being a man. Don't we need yet another relation to link Socrates, the quality, and the inherence relation? But then don't we need yet another relation to link it to those three things? We appear to face an infinite regress.

Individualizers are odd entities—sometimes called "bare particulars" in the West—that are over and above a thing's properties and relations and thus seem to be unobservable and unknowable. But without them, how can one distinguish two qualitatively identical things? (Contemporary American philosopher Max Black devises a puzzle of a universe consisting of nothing but two qualitatively identical black iron spheres. They have the same properties, and their relations to each other are completely symmetrical. So how can they differ? A universe with one sphere does as well—the two halves are qualitatively identical and symmetrically related.) Finally, absences or lacks are especially peculiar things to count among the things in the world. Yet we can sensibly talk about the dog that didn't bark in the nighttime, or the questions the professor did not ask on the exam.

In all these cases, we get a puzzle like that facing platonism. If we accept entities like inherences, universals, individualizers, and absences as inhabiting the world, how do we have knowledge of them? We evidently do not experience them directly. On the other hand, if we do not accept such entities, how do we make sense of sentences that seem to refer to them? This dilemma confronts any categorical framework.

Substance

To return to Aristotle, we must say something about how the categories relate. The most important relation is that all the other categories depend on substance. We can speak of Socrates being six feet tall, being wise, being greater than Thales, being in Athens, lying down yesterday, being puzzled at a proposed definition, questioning and being questioned. But combinations of other categories (for example, 'wise in Athens puzzled') make no sense. Qualities, quantities, actions, affections, relations, and so on, are always qualities, quantities, etc., *of substances.*

What do all the senses in which a thing can be said to be have in common?

> There are many senses in which a thing may be said to 'be', but all that 'is' is related to one central point, one definite kind of thing, and is not said to 'be' by a mere ambiguity. Everything which is healthy is related to health, one thing in the sense

> that it preserves health, another in the sense that it produces it, another in the sense that it is a symptom of health, another because it is capable of it. . . . So, too, there are many senses in which a thing is said to be, but all refer to one starting-point; some things are said to be because they are substances, others because they are affections of substance, others because they are a process towards substance, or destructions or privations or qualities of substance, or productive or generative of substance, or of things which are relative to substance, or negations of one of these things or of substance itself. (IV, 2)[13]

There are many senses in which something may be said to be, but all center on a *focal meaning* of 'being', namely, substance. What is, in the primary sense, is substance. So a chief task of metaphysics is explaining the nature of substance.

> As, then, there is one science which deals with all healthy things, the same applies in the other cases also. For not only in the case of things which have one common notion does the investigation belong to one science, but also in the case of things which are related to one common nature; for even these in a sense have one common notion. It is clear then that it is the work of one science also to study the things that are, qua being.—But everywhere science deals chiefly with that which is primary, and on which the other things depend, and in virtue of which they get their names. If, then, this is substance, it will be of substances that the philosopher must grasp the principles and the causes. (IV, 2)

What is substance? Aristotle gives various criteria. But most importantly a substance is a 'this': it is an answer to the question, What is it? If we ask what a thing is, we do not expect to be told, It's white, or It's sitting down, or It's in Texas, but It's a cat, or It's Socrates. A substance such as Socrates is always a substance of a certain kind, falling under a species (a specific kind, such as human being) and a genus (a broader kind, such as animal). Every substance is a 'this' and a 'such'. Thus, substance is what exists in the primary and unqualified sense. When we ask, What is there? the most obvious answer is, Substances.

> There are several senses in which a thing may be said to 'be', as we pointed out previously in our book on the various senses of words; for in one sense the 'being' meant is 'what a thing is' or a 'this', and in another sense it means a quality or quantity or one of the other things that are predicated as these are. While 'being' has all these senses, obviously that which 'is' primarily is the 'what', which indicates the substance of the thing. For when we say of what quality a thing is, we say that it is good or bad, not that it is three cubits long or that it is a man; but when we say what it is, we do not say 'white' or 'hot' or 'three cubits long', but 'a man' or 'a 'god'. And all other things are said to be because they are, some of them, quantities of that which is in this primary sense, others qualities of it, others affections of it, and others some other determination of it. . . . Therefore that which is primarily, i.e. not in a qualified sense but without qualification, must be substance. (VII, 1)

---

[13] This and subsequent quotations from Aristotle, unless otherwise noted, are from *Metaphysics*, translated by W. D. Ross (Oxford: Clarendon, 1924).

A substance is a 'this such'; it is what a thing is. A substance, in other words, is a subject. We predicate things of it (The cat is an animal); other things can be present in it (The cat is sleeping). But we never predicate a substance of anything else, or speak of a substance as present in something else. Aristotle distinguishes two kinds of substance: *primary* substances, individual objects, and *secondary* substances, species or genera—in short, kinds.

What is the difference between primary and secondary substances?

> Substance, in the truest and primary and most definite sense of the word, is that which is neither predicable of a subject nor present in a subject; for instance, the individual man or horse. But in a secondary sense those things are called substances within which, as species, the primary substances are included; also those which, as genera, include the species. For instance, the individual man is included in the species 'man', and the genus to which the species belongs is 'animal'; these, therefore—that is to say, the species 'man' and the genus 'animal'—are termed secondary substances.[14]

Aristotle goes on to explain the priority of substance over the other categories:

> Everything except primary substances is either predicable of a primary substance or present in a primary substance. This becomes evident by reference to particular instances which occur. 'Animal' is predicated of the species 'man', therefore of the individual man, for if there were no individual man of whom it could be predicated, it could not be predicated of the species 'man' at all. Again, colour is present in body, therefore in individual bodies, for if there were no individual body in which it was present, it could not be present in body at all. Thus everything except primary substances is either predicated of primary substances, or is present in them, and if these last did not exist, it would be impossible for anything else to exist. . . . [P]rimary substances are most properly so called, because they underlie and are the subjects of everything else.[15]

This is strikingly similar to the account given in the *Vaisesika Sutra*. Substances are subjects of attributes and actions, but they are never subjects of substances.

> It possesses action and attribute, it is a combinative cause—such (is) the mark of substance.
>
> Inhering in substance, not possessing attribute, not an independent cause in conjunctions and disjunctions—such is the mark of attribute.
>
> Residing in one substance only, not possessing attribute, an independent cause of conjunctions and disjunctions—such is the mark of action.[16]

Primary substances are individual objects, physical things such as tables and chairs, people and penguins, "cabbages and kings," as well as physical parts of them and wholes comprising them.

---

[14] Aristotle, *Categories,* 5, translated by E. M. Edghill, from *The Basic Works of Aristotle* (New York: Random House, 1941).

[15] Aristotle, *Categories,* 5, translated by E. M. Edghill, from *The Basic Works of Aristotle* (New York: Random House, 1941).

[16] *The Vaisesika Sutras of Kanada,* translated by Nandalal Sinha, in *The Sacred Books of the Hindus,* Volume VI (Allahabad: Panini office, 1923).

> Substance is thought to belong most obviously to bodies; and so we say that not only animals and plants and their parts are substances, but also natural bodies such as fire and water and earth and everything of the sort, and all things that are either parts of these or composed of these (either of parts or of the whole bodies), e.g. the physical universe and its parts, stars and moon and sun. (VII, 2)

Aristotle characterizes each substance as a 'this such'—a thing of which other things are predicated—but substances are never predicated of anything else. There are other criteria by which we may recognize substances. First, there are no degrees of substance in the way there are degrees of quantity, quality, relation, and so on. A cat may be more or less white or old or more or less far away, but it cannot be more or less a cat. Socrates may be a little angry or very wise, a little greater than Thales or a lot, a little puzzled or very impressed, but he cannot be a little bit man or very Socrates.

> Substance, again, does not appear to admit of variation of degree. I do not mean by this that one substance cannot be more or less truly substance than another, for it has already been stated that this is the case; but that no single substance admits of varying degrees within itself. For instance, one particular substance, 'man', cannot be more or less man either than himself at some other time or than some other man. One man cannot be more man than another, as that which is white may be more or less white than some other white object, or as that which is beautiful may be more or less beautiful than some other beautiful object. The same quality, moreover, is said to subsist in a thing in varying degrees at different times. A body, being white, is said to be whiter at one time than it was before, or, being warm, is said to be warmer or less warm than at some other time. But substance is not said to be more or less that which it is: a man is not more truly a man at one time than he was before, nor is anything, if it is substance, more or less what it is. Substance, then, does not admit of variation of degree.[17]

Second, substances admit contrary qualities, while things of other categories do not. Socrates may be sitting one moment and lying down the next. He may go from being angry to being puzzled to being impressed. In short, substances can change qualities, relations, positions, and so on. Things of other categories cannot change in that way.

> The most distinctive mark of substance appears to be that, while remaining numerically one and the same, it is capable of admitting contrary qualities. From among things other than substance, we should find ourselves unable to bring forward any which possessed this mark. Thus, one and the same colour cannot be white and black. Nor can the same one action be good and bad: this law holds good with everything that is not substance. But one and the selfsame substance, while retaining its identity, is yet capable of admitting contrary qualities. The same individual person is at one time white, at another black, at one time warm, at another cold, at one time good, at another bad. This capacity is found nowhere else. . . . it is the peculiar mark of substance that it should be capable of admitting contrary qualities; for it is by itself changing that it does so. . . .

[17] Aristotle, *Categories,* 5, translated by E. M. Edghill, from *The Basic Works of Aristotle* (New York: Random House, 1941).

> To sum up, it is a distinctive mark of substance, that, while remaining numerically one and the same, it is capable of admitting contrary qualities, the modification taking place through a change in the substance itself.[18]

The same river, then, can be cold at one time and warm at another; calm in one spot and turbulent at another; full after a rain and low after a drought; and so on. It can even consist of different parts at different times. It is nevertheless the same river.

How is this possible? The matter constituting the river can change. The quantity of water in the river, the qualities the water possesses (warm or cold, clean or dirty), the actions (flooding) or affections (being dredged, being sailed upon) can all change while the river remains the same. Aristotle explains this by appealing to the river's **essence.** Certain properties are **essential** to the river; if the river loses them, it ceases to be that river any longer. Other properties are *accidental* to it. The river can lose those properties while remaining the same river. In general, a property is essential to a thing, or kind of thing, when it is necessary to it; without the property, it would not be that thing (or kind of thing).

> Things are said to 'be' (1) in an accidental sense, (2) by their own nature. (1) In an accidental sense, e.g. we say 'the righteous doer is musical', and 'the man is musical', and 'the musician is a man', just as we say 'the musician builds', because the builder happens to be musical or the musician to be a builder; for here 'one thing is another' means 'one is an accident of another'. . . . Thus when one thing is said in an accidental sense to be another, this is either because both belong to the same thing, and this is, or because that to which the attribute belongs is, or because the subject which has as an attribute that of which it is itself predicated, itself is.
>
> (2) The kinds of essential being are precisely those that are indicated by the figures of predication; for the senses of 'being' are just as many as these figures. Since, then, some predicates indicate what the subject is, others its quality, others quantity, others relation, others activity or passivity, others its 'where', others its 'when', 'being' has a meaning answering to each of these. (IV, 7)

A thing has a property essentially if it has it by its own nature, that is, by virtue of itself, by virtue of being the very thing it is. Aristotle's phrase for the essence is "what it is to be" a thing. What is essential to Socrates? That is to ask what it is to be Socrates. Most Western philosophers have assumed that being human is essential to Socrates; if something were not human, it could not be Socrates. Hindu and Buddhist philosophers, insisting on the possibility of reincarnation and the transmigration of souls, have often thought that humanity is not essential to Socrates; he might be a pig or a cow in another life. Some have suggested that having the particular parents he had was essential to Socrates; he could not have been the son of Karl Marx or Margaret Thatcher. But clearly many of Socrates's properties are accidental to him. He might easily have failed to be the teacher of Plato, for example, if Plato had decided to study with Protagoras instead. But he would still have been Socrates.

What is an essence, according to Aristotle?

> The essence of each thing is what it is said to be propter se [by virtue of itself]. For being you is not being musical, since you are not by your very nature musical.

[18] Aristotle, *Categories,* 5, translated by E. M. Edghill, from *The Basic Works of Aristotle* (New York: Random House, 1941).

> What, then, you are by your very nature is your essence. . . . The formula, therefore, in which the term itself is not present but its meaning is expressed, this is the formula of the essence of each thing. (VII, 4)

If we could give a definition of 'Socrates', that would express Socrates's essence. Aristotle doubts, however, that we can do this. So, he doubts that there are essences of individual, primary substances. Medieval philosophers would later refer to such individual essences as **haecceities**—"this-nesses." Similarly, if we could give a definition of 'river', that would express what is essential to being a river. The definition tells us what a thing is by telling us what it is to be that thing.

> Clearly, then, definition is the formula of the essence, and essence belongs to substances either alone or chiefly and primarily and in the unqualified sense. (VII, 5)

So, although it is difficult to say what Socrates's essence is, it is somewhat easier to say what the essence of man or river or gold is. Aristotle defines a human being as a rational animal, for example. Being an animal and being capable of rationality are essential to being human, he contends; everything that does not follow from these is accidental to it.

The question, What is there? thus leads, for Aristotle, to questions about substances and their natures. That in turn leads us to questions about essences. In the process, an interesting transformation takes place. We begin by thinking of a substance as an individual thing. We analyze it as having qualities, standing in relations, acting, being acted upon, etc., and finally as consisting of matter and form. In one sense, we think of a substance as a combination of matter and form. Yet we notice that the Colorado can contain different (or fewer or more) water molecules without becoming a different river. Socrates can lose or gain weight without becoming a different person. So in another sense we do not want to identify the substance with either its matter or the combination of form and matter it comprises. Instead, we identify it with its form, specifically with its essence, which explains how it can remain the *same* object despite changing matter, qualities, quantities, relations, and so forth.

Aquinas

St. Thomas Aquinas (1224–1274; see Chapter 2) develops Aristotle's theory further. Aquinas stresses the role of essences as causes. Aristotle treats essences as causes and mentions them in his famous account of the four causes:

> Evidently we have to acquire knowledge of the original causes (for we say we know each thing only when we think we recognize its first cause), and causes are spoken of in four senses. In one of these we mean the substance, i.e. the essence (for the 'why' is reducible finally to the definition, and the ultimate 'why' is a cause and principle); in another the matter or substratum, in a third the source of the change, and in a fourth the cause opposed to this, the purpose and the good (for this is the end of all generation and change). (I, 3)

As this is often expressed, Aristotle distinguishes four kinds of **causes** or explanations: *formal, material, efficient,* and *final.* To illustrate the difference, suppose we ask why

Socrates is human. A formal explanation relies on an essence or definition: Socrates is human because he is a rational animal. A material explanation relies on matter: Socrates is human because he has a certain biochemical composition. An efficient explanation relies on a causal chain of events: Socrates is human because his parents were human and produced him in the usual way. And a final explanation relies on some goal, purpose, or function that Socrates serves, having the form, "Socrates is human in order to . . ."

Aquinas places the causal role of essences on center stage, using the term **quiddity** as well as 'essence'. 'Quiddity' translates the Latin *quidditas,* literally, "whatness," which in turn is meant to capture the Greek phrase meaning "what it is." A quiddity is what in reality a definition corresponds to; it is a definition *in re.* The **nature** of a thing is what makes it what it is; it is that by virtue of which a thing is what it is—a human, a river, a building, or whatever. The nature of a thing not only explains why it is what it is; it is also what we grasp in thinking about the thing. We know objects by grasping their essences. So an essence not only makes something what it is but also makes it knowable. Aquinas follows Aristotle in identifying the essence of a thing with both its quiddity and its nature.

According to Aquinas, what is an essence? A quiddity? A nature?

> Since the definition indicating what a thing is signifies that through which the thing is placed in its genus or species, philosophers have swapped the term 'essence' for the term 'quiddity'. The Philosopher [Aristotle] frequently calls this 'what it is to be a thing'; that is, what makes a thing what it is. It is also called 'form', because form signifies the determination of each thing, as Avicenna says. Another term used for this is 'nature', in the first of the four senses marked by Boethius: anything is called a nature which the intellect can grasp in any way. For nothing is intelligible except through its definition and essence. Thus the Philosopher, too, says that every substance is a nature. Yet the term 'nature' in this sense seems to mean the essence of a thing as governing its characteristic operation, for nothing lacks a characteristic operation. In fact, the term 'quiddity' is taken from what is signified by the definition. But 'essence' is used because through it, and in it, a being has being. (1, 4)[19]

That is, according to both Aristotle and Aquinas, these are the same:

> the essence of x = the properties necessary to x, without which x would not be what it is
> the quiddity of x = what corresponds to x's definition in the world
> the nature of x = what makes x what it is

Aquinas distinguishes simple from composite substances. Simple substances such as God are primary, the causes of composite substances. But we have easier access to composite substances, which are all around us.

What are simple substances? Composite substances? How do they relate to each other?

> In fact, some substances are simple and some composite, and essence is in both. But it is in simple substances in a truer and finer way, because they also have being

[19] This and subsequent quotations from Aquinas are from St. Thomas Aquinas, *De Ente et Essentia (On Being and Essence),* my translation.

> in a finer way. They are causes of those that are composite. At least this is true of the first simple substance, which is God. But because the essences of these substances are more hidden from us, we must start with the essences of composite substances; learning is easier if we begin with what is easier. (1, 6)

Individual objects, which are composite substances, are composed of matter and form. What is the relation of the essence to that composite? As we have seen, the essence is generally not a matter of matter, for humans, rivers, etc., can undergo a change of matter while remaining the same thing. So, essence must involve form. But it is not form alone. It must include both.

What is Aquinas's conclusion? Reconstruct his argument for it.

> In composite substances we find form and matter, as we find soul and body in man. But we cannot call either one of these alone the essence. That the matter alone of a thing is not its essence is plain, for through its essence a thing is knowable and arranged in its species or genus. But matter is not a principle of knowledge, and it does not determine a thing's genus or species; what something actually is does that. Neither can we call the form alone of a composite substance its essence, however strongly some strive to assert this. What we have said shows that the essence is what is signified by the definition of a thing. Now the definition of natural substances includes not only form but also matter. Otherwise, definitions in physics and in mathematics would not differ. Nor can we say that the definition of a natural substance includes matter as something added to its essence or outside its essence. This is the kind of definition proper to accidents, which do not have a perfect essence. Their definition must include their subject, which is outside their genus. It is evident, therefore, that essence comprises both matter and form. (2, 1)

Aquinas identifies the essence of a composite substance with the composite of its matter and form:

Aquinas here develops two additional arguments. What are they?

> It remains, then, that in the composite substances the term 'essence' signifies the composite of matter and form. . . . This is reasonable, too, for the being that a composite substance has is not the being of the form alone nor of the matter alone but of the composite. It is essence according to which a thing is said to be. So the essence, according to which a thing is called a being, is neither the form alone nor the matter alone, but both, although form alone is in its own way the cause of its being. We see in other things composed of several principles that they do not take their name from one of these principles alone, but from all together. This is clear in tastes: Sweetness is caused by the action of heat [form] dissolving moisture [matter]. Although in this way heat is the cause of sweetness, a body is not called sweet from its heat but from its taste, which includes heat and moisture. (2, 3)

Matter, then, is crucially involved in essences of composite substances. But it is **undesignated matter,** for example, "flesh and blood," not **designated matter,** "this flesh and that blood." A human being is a rational animal—rationality and animality in the appropriate kind of matter, namely, flesh and blood. The distinction between designated and undesignated matter is important, for matter is the **principle of individuation;** it is what makes one object differ from another. Socrates and Protagoras have the same essence—both are rational animals in flesh and blood—but differ because they have different matter. Socrates is rationality and animality in *this* flesh and blood; Protagoras is rationality and animality in *that* flesh and blood.

To put this differently, matter enters into the essence of things, but only generically. A human being is a certain form in a certain kind of matter. A particular human being such as Socrates is that form in a particular piece of matter.

PRIMARY AND SECONDARY QUALITIES

Aristotle's theory of substance dominated metaphysics for centuries, becoming known, in the form in which Aquinas and other medieval philosophers developed it, as the *philosophia perennis,* the perennial philosophy. But gradually the progress of science disrupted its view of objects. By the seventeenth century, the **atomic theory** of matter became generally accepted by the scientific community. The theory was still in a primitive form, little advanced from where Democritus and other ancient atomists had left it. But it nonetheless forced a rethinking of the nature of objects.

The argument itself is simple, going back to ancient times. A clear expression of it occurs in the works of the Indian Buddhist philosopher Dignaga (c. 450), who argues for *idealism,* the thesis that everything is mind-dependent. We will return to his overall theory in the next section. For now, however, it is enough to consider his argument that things are not as they appear.

> Though atoms serve as causes of the consciousness (*vijñapti*) of the sense-organs, they are not its actual objects like the sense organs; because the consciousness does not represent the image of the atoms.
>
> The consciousness does not arise from what is represented in it.
> Because they do not exist in substance just like the double moon.
> Thus both the external things are unfit to be the real objects of consciousness.[20]

If the atomic theory is right, then external objects are not at all as they appear. A table, for example, appears to be solid, stationary, and brown. In fact, however, it is mostly empty space, with a large number of tiny particles—which themselves have no color—moving very rapidly. What we see, in other words, differs greatly from what is actually there, causing our sense organs to react as they do. Our brains construct an image of the world that is useful to us and helps us survive but bears little resemblance to the world as it actually is.

In Aristotle's picture of perception, objects serve as the causes of perception, which are then represented in consciousness. So, the *causes* of perception and the *objects* of perception are the same. Dignaga points out that, on the atomic theory, that is not so. He distinguishes two kinds of objects: what he calls **actual objects** (***alambana***) and what he calls simply objects, or **internal objects** (***artha***). Actual objects are the causes of our perceptions; internal objects are what they are (or appear to be) perceptions *of.* The actual objects, the causes of perception, are atoms; the internal objects are not. We do not see atoms; what we see is an effect of perception, not its cause. So what we see does not exist in reality; it is "just like the double moon," an illusion.

Dignaga is happy to draw the conclusion that our experiences of the external world are one and all illusory. But many philosophers have tried to distinguish some

[20] Dignaga, *Dignaga's Alambanapariksa [The Investigation of the Object of Awareness],* translated by N. Aiyaswami Sastri (Madras: Adyar, 1942), 1–2d.

features of our experiences that really reflect the way the world is from those that arise from the activity of our sense organs and our brains. René Descartes (1596–1650; see Chapter 2), for example, begins with a commonsense, Aristotelian picture of how we think of external objects:

What persuaded Descartes that there were objects outside him?

> And outside myself, in addition to the extension, shape, and motions of bodies, I sensed in them hardness, heat, and all other tactile qualities. I also sensed light, color, scents, tastes, and sounds; their variety let me distinguish the sky, the earth, the sea, and the rest in turn. And certainly, considering the ideas of all these qualities which presented themselves to my mind—and which alone I sensed properly or immediately—it was not without reason that I thought I sensed things plainly different from my thought, namely bodies that produced those ideas. For I experienced that these ideas came to me without my consent; I could not sense any object, however much I might want to, unless it were present to my sense organs. I could not *not* sense it when it was present. And because the ideas I received through the senses were much more lively, more vivid, and even in their own way more distinct than any of those I could deliberately frame in meditation or found impressed on my memory, it seemed they could not have proceeded from my mind; they must have come from other things. Having acquaintance with those only through the ideas themselves, nothing came to mind but that they were similar. And because I remembered that I had made use of my senses before my reason, and saw that the ideas I formed of myself were not as clear as those I perceived through the senses, and that they were for the most part made up of such parts, I easily persuaded myself that, plainly, I had no idea in my intellect that I had not previously had in sensation.[21]

We naturally assume, then, that the objects causing our experiences are as they seem to be; we assume that they are similar to the ideas and sensations they cause in us. But we cannot hold that assumption for very long. We are prone to too many illusions and mistakes.

What arguments does Descartes give for doubting the existence of external objects?

> Afterwards, to be sure, many experiences shook, little by little, all the faith I had in my senses. From time to time I saw that towers that looked round from far away appeared square close up, and that colossal statues standing on the summits of these towers did not look large at all when viewed from the ground. And so in countless other cases I found mistakes in judgments founded on the external senses. And not only the external senses, but also the internal. Is there anything more intimate than pain? And yet I have heard from some persons whose arms or legs have been cut off that they sometimes seemed to feel pain in the part that was amputated. This made me think that I could not be quite sure that it was a certain member that pained me, even if I felt pain in it. And to those grounds of doubt I have lately added two other very general ones. The first: I never have believed myself to sense anything while awake that I cannot also sometimes believe myself to sense while asleep. Since I do not think that the things I seem to sense in sleep come to me from

[21]This and subsequent quotations from Descartes are from René Descartes, *Meditations,* VI, my translation.

> things outside of me, I do not see any reason why I should have this belief about things I seem to sense while awake. The other: Being still ignorant—or rather supposing myself to be ignorant—of the author of my origins, I saw nothing to stand in the way of my having been constituted by nature to be deceived even about the things that seem to me to be most true. As for the reasons that persuaded me of the truth of sensible things, I answered them without difficulty. For since nature seemed to impel me toward many things from which reason repelled me, I did not think I should put much faith in the teachings of nature. And although the perceptions of the senses do not depend on my will, I did not think I should for that reason conclude that they proceeded from things different from myself, since I might possibly have some faculty—not yet known to me—that produced them.

Illusion, then, tempts us to conclude that we know nothing about how the outside world might be in reality. But, for reasons we have seen in Chapter 2, Descartes is unwilling to go so far:

> But now, when I begin to know myself and the author of my origins better, I do not think that I should casually admit everything I seem to have in the senses. But, on the other hand, neither should I call them all into doubt.

But how do we distinguish the aspects of our perceptions that reflect the way the world really is from those that arise solely from our own nervous system? We can deduce that external objects exist from the fact that God is good and would not systematically deceive us. But we can trust as reflecting the way things really are only what we perceive clearly and distinctly. Descartes maintains that we can perceive clearly and distinctly only the *mathematical* properties of objects, such as extension (size, shape) and motion. Only they can be trusted as reflecting the true nature of things.

> But, since God is no deceiver, it is quite clear that He does not send these ideas to me directly and by Himself nor indirectly by means of some creature containing their objective reality eminently but not formally. For He plainly has given me no faculty to recognise this. On the contrary, He has given me a great propensity to believe that they are sent to me by corporeal objects. I do not see how He could be understood as anything but a deceiver if these ideas were produced by something other than corporeal objects. It follows that corporeal things exist. Still, perhaps they do not exist exactly as I grasp them by the senses, this grasp by the senses is in many cases very obscure and confused. But at least they are everything I clearly and distinctly understand them to be—that is, everything that, generally speaking, is an object of pure mathematics.

Other characteristics of objects, however, are untrustworthy. It is not that colors, sounds, scents, taste, heat, texture, etc., are random; our perceptions are systematic and regular enough that we can infer that we are responding to something in the object. But we have no reason to believe that the object itself is in these respects as we perceive it to be.

> Moreover, nature teaches me that various other bodies exist around mine. Some are to be pursued; others, shunned. And certainly from the fact that I sense very different colors, sounds, scents, tastes, heat, hardness, and the like, I rightly conclude

> that something in the bodies from which all these various sense-perceptions come corresponds to these variations, even if perhaps they do not resemble them.

For example,

> And although, coming near the fire, I feel heat, and, coming a little too near, I even feel pain, there is no reason to think that something in the fire resembles heat any more than that something in it resembles pain. There is only reason to think that there is something in it—whatever it may eventually turn out to be—that produces in us these sensations of heat or of pain.

Descartes thus refines Dignaga's argument in the following way. We have reason to believe that the objects of our perception really do exist and really do serve as the causes of our perceptions. But we also have reason to believe that they differ in important ways from our perceptions of them. In some respects—corresponding to the mathematical properties of the objects—we perceive objects as they really are. In other respects, we respond to features of the objects in ways that are not similar to those features at all.

John Locke (1632–1704; see Chapter 3) puts this distinction in its now-standard form, as a distinction between the primary and secondary qualities of objects. First, he explains what a quality is:

What is a quality, according to Locke?

> Whatsoever the mind perceives in itself, or is the immediate object of perception, thought, or understanding, that I call idea; and the power to produce any idea in our mind, I call quality of the subject wherein that power is. Thus a snowball having the power to produce in us the ideas of white, cold, and round,—the power to produce those ideas in us, as they are in the snowball, I call qualities; and as they are sensations or perceptions in our understandings, I call them ideas; which ideas, if I speak of sometimes as in the things themselves, I would be understood to mean those qualities in the objects which produce them in us. (II, VIII, xx)[22]

He then distinguishes two kinds of qualities. **Primary qualities** are inseparable from body; atoms have them. They are the qualities matter has according to the atomic theory of matter. Primary qualities, as we shall see, produce certain simple ideas in us—ideas of solidity, extension, figure, motion, and number—that really correspond to the way things are.

> Qualities thus considered in bodies are, First, such as are utterly inseparable from the body, in what state soever it be; and such as in all the alterations and changes it suffers, all the force can be used upon it, it constantly keeps; and such as sense constantly finds in every particle of matter which has bulk enough to be perceived; and the mind finds inseparable from every particle of matter, though less than to make itself singly be perceived by our senses: v.g. Take a grain of wheat, divide it into two parts; each part has still solidity, extension, figure, and mobility: divide it again, and it retains still the same qualities; and so divide it on, till the parts become insensible; they must retain still each of them all those qualities. For division

[22] This and subsequent quotations from Locke are from John Locke, *An Essay Concerning Human Understanding* (London: printed for Tho. Basset, 1690).

> (which is all that a mill, or pestle, or any other body, does upon another, in reducing it to insensible parts) can never take away either solidity, extension, figure, or mobility from any body, but only makes two or more distinct separate masses of matter, of that which was but one before; all which distinct masses, reckoned as so many distinct bodies, after division, make a certain number. These I call original or primary qualities of body, which I think we may observe to produce simple ideas in us, viz. solidity, extension, figure, motion or rest, and number.

Secondary qualities are effects of primary qualities on our sense organs and nervous systems. They do not resemble the ideas they produce in us.

What is a secondary quality?

> Secondly, such qualities which in truth are nothing in the objects themselves but power to produce various sensations in us by their primary qualities, i.e. by the bulk, figure, texture, and motion of their insensible parts, as colours, sounds, tastes, &c. These I call secondary qualities.

There are also qualities that are *powers* to cause other objects to produce sensations in us (such as the power of fire to produce a new color in clay); to cause other objects to cause other objects to produce sensations in us (such as the power of a spark to cause such a fire), and so on.

How do qualities in objects produce sensations in us? The answer is given by the atomic theory.

> The next thing to be considered is, how bodies produce ideas in us; and that is manifestly by impulse, the only way which we can conceive bodies to operate in.
>
> If then external objects be not united to our minds when they produce ideas therein; and yet we perceive these original qualities in such of them as singly fall under our senses, it is evident that some motion must be thence continued by our nerves, or animal spirits, by some parts of our bodies, to the brains or the seat of sensation, there to produce in our minds the particular ideas we have of them. And since the extension, figure, number, and motion of bodies of an observable bigness, may be perceived at a distance by the sight, it is evident some singly imperceptible bodies must come from them to the eyes, and thereby convey to the brain some motion; which produces these ideas which we have of them in us.

This story, however primitive in the form Locke tells it, indicates the relation between primary and secondary qualities. Our ideas are produced by qualities of objects by way of impulses: tiny particles (or waves) from the object strike our sense organs, which respond by sending neural impulses to the brain. That explanation makes reference only to the primary qualities of the object (and of our bodies). So, the ideas we have depend solely on the primary qualities of objects. Secondary qualities thus depend on primary qualities.

> What I have said concerning colours and smells may be understood also of tastes and sounds, and other the like sensible qualities; which, whatever reality we by mistake attribute to them, are in truth nothing in the objects themselves, but powers to produce various sensations in us; and depend on those primary qualities, viz. bulk, figure, texture, and motion of parts as I have said.

It follows that the primary qualities produce ideas that resemble them, but secondary qualities do not. Secondary qualities are **response-dependent:** to have one is simply to generate a certain kind of response in a perceiver. They are "just like the double moon," in Dignaga's words; they are in the object only as powers to affect our sense organs in certain ways, not in the way they appear to be.

> From whence I think it easy to draw this observation, that the ideas of primary qualities of bodies are resemblances of them, and their patterns do really exist in the bodies themselves, but the ideas produced in us by these secondary qualities have no resemblance of them at all. There is nothing like our ideas, existing in the bodies themselves. They are, in the bodies we denominate from them, only a power to produce those sensations in us: and what is sweet, blue, or warm in idea, is but the certain bulk, figure, and motion of the insensible parts, in the bodies themselves, which we call so.

Indeed, if our sense organs were more powerful than they are—or if we artificially supplement them, by looking through a microscope, for example—we would see something very different from what we see now. Things would still have extension, figure, and motion, and we could still count them, but their colors, textures, etc., would be very different.

> The now secondary qualities of bodies would disappear, if we could discover the primary ones of their minute parts. Had we senses acute enough to discern the minute particles of bodies, and the real constitution on which their sensible qualities depend, I doubt not but they would produce quite different ideas in us: and that which is now the yellow colour of gold, would then disappear, and instead of it we should see an admirable texture of parts, of a certain size and figure. This microscopes plainly discover to us; for what to our naked eyes produces a certain colour, is, by thus augmenting the acuteness of our senses, discovered to be quite a different thing; and thus altering, as it were, the proportion of the bulk of the minute parts of a coloured object to our usual sight, produces different ideas from what it did before. (II, XXIII, 11)

In keeping with his distinction between primary and secondary qualities, Locke distinguishes two kinds of essences: real and nominal. As we have seen, Aquinas and other Aristotelians have identified three things:

> the essence of *x* = the properties necessary to *x*, without which *x* would not be what it is
> the quiddity of *x* = what corresponds to *x*'s definition in the world
> the nature of *x* = what makes *x* what it is

This makes good sense as long as we hold that objects are as they appear to be. The atomic theory, however, breaks apart the notion of essence into at least two notions. The quiddity of a thing or kind, which we can express in a definition—and which Locke therefore dubs a **nominal essence**—generally makes use of secondary qualities. We might define water, for example, as a tasteless, odorless, clear liquid occupying over two-thirds of the earth's surface. Or, we might define gold as a shiny, malleable yellow or white metal of great value. These definitions use secondary qualities: *taste-*

less, odorless, clear, shiny, malleable, yellow or white, of great value. But, in the atomic theory, these definitions do not express the nature of water or gold; the properties they mention do not make water or gold what they are. Water has the qualities it does because it is H_2O. Gold has its properties because it has atomic number 79. The nature of a thing or kind—what Locke dubs its **real essence**—is thus given by the atomic theory. It stems from the **real internal constitution** of the object or kind.

Nominal essences are the abstract ideas for which general terms stand. They are creatures of the understanding, that is, our power to draw distinctions. We may craft our ideas as we please, although we generally try to mark common divisions we find in experience.

> That then which general words signify is a sort of things; and each of them does that, by being a sign of an abstract idea in the mind; to which idea, as things existing are found to agree, so they come to be ranked under that name, or, which is all one, be of that sort. Whereby it is evident that the [nominal] essences of the sorts, or, if the Latin word pleases better, species of things, are nothing else but these abstract ideas . . . it follows, that the abstract idea for which the name stands, and the essence of the species, is one and the same. From whence it is easy to observe, that the essences of the sorts of things, and, consequently, the sorting of things, is the workmanship of the understanding that abstracts and makes those general ideas. (III, III, 12)

But real essences are different. We are not free to craft them as we please. They stem from the real internal constitutions of things and correspond to natural kinds, kinds that are in nature, not merely creatures of the understanding.

What is a real essence?

> The particular parcel of matter which makes the ring I have on my finger is forwardly by most men supposed to have a real essence, whereby it is gold; and from whence those qualities flow which I find in it, viz. its peculiar colour, weight, hardness, fusibility, fixedness, and change of colour upon a slight touch of mercury, &c. This essence, from which all these properties flow, when I inquire into it and search after it, I plainly perceive I cannot discover: the furthest I can go is, only to presume that, it being nothing but body, its real essence or internal constitution, on which these qualities depend, can be nothing but the figure, size, and connexion of its solid parts; of neither of which having any distinct perception at all can I have any idea of its essence: which is the cause that it has that particular shining yellowness; a greater weight than anything I know of the same bulk; and a fitness to have its colour changed by the touch of quicksilver. (II, XXXI, 7)

The real essence is that on which the other properties of objects of a certain kind depend. Locke doubts whether we can have knowledge of it. The state of atomic theory in his day no doubt justified those worries. Now, however, we have scientific theories capable of giving real essences real explanatory power. Locke could only envision such a state of affairs in a distant future, when, he held, our conception of objects—and indeed of ourselves—would change dramatically.

> For, though perhaps voluntary motion, with sense and reason, joined to a body of a certain shape, be the complex idea to which I and others annex the name man, and so be the nominal essence of the species so called: yet nobody will say that

> complex idea is the real essence and source of all those operations which are to be found in any individual of that sort. The foundation of all those qualities which are the ingredients of our complex idea, is something quite different: and had we such a knowledge of that constitution of man, from which his faculties of moving, sensation, and reasoning, and other powers flow, and on which his so regular shape depends, as it is possible angels have, and it is certain his Maker has, we should have a quite other idea of his essence than what now is contained in our definition of that species, be it what it will: and our idea of any individual man would be as far different from what it is now, as is his who knows all the springs and wheels and other contrivances within of the famous clock at Strasburg, from that which a gazing countryman has of it, who barely sees the motion of the hand, and hears the clock strike, and observes only some of the outward appearances. (III, VI, 3–4)

IDEALISM

Dignaga, as we saw, takes the atomic theory as his starting point, and distinguishes two kinds of objects: what he calls actual objects (*alambana*) and what he calls simply objects, or internal objects (*artha*). Actual objects are the causes of our perceptions, namely atoms; internal objects are what they are (or appear to be) perceptions *of*. We cannot identify the causes of perception with the objects of perception in all respects, for the objects of our perception have various secondary qualities—color, scent, taste, texture—that their atomic parts do not have. Descartes and Locke insist that primary qualities are as they appear to be; objects in the world really do have extension, figure, and motion, for atomic theory tells us that their parts have such properties. Dignaga himself, however, found this position unsatisfying. *All* qualities, he contends, are "just like the double moon"; all are response-dependent.

Dignaga argues, therefore, that actual objects, atoms, cannot be taken as real objects of consciousness or constituents in the world. Part of his argument seems to depend on the primitive state of atomic theory in fifth-century India. He cannot see how atomic theory could explain why we sometimes see a cloth and other times a pot, for "the atoms are absolutely identical in their dimensions." But the more serious argument is that we can know the external world only through our sense organs. Thus, we can know an object only to the extent that it becomes an internal object:

> It is the object (*artha*) which exists internally in knowledge itself as a knowable aspect and which appears to us as if it exists externally.
>
> Because consciousness is the essence and that acts as the condition.[23]

We know objects only as *artha,* internal objects of awareness. Inescapably, they are constituted by consciousness; they are essentially objects of consciousness. Consciousness is the condition of their existence. We cannot know anything of objects, then, except as they are conditioned by consciousness.

---

[23] Dignaga, *Dignaga's Alambanapariksa [The Investigation of the Object of Awareness],* translated by N. Aiyaswami Sastri (Madras: Adyar, 1942), 6a–d.

This is the central argument for *idealism,* the view that everything is mind-dependent. The idealist typically argues that

1. We can know a thing only by making it an object of consciousness.
2. Any object of consciousness is conditioned by consciousness.
3. So we can know only what is conditioned by consciousness.
4. But anything conditioned by consciousness is mind-dependent.
5. So we can know only what is mind-dependent.
6. We have reason to believe something exists only if we can have knowledge of it.
7. So we have reason to believe that a thing exists only if it is mind-dependent.

This is common in Indian philosophy, not only among Buddhists such as Dignaga, but among Hindus as well. *Vedanta* is an Indian philosophical school with its roots in the *Upanishads,* which are among the oldest texts in Sanskrit (dating to about 900 B.C.E.; see Chapter 4). The Upanishads center on metaphysics: What is ultimate reality? How does it relate to the world? How can it be known? The ultimate reality is *Brahman.* All Vedanta is Brahman-centered.

Some Vedantins take Brahman to be God; others see it as an impersonal ground of Being. But the crucial division is between those who identify the self (*atman*) with Brahman and those who do not. Dualists maintain that the self and Brahman are distinct—the knower is not identical with God or the ground of all being—and that the self's ability to know Brahman is limited. Nondualists, called Advaita Vedantins, hold that the self and Brahman are one and the same. In their view, in the mystical knowledge of Brahman one knows the One, the Sole True Existent, whose nature is perfect being, consciousness, and bliss—and "Thou art that!" The nondualist view plainly is idealist. Everything is mind-dependent, for the ground of all being is the self, mind.

The most famous Advaita Vedantin is the South Indian philosopher Sankara (788–820), its founder. Sankara defends the dualism between mind and body, the existence of many minds, the thesis that physical objects are mind-independent, and the thesis that there is one God, distinct from the self—all at the level of our commonsense view of the world.

> It is a matter not requiring any proof that the object and the subject . . . which are opposed to each other as much as darkness and light are, cannot be identified. All the less can their respective attributes be identified.[24]

He then rejects the commonsense view as incompatible with scripture and with enlightenment experience. Our commonsense view of the world is thoroughly dualist and realist, he maintains, but it is inaccurate; it does not reflect the true nature of reality. In truth, there is only one thing—the ultimate reality, Brahman—and everything else is illusion.

> In their literal, superficial meaning, 'Brahman' and 'Atman' have opposite attributes, like the sun and the glow-worm, and king and his servant, the ocean and the well, or Mount Meru and the atom. Their identity is established only when they

[24]Sankara, *Brahmasutra Commentary,* from *The Vedanta Sutras of Badarayana,* translated by George Thibant (Sacred Books of the East, 1890).

> are understood in their true significance, and not in a superficial sense. . . . this apparent opposition is caused by Maya [illusion] and her effects. It is not real, therefore, but superimposed.[25]

Idealists are **monists**, philosophers who maintain that there is ultimately only one kind of thing. (Idealists, for example, hold that everything is mental. *Materialists* hold that everything is material. *Physicalists* hold that everything is physical.) They sometimes take the further step of holding not only that there is only one *kind* of thing, but that there is only one *thing*. Sankara and subsequent Advaita Vedantins do exactly that. Brahman is that one thing—the one ultimate reality of which everything else is merely appearance.

> The wise men of true discrimination understand that the essence of both Brahman and Atman is Pure Consciousness, and thus realize their absolute identity.[26]

Sankara's key concept is **superimposition**, which he defines as

> The apparent presentation, in the form of remembrance, to consciousness of something previously observed, in some other things. . . . [in other words,] the apparent presentation of the attributes of one thing in another thing.[27]

This is what we do routinely and even reasonably in our ordinary lives. We attribute properties of ourselves to the world and properties of the world to ourselves. We attribute properties of Brahman to a wide variety of things, including ourselves. Thus we become trapped in ignorance. Through study, we can learn to escape ignorance and see the true reality.

Berkeley and Hume

As we saw in Chapter 4, idealism has been popular in other traditions as well, including Zen Buddhism and neo-Confucianism. Rarely, however, do the idealists in those traditions offer arguments that are more sophisticated than the argument in Dignaga. Sometimes, however, idealists have gone beyond that, arguing that the core concepts of a realist understanding of the world are ultimately incoherent. That is the strategy of the Indian philosopher Sriharsa (c. 1150), an Advaitin who critiques Nyaya conceptions of objects, identity, and difference. It is also the strategy of George Berkeley (1685–1753), Irish philosopher and bishop, contemporary of Leibniz, Voltaire, Handel, and Bach. Berkeley graduated from Trinity College, Dublin, at nineteen, was appointed Fellow, and wrote most of his important philosophical works by the time he was twenty-eight. In his forties, he spent four years in Rhode Island, hoping for funds from King George II to establish a college in Bermuda. His plans fell through, and he returned to Ireland to become Bishop of Cloyne at age forty-nine.

---

[25] Sankara, from *Shankara's Crest-Jewel of Discrimination: Viveka-Chudamani,* translated by Swami Prabhavananda and Christopher Isherwood (Hollywood: Vedanta Press, 1947, 1975).

[26] Sankara, from *Shankara's Crest-Jewel of Discrimination: Viveka-Chudamani,* translated by Swami Prabhavananda and Christopher Isherwood (Hollywood: Vedanta Press, 1947, 1975).

[27] Sankara, *Brahmasutra Commentary,* from *The Vedanta Sutras of Badarayana,* translated by George Thibant (Sacred Books of the East, 1890).

Unlike Sankara, who argues that common sense is realist and that idealism must supplant common sense, Berkeley sees idealism as the best *defense* of common sense against skepticism. He argues that the notions of an object propounded by Descartes and especially Locke make no sense. Moreover, he contends that the distinction between primary and secondary qualities is ill-grounded. In effect, he argues, *every* quality is a secondary quality. We have no basis for thinking that any of our ideas correspond to some mind-independent reality. Further, our ideas of primary qualities are supposed to resemble the qualities themselves. But we have no access to the qualities apart from our ideas of them. We have no way of assessing resemblance. So two of Berkeley's chief arguments for idealism are (1) an attack on the idea of primary qualities and (2) an attack on the idea of substance.

Berkeley rejects primary qualities, for he notes that our perceptions of length, width, height, etc., vary, while objects remain unchanged. To argue for idealism, Berkeley writes a series of dialogues between Hylas, who defends Locke, and Philonous, who speaks for Berkeley. Philonous employs the arguments for recognizing certain qualities as secondary and uses them against primary qualities. The underlying principle of those arguments, as David Hume (1711–1776; see Chapter 3) notes, is "when different impressions of the same sense arise from any object, every one of these impressions has not a resembling quality existent in the object."[28]

Why does Berkeley conclude that even primary qualities are not really in objects?

PHIL. Again, have you not acknowledged that no real inherent property of any object can be changed without some change in the thing itself?

HYL. I have.

PHIL. But, as we approach to or recede from an object, the visible extension varies, being at one distance ten or a hundred times greater than another. Doth it not therefore follow from hence likewise that it is not really inherent in the object?

HYL. I own I am at a loss what to think.

PHIL. Your judgment will soon be determined, if you will venture to think as freely concerning this quality as you have done concerning the rest. Was it not admitted as a good argument, that neither heat nor cold was in the water, because it seemed warm to one hand and cold to the other?

HYL. It was.

PHIL. Is it not the very same reasoning to conclude, there is no extension or figure in an object, because to one eye it shall seem little, smooth, and round, when at the same time it appears to the other, great, uneven, and regular?

HYL. The very same. But does this latter fact ever happen?

PHIL. You may at any time make the experiment, by looking with one eye bare, and with the other through a microscope.[29]

Moreover, the very distinction between primary and secondary qualities matters because of the supposed link between our ideas of primary qualities and the qualities

[28] David Hume, *A Treatise of Human Nature* (London: printed for John Noon, 1739), I, 512.

[29] George Berkeley, *Three Dialogues Between Hylas and Philonous, The Design of which Is Plainly to Demonstrate the Reality and Perfection of Human Knowledge, The Incorporeal Nature of the Soul, and the Immediate Providence of a Deity in Opposition to Sceptics and Atheists: Also to Open a Method for Rendering the Sciences More Easy, Useful, and Compendious* (London: printed for G. James and H. Clements, 1713).

themselves. Our ideas are supposed to resemble the things; in respect of primary qualities, at least, we see things as they really are. Berkeley finds this unintelligible. We have access to nothing but our own ideas. So we have no good reason for thinking external objects exist at all or are anything but our own ideas. And we have no way of comparing our ideas to the actual qualities in things to see whether there is any resemblance or not.

PHIL. I ask you, whether the things immediately perceived are other than your own sensations or ideas? . . .

HYL. To speak the truth, Philonous, I think there are two kinds of objects:—the one perceived immediately, which are likewise called ideas; the other are real things or external objects, perceived by the mediation of ideas, which are their images and representations. Now, I own ideas do not exist without the mind; but the latter sort of objects do. I am sorry I did not think of this distinction sooner; it would probably have cut short your discourse.

PHIL. Are those external objects perceived by sense or by some other faculty?

HYL. They are perceived by sense.

PHIL. How? Is there any thing perceived by sense which is not immediately perceived?

HYL. Yes, Philonous, in some sort there is. For example, when I look on a picture or statue of Julius Caesar, I may be said after a manner to perceive him (though not immediately) by my senses.

PHIL. It seems then you will have our ideas, which alone are immediately perceived, to be pictures of external things: and that these also are perceived by sense, inasmuch as they have a conformity or resemblance to our ideas?

HYL. That is my meaning.

PHIL. And, in the same way that Julius Caesar, in himself invisible, is nevertheless perceived by sight; real things, in themselves imperceptible, are perceived by sense.

How does Philonous argue that we perceive nothing but our own ideas?

HYL. In the very same.

PHIL. Tell me, Hylas, when you behold the picture of Julius Caesar, do you see with your eyes any more than some colours and figures, with a certain symmetry and composition of the whole?

HYL. Nothing else.

PHIL. And would not a man who had never known anything of Julius Caesar see as much?

HYL. He would.

PHIL. Consequently he hath his sight, and the use of it, in as perfect a degree as you?

HYL. I agree with you.

PHIL. Whence comes it then that your thoughts are directed to the Roman emperor, and his are not? This cannot proceed from the sensations or ideas of sense by you then perceived; since you acknowledge you have no advantage over him in that respect. It should seem therefore to proceed from reason and memory: should it not?

HYL. It should.

PHIL. Consequently, it will not follow from that instance that anything is perceived by sense which is not immediately perceived. Though I grant we may, in one acceptation, be said to perceive sensible things mediately by sense: that is, when, from a frequently perceived connexion, the immediate perception of ideas by one sense suggests to the mind others, perhaps belonging to another sense, which are wont to be connected with them. For instance, when I hear a coach drive along the streets, immediately I perceive only the sound; but, from the experience I have had that such a sound is connected with a coach, I am said to hear the coach. It is nevertheless evident that, in truth and strictness, nothing can be heard but sound; and the coach is not then properly perceived by sense, but suggested from experience. So likewise when we are said to see a red-hot bar of iron; the solidity and heat of the iron are not the objects of sight, but suggested to the imagination by the colour and figure which are properly perceived by that sense. In short, those things alone are actually and strictly perceived by any sense, which would have been perceived in case that same sense had then been first conferred on us. As for other things, it is plain they are only suggested to the mind by experience, grounded on former perceptions. But, to return to your comparison of Caesar's picture, it is plain, if you keep to that, you must hold the real things, or archetypes of our ideas, are not perceived by sense, but by some internal faculty of the soul, as reason or memory. I would therefore fain know what arguments you can draw from reason for the existence of what you call real things or material objects. Or, whether you remember to have seen them formerly as they are in themselves; or, if you have heard or read of any one that did.

HYL. I see, Philonous, you are disposed to raillery; but that will never convince me.

PHIL. My aim is only to learn from you the way to come at the knowledge of material beings. Whatever we perceive is perceived immediately or mediately: by sense, or by reason and reflexion. But, as you have excluded sense, pray shew me what reason you have to believe their existence; or what medium you can possibly make use of to prove it, either to mine or your own understanding.

The notion of resemblance, then, makes no sense. We perceive ideas. We can say when one idea resembles another idea. But we cannot say whether an idea resembles something else, for we never encounter anything else.

PHIL. But neither is this all. Which are material objects in themselves—perceptible or imperceptible?

HYL. Properly and immediately nothing can be perceived but ideas. All material things, therefore, are in themselves insensible, and to be perceived only by our ideas.

PHIL. Ideas then are sensible, and their archetypes or originals insensible?

HYL. Right.

PHIL. But how can that which is sensible be like that which is insensible? Can a real thing, in itself invisible, be like a colour; or a real thing, which is not audible, be like a sound? In a word, can anything be like a sensation or idea, but another sensation or idea?

HYL. I must own, I think not.

As he puts it in the *Principles of Human Knowledge,*

But, say you, though the ideas themselves do not exist without the mind, yet there may be things like them, whereof they are copies or resemblances, which things exist without the mind in an unthinking substance. I answer, an idea can be like nothing but an idea; a colour or figure can be like nothing but another colour or figure. If we look but never so little into our thoughts, we shall find it impossible for us to

> conceive a likeness except only between our ideas. Again, I ask whether those supposed originals or external things, of which our ideas are the pictures or representations, be themselves perceivable or no? If they are, then they are ideas and we have gained our point; but if you say they are not, I appeal to any one whether it be sense to assert a colour is like something which is invisible; hard or soft, like something which is intangible; and so of the rest.[30]

Locke's position, Berkeley thus insists, leads inevitably to skepticism. Hume agrees, maintaining that our commonsense picture of the world, when analyzed, leads directly to skepticism. He echoes Berkeley's argument:

Why can we not tell whether an idea resembles something in the object?

> It is a question of fact, whether the perceptions of the senses be produced by external objects, resembling them: how shall this question be determined? By experience surely; as all other questions of a like nature. But here experience is, and must be entirely silent. The mind has never anything present to it but the perceptions, and cannot possibly reach any experience of their connexion with objects. The supposition of such a connexion is, therefore, without any foundation in reasoning.[31]

Berkeley also attacks Locke's idea of substance. Locke himself admits that there is little content to the idea. His concept is not Aristotle's, which is primarily the concept of an object. Substance, for Locke, is a substratum in which the qualities of objects inhere:

What is substance, according to Locke?

> The mind being, as I have declared, furnished with a great number of the simple ideas, conveyed in by the senses as they are found in exterior things, or by reflection on its own operations, takes notice also that a certain number of these simple ideas go constantly together; which being presumed to belong to one thing, and words being suited to common apprehensions, and made use of for quick dispatch, are called, so united in one subject, by one name; which, by inadvertency, we are apt afterward to talk of and consider as one simple idea, which indeed is a complication of many ideas together: because, as I have said, not imagining how these simple ideas can subsist by themselves, we accustom ourselves to suppose some substratum wherein they do subsist, and from which they do result, which therefore we call substance. (II, XXIII, 1)

Yet, under analysis, there turns out to be little that we can say about it. Aristotle had contemplated such an understanding of substance as matter, and concluded that it was not viable—in fact, he called it "crazy". Locke almost admits as much:

> So that if any one will examine himself concerning his notion of pure substance in general, he will find he has no other idea of it at all, but only a supposition of he knows not what support of such qualities which are capable of producing simple ideas in us; which qualities are commonly called accidents. If any one should be asked, what is the subject wherein colour or weight inheres, he would have nothing to say, but the solid extended parts; and if he were demanded, what is it that solidity and extension adhere in, he would not be in a much better case than the

[30] George Berkeley, *Principles of Human Knowledge* (London: Hull, A. Brown, and Sons, 1710, 1937), 8.
[31] David Hume, *An Enquiry Concerning Human Understanding* (London: printed for A. Millar, 1758), X.

> Indian before mentioned who, saying that the world was supported by a great elephant, was asked what the elephant rested on; to which his answer was—a great tortoise: but being again pressed to know what gave support to the broad-backed tortoise, replied—something, he knew not what. And thus here, as in all other cases where we use words without having clear and distinct ideas, we talk like children: who, being questioned what such a thing is, which they know not, readily give this satisfactory answer, that it is something: which in truth signifies no more, when so used, either by children or men, but that they know not what; and that the thing they pretend to know, and talk of, is what they have no distinct idea of at all, and so are perfectly ignorant of it, and in the dark. The idea then we have, to which we give the general name *substance,* being nothing but the supposed, but unknown, support of those qualities we find existing, which we imagine cannot subsist *sine re substante,* without something to support them, we call that support *substantia;* which, according to the true import of the word, is, in plain English, standing under or upholding. (II, XXIII, 2)

Berkeley's argument against substance relies on Locke's admission that the idea is virtually content-free. But he also uses the argument against primary qualities to contend that the idea of substance or matter is self-contradictory.

Why is the idea of corporeal substance self-contradictory, according to Berkeley?

> But it is evident from what we have already shown, that extension, figure, and motion are only ideas existing in the mind, and that an idea can be like nothing but another idea, and that consequently neither they nor their archetypes can exist in an unperceiving substance. Hence, it is plain that that the very notion of what is called Matter or corporeal substance, involves a contradiction in it.[32]

David Hume continues the attack: How could we obtain an idea of substance as the ground in which qualities of objects inhere? Our ideas correspond to the qualities; by definition they cannot correspond to anything else.

> I wou'd fain ask those philosophers, who found so much of their reasonings on the distinction of substance and accident, and imagine we have clear ideas of each, whether the idea of substance be deriv'd from the impressions of sensation or of reflection? If it be convey'd to us by our senses, I ask, which of them; and after what manner? If it be perceiv'd by the eyes, it must be a colour; if by the ears, a sound; if by the palate, a taste; and so of the other senses. But I believe none will assert, that substance is either a colour, or sound, or a taste. The idea, of substance must therefore be deriv'd from an impression of reflection, if it really exist. But the impressions of reflection resolve themselves into our passions and emotions: none of which can possibly represent a substance. We have therefore no idea of substance, distinct from that of a collection of particular qualities, nor have we any other meaning when we either talk or reason concerning it.[33]

Berkeley also offers positive arguments of his own. The most famous rests on the idea that we can perceive and know nothing but our own ideas.

[32] George Berkeley, *Principles of Human Knowledge* (London: Hull, A. Brown, and Sons, 1710, 1937), 9.
[33] David Hume, *A Treatise of Human Nature* (London: printed for John Noon, 1739), VI, 1.

> It is indeed an opinion strangely prevailing amongst men, that houses, mountains, rivers, and in a word all sensible objects, have an existence, natural or real, distinct from their being perceived by the understanding. But, with how great an assurance and acquiescence soever this principle may be entertained in the world, yet whoever shall find in his heart to call it in question may, if I mistake not, perceive it to involve a manifest contradiction. For, what are the fore-mentioned objects but the things we perceive by sense? and what do we perceive besides our own ideas or sensations? and is it not plainly repugnant that any one of these, or any combination of them, should exist unperceived?[34]

Interestingly, Berkeley takes this to be completely obvious:

How does Berkeley argue that to be is to be perceived?

> Some truths there are so near and obvious to the mind that a man need only open his eyes to see them. Such I take this important one to be, viz., that all the choir of heaven and furniture of the earth, in a word all those bodies which compose the mighty frame of the world, have not any subsistence without a mind, that their being is to be perceived or known; that consequently so long as they are not actually perceived by me, or do not exist in my mind or that of any other created spirit, they must either have no existence at all, or else subsist in the mind of some Eternal Spirit—it being perfectly unintelligible, and involving all the absurdity of abstraction, to attribute to any single part of them an existence independent of a spirit. To be convinced of which, the reader need only reflect, and try to separate in his own thoughts the being of a sensible thing from its being perceived.
>
> From what has been said it follows there is not any other Substance than Spirit, or that which perceives. But, for the fuller proof of this point, let it be considered the sensible qualities are colour, figure, motion, smell, taste, etc., i.e. the ideas perceived by sense. Now, for an idea to exist in an unperceiving thing is a manifest contradiction, for to have an idea is all one as to perceive; that therefore wherein colour, figure, and the like qualities exist must perceive them; hence it is clear there can be no unthinking substance or substratum of those ideas.[35]

Hume characteristically puts the argument succinctly:

> A like reasoning will account for the idea of external existence. We may observe, that 'tis universally allow'd by philosophers, and is besides pretty obvious of itself, that nothing is ever really present with the mind but its perceptions or impressions and ideas, and that external objects become known to us only by those perceptions they occasion. To hate, to love, to think, to feel, to see; all this is nothing but to perceive.
>
> Now since nothing is ever present to the mind but perceptions, and since all ideas are deriv'd from something antecedently present to the mind; it follows, that 'tis impossible for us so much as to conceive or form an idea of any thing specifically different from ideas and impressions. Let us fix our attention out of ourselves as much as possible: Let us chase our imagination to the heavens, or to the utmost limits of the universe; we never really advance a step beyond ourselves, nor can

---

[34] George Berkeley, *Principles of Human Knowledge* (London: Hull, A. Brown, and Sons, 1710, 1937), 4.
[35] George Berkeley, *Principles of Human Knowledge* (London: Hull, A. Brown, and Sons, 1710, 1937), 4.

> conceive any kind of existence, but those perceptions, which have appear'd in that narrow compass.[36]

He, too, considers this obvious:

> These are the obvious dictates of reason; and no man, who reflects, ever doubted, that the existences, which we consider, when we say, this house and that tree, are nothing but perceptions in the mind, and fleeting copies or representations of other existences, which remain uniform and independent.[37]

As Berkeley puts his conclusion, ***esse est percipi***—to be is to be perceived. We have no access to anything but what is before the mind. A thing can exist, therefore, only if it can be perceived. Indeed, he goes further: A thing can exist only if it *is* perceived. He finds the idea of an unperceived object absurd.

> But say you, surely there is nothing easier than to imagine trees, for instance, in a park, or books existing in a closet, and nobody by to perceive them. I answer, you may so, there is no difficulty in it: but what is all this, I beseech you, more than framing in your mind certain ideas which you call *books* and *trees,* and at the same time omitting to frame the idea of anyone that may perceive them? But do not you your self perceive or think of them all the while? This therefore is nothing to the purpose. . . . it is necessary that you conceive them existing unconceived or unthought of, which is a manifest repugnancy.[38]

But if to be is to be perceived, what happens to the books in my room when I walk out of it, and am no longer there to perceive them? When I fall asleep, and neither perceive nor even think of them? Do they go out of existence, as my perceptions and thoughts do? No, Berkeley says—but only because *God* perceives them.

Kant

We have already discussed the views of Immanuel Kant (1724–1804; see Chapter 3). Kant is an idealist, though of a peculiar kind. He calls himself a *transcendental idealist* because he holds that the transcendental unity of apperception—the ground of all our perceptions and thoughts being *ours*—is an objective condition of all knowledge. His argument is a greatly elaborated version of that advanced by Dignaga (although they were unaware of each other's work). We can know objects only insofar as they relate to the transcendental unity. Truth, objectivity, and existence thus become fundamentally epistemic notions. The same holds of all the modalities—possibility, truth or existence, and necessity—for all have the same function of relating a judgment to the understanding. Metaphysics is inseparable from epistemology; the root notions of metaphysics are all, in the end, epistemological notions.

Just as Dignaga distinguishes actual objects, the causes of perception, from the internal objects of our perceptions, so Kant distinguishes things-in-themselves,

---

[36] David Hume, *A Treatise of Human Nature* (London: printed for John Noon, 1739), VI.
[37] David Hume, *An Enquiry Concerning Human Understanding* (London: printed for A. Millar, 1758), X.
[38] George Berkeley, *Principles of Human Knowledge* (London: Hull, A. Brown, and Sons, 1710, 1937), 23.

noumena—things as they actually exist, unconditioned by our perceiving or thinking about them—from *objects of experience,* also called *appearances* or *phenomena,* which are objects as they appear to us. Kant denies that we can have knowledge of noumena. Indeed, we never encounter things-in-themselves; everything we perceive or conceive has been conditioned by our faculties of perception and thought. Sensibility, our faculty of perception, imposes the form of space and time on objects perceived. The understanding, the faculty of thought, imposes the categories, which give our thoughts logical form. We can speak of objects or events causing other objects or events; we can speak of things existing or failing to exist. But we thereby speak solely of appearances. The categories apply only to things as conditioned by sensibility and understanding. We cannot legitimately apply them to things-in-themselves. So, we cannot even say that that there *are* things-in-themselves. Much less can we say that they *cause* us to perceive what we perceive. Like Dignaga, then, Kant begins with the distinction between actual objects (things-in-themselves) as causes of our perceptions and internal objects (appearances) that those perceptions are about. But, like Dignaga, he finds that he can say nothing about actual objects; we have access only to things as conditioned by our modes of knowledge.

So far, Kant seems to be a classic idealist. But he is concerned to distance himself from Berkeley, even entitling one section of the *Critique of Pure Reason* "The Refutation of Idealism." It is worth considering his argument against Berkeley, to see in what sense Kant considers himself to be an idealist.

Kant argues for the following proposition, which he calls a "theorem":

> THEOREM
>
> The simple but empirically determined consciousness of my own existence proves the existence of external objects in space.[39]

This immediately distinguishes Kant from Berkeley and Hume, who find the existence of external objects not only unprovable but absurd. Kant's argument:

Why must there be something outside me, according to Kant?

> PROOF
>
> I am conscious of my own existence as determined in time. All determination in regard to time presupposes the existence of something permanent in perception. But this permanent something cannot be something in me, for the very reason that my existence in time is itself determined by this permanent something. It follows that the perception of this permanent existence is possible only through a thing without me and not through the mere representation of a thing without me. Consequently, the determination of my existence in time is possible only through the existence of real things external to me. Now, consciousness in time is necessarily connected with the consciousness of the possibility of this determination in time. Hence it follows that consciousness in time is necessarily connected also with the

[39] This and subsequent quotations from Kant are from Immanuel Kant, *Critique of Pure Reason,* translated by J. M. D. Meiklejohn (New York: Colonial Press, 1899). Throughout, any emphasis in the quotations is Kant's; the pagination is that of the original first [A] and second [B] editions. I have replaced 'analytical' and 'synthetical' with 'analytic' and 'synthetic'; 'cognize' and 'cognition' with 'know' and 'knowledge'; and 'conception' with 'concept' to accord with common usage.

> existence of things without me, inasmuch as the existence of these things is the condition of determination in time. That is to say, the consciousness of my own existence is at the same time an immediate consciousness of the existence of other things without me.

Remarking on this proof, Kant writes,

> For experience contains, in addition to the thought of something existing, intuition, and in this case it must be internal intuition, that is, time, in relation to which the subject must be determined. But the existence of external things is absolutely requisite for this purpose, so that it follows that internal experience is itself possible only mediately and through external experience.

Intuition, recall, is sensation or reflection. Kant is making a point against Descartes, urging that reflection depends on sensation; if we have no sensations, there is nothing on which to reflect. (That doesn't mean we can't have hallucinations, or simply imagine things that don't exist. We can. But reflection and imagination, in general, depend on sensation, in general. If we had no faculty of sensation at all, we would have no material for reflection or imagination.) That matters, for sensation is sensation *of* something—something outside the mind. It is a mistake, therefore, to think that we have nothing in the mind but perceptions or ideas and to conclude from that the objects of experience are merely ideas. Sensations may be mental, but they are sensations *of* something, and what they are *of* is an external object. Kant thus refutes Berkeley's positive argument for idealism.

He also defends the idea of substance or matter against the assaults of Berkeley and Hume:

> We find that we possess nothing permanent that can correspond and be submitted to the concept of substance as intuition, except matter. This idea of permanence is not itself derived from external experience but is an a priori necessary condition of all determination of time, consequently also of the internal sense in reference to our own existence, and that through the existence of external things.

Recall Chapter 3: Finding no experience from which the ideas of universality and necessary connection can be derived, Kant postulates them as a priori necessary conditions of experience. We do not abstract them from experience; they are an in-born part of our mental toolbox. The same is true of substance as the ground in which the qualities of objects inhere. We have experience only of the qualities; we do not perceive anything underlying them. Still, we organize our perceptions and thoughts around objects. That must then reflect a basic organizing principle of our thinking. Hume would agree, to an extent; the concepts of causality and substance, he would say, are not in the world, but in us. Kant turns this around: They are in the world *because* they are in us.

We can now see that Kant refutes idealism only in a Pickwickian sense. Berkeley and Hume are wrong to think that the ideas of substance and matter are incoherent or empty; those concepts are perfectly sensible and in fact are necessary conditions of the possibility of experience. But they do not come to us from the world. We impose them on the world. They are part of the innate equipment of the understanding. The idea of substance, moreover, includes permanence. So, *esse* is not *percipi:* to be is not to be perceived. But Kant still requires a connection with perception. ***Esse est posse percipi:*** To be is to be *perceivable.*

> For in the understanding alone is the unity of experience, in which all perceptions must have their assigned place, possible. In addition to accordance with the formal conditions of experience, the understanding requires a connection with some perception; but that which is connected with this perception is real, even although it is not immediately perceived.

We thus do not have to invoke God to show that our books do not disappear when we leave the room. The books can be perceived, even if they are not being perceived at the moment. That is a significant divergence from Berkeley. But Kant's view remains within the general framework of idealism. To be is to be capable of being perceived. To be, in other words, is to be capable of being brought into connection with the understanding. The general point is that 'is', 'exists', 'is possible', 'is necessary', and so on all relate objects to *us.*

What do we predicate of a thing when we say that it exists, according to Kant?

> The principles of modality are, however, not objectively synthetic, for the predicates of possibility, reality, and necessity do not in the least augment the concept of that of which they are affirmed, inasmuch as they contribute nothing to the representation of the object. But as they are, nevertheless, always synthetic, they are so merely subjectively. That is to say, they have a reflective power, and apply to the concept of a thing, of which, in other respects, they affirm nothing, the faculty of knowledge in which the concept originates and has its seat. So that if the concept merely agree with the formal conditions of experience, its object is called possible; if it is in connection with perception, and determined thereby, the object is real; if it is determined according to concepts by means of the connection of perceptions, the object is called necessary. . . .
>
> The principles of modality therefore predicate of a concept nothing more than the procedure of the faculty of knowledge which generated it. . . . reality is the conjunction of the thing with perception.

To say that something exists, then, is simply to say that it is perceivable: "Reality is the conjunction of the thing with perception." When Kant says, therefore, that external objects exist, he is saying that external objects are perceivable. He is relating those objects to a faculty of knowledge. And, as related to a faculty of knowledge, those objects are conditioned by sensibility and understanding. So, we perceive things existing in space and time, and conforming to the categories, the pure concepts of the understanding in terms of which we constitute objects. In short, we do not perceive things-in-themselves; we perceive things as our faculties of knowledge condition them. That is, Kant here proves the existence of phenomena, appearances, objects of experience—what Dignaga called internal objects—rather than *actual* objects, things-in-themselves. Appearances are projected by the mind in accord with the categories. It is significant that Kant's categories are not sorts of objects but concepts.

REALISM

Idealism is the view that everything is mind-dependent. **Realism,** in contrast, holds that some things are mind-independent. In particular, one is a *realist about* something if one holds that it exists independently of mind. Aristotle, as we have seen, presents a classically realist theory, and offers what remains one of the strongest arguments for realism:

> And, in general, if only the sensible exists, there would be nothing if animate things were not; for there would be no faculty of sense. Now the view that neither the sensible qualities nor the sensations would exist is doubtless true (for they are affections of the perceiver), but that the substrata which cause the sensation should not exist even apart from sensation is impossible. For sensation is surely not the sensation of itself, but there is something beyond the sensation, which must be prior to the sensation; for that which moves is prior in nature to that which is moved, and if they are correlative terms, this is no less the case. (IV, 5)

Dignaga, for example, defines actual objects as the causes of perception. In the end he argues that we have no reason to think they exist, for we cannot perceive them except as conditioned by our faculties of knowledge. Kant too speaks of sensibility receiving data from things-in-themselves, at one point in the first edition of the *Critique* slipping into talking about noumena as causes of perception. But he too finds that we have no way of experiencing them. He concludes not that they do not exist or even that we have no reason to assume they exist, but that existence and causation, as features of objects of experience conditioned by the categories, cannot meaningfully be applied to them. Things-in-themselves lie beyond the bounds of possible experience; we can say nothing about them. Small wonder that Kant's successor Georg Wilhelm Friedrich Hegel (1770–1831), the great German idealist, found Kant's talk of things-in-themselves useless and discarded the concept. But Aristotle offers an argument that there are things-in-themselves. Say that they are the causes of perception. Sensations, as Kant notes, are sensations *of* something. But that something must be prior to and independent of the sensation itself. If I perceive a cat, for example, I have a sensation, which is of something that exists quite independently of my sensation of it. The cat's existence does not depend on my perceiving it. Nor does it depend on the possibility of my perceiving it. The cat would exist just as well if I were blind or dead.

Argentinean writer Jorge Luis Borges (1899–1986) makes a similar argument more elegantly. He imagines a world, Tlön, that is thoroughly idealist:

> Hume noted for all time that Berkeley's arguments did not admit the slightest refutation nor did they cause the slightest conviction. This dictum is entirely correct in its application to the earth, but entirely false in Tlön. The nations of this planet are congenitally idealist. Their language and the derivations of their language—religion, letters, metaphysics—all presuppose idealism. The world for them is not a concourse of objects in space; it is a heterogeneous series of independent acts.[40]

[40]Jorge Luis Borges, "Tlön, Uqbar, Orbis Tertius," in *Labyrinths* (New York: New Directions, 1962), 8.

The languages of Tlön contain no nouns (for example, "moon"), for there are no real objects; there are only verbs ("It mooned") and adjectives ("round airy-light on dark"). There is no science except psychology. An eleventh-century heresiarch (that is, founder of a heresy, materialism) put forth a paradox seeming to show the existence of mind-independent objects:

> *On Tuesday, X crosses a deserted road and loses nine copper coins. On Thursday, Y finds in the road four coins, somewhat rusted by Wednesday's rain. On Friday, Z discovers three coins on the road. On Friday morning, X finds two coins in the corridor of his house.* The heresiarch would deduce from this story the reality—i.e., the continuity—of the nine coins which were recovered. *It is absurd* (he affirmed) *to imagine that four of the coins have not existed between Tuesday and Thursday, three between Tuesday and Friday afternoon, two between Tuesday and Friday morning. It is logical to think they have existed—at least in some secret way, hidden from the comprehension of men—at every moment of those three periods.*

Aristotle holds that the coins *must* have existed; Borges, only that it is *logical* to assume their existence. Realism, we might say, is the simplest explanation of the experiences we have. We have no direct experience of how things are unperceived; by definition, we perceive things as perceived. Perhaps they exist only when we perceive them. Perhaps they do not obey the laws of causation or even the laws of logic when we are not watching them. But it is far more reasonable and far simpler to assume that they continue to exist independently of us. Borges's story of Tlön shows how radically we would have to rethink our approach to the world if we truly believed that reality were dependent on mind and that to be is to be perceived. In the remainder of this chapter, we will consider three variants of realism, all of which rest on arguments similar to those of Aristotle and Borges.

Wang Fuzhi (Wang Fu-chih)

Wang Fuzhi (Wang Fu-chih; 1619–1692), a Chinese materialist and realist, was a contemporary of Descartes, Hobbes, and Newton. Working half a world away from them, without any contact with them or the scientific community that shaped their thought, he nevertheless advanced a materialism reminiscent of that of Hobbes. He attacked neo-Confucianism, which by then had become a form of idealism, from a strikingly modern perspective.

The son of a scholar, Wang Fuzhi got his civil service degree at twenty-three. Shortly afterward, he raised and led a militia trying to save the Ming emperor from the invading Manchus. At thirty-three, having been defeated, he retired and devoted himself to writing. Only in the nineteenth and twentieth centuries has his work been recognized and appreciated. He is now regarded as the initiator of Chinese philosophy's modern era.

Wang Fuzhi attacks neo-Confucianism, which holds that things are composed of **principle** (***li***) and **material force** (***chi***). The distinction is strikingly similar to that between form and matter in Aristotelian metaphysics. Neo-Confucians take principle as prior to and independent of material force. Indeed, the philosophy of the great Chinese neo-Confucian philosopher Zhuxi (Chu Hsi; 1130–1200), who maintained the independence of principle and material force, proved vulnerable to the idealistic attack of Wang Yangming (1472–1529; see Chapter 8) for precisely this reason. Just as Berkeley and Hume attack Locke's idea of substance as playing no important role, so Wang Yangming attacks Zhuxi's notion of material force as empty. Wang Yangming is happy to reduce everything to principle, which he locates within the mind.

But Wang Fuzhi rejects the priority of principle that earlier neo-Confucians assume. For him, principle depends on material force. We should think of principle, he maintains, not as an abstract law or set of laws but as the concrete order of the world—the arrangement of material objects. The Great Ultimate, the Principle of Nature or Heaven, and other abstractions of earlier neo-Confucian thought Wang likewise reduces to the concrete and material. "The world," Wang Fuzhi insists, "consists only of concrete things." [41]

Wang Fuzhi plays on the similar sound of two distinct Chinese words, written with distinct characters. *Chi* appears as "material force," in the sense of the earlier neo-Confucians. It is akin to matter and substance in Western philosophy but with the dynamic character of force or energy as well. *Chi* also appears as "concrete things," tangible objects. Concrete things have both principle and material force. Principle, however, has no independent status. There are only concrete entities. They have the principles they do because of the arrangements of their material parts.

> Principle depends on material force. When material force is strong, principle prevails. . . . All products in the world are results of refined and beautiful material force. . . .
>
> At bottom principle is not a finished product that can be grasped. It is invisible. The details and order of material force is principle that is visible. Therefore the first time there is any principle is when it is seen in material force. After principles have thus been found, they of course appear to become tendencies. We see principle only in the necessary aspects of tendencies.

Wang Fuzhi's view is thus akin to Locke's in many ways. Things have a real internal constitution that gives them the observable properties they have. Principle depends on material force just as, for Locke, secondary qualities depend on primary qualities and on real essences.

Wang Fuzhi has three arguments for his realism. The first, akin to Aristotle's, rests on the causal structure of the world. The world as it appears has a causal structure; there are causes and effects in regular, discernible patterns. Perception itself is part of that structure.

> All functions in the world are those of existing things. From their functions I know they possess substance. Why should we entertain any doubt? Function exists to become effect, and substance exists to become nature and feelings. Both substance and function exist, and each depends on the other to be concrete. Therefore all that fills the universe demonstrates the principle of mutual dependence.

---

[41] This and subsequent quotations from Wang Fuzhi are from *The Surviving Works of Wang Fu-chih,* in Wing-tsit Chan (ed.), *A Source Book in Chinese Philosophy* (Princeton: Princeton University Press, 1963).

The second argument attacks the standard argument for idealism. Idealists typically infer the nonexistence of mind-independent objects from their imperceptibility. Idealists assume that to be is to be perceived or at least perceivable. But why should we accept that? What licenses the inference from 'X cannot be perceived' to 'X does not exist'?

> Because the eye cannot see a thing or the ear cannot hear it, people hastily say that it does not exist. They are obscured because they follow their inferior faculties (eye and ear). Good and evil can be seen and heard but that which produces good and evil cannot be seen or heard. Therefore people hastily say that there is neither good nor evil.

Indeed, given Wang Fuzhi's account of material force, we would expect that the causes of observable things are typically not themselves observable. But that does not make them unreal. Indeed, the observable depends on them, which makes them more real than what we can observe.

Finally, Wang Fuzhi criticizes Buddhism and its doctrine of no-self. As we saw in Chapter 4, the arguments against the self parallel arguments against the existence of material objects (for example, King Milinda's chariot). So, arguments against the self and arguments against substance stand or fall together. But Wang Fuzhi finds arguments against the self—no pun intended—self-defeating.

> Those who speak of non-self do so from the point of view of the self. If there were no self, who is going to deny the self? It is obvious that to speak of non-self is to utter extravagant and evasive words.

Wang Fuzhi's materialism leads him to reject the ethical outlooks of both Zhuxi and Wang Yang-Ming. They, following Mencius, see desire as clouding the otherwise clear mirror of the mind. That clarity however relies on principle: the moral mind is the assemblage of principles that constitute the Nature. Consequently Wang Fuzhi rejects the image of the mind as mirror. He also rejects the idea that right action consists in putting principle before desire. His materialism might suggest that he has no place for ethics at all; but—he argues instead—the Way, like principle in general, depends on material force. Moral principle does not stand opposed to desire; it depends on and is found in desire. Wang Fuzhi takes from Daoism the idea that things naturally tend toward improvement, and that—to put the point in neo-Confucian language—principle is inherently good. This injects the realm of values into his materialistic system. Unlike the Daoists, however, Wang Fuzhi does not deduce an ethics of noninterference. People must make choices and in making them should strive for the Mean (see Chapter 7). Desire in itself is not wrong but stems from material force:

> . . . Wherever human desires are found, the Principle of Nature is found.

American Realism

Due to the arguments of Berkeley, Hume, Kant, and Hegel, idealism swept throughout Europe and the United States during the nineteenth century. The dawn of a new century, however, brought forth a rebirth of realism in England and America. Six influential American philosophers—Edwin Holt, Walter Marvin, William Pepperel Montague, Ralph Barton Perry, Walter Pitkin, and E. G. Spaulding—published "The Program and First Platform of Six Realists" in 1910 to announce their opposition to the dominant idealist and pragmatist camps. While short on argument, the paper is nevertheless a classic statement of realism.

What is realism?

> HOLT:
>
> 1. The entities (objects, facts, *et caet.*) under study in logic, mathematics, and the physical sciences are not mental in any usual or proper meaning of the word 'mental'.
> 2. The being and nature of these entities are in no sense conditioned by their being known.
>
> MONTAGUE:
>
> 1. Realism holds that things known may continue to exist unaltered when they are not known, or that things may pass in and out of the cognitive relation without prejudice to their reality, or that the existence of a thing is not correlated with or dependent upon the fact that anybody experiences it, perceives it, conceives it, or is in any way aware of it.[42]

Montague criticizes three arguments in favor of idealism, claiming that each rests on a fallacy. He attacks the argument that the mind can have for its direct object only its own ideas or states as wrongheaded: "A knowing process is never its own object, but is rather the means by which some other object is known." He criticizes (what he takes to be) Berkeley's argument, which starts from a truism, "We can only know that objects exist, when they are known," and infers an absurdity: "We know that objects can only exist when they are known." In general, Montague says, idealists note correctly that we can gain knowledge of the world only through experience but incorrectly infer that "the objects known are constructs or products of our perceptual experience."

Recall the argument for idealism that we considered earlier:

1. We can know a thing only by making it an object of consciousness.
2. Any object of consciousness is conditioned by consciousness.
3. So we can know only what is conditioned by consciousness.
4. But anything conditioned by consciousness is mind-dependent.
5. So we can know only what is mind-dependent.
6. We have reason to believe something exists only if we can have knowledge of it.
7. So we have reason to believe that a thing exists only if it is mind-dependent.

The six realists focus their attack on premises 2 and 4. We have no reason to believe that objects of consciousness are conditioned by consciousness. Indeed, they directly deny it.

This gets them into trouble and earns their view the moniker *naive realism,* for they hold, in Perry's words, that "physical nature, for example is, under certain circumstances, directly present in consciousness." The stereotype of the view, at any

[42] This and subsequent quotations from the six realists are from E. B. Holt, et al., "The Program and First Platform of Six Realists," *Journal of Philosophy* 7, 1910.

rate, is that according to the realists the object of perception is not a representation but the object itself. If so, however, how can we ever be mistaken? How is error possible? And how can we reconcile this view with the atomic theory of matter, which implies that the objects of experience are not what they seem?

To some extent, this complaint is unfair. Perry prefaces his remark about direct presence in consciousness with the caution,

> The object or content of consciousness is any entity in so far as it is responded to by another entity in a specific manner exhibited by the reflex nervous system.

And he then continues:

> The specific response which determines an entity to be content of consciousness, does not directly modify such entities otherwise than to endow them with this content status. In other words, consciousness selects from a field of entities which it does not create.

The picture, then, is this. An object—a cat, say—affects our organs of sense. As a result, information is sent to our central nervous system, resulting in a perception. The form that perception takes depends on the nervous system, and may differ in various ways from the object itself. Our sensation of the cat may have features not present in the cat itself. Nevertheless, it is a perception *of that object.* The cat does not change as a result of our perceiving it. It is not constituted by our perception of it. As Spaulding puts it, "the entity is, in its being, behavior, and character, independent of the knowing."

The crux of the realist critique of idealism, then, is the attack on premises 1, 2, and 4 jointly. We cannot maintain that we can know objects only by making them objects of consciousness; that they are thereby conditioned; and that any object conditioned by consciousness is mind-dependent. The idealist argument relies on an ambiguity in 'object of consciousness'—the same ambiguity that Dignaga notes by distinguishing actual objects from internal objects. We can know an actual object such as a cat only by making it an object of consciousness—by having a corresponding internal object. Consciousness conditions something in this process, since what we perceive differs in some ways from the object itself. But the *cat* is not conditioned; it does not change. The *internal object* is conditioned. It, if anything, thus becomes mind-dependent. Thus interpreted, the idealist's argument shows that internal objects are mind-dependent—which no realist would want to deny—but shows nothing whatever about actual objects, what Kant dubs "things-in-themselves." The realist can continue to hold that they are mind-independent. Moreover, the idealist claim that they cannot be known is absurd: they *are* known, precisely through the cognitive process just described. We are not in any sense trapped inside our own heads. As Montague concludes,

> Cognition belongs to the same world as that of its objects. It has its place in the order of nature. There is nothing transcendental or supernatural about it.

Here, then, is another way to see the realists' argument. Locke distinguishes real from nominal essences. The nominal essence, which corresponds to a definition, is a creature of the understanding. But the real essence is not; it stems from the real internal constitution of an object. It determines the object's properties; it makes the object what it is. Aristotle and Aquinas hold that we know a sort of object by grasping its essence. Once we distinguish real from nominal essence, however, we must ask, Which essence? Idealists such as Kant argue, in effect, that we have no choice but to grasp the nominal essence. It is intelligible, for we construct it. The real essence lies beyond experience; we cannot know it. The realists' response is that we study knowledge just as we study any other phenomenon in nature. Our scientific theories give us accounts of what makes objects what they are. We have explanations of the properties of water and gold based on their microphysical constitutions. Similarly, we have accounts of the human cognitive system. We know things in the fullest sense by grasping real essences. We do not perceive them directly—but that does not prevent us from having knowledge of them. We know them through scientific method: We construct hypotheses, test them against experience, revise our hypotheses, and test again. The atomic theory of matter is precisely an account of the real essences of things. The causes of our perceptions, then, are not inaccessible to us, even though they are inaccessible to our sense organs. We know about them by means of natural science.

Bertrand Russell

British philosopher Bertrand Russell (1872–1970; see Chapter 1), following his Cambridge colleague G. E. Moore (1873–1958), also grew disaffected with idealism. Moore argued that its central argument relies on an equivocation in a way similar to that just outlined. Russell notes the importance of the question of the existence of external, mind-independent objects. If they do not exist, we have no reason to think that there is anything or anyone else in the universe:

> We shall be left alone in a desert—it may be that the whole outer world is nothing but a dream, and that we alone exist.[43]

Russell points out, not only the significance of the issue, but also the number of things a mind-independent universe explains that the idealist would need to explain separately. Smith and Jones both look at the cat; they have cat-type sensations. We want to say that they see the *same* cat, and that these sensations are of the *same thing.* If there is a mind-independent cat they both see, this is easy. But, on idealist premises, how do we explain that Smith's sensation and Jones's sensation are of the same object? The same problem occurs when one person sees something at different times. Smith sees the cat. She looks away, then turns to see the cat again. We want to say that her sensations are of the same cat. But if there is no cat independently of her sensations, how do we explain that? Moreover, the sensations of the cat relate to each other in lawlike ways. We see the cat become bored, stretch, fall asleep, wake up, get hungry, eat, etc. If the cat has no independent existence, however, how do we explain the connections among these various perceptions? And the complexity of the relations of the cat's perceived states is nothing compared to the complexity of those of another human being.

There is no logical contradiction in the idea that we alone exist and that everything is really a dream. But, Russell says, it is a bizarre and vastly more complicated

---

[43] Bertrand Russell, *The Problems of Philosophy.* (London: Williams and Norgate, 1912).

hypothesis than "the common-sense hypothesis that there really are objects independent of us, whose action on us causes our sensations." The belief that there are mind-independent physical objects is *instinctive,* Russell says; it is not the product of metaphysical argument but part of our commonsense view of the world. We sometimes have reason to reject instinctive beliefs. Einstein's theory of relativity, for example, implies that many of our commonsense beliefs about objects, lengths, and so on are strictly speaking incorrect. But it takes very powerful arguments for us to reject those beliefs. And even then we seek to explain why we hold such beliefs and have managed to survive in the world for millennia while doing so. Dignaga, Berkeley, Hume, Kant, and other idealists have provided no such arguments. Russell here makes a recommendation that applies across the board, not just in metaphysics: Other things being equal, use common sense.

SUMMARY

The central task of metaphysics is to explain what the world is, what it consists of, and how its constituents relate to each other. Plato insists that abstract forms are more real than the objects of the senses. Aristotle, Aquinas, and Indian metaphysicians of the Vaisesika school put their emphasis on individual substances. Descartes and Locke distinguish primary qualities such as extension and motion, which are objective, from secondary qualities such as colors and sounds, which are response-dependent and best understood as powers to produce certain sensations. Idealists such as Dignaga, Sankara, Berkeley, and Kant reject this distinction, finding everything to be response-dependent (and thus mind-dependent). Finally, realists such as Wang Fuzhi, E. B. Holt, William Pepperel Montague, and Bertrand Russell defend our commonsense conception of the world as existing independently of us.

REVIEW QUESTIONS

1. How does Plato's image of the divided line relate to the cave allegory?
2. How do Philo, Origen, and Augustine develop Plato's theory? What role does God play in each?
3. What is a substance, according to Aristole?
4. Compare the Vaisesika theory of categories with Aristotle's.
5. What is an essential property? What is essential to human beings? To you?
6. What is a thing's essence? Its quiddity? Its nature? Are they the same, according to Aristotle and Aquinas? Do you agree?
7. Explain Dignaga's distinction between actual and internal objects, and compare it to Kant's distinction between phenomena and noumena.
8. How does Locke distinguish primary from secondary qualities? What objections do Berkeley and Hume raise against that distinction?
9. Explain Locke's distinction between real and nominal essences. How does it relate to Aquinas's distinction between essence, quiddity, and nature?

10. What is realism? Describe and evaluate the arguments for it advanced by Aristotle, Borges, Wang Fuzhi, Russell, and the American realists.

Terms for Review

actual object (*alambana*) The cause of a perception; in Dignaga, atoms.
***alambana* (actual object)** The cause of a perception; in Dignaga, atoms.
***artha* (internal object)** What a perception is (or appears to be) a perception *of.*
atomic theory The theory that observable physical objects are made up of microscopic atoms in various combinations.
category In Aristotle, a general kind of thing to which linguistic expressions refer. In Kant, a pure concept of the understanding; an innate cognitive ability of a very general kind; a possible logical form of an object.
cause Aristotle distinguishes four kinds of causes or explanations: *formal,* relying on essence or definition (Socrates is human because he is a rational animal); *material,* relying on matter (Socrates is human because he has a certain bio-chemical composition); *efficient,* relying on a causal chain of events (Socrates is human because his parents were human and produced him in the usual way); and *final,* relying on some goal, purpose, or function (Socrates is human in order to . . .).
***chi* (material force)** In neo-Confucianism, something akin to matter but with the dynamic character of force or energy. *Chi* is also used for material objects, that is, concrete, tangible things.
conceptualism The view that universals are mind-dependent.
designated matter A specific bit of matter, for example, “this flesh and that blood.”
esse est percipi To be is to be perceived; a primary thesis of Berkeley.
esse est posse percipi To be is to be perceivable; a consequence of Kant’s transcendental idealism.
essence The properties necessary to a thing, without which it would not be what it is.
essential property A property necessary to a thing or kind of thing; without the property, it would not be that thing (or kind of thing).
forms In Plato, abstract universals that exist independently of us. They make things what they are, and they enable us to think about things as they are.
haecceity Individual essence; “this-ness.”
illumination In Augustine, what enables us to know the forms. God illumines the intelligible world, making it intelligible to us.
internal object (*artha*) What a perception is (or appears to be) a perception *of.*
***li* (principle)** In neo-Confucianism, something (akin to form) prior to and independent of material force.
material force (*chi*) In neo-Confucianism, something akin to matter but with the dynamic character of force or energy.
monism The view that there is ultimately only one fundamental kind of stuff.
nature What makes a thing what it is; it is that *by virtue of which* a thing is what it is—a human, a river, a building, or whatever. The nature of a thing not only explains why it is what it is; it is also what we grasp in thinking about the thing.
nominal essence In Locke, the quiddity of a thing or kind of thing, that is, what a definition of it would express. It generally makes use of secondary qualities.

nominalism The view that universals do not exist at all, that everything is particular.

ontology The study of what there is.

particular A thing that cannot have multiple instances.

primary quality A property inseparable from body; the qualities matter has according to the atomic theory of matter.

principle (*li*) In neo-Confucianism, something (akin to form) prior to and independent of material force.

principle of individuation What makes one object differ from another; in Aquinas, designated matter.

quiddity From the Latin *quidditas*, literally, "whatness," which in turn is meant to capture the Greek phrase meaning "what it is." A quiddity is what, in reality, a definition corresponds to; it is a definition *in re* (in the thing). The quiddity of *x* is what corresponds to *x*'s definition in the world.

real essence In Locke, the nature of a thing; that which makes it what it is. It stems from the real internal constitution of the object or kind.

real internal constitution In Locke, the internal structure of a thing or kind according to the atomic theory of mattter.

realism (or platonism) The view that universals are real and mind-independent.

realism The view that something exists independently of mind.

response-dependent quality A quality that consists in generating a certain kind of response in a perceiver.

secondary quality Effects of primary qualities on our sense organs and nervous systems.

superimposition In Sankara, "The apparent presentation, in the form of remembrance, to consciousness of something previously observed, in some other things. . . . [in other words,] the apparent presentation of the attributes of one thing in another thing."

undesignated matter Matter in general, for example, "flesh and blood."

universal An object that may be *multiply instantiated*, that is, have instances at different times and places.

For Further Reading

For readings on Plato, Aquinas, and Russell, see Chapter 1; on Augustine and Descartes, Chapter 2; on Locke, Hume, Kant, and Indian philosophies, Chapter 3.

The standard work on Philo is Harry A. Wolfson, *Philo: Foundations of Religious Philosophy in Judaism, Christianity, and Islam* (Cambridge: Harvard University Press, 1947). On Origen, see Henry Chadwick, *Early Christian Thought and the Classical Tradition* (Oxford: Clarendon, 1966); Joseph Trigg, *Origen* (New York: Routledge, 1998); and Peter Widdicombe, *The Fatherhood of God from Origen to Athanasius* (Oxford: Clarendon Press, 1994).

There is a vast literature on Aristotle. Good places to start are W. D. Ross, *Aristotle* (London: Methuen, 1923); Jonathan Barnes, *Aristotle* (Oxford: Oxford University Press, 1982); Terrance Irwin, *Aristotle's First Principles* (Oxford: Oxford University

Press, 1988); and Jonathan Barnes (ed.), *The Cambridge Companion to Aristotle* (Cambridge: Cambridge University Press, 1995).

On Berkeley, see Jonathan Bennett, *Locke, Berkeley, Hume: Central Themes* (Oxford: Oxford University Press, 1971); G. J. Warnock, *Berkeley* (London: Penguin, 1953); George Pitcher, *Berkeley* (London: Routledge and Kegan Paul, 1977); and J. O. Urmson, *Berkeley* (Oxford: Oxford University Press, 1982).

I know that He exists.
Somewhere—in Silence—
He has hid his rare life
From our gross eyes.
—Emily Dickinson, 338

CHAPTER 6

God

Few philosophical issues interest ordinary people more than the one that forms the title of this chapter. Indeed, many people first enter philosophy by trying to address it. Many of the world's greatest philosophers, having it as a central motivation, try to give rational arguments for or against God's existence. Others see their chief task as explicating what God is or outlining what we can and cannot know about God. Of course, many people see religious belief as a matter of faith alone; they deny that any purely rational arguments can justify or contradict belief in God. Immanuel Kant, for example, said that he denied knowledge to make room for faith. But many religious thinkers, like Emily Dickinson in the poem on the left, hold that we can know or at least have good reason to believe that God exists. Other thinkers contend that the existence of evil in the world shows that God does not exist. Even those who see belief in God as a matter of faith alone find it important to understand—to the extent human beings can understand—who or what God is and how the world can exhibit intricate design, shining beauty, and horrific evil all at once.

WHAT IS RELIGION?

In the early dialogues, Socrates asks what courage or friendship or piety or self-control are. Someone gives him an example. In the *Laches,* for example, Socrates asks what courage is, and Laches responds, "Staying at your post and not running away." (See Chapter 7.) This does not satisfy Socrates. He wants to know what makes this an instance of courage.

Similarly, we might ask, What is religion? Everyone will agree on many examples. Everyone will agree, that is, that Judaism, Christianity, and Islam are religions. Almost everyone will agree that Hinduism, Buddhism, Confucianism, Daoism, Shinto, and various African and Native American tribal belief systems are religions. But what do they all have in common? What makes them all religions? It is surprisingly hard to say.

We might list various things that religions seem to have in common. The first problem we encounter is that, while most religions have most of these features, few have all of them. The second and more fundamental is, What goes on the list? Religions have infinitely many things in common; how do we decide which are important? We might begin by observing that religions are systems of belief and practice. A religious person believes certain things and does certain things. Some religions stress belief, while others stress action. Some assign them very different roles. But all religions seem to involve both belief and practice.

We might continue by listing some things that religious people from various traditions find central: belief in a supernatural being, a being who transcends the world (for example, God); belief in intelligent beings superior to humans (for example, angels or ancient Greek or Roman gods on Mount Olympus); belief in an afterlife; belief in a moral code; belief that the moral code is endorsed and enforced by a superior being; practices of prayer, worship, and ritual; and respect for sacred stories or writings containing revealed truths. Do all the religions listed above share these features? Answering these questions sometimes requires making difficult judgments. Still, we might express the overall picture of some main religions in a table:

	Judaism	*Christianity*	*Islam*	*Hinduism*	*Buddhism*	*Confucianism*	*Daoism*	*Tribal rel.*	*Olympian*
Supernatural being	Y	Y	Y	Y?	N	?	Y?	Y?	N
Superior being	Y	Y	Y	Y	N	?	Y	Y	Y
Afterlife	Y	Y	Y	?	?	?	?	Y	Y
Morality	Y	Y	Y	Y	Y	Y	Y	?	N
Sanction	Y	Y	Y	Y	N	?	?	N	N
Worship	Y	Y	Y	Y	Y	Y	Y	?	Y
Sacred texts	Y	Y	Y	Y	Y	Y	Y	?	Y

There is an obvious oversimplification here; tribal religions vary considerably, and different sects of various religions differ from others on some of these points. Still, we can see that nothing figures in *all* these religions. Only worship rituals and sacred texts figure in everything other than tribal religion. It is tempting, then, to define religion in terms of worship or sacred texts. We might, for example, say that a religion is a system of beliefs and practices that includes worship as an integral part. But that seems peculiar for several reasons. First, many people of various faiths consider themselves religious although they do not participate in worship. They may believe in God, for example, without going to church. Second, what is worship? If we define religion in terms of religious practice, then what makes a practice religious? How does going to church differ from going to the post office, to the grocery store, to a concert, to a baseball game, or to school? It is not clear that we can answer that question without referring to beliefs and what those beliefs are about.

The same problems afflict any attempt to define religion in terms of respect for sacred and revealed texts. We must allow for myths, stories, legends, and the like to account for the fact that in some cultures the sacred texts are transmitted orally rather than in writing. This seems to capture all the major religions, including many tribal religions (although, as always, it is dangerous to generalize). But we encounter the same problem as in defining religion in terms of worship. What makes a text sacred? How do the Torah, the Bible, the Koran, the sermons of the Buddha, the *Analects,* and the *Dao de Jing* differ from Plato's *Republic,* the plays of Shakespeare, or *A Thousand and One Nights*? We seem to be back where we started.

Beliefs

Yet trying to define religion in terms of belief also generates puzzles, such as the following four:

1. Suppose we say that a religion is a system of beliefs and practices centered on belief in the existence of God, a supernatural, all-knowing, all-powerful being. That

fits Judaism, Christianity, and Islam well. But it is not a good fit with Hinduism and Daoism. As we shall see in the next section, Brahman and the Dao share some features of the Judeo-Christian-Muslim God but not others. Brahman and the Dao, for example, are omnipresent and underlie everything that is. But it is not clear whether they are supernatural, all-knowing, or all-powerful. On some conceptions, at any rate, each is more like a *substratum* than a *ruler* of the world.

This definition, moreover, does not fit the other religions in our table at all. Theravada Buddhism denies the existence of any supernatural being. Confucius refuses to speak of the Ways of Heaven. No Greek or Roman god is all-powerful. And tribal religions vary on whether there is any supreme being.

2. We might capture Hinduism, ancient Greek and Roman religion, and some tribal religions by saying that religion is a system of beliefs and practices centered on the existence of one or more intelligent, superior beings. But that still omits Buddhism and Confucianism, while leaving the status of Daoism unclear. There are scholars—and indeed practicing Buddhists, Confucians, and Daoists—who would say that this is an appropriate omission, for those systems should be viewed as philosophies rather than religions. Certainly there are philosophical systems associated with them. But if we treat Buddhism, Confucianism, and Daoism as philosophies only, we cannot understand their rituals of prayer and worship. Nor can we understand why Buddhists, Confucians, and Daoists treat their basic texts as sacred. Platonists, Aristotelians, Kantians, and other philosophical schools subscribe to a system of philosophical beliefs, but they do not construct temples to their favorite philosopher or consider his writings sacred. So viewing Buddhism, Confucianism, and Daoism solely as philosophies seems to omit something very important.

3. We might define religion in terms of adherence to a moral code. But it is hard to discern any morality in the behavior of the Olympian gods and goddesses. And the myths and stories of some tribal religions seem independent of any moral code. Many myths and stories, for example, concern the creation of the world, the creation of human beings, or the origin of death. Often there is no evident moral significance to these stories. Just as frequently, they involve superior beings behaving in immoral ways. Moreover, as we shall see in Chapters 7 and 8, secular philosophers have advanced many different moral codes. It would be strange to make them all religious by definition. If we define religion in terms of a moral code backed by divine sanction, then we can exclude these secular moralities. But we also exclude Buddhism, some tribal religions, and ancient Greek and Roman religion, while leaving the status of Confucianism and Daoism in doubt.

4. We might define religion in terms of belief in an afterlife. But some religions, such as Confucianism or Daoism, decline to speculate on the afterlife (officially, at any rate, in their sacred texts, although some beliefs about life after death have sprouted informally from them). Others, such as Hinduism and Buddhism, speak of reincarnation, which implies an afterlife, but a "this-worldly" one: eventually the process of rebirth ends. But these religions speak of the final afterlife—after the entire series of births and rebirths—as liberation from the cycle of birth and death as an

extinguishing, or in terms of metaphors such as "rain falling into a river." It is not clear to what extent we survive *as individuals* after death in such views.

Attitudes

We might seek to define religion not in terms of the beliefs or practices they involve but in terms of the attitudes of those who partake in them. German Romantic philosopher Friedrich Schleiermacher (1768–1834), the founder of hermeneutics and religious studies, outspoken advocate of women's rights, translator of Plato, and co-founder of the University of Berlin, pioneered this approach. He suggests that religious beliefs and practices are those accompanied by a *feeling of utter dependence.* This does seem to capture something important that all religions have in common. We worship something we think to be greater than ourselves, on whom we depend.

Still, we might worry that Schleiermacher's definition is too broad. Small children may feel utterly dependent on their parents, but do they worship them? Adults may feel utterly dependent on a spouse, a boss, a doctor, a judge, or an IRS auditor without the presence of anything religious. Moreover, Schleiermacher's definition makes religiosity a purely subjective matter. But if God exists, demands adherence to a moral code, and so on, that seems to have religious significance no matter how we feel about it.

German theologian Rudolf Otto (1869–1937), founder of the comparative study of religions, traveled extensively in Asia before settling down in a Chair of Theology at Marburg. Otto agrees with Schleiermacher that one must begin by defining the religious attitude. He criticizes attempts to understand religion in purely rational terms. But he thinks Schleiermacher misses the most important feature of that attitude. What distinguishes religious feelings from all others, he holds, is *the idea of the holy:* an awareness of what he calls the **numinous,** the holy. This attitude cannot be defined in other terms. The "numinous state of mind," he writes,

> is perfectly *sui generis* and irreducible to any other; and therefore, like every primary and elementary datum, while it admits of being discussed, it cannot be strictly defined. There is only one way to help another to an understanding of it. He must be guided and led on by consideration and discussion of the matter through the ways of his own mind, until he reach the point at which 'the numinous' in him perforce begins to stir, to start into life and into consciousness. . . . In other words our *X* cannot, strictly speaking, be taught, it can only be evoked, awakened in the mind; as everything that comes 'of the spirit' must be awakened.[1]

So Otto sets out to try to stir this feeling in the minds of his readers.

> The reader is invited to direct his mind to a moment of deeply felt religious experience, as little as possible qualified by other forms of consciousness. Whoever cannot do this, whoever knows no such moments in his experience, is requested no read no farther. . . . (8)

[1] This and subsequent passages from Rudolf Otto are from *The Idea of the Holy* (London: Oxford University Press, 1923), 7.

He compares one who cannot recall any religious experience to one who has never had aesthetic experience—has never appreciated a work of art or music or even admired a beautiful sunset. Such a person is not to blame, but there is nothing to be gained by trying to discuss art with him or her. Similarly, the person without religious experience is not to blame, but there is nothing to be gained by discussing religion with him or her. As an example of religious experience, he cites American philosopher William James (1842–1910; see Chapter 1):

> The perfect stillness of the night was thrilled by a more solemn silence. The darkness held a presence that was all the more felt because it was not seen. I could not any more have doubted that *He* was there than that I was. Indeed, I felt myself to be, if possible, the less real of the two.[2]

Otto analyzes religious experience as having several elements: (a) *awefulness:* a shudder, a feeling of trembling, of awe, even of dread; (b) *overpoweringness:* a feeling of utter dependence, as Schleiermacher has it; an appreciation of the overwhelming majesty of God; (c) *energy:* a feeling of vitality and urgency; and, most importantly, (d) *the wholly other:* a feeling of mystery, amazement, astonishment:

> Taken in the religious sense, that which is 'mysterious' is—to give it perhaps the most striking expression—the 'wholly other' . . . , that which is quite beyond the sphere of the usual, the intelligible, and the familiar, which therefore falls quite outside the limits of the 'canny', and is contrasted with it, filling the mind with blank wonder and astonishment. (26)

In this view, religion is a system of beliefs and practices accompanied by religious experience.

German-born American philosopher and theologian Paul Tillich (1886–1965) proposes another influential definition of religion. Tillich was ordained a minister in the Prussian Evangelical Church at age twenty-six and shortly thereafter served as a German army chaplain during World War I. He taught at a variety of German universities before being fired by the Nazis in 1933. He came to the United States and taught at Columbia, Union Theological Seminary, Harvard, and the University of Chicago. Tillich, following Schleiermacher and Otto, defines religion in subjective terms. That is, he holds that whether a system of beliefs and practices is religious depends on the attitudes of those participating in it. The characteristic religious attitude, Tillich says, is **faith.** But what is faith? He identifies it with **ultimate concern.**

What does Tillich mean by 'ultimate concern'?

> Faith is the state of being ultimately concerned: the dynamics of faith are the dynamics of man's ultimate concern. Man, like every living being, is concerned about many things, above all about those which condition his very existence, such as food and shelter. But man, in contrast to other living beings, has spiritual concerns—cognitive, aesthetic, social, political. Some of them are urgent, often extremely urgent, and each of them as well as the vital concerns can claim ultimacy for a human life or the life of a social group. If it claims ultimacy it demands the total surrender of him who accepts this claim, and it promises total fulfillment even if all other claims have to be subjected to it or rejected in its name.[3]

[2] William James, *Varieties of Religious Experience* (New York: Longmans, Green, 1902).

[3] This and subsequent quotations from Paul Tillich are from *The Dynamics of Faith* (New York: Harper and Row, 1957), 1.

An ultimate concern, then, is more than something you care about deeply. It demands your total surrender; you are willing to give up everything else for it. And it promises total fulfillment, even if you do give up everything else.

Tillich sees religion as essentially symbolic. In faith, a finite being expresses its awareness of an infinite being, a "wholly other" on which it depends. The finite being cannot comprehend the infinite; at best it can seek symbols of it.

> Man's ultimate concern must be expressed symbolically, because symbolic language alone is able to express the ultimate. . . . Symbols have one characteristic in common with signs; they point beyond themselves to something else. (41)

But symbols differ from signs, for they participate in what they symbolize. (The flag that symbolizes a country, for example, is also part of its history.) Symbols "open up levels of reality which otherwise are closed to us" (42). We cannot produce them intentionally; they stem from the unconscious and are not merely conventional. Finally, they grow when the situation is ripe for them and die when change makes them unnecessary or unsuccessful. On Tillich's view, then, every religion exhibits faith, ultimate concern, and symbolism.

CONCEPTS OF GOD

If Otto and Tillich are right, then all religions inspire religious experience—feelings of awe and wonder at something wholly other—and faith, an ultimate concern that we can express fully only through symbolism. The major world religions do seem to share these features. Most of them, moreover, have a concept of God, a supernatural being toward whom religious feelings are directed. God is the "wholly other," the object of ultimate concern, the one in whom the religious person has faith. But what is God? In Tillich's view, we can express God's nature only through symbols, for our finite minds cannot grasp God's infinite reality. Indeed, religions adopt various symbols for God, which play important roles in religious belief and practice. Through those symbols, and through what sacred texts say about God, we can isolate several distinct concepts of God.

Classical Theism

The **classical Western concept of God** is that of **classical theism:** a being who is almighty (omnipotent), all-knowing (omniscient), eternal, omnipresent, transcendent, and compassionate. The Jewish scriptures, which constitute the Christian Old Testament, express such a concept of God, as do the Christian New Testament and the Koran:

> OMNIPOTENCE
>
> When Abram was ninety-nine years old the Lord appeared to Abram, and said to him, "I am God Almighty; walk before me, and be blameless." (*Genesis* 17:1)
>
> Jesus looked at them and said, "With men it is impossible, but not with God; for all things are possible with God." (*Mark* 10:27)
>
> God is the Creator of everything, and He is the One, the Omnipotent. (*Sura* 13)

OMNISCIENCE

. . . he looks to the ends of the earth, and sees everything under the heavens. (*Job* 28:24)

So God makes clear to you His signs; and God is All-knowing, All-wise. (*Sura* 24)

ETERNITY

For thus says the high and lofty One who inhabits eternity, whose name is Holy. . . . (*Isaiah* 57:15)

There is no God but He, the Living, the Everlasting. (*Sura* 2)

OMNIPRESENCE

Whither shall I go from thy Spirit? Or whither shall I flee from thy presence? If I ascend to heaven, thou art there! If I make my bed in Sheol, thou art there! (*Psalms* 139:7–8)

Him who created the earth and the high heavens; the All-compassionate sat himself upon the Throne; to Him belongs all that is in the heavens and the earth and all that is between them, and all that is underneath the soil. (*Sura* 2)

TRANSCENDENCE

To whom then will you liken God, or what likeness compare with him? . . . To whom then will you compare me, that I should be like him? Says the Holy One. (*Isaiah* 40:18, 25)

He is God; there is no god but He. He is the King, the All-holy, the All-peaceable, the All-faithful, the All-preserver, the All-mighty, the All-compeller, the All-sublime. . . . (*Sura* 59)

COMPASSION

For the mountains may depart and the hills be removed, but my steadfast love shall not depart from you, and my covenant of peace shall not be removed, says the Lord, who has compassion on you. (*Isaiah* 54:10)

For God so loved the world that he gave his only son, that all who believe in him might not perish, but have eternal life. (*John* 3:16)

The All-merciful has taught the Koran. He created man and He has taught him the Explanation. . . . (*Sura* 55)

The classical conception is common to almost all the philosophers to be discussed in later sections of this chapter. It is adopted and elaborated by Jewish philosophers such as Philo and Maimonides; Christian philosophers such as Anselm and Aquinas; and Islamic philosophers such as Avicenna and Averroës. Most philosophical debate concerning the existence of God has centered on classical theism and its classical conception of God.

Interestingly, African tribal religions largely share the classical concept of God. They have a very different concept of religion—worship, for example, plays no significant role, and ancestors and spirits of various kinds do—but the concept of God strikes Western ears as familiar. Kwasi Wiredu, a contemporary philosopher from Ghana, writes:

> African worldviews usually, though not invariably, feature a supreme being who is responsible for the world order. Generally, that being is explicitly conceived to be omniscient, omnibenevolent and, subject to a rider to be entered in due course, omnipotent. . . . A sense of dependency, trust, and unconditional reverence is almost everywhere evident in African attitudes to the supreme being.[4]

Classical theism, then, is not only a Western concept, though its best-known elaborations are Western.

Other Concepts of God

Other religions have somewhat different conceptions of God. And dissidents have expressed different conceptions even within Judaism, Christianity, and Islam. Perhaps the most common and influential nonclassical conception has been the **via negativa,** the "negative way" of presenting the nature of God. According to mystical theologians, it is misleading to speak of God as almighty, all-knowing, compassionate, and so on. We understand power, knowledge, and compassion in finite terms as applying to people and things. But God's power, knowledge, and compassion are infinite. The classical theist holds that we can understand infinite power, knowledge, and compassion by analogy with the finite instances of the notions that we encounter. The mystic denies it: We cannot say anything about God in a literal and fully meaningful way because God transcends everything we can say. God's nature is ineffable; it lies beyond the power of language. The most we can do is say what God is *not.* We must take scriptural and philosophical descriptions of God as poetic evocations pointing our minds toward God's indescribable nature. Tillich recognizes the power of this view in saying that all religion relies on symbols, for no one can adequately put God into words.

Deism is the view that God exists and created the world but has had no further interaction with it. Deists differ from classical theists in denying the possibility of miracles. In the deist conception, God created the world and established its laws but then has allowed those laws to operate without intervention. This contradicts Judaism, Christianity, and Islam, for all depend on miracles—at the very least, the miracle of divine revelation (to Moses, Jesus, or Mohammed, for example). Moses, Elijah, Elisha, and Jesus all work miracles; Elisha and Jesus even bring people back from the dead. Jesus himself is resurrected from the dead. Without these miracles, ideas of God's revelation and relationship with the world have little content. Deism also makes a practical difference, for prayer and worship are hard to understand if God does not interact with the world.

Pantheism holds that God is everything; that is, that God exists and moreover is the *only* thing that exists. **Panentheism** holds that everything is God, but that God

[4] This and subsequent quotations from Wiredu are from "African Religions from a Philosophical Point of View," in P. Quinn and C. Taliaferro (ed.), *A Companion to the Philosophy of Religion* (Cambridge: Blackwell, 1997), 34–42.

also transcends the world. These positions sound similar. Both identify God with the totality of what exists. But in fact they have very different implications. The pantheist, contending that God is everything, in effect identifies God and nature. The pantheist thus denies that God transcends the universe. Indeed, for the pantheist, God just *is* the universe. The panentheist, however, maintains that God transcends the universe. God includes everything that is, so God includes nature. But God includes much more besides. Again, this makes a practical difference. If God is nature, then prayer and worship have little or no role to play; at most they amount to an aesthetic appreciation of the beauty and power of nature and nothing more. But if God includes but transcends nature, prayer and worship may play their traditional roles. It can still make sense to think of God as listening to our prayers and responding to them. It can make sense to think of God as reacting to worship and praise.

In short, prayer and worship, in the traditional picture, are important activities because God both transcends and interacts with the world. The deist denies interaction; the pantheist denies transcendence. For both, therefore, prayer and worship lose significance.

Though deism, pantheism, and panentheism have been important dissident conceptions of God, no major world religion employs them. Nevertheless, Hinduism, Confucianism, and Daoism advance conceptions of God that differ from that of classical theism.

Hinduism

Hinduism contains more variation in conceptions of God than any Western religion. The term 'Hindu' is not Sanskrit in origin; no one described him- or herself as a Hindu until relatively recently. Hinduism comprises various traditional Indian religious views that have certain practices in common but differ considerably in their concepts of God. We have examined Advaita Vedanta, with its stress on Brahman as the one reality underlying everything, in Chapters 4 and 5. Some Hindus are **atheists,** holding that there is no supernatural being. Some Hindus consider themselves **polytheists,** believers in more than one god. Others consider themselves **monotheists,** believers in one God. But the mainstream Hindu conception is something between these two. It is generally called **henotheism:** the view that there is one God who takes many forms. There are various gods and goddesses, but all are forms of a single God.

The *Rg Veda,* the oldest text in Sanskrit, is more than 3000 years old. It advances a henotheistic concept of God:

> They have styled Him Indra (the Chief of the Gods), Mitra (the Friend), Varuna (the Venerable), Agni (Fire), also the celestial, great-winged Garutma; for although one, poets speak of Him diversely; they say Agni, Yama (Death), and Matarisvan (Lord of breath). (1.164.46)[5]

[5] This and subsequent passages from the *Rg Veda* are from *Rg Veda,* translated by Swami Prakash Sarasvati and Satyakam Vidyaalanakr, quoted in Stephen H. Phillips (ed.), *Philosophy of Religion: A Global Approach* (Fort Worth: Harcourt Brace, 1996).

All these gods exist; they are not mere illusion. (Some Hindus, however, hold that they are illusion, and that only one God, Brahman, is real.) But they are nevertheless diverse appearances of one God, "the divine architect, the impeller of all, the multiform" (3.55.19):

> The ten hundreds stand there as one; I have beheld the most excellent form of the gods. (5.62.1)
>
> His steady light, swifter than the mind, stationed throughout the moving world, indicates the way to happiness. All the gods are of one accord and one intention; they proceed unobstructed according to a single Will. (6.9.5)

The *Bhagavad Gita* (see Chapter 4) also propounds henotheism. Krishna tells Arjuna,

How do the various Hindu gods and goddesses relate to each other?

> Even those who are devotees of other gods,
> And worship them permeated with faith,
> It is only me, son of Kunti, that even they
> Worship, (tho) not in the enjoined fashion.
> For I of all acts of worship
> Am both the recipient and the Lord. . . . (9.23–24a)[6]

Arjuna recognizes Krishna as the "Lord of Gods":

> O infinite Lord of Gods, in whom the world dwells,
> Thou the imperishable, existent, non-existent, and beyond both!
> Thou art the Primal God, the Ancient Spirit,
> Thou art the supreme resting-place of this universe;
> Thou art the knower, the object of knowledge, and the highest station,
> By Thee the universe is pervaded, Thou of infinite form! (11.37b–38)

Arjuna also seems to advance a version of panentheism, for he sees all other gods and everything else in Krishna:

> I see the gods in Thy body, O God,
> All of them, and the hosts of various kinds of beings too,
> The Creator sitting on the lotus-seat,
> And the seers all, and the divine serpents.
> With many arms, bellies, mouths, and eyes,
> I see Thee, infinite in form on all sides. . . . (11.15–16a)

Thus, Hindus may worship a variety of gods and goddesses—such as Vishnu, Shiva, Brahma, Parvati, and Ganesha—while still maintaining that there is one God. All the gods and goddesses are manifestations of the single but multiform divine being. Believers may choose to worship those manifestations they find most meaningful. The various gods and goddesses do not compete with each other, and devotees of one have no objection to the worship of others.

---

[6]This and further passages from the *Bhagavad Gita* are from *The Bhagavad Gita,* translated and interpreted by Franklin Edgerton (Cambridge: Harvard University Press, 1944).

Confucianism

Kong Fuzi (K'ung Fu-Tzu)—Grand Master Kong, or, as he became known in the West, Confucius (551–479 B.C.E.)—was a contemporary of Lao Tzu, the Buddha, Aesop, Thales, and many of the Biblical prophets. He was completely self-educated. Living in a time of great political and intellectual upheaval, he rose from poverty and obscurity to become the most influential and revered person in the history of China.

There is little to say about the Confucian conception of God because Confucius declines to say anything about God or Heaven. As we shall see in Chapter 7, he presents a rich ethical theory centered on the idea of virtue. But he takes pains not to speculate on human nature itself or the ways of Heaven.

> 5:12 Zi-kong said, "We may hear the Master on letters and culture. But we may not hear him on human nature and the way of Heaven."

The distinction here is between nature and nurture. Confucius speaks to his students about the aspects of their character developed through nurture. This they can affect. But he does not speak of human nature itself. Similarly, he speaks about culture and government, aspects of the world humans can affect. But he does not speak about the ways of Heaven. Indeed, he acts as if inquiry into things that transcend the world is pointless:

> 11:11 Qi Lu asked about serving the spirits. The Master said, "If you can't serve men, how can you serve spirits?" Qi Lu added, "I venture to ask about death." Confucius answered, "If you don't know about life, how can you know about death?"

Confucius's thought is a form of **humanism**, the view that value is to be defined in purely human terms. He does refer to the ways of Heaven and the decrees of Heaven, but they play no role in his account of virtue. Indeed, he directly denies that they should play a role:

> 15:28 The Master said, "The value of the Way depends on man; the value of man doesn't depend on the Way."

Consequently, it makes little difference whether any superior being endorses or enforces morality. Morality stands on its own without such sanction. Confucius, in referring to Heaven, makes it clear he thinks there is some superior realm. But he seems to consider it unknowable.

Daoism

Laozi (Lao Tzu), a contemporary of Confucius and the Buddha in the sixth century B.C.E., founded Daoism (Taoism). According to legend, he composed the *Dao-de-Jing (Tao-te-Ching)*, literally, the "Way-Virtue-Classic," upon his retirement, although many scholars believe that several people compiled the book over roughly two centuries.

Confucius, in elaborating his account of the superior person, refuses to say anything about human nature, the nature of the universe, or God. He treats *Dao,* the Way, as a purely ethical concept: the right way to live. Laozi, in contrast, begins with metaphysical speculation about *Dao,* which he takes as the way the universe works and identifies with the One, which underlies everything (in Laozi's language, "the ten thousand things") but admits no description. Laozi speaks of it as natural and eternal but also as changing and spontaneous. In itself it lacks any moral dimension. Throughout the *Dao-de-Jing,* however, he makes it clear that language is inadequate to describe the One. At most, language can suggest or evoke it.

What qualities does Laozi attribute to Dao?

1

The Dao that can be trodden is not the eternal Dao.
The name that can be named is not the eternal name.
Nameless, it is the origin of heaven and earth.
Named, it is the mother of ten thousand things.

4

The Dao is the emptiness of a bowl; beware fullness.
Deep and unfathomable, it seems to be the ancestor of ten thousand things.
Blunt the sharp, unravel the knots, temper the bright, and become dark.
The Dao is pure and still.

5

Heaven and earth are not benevolent [*ren*];
They treat the ten thousand things like straw dogs.
The sage is not benevolent;
He treats the people like straw dogs.

16

Reach the height of Emptiness; strive for stillness.
Ten thousand things flourish together and then return.
Things grow luxuriously and then return to the root.
To return to the root is to achieve stillness,
To achieve stillness is to reach the goal.

25

There was something indefinite existing before heaven and earth.
Still, formless, alone, unchanging,
Reaching everywhere without becoming exhausted,
It may be called the mother of ten thousand things.

I do not know its name; I call it Dao.
If pressed, I call it "great."
"Great," it flows constantly.
Flowing, it goes far away.
Far away, it returns.

Therefore Dao is great,
Heaven is great,
Earth is great,
The king is also great.
In the universe four are great,
And the king is one of them.

Humans take their law from the earth,
Earth takes its law from heaven;
Heaven takes its law from Dao,
Dao takes its law from what it is.[7]

The Dao, "the mother of ten thousand things," is remarkably like Brahman. It underlies everything that exists. It cannot be perceived directly but can be known by its works; everything that happens is the work of the Dao. The Dao fits classical theism in some ways; it is omnipresent and eternal. To say that it is all-powerful, however, seems misleading. From one point of view it is true; the Dao can do anything that can be done, for everything that happens is the work of the Dao. From another point of view, however, it strikes a wrong note; the Dao has no will. For that reason, 'all-knowing' fits the Dao even less. And Laozi denies that the Dao is compassionate; it treats "the ten thousand things like straw dogs."

One way to see the contrast between the Dao (and Brahman) and the classical Western concept of God centers on personhood. The Western concept treats God as analogous to a person. God creates, loves, becomes angry, shows compassion, rewards and punishes, and so on. God, like a person, has intelligence, emotions, and a will. The Dao does not. The Dao is great but is utterly unlike a person.

A PRIORI ARGUMENTS FOR GOD'S EXISTENCE

Over the centuries, philosophers have advanced many arguments for God's existence. They fall into three main groups:

1. A priori arguments
   a. Arguments from thought
   b. Ontological arguments
2. A posteriori arguments
   a. Cosmological arguments
   b. Arguments from design (teleological arguments)
3. Practical arguments

Let's consider each in turn.

A priori arguments try to establish the existence of God independently of experience. They seek to show that God must exist no matter what the world and our experience of it are like.

The Argument from Thought

The last section investigated the concept of God. Some might deny that there is any such concept, that they at any rate do not have it, or that it is ultimately incoherent. But even many atheists would agree to having a concept of God; they would just deny

[7] This and subsequent selections from Laozi are from *The Texts of Taoism*, translated by James Legge (Oxford: Oxford University Press, 1891). I have altered the translation significantly to bring out the poetic quality of the original and to accord with the Pinyin system.

that it corresponds to anything in the world. If there is such a concept, where do we get it? Where does it come from?

Concept empiricists (see Chapter 3) contend that all concepts capable of applying to things in the world come from experience. The concept of God, however, does not *seem* to come from experience. Religious traditions differ on whether it is possible to experience God in this lifetime. But even Moses, "whom the Lord knew face to face," according to *Deuteronomy* 34:10, had a concept of God before he encountered the burning bush or ascended Mt. Sinai. This is a traditional argument for rejecting concept empiricism. Since we have a first-order concept of God, and it does not come from experience, some first-order concepts must be a priori.

The **argument from thought** takes this reasoning one step further. If our capacity to think of God does not come from experience, it must be innate. But where could this inborn capacity have come from? Only from God. Our concept of God is a concept of a perfect being. We never encounter perfection, but our idea must have its origin in something perfect. Just as our idea of *green* has its origin in green things, our idea of perfection must have its origin in something perfect—God.

French philosopher René Descartes (1596–1650; see Chapter 2) presents the most influential and sophisticated version of the argument from thought in the third *Meditation:*

> But another way occurs to me to inquire whether anything of which I have ideas exists outside of me. To be sure, to the extent that ideas are merely certain modes of thought, I recognize no inequality among them. All appear to come from me in the same manner. But to the extent that one represents one thing and another represents another, it is clear that they are very different. No doubt those standing for substances [that is, nouns] are something more, and contain, so to speak, more objective reality than those that simply represent modes or accidents [that is, adjectives, verbs, and adverbs]. That idea again by which I understand a supreme God, eternal, infinite, omniscient, omnipotent, and Creator of all things besides Himself, surely has more objective reality in itself than those ideas standing for finite substances.[8]

Descartes's main premise is that a cause has at least as much reality as its effect.

What is Descartes's conclusion? Why does he think it follows?

> Now it is evident by the natural light that there must at least be as much reality in the efficient and total cause as in its effect. For, I beg you, where could the effect get its reality, if not from its cause? And how could the cause give it, if it did not have it? It follows, not only that something cannot arise from nothing, but also that what is more perfect—that is, what contains more reality—cannot arise from the less perfect.

If we apply this to ideas, we can put the point this way: the cause of the idea of X must have at least as much reality as X. Descartes speaks of things in the world as having **actual** or **formal reality.** The contents of our ideas—their objects, what our ideas are *about*—have **objective reality.** Because today we call things objective when they do *not* depend on our own states of mind, Descartes's usage is confusing. When he attributes objective reality to something, he means to say it is an object of thought, an

[8]This and subsequent selections from Descartes are from the *Meditations,* my own translation.

intentional object, in German philosopher Franz Brentano's (1838–1917) phrase. Such objects may or may not have actual or formal reality; we can think of things that do not exist. (Famous examples include Pegasus, the golden mountain, and the round square cupola on Berkeley College.) In short, Descartes means by 'objective' something very close to what we mean by 'subjective'.

> And this is not only transparently true of those effects having actual or formal reality, but also of the ideas having merely objective reality. For example, some stone that did not exist before cannot now begin to be unless produced by something that has, formally or eminently, all that is in the stone. Neither can heat be produced in a subject that was not hot unless by something of an order at least as perfect as heat, and so on. But further, I cannot have the idea of heat or of a stone unless it has been put into me by some cause that has in it at least as much reality as I conceive to be in the heat or the stone. For although this cause does not transfer any of its actual or formal reality to my idea, it should not on that account be thought less real. But the nature of an idea is such that it demands no formal reality other than that which it borrows from my thought, of which it is a mode. But for an idea to contain this or that objective reality, it must surely derive it from some cause that has at least as much formal reality as the idea contains objective reality. For if we think that something is to be found in an idea that is not in its cause, it must therefore arise from nothing. But however imperfect this mode of being may be, by which a thing is objectively in the understanding by way of an idea, it is certainly not nothing; consequently, it cannot come from nothing.

How does Descartes's principle apply to a stone? To heat? To an idea?

The cause of an idea must contain at least as much formal reality as the idea contains objective reality. We do not, in other words, derive our ideas from nothing. We get the idea of fire from fire. We get the idea of red from red things. Our ideas may be imperfect copies of the originals; our idea of fire, for example, does not capture the full richness and complexity of fire itself. The key point, however, is that our idea does not contain more richness and complexity than the thing itself.

> Nor should I surmise that, since the reality that I consider in my ideas is only objective, it is not essential that this reality should be formally in the causes of these ideas, but that it is enough if it is in them objectively. For just as this objective mode of being pertains to ideas by their nature, so does the formal mode of being pertain to the causes of those ideas—at least the first and principal ones—by their nature. And although one idea may be born from another idea, that cannot proceed into infinity. In the end we must reach a first idea, whose cause is an archetype, which contains formally all the reality objectively in the idea. Thus it is transparent to me, by the light of nature, that the ideas in me are like images, which can easily fall short of the perfection of the things from which they are taken, but which cannot contain anything greater or more perfect.

Now, if I have an idea that has more reality than any original I can find within me, the original must be outside me.

> And the longer and the more carefully I examine all these things, the more clearly and distinctly I recognize their truth. But what should I finally conclude? If the objective reality of any one of my ideas is so great that it is certainly not in me, either formally or eminently, and consequently I cannot myself be its cause, it necessarily

> follows that I am not alone in the world, but that some other thing—the cause of this idea—exists. In fact, if no such idea is found in me, I plainly have no argument to restore my confidence in the existence of any being beyond myself; for I have investigated everything most diligently and so far have been able to find nothing else.

The idea of God, then, must have come from something with at least as much reality as God; since nothing has as much reality as God, our idea must have come from God.

Why could a finite being not be the source of the idea of an infinite substance?

> And so there remains only the idea of God. I must consider whether it is something [that] could not have sprung from me myself. By the name 'God' I understand a substance that is infinite, independent, most-knowing, most-powerful, and by which I myself and everything else that exists—if anything else does exist—have been created. In fact all these are such that the more diligently I attend to them, the less do they seem capable of springing from me alone. Hence, we must conclude that God necessarily exists.
>
> The idea of substance is within me because I am a substance. Nevertheless I would not have the idea of an infinite substance—since I am finite—if it had not proceeded from some substance which was veritably infinite.

Scottish philosopher David Hume (1711–1776) and German philosopher Ludwig Feuerbach (1804–1872), among others, have objected that we can account for the origin of our idea of the infinite without assuming an infinite cause. We encounter finite things, and we have the idea of negation. Surely, they contend, we can combine them to form the idea of the infinite. Not so, Descartes argues:

> Nor should I think that, just as I perceive rest and darkness by the negation of movement and light, I perceive the infinite not by a true idea, but only by negating the finite. For, on the contrary, I understand that there is manifestly more reality in infinite substance than in finite, and therefore that in some way I have in me the perception of the infinite earlier than the finite—that is, the perception of God before that of myself. For how could I understand myself as doubting and desiring—that is, as lacking something—and as not being wholly perfect, if no idea of a more perfect Being were in me, in comparison with which I might recognise my own defects?

Descartes here tries to shift the burden of proof to his opponent. He can explain our recognition of our own imperfection, expressed explicitly in our awareness of our own finite nature and implicitly in doubt and desire. Can his opponent do so as well? One might try to argue that doubt and desire are basic or rest on feelings of insecurity, hunger, frustration, and so on, that are basic. One might also accept that doubt and desire presuppose an idea of something better without agreeing that they presuppose the idea of something better than anything else could possibly be. We recognize that numbers like 100 are finite by recognizing that there are larger numbers, not by having the idea of an infinite number already in mind.

Perhaps the idea of God is incoherent or confused or corresponds to nothing in the world. Again, Descartes argues, not so:

> It cannot be said that perhaps this idea of God is materially false and so could come from nothing, as with ideas of heat, cold and the like. On the contrary, this idea is

> utterly clear and distinct. It contains more objective reality than any other. Nothing is in itself truer or less to be suspected of falsehood. This idea of a Being of the highest perfection and infinity is utterly true. For although, perhaps, we can imagine that such a Being does not exist, we cannot nevertheless imagine that His idea represents nothing real to me, as I have said of the idea of cold. This idea is also utterly clear and distinct; all that I conceive clearly and distinctly as real and true, and as conveying some perfection, is wholly contained in it. That I do not comprehend the infinite does not stand in the way of this. Nor do the countless other things in God that I do not comprehend, and perhaps cannot even grasp in any way in thought. For it is of the nature of the infinite that I, who am finite, do not comprehend it. It is enough that I understand this, and judge that all things I clearly perceive and know to convey some perfection—and perhaps countless others of which I am ignorant—are in God formally or eminently. The idea I have of Him is thus the most true, most clear, and most distinct of all that are in me.

Descartes's principle of method undergirds the argument: Everything that I perceive clearly and distinctly must be true. The idea of God cannot be a human imperfection that reflects no corresponding reality; the idea is clear and distinct and must therefore reflect the world accurately.

What is true of our idea of God is true of us. We could not exist if it were not for God's causation and active support.

> Indeed, all this is obvious to anyone who concentrates diligently using the light of nature. But when I concentrate less, and images of sensible things blunt my mind's edge, it is not so easy to remember why the idea of a being more perfect than I necessarily proceeded from something that was really more perfect. Thus I would like to inquire further whether I, who have this idea, could exist if no such being existed.

The idea of God, then, is a priori, and only God could have placed it in us.

> The only thing left is to examine how I have received this idea from God. For I have not drawn it from the senses. It never comes to me unexpectedly, as ideas of sensible things usually do when these things present themselves—or seem to present themselves—to the external organs of my senses. Nor have I invented it, for plainly I cannot subtract anything from it or add anything to it. Consequently, the only thing left is that it is innate in me, just as the idea of myself is innate in me.

What alternatives does Descartes consider? Are they exhaustive?

Descartes's argument, as we saw a moment ago, relies on his principle that everything I perceive clearly and distinctly is true. But how do I know that? In the course of the *Meditations,* he first announces the principle as a generalization from the *cogito.* But it will not do to argue that *everything* I clearly and distinctly perceive is true on the ground that *one* thing, that I exist, is something I clearly and distinctly perceive that must be true.

In the end, Descartes's answer is that God is good and cannot be a deceiver. I can trust my senses in most contexts. I can trust the clear and distinct ideas that inhabit my mind innately. God, being perfect, must be good and surely would not have ordered the world so that my mind would systematically mistake its nature.

Most philosophers have found this answer deeply unsatisfying. We can trust our clear and distinct ideas, because God exists, is good, and so could not be a deceiver. But the argument for God's existence depends on the premise that we can trust our clear and distinct ideas! The argument is circular. In fact, it is known as the Cartesian circle. Little wonder that Descartes sought another argument for God's existence that would not require prior trust in clear and distinct ideas.

The Ontological Argument

Descartes turned to a second argument for God's existence that depends on God's perfection in a different way. Anselm of Canterbury (1033–1109), an Italian who was educated in France, joined the Benedictine order, and eventually became Archbishop of Canterbury, presented two versions of the argument. Extending Augustine's definition of God as "something than which nothing more excellent or sublime exists," Anselm defines God as "that, the greater than which cannot be thought," that is, the greatest conceivable being, the greatest thing you could possibly think of.

How do we know that the greatest conceivable being does not exist in the understanding alone?

> Even the Fool . . . is forced to agree that something, the greater than which cannot be thought, exists in the intellect, since he understands this when he hears it, and whatever is understood is in the intellect. And surely that, the greater than which cannot be thought, cannot exist in the intellect alone. For if it exists solely in the intellect, it can be thought to exist in reality, which is greater. If, then, that, the greater than which cannot be thought, exists in the intellect alone, this same being, than which a greater cannot be thought, is that than which a greater can be thought. But surely this is impossible. Therefore, there can be absolutely no doubt that something, the greater than which cannot be thought, exists both in the intellect and in reality.[9]

God not only exists but exists necessarily. Atheism is not only false but incoherent; God cannot even be thought not to exist.

> Certainly, this being so truly exists that it cannot even be thought not to exist. For something can be thought to exist that cannot be thought not to exist, and this is greater than whatever can be thought not to exist. Hence, if that, the greater than which cannot be thought, can be thought not to exist, then that, the greater than which cannot be thought, is not the same as that, the greater than which cannot be thought, which is absurd. Therefore, something, the greater than which cannot be thought, exists so truly that it cannot even be thought not to exist.
>
> And You are this being, O Lord, our God. You exist so truly, Lord my God, that You cannot even be thought not to exist. And this is as it should be. For, if a mind could think of something better than You, the creature would rise above its creator and judge its creator, and that is completely absurd. In fact, everything else, except You alone, can be thought not to exist. You alone, then, of all things most truly exist, and therefore of all things possess existence to the highest degree; for anything else does not exist as truly, and possesses existence to a lesser degree.

If God is the greatest thing you could possibly think of, Anselm contends, God must exist; He cannot even be thought not to exist. Suppose He did not exist. Then it would be possible to think of something greater—namely, something just like God but that

[9] Anselm, *Proslogion,* my translation.

really existed. But then God would not be the greatest thing you could possibly think of after all, contradicting the definition of 'God'. Similarly, suppose you could conceive of God's nonexistence. Then you could think of something greater—namely, something just like God, but existing necessarily. Again, that would contradict the definition of 'God', because God would not be the greatest thing you could think of.

Descartes, who advanced the argument from thought in his third *Meditation,* only to run around in the Cartesian circle, advances the **ontological argument** in his fifth *Meditation* in an especially elegant form:

> Although it is not necessary that I happen upon any thought of God, nevertheless, as often as I would like to think of a being first and supreme—and bring forth the idea of God as if from the warehouse of my mind—it is necessary that I attribute all perfections to it, even though I do not then enumerate them all, nor attend to them one by one. This necessity plainly suffices so that afterwards, when I notice that existence is a perfection, I rightly conclude that a first and supreme being exists.

Descartes's argument is straightforward:

> God has all perfections.
> Existence is a perfection.
> Therefore, God exists.

This argument purports to show the existence of God from nothing more than the concept of God. It is plainly valid, and the first premise is just a definition of 'God'.

So the only way to challenge the argument is to challenge its second premise, that existence is a perfection. It does sound odd. Surely someone can become better by learning more, becoming more virtuous, becoming stronger, developing talents, and so on. But it sounds bizarre to say that someone can become better by existing. Conversely, people can become worse by forgetting things, growing weaker, indulging vices, etc., but can they become worse by not existing? Existence does not seem to be a kind of excellence. This is at the heart of Kant's objection to the ontological argument:

> I simply ask you, whether the proposition, that *this* or *that thing* (which, whatever it may be, I grant you as possible) *exists,* is an analytic or synthetic proposition? If the former, then by its existence you add nothing to your thought of the thing; but in that case, either the thought within you would be the thing itself, or you have presupposed existence, as belonging to possibility, and have according to your own showing deduced existence from internal possibility, which is nothing but a miserable tautology. . . . If, on the contrary, you admit, as every sensible man must do, that every proposition involving existence is synthetic, how can you say that the predicate of existence does not admit of removal without contradiction, a distinguishing property which is peculiar to analytic propositions only, the very character of which depends on it? [10]

Why, according to Kant, can't 'God exists' be an analytic truth?

Kant argues that the conclusion, 'God exists' is either analytic or synthetic. If it is analytic, it tells us nothing about the world but only about our own linguistic usage; it is

[10] This and subsequent quotations from Kant are from Immanuel Kant, *Critique of Pure Reason,* rev. 2nd edition, translated by Max Müller (London: Macmillan, 1927). I have altered a few terms to coincide with the terminology used in the rest of this book ('analytical' to 'analytic', for example).

"nothing but a miserable tautology," for it tells us only that we would not call something 'God' unless it existed. If it is synthetic, as Kant thinks it is—existence is never just a matter of logic—then it really tells us something about the world but cannot be established by this kind of a priori argument, for there is no contradiction in the contrary statement that God does not exist.

The key, Kant says, is that 'exists' is not a real predicate. It cannot enlarge a concept:

> *Being* is evidently not a real predicate, or a concept of something that can be added to the concept of a thing. It is merely an admission of a thing, and of certain determinations in it. Logically, it is merely the copula of a judgment. The proposition, *God is almighty,* contains two concepts, each having its object, namely, God and almightiness. The small word *is,* is not an additional predicate, but only serves to put the predicate *in relation to* the subject. If, then, I take the subject (God) with all its predicates (including that of almightiness), and say, *God is,* or there is a God, I do not put a new predicate to the concept of God, but I only put the subject by itself, with all its predicates, in relation to my concept, as its object.

Since existence is not a real predicate, it is not a perfection. So the second premise of Descartes's argument is false, and the argument itself is unsound.

Kant's objection is subtler than it seems at first glance. He contends that existential statements are synthetic. Now as he defines the terms, analytic statements have predicates that are contained in their subjects. 'Bachelors are unmarried', for example, is analytic; the concept of bachelor includes the concept of being unmarried. Synthetic statements have predicates that are not contained in their subjects but instead add something to them. 'Bachelors are unhappy' is synthetic, for the concept of bachelor does not contain the concept of unhappiness. Now Kant insists that 'exists' is not a real predicate; it cannot enlarge a concept. But if so, how can existence statements be synthetic?

'Exists', evidently, adds something to a concept without enlarging it.

How could one put Kant's point using Descartes's terminology of 'formal' and 'objective' reality?

> And thus the real does not contain more than the possible. A hundred real dollars do not contain a penny more than a hundred possible dollars. For as the latter signify the concept, the former the object and its position by itself, it is clear that, in case the former contained more than the latter, my concept would not express the whole object, and would not therefore be its adequate concept. In my financial position no doubt there exists more by one hundred real dollars, than by their concept only (that is, their possibility), because in reality the object is not only contained analytically in my concept, but is added to my concept (which is a determination of my state), synthetically; but the conceived hundred dollars are not in the least increased through the existence which is outside my concept.

What 'exists' adds to a concept, in other words, is not *content* but something outside the realm of concepts, an *object* corresponding to it. 'Existing dollar' is not like 'silver dollar'; 'existing' modifies 'dollar' in a different way. It does not describe the dollar but instead says that it corresponds to something in reality. To take a different example: imagine listing the qualities you would like in a spouse. You might say you want someone who is kind, considerate, attractive, responsible, funny, and so on. Do you add anything if you say, "Oh! I also want someone who *exists*"? No. Existence does not contribute content to any concept. So, it cannot be part of the content of the concept of God. That is why all existence statements are synthetic. That is also why the ontological proof fails, for 'exists' ascribes to the concept of God an object corresponding to the concept, and no examination of a concept, even the concept of God, can tell us whether something in reality corresponds to the concept or not.

Charles Hartshorne, Norman Malcolm, and Alvin Plantinga have advanced contemporary versions of the ontological argument that try to avoid Kant's objection. Here is a simple version:

> It is possible that God exists.
> If God exists, He exists necessarily.
> Therefore, God exists necessarily.

The first premise rests on the coherence of the concept of God. There is no contradiction in the idea of a perfect being. The second rests on the impossibility of God's existing purely as a matter of chance, or as dependent on something else. If God exists, He is self-subsistent, not depending on any thing or circumstance.

Does the conclusion follow? It depends on the logic of 'necessarily' and 'possible'. Logicians agree about most principles involving these terms, but they disagree about principles involving "nested modalities," such as "If it is possible that God exists necessarily, then God does exist necessarily," or, equivalently, "If it is possible that God exists, then it is necessarily possible that God exists." According to the most popular *modal* logic—that is, logic of possibility and necessity—among contemporary philosophers, called S5, and according to the logic of modality that Descartes and Kant both took for granted, there are only six modalities: truth, falsehood, possibility, impossibility, necessity, and non-necessity. That means that any statement must be necessarily true, contingently true, contingently false, or necessarily false; there are no other options. In such a logic, the above argument is valid. There remains the question, Is it sound? That logic cannot answer.

A POSTERIORI ARGUMENTS

Many philosophers—St. Thomas Aquinas (1225–1274; see Chapter 1), for example—have been skeptical of a priori arguments for the existence of God. They have agreed with Kant that existence is not merely a matter of logic and that God's existence cannot be demonstrated on the basis of thought alone. But they have found in the world and our experience of it reasons to believe that God exists. The arguments they advance on the basis of experience are a posteriori.

A posteriori arguments fall into two groups: **cosmological arguments,** which turn on the idea that the origin of the universe must have some ultimate explanation, and **teleological arguments,** or **arguments from design,** which find in nature's intricate design a reason to believe in God.

Cosmological Arguments

Aristotle drafted the first cosmological argument, contending that there must have been a "prime mover" for the universe. His argument, however, is highly complex, and depends on showing that the "first sphere of heaven" revolves eternally in a circular path. Various early church fathers—notably Athenian philosopher Marcianus Aristides (second century)—tried to simplify the argument. And simple versions occur in the works of the great Indian philosopher Udayana (c. 1000), who unified two long-running realist schools, Vaisesika (particularism) and Nyaya (logic):

> 1. Argument from effects
>
> Things like the earth must have a cause.
> Because they are effects.
> Like a pot.
>
> By having a cause I mean active production by someone possessed of the intent to produce, and a direct knowledge concerning the matter from which the production is to be.[11]

But it was in the medieval period that Muslim, Jewish, and Christian philosophers devoted serious attention to the cosmological argument as the most important and reliable way of establishing God's existence.

St. Thomas Aquinas The classic place to find a posteriori arguments for God's existence is the *Summa Theologica* of St. Thomas Aquinas. Aquinas advances five a posteriori arguments for God's existence, three of which are versions of the cosmological argument:

> The first and most obvious way is based on change. Certainly, our senses show us that some things in the world are changing. Now anything changing is changed by something else. For nothing changes except what can but does not yet have some actuality; something that causes change has that actuality already. For to cause change is to bring into being what was before only potential, and only something that already is can do this. Thus, fire, which is actually hot, causes wood, which can be hot, to become actually hot, and so causes change in the wood. Now it is impossible for the same thing to be simultaneously actually F and potentially F, though it can be actually F and potentially G: The actually hot cannot at the same time be potentially hot, though it can be potentially cold. It is therefore impossible for something undergoing a change to cause itself to undergo that very change. It follows that anything changing must be changed by something else. If this other thing is also changing, it is being changed by another thing, and that by another. Now this does not go on to infinity, or else there would be no first cause of the change and, consequently, no other changes. The intermediate causes will not produce change unless they are affected by the first change, just as a stick does not move unless moved by a hand. Therefore, it is necessary to arrive at some first cause of change, itself changed by nothing, and this all understand to be God.[12]

Every change has a cause other than itself. There cannot be an infinite regress of causes, however, for, if there were, the causal conditions of subsequent changes could never

---

[11] Udayana, from *Udayana's Nyayakusumanjali,* translated by José Pereira, in *Hindu Theology: A Reader* (New York: Doubleday, 1976).

[12] This and subsequent quotations from Thomas Aquinas are from *Summa Theologica.* The translations are my own.

have been fulfilled. So, there must have been a first cause—what Aristotle calls the **prime mover.** And that, Aquinas asserts, is God.

The second variant is almost a restatement of the first:

> The second way is based on the nature of causation. In the observable world, causes are to be found ordered in series; we never observe, or even could observe, something causing itself, for this would mean it preceded itself, and this is impossible. Such a series of causes, however, must stop somewhere. For in all series of causes, an earlier member causes an intermediate, and the intermediate a last (whether the intermediate be one or many). If you eliminate a cause you also eliminate its effects. Therefore there can be neither a last nor an intermediate cause unless there is a first. But if the series of causes goes on to infinity, and there is no first cause, there would be neither intermediate causes nor a final effect, which is patently false. It is therefore necessary to posit a first cause, which all call 'God'.

Call the current state of the world *a*. It must have had a cause. That cause must have been earlier than *a*, and something other than *a* itself. Call it *b*. But then *b* must have had some other cause, *c*, and so on. The chain of causes (*a, b, c, . . .*) cannot be infinite; so, there must have been a first cause, God.

Many objections have been raised to this argument. Two are especially obvious. First, why can't the chain of causes be infinite? Aquinas provides little supporting argument: "If you eliminate a cause you also eliminate its effects. Therefore there can be neither a last nor an intermediate cause unless there is a first." But this seems to miss the point. No one suggests eliminating a cause. The question is why each cause cannot have some further cause (or even, as Averroës suggests, why the chain of causes cannot loop back on itself). Aquinas offers no answer. Second, why call the first cause God?

Islamic philosophers, in the two centuries before Aquinas, developed sophisticated versions of the cosmological argument meant to answer these objections. Before turning to them, however, let's consider one more a posteriori argument in Aquinas:

Why is something necessary, according to Aquinas?

> The third way depends on what is possible and necessary, and goes like this. We observe in things something that can be, and can not be, for we observe them springing up and dying away, and consequently being and not being. Now not everything can be like this, for whatever can not be, once was not. If all things could not be, therefore, at one time there was nothing. But if that were true there would be nothing even now, because something that does not exist can be brought into being only by something that already exists. So, if there had been nothing, it would have been impossible for anything to come into being, and there would be nothing now, which is patently false. Not all things, therefore, are possible but not necessary; something is necessary. Now what is necessary may or may not have its necessity caused by something else. It is impossible to go on to infinity in a series of necessary things having a cause of their necessity, just as with any series of causes. It is therefore necessary to posit something that is itself necessary, having no other cause of its necessity, but causing necessity in everything else.

This argument relies on the premise that "If all things could not be, therefore, at one time there was nothing." This might be an equivocation; "all things could not be" could mean either that each thing is such that it might not exist—a reasonable claim, if all things are contingent—or that it is possible for nothing to exist, that is, for everything to fail to exist all at once. *That* does not follow from anything Aquinas has said. So, the argument may rest on a simple fallacy.

Aquinas may, however, have had in mind the following argument. Suppose each thing is contingent and so might at some point fail to exist. If there were an infinite series of events stretching back into the past, all possibilities would have been realized at some point in the past; and among those is the situation in which the contingent things cease to exist all at once. That, however, would have made it impossible for anything to exist now. So, the existence of some things now shows that such a thing never happened, and, thus, that the series of causes cannot be infinite.

Reconstructed in this way, the argument faces two problems. First, that each thing might not exist does not establish that everything might fail to exist all at once, for the existence of things might not be independent issues. Maybe *a* might fail to exist, because it could be replaced by *b,* and likewise *b* might fail to exist, being replaced by *a*. Aquinas needs the assumption that one thing's nonexistence never requires the existence of something else. Second, the idea that an infinite past would have realized every possible circumstance seems to rest on an intuitive but sloppy conception of infinity. Consider the infinite series of numbers < 2, 4, 6, 8, . . . >. It is infinite, but it does not contain every number. Similarly, a sequence of events could be infinite without containing every possible event.

Avicenna Islamic and Jewish theologians developed innovative and important versions of the cosmological argument in the two centuries before Aquinas. Avicenna (Abu All al-Husayn ibn Abd Allah ibn Sina, 980–1037; see Chapter 3) was born in Persia near Bukhara (in present-day Uzbekistan), son of the provincial governor. A prodigy, he had memorized the Koran by the age of ten and had a reputation as a physician at the court of the ruling Samanid family while still in his teens. He articulated the cosmological argument in a form that shaped subsequent discussion of it in the Islamic world.

Al-Farabi (Abu Nasr Muhammad al-Farabi, 870?–950), of Turkish descent but also born in what is now Uzbekistan, presents a version of the argument that follows Aristotle closely. He begins his metaphysics by defining God as "the First Cause of the existence of all the other existents," ultimately responsible for the existence of everything else. Avicenna, in contrast, begins by defining God as the Necessary Being. He analyzes the nature of substance, contrasts necessity with contingency, and then demonstrates the nature of the Necessary Being.

> Whatever has being must either have a reason for its being, or have no reason for it. If it has a reason, then it is contingent. . . . If on the other hand it has no reason for its being in any way whatsoever, then it is necessary in its being. This rule having been confirmed, I shall now proceed to prove that there is in being a being which has no reason for its being.
>
> Such a being is either contingent or necessary. If it is necessary, then the point we sought to prove is established. If on the other hand it is contingent, that which is contingent cannot enter upon being except for some reason which sways the scales in favour of its being and against its not-being. If the reason is also contingent, then there is a chain of contingents linked one to the other, and there is no being at all; for this being which is the subject of our hypothesis cannot enter into

> being so long as it is not preceded by an infinite succession of beings, which is absurd. Therefore contingent beings end in a Necessary Being.[13]

Avicenna's argument depends on the impossibility of an infinite regress. If there is no necessary being, then everything is contingent, having a reason for its existence. So, *a* exists because of *b; b,* because of *c; c,* because of *d;* and so on. But that means that *a* could not exist unless preceded by "an infinite succession of beings," *b, c, d,* and so on. But such an infinite regress is impossible; if an infinite number of things had to exist in order for *a* to exist, *a* could never exist. But some things do exist. (This is the a posteriori premise.) So, there must be a necessary being.

Al-Ghazali Avicenna's cosmological argument appears in European philosophy as Aquinas's third way. It prompted many debates in Islamic circles. The argument's chief critic was Abu Hamid Muhammad al-Ghazali (1058–1111), known to medieval philosophers in the West as Algazel. He was born in a village, Ghazaleh, near Tus in Khorasan, now northeastern Iran. He became a professor and rector at Nizamiya University in Baghdad but resigned to live the ascetic life of a Sufi mystic.

Most of al-Ghazali's philosophical work attacks the possibility of metaphysical knowledge and more generally the utility of reason. In *The Incoherence of the Philosophers,* he tries to refute many standard philosophical views and the arguments that al-Farabi, Avicenna, and other philosophers use to support them. In particular, al-Ghazali argues that the philosophers have been unsuccessful in trying to show that God exists. He uses philosophical arguments to try to demonstrate that philosophical argument on religious subjects is pointless. Averroës (ibn Rushd; 1126–1198), who attacks *The Incoherence of the Philosophers* in *The Incoherence of the Incoherence,* contends that this strategy is thus hopelessly paradoxical. But al-Ghazali's work lies within the tradition of philosophical skepticism. Skeptics try to show that some kinds of alleged knowledge are unreliable or unjustifiable. They often use reason to undermine the claims of reason. In itself this is not paradoxical. Reason may lead to contradictory conclusions, for example, or may show itself to be unreliable. Only if skeptics claim certainty within the realm they subject to attack—a kind of certainty they themselves deem impossible—does their general method seem troublesome. Al-Ghazali does claim a kind of certainty based on communion with God. That, however, is achieved not through reason but through mystical insight.

Al-Ghazali's assault on the cosmological argument is straightforward. The argument depends on the impossibility of an infinite regress. But that premise is not obvious; where is the argument for it?

> It does not behoove you to say that an infinite regress of causes is impossible. For, we will say, do you know it as a matter of immediate inference necessitated by reason, or through some deductive argument?[14]

It cannot be immediate (that is, self-evident), al-Ghazali argues, for even such defenders of the cosmological argument as Aristotle, al-Farabi, and Avicenna hold that

---

[13] Avicenna, *On the Nature of God,* from *Avicenna on Theology,* translated by Arthur J. Aiberry (London: John Murray, 1951).

[14] This and subsequent passages from al-Ghazali are from *Al-Ghazali's Tahafut al-Falasifah* (*Incoherence of the Philosophers*), translated by Sabih Almad Kamali (Lahore: Pakistan Philosophical Congress, 1963).

the world or certain portions of it are eternal. In any case it is not obvious on its face. So it must be the conclusion of an argument.

Al-Ghazali imagines an argument for it, which goes like this. Suppose that there were an infinite regress of causes or reasons for being, so that *a* exists because of *b*, which exists because of *c*, etc. The whole series (*a, b, c, . . .*) would have to be necessary or contingent. But it can be neither. The idea of a necessary being made up of contingent beings is absurd, while the idea of the series depending on something outside itself is also absurd, since each element of the series depends on subsequent elements and nothing else.

Al-Ghazali rejects this argument. He sees no problem with the idea of a necessary being made up of contingent beings:

Explain al-Ghazali's analogy.

> And we do not admit that it is absurd. To call it absurd is like one's saying that something eternal made up of temporal events is impossible. To the philosophers, Time *is* eternal; whereas individual spherical revolutions are temporal. And each individual revolution has a beginning; whereas the aggregate of those revolutions has no beginning. Therefore, that which has no beginning *is* made up of those which have. And the predicate of having a beginning in time is truly applicable to individual revolutions, but not to their aggregate. Similarly, therefore, (in the case of the causes and their aggregate) it will be said that each cause has a cause, but the aggregate of these causes has no cause. For all that can be truly said of the individuals cannot similarly be said of their aggregate.

The cosmological argument, then, fails, because the necessary being—the being having no reason for its being—whose existence it demonstrates may just be the world and its sequence of temporal events. The principles we use to reason about temporal events, moreover, may not apply to the world as a whole.

Averroës Averroës (ibn Rushd; 1126–1198), born in Córdoba, Spain, himself became a judge in Seville and then Córdoba, eventually, like his father and grandfather before him, becoming chief judge. He was also an immensely influential philosopher who wrote many commentaries on Aristotle and tried to harmonize religion and philosophy.

In *The Incoherence of the Incoherence,* Averroës attacks al-Ghazali's critiques of philosophical arguments and his implicit assertion that reason cannot discover religious truth. He agrees with al-Ghazali that Avicenna's proof does not work as it stands. It runs together two notions of 'cause' or 'for a reason':

> There are two kinds of agent: (1) the agent to which the object which proceeds from it is only attached during the process of its becoming; once this process is finished, the object is not any more in need of it—for instance, the coming into existence of a house through the builder; (2) the agent from which nothing proceeds but an act which has no other existence than its dependence on it. The distinctive mark of this act is that it is convertible with the existence of its object, i.e. when the act does not exist the object does not exist, and when the act exists the object exists—they are inseparable.[15]

[15]This and subsequent quotations from Averroës are from *Averroës' Tahafut al Tahafut* (*The Incoherence of the Incoherence*), translated by Simon van den Bergh (London: Luzac & Co., 1954).

We may think of causation, then, in two different ways. A cause may precede its effect in time and bring it into being, as a builder constructs a house or a swing of a bat propels a baseball over the fence. But an effect may also depend on a cause in a different way. A desk, for example, may be thirty inches high because its legs are 28 inches long and its top is two inches thick. But the length of the legs, the thickness of the top, and the height of the desk are not events, and their relation is not one of temporal precedence. The sense in which the height of the desk depends on the length of its legs and the thickness of its top, Averroës holds, is precisely the sense in which the world depends on God.

That means that 'contingent' and 'necessary' are ambiguous. We may call something contingent if it is the effect of a temporally preceding cause; the contingent, in this sense, is what has a causal explanation. The necessary, in this sense, is what cannot be explained causally. But we may also call something contingent in another sense if it depends on something else and necessary if it does not.

Averroës sees in al-Ghazali's criticism the seeds of a successful argument:

> Contingent existents must of necessity have causes which precede them, and if these causes again are contingent it follows that they have causes and that there is an infinite regress; and if there is an infinite regress there is no cause, and the contingent will exist without a cause, and this is impossible. Therefore the series must end in a necessary cause, and in this case this necessary cause must be necessary through a cause or without a cause, and if through a cause, this cause must have a cause and so on infinitely, and if we have an infinite regress here, it follows that what was assumed to have a cause has no cause, and this is impossible. Therefore the series must end in a cause necessary without a cause, i.e. necessary by itself, and this necessarily is the necessary existent.

To be precise, let's restrict 'contingent' and 'necessary' to the first sense delineated above (that is, 'having a cause' and 'not having a cause') and use 'dependent' and 'independent' for the second. Al-Ghazali holds that a necessary being could be made up of contingent beings. So, he concludes, Avicenna's cosmological argument shows little, for the being without a reason for its own being might just be the universe, the totality of contingent beings itself. Averroës, in effect, agrees. He maintains, however, that we can apply the same form of argument to the necessary being—that is, the being having no causal explanation—but using the other sense of 'contingent' and 'necessary'. The being having no causal explanation may be dependent or independent. There cannot be an infinite regress of dependence, or the conditions on which the necessary being depends could never be satisfied. So, there must be something that is necessary in both senses—that has no causal explanation and depends on nothing else.

Could this necessary being just be the universe? No. Averroës's argument depends on a further argument that the world must be eternal and, in particular, that the natural kinds of things in the universe (which he calls, using Aristotle's term, the *genera*) are eternal. That argument is too complicated to trace here. But Averroës uses its conclusion to argue that anything on which the eternal depends must be infinite, as only God can be:

> . . . the man who does not acknowledge infinite causes cannot prove the existence of an eternal first cause, since it is the existence of infinite effects which demands

> the necessity of an eternal cause from which the infinite causes acquire their existence; for if not, the genera, all of whose individuals are temporal, would be necessarily finite. And in this and no other way can the eternal become the cause of temporal existents, and the existence of infinite temporal existents renders the existence of a single eternal first principle necessary, and there is no God but He. . . .

Averroës's argument, then, relies on a principle familiar from Descartes's argument from thought, that the cause must contain at least as much reality as the effect. The world is in some respects infinite; thus the cause of the world must be infinite as well. It remains puzzling, however, why this infinite cause must be God.

Leibniz Gottfried Wilhelm von Leibniz (1646–1716; see Chapter 3), a German philosopher, mathematician, and statesman, was a contemporary of John Locke, George Berkeley, Alexander Pope, and Johann Sebastian Bach. He put the cosmological argument in a form that shows Averroës's influence. It rests on a basic principle of Leibniz's rationalistic philosophy, the principle of sufficient reason:

> . . . *nothing happens without a sufficient reason;* that is to say, that nothing happens without its being possible for him who should sufficiently understand things, to give a reason sufficient to determine why it is so and not otherwise.[16]

This principle is very broad, implying that every event has a cause, that nothing happens purely by chance, that everything can be explained, and that the universe is ultimately intelligible, existing for a reason.

> Now this sufficient reason for the existence of the universe cannot be found *in the series of contingent things,* that is, of bodies and of their representation in souls; for matter being indifferent in itself to motion and to rest, and to this or another motion, we cannot find the reason of motion in it, and still less of a certain motion. And although the present motion which is in matter, comes from the preceding motion, and that from still another preceding, yet in this way we make no progress, try as we may; for the same question always remains. Thus it must be that the sufficient reason, which has no need of another reason, be outside this series of contingent things and be found in a substance which is the cause, or which is a necessary being, carrying the reason of its existence within itself; otherwise we still should not have a sufficient reason in which we could rest. And this final reason of things is called *God.*

By the principle of sufficient reason, everything exists for a reason—including the entire series of contingent causes. Take the entire history of the universe, finite or infinite, and ask why *it* exists. Why is there something rather than nothing? Why is *this* particular history actual? There must be a sufficient reason for the entire universe.

---

[16]This and subsequent passages from Leibniz are from Gottfried Wilhelm von Leibniz, *Monadology,* from *The Monadology and Other Philosophical Writings,* translated by Robert Latta (Oxford: Oxford University Press, 1898).

And that is God. It cannot be the universe itself, or anything material, because matter is indifferent to existence or nonexistence. It must be something outside the realm of the material, temporal world that explains the existence of everything else. There must, in other words, be something spiritual that explains the existence of everything, spiritual and material. And that can only be God.

Design Arguments

The most familiar arguments for God's existence, and the ones that motivate religious belief for many people, are arguments from design. The universe is filled with beauty and wonder; it displays a remarkable intricacy and harmony. Could such a universe have happened by accident?

Versions of this argument appear in the works of the early church fathers. Aquinas puts it in a highly influential form:

> The fifth way is based on the rule-governed character of nature. The ordering of actions toward an end is observed in all bodies obeying natural laws, even when they lack awareness. For their behavior hardly ever varies, and will practically always turn out well; this shows that they truly tend toward a goal, and do not merely hit it by accident. Nothing, however, that lacks awareness tends toward a goal, except under the direction of someone aware and intelligent. The arrow, for example, requires an archer. All things in nature, therefore, are directed toward a goal by someone intelligent, and this we call 'God'.

There is a subtle ambiguity in Aquinas's argument. It begins straightforwardly enough:

> All bodies obey natural laws.
> All bodies obeying natural laws act toward an end.
> Therefore, all bodies act toward an end. (Including those that lack awareness.)
> Things lacking awareness act toward a goal only under the direction of someone aware and intelligent.
> Therefore, all things lacking awareness act under the direction of someone aware and intelligent.

The conclusion is ambiguous. If the argument is to be valid, it must mean that each unconscious thing must act under someone's direction. But there may be different directors for different objects. The arrow may be propelled toward a goal by the archer; the football, by the quarterback; the airplane, by the pilot; and so on. But Aquinas seems to read it as saying that all unconscious things are directed by the same conscious, intelligent being, namely, God. And that does not follow at all.

Perhaps this interpretation gives Aquinas too little credit. When he speaks of "all things in nature" in the conclusion, he may have in mind all things taken together—that is, the universe as a whole. The universe as a whole lacks awareness. So, perhaps he means to extend the argument as follows:

> All things lacking awareness act under the direction of someone aware and intelligent.

The universe as a whole lacks awareness.
Therefore, the universe as a whole acts under the direction of someone aware and intelligent—namely, God.

In that form, the argument is valid. The first premise, however, may or may not be true.

For various reasons, Aquinas's fifth way did not convince many people; subsequent philosophers took the cosmological argument much more seriously. But in the eighteenth century, English philosopher William Paley (1743–1805), who taught at Cambridge and became archdeacon of Carlisle, put the argument in a rhetorically more powerful form. (Note the implicit criticism of the cosmological argument in the first sentence!)

How does Paley implicitly criticize the cosmological argument?

> In crossing a heath, suppose I pitched my foot against a *stone,* and were asked how the stone came to be there; I might possibly answer, that, for anything I knew to the contrary, it had lain there forever: nor would it perhaps be very easy to show the absurdity of this answer. But suppose I had found a *watch* upon the ground, and it would be inquired how the watch happened to be in that place: I should hardly think of the answer which I had given before, that, for anything I knew, the watch might always have been there. Yet why should not this answer serve for the watch as well as for the stone? Why is it not as admissible in the second case, as in the first?
>
> For this reason, and for no other, viz. that, when we come to inspect the watch, we perceive (what we could not discover in the stone) that its several parts are framed and put together for a purpose, e.g., that they are so formed and adjusted as to produce motion, and that motion so regulated as to point out the hour of the day; that if the different parts had been differently shaped from what they are, of a different size from what they are, or placed after any other manner, or in any other order . . . either no motion at all would have been carried on in the machine, or none which would have answered the use that is now served by it. . . . The inference, we think, is inevitable; that the watch must have had a maker; that there must have existed, at sometime, and at some place or other, an artificer or artificers, who formed it for the purpose which we find it actually to answer; who comprehended its construction, and designed its use.[17]

Finding a watch, we infer from the intricacy and success of its design that it had a maker. The inference is not strictly speaking deductive; it *might* have been the result of an accident. But that is very unlikely. Almost certainly, it had a maker. It does not matter, Paley continues, if the watch does not keep time perfectly, or seems to have extraneous parts. Nor does it matter if the watch after a time produces other watches. That, in fact, would only increase the impressiveness of the maker's design.

What is true of the watch is also true of the universe.

How are the watch and the universe analogous?

> . . . every indication of contrivance, every manifestation of design, which existed in the watch, exists in the works of nature; with the difference, on the side of na-

[17] This and subsequent quotations from William Paley are from *Natural Theology* (London: printed for R. Faulder, 1804).

> ture, of being greater and more, and that in a degree which exceeds all computation. I mean, that the contrivances of nature surpass the contrivances of art, in the complexity, subtlety, and curiosity of the mechanism; and still more, if possible, do they go beyond them in number and variety; yet, in a multitude of cases, are not less evidently mechanical, not less evidently contrivances, not less evidently accommodated to their end, or suited to their office, than are the most perfect productions of human ingenuity.

Not only does the entire universe display the kind of order that leads us to infer that it had a maker; certain parts of the universe, for example, the ear or eye, also display that kind of order and would point to the existence of a maker even if the universe as a whole were chaotic:

> Were there no example in the world of contrivance, except that of the eye, it would be alone sufficient to suppose the conclusion which we draw from it, as to the necessity of an intelligent Creator. . . . If other parts of nature were inaccessible to our inquiries, or even if other parts of nature presented nothing to our examination but disorder and confusion, the validity of this example would remain the same. If there were but one watch in the world, it would not be less certain that it had a maker. . . . The argument is cumulative, in the fullest sense of that term. The eye proves [divine agency] without the ear; the ear without the eye. The proof in each example is complete; for when the design of the part, and the conduciveness of its structure to that design is shown, the mind may set itself at rest; no future consideration can detract anything from the force of the example.

Contemporary debate about the argument from design centers on Charles Darwin's theory of evolution, which tries to show that the apparent design of the world is only apparent. Evolutionary theory, that is, tries to show that random mutation and natural selection (the "survival of the fittest") can explain the development of design. The prospects for success of the program of evolutionary theory raise difficult biological questions that we cannot address here. Philosophically, however, the classic attack in the argument from design occurs in David Hume's *Dialogues Concerning Natural Religion.* The argument's defender in the *Dialogues,* Cleanthes, summarizes it elegantly:

> Contemplate the whole world and every part of it: You will find it to be nothing but one great machine, subdivided into an infinite number of lesser machines, which again admit of subdivisions to a degree beyond what human senses and faculties can trace and explain. All these various machines, and even their most minute parts, are adjusted to each other with an accuracy which ravages into admiration all men who have ever contemplated them. The curious adapting of means to ends, throughout all nature, resembles exactly, though it much exceeds, the productions of human contrivance; of human design, thought, wisdom, and intelligence. Since therefore the effects resemble each other, we are led to infer, by all the rules of analogy, that the causes also resemble, and that the Author of Nature is somewhat similar to the mind of man, though possessed of much larger faculties, proportioned to the grandeur of the work which he has executed. By this argument *a posteriori,* and

> by this argument alone, do we prove at once the existence of a Deity and his similarity to human mind and intelligence.[18]

Philo, the *Dialogues*'s skeptic, attacks the argument on several grounds. First, he objects, the analogy is not that strong. Kant later extends this objection to a claim that, in general, we cannot extend principles that apply to the things we experience to things beyond the realm of all possible experience, like the creation of the world.

> If we see a house, Cleanthes, we conclude, with the greatest certainty, that it had an architect or builder because this is precisely that species of effect which we have experienced to proceed from that species of cause. But surely you will not affirm that the universe bears such a resemblance to a house that we can with the same certainty infer a similar cause, or that the analogy is here entire and perfect. The dissimilitude is so striking that the utmost you can here pretend to is a guess, a conjecture, a presumption concerning a similar cause. . . .

Philo also complains that the order we find in the universe may be self-generated; the universe may contain its own principles of self-organization (as Darwin's theory of evolution, for example, would later suggest that it does).

> . . . order, arrangement, or the adjustment of final causes, is not of itself any proof of design, but only so far as it has been experienced to proceed from that principle. For aught we can know *a priori,* matter may contain the source or spring of order originally within itself, as well as mind does; and there is no more difficulty conceiving that the several elements, from an internal unknown cause, may fall into the most exquisite arrangement, than to conceive that their ideas, in the great universal mind, from a like internal unknown cause, fall into that arrangement.

Cleanthes is not convinced; he compares the universe to a library:

> Suppose that there is a natural, universal, invariable language, common to every individual of the human race, and that books are natural productions which perpetuate themselves in the same manner with animals and vegetables, by descent and propagation. . . .
>
> Suppose, therefore, that you enter into your library thus peopled by natural volumes containing the most refined reason and most exquisite beauty. Could you possibly open one of them and doubt that its original cause bore the strongest analogy to mind and intelligence?

Philo then sharpens his attack by pointing out that taking the analogy between the universe and products of human invention seriously leads to some disturbing consequences:

What disturbing consequences does the analogy between the universe and a machine have, according to Philo?

> First, by this method of reasoning you renounce all claim to infinity in any of the attributes of the Deity. For, as the cause ought only to be proportioned to the effect,

[18] This and subsequent quotations from David Hume are from *Dialogues Concerning Natural Religion* (London, 1779), Part II.

> and the effect, so far as it falls under our cognizance, is not infinite: What pretensions have we, upon your suppositions, to ascribe that attribute to a Divine Being? . . .
>
> Secondly, you have no reason, on your theory, for ascribing perfection to the Deity, even in his finite capacity; or for supposing him free from every error, mistake, or incoherence, in his undertakings. There are many inexplicable difficulties in the works of Nature. . . . At least, you must acknowledge that it is impossible for us to tell, from our limited views, whether this system contains any great faults or deserves any considerable praise if compared to other possible and even real systems. Could a peasant, if the *Aeneid* were read to him, pronounce that poem to be absolutely faultless, or even assign to it its proper rank among the productions of human wit, he who had never seen any other production?
>
> But were this world ever so perfect a production, it must still remain uncertain whether all the excellences of the work can justly be ascribed to the workman. If we survey a ship, what an exalted idea must we form of the ingenuity of the carpenter who framed so complicated, useful, and beautiful a machine? And what surprise must we feel when we find him a stupid mechanic who imitated others, and copied an art which, through a long succession of ages, after multiplied trials, mistakes, corrections, deliberations, and controversies, had been gradually improving? Many worlds might have been botched and bungled, throughout an eternity, ere this system was struck out; much labor lost; many fruitless trials made; and a slow but continued improvement carried on during infinite ages in the art of world-making. In such subjects, who can determine where the truth, nay, who can conjecture where the probability lies, amidst a great number of hypotheses which may be proposed, and a still greater which may be imagined?
>
> And what shadow of an argument, continued Philo, can you produce from your hypothesis to prove the unity of the Deity? A great number of men join in building a house or a ship, in rearing a city, in framing a commonwealth; why may not several deities combine in contriving and framing a world?

Why, moreover, should we think that the world is more like a machine than an animal or vegetable?

> If the universe bears a greater likeness to animal bodies and to vegetables than to the works of human art, it is more probable that its cause resembles the cause of the former than that of the latter, and its origin ought rather to be ascribed to generation or vegetation than to reason or design.

Philo concludes with a generally skeptical form of argument. In the absence of data, many hypotheses are possible (variability), and we have no way to choose (undecidability).

> . . . we have no *data* to establish any system of cosmogony. Our experience, so imperfect in itself and so limited both in extent and duration, can afford us no probable conjecture concerning the whole of things. But if we must needs fix on some hypothesis, by what rule, pray, ought we to determine our choice?

Hume thus leaves us with skepticism concerning our ability to prove God's existence, or even to know anything beyond the realm of our own experience.

PRACTICAL ARGUMENTS

So far we have been considering theoretical arguments for God's existence. But some of the most influential arguments for the existence of God are **practical arguments,** insisting that belief in God is inevitable or at least rational.

Pascal's Wager

The best-known practical argument for God's existence is **Pascal's wager,** developed by Blaise Pascal (1623–1662), a French philosopher and mathematician who was a contemporary of Descartes and a member of the Port-Royal Academy. Pascal, despairing of any attempt to prove God's existence theoretically, thinks of the person trying to decide whether or not to believe in God as someone about to make a bet:

> Let us then examine this point, and say, "God is, or He is not." But to which side shall we incline? Reason can decide nothing here. There is an infinite chaos which separated us. A game is being played at the extremity of this infinite distance where heads or tails will turn up. What will you wager? According to reason, you can do neither one thing nor the other; according to reason, you can defend neither of the propositions.[19]

You must place your bet, that is, under conditions of total uncertainty; you cannot know whether God exists or not, or even where the probabilities lie. And you cannot refuse to bet; you must believe in God or decline to believe in Him. What should you do?

> Let us weigh the gain and the loss in wagering that God is. Let us estimate these two chances. If you gain, you gain all; if you lose, you lose nothing. Wager, then, without hesitation that He is.

Here, in short, is the situation facing you:

Pascal's Wager

	You believe	*You do not believe*
God exists	Heaven, Virtue	Hell
God does not exist	Virtue	Nothing

If you believe, and God exists, you earn the eternal rewards of Heaven. If God does not exist, you still benefit:

Why would even an erroneous faith be beneficial?

> Now what harm will befall you in taking this side? You will be faithful, humble, grateful, generous, a sincere friend, truthful. Certainly you will not have those poisonous pleasures, glory and luxury; but will you not have others? I will tell

[19] This and subsequent quotations from Blaise Pascal are from *Thoughts,* translated by W. F. Trotter (New York: P. F. Collier and Son, 1910), 233.

> you that you will thereby gain in this life, and that, at each step you take on this road, you will see so great certainty of gain, so much nothingness in what you risk, that you will at last recognize that you have wagered for something certain and definite, for which you have given nothing.

In short, believing in God develops virtues, whether or not God exists. If He exists, it additionally yields the infinite benefit of Heaven. There is nothing to lose and everything to gain. (This assumes that God admits believers into Heaven even if they believe for self-interested reasons. Rabi'a al-'Adawiyya [d. 801; see Chapter 3], among others, would doubt this.)

In contrast, failing to believe can result in no benefit whatever. If God exists, it earns one the eternal punishments of Hell. If God does not exist—or if the traditional picture of Hell is mistaken—then it yields nothing: no reward, no punishment. There is nothing to gain and everything to lose.

Placing a bet that God does not exist, then, cannot win, and placing a bet that God exists cannot lose. Pascal concludes that faith in God is rational, even if God's existence cannot be given rational proof.

Pascal's wager seems to clash with a modern, scientific sensibility, for it urges that it is rational to believe in God's existence even in the total absence of evidence. But can it ever be rational to believe in something without any supporting evidence? Hume, for example, answers no:

> All that belongs to human understanding, in this deep ignorance and obscurity, is to be skeptical or at least cautious, and not to admit of any hypothesis whatever, much less of any which is supported by no appearance of probability.[20]

But American pragmatist William James (1842–1910; see Chapter 1) argues that this attitude is so restrictive that it is itself irrational.

> Scepticism, then, is not avoidance of option; it is option of a certain particular kind of risk. *Better risk loss of truth than chance of error*—that is your faith-vetoer's exact position. He is actively playing his stake as much as the believer is; he is backing the field against the religious hypothesis, just as the believer is backing the religious hypothesis against the field. To preach scepticism to us as a duty until "sufficient evidence" for religion be found, is tantamount therefore to telling us, when in presence of the religious hypothesis, that to yield to our fear of its being error is wiser and better than to yield to our hope that it may be true. It is not intellect against all passions, then; it is only intellect with one passion laying down its law. And by what, forsooth, is the supreme wisdom of this passion warranted? Dupery for dupery, what proof is there that dupery through hope is so much worse than dupery through fear?[21]

There is no *argument,* in short, for refusing to believe in the absence of supporting evidence. In fact, the modern, skeptical attitude, by excluding certain possibilities at the outset, is itself irrational:

---

[20] David Hume, *Dialogues Concerning Natural Religion* (London, 1779), Part XI (Philo speaking).

[21] William James, "The Will to Believe," in *The Will to Believe and Other Essays in Popular Philosophy* (New York: Longmans, Green, 1896).

> If the [religious] hypothesis *were* true in all its parts . . . then pure intellectualism, with its veto on our making willing advances, would be an absurdity; and some participation of our sympathetic nature would be logically required. I, therefore, for one, cannot see my way to accepting the agnostic rules of truth-seeking, or willfully agree to keep my willing nature out of the game. I cannot do so for this plain reason, that *a rule of thinking which would absolutely prevent me from acknowledging certain kinds of truth if those kinds of truth were really there, would be an irrational rule.*

We want to believe what is true but also avoid believing what is false. Adopting a skeptical attitude and refusing to believe until we have supporting evidence helps us avoid falsehood, but it can also keep us from believing truths. Being gullible can help us believe truths, but also sets us up to believe falsehoods. We must somehow find a proper mean between these extremes. Now, if religious truths were the only ones we might miss by adopting a skeptical stance, we might insist that the attitude is reasonable and that there are no grounds for making an exception for religion. (Although an attitude that might preclude believing that there is a God, that the universe has a purpose, and so on, if these things are true, is already problematic!) But James points out that skepticism risks missing other truths of real practical import. What kind of evidence do we have for thinking that murder is wrong? That generosity and kindness are virtues? That we have free will? Or, for that matter, as Hume himself shows, that the future will resemble the past? Applying a skeptical attitude across the board rules out not only religion but morality, action, and prediction.

The Moral Argument

The idea that religion and morality hang together lies behind the other influential practical argument for God's existence, that of Immanuel Kant: the moral argument. Kant, as we have seen, denies that any theoretical proof of God's existence is possible. Nevertheless, he thinks, we cannot live and act except on the assumption that God exists. There is in this respect a perfect analogy between God's existence and human freedom. Theoretically, Kant believes, we cannot establish either that humans have free will or that all our actions are determined. Nonetheless, we cannot act as if all our actions are determined; we find ourselves having to believe, practically, in our own free will in order to function. Similarly, although we cannot demonstrate that God does or does not exist, we find ourselves having to believe in God to make sense of our lives and, in particular, of morality.

> . . . everyone has a ground to hope for happiness in the measure in which he has rendered himself by his conduct worthy of it. . . . [N]either the nature of the things of the world nor the causality of the actions themselves and their relation to morality determine how the consequences of these actions will be related to happiness. The alleged necessary connection of the hope of happiness with the necessary endeavor to render the self worthy of happiness cannot therefore be known through reason. It can be counted upon only if a Supreme Reason, that governs according to moral rules, be likewise posited as underlying nature as its cause.
>
> . . . we must assume that moral world [in which happiness stands in exact relation with morality, that is, with worthiness to be happy] to be a consequence

> of our conduct in the world of sense (in which no such connection between worthiness and happiness is exhibited), and therefore to be for us a future world. Thus God and a future life are two postulates which, according to the principles of pure reason, are inseparable from the obligation which that same reason imposes upon us.[22]

In this world, bad things happen to good people, while the wicked prosper. Why, then, should we strive to be good? Being moral is rational only if it is rewarded. Since that evidently does not happen in this life—Kant will have none of Plato's optimism on this score!—it must happen in another life. In short, there must be an afterlife, and there must be a God who dispenses justice in it. Otherwise, morality is nonsense. As one of Fyodor Dostoyevsky's characters contends, "If God does not exist, then everything is permitted."

THE PROBLEM OF EVIL

Kant takes the injustice of this world as evidence for God's existence and for God's justice in an afterlife. Other philosophers, however, have seen in the world's injustice, evil, and misfortune an argument against God's existence. The argument has its origins in the ancient Greek philosopher Epicurus (341–270 B.C.E.) but finds its clearest expression in the words of Hume's Philo:

> His power, we allow, is infinite; whatever he wills is executed: But neither man nor any other animal is happy; therefore he does not will their happiness. His wisdom is infinite; He is never mistaken in choosing the means to any end; But the course of nature tends not to human or animal felicity: Therefore, it is not established for that purpose. Through the whole compass of human knowledge there are no inferences more certain and infallible than these. In what respect, then, do his benevolence and mercy resemble the benevolence and mercy of men?
>
> *Epicurus'* old questions are yet unanswered.
>
> Is he willing to prevent evil, but not able? then he is impotent. Is he able, but not willing? then he is malevolent. Is he both able and willing? whence then is evil?[23]

Hume's argument (the **argument from evil**) purports to show that God is either unwilling or unable to prevent evil. If God were omnipotent (all-powerful), omniscient (all-knowing), and entirely good, however, then God would be both willing and able to prevent evil. So, the existence of evil shows that God does not exist—or, at least, that God does not have the properties that most religions attribute to Him.

The world's great religions, of course, have long recognized the enigma posed by the existence of evil. The reflections of the Buddha were prompted by his encounter

[22] Immanuel Kant, *Critique of Pure Reason,* translated by Norman Kemp Smith (New York: St. Martin's, 1929), 638–639.

[23] David Hume, *Dialogues Concerning Natural Religion* (London, 1779), Part X.

with the three evils of sickness, old age, and death. The book of Job wrestles with the problems posed by a good person's suffering. How can God's goodness and power be reconciled with the existence of suffering?

Providence

Saint Augustine (354–430; see Chapter 2) formulates the classic Christian response. His solution to the **problem of evil** has three main components. All attack Hume's premise that, if God is not willing to prevent evil, He is malevolent.

The first component is that we must judge the universe as a whole, not part by part, for the excellence of the whole may depend on parts that, taken alone, do not seem good:

> By the Trinity, thus supremely and equally and unchangeably good, all things were created; and these are not supremely and equally and unchangeably good, but yet they are good, even taken separately. Taken as a whole, however, they are very good, because their *ensemble* constitutes the universe in all its wonderful order and beauty.[24]

A good life, for example, is not one that contains no adversity, but rather one that contains adversity overcome. A universe with some evil may be better than one without any evil at all. It must therefore be good that there is some evil:

> Nor can we doubt that God does well even in the permission of what is evil. For He permits it only in the justice of His judgment. And surely all that is just is good. Although, therefore, evil, in so far as it is evil, is not a good; yet the fact that evil as well as good exists, is a good.

By itself, this seems hard to swallow. Why is it good that there are murders, wars, famines, and earthquakes? But theologians have developed it into the doctrine of the general providence of God. When Job challenges God, He responds:

> Where wast thou when I laid the foundations of the earth? declare, if thou hast understanding.
>
> Who hath laid the measures thereof, if thou knowest? or who hath stretched the line upon it?
>
> Whereupon are the foundations thereof fastened? or who laid the corner stone thereof;
>
> When the morning stars sang together, and all the sons of God shouted for joy? (*Job* 38:4–7)

God, that is, established the universe and the natural laws that govern it. Those laws make possible the stars, the moon, the earth's green fields, blue seas, and purple mountains, and everything that brings joy to human hearts. They make possible the arts of medicine, engineering, and, in short, the entire array of human achievements. But

[24] This and subsequent passages from St. Augustine, unless otherwise noted, are from *The Enchiridion*, from *The Works of Aurelius Augustine*, Volume X (Edinburgh: T & T Clark, 1883), Chapter X.

the same laws also make possible murders, wars, famines, and earthquakes. Could God have crafted laws for the universe that would have made possible the good things without also making possible the bad? Or perhaps permit frequent violations of the laws to prevent the bad without thereby disrupting the good? It is not obvious that He could have. Leibniz, in fact, argued that He could not have; this is the best of all possible worlds, Leibniz contended, despite its obvious defects, for any attempt to improve it would produce side effects that are even worse.

The second part of Augustine's solution is the doctrine that evil is the absence of good, advocated first by the neo-Platonic philosopher Plotinus (204–270), who was of Greek ancestry, was born in Egypt, was educated in Alexandria, and taught for twenty-six years in Rome. As Augustine puts it:

> And in the universe, even that which is called evil, when it is regulated and put in its own place, only enhances our admiration of the good; for we enjoy and value the good more when we compare it with the evil. For the Almighty God, who, as even the heathen acknowledge, has supreme power over all things, being Himself supremely good, would never permit the existence of anything evil among His works, if He were not so omnipotent and good that He can bring good even out of evil. For what is that which we call evil but the absence of good?

This allows Augustine to say that God does not create evil, for evil is not a thing; it is simply a lack, a thing's failure to be better.

Free Will

The third part of Augustine's solution is the corruptibility of things—in particular, human beings, who can exercise their free wills to do evil. God, for reasons we do not understand, created human beings with the capacity to make choices. People can do good but can also do evil. Undoubtedly, much evil can be explained as the result of free human choices. In the twentieth century, for example, over 100 million people were killed by their own governments. The litany of such horrors is overwhelming: The Armenian genocide, Stalin's forced famine in the Ukraine, Hitler's death camps, the Gulag archipelago, and Pol Pot's murder of a third of the Cambodian population are only the best-known examples. Tens of millions more have been killed in wars. These are human acts for which human beings are responsible.

Nevertheless, it appears that free will cannot explain everything. Some kinds of evil are not the result of human choice. Hurricanes, tornadoes, earthquakes, and diseases strike the just and the unjust independently of human acts of will. The bubonic plague, for example, killed over half the population of Europe in the sixteenth and seventeenth centuries. The Great Plague of London of 1665 killed 68,596 people, more than a third of the city's residents, in just four months. The Lisbon earthquake of 1755 killed over 30,000 people and did much to undermine faith in God during the Enlightenment. In some works, Augustine argues that these are products of human action in the sense that they are part of the punishment for original sin, that is, for Adam and Eve's disobedience in the Garden of Eden. In other places, however, he holds that such natural evils can hardly be blamed on the freedom of the human will.

What does the example of the two infants show, according to Augustine?

> For example, when of two infants, whose cases seem in all respects alike, one is by the mercy of God chosen to Himself, and the other is by His justice abandoned (wherein the one who is chosen may recognize what was of justice due to himself, had not mercy intervened); why, of these two, the one should have been chosen rather than the other, is to us an insoluble problem. And again, why miracles were not wrought in the presence of men who would have repented at the working of miracles, while they were wrought in the presence of others who, it was known, would not repent.

Augustine remains discontent with a free-will defense for a different reason as well:

> Who made me? Surely it was my God, who is not only good but Goodness itself. How, then, do I come to possess a will that can choose to do wrong and refuse to do good, thereby providing a just reason why I should be punished? Who put this will into me? Who sowed this seed of bitterness in me, when all that I am was made by my God, who is Sweetness itself? If it was the devil who put it there, who made the devil? If he was a good angel who became a devil because of his own wicked will, how did he come to possess the wicked will which made him a devil, when the Creator, who is entirely good, made him a good angel and nothing else?[25]

In short, even if evil results from human free choice, isn't God responsible for giving humans the ability and the will to choose evil? Adam and Eve may have eaten the fruit of the tree in the garden, but God gave them the opportunity and the propensity to eat it. Augustine feels uncomfortable assigning responsibility either to humans or to God; to seek the root of an evil choice "is as if one sought to see darkness, or hear silence."[26] In the end, freedom is unanalyzable: "What cause of willing can there be which is prior to willing?"[27] God did not corrupt Adam and Eve—but he made them corruptible.

Even corruptible things are good, Augustine affirms:

> All things that exist, therefore, seeing that the Creator of them all is supremely good, are themselves good. But because they are not, like their Creator, supremely and unchangeably good, their good may be diminished and increased. But for good to be diminished is an evil, although, however much it may be diminished, it is necessary, if the being is to continue, that some good should remain to constitute the being. For however small or of whatever kind the being may be, the good which makes it a being cannot be destroyed without destroying the being itself. An uncorrupted nature is justly held in esteem. But if, still further, it be incorruptible, it is undoubtedly considered of still higher value. When it is corrupted, however, its corruption is an evil, because it is deprived of some sort of good. For if it be deprived

[25] Augustine, *Confessions,* translated by R. S. Pine-Coffin (Harmondsworth: Penguin, 1961), Book VII, 137.

[26] Augustine, *City of God,* in P. Schaff and A. Roberts (ed.), *The Nicene and Post-Nicene Fathers of the Christian Church* (New York: Christian Literature Company, 1890), XII, 7.

[27] Augustine, *Free Will,* in P. Schaff and A. Roberts (ed.), *The Nicene and Post-Nicene Fathers of the Christian Church* (New York: Christian Literature Company, 1890), III, xvii, 49.

> of no good, it receives no injury; but it does receive injury, therefore it is deprived of good. Therefore, so long as a being is in process of corruption, there is in it some good of which it is being deprived; and if a part of the being should remain which cannot be corrupted, this will certainly be an incorruptible being, and accordingly the process of corruption will result in the manifestation of this great good. But if it do not cease to be corrupted, neither can it cease to possess good of which corruption may deprive it. But if it should be thoroughly and completely consumed by corruption, there will then be no good left, because there will be no being. Wherefore corruption can consume the good only by consuming the being. Every being, therefore, is a good; a great good, if it cannot be corrupted; a little good, if it can: but in any case, only the foolish or ignorant will deny that it is a good. And if it be wholly consumed by corruption, then the corruption itself must cease to exist, as there is no being left in which it can dwell.[28]

"Therefore," as Augustine puts it in the *Confessions,* "whatever is, is good." Evil is not a thing, something God created or even chosen by free human beings in its own right. Humans choose evil by choosing a lesser good over a greater good. Stalin, for example, valued his own power over the lives and freedom of millions of people. Pol Pot similarly valued his own vision of society over millions of lives. Adam and Eve valued the fruit of the tree—and its consequence, the knowledge of good and evil—over obedience to God. From Augustine's perspective, these acts involved not choosing evil over good but choosing a minor good at the cost of a vastly greater good.

Hinduism and Buddhism

Hinduism and Buddhism offer very different reactions to the problem of evil. Both take evil as a major concern and motivation. But the solutions they propose bear little similarity to Western solutions.

Hinduism confronts the problem of evil on several levels. The *Bhagavad Gita,* a small portion of a long epic, the *Mahabharata,* considers an impending war. The *Mahabharata*'s story centers on a conflict over the succession to the throne in the ancient civilization along the Ganges River. Five brothers are the principal "good guys" with a just claim on the throne, but many noble sages and heroes fight against them. Krishna, prince of a neighboring state, joins the battle as charioteer for the third brother, a champion archer named Arjuna. The *Gita,* a dialogue between Krishna and Arjuna (Everyman), occurs moments before the battle begins. Even if war is justified, it carries immense costs; it is a great source of suffering even under the best of circumstances. Arjuna, for that very reason, wonders whether it is right for him to fight. He looks across the battle line at his friends and kin and cannot face the prospect of killing them. He sinks down in his chariot, paralyzed about what to do.

> No good do I see in killing my own family in battle. I desire not victory, nor rule, nor pleasures, Krishna; what is power to us, enjoyments, or life, Govinda? Those

[28] Augustine, *The Enchiridion,* from *The Works of Aurelius Augustine,* Volume X (Edinburgh: T & T Clark, 1883), Chapter XII.

> who make rulership desirable for us, and enjoyments and pleasures, it is they that are arrayed in battle against us, abandoning life and wealth. Teachers, fathers, sons, grandfathers, uncles, in-laws—these I do not wish to kill even if it means that I must die, Krishna—not even to rule the three worlds, why then for the earth?[29]

Krishna reveals himself as God incarnate and provides a religious and mystical answer to Arjuna's ethical crisis. He urges Arjuna to fight, assuring him that fighting is his religious duty. We will discuss this further and more extensively in Chapter 8. Now, however, one aspect of Krishna's answer is especially important. He tells Arjuna not to worry about killing his relatives and countrymen, because the soul is immortal and cannot be destroyed:

> This embodied (soul) is eternally unslayable
> In the body of every one, son of Bharata;
> Therefore all beings
> Thou shouldst not mourn.[30]

Krishna's answer to Arjuna might seem to miss the point. Many people who believe that we have eternal souls nevertheless think that killing is bad. Pain, suffering, and death matter even if they do not destroy a soul. But Krishna relies on the Hindu conception of the self outlined in Chapter 4. He assumes reincarnation. The soul, finding one body no longer of use, steps off that chariot and waits for another. So, anyone Arjuna kills in battle will simply await another reincarnation. That is not to say that suffering and death have no meaning. But they have a different and less serious meaning than they do in other conceptions of the soul. If you find life terrible, don't worry; you'll have another chance.

More generally, everything is illusion; suffering and death are unreal. The world as it appears to us is *maya,* illusion; the evil that it contains is not ultimately real. The ultimate reality is Brahman, and Brahman neither changes nor suffers. We tend to think of the objects of our experience, and our pleasures and pains, as real. But they are only fleeting expressions of a deeper reality. That is not to say that people do not really feel pain or die; they do. Pain and death are real in a sense, but it is the sense in which appearances are real. The underlying reality suffers no harm at all.

We can see Hinduism, therefore, as offering a twofold response to the argument from evil in Epicurus and Hume. First, Brahman is a reality underlying everything, not a being with a will. Brahman cannot accurately be described as either all-good or all-powerful. So, the argument as stated does not apply to Brahman. Second, the general pattern of argument is that the existence of evil is incompatible with the existence of God. Epicurus and Hume contend that, since evil exists, God does not. The *Gita* turns this around; since God exists, evil does not. Apparent evil is illusory.

Buddhism responds to evil in yet another way. The argument of Epicurus and Hume does not apply to Buddhism, since it postulates no supernatural being. Nevertheless the problem of evil is at the forefront of Buddhist thought. This is not the place to consider Buddhism in detail; we have discussed the Buddhist concept of the self in

---

[29] The *Bhagavad Gita,* translated by Stephen H. Phillips.

[30] The *Bhagavad Gita,* translated and interpreted by Franklin Edgerton (Cambridge: Harvard University Press, 1944).

Chapter 4 and will treat Buddhist ethics in Chapters 7 and 8. Here it is enough to recall that the Buddha's spiritual crisis was brought about by his encounter with suffering (specifically, old age, disease, and death). How can we understand and respond to a world containing evils such as "old age, death, sorrow, lamentation, misery, grief, and despair"?[31] That is the central question of Buddhism.

The Buddha bases his response on Four Noble Truths:

1. Life is painful (*dukkha*). This noble truth characterizes the symptom of the human condition: Life is painful, dislocated, out of joint.

> 1. Now this, O monks, is the noble truth of pain: birth is painful, old age is painful, sickness is painful, death is painful, sorrow, lamentation, dejection, and despair are painful. Contact with unpleasant things is painful, not getting what one wishes is painful. In short the five *khandhas* of grasping are painful.[32]

2. The root of pain is desire, attachment, or personal clinging (*tanha*). This gives the diagnosis: Selfish desire, craving, is the cause of suffering.

> 2. Now this, O monks, is the noble truth of the cause of pain: that craving which leads to rebirth, combined with pleasure and lust, finding pleasure here and there, namely, the craving for passion, the craving for existence, the craving for non-existence.

3. There is a way to eliminate desire and thereby eliminate suffering, namely *nirvana* experience. This gives the prognosis: There is a way to eliminate suffering. To eliminate suffering, eliminate desire.

> 3. Now this, O monks, is the noble truth of the cessation of pain: the cessation without a remainder of that craving, abandonment, forsaking, release, nonattachment.

4. The way to this supreme good is the Eightfold Noble Path: right thought, right resolve, right speech, right conduct, right livelihood, right effort, right mindfulness, and right concentration or meditation. The Eightfold Path is the Buddha's prescription: To eliminate desire, follow the Eightfold Path.

> 4. Now this, O monks, is the noble truth of the way that leads to the cessation of pain: this is the noble Eightfold Path, namely, right views, right intention, right speech, right action, right livelihood, right effort, right mindfulness, right concentration. . . .

We will examine the Buddha's Eightfold Path in detail in Chapter 8. It is the heart of Buddhist ethics. But the Four Noble Truths may be seen as the Buddha's solution to

---

[31] The *Majjhima-Nikaya*, translated by Henry Clarke Warren, in *Buddhism in Translations* (Cambridge: Harvard University Press, 1896).

[32] "The First Sermon," in Edward J. Thomas, *The Life of Buddha as Legend and History* (New York: Alfred A. Knopf, Inc., 1927).

the problem of evil. There is undoubtedly evil in the world; it is fully real. People suffer, grow old, and die. But we can learn to eliminate pain by eliminating desire. Why, after all, do pain, infirmity, and death cause us suffering? It is because we want to feel good. We want to be active. We want above all to live. The world thus does not match our desires, and suffering results from the mismatch. So, we must either change the world or change ourselves. Prospects for eliminating pain, aging, illness, and death look only slightly better in our day than they did in Buddha's day. So, the best route is to change ourselves, giving up our desires for pleasure, activity, and life.

SUMMARY

What is religion? Is there a God? If so, what is God like? Can we advance any rational arguments for or against belief in God? These questions have central importance in a wide range of philosophical traditions. But those traditions offer very different answers. Some adopt a classical concept of God as almighty, all-knowing, eternal, and compassionate. Others, such as Daoism, treat God as an impersonal ground of being, something that underlies everything but has no will of its own. Hinduism treats God as one but as having many forms, comprising many different gods and goddesses.

Philosophers argue for God's existence on a priori as well as a posteriori grounds. If God did not exist, they ask, how could we have acquired an idea of God? How could the universe have begun? On what could it depend? What could explain its beauty and order? But others argue against God's existence: If God is all-good and all-powerful, they ask, why is there evil? Why do people suffer and die? Philosophical traditions answer these questions very differently as well.

REVIEW QUESTIONS

1. Can one define religion in terms of beliefs? In terms of practices? Why or why not?
2. Compare the definitions of religion offered by Schleiermacher, Otto, and Tillich. Does one have an advantage over the others, in your view?
3. How do the conceptions of God found in Hinduism, Confucianism, and Daoism differ from the classical Western conception of God?
4. Explain Descartes's argument from thought. What is the Cartesian circle?
5. What is the ontological argument? How does Kant criticize it? Do you find his criticism persuasive?
6. Compare the cosmological arguments of Aquinas and Avicenna. Are there important differences between these arguments, or do they stand or fall together?
7. Discuss al-Ghazali's criticism of Avicenna's ontological argument. How do Averroës and Leibniz respond to that criticism? Do they succeed in answering al-Ghazali?
8. What is the design argument? Explain and assess Hume's critique of it.

9. Describe Pascal's wager. Does it give a compelling reason for believing in God?
10. What is the problem of evil? Discuss and evaluate an attempted solution.

Terms for Review

argument from design The argument that the universe, like a watch or other machine, shows such a beauty and coordination of parts that it must be the product of a creator. Also called the teleological argument.

argument from evil The argument that, if God were omnipotent (all-powerful), omniscient (all-knowing), and entirely good, God would be both willing and able to prevent evil. So the existence of evil shows that God does not exist—or, at least, that God does not have the properties that most religions attribute to Him.

argument from thought The argument that God exists, because only God could be the source of our idea of God.

atheism The view that there is no supernatural being.

classical theism The view that there exists an almighty (omnipotent), all-knowing (omniscient), eternal, omnipresent, transcendent, and compassionate God.

classical Western concept of God The concept of a being who is almighty (omnipotent), all-knowing (omniscient), eternal, omnipresent, transcendent, and compassionate.

cosmological argument The argument that God exists as a first cause of the universe or necessary being on which all other beings depend.

deism The view that God exists and created the world but has had no further interaction with it.

faith According to Tillich, the state of being ultimately concerned; the defining attitude of the religious person.

formal (actual) reality In Descartes, the reality of objects in the actual world.

henotheism The view that there is one God who takes many forms. There are various gods and goddesses, but all are forms of a single God.

humanism The view that value is to be defined in purely human terms.

intentional object An object of thought.

monotheism The view that there is exactly one God.

moral argument The argument that morality compels belief in God; recognizing injustice, we must think God exists and will right these injustices in the afterlife.

numinous The holy.

objective reality In Descartes, the reality of the contents of our ideas—their objects, what our ideas are *about*. Since we now call things objective when they do *not* depend on our own states of mind, Descartes's usage is confusing. When he attributes objective reality to something, he means to say it is an object of thought, an *intentional object*.

ontological argument The argument that God, being perfect, must exist necessarily, for necessary existence is better than contingent existence, which is better than nonexistence.

panentheism The view that everything is God but that God also transcends the world.

pantheism The view that God is everything; that is, that God exists and moreover is the *only* thing that exists. The pantheist, contending that God is everything, in effect identifies God and nature. The pantheist thus denies that God transcends the universe. Indeed, for the pantheist, God just *is* the universe.

Pascal's wager The argument that it is rational to believe in God, for the believer wins all if God exists and loses nothing if there is no God.

polytheism The view that there is more than one god.

practical argument An argument with a practical conclusion, that is, a conclusion about what ought to be done; or, in the philosophy of religion, an argument that belief in God is inevitable or at least rational.

prime mover The first cause, for Aristotle. Every change has a cause other than itself. There cannot be an infinite regress of causes, however; so there must have been a first cause.

problem of evil The problem posed by the argument from evil: How can God let bad things happen to good people?

teleological argument The argument that the universe, like a watch or other machine, shows such a beauty and coordination of parts that it must be the product of a creator. Also called the argument from design.

ultimate concern Something you care about deeply. It demands your total surrender; you are willing to give up everything else for it. And it promises total fulfillment, even if you do give up everything else.

via negativa The "negative way" of presenting the nature of God by saying what God is not.

For Further Reading

Huston Smith, in *The Religions of Man* (New York: Harper and Row, 1965), gives a majestic if slightly outdated overview of the major world religions. An excellent recent treatment of major Asian religions is Patrick Bresnan, *Awakening: An Introduction to the History of Eastern Thought* (Upper Saddle River: Prentice-Hall, 1999). Ninian Smart's *The Religious Experience of Mankind* (New York: Scribner's, 1976) is a detailed study, as is Mircea Eliade's classic *A History of Religious Ideas* (Chicago: University of Chicago Press, 1978).

A fine multicultural introduction to the philosophy of religion is Stephen H. Phillips (ed.), *Philosophy of Religion: A Global Approach* (Fort Worth: Harcourt Brace, 1996). Texts for many of the sources discussed in this chapter may be found in Daniel Bonevac and Stephen Phillips (ed.), *Understanding Non-Western Philosophy* (Mountain View: Mayfield, 1993).

On Judaism, Louis Finkelstein, *The Jews: Their History, Culture, and Religion* (New York: Harper, 1960), presents a rich scholarly study, and Jacob Neusner, *The Way of the Torah* (Belmont: Wadsworth, 1979), offers an introductory treatment. Harry Wolfson has written two classic treatments of Christianity and Islam: *The Philosophy of the Church Fathers* (Cambridge: Harvard University Press, 1970) and *The Philosophy of the Kalam* (Cambridge: Harvard University Press, 1976).

On arguments for God's existence, see William Lane Craig, *The Cosmological Argument from Plato to Leibniz* (New York: Barnes and Noble, 1980) and *The Kalam Cosmo-*

logical Argument (London: Macmillan, 1969); John Hick (ed.), *The Existence of God* (New York: Macmillan, 1964); Anthony Kenny, *The Five Ways: Saint Thomas Aquinas' Proofs of God's Existence* (London: Routledge and Kegan Paul, 1969); Alvin Plantinga, *The Nature of Necessity* (Oxford: Oxford University Press, 1974); and Richard Swinburne, *The Existence of God* (Oxford: Clarendon, 1979). On the problem of evil, see Nelson Pike (ed.), *God and Evil: Readings on the Theological Problem of Evil* (Englewood Cliffs: Prentice-Hall, 1964) and Marilyn McCord Adams and Robert Merrihew Adams (ed.), *The Problem of Evil* (New York: Oxford University Press, 1990).

She knows what maddens us is what we ought
To be and never are. She also knows
How little what we are is what we are.
—John Burt, "Rich Blind Minotaur Led by a Girl"

C H A P T E R 7

Virtue

Philosophy is the pursuit of wisdom. Ethics is specifically the pursuit of *practical* wisdom, good judgment about action, about what to do and how to live one's life. It is a practical discipline, focusing on such questions as

What should I do?
What kind of life should I lead?
What kind of person should I try to become?
How can I tell right from wrong?
What obligations do I have to other people and to myself?
When am I justified in criticizing or praising others?
When are they justified in criticizing or praising me?

Philosophers writing on ethics try to answer at least some of these questions.

Ethics is *normative* rather than descriptive; it deals with the way the world ought to be, not merely with the way the world is. Ethical assertions typically contain **prescriptive** or **normative terms** such as 'ought', 'should', 'good', 'bad', 'may', duty', 'responsible', and 'obligation'. Sometimes they take the imperative mood ("Thou shalt not steal," for example). Ethical assertions do not merely describe the facts; they evaluate them.

People agree about many issues in ethics. Virtually everyone agrees that torturing innocent children is wrong and that helping those in dire need is admirable. But as controversies over such issues as abortion and the death penalty indicate, people do not agree about everything. Especially when they disagree, people press each other to justify their positions. That leads directly to ethical philosophy, the systematic evaluation of moral intuitions and assertions. Usually, to justify a particular moral judgment—"The conspirators were right to try to assassinate Hitler," for example—we appeal to general moral principles such as "One ought to save lives" or "One ought to prevent injustice." But these principles and their scopes can also become matters of dispute.

To try to justify moral principles as well as particular moral judgments is to construct a moral theory. Moral theories are systematic attempts to provide and justify answers to questions such as 'What should I do?' and 'What kind of person should I try to become?' Most modern moral theories take the former question as basic. They focus on action and try to distinguish right from wrong in principled ways. They then define a good person as one who tends to do the right thing.

Most ancient theories, in contrast, focus instead on the question, What kind of person should I try to become? and try to distinguish good from bad character traits. Good traits are **virtues;** bad traits, **vices.** Such theories then define good actions as those that good people tend to perform. Because the issue of virtue is central to these theories, their approach to ethics is called **virtue ethics.** But any ethical theory, wherever it starts, must in the end provide a theory of virtues.

PLATO

Plato (427–347 B.C.E.; see Chapter 1), student of Socrates, teacher of Aristotle, and the first great systematic philosopher, develops two accounts of virtue. In his early dialogues, such as the *Apology, Euthyphro,* or *Laches,* Socrates appears as a character and treats virtue as a kind of knowledge. He subtly argues that the virtues are ultimately one. Probably these views are close to those of the historical Socrates. In the *Republic,* from Plato's middle period, he treats the soul as having three parts or aspects. As we saw in Chapter 4, he thinks of the soul as divided between rational, appetitive, and spirited elements. Virtue is a proper balance of the parts. This theory seems to be distinctively Plato's.

The Unity of the Virtues

Plato's early dialogues are essentially plays; Plato never speaks in his own voice. The central character is Socrates, Plato's teacher. (The relation of the character to the historical Socrates is a matter of some dispute.) Socrates typically encounters a small group of people involved in a discussion, one of whom eventually makes a claim about someone having or lacking a certain virtue: courage, self-control, piety, or beauty, for example. Socrates then asks, "What is courage?" (or self-control, or piety, etc.). Someone typically gives an example, and Socrates points out that an example is not a definition. The person then proposes a definition, and Socrates shows that it is either too broad (including things that do not fall under the term) or too narrow (failing to include things that do fall under the term). The interlocutor amends the definition, or someone else proposes a different one, and the process continues. Socrates never advances his own definition. He professes to have no answers, but maintains that wisdom begins with recognition of one's own ignorance. A wise person realizes how little he or she knows.

In the *Laches,* for example, the initial conversation concerns educating young people. Socrates points out that the young should be raised to be virtuous, and everyone agrees. But what, he asks, is virtue? To make the question easier, he proposes to examine a particular virtue, courage. Laches, a Greek general, proposes a definition.

> SOCRATES. Then, Laches, suppose that we first set about determining the nature of courage, and in the second place proceed to enquire how the young men may attain this quality by the help of studies and pursuits. Tell me, if you can, what is courage.
>
> LACHES. Indeed, Socrates, I see no difficulty in answering; he is a man of courage who does not run away, but remains at his post and fights against the enemy; there can be no mistake about that.[1]

[1] This and subsequent selections are from Plato, *Laches,* translated by Benjamin Jowett, in *The Dialogues of Plato* (Oxford: Clarendon, 1898).

But this, Socrates observes, is only one kind of courage. Soldiers may display courage in many other ways. And there is more to courage than the bravery of the soldier. So, Laches's definition is far too narrow. Socrates poses the question again.

How do Socrates's examples show the inadequacy of Laches's proposed definition of courage?

SOCRATES. Very good, Laches; and yet I fear that I did not express myself clearly; and therefore you have answered not the question which I intended to ask, but another.

LACHES. What do you mean, Socrates?

SOCRATES. I will endeavour to explain; you would call a man courageous who remains at his post, and fights with the enemy?

LACHES. Certainly I should.

SOCRATES. And so should I; but what would you say of another man, who fights flying, instead of remaining?

LACHES. How flying?

SOCRATES. Why, as the Scythians are said to fight, flying as well as pursuing; and as Homer says in praise of the horses of Aeneas, that they knew "how to pursue, and fly quickly hither and thither"; and he passes an encomium on Aeneas himself, as having a knowledge of fear or flight, and calls him "an author of fear or flight."

LACHES. Yes, Socrates, and there Homer is right: for he was speaking of chariots, as you were speaking of the Scythian cavalry, who have that way of fighting; but the heavy-armed Greek fights, as I say, remaining in his rank.

SOCRATES. And yet, Laches, you must except the Lacedaemonians at Plataea, who, when they came upon the light shields of the Persians, are said not to have been willing to stand and fight, and to have fled; but when the ranks of the Persians were broken, they turned upon them like cavalry, and won the battle of Plataea.

LACHES. That is true.

SOCRATES. That was my meaning when I said that I was to blame in having put my question badly, and that this was the reason of your answering badly. For I meant to ask you not only about the courage of heavy-armed soldiers, but about the courage of cavalry and every other style of soldier; and not only who are courageous in war, but who are courageous in perils by sea, and who in disease, or in poverty, or again in politics, are courageous; and not only who are courageous against pain or fear, but mighty to contend against desires and pleasures, either fixed in their rank or turning upon their enemy. There is this sort of courage—is there not, Laches?

LACHES. Certainly, Socrates.

SOCRATES. And all these are courageous, but some have courage in pleasures, and some in pains: some in desires, and some in fears, and some are cowards under the same conditions, as I should imagine.

LACHES. Very true.

SOCRATES. Now I was asking about courage and cowardice in general. And I will begin with courage, and once more ask, What is that common quality, which is the same in all these cases, and which is called courage?

Laches tries again:

LACHES. I should say that courage is a sort of endurance of the soul, if I am to speak of the universal nature which pervades them all.

Laches's second definition is that courage is a sort of endurance of the soul. Now it is not clear that this is a definition at all. What sort of endurance is courage? Socrates makes just this point.

> SOCRATES. . . . I cannot say that every kind of endurance is, in my opinion, to be deemed courage. Hear my reason: I am sure, Laches, that you would consider courage to be a very noble quality.
>
> LACHES. Most noble, certainly.
>
> SOCRATES. And you would say that a wise endurance is also good and noble?
>
> LACHES. Very noble.
>
> SOCRATES. But what would you say of a foolish endurance? Is not that, on the other hand, to be regarded as evil and hurtful?
>
> LACHES. True.
>
> SOCRATES. And is anything noble which is evil and hurtful?
>
> LACHES. I ought not to say that, Socrates.
>
> SOCRATES. Then you would not admit that sort of endurance to be courage—for it is not noble, but courage is noble?
>
> LACHES. You are right.
>
> SOCRATES. Then, according to you, only the wise endurance is courage?
>
> LACHES. True.

Now, Socrates shows that defining courage as wise endurance of the soul does not work either. It is too broad; it counts too many things as courage.

What is the point of Socrates's examples here? What dilemma do they force Laches to confront?

> SOCRATES. But as to the epithet "wise,"—wise in what? In all things small as well as great? For example, if a man shows the quality of endurance in spending his money wisely, knowing that by spending he will acquire more in the end, do you call him courageous?
>
> LACHES. Assuredly not.
>
> SOCRATES. Or, for example, if a man is a physician, and his son, or some patient of his, has inflammation of the lungs, and begs that he may be allowed to eat or drink something, and the other is firm and refuses; is that courage?
>
> LACHES. No; that is not courage at all, any more than the last.

Worse, it often appears that the person who endures foolishly is braver than the person who endures wisely.

> SOCRATES. Again, take the case of one who endures in war, and is willing to fight, and wisely calculates and knows that others will help him, and that there will be fewer and inferior men against him than there are with him; and suppose that he has also advantages of position; would you say of such a one who endures with all this wisdom and preparation, that he, or some man in the opposing army who is in the opposite circumstances to these and yet endures and remains at his post, is the braver?
>
> LACHES. I should say that the latter, Socrates, was the braver.
>
> SOCRATES. But, surely, this is a foolish endurance in comparison with the other?
>
> LACHES. That is true.
>
> SOCRATES. Then you would say that he who in an engagement of cavalry endures, having the knowledge of horsemanship, is not so courageous as he who endures, having no such knowledge?

LACHES. So I should say.

SOCRATES. And he who endures, having a knowledge of the use of the sling, or the bow, or of any other art, is not so courageous as he who endures, not having such a knowledge?

LACHES. True.

SOCRATES. And he who descends into a well, and dives, and holds out in this or any similar action, having no knowledge of diving, or the like, is, as you would say, more courageous than those who have this knowledge?

LACHES. Why, Socrates, what else can a man say?

SOCRATES. Nothing, if that be what he thinks.

LACHES. But that is what I do think.

SOCRATES. And yet men who thus run risks and endure are foolish, Laches, in comparison of those who do the same things, having the skill to do them.

LACHES. That is true.

SOCRATES. But foolish boldness and endurance appeared before to be base and hurtful to us.

LACHES. Quite true.

SOCRATES. Whereas courage was acknowledged to be a noble quality.

LACHES. True.

SOCRATES. And now on the contrary we are saying that the foolish endurance, which was before held in dishonour, is courage.

LACHES. Very true.

SOCRATES. And are we right in saying so?

LACHES. Indeed, Socrates, I am sure that we are not right.

Laches at this point admits puzzlement. His friend Nicias tries to help:

NICIAS. I have often heard you say that "Every man is good in that in which he is wise, and bad in that in which he is unwise."

SOCRATES. That is certainly true, Nicias.

NICIAS. And therefore if the brave man is good, he is also wise.

Nicias is saying that courage is a kind of wisdom. This astounds Laches. But Socrates encourages Nicias, and asks what kind of wisdom he has in mind.

NICIAS. I mean to say, Laches, that courage is the knowledge of that which inspires fear or confidence in war, or in anything.

Socrates and Laches object that this is too narrow, for it excludes the courage of animals.

SOCRATES. Then tell me, Nicias, or rather tell us, for Laches and I are partners in the argument: Do you mean to affirm that courage is the knowledge of the grounds of hope and fear?

NICIAS. I do.

SOCRATES. And not every man has this knowledge; the physician and the soothsayer have it not; and they will not be courageous unless they acquire it—that is what you were saying?

NICIAS. I was.

SOCRATES. Then this is certainly not a thing which every pig would know, as the proverb says, and therefore he could not be courageous.

NICIAS. I think not.

SOCRATES. Clearly not, Nicias; not even such a big pig as the Crommyonian sow would be called by you courageous. And this I say not as a joke, but because I think that he who assents to your doctrine, that courage is the knowledge of the grounds of fear and hope, cannot allow that any wild beast is courageous, unless he admits that a lion, or a leopard, or perhaps a boar, or any other animal, has such a degree of wisdom that he knows things which but a few human beings ever know by reason of their difficulty. He who takes your view of courage must affirm that a lion, and a stag, and a bull, and a monkey, have equally little pretensions to courage.

LACHES. Capital, Socrates; by the gods, that is truly good. And I hope, Nicias, that you will tell us whether these animals, which we all admit to be courageous, are really wiser than mankind; or whether you will have the boldness, in the face of universal opinion, to deny their courage.

But Nicias defends his definition by drawing a distinction. Courage is more than fearlessness.

How does courage differ from fearlessness?

NICIAS. Why, Laches, I do not call animals or any other things which have no fear of dangers, because they are ignorant of them, courageous, but only fearless and senseless. Do you imagine that I should call little children courageous, which fear no dangers because they know none? There is a difference, to my way of thinking, between fearlessness and courage. I am of opinion that thoughtful courage is a quality possessed by very few, but that rashness and boldness, and fearlessness, which has no forethought, are very common qualities possessed by many men, many women, many children, many animals. And you, and men in general, call by the term "courageous" actions which I call rash;—my courageous actions are wise actions.

Socrates now attacks the definition in a different way. He argues that, on this account, courage is not just one of the virtues but all of virtue. He begins by noting that hope and fear are directed toward the future.

SOCRATES. You remember that we originally considered courage to be a part of virtue.

NICIAS. Very true.

SOCRATES. And you yourself said that it was a part; and there were many other parts, all of which taken together are called virtue.

NICIAS. Certainly.

SOCRATES. Do you agree with me about the parts? For I say that justice, temperance, and the like, are all of them parts of virtue as well as courage. Would you not say the same?

NICIAS. Certainly.

SOCRATES. Well then, so far we are agreed. And now let us proceed a step, and try to arrive at a similar agreement about the fearful and the hopeful. I do not want you to be thinking one thing and myself another. Let me then tell you our opinion, and if we are wrong you shall set us right. In our opinion the terrible and the hopeful are the things which do and do not create fear, and fear is not of the present, nor of the past, but is of future and expected evil. Do you not agree to that, Laches?

LACHES. Yes, Socrates, entirely.

SOCRATES. That is my view, Nicias; the terrible things, as I should say, are the evils which are future; and the hopeful are the good or not evil things which are future. Do you or do you not agree with me?

NICIAS. I agree.

SOCRATES. And the knowledge of these things you call courage?

NICIAS. Precisely.

But there is no division between wisdom about the past, wisdom about the present, and wisdom about the future; the same quality of good judgment underlies all of them. So, knowledge of the grounds of hope and fear is just knowledge of good and evil, which is virtue in general.

SOCRATES. I will tell you. He [Laches] and I have a notion that there is not one knowledge or science of the past, another of the present, a third of what is likely to be best and what will be best in the future; but that of all three there is one science only: for example, there is one science of medicine which is concerned with the inspection of health equally in all times, present, past, and future; and one science of husbandry in like manner, which is concerned with the productions of the earth in all times. As to the art of the general, you yourselves will be my witnesses that he has an excellent foreknowledge of the future, and that he claims to be the master and not the servant of the soothsayer, because he knows better what is happening or is likely to happen in war: and accordingly the law places the soothsayer under the general, and not the general under the soothsayer. Am I not correct in saying so, Laches?

LACHES. Quite correct.

SOCRATES. And do you, Nicias, also acknowledge that the same science has understanding of the same things, whether future, present, or past?

Why, according to Socrates, does Nicias's definition of courage as the knowledge of the fearful and hopeful make courage all rather than a part of virtue?

NICIAS. Yes, indeed Socrates; that is my opinion.

SOCRATES. And courage, my friend, is, as you say, a knowledge of the fearful and of the hopeful?

NICIAS. Yes.

SOCRATES. And the fearful, and the hopeful, are admitted to be future goods and future evils?

NICIAS. True.

SOCRATES. And the same science has to do with the same things in the future or at any time?

NICIAS. That is true.

SOCRATES. Then courage is not the science which is concerned with the fearful and hopeful, for they are future only; courage, like the other sciences, is concerned not only with good and evil of the future, but of the present and past, and of any time?

NICIAS. That, as I suppose, is true.

SOCRATES. Then the answer which you have given, Nicias, includes only a third part of courage; but our question extended to the whole nature of courage: and according to your view, that is, according to your present view, courage is not only the knowledge of the hopeful and the fearful, but seems to include nearly every good and evil without reference to time. What do you say to that alteration in your statement?

NICIAS. I agree, Socrates.

SOCRATES. But then, my dear friend, if a man knew all good and evil, and how they are, and have been, and will be produced, would he not be perfect, and wanting in no virtue, whether justice, or temperance, or holiness? He would possess them all, and he would know which were dangers and which were not, and guard against them whether they were supernatural or natural; and he would provide the good, as he would know how to deal both with gods or men.

NICIAS. I think, Socrates, that there is a great deal of truth in what you say.

SOCRATES. But then, Nicias, courage, according to this new definition of yours, instead of being a part of virtue only, will be all virtue?

NICIAS. It would seem so.

SOCRATES. But we were saying that courage is one of the parts of virtue?

NICIAS. Yes, that was what we were saying.

SOCRATES. And that is in contradiction with our present view?

NICIAS. That appears to be the case.

SOCRATES. Then, Nicias, we have not discovered what courage is.

NICIAS. We have not.

This is a common theme in the early dialogues. Every particular virtue turns out to be indistinguishable from the knowledge of good and evil, which, Socrates asserts, is virtue in general. He then declares defeat. But another way to view the result is that, at root, the virtues are all identical. Socrates seems to be relying on a thesis of **the unity of the virtues;** courage, wisdom, self-control, justice, piety, and so on are really the same thing. Moreover, he takes virtue to be a kind of knowledge—the knowledge of good and evil, of right and wrong, of what to pursue and what to avoid. At least part of that virtue lies in the pursuit of its definition.

The view that virtue is a kind of knowledge has an important consequence: weakness of will is either impossible or irrelevant. Paul gives the classic characterization of weakness of will in his letter to the Romans:

> For that which I do I allow not: for what I would, that do I not; but what I hate, that I do. If then I do that which I would not, I consent unto the law that it is good. . . . for to will is present with me; but how to perform that which is good I find not. For the good that I would I do not; but the evil which I would not, that I do. (*Romans* 7 : 15–19)

Weakness of will, in short, is knowing the better and doing the worse. It is knowing what you ought to do and nevertheless not doing it. The smoker who knows she ought to quit but can't and the dieter who knows he shouldn't eat the cake but does it anyway both display weakness of will.

If virtue is simply a matter of knowing good and evil, however, weakness of will is unintelligible. For then virtue is *knowing* the better; someone who knows the better and does the worse would be virtuous. But that seems absurd. As philosophers such as Aristotle and Kant have stressed, self-control, strength of character, and will power are themselves virtues.

Turning this around, on Socrates's view, all vice is ignorance. But we do not tend to think that the person who is weak of will is simply ignorant. The only way to defend the thesis that virtue is knowledge is to maintain either that weakness of will is impossible or that the person displaying weakness of will is ignorant in some significant way. But neither option seems very plausible. Cases of weakness of will are commonplace. And they do not seem to involve ignorance. The sinner trying to reform may be all too aware of the evils of sin.

The Balance of the Soul

Plato offers a very different account of virtue in the *Republic,* where Socrates (the character) for the first time offers his own definition of a virtue. The question is, What is justice? Socrates answers, "Doing one's own"—an answer that rests on an analysis both of the state and of the soul. According to Plato, each has three parts: the rational, the appetitive, and the spirited. A person is just when his or her soul is in balance, when, that is, each part of the soul is playing its proper role.

> And a State was thought by us to be just when the three classes in the State severally did their own business; and also thought to be temperate and valiant and wise by reason of certain other affections and qualities of these same classes?
>
> True, he said.
>
> And so of the individual; we may assume that he has the same three principles in his own soul which are found in the State; and he may be rightly described in the same terms, because he is affected in the same manner?
>
> Certainly, he said.[2] (435c)

Consider a case of conflict, in which the person who has will power resists his desires and the person who is weak of will gives in to them. A person in such a situation seems to be at war with himself. There must, then, be different parts of the soul (aspects of the personality, parts of the self) that are fighting each other.

How is Socrates arguing that the soul contains distinct rational and appetitive elements?

> And might a man be thirsty, and yet unwilling to drink?
>
> Yes, he said, it constantly happens.
>
> And in such a case what is one to say? Would you not say that there was something in the soul bidding a man to drink, and something else forbidding him, which is other and stronger than the principle which bids him?
>
> I should say so.
>
> And the forbidding principle is derived from reason, and that which bids and attracts proceeds from passion and disease?
>
> Clearly.
>
> Then we may fairly assume that they are two, and that they differ from one another; the one with which a man reasons, we may call the rational principle of the

[2]This and subsequent selections are from Plato, *Republic,* translated by Benjamin Jowett, in *The Dialogues of Plato* (Oxford: Clarendon, 1898).

soul, the other, with which he loves and hungers and thirsts and feels the flutterings of any other desire, may be termed the irrational or appetitive, the ally of sundry pleasures and satisfactions?

Yes, he said, we may fairly assume them to be different. (439d)

The soul, then, contains a rational principle and an appetitive principle. There is also a third passionate or spirited principle. It cannot be identified with appetite:

What forces us to recognize a third, spirited element, according to Socrates?

Then let us finally determine that there are two principles existing in the soul. And what of passion, or spirit? Is it a third, or akin to one of the preceding?

I should be inclined to say—akin to desire.

Well, I said, there is a story which I remember to have heard, and in which I put faith. The story is, that Leontius, the son of Aglaion, coming up one day from the Piraeus, under the north wall on the outside, observed some dead bodies lying on the ground at the place of execution. He felt a desire to see them, and also a dread and abhorrence of them; for a time he struggled and covered his eyes, but at length the desire got the better of him; and forcing them open, he ran up to the dead bodies, saying, Look, ye wretches, take your fill of the fair sight.

I have heard the story myself, he said.

The moral of the tale is, that anger at times goes to war with desire, as though they were two distinct things.

Yes; that is the meaning, he said.

And are there not many other cases in which we observe that when a man's desires violently prevail over his reason, he reviles himself, and is angry at the violence within him, and that in this struggle, which is like the struggle of factions in a State, his spirit is on the side of his reason;—but for the passionate or spirited element to take part with the desires when reason decides that she should not be opposed, is a sort of thing which, I believe, you never observed occurring in yourself, nor, as I should imagine, in any one else?

Certainly not. (439e–440c)

Nor can it be identified with reason:

Yes, I replied, if passion, which has already been shown to be different from desire, turn out also to be different from reason.

But that is easily proved:—We may observe even in young children that they are full of spirit almost as soon as they are born, whereas some of them never seem to attain to the use of reason, and most of them late enough.

Excellent, I said, and you may see passion equally in brute animals, which is a further proof of the truth of what you are saying. And we may once more appeal to the words of Homer, which have been already quoted by us,

"He smote his breast, and thus rebuked his soul";

> for in this verse Homer has clearly supposed the power which reasons about the better and worse to be different from the unreasoning anger which is rebuked by it. (441a–c)

There are, then, three parts of the soul—the rational, appetitive, and spirited elements (or, in other words, reason, desire, and will)—each of which has an essential role to play. In a just person, each element plays its proper role. The rational element rules over the other two, restraining both desires and passions.

On this account, it is easy to explain weakness of will, which poses problems for Socrates's view. A person may face a conflict between reason and desire, between reason and passion, between passion and desire. She may know which ought to triumph. But she may or may not be strong enough to make it triumph. The smoker, for example, may know it would be best for her to quit smoking. Her rational element directs her to stop. But her appetitive element calls for her to smoke. If she is strong, the rational element wins. If not, the appetitive element does.

Plato, in short, offers us two theories of virtue. In his early dialogues, Socrates treats the virtues as unified. Virtue is a kind of knowledge, specifically, the knowledge of good and evil. That makes weakness of will impossible or irrelevant. In the *Republic,* Plato puts forward an account of virtue as a balance of the soul. A person is virtuous when reason, desire, and will each play their proper role. That makes weakness of will easy to understand; it occurs when reason loses a conflict with desire or will.

ARISTOTLE

Aristotle (384–322 B.C.E.; see Chapter 1), student of Plato, tutor of Alexander the Great, and contemporary of Demosthenes and Euclid, develops the classic theory of virtue in the Western philosophical tradition. He distinguishes **intrinsic goods,** which are desired for their own sake, from **instrumental goods,** which are desired as means to other things. To justify any answers to questions of justification, we must appeal to intrinsic goods. Suppose that someone asks why you are reading this book.

"Because it's required for my philosophy course," you answer.

"But why do what's required?"

"I want to get a good grade."

"Why do you want a good grade?"

"I want a good GPA."

"Why?"

"It will help me get a job."

"Why do you want a job?"

"I want money."

"Why?"

"I want things money can buy!"

"Why do you want them?"

To stop the chain of questions, you must appeal to something that is *intrinsically* good. Every time you appeal to an instrumental good, the questioner can ask in turn why you want it. The chain of answers cannot loop back on itself in a circle:

"I want money."

"Why?"
"I want things money can buy!"
"Why?"
"So I can sell them to get money!"

That is plainly absurd. Nor can the chain go on forever:

"I want money."
"Why?"
"I want things money can buy!"
"Why?"
"So I can sell them to get even more money!"
"Why do you want *more* money?"
"So I can buy more things and then sell them to make even *more*. . . ."

This is no justification; it is what Aristotle calls an **infinite regress.** Anything good for the sake of something else invites a further question.

To respond to questions asking for justification successfully, we must invoke something good for its own sake.

> Let us resume our inquiry and state, in view of the fact that all knowledge and every pursuit aims at some good, what it is that we say political science aims at and what is the highest of all goods achievable by action. Verbally there is very general agreement; for both the general run of men and people of superior refinement say that it is happiness, and identify living well and doing well with being happy; but with regard to what happiness is they differ, and the many do not give the same account as the wise.[3]

Aristotle contends that people desire only one thing for its own sake and never for the sake of something else: *happiness.*

> Let us again return to the good we are seeking, and ask what it can be. It seems different in different actions and arts; it is different in medicine, in strategy, and in the other arts likewise. What then is the good of each? Surely that for whose sake everything else is done. In medicine this is health, in strategy victory, in architecture a house, in any other sphere something else, and in every action and pursuit the end; for it is for the sake of this that all men do whatever else they do. Therefore, if there is an end for all that we do, this will be the good achievable by action, and if there are more than one, these will be the goods achievable by action. So the argument has by a different course reached the same point; but we must try to state this even more clearly. Since there are evidently more than one end, and we choose some of these (e.g. wealth, flutes, and in general instruments) for the sake of something else, clearly not all ends are final ends; but the chief good is evidently something final. Therefore, if there is only one final end, this will be what we are seeking, and if there are more than one, the most final of these will be what we are seeking. Now we call that which is in itself worthy of pursuit more final than that which is worthy of pursuit for the sake of something else, and that which is never desirable

[3]This and subsequent selections from Aristotle are from the *Nicomachean Ethics,* translated by W. D. Ross, in *Aristotle* (Oxford: Clarendon Press, 1908).

> for the sake of something else more final than the things that are desirable both in themselves and for the sake of that other thing, and therefore we call final without qualification that which is always desirable in itself and never for the sake of something else.

Any series of requests for justifications leads eventually to the response, "Because I want to be happy!" If someone persists in asking why, there is nothing more to say. Happiness (in Greek, ***eudaimonia***) is desirable for its own sake, never for the sake of something else.

How does Aristotle argue that happiness is the end of action?

> Now such a thing happiness, above all else, is held to be; for this we choose always for self and never for the sake of something else, but honour, pleasure, reason, and every virtue we choose indeed for themselves (for if nothing resulted from them we should still choose each of them), but we choose them also for the sake of happiness, judging that by means of them we shall be happy. Happiness, on the other hand, no one chooses for the sake of these, nor, in general, for anything other than itself. From the point of view of self-sufficiency the same result seems to follow; for the final good is thought to be self-sufficient. . . . the self-sufficient we now define as that which when isolated makes life desirable and lacking in nothing; and such we think happiness to be; and further we think it most desirable of all things, without being counted as one good thing among others—if it were so counted it would clearly be made more desirable by the addition of even the least of goods; for that which is added becomes an excess of goods, and of goods the greater is always more desirable. Happiness, then, is something final and self-sufficient, and is the end of action.

What is happiness? We tend to think that people are happy when they feel good. Aristotle would agree that happiness has something to do with feelings. But that is only part of the story. To be happy, for Aristotle, is to succeed at life; to flourish; to be fulfilled; to *live well.*

What is it to live well? Some people—according to some feminist philosophers, especially men—tend to think of success, of living well, in purely material terms, as having a big house and lots of toys. Aristotle thinks that material well-being and outright luck are important factors; it's hard to be happy, he points out, if you are starving or if your loved ones have been killed. But there is more to happiness than prosperity and luck. What more is required to live well? Aristotle's answer relies on the idea that human beings have a *function.* Just as a good knife cuts well, and a good teacher teaches well, a good person fulfills the function of a human being well.

But what is the function of a person? According to Aristotle, it is what is most distinctive of human beings. It is what distinguishes us from other animals. As philosophers over the ages have pointed out, we differ from other animals in many ways: we use language; we can conceive of beings such as God, who are greater than anything we experience; we buy and sell; we control what Marx calls "the means of production"; and, as humorist Dave Barry notes, we are not afraid of vacuum cleaners. Dogs and cats do not talk, pray, trade, or farm. But what underlies all these differences is our ability to reason. Undoubtedly, other animals have some cognitive abilities; they learn to trot into the kitchen at the sound of the can opener. In general, they act rationally in some respects. It is not easy to say what is distinctive about human reason that enables us to do the things we alone can do. But whatever it is, it enables us not only to act rationally in particular situations but also to construct rational plans for our lives. That, Aristotle contends, is our function: to live according to a rational plan.

A good person acts in accordance with virtue, and to act virtuously is to act in accordance with a rational plan. A good person consistently does the right thing at the right time, in the right way, and for the right reason. There is no rule for becoming good or for distinguishing good from bad, right from wrong; a person of practical wisdom has a highly refined ability to draw the right distinctions and tell right from wrong.

What, according to Aristotle, is the function of a human being? How does he argue for this conclusion? How does it help us to understand virtue?

> Presumably, however, to say that happiness is the chief good seems a platitude, and a clearer account of what it is still desired. This might perhaps be given, if we could first ascertain the function of man. For just as for a flute-player, a sculptor, or an artist, and, in general, for all things that have a function or activity, the good and the 'well' is thought to reside in the function, so would it seem to be for man, if he has a function. Have the carpenter, then, and the tanner certain functions or activities, and has man none? Is he born without a function? Or as eye, hand, foot, and in general each of the parts evidently has a function, may one lay it down that man similarly has a function apart from all these? What then can this be? Life seems to be common even to plants, but we are seeking what is peculiar to man. Let us exclude, therefore, the life of nutrition and growth. Next there would be a life of perception, but it also seems to be common even to the horse, the ox, and every animal. There remains, then, an active life of the element that has a rational principle; of this, one part has such a principle in the sense of being obedient to one, the other in the sense of possessing one and exercising thought. And, as 'life of the rational element' also has two meanings, we must state that life in the sense of activity is what we mean; for this seems to be the more proper sense of the term. Now if the function of man is an activity of soul which follows or implies a rational principle, and if we say 'so-and-so-and 'a good so-and-so' have a function which is the same in kind, e.g. a lyre, and a good lyre-player, and so without qualification in all cases, eminence in respect of goodness being added to the name of the function (for the function of a lyre-player is to play the lyre, and that of a good lyre-player is to do so well): if this is the case, and we state the function of man to be a certain kind of life, and this to be an activity or actions of the soul implying a rational principle, and the function of a good man to be the good and noble performance of these, and if any action is well performed when it is performed in accordance with the appropriate excellence: if this is the case, human good turns out to be activity of soul in accordance with virtue, and if there are more than one virtue, in accordance with the best and most complete.
>
> But we must add 'in a complete life.' For one swallow does not make a summer, nor does one day; and so too one day, or a short time, does not make a man blessed and happy.

How does a person become virtuous? How, in other words, can someone become practically wise? Not by abstract thought, Aristotle says, but by doing virtuous things. One becomes good not by intellectual discovery but by apprenticeship to good role models.

> Virtue, then, being of two kinds, intellectual and moral, intellectual virtue in the main owes both its birth and its growth to teaching (for which reason it requires experience and time), while moral virtue comes about as a result of habit, whence also its name (*ethike*) is one that is formed by a slight variation from the word *ethos* (habit). From this it is also plain that none of the moral virtues arises in us by nature; for nothing that exists by nature can form a habit contrary to its nature. For instance the stone which by nature moves downwards cannot be habituated to move upwards, not even if one tries to train it by throwing it up ten thousand times; nor can fire be habituated to move downwards, nor can anything else that by nature behaves in one way be trained to behave in another. Neither by nature, then, nor contrary to nature do the virtues arise in us; rather we are adapted by nature to receive them, and are made perfect by habit.

"Assume a virtue if you have it not," Shakespeare's Polonius advises; Aristotle agrees. If you do brave things, for example—initially, by forcing yourself to do them, by imitating a brave person, by pretending to be brave—you gradually develop the habit of doing brave things. When the habit is ingrained to the point of being second nature, you are brave. In general, people become good by doing good things.

How can people become virtuous? What role should law play in this process?

> . . . the virtues we get by first exercising them, as also happens in the case of the arts as well. For the things we have to learn before we can do them, we learn by doing them, e.g. men become builders by building and lyreplayers by playing the lyre; so too we become just by doing just acts, temperate by doing temperate acts, brave by doing brave acts.
>
> This is confirmed by what happens in states; for legislators make the citizens good by forming habits in them, and this is the wish of every legislator, and those who do not effect it miss their mark, and it is in this that a good constitution differs from a bad one.
>
> Again, it is from the same causes and by the same means that every virtue is both produced and destroyed, and similarly every art; for it is from playing the lyre that both good and bad lyre-players are produced. And the corresponding statement is true of builders and of all the rest; men will be good or bad builders as a result of building well or badly. For if this were not so, there would have been no need of a teacher, but all men would have been born good or bad at their craft. This, then, is the case with the virtues also; by doing the acts that we do in our transactions with other men we become just or unjust, and by doing the acts that we do in the presence of danger, and being habituated to feel fear or confidence, we become brave or cowardly. The same is true of appetites and feelings of anger; some men become temperate and good-tempered, others self-indulgent and irascible, by behaving in one way or the other in the appropriate circumstances. Thus, in one word, states of character arise out of like activities. This is why the activities we exhibit must be of a certain kind; it is because the states of character correspond to the differences between these. It makes no small difference, then, whether we form habits of one kind or of another from our very youth; it makes a very great difference, or rather all the difference.

A good person, we've seen, does the right thing at the right time, in the right way, and for the right reason. Virtue is thus a mean between extremes. The ability to find that mean Aristotle calls **practical wisdom** (*phronesis*). To fear too much is cowardly, but to fear too little is rash. Someone who forgets a bungee cord and leaps into a river with construction cable tied around his ankle is not brave but foolish. Courage is fearing what ought to be feared when it ought to be feared to the extent that it ought to be feared, and for the appropriate reason.

> First, then, let us consider this, that it is the nature of such things to be destroyed by defect and excess, as we see in the case of strength and of health (for to gain light on things imperceptible we must use the evidence of sensible things); both excessive and defective exercise destroys the strength, and similarly drink or food which is above or below a certain amount destroys the health, while that which is proportionate both produces and increases and preserves it. So too is it, then, in the case of temperance and courage and the other virtues. For the man who flies from and fears everything and does not stand his ground against anything becomes a coward, and the man who fears nothing at all but goes to meet every danger becomes rash; and similarly the man who indulges in every pleasure and abstains from none becomes self-indulgent, while the man who shuns every pleasure, as boors do, becomes in a way insensible; temperance and courage, then, are destroyed by excess and defect, and preserved by the mean.
>
> But not only are the sources and causes of their origination and growth the same as those of their destruction, but also the sphere of their actualization will be the same; for this is also true of the things which are more evident to sense, e.g. of strength; it is produced by taking much food and undergoing much exertion, and it is the strong man that will be most able to do these things. So too is it with the virtues; by abstaining from pleasures we become temperate, and it is when we have become so that we are most able to abstain from them; and similarly too in the case of courage; for by being habituated to despise things that are terrible and to stand our ground against them we become brave, and it is when we have become so that we shall be most able to stand our ground against them.

Right and wrong are defined in terms of virtue: an act is good if it is something a virtuous person would do.

> Actions, then, are called just and temperate when they are such as the just or the temperate man would do; but it is not the man who does these that is just and temperate, but the man who also does them as just and temperate men do them. It is well said, then, that it is by doing just acts that the just man is produced, and by doing temperate acts the temperate man; without doing these no one would have even a prospect of becoming good.

We can think of virtues, for Aristotle, as corresponding to human drives and emotions. A virtue *constrains* a drive or emotion—at the right times, in the right ways, and for the right reasons.

Why is virtue a kind of mean?

> . . . the virtue of man also will be the state of character which makes a man good and which makes him do his own work well.
>
> . . . virtue must have the quality of aiming at the intermediate. I mean moral virtue; for it is this that is concerned with passions and actions, and in these there is excess, defect, and the intermediate. For instance, both fear and confidence and appetite and anger and pity and in general pleasure and pain may be felt both too

much and too little, and in both cases not well; but to feel them at the right times, with reference to the right objects, towards the right people, with the right motive, and in the right way, is what is both intermediate and best, and this is characteristic of virtue. Similarly with regard to actions also there is excess, defect, and the intermediate. Now virtue is concerned with passions and actions, in which excess is a form of failure, and so is defect, while the intermediate is praised and is a form of success; and being praised and being successful are both characteristics of virtue. Therefore virtue is a kind of mean, since, as we have seen, it aims at what is intermediate. . . .

Virtue, then, is a state of character concerned with choice, lying in a mean, i.e., the mean relative to us, this being determined by a rational principle, and by that principle by which the man of practical wisdom would determine it. Now it is a mean between two vices, that which depends on excess and that which depends on defect. . . .

Any virtue, then, has two related vices. One consists in not constraining the drive or emotion enough, the other, in constraining it too much. These are the virtues and vices Aristotle describes:

Drive or Emotion	*Too Unconstrained*	*Virtuous*	*Too Constrained*
fear	cowardly	courageous	rash
pleasure	self-indulgent	self-controlled	insensitive
material goods	stingy	generous	extravagant
spending	grudging, mean	tasteful	vulgar, profligate
self-esteem	vain	high-minded	small-minded
drive for honor	ambitious	[nameless]	unambitious
anger	short-tempered	gentle	apathetic
social relations	obsequious	friendly	grouchy
boasting	boastful	truthful	self-depreciating
humor	clownish	witty	boorish

In sum, all virtues are means between constraining a drive too much and not enough. To act as we ought is to find that mean. Correct action therefore requires practical wisdom.

CONFUCIUS

Kong Fuzi, Confucius (551–479 B.C.E.; see Chapter 6) presents an ethics of virtue almost 200 years before Aristotle. It has much in common with Aristotle's theory; nevertheless, Confucius presents a different list of virtues, which has a different structure. Confucian doctrine is sometimes summarized as **ethical humanism.** Like Aristotle, Confucius begins with the question, What kind of person should I try to become? and centers his answer on the concept of virtue (***ren***). He transforms the traditional notion of a superior person, *junzi,* literally, "child of a ruler," a person of superior social standing, into the notion of a morally upright person, a person of superior *character.* The idea that human excellence is a function of character—rather than birth, upbringing, social position, wealth, power, or even achievement—was revolutionary.

Confucius contrasts selfishness, a desire for personal gain, with righteousness (*yi* or *i*), a desire to do what is right just because it is right. The superior person does the right thing for the right reason—because it is the right thing to do—not in order to get something else. In other words, the superior person treats the good as intrinsically valuable.

What do these characterizations of the superior person have in common?

1:14. The Master said, "A superior person doesn't seek gratification or comfort. He's earnest in what he does; he's careful in speech. He associates with people of principle to set himself right. Such a person truly loves to learn."

2:13. Zi-kong asked what constituted the superior person. The Master said, "He acts before he speaks, and then speaks as he acts."

4:10. The Master said, "The superior person in the world is not for anything or against anything; he follows what is right."

4:11. The Master said, "The superior person thinks of virtue; the small person thinks of comfort. The superior person thinks of the law; the small person thinks of favors."

4:15. The Master said, "Shen, my doctrine is one thread." Zeng replied, "Yes." The Master went out, and the other disciples asked, "What do his words mean?" Zeng said, "Our Master's doctrine is to be true to the principles of our nature and to exercise them benevolently toward others—this and nothing more."

4:16. The Master said, "The superior person's mind is conversant with righteousness [*yi*]; the inferior person's mind is conversant with gain."

14:30. The Master said, "The way of the superior person is threefold, but I am not equal to it. Virtuous [*ren*], he is free from anxieties; wise, he is free from perplexities; bold, he is free from fear." Zi-kong said, "Master, that's you."[4]

In developing an ethics of character, Confucius elaborates a system of virtues around "one thread" (4:15, 15:2): "to be true to the principles of our nature and to exercise them benevolently toward others." It may sound as if that one thread comprises two different strands. For Confucius, however, thought and action are intimately linked; being true to the principles of our nature and exercising them in helping others come to the same thing. "One whose mind is set on virtue will not practice wickedness," Confucius says (4:4); people's characters are revealed by what they do (2:10). Because *ren,* virtue, involves both being true to the principles of our nature and acting benevolently toward others, *ren* has often been translated as "humanity" or "benevolence."

2:10. The Master said, "See what a person does. Mark his motives. Examine his habits. How can anyone conceal his character? How can anyone conceal his character?"

2:24. The Master said, ". . . To see what is right and not do it is cowardice."

4:7. The Master said, "People's faults often reveal their character. By observing someone's character, you may know him to be virtuous."

Virtue leads us to restrain ourselves and act properly. Virtue stems from knowledge; we must "know what to love and hate in others" (4:3) by knowing "what is right in ourselves" (6:28).

---

[4] This and subsequent selections from Confucius are from *The Analects,* in *The Four Books,* translated by James Legge, originally published in *The Chinese Classics,* Volume I (Oxford: Clarendon Press, 1893). I have altered the translation significantly to improve readability and to accord with the Pinyin system.

What are the five chief virtues, according to Confucius?

4:3. The Master said, "Only the truly virtuous [*ren*] know what to love or hate in others."

4:17. The Master said, "When we see people of worth, we should think of equaling them; when we see people of a contrary character, we should turn inward and examine ourselves."

6:28. Zi-kong said, "What would you say about someone who benefits people extensively and helps everyone? May he be called perfectly virtuous [*ren*]?" The Master said, "Why only virtuous? Must he not have the qualities of a sage? Even Yao and Shun [legendary rulers who lived as much as two millennia earlier] weren't like this. Someone of perfect virtue [*ren*], wishing to establish himself, establishes others; wishing to enlarge himself, enlarges others. To be able to judge others by what is right in ourselves is the art of virtue [*ren*]."

17:6. Zi-Qang asked Confucius about perfect virtue [*ren*]. Confucius said: "To be able to practice five things everywhere under Heaven constitutes perfect virtue." He begged to know what they were, and was told, "Seriousness, generosity, sincerity, diligence, and kindness. If you're serious, you won't be treated with disrespect. If you're generous, you'll win all hearts. If you're sincere, you'll be trusted. If you're diligent, you'll accomplish much. If you're kind, you'll enjoy the service of others."

One of the most striking and distinctive features of Confucius's theory of virtue is his idea that different virtues pertain to different relationships. There are virtues to be displayed toward other people in general, virtues to be displayed to friends and family, and virtues to exhibit to oneself. All are important, but all rest on the virtues of the self, which are central to virtue in general. The contrast between relations to others, relations to family and friends, and relations to the self structures the first part of the *Analects*. The very first section contrasts relations to the self (in learning), to friends, and to strangers.

1:1. The Master said, "Isn't it pleasant to learn and to apply what you've learned? Isn't it delightful to have friends coming from far away? Isn't he a person of complete virtue who doesn't get angry that others don't recognize him?"

The next sections continue the contrast, while making it clear that virtue in relation to family and friends underlies virtue in relation to strangers (1:2) and that virtue in relation to oneself underlies virtue as a whole (1:8).

1:2. Yu said, "Few filial and fraternal people like to offend their superiors, and nobody who doesn't like to offend superiors likes to stir up rebellion. The superior person attends to the root of things. From the root grows the Way [*Dao*]. Filial piety and fraternal submission are the root of benevolence [*ren*]."

1:4. Zeng said, "Every day I examine myself on three points: whether, with others, I may have been unfaithful; whether, with friends, I may have been untrustworthy; whether I may have failed to master and practice the instructions of my teacher."

1:6. The Master said, "A youth at home should be filial; abroad, respectful to elders. He should be earnest and truthful. He should overflow with love to all and cultivate the friendship of the good. When he has time and opportunity after doing these things, he should study."

1:7. Zi-Xia said, "If someone turns from the love of beauty to a sincere love of virtue; if he can serve his parents with all his strength; if he can serve his prince with his life; if his words to his friends are sincere; although people say he has not learned, I will certainly say that he has."

1:8. The Master said, "A scholar who is not serious will not be venerated, and his learning will not be solid. Hold faithfulness and sincerity as first principles. Have no friends not equal to yourself. When you have faults, do not be afraid to abandon them."

The basic virtues toward others are faithfulness and the five key components of *ren:* seriousness, generosity, sincerity, diligence, and kindness. The chief principle for dealing with other people is ***zhong,*** reciprocity (sometimes translated "altruism" or "likening to oneself"): "What you do not want done to yourself, do not do to others" (5:11, 12:2, 15:23). (This so-called "Silver Rule" is a logically weaker cousin of the Golden Rule: "What you would have others do unto you, do so unto them.") Repay kindness with kindness, Confucius advises, and injury with justice (14:36).

What is the principle of reciprocity? How does it underlie the five chief virtues?

5:11. Zi-kong said, "What I don't want others to do to me, I also want not to do to others."

6:24. Zai Wu asked, "A benevolent person, told 'Someone is in the well,' will go in after him, I suppose." Confucius said, "Why should he? A superior person may be made to go into the well, but not to go down into it. One may impose upon him, but not make a fool of him."

12:2. Zhong-kong asked about perfect virtue [*ren*]. The Master said, "When you travel, act as if you were receiving a great guest. Employ the people as if you were assisting at a great sacrifice. Don't do to others what you wouldn't want done to yourself. Then no one in the country or in your family will complain about you."

14:36. Someone said, "What do you say about the principle of repaying injury with kindness?" The Master said, "How then will you repay kindness? Repay kindness with kindness and injury with justice."

15:23. Zi-kong asked, "Is there one word to serve as a rule for practice throughout life?" Confucius said, "It is *reciprocity.* What you don't want done to yourself, don't do to others."

Confucius's saying here stands in sharp contrast with both the *lex talionis,* "an eye for an eye, a tooth for a tooth," and with the Christian emphasis on "walking the extra mile," that is, repaying injury with kindness:

> Ye have heard that it hath been said, An eye for an eye, and a tooth for a tooth: But I say unto you, That ye resist not evil: but whosoever shall smite thee on thy right cheek, turn to him the other also. And if any man will sue thee at the law, and take away thy coat, let him have thy cloak also. And whosoever shall compel thee to go a mile, go with him twain. (*Matthew* 5:38–41)

Confucius advocates an ethic of justice, not one of retaliation ("an eye for an eye") or of mercy.

The virtues we have discussed so far apply to dealings with family and friends. But there are also virtues special to those relationships that both underlie and override more general obligations. Confucius stresses two: **filial piety** (***xiao***), obedience, reverence, and service to one's parents and elders; and **fraternal submission**, service and trustworthiness to one's equals. These virtues are roots of *ren*. We learn how to treat others by learning how to interact with those closest to us.

> 2:5. Meng I asked what filial piety was. The Master said, "Not being disobedient." As Fan Qi was driving him, the Master said, "Mang-sun asked me what filial piety was, and I answered, 'Not being disobedient.'" Fan Qi said, "What did you mean?" The Master replied, "Parents, when alive, should be served according to propriety. When dead, they should be buried according to propriety and sacrificed to according to propriety."
>
> 13:18. The Duke of Sheh told Confucius, "Some of us are upright. If our father had stolen a sheep, we'd bear witness to it." Confucius said, "In my country the upright are different. The father conceals the misconduct of the son, and the son conceals the misconduct of the father. Uprightness is to be found in this."

Another ancient Chinese philosopher, Mozi (Mo Tzu), argued that people's preference for friends and family over strangers is unjust. Confucius and Plato discuss a kind of case on which Mozi and Confucius disagree: Suppose you have reason to believe that your own parents have committed a crime. Should you turn them in? Testify against them? Answer the police's questions? Presumably you would be obliged to do these things if they were not your parents. So, unless family relations have special moral status, it seems the answers to these questions should be yes. Confucius's division between virtues in relation to friends and family and virtues in relation to strangers, however, leads him to say no. Your obligations to family override obligations to strangers.

This might seem to make Confucius's approach contradict Western notions of justice. To some extent, it does. Western theories of justice are closer to Mozi than to Confucius. But two points are worth keeping in mind. First, Socrates, confronted with a similar situation in the *Euthyphro*, agrees with Confucius. He plainly doubts Euthyphro's decision to prosecute his father for having allowed a slave accused of murder to die while he went to get the proper official. So there are Western parallels to Confucius's view. Second, Confucius is speaking here of someone acting as a private citizen; government officials should not put family obligations above the obligations of their offices.

Most fundamental of all are the virtues of the self. In this respect Confucius and Socrates surely agree that "the unexamined life is not worth living." Knowledge leads to virtuous thought, which leads to virtuous feelings, which leads in turn to virtuous action.

1. *Knowledge:* The superior person knows the Way (***Dao***), the right way to act, but also loves learning; without the love of learning, virtues easily transform into their opposites.

2. *The Virtues of Thought:* Sincerity and humility are virtues we exhibit to ourselves. They underlie all other virtues. To us, it sounds odd to speak of being sincere or humble with oneself. But we are insincere with others if we do not mean what we say to them; we are insincere with ourselves if we do not mean what we say to ourselves. Insincerity with oneself, in other words, amounts to self-deception. So

sincerity to oneself is a form of self-knowledge, of knowing what one thinks and wants and knows.

3. *The Virtues of Feeling:* For Confucius, it is not enough to know the Way; one must also love and delight in the Way. The virtuous person not only does the right thing but wants to do it.

4. *The Virtues of Action:* The five basic virtues are those of *ren.* The virtuous person is benevolent, kind, generous, and above all balanced, observing the Mean in all things. But Confucius adds other characteristics: he describes the superior person as careful, slow in speech, mild, at ease, composed, warm, satisfied, earnest, respectful, dignified, majestic, and open-minded.

Confucius, like Aristotle, thinks of virtue as a mean between extremes; the properly generous person, for example, gives appropriately, neither too much nor too little, to the right person in the right circumstances. Though Confucius does not do so explicitly (except in 17:8; see excerpt following), we might think of Confucian virtues as means between vices, just as in Aristotle:

FIVE VIRTUES OF *REN:*

Too little	*Right amount*	*Too much*
frivolous	serious	somber
stingy	generous	profligate
insincere	sincere	reckless
lazy	diligent	"workaholic"
mean, indifferent	kind	indulgent
small-minded	*ren*	simplicity

OTHER CONFUCIAN VIRTUES:

Too little	*Right amount*	*Too much*
disrespectful	respectful	bustling
careless	cautious	timid
diffident	bold	insubordinate
devious	straightforward	rude
weak	strong	extravagant

Also, as in Aristotle, the superior person is at ease with virtue. Proper conduct becomes habitual. It becomes second nature. The superior person not only has strength of will but also avoids inner conflict, for he or she desires to do what is right.

What is the key to finding the virtuous mean between extremes?

2:4. At fifteen, I had my mind bent on learning. At thirty, I stood firm. At forty, I had no doubts. At fifty, I knew the decrees of Heaven. At sixty, my ear obeyed truth. At seventy, I could follow what my heart desired without transgressing what was right."

4:2. The Master said, "Those without virtue can't abide long in a condition of poverty and hardship—or in a condition of enjoyment. The virtuous are at ease with virtue [*ren*]; the wise desire virtue."

6:18. The Master said, "Those who know the Way aren't equal to those who love it, and those who love it aren't equal to those who delight in it."

6:27. The Master said, "Perfect is the virtue that accords with the Constant Mean! For a long time, its practice has been rare among the people."

17:8. The Master said, "Yu, have you heard the six things followed by the six confusions?" Yu replied, "I haven't." "Sit down and I'll tell you. The love of benevolence without the love of learning leads to an ignorant simplicity. The love of knowledge without the love of learning leads to dissipation of mind. The love of sincerity without the love of learning leads to recklessness. The love of straightforwardness without the love of learning leads to rudeness. The love of boldness without the love of learning leads to insubordination. The love of strength of character without the love of learning leads to extravagance."

To become virtuous, in Confucius's view, one must associate with the right people (1:8), examine oneself, and above all act with **propriety**, the observance of proper rites, ceremonies, and principles. The word he uses is ***li***, which originally referred to religious sacrifice. In Confucius's hands, it comes to mean ceremony, rite, ritual, decorum, propriety, principle, and proper form or custom. Most often, Confucius uses *li* to refer to traditional social rules and practices. All three aspects of *li* are important. The rules of propriety are traditional: they are mandated by custom and connect us with the past, embodying the wisdom of generations of people who have faced situations similar to those we face. The rules of propriety are social: they concern relations between people in society and constitute a significant part of the social order. Finally, the rules of propriety are rules or practices: they govern how people should behave in certain circumstances. Many features of propriety arise from particular social relations—of parent to child, for example, or friend to friend—but some, such as the rule of reciprocity, are universal.

Propriety is a crucial component of virtue, for it establishes character. We train ourselves, developing good habits, by obeying the rules of propriety. To become truly virtuous, propriety must become habitual; we must develop a natural ease with, and even love, the rules of propriety (1:12). As in Aristotle, the superior person not only does the right thing but wants to do it, is "at ease with virtue" (4:2).

1:12. Yu said, "In practicing propriety, a natural ease is best. This is the excellence of the ancient kings, and in things small and great we follow them. Yet it is not to be observed in all cases. Anyone who knows and manifests such ease must regulate it by propriety."

The role of the love of learning in 17:8 is here ascribed to propriety. Is this an inconsistency?

2:3. The Master said, "If the people are led by laws and restrained by punishments, they will try to avoid them without any sense of shame. If they are led by virtue and restrained by propriety, they will have a sense of shame and become good."

8:2. The Master said, "Respectfulness without propriety becomes laborious bustle. Caution without propriety becomes timidity. Boldness without propriety becomes insubordination; straightforwardness without propriety becomes rudeness."

12:1. Yen Yuan asked about perfect virtue [*ren*]. The Master said, "To subdue oneself and return to propriety is virtue. If a man can subdue himself and return to propriety for one day, all under heaven will ascribe virtue to him. Is the practice of virtue from oneself alone, or does it depend on others?" Yen Yuan said, "I want to ask about these steps." The Master replied, "Don't look at what is contrary to propriety; don't listen to what is contrary to propriety; don't speak what is contrary to propriety; don't make a move that is contrary to propriety."

15:17. The Master said, "The superior person takes righteousness [*yi*] to be essential. He practices it according to propriety. He brings it forth in humility. He completes it with sincerity. This is indeed a superior person."

Confucius thus offers a theory of virtue that parallels Aristotle's theory in many respects. Virtue is a kind of mean; it arises from habit. The virtuous person not only does the right thing but has no desire to do anything else. Confucius distinguishes virtues of the self—most centrally, virtues of knowledge, followed by virtues of thought and virtues of action—which underlie virtue in general. There are also virtues to be exhibited toward family and friends, most importantly filial piety and fraternal submission, as well as virtues toward strangers. Confucius summarizes the last in his principle of reciprocity: "What you do not want done to yourself, do not do to others."

LAOZI (LAO TZU)

Laozi (Lao Tzu), a contemporary of Confucius and the Buddha in the sixth century B.C.E. (see Chapter 6), founded Daoism (Taoism), which opposes Confucianism in many respects. Confucius emphasizes traditional social rules, activity, and social relationships; Laozi stresses nonconformity, tranquility, and individual transcendence. But Laozi, too, can be seen as outlining an ethics of character. Daoist virtues, however, differ strikingly from those advocated by Confucius or Aristotle.

Confucius, in elaborating his account of the superior person, refuses to say anything about human nature, the nature of the universe, or God. He treats *Dao,* the Way, as a purely ethical concept: the right way to live. Laozi, in contrast, begins with metaphysical speculation about *Dao,* which he takes as the way the universe works and identifies with the One, which underlies everything but admits no description. (See Chapter 6.) Laozi nevertheless takes the *Dao* as having moral force. *Dao,* embodied in an individual thing, is the thing's ***de***—its power, force, nature, character, or virtue.

The features of the vast De,
Follow entirely from Dao.

It is an active principle guiding the thing. It also determines what the thing ought to do and be. The excellence of a thing thus stems from its *Dao.*

51

Dao produces ten thousand things, and De nourishes them.
Their natures give them form, and circumstances complete them.

The ten thousand things respect Dao and exalt De,
Not by decree, but spontaneously.

Thus Dao produces,
De nourishes, grows, nurtures, matures, maintains, and covers.
It produces without claiming possession,
Supports without vaunting itself,

Matures without controlling,
This is called the dark De.[5]

This twofold character of *de*—power and virtue, or, in different terminology, guiding and regulating principle—leads to the distinctive ethical principles of Daoism. What a thing is and what it ought to be are intertwined. Things naturally tend toward what they ought to be. *De* flows both from and toward the Dao.

Laozi therefore advocates inaction. If things naturally tend toward what they ought to be, we should leave them alone; our interference is more likely to do harm than good. Laozi therefore recommends weakness, simplicity, and tranquility. It often seems that he recommends passivity and laziness. But the inaction (***wuwei***) he recommends is that of letting nature take its course. We should let the guiding principles of things guide them without interference. The Dao flows naturally, spontaneously, underpinning a world in which things naturally tend toward what they ought to be. The coincidence of guiding and regulating principles in *de* means that things naturally tend to their own states of excellence. Interference with this natural process prevents them from attaining excellence. The individual should adopt a policy of noninterference.

2

Therefore the sage manages affairs without acting, and teaches without speech.
Ten thousand things spring up and show themselves,
They grow and he does not claim them,
They mature and he does not expect reward.
The sage accomplishes without resting on his laurels.
He works imperceptibly, so his power continues.

Many of Laozi's sayings sound paradoxical. What, for example, does it mean to 'act without acting'?

63

Act without acting,
Manage affairs without trouble,
Taste without tasting.
Consider the small great, the few many.
Repay injury with De.

Plan difficult things while they are easy.
Accomplish great things while they are small.
Difficult things of the world start easy.
Great things of the world start small.
Because the sage never does great things,
He can accomplish great things.

He who promises lightly keeps few promises.
He who thinks things easy finds them difficult.
Therefore the sage takes even easy things to be difficult,
So that they are not difficult.

---

[5] This and subsequent selections from Laozi are from the *Dao de Jing*, in *The Texts of Taoism*, translated by James Legge (Oxford: Oxford University Press, 1891). I have altered the translation significantly to bring out the poetic quality of the original and to accord with the Pinyin system.

Note the criticism of Confucius's saying, "Repay kindness with kindness, and injury with justice." Laozi tells us to repay injury with *de*. What does this mean? To construe it as saying we should repay injury with virtue makes it true but uninformative. It is important to remember that *de* is natural, something that flows from the world's order. Laozi seems to be saying, then, that we should not worry about what to do to repay injury; do whatever comes naturally.

One might object to the Daoist picture as follows: "The Daoist argument for noninterference rests on an ambiguity in the claim that things naturally tend toward what they ought to be. (a) It might mean that apples, for example, are typically good—that is, that we count defective apples as atypical. That seems true for apples, but dubious for murderers or mistakes. In any case, it implies nothing about interference or noninterference. (b) It might also mean that things taken individually naturally tend toward what they ought to be. This might entail noninterference, but it seems absurd; worm-ridden apples do not tend to become whole again." That is certainly right. But the Daoist case for noninterference rests partly on the assumption that *people* are naturally good. Things naturally tend toward what they ought to be, and so do people. Consequently, for normal people, at any rate, becoming good requires no special effort. Relax; you will naturally tend toward what is good.

This leads Laozi to a theory of virtue strikingly different from that presented by Aristotle or Confucius. Laozi criticizes Confucian ideas directly in various passages, maintaining that virtue (*ren*), righteousness (*yi*), and propriety (*li*) are signs of desperation and decline. All result from self-examination and training. But if our guiding and regulating principles converge—if people, that is, naturally tend to be good, and become what they ought to be—then none of this is necessary. We do not need to examine ourselves unless there is something wrong with us. We do not need to be trained unless something has disrupted our natural tendencies.

How is Laozi criticizing Confucius?

18

When the great Dao ceases to be observed,
There are benevolence [*ren*] and righteousness [*i*].

When wisdom and cleverness appear,
There is great hypocrisy.

When the six kinships are not in harmony,
There is filial piety.

When the nations and clans fall into disorder,
There are loyal ministers.

19

Renounce sagacity, discard wisdom,
People will profit a hundredfold.

Renounce benevolence [*ren*], discard righteousness [*i*],
People will again practice filial piety.

Renounce artistry, discard profit-seeking,
There will be no robbers and thieves.

These three pairs adorn inadequacy.
Therefore, let there be the advice:
Look to the undyed silk, hold on to the uncarved wood [*pu*],
Reduce your selfishness and your desires.

38

Those of high De do not display De, so they have De.
Those of low De cling to De, so they lack De.

Those of high De do not act, for they have no need to.
Those of low De act, and need to.

Those of high benevolence [*ren*] act, but have no need to.
Those of high righteousness [*i*] act, and need to.

Those of high propriety [*li*] act, but, getting no response,
Bare their arms and march.

Thus when Dao is lost, De appears.
When De is lost, benevolence [*ren*] appears.
When benevolence [*ren*] is lost, righteousness [*i*] appears.
When righteousness [*i*] is lost, propriety [*li*] appears.

Propriety [*li*] is the thin edge of loyalty and good faith,
And the beginning of disorder;
Intelligence is the flower of Dao,
And the beginning of stupidity.

Great people abide in the solid and reject the flimsy;
Abide in the fruit and not in the flower.
Thus they put away one and choose the other.

Laozi advocates virtues of inactivity, passivity, humility, and spontaneity. Above all, we are to act naturally. He advises acceptance rather than desire, cooperation rather than competition, understanding rather than knowledge.

8

The highest excellence is like water,
Which benefits all things, without contending with any.

10

In concentrating your breath to make it soft,
Can you become like a baby?

In cleansing your mind of the dark,
Can you make it spotless?

In loving the people and governing the state,
Can you practice inaction?

In opening and shutting heaven's gate,
Can you be the female?

In understanding all,
Can you be without knowledge?

To produce, to nourish, to produce without claiming,
To act without boasting, to preside without control,
This is called the dark virtue.

The Daoist ideal is the uncarved block (***pu***), which simply is what it is and does not try to be anything else. It avoids superfluous actions and makes no attempt to go beyond what it is and ought to be (its nature, *de*) by cultivating an excess or artificial nature (***yu de***).

What does the uncarved wood represent?

37

Dao does nothing, yet there is nothing it does not do.
If kings and princes can hold to it,
The ten thousand things will transform themselves.

If I desire this transformation,
I will express it by the nameless uncarved wood.
The nameless uncarved wood has no desires.
Without desire, at rest and still,
The ten thousand things will order themselves.

57

Therefore a sage says:
I do nothing, and the people transform themselves.
I love stillness, and the people correct themselves.
I have no business, and the people prosper themselves;
I have no ambition, and the people attain the uncarved wood themselves.

Similarly, because we cannot describe the Dao, we should not seek enlightenment through language. In thinking, we draw distinctions. Language, reason, reflection, and other forms of intellectual activity thus lead us away from the ultimate truth, from recognizing the world's unity.

Daoism is therefore anti-intellectual. Ordinarily, we think in order to understand. We reflect in order to answer questions arising from reason or experience. For Confucius, knowledge is the root of all virtue. Even those who would not go quite so far as that—Aristotle, for example—think that knowledge is good and a vital component of practical wisdom.

In Laozi's view, however, thinking leads us away from understanding. We understand most clearly when we set reason, language, and thinking aside.

20

Renounce learning and have no troubles.
Yes and no, how far apart are they?
Good and evil, how far apart are they?

47

Without stepping out the door, understand all under the sky.
Without looking out the window, see the Dao of Heaven.
The farther you go out, the less you know.

Therefore sages know without travelling,
Name things without seeing them,
Accomplish without trying.

56

One who knows does not speak,
One who speaks does not know.

71

From knowing to not knowing is best.
From not knowing to knowing is sickness.
By being sick of sickness, you keep from being sick.

This anti-intellectual aspect of Daoism has had significant influence on the Chinese and Japanese form of Buddhism known as Zen, discussed in Chapter 4.

BUDDHIST VIRTUES

The Buddha (563–483 B.C.E.; see Chapter 4), a contemporary of Confucius and Laozi, lived in the Ganges valley in what is now Nepal. Although he did not write anything, his disciples kept records of his teachings and sermons, compiling a vast canon of literature. The southern branch of Buddhism, Theravada Buddhism, rests its conception of virtue on that "Southern Canon." Its ideal is to become an *arhat* (a saint, also called a ***Pratyekabuddha*** in the *Sutra* to follow), one who loses all individuality in universal, impersonal bliss. The northern branch of Buddhism, Mahayana Buddhism, recognizes a distinct and later literature as sacred. Its ideal is the ***bodhisattva,*** "one who has achieved the goal," who, unlike the *arhat,* turns back from the final bliss to help others attain it.

The next chapter details the central ethical teachings of the Buddha as presented in the Southern Canon. This chapter focuses on the Mahayana theory of virtue developed in the Northern Canon. Mahayana Buddhists sometimes tell a story to illustrate the difference between the *arhat* and the *bodhisattva* and thus between Theravada and Mahayana Buddhism. Four travelers in the desert, about to collapse of thirst, find what appears to be an oasis. But it has a tall wall around it. One offers to climb the wall and report what he finds. He disappears over the wall, and does not call out or come back. The same happens with the second. The third climbs the wall and sees that it is indeed an oasis. He climbs back down and helps boost the fourth over the wall. The fourth calls to him, "Come on!" But he answers, "You go ahead. I'm going to look for others who might be lost in the desert, and direct them here." Three of the four are *arhats,* who seek their own fulfillment in the oasis. The one who glimpses the oasis but resists entering in order to help others find it as the *bodhisattva.*

Mahayanists try to attain six virtues, or "perfections" (***paramitas***) possessed by the Buddha. These enable them to promote the welfare of all beings. Thus the Mahayana sect is more world-affirming than Theravada Buddhism; it aims to develop individual perfections rather than to extinguish the self in otherworldly bliss. Mahayanists do not deny doctrines of the Southern Canon so much as construe them as the Buddha's way to help people who are not yet ready to appreciate higher truths. In effect, they urge us to look at what the Buddha *did* as well as what he *said*. The Buddha himself exemplifies the ideal of the *bodhisattva*, someone who seeks the enlightenment of all. The Buddha did not simply disappear into nirvana; he spent many years preaching to help others attain the enlightenment that he had achieved.

> Here a Bodhisattva, who courses towards enlightenment, and has stood firmly in the perfection of giving, gives a gift not for the sake of a limited number of beings, but, on the contrary, for the sake of all beings. And in the same spirit he practices the other perfections.[6]

The six perfections the *bodhisattva* achieves are (1) charity, (2) good moral character (which amounts to concern for others rather than oneself), (3) patience (which involves peace in the face of anger or desire), (4) energy or vigor (for striving for the good), (5) deep concentration, and (6) wisdom.

> [1] . . . the perfection of giving of a Bodhisattva, who courses in perfect wisdom and gives gifts, consists in that, with attentions associated with the knowledge of all modes, he turns over to full enlightenment that gift which he gives, after he has made that wholesome root (which results from the act of giving) common to all beings.

The *bodhisattva*, that is, is generous, giving to others not just material goods but spiritual gifts that help them toward enlightenment. The benefits of the gift bounce back on the *bodhisattva*, who becomes more deserving of enlightenment as a result of his or her generosity.

> [2] His perfection of morality consists in that, with his whole attention centred on the knowledge of all modes, he shuns the attentions of Disciples and Pratyekabuddhas. . . .

The *bodhisattva*, that is, concentrates on knowing and helping others. He or she is not in it for the money, or fame, or attention, or gratitude, or respect. In fact the *bodhisattva* has no need of any of these. The *bodhisattva* keeps his or her eyes on the prize of enlightenment without being distracted. But the perfection of morality is more than single-mindedness. The *bodhisattva* is fully compassionate, caring deeply for others. The Disciples and Pratyekabuddhas seek their own enlightenment. They want to eliminate their own suffering. To the extent that you share that perspective and have similar thoughts, you seek your own good rather than that of others. The Disciples and Pratyekabuddhas, in short, are selfish. So is anyone who craves attention, fame, money, respect, or gratitude. The *bodhisattva* is unselfish, desiring the good of others as much as his or her own good.

> [3] his perfection of patience in the enduring of those dharmas, in his willingness to find pleasure in them, in his ability to tolerate them. . . .

The *bodhisattva* is willing to tolerate his or her duties, indeed, finds pleasure in them. Aristotle and Confucius hold that the virtuous person not only does the right thing but also *wants* to do it. The Mahayana ideal does not go quite so far. The *bodhisattva*, valuing enlightenment above all else, cannot help but feel the pull of enlightenment beckoning him or her. So we cannot expect the *bodhisattva* to want to do the best thing

---

[6] This and subsequent selections in this section are from *The Large Sutra on Perfect Wisdom*, edited and translated by Edward Conze (Berkeley: University of California Press, 1975).

without having any contrary desire. The *bodhisattva* is bound to want his or her own enlightenment to some degree. But the *bodhisattva* is patient enough to postpone his or her own gratification for the benefit of others and even finds pleasure in doing so.

> [4] his perfection of vigour in the indefatigability with which he continues to dedicate his wholesome roots to full enlightenment, after he has made them common to all beings. . . .

The *bodhisattva* works tirelessly for the enlightenment of others, thus keeping to the Eightfold Path (see Chapter 8), which requires right effort. This requires being as steady as an ox, working constantly to overcome desire and inclination.

> [5] his perfection of concentration in his one-pointedness of thought when he gives a gift, so that, when he dedicates that wholesome root to enlightenment, after he has made it common to all beings, he gives, through keeping his whole attention centred on the knowledge of all modes, no opportunity to a Disciple-thought or a Pratyekabuddhas-thought.

Why is being "centred on the knowledge of all modes" important?

This reflects another step on the Eightfold Path: right mindfulness. Thought and action are intimately linked; you cannot eliminate selfish desire in your behavior without overcoming it mentally. Only by thinking correctly can you hope to act correctly and escape suffering. The *bodhisattva* has a special temptation over and above those that afflict the rest of us; he or she can choose enlightenment for him- or herself over enlightenment for others. So, the *bodhisattva* must guard especially carefully against "Pratyekabuddhas-thought," that is, his or her own desire for enlightenment.

> [6] His perfection of wisdom consists in that he sets up the notion that everything is made of illusion and in that he gets at no giver, recipient, or gift.

This relates to the final step on the Eightfold Path, right concentration. The *bodhisattva* who has this perfection is enlightened; he or she understands the essential unity between mind and world. He or she has seen through the illusion of a separate ego, recognizing that there is no self. (See Chapter 4.) To desire his or her own bliss apart from the bliss of everyone is to fall into the trap of thinking that there is a separate self. The only way to achieve true liberation is to achieve liberation for everyone.

These virtues entail others. Anyone who exhibits the six perfections places the good of others above his or her own good. Consequently, the *bodhisattva* is also friendly, compassionate, sympathetic, and impartial, taking joy in the joy of others. In short, the *bodhisattva* is thoroughly altruistic.

> A Bodhisattva enters the concentration of friendliness, and strives to save all beings. He enters the concentration on compassion, and directs pity and compassion towards beings. He enters the concentration on sympathetic joy, and resolves to make beings rejoice. He enters into the concentration on impartiality, and "extends" to beings the extinction of the outflows.

How can the *bodhisattva* seek the enlightenment of *all* without seeking his or her own enlightenment? The key is concentration. The *bodhisattva* remains directed toward others, seeking joy and enlightenment for them while overcoming his own desires. He seeks these things for others, but "he does not relish them, is not captivated by them." In short, the *bodhisattva* seeks enlightenment for himself only insofar as he is included in "all beings"; he detaches himself from a personal desire for enlightenment.

The Mahayana wisdom literature thus puts forward a conception of virtue that, while distinctly Buddhist, resembles Christian virtues in many ways. The *bodhisattva* sacrifices the quest for his own good to seek the good of others.

The Theravada Buddhist, however, has a response to this ideal. One could argue that the ethical ideal of the *bodhisattva* undermines itself: If the *bodhisattva* helps others toward enlightenment, he or she in effect helps them to become *arhats,* not *bodhisattvas.* So, the good *bodhisattva* will teach Theravada, not Mahayana, Buddhism.

From a Mahayana perspective, this response falls into a trap. To achieve enlightenment, one must eliminate cravings—selfish desires—including the desire for enlightenment itself. The best way to lead people to enlightenment, therefore, is to teach them the *bodhisattva* ideal. Teaching them to be *arhats* encourages them to subjugate most desires to a desire for enlightenment, not to eliminate desire itself.

MODERN VARIANTS OF VIRTUE ETHICS

Concern with action and rules for distinguishing right from wrong action dominated ethics in the seventeenth, eighteenth, and nineteenth centuries. Over the past thirty years, however, the ethics of character has returned to center stage in philosophy. Various writers have found in Aristotle a theory that focuses on the central questions of human life.

Care

That is not to say, however, that contemporary philosophers have accepted all aspects of Aristotle's theory. Feminists such as Nel Noddings and Rita Manning, in particular, have questioned Aristotle's list of virtues. Aristotle describes a virtuous person as courageous, self-controlled, generous, magnificent, high-minded, ambitious to the proper degree, gentle, friendly, truthful, and witty. That, they contend, describes not a virtuous *person* but a virtuous *man*—specifically a virtuous, upper-class officer or nobleman in ancient Greece. Aristotle's virtues are masculine, even military, virtues. Just as Laozi rejects Confucius's account of virtues as masculine and argues instead for traditional feminine virtues, some contemporary feminists argue that the ethics of character must incorporate, or even rest primarily upon, virtues often seen as the virtues of women—especially caring for others. In this respect, they hold a conception of virtue similar to that of Mahayana Buddhism. Contemporary American philosopher Rita Manning, for example, writes,

What is the difference between caring and caring for?

> An ethic of caring, as I shall defend it, includes two elements. First is a disposition to care. This is a willingness to receive others, a willingness to give the lucid attention to the needs of others which filling these needs appropriately requires. . . .
>
> . . . I am also obligated to care for. (I am following Noddings in using "care for" to indicate caring as expressed in action.) In the paradigm case, caring for involves acting in some appropriate way to respond to the needs of persons, and animals, but can also be extended to responding to the needs of communities, values, or objects. . . .[7]

[7] Rita Manning, "Just Caring," in Eve Browning Cole and Susan Coultrap McQuinn (eds.), *Explorations in Feminist Ethics: Theory and Practice* (Bloomington: Indiana University Press, 1992), 45–54.

In other words, we must be caring people generally and must put our sensitivity to the needs of others into practice.

Why should we be caring? Manning's answer is simple. Others need care; relationships depend on care; and care that is never put into practice withers. As she observes, "human lives devoid of caring impulses and responses would be nasty, brutish, short, and lonely."

Just as in Aristotle, virtue is a mean between extremes. It is not good to be selfish, but neither is it good to be completely self-sacrificing. Just as a generous person gives the right amount in the right way in the right circumstances and for the right reason, a caring person gives of him- or herself to the right degree in the right way in the right circumstances and for the right reason. We are not required to become martyrs any more than we are required to be profligate with what we have.

> . . . I have a prima facie obligation to care for when I come across a creature in need who is unable to meet that need without help, when my caring is part of a reciprocal relationship, or when indicated as part of my role responsibility [e.g., as parent or nurse]. My actual obligation rests on the seriousness of the need, my assessment of the appropriateness of filling the need, and my ability to do something about filling it. But I must also recognize that I am a person who must be cared for and that I must recognize and respond to my own need to be cared for.

We might correspondingly make up a list of virtues and vices based on Aristotelian principles but sketching a very different portrait of a good person:

Drive or Emotion	*Too Unconstrained*	*Virtuous*	*Too Constrained*
selfishness	selfish	caring	selfless
love	slavishly devoted	loving	cold
suspicion	suspicious	trusting	foolish
pity	[nameless]	compassionate	merciless
hurt	vengeful	forgiving	unassertive

These too are important virtues, which deserve a place in any adequate account of what it is to be a good person.

An emphasis on the virtues of care naturally raises questions about the relation between caring and justice. Confucius and Plato, we have seen, discuss the conflict between the two. They envision a case in which a family member commits a crime. Should you turn him or her in to the police? Interestingly, both say no; family relations take precedence over the demands of justice. Sometimes, they are surely right. Jones should not call the police to report that his sister drove at 38 mph in a 35-mph zone.

Presumably, however, it depends on how close the relation is and how serious the crime is. If I find that someone has been embezzling money from the company and then learn, on further investigation, that the guilty party is a second cousin of mine, my obligation to tell the authorities still seems strong. Consider, too, the case of the Unabomber, who killed several people and maimed several others. His brother read his manifesto in the newspaper, recognized certain phrases, and alerted the authorities. Surely he was right to do so. Lives were in the balance.

Of course, caring extends far beyond family members. So we can raise similar issues with respect to other kinds of relationships. Sometimes care will take precedence over justice; sometimes the reverse will hold. Resolving such conflicts requires thinking carefully about the stakes on both sides and about whether you have any special obligations that require impartiality. Judges, for example, must put the demands of justice and equal treatment over caring. They should not hand out one sentence for friends and acquaintances and another, harsher sentence for strangers.

But Manning suggests two further complications in the relationship between caring and justice. First, even a judge ought to care about the person being sentenced as well as that person's victims. It is not clear that we can make sense of justice, even in that paradigm case, without thinking about what would be best for the criminal, the victim, the victim's friends and family, and the rest of society. So it is dangerous to isolate questions of justice from questions of caring. Second, caring is important in part because we *need* care. If justice demands that our needs be met—and it does in some conceptions of justice (see Chapter 9)—then justice demands that we receive a certain level of care.

Conflict

Contemporary British philosopher Philippa Foot advances another worry about the ethics of character: virtues may come into conflict with one another. Aristotle, Confucius, and Laozi all give the impression that a superior person has all the virtues. Even if we cannot achieve perfection, there is an ideal of perfect virtue—Confucius's sage—to which we can aspire. Human beings have a coherent function; we can fulfill that function more or less well. On this conception, the virtues form a harmonious whole. Perhaps, as Plato sometimes suggests, the virtues even interconnect so that to have one virtue completely would be to have them all.

Perhaps, however, the virtues conflict with each other. Perhaps having one virtue precludes having certain others. Prudence and altruism might both be virtues, for example, but pursuing one's own self-interest can conflict with pursuing the welfare of others. Truthfulness and caring may conflict; it may be best for my friend that I not tell her the truth. There may be circumstances in which I cannot be both courageous and gentle, high-minded and friendly, cautious and bold, respectful and straightforward, loving and forgiving. It is not just that Aristotelian virtues may conflict with feminist virtues or that Confucian virtues may conflict with Daoist ones. One may be forced to choose among virtues even in the same theory of virtues. This may be due to bad luck, that is, to facing an unusual and unfortunate situation. But Foot worries that it also may be that one can develop certain virtues only by developing vices that inevitably go along with them. There is

What does it mean to say that the virtues conflict?

> inevitable loss involved in a choice between values: when one really good thing which the man of virtue must cherish has to be sacrificed for another, a loss that is often reflected in a conflict of *oughts* or *obligations* but is not described simply by talking about such conflicts. . . . [S]o far from forming a unity in the sense that Aristotle or Aquinas believed that they did, the virtues actually conflict with each other: which is to say that if someone has one of them he inevitably fails to have some other. . . . [He] can only become good in one way by being bad in another, as if e.g., he could only rein in his ruthless desires at the cost of a deep malice against

himself and the world; or as if a kind of dull rigidity were the price of refusing to do what he himself wanted at whatever cost to others.[8]

In Aristotle's view, sorting out what to do in which circumstances is the task of practical reason. A person with practical wisdom is good at finding the mean. We can extend this idea to conflicts among virtues; a person with practical wisdom is good at seeing which virtues take precedence over others under which circumstances. Practical wisdom thus consists not only in seeing what a virtue—say, courage—requires, but also how to compare the demands of courage to the demands of other virtues. If developing a virtue entails developing vices along with it, practical reason will have to illuminate not only the conflicts that result but also whether it is worth it to develop the virtue in the first place.

Virtue, Luck, and Responsibility

Suppose, as Aristotle says, that living well depends in part on good fortune. It is hard to be happy without a certain level of material well-being. Thirst, hunger, cold, and disease are enemies of happiness. It is also hard to be happy without friends and loved ones or with friends and loved ones who are suffering or dead. To some extent, then, living well requires luck.

It also requires luck in a more fundamental and pervasive sense. It is hard to become virtuous in an environment hostile to virtue. To become good, Aristotle says, people who train us to form the right habits of thought and action must bring us up under the right laws. Like plants, we require nurturing to grow. A good person is lucky not only to have enough food, drink, companionship, health, and so on to live well but also to have been born into a situation that encouraged him or her to flourish.

As contemporary American philosopher Martha Nussbaum points out, however, that creates a problem. We think of virtues not only as goals but also as measures of human excellence. We praise people for being virtuous and hold them responsible for their vices. If flourishing is partly a matter of luck, however, this makes no sense; we might as well praise lottery winners and condemn losers. But these are morally neutral events, deserving neither praise nor blame. How can we hold people accountable for their characters? We tend to think that people can be held responsible for their characters. We think it is worth answering the question, What kind of person should I be? for people have the power to develop certain traits of character and avoid others.

But we depend on external circumstances in a bewildering variety of ways. To achieve excellence, we must be born with enough ability, be raised in a nurturing environment, avoid disasters of various kinds, enter into the right kinds of relationships with other human beings, and so on. We depend on others—friends, family, loved ones, teachers, colleagues, etc.—both for what they can do for us and for their own sakes. This, however, raises the questions:

> . . . To what extent *can* we distinguish between what is up to the world and what is up to us, when assessing a human life? To what extent *must* we insist on funding these distinctions, if we are to go on praising as we praise?[9]

---

[8] Philippa Foot, "Moral Realism and Moral Dilemma," *The Journal of Philosophy* 80 (1983): 370–98, 396–97.

[9] Martha Nussbaum, *The Fragility of Goodness* (Cambridge: Cambridge University Press, 1986).

These questions are important, for happiness and virtue stem from a mixture of luck and effort. From Aristotle's point of view, we can become good only if we are fortunate enough to grow up and live under the right conditions—*and* only if we work to train ourselves to have the right habits. Our characters result from our inborn traits, from influences of our environments, and from our own efforts. To know for what we should be held responsible, we must be able to distinguish these components. If we cannot, then thinking of ethics in terms of traits of character may be unhelpful.

Human excellence is partly the result of our own striving but partly a result of external influences. You need only ask yourself, "What would I be like—what kind of person would I be—if I had been born poor, disabled, or hideously ugly? If I had been born into a family of shepherds in Mongolia or Bushmen in the Kalahari?" to realize how fragile, how contingent, how dependent on external circumstances many features of our lives and characters are. Under any of those circumstances, you might still be able to flourish, but the virtues you would have been able to develop would almost certainly be different from the ones you actually have.

Which virtues depend on vulnerability?

> . . . part of the peculiar beauty of *human* excellence just *is* its vulnerability. . . . Human excellence is . . . something whose very nature it is to be in need, a growing thing in the world that could not be made invulnerable and keep its own peculiar fineness. (The hero Odysseus chose the mortal love of an aging woman over Calypso's unchanging splendor.) The contingencies that make praise problematic are also, in some as yet unclear way, constitutive of that which is there for praising.

Our lives and characters are nevertheless not entirely the product of chance. We engrain in ourselves habits that are not parts of our nature but which in time become second nature. We are able to use reason to understand and direct our lives. We are not completely at the mercy of external forces; we are not leaves being blown about by the wind or even plants who can do nothing more than turn slowly toward the sun. To what extent, however, can we escape the contingency and vulnerability not only of what we have but also of who we are? Can we take enough control of our lives to be held responsible for what we are and become while retaining the beauty that arises from human vulnerability?

> We have reason. We are able to deliberate and choose, to make a plan in which ends are ranked, to decide actively what is to have value and how much. All this must count for something. If it is true that a lot about us is messy, needy, uncontrolled, rooted in the dirt and standing helplessly in the rain, it is also true that there is something about us that is pure and purely active, something that we could think of as 'divine, immortal, intelligible, unitary, indissoluble, ever self-consistent and invariable'. It seems possible that this rational element in us can rule and guide the rest, thereby saving the whole person from living at the mercy of luck.

We can be held responsible for who we are to the extent that who we are is the product of our own reasoning and striving rather than mere chance. We naturally seek to reduce our own vulnerability by becoming self-sufficient through the use of reason. But Nussbaum worries that self-sufficiency is not only unattainable but also undesirable. To avoid dependence on external factors, we would have to avoid having friends, falling in love, becoming attached to places and things, and other parts of a good life.

Moreover, the richer our lives—the more things we care about—the more likely those things are to come into conflict. It is possible to avoid work–family conflicts, for example, by not having a family or by not having a job. It is possible to avoid conflicts between friends by having only one friend. But a life without the possibility of conflict seems impoverished. We rationally value many things, people, and activities, even though that increases our vulnerability. Yet we do not want to embrace richness and conflict without reserve; conflict always has a cost, and sometimes the cost is high—in the case of tragedy, more than we can bear. We must balance self-sufficiency and vulnerability. Both are essential to human flourishing. If Aristotle is right that happiness—living well—is our primary end, then the very things vital to achieving it place it most at risk.

SUMMARY

Two fundamental questions of ethics are, What should I do? and What kind of person should I be? Some philosophers take the latter question as fundamental. Whatever its status, however, all ethical theories need to answer it. Philosophers in different traditions have done so in different ways, stressing the importance of different virtues. Nevertheless, there are some striking parallels. Aristotle and Confucius, for example, agree that virtues are means between extremes. Mahayana Buddhists and contemporary feminists take concern for others to play a central role. Most theories of virtue assume that one could have them all, at least in principle. But Philippa Foot questions that, worrying that one may be able to develop some virtues only at the expense of others. Finally, Martha Nussbaum sees our talk of virtues as resting on the assumption that we can distinguish the aspects of our characters for which we are responsible from those that result from luck. We may not be able to do that; indeed, our peculiarly human excellence depends partly from our dependence on circumstances outside us.

REVIEW QUESTIONS

1. Explain Socrates's thesis of the unity of the virtues. Why does it make weakness of will impossible or irrelevant?
2. Explain Plato's theory of virtue in the *Republic*. How does it differ from the view Socrates advances in the early dialogues? How does it relate to Plato's chariot analogy discussed previously in Chapter 4?
3. Discuss Aristotle's concept of happiness. How is happiness connected to virtue?
4. How, according to Aristotle, can we attain virtue? Contrast his view with Plato's views in the early dialogues and in the *Republic*.
5. What is the most important virtue in Confucius's theory? Defend your view.
6. How are Aristotle's and Confucius's views of virtue similar? How do they differ?
7. Contrast Laozi's conception of virtue with that of Aristotle, Confucius, or Mahayana Buddhism.
8. In what sense, if any, is Manning's ethics of care a critique of Aristotelian ethics?

9. Do you think that Foot is right that the virtues conflict with one another? If there were such conflict, what implications would it have?

10. To what extent does Nussbaum's stress on the fragility of virtue challenge Aristotle's account of the virtues? To what extent does it complement it? Would the same hold true of the accounts of virtues given by Plato, Confucius, and Laozi?

Terms for Review

artificial nature (*yu de*) In Laozi, a defect exhibited by anything that strives to be something other than what it is.

bodhisattva "One who has achieved the goal," who, unlike the *arhat,* turns back from the final bliss to help others attain it.

Dao In Confucius, the Way or Path; the proper way to live. In Laozi, the way the universe works; the One, which underlies everything but admits no description.

de A thing's power, force, nature, character, or virtue; *Dao* embodied in a particular thing.

ethical humanism The view that value is to be defined in purely human terms.

eudaimonia Happiness; flourishing; living well. In Aristotle, it is the only thing desirable for its own sake, never for the sake of something else.

excess nature (*yu de*) In Laozi, a defect exhibited by anything that strives to be something other than what it is.

filial piety (*xiao*) Obedience, reverence, and service to one's parents and elders.

fraternal submission Service and trustworthiness to one's equals.

inaction (*wuwei*) In Laozi, the policy of letting nature take its course.

infinite regress In Aristotle, the answering of a question of justification with an instrumental good rather than an intrinsic good—which merely invites further question.

instrumental goods Things desired as means to other things.

intrinsic goods Things desired for their own sake.

***li* (propriety)** The observance of proper rites, ceremonies, and principles.

normative term A term such as 'ought', 'should', 'good', 'bad', 'may', duty', 'responsible', and 'obligation', that speaks of how things should be or what ought to be done.

paramita One of the six virtues or perfections possessed by the Buddha.

***phronesis* (practical wisdom)** The ability to find the mean between extremes and thus act virtuously.

practical wisdom (*phronesis*) The ability to find the mean between extremes and thus act virtuously.

Pratyekabuddha An *arhat,* a saint who achieves enlightenment. But the term as used in Mahayana literature is pejorative; the *arhat* does not display the virtues of the *bodhisattva.*

prescriptive term A term such as 'ought', 'should', 'good', 'bad', 'may', duty', 'responsible', and 'obligation', that speaks of how things should be or what ought to be done.

propriety (*li*) The observance of proper rites, ceremonies, and principles.

***pu* (uncarved block)** In Laozi, something that is what it is and does not try to be anything else.

ren In Confucius, virtue, humanity, or benevolence; it involves both being true to the principles of our nature and acting benevolently toward others.

uncarved block (*pu*) In Laozi, something that is what it is and does not try to be anything else.

unity of the virtues The view that courage, wisdom, self-control, justice, piety, and so on are really the same thing.

vice A bad character trait.

virtue A good character trait.

virtue ethics A system of ethics taking the issue of virtue as central.

weakness of will Knowing the better and doing the worse; knowing what you ought to do and nevertheless not doing it.

***wuwei* (inaction)** In Laozi, the policy of letting nature take its course.

***xiao* (filial piety)** Obedience, reverence, and service to one's parents and elders.

***yu de* (excess or artificial nature)** In Laozi, a defect exhibited by anything that strives to be something other than what it is.

zhong Reciprocity (sometimes translated "altruism" or "likening to oneself"): "What you do not want done to yourself, do not do to others" (Confucius).

For Further Reading

On Plato, see Terence Irwin, *Plato's Moral Theory: The Early and Middle Dialogues* (Oxford: Clarendon Press, 1977) and *Plato's Ethics* (New York: Oxford University Press, 1995). On Aristotle's ethics, see *Essays on Aristotle's Ethics,* edited by Amelie Oksenberg Rorty (Berkeley: University of California Press, 1980).

Wing-tsit Chan (ed.), *A Source Book in Chinese Philosophy* (Princeton: Princeton University Press, 1973), is an outstanding overview of Chinese philosophy with many original sources. On Confucius, see David Hall and Roger Ames, *Thinking Through Confucius* (Albany: State University of New York Press, 1987). An entertaining introduction to Daoism is Benjamin Hoff, *The Tao of Pooh* (New York: Penguin Books, 1983). On both, see A. C. Graham, *Disputers of the Tao* (LaSalle: Open Court, 1989).

On contemporary virtue ethics, see Philippa Foot, *Virtues and Vices and Other Essays in Moral Philosophy* (Berkeley: University of California Press, 1978); Alasdair Macintyre, *After Virtue* (Notre Dame: University of Notre Dame Press, 1980); *How Should One Live?* edited by Roger Crisp (Oxford: Clarendon Press, 1996); *Virtue Ethics,* edited by Roger Crisp and Michael Slote (Oxford: Oxford University Press, 1997); Michael Slote, *From Morality to Virtue* (New York: Oxford University Press, 1992).

On specifically feminist ethics, see Annette C. Baier, *Moral Prejudices* (Cambridge: Harvard University Press, 1994); Peta Bowden, *Caring* (London: Routledge, 1997); Grace Clement, *Care, Autonomy, and Justice* (Boulder: Westview Press, 1996); Marilyn Friedman, *What Are Friends For?* (Ithaca: Cornell University Press, 1993); Daryl Koehn, *Rethinking Feminist Ethics* (London: Routledge, 1998); and Selma Sevenhuijsen, *Citizenship and the Ethics of Care* (London: Routledge, 1998).

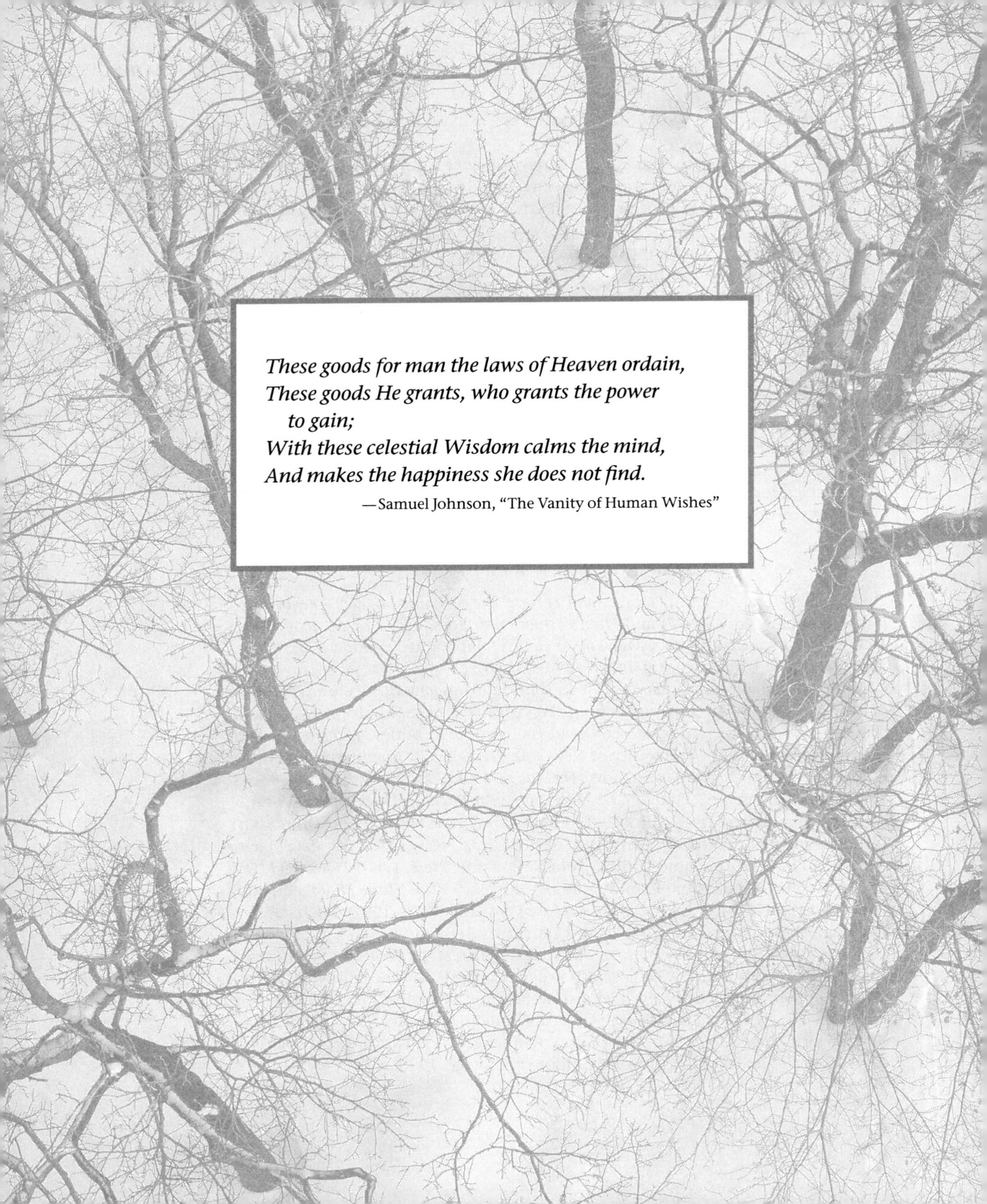

These goods for man the laws of Heaven ordain,
These goods He grants, who grants the power
to gain;
With these celestial Wisdom calms the mind,
And makes the happiness she does not find.

—Samuel Johnson, "The Vanity of Human Wishes"

CHAPTER 8

Right and Wrong

One of the basic questions of ethics is, What should I do? We use ethics to guide us in making decisions. We evaluate actions as right or wrong. But how can we tell the difference between right and wrong? What makes right actions right and wrong actions wrong?

These last two questions, though related, are not equivalent. The first asks for a *practical test* for telling whether something is right or wrong. The second asks what rightness and wrongness *are*. We had practical tests for recognizing water long before knowing that water is H_2O. We still use them. Similarly, we could devise a practical test for telling right from wrong without knowing what right and wrong really are. And we could know what they are without having a practical test for distinguishing them.

In Western and non-Western philosophical traditions, there are four traditional ways of distinguishing right from wrong:

1. *Reason.* Many philosophers hold that we can distinguish right and wrong by reasoning. They hold that morality consists in putting one's desires under the control of reason. The difference between right and wrong, in this view, amounts to the difference between rationality and irrationality.

2. *Happiness.* Aristotle, as we have seen, holds that happiness is the one thing that human beings seek for its own sake and never for the sake of something else. Many philosophers go one step further to maintain that we can distinguish right from wrong in terms of effects on human happiness (or, more generally, the happiness of sentient beings). Roughly, right actions contribute to happiness, while wrong actions detract from it.

3. *Conscience.* Many philosophers think that conscience is the best practical ethical test. They have spoken of a moral sense, likening ethical thinking to perception and right and wrong to perceptual qualities of objects. Just as our eyes distinguish colors and our ears distinguish sounds, our feelings distinguish moral qualities.

4. *God.* Ethics is part of philosophy, but it is also a part of religion; every major world religion includes rules for living such as the Ten Commandments or the Golden Rule. Some philosophers have correspondingly argued that God distinguishes right from wrong. What God commands or allows is right; what God forbids is wrong. We know what God commands by way of Holy Scripture, which details rules to use as a practical ethical test.

REASON

Many philosophers see moral decision as a battle between reason and desire. They hold that morality consists in putting one's desires under the control of reason, giving in to desire only when it is reasonable to do so. To do the right thing is thus to behave rationally. To do the wrong thing is to behave irrationally. One of the strengths of this view is that it explains why someone ought to be moral: It is *rational* to be moral.

The Buddha

The earliest form of a moral theory based on the control of desire is Buddhism. Among the most important teachings presented in Early Buddhism are the Four Noble Truths (see Chapter 6):

1. Life is painful.
2. The root of pain is desire.
3. It is possible to eliminate pain by eliminating desire.
4. The Noble Eightfold Path eliminates desire.

The Pali term for pain (or suffering) is ***dukkha.*** It is the term used for dislocated joints and broken axles. It thus has the connotation not only of pain but of being broken, out of place, out of joint. Desire puts life out of joint. Eliminating it can restore life to its proper place and lead to the highest good.

The way to this supreme good is the **Noble Eightfold Path:** right thought, right resolve, right speech, right conduct, right livelihood, right effort, right mindfulness, and right concentration or meditation.

> 4. Now this, O monks, is the noble truth of the way that leads to the cessation of pain: this is the noble Eightfold Path, namely, right views, right intention, right speech, right action, right livelihood, right effort, right mindfulness, right concentration. . . .[1]

To eliminate desire, follow the Eightfold Path, which constitutes "the Middle Way, which gives sight and knowledge, and tends to calm, to insight, enlightenment, *nirvana.*" It has eight components:

1. *Right views.* To eliminate desire, you must know something—in particular, the four noble truths. You must understand your condition and come to the proper diagnosis.

What must one know about desire?

> 136. A fool does not know when he commits his evil deeds; but the wicked man burns by his own deeds, as if by fire.
>
> 141. Not nakedness, not platted hair, not dirt, not fasting, or lying on the earth, not rubbing with dust, not sitting motionless, can purify a mortal who has not overcome desires.

[1] "The First Sermon," in Edward J. Thomas, *The Life of Buddha as Legend and History* (New York: Alfred A. Knopf, Inc., 1927).

186. There is no satisfying desires, even by a shower of gold pieces; he who knows that desires have a short taste and cause pain, he is wise.

190. He who takes refuge with Buddha, the Law, and the Church; he who, with clear understanding, sees the four holy truths:

191. These four holy truths are: suffering, the origin (*Samudaya*) of suffering (*Dukkha*), the destruction (*Nirodha*) of suffering, and the eightfold holy way (*Marga*) that leads to the quieting of suffering.

192. That is the safe refuge, that is the best refuge; having gone to that refuge, a man is delivered from all suffering.[2]

2. *Right intention.* To eliminate desire, you must not only understand your condition but want to eliminate suffering by eliminating desire. You must want to do the right thing and liberate yourself.

116. If a man would hasten towards the good, he should keep his thought away from evil; if a man does what is good slothfully, his mind delights in evil.

3. *Right speech.* You must tell the truth, to others and to yourself. You must also be charitable, recognizing that everyone suffers from the same disease. Lying both stems from and encourages ***tanha,*** selfish desire.

306. He who says what is not, goes to hell; he who, having done a thing, says he hasn't done that thing, also goes to hell. After death, both are equal: they are men with evil deeds in the next world.

4. *Right action.* You must overcome selfish desire. In particular, there are five moral precepts you must obey: (a) Do not kill; (b) Do not steal; (c) Do not lie; (d) Do not be unchaste; and (e) Do not drink. Lying, killing, stealing, drinking, and lust all stem from selfish desire and further promote it.

183. Not to commit any sin, to do good, and to purify one's mind, that is the teaching of the Awakened.

185. Not to blame, not to strike, to live restrained under the law, to be moderate in eating, to sleep and sit alone, and to dwell on the highest thoughts—this is the teaching of the Awakened.

368. The Bhikshu who acts with kindness, who is calm in the doctrine of Buddha, will reach the quiet place (*Nirvana*), cessation of natural desires, and happiness.

5. *Right livelihood.* You must choose an occupation that promotes life and enables you to overcome selfish desire. Certain occupations encourage violations of the above moral precepts. In particular, the Buddha denounces poison peddlers, slave dealers, prostitutes, butchers, brewers, arms makers, tax collectors, and caravan traders—the last, evidently, because a business without a fixed abode is likely to cheat its customers.

66. Fools of little understanding have themselves for their greatest enemies, for they do evil deeds which must bear bitter fruits.

---

[2] The *Dhammapada,* translated by Max Müller (Oxford: Clarendon Press, 1881).

69. As long as the evil deed done does not bear fruit, the fool thinks it is like honey; but when it ripens, then the fool suffers grief.

6. *Right effort.* Selfish desire stems from human nature. Overcoming it requires constant effort. You must be as steady as an ox, working constantly against your own natural inclinations.

Why are good deeds difficult?

121. Let no man think lightly of evil, saying in his heart, It will not come near to me. Even by the falling of water-drops is a water-pot filled; the fool becomes full of evil, even if he gathers it little by little.

122. Let no man think lightly of good, saying in his heart, It will not come near to me. Even by the falling of water-drops is a water-pot filled; the wise man becomes full of good, even if he gathers it little by little.

145. Canal-makers lead the water; archers bend the arrow; carpenters bend a log of wood; good people fashion themselves.

163. Bad deeds, and deeds hurtful to ourselves, are easy to do; what is beneficial and good, that is very difficult to do.

7. *Right mindfulness.* Thought and action are intimately linked; you cannot eliminate selfish desire in your behavior without overcoming it mentally. Only by thinking correctly can you hope to act correctly and escape suffering.

1. All that we are is the result of what we have thought: it is founded on our thoughts, it is made up of our thoughts. If a man speaks or acts with an evil thought, pain follows him, as the wheel follows the foot of the ox that draws the carriage.

2. All that we are is the result of what we have thought: it is founded on our thoughts, it is made up of our thoughts. If a man speaks or acts with a pure thought, happiness follows him, like a shadow that never leaves him.

33. As an archer makes his arrow straight, so a wise man makes straight his trembling and unsteady thought, which is difficult to guard and difficult to hold back.

35. It is good to tame the mind, which is difficult to hold in and flighty, rushing wherever it wishes; a tamed mind brings happiness.

36. Let the wise man guard his thoughts, for they are difficult to perceive, very artful, and they rush wherever they wish: thoughts well guarded bring happiness.

8. *Right concentration.* In the final analysis, only a new mode of experience can allow you to escape selfish desire. You must attain enlightenment, seeing past the boundaries of your self and recognizing the unity between your mind and the world.

What does enlightenment involve?

153, 154. Looking for the maker of this tabernacle, I shall have to run through a course of many births, so long as I do not find him; and painful is birth again and again. But now, maker of the tabernacle, you have been seen; you shall not make up this tabernacle again. All your rafters are broken, your ridge-pole is sundered; the mind, approaching the Eternal has attained to the extinction of all desires.

160. The self is the master of the self, for who else could be its master? With the self well subdued, a man finds a master such as few can find.

> 202. There is no fire like passion; there is no losing throw like hatred; there is no pain like this body; there is no happiness higher than stillness.
>
> 369. O Bhikshu, empty this boat! If emptied, it will go quickly; having cut off passion and hatred, you will go to Nirvana!
>
> 370. Cut off the five senses, leave the five senses, rise above the five senses. A Bhikshu who has escaped from the five chains (i.e., the five senses) is called *Oghatinna:* "saved from the flood."

The Hindu conception of the self, as we saw in Chapter 4, strikingly resembles Plato's image of the divided self. Imagine the soul as a passenger in a chariot (the body), driven by reason, with desire and emotion (Plato) or desire and the senses (Hinduism) as the horses and the world as the road. The Buddha revises this image, but only by arguing that there is no soul; there is no self over and above reason, desire, the senses, and the body. The conception of "reason" in Hinduism and Buddhism is broader than in Plato and other Western philosophers. Ethically, however, this makes little difference. In Hinduism, Buddhism, and Plato, right action consists of subjugating appetite, emotion, and the senses to proper control.

Immanuel Kant

Immanuel Kant (1724–1804), like Aristotle, begins with the question of intrinsic good. What is good always for its own sake and never for the sake of something else? In Kant's language, what is good without qualification?

> Nothing can possibly be conceived in the world, or even out of it, which can be called good, without qualification, except a good will. Intelligence, wit, judgment, and the other talents of the mind, however they may be named, or courage, resolution, perseverance, as qualities of temperament, are undoubtedly good and desirable in many respects; but these gifts of nature may also become extremely bad and mischievous if the will which is to make use of them, and which, therefore, constitutes what is called character, is not good. It is the same with the gifts of fortune. Power, riches, honour, even health, and the general well-being and contentment with one's condition which is called happiness, inspire pride, and often presumption, if there is not a good will to correct the influence of these on the mind, and with this also to rectify the whole principle of acting and adapt it to its end. The sight of a being who is not adorned with a single feature of a pure and good will, enjoying unbroken prosperity, can never give pleasure to an impartial rational spectator. Thus a good will appears to constitute the indispensable condition even of being worthy of happiness.[3]

Why are intelligence and happiness not good without qualification, in Kant's view?

The only unqualified good is a good will. Virtues, material things, power, and even happiness are not good if pressed into service for the wrong end. An "impartial rational spectator," as Kant puts it, would never delight in the courage, wealth, power, or happiness of an evil tyrant. What matters from a moral point of view is not

[3] Immanuel Kant, *Fundamental Principles of the Metaphysic of Morals,* translated by Thomas Kingsmill Abbott (New York: Longmans, Green, 1926).

happiness but worthiness to be happy. That is a matter of the heart, not of happiness, virtue, or any external sign. Even without any of those things, a good will,

> like a jewel, . . . would still shine by its own light, as a thing which has its whole value in itself. Its usefulness or fruitfulness can neither add nor take away anything from this value. It would be, as it were, only the setting to enable us to handle it the more conveniently in common commerce, or to attract to it the attention of those who are not yet connoisseurs, but not to recommend it to true connoisseurs, or to determine its value.

What makes a will good, Kant says, is acting on the basis of universal considerations rather than subjective, particular determinations: "the proper and inestimable worth of an absolutely good will consists just in this, that the principle of action is free from all influence of contingent grounds." Take a paradigm case of a good action—Smith, at significant risk to her own life, jumping into an icy river to save someone calling for help. Why does she do it? The act truly has moral worth, Kant says, if she does it to save a life or, more generally, to help someone in distress. These are universal considerations that apply no matter who Smith is, what kind of person she is, what she wants, likes, or dreams, or whom she is trying to save. It lacks moral worth, however, if she does it just to show off for some bystanders, just because the person in trouble is a friend, or just because she is feeling warm and the thought of a plunge into the river sounds invigorating. These considerations are subjective, depending on her state of mind. They are also particular, in that they relate to specific aspects of the circumstances that have no moral relevance. A person manifests a good will and acts in a way that has moral worth when he or she acts from *duty,* out of respect for the moral law.

In distinguishing right from wrong actions, we might try developing a criterion concerning actions themselves. Focusing on actions alone, however, tends to produce lists of obligatory or proscribed kinds of action. In short, it produces collections of moral rules, such as Buddhism's "Do not kill, steal, lie, lust, or drink" or the Ten Commandments. It remains to ask what the acts specified in the rules have in common. What is it about killing, stealing, lying, lusting, and drinking, for example, that makes them all impermissible? Ethical theories fall into two camps, depending on how they answer that sort of question. **Consequentialism** holds that all moral value rests ultimately on the consequences of actions. So consequentialists distinguish right from wrong acts by their effects. **Deontological theories** maintain that moral value rests at least in part on something other than the consequences of actions. So deontologists distinguish right from wrong acts—in part, at any rate—by considering something other than their effects, usually the intentions, motives, or states of character lying behind them.

One might think of an act as stemming from someone's character by way of a motive and an intention and then as having a certain result.

Character → Motive → Intention → Action → Consequences

Smith, for example, has a courageous and generous character; hearing cries for help, her motive is to save someone in trouble; her intention is to jump into the river, swim to that person, and pull him to shore; the result depends on whether or not she succeeds. Consequentialists judge acts by their results, or at least their expected results.

(We would not fault Smith for failing for unforeseeable reasons, for example.) In short, they judge acts by what happens or might reasonably be expected to happen later. Deontologists judge acts by what precedes them: the character of the agent or of someone who would tend to do that sort of act (as in Aristotle); the motive underlying the act; or the agent's intention.

The moral quality of an act, Kant maintains, does not depend on consequences. We judge Smith's action admirable even if she fails to save the person crying for help—even, indeed, if she herself perishes in the attempt. Kant's theory is thus deontological and in a strong form: consequences play no role whatever. Morality

> concerns not the matter of the action, or its intended result, but its form and the principle of which it is itself a result; and what is essentially good in it consists in the mental disposition, let the consequence be what it may.

We judge acts as right or wrong, in other words, according to the agent's intentions. The **maxim** of an act is "a subjective principle of action," a rule it falls under that reflects the agent's intention but abstracts from morally irrelevant details. Smith's intention is to jump into the river, swim to the person in danger of drowning, and pull him to safety. Most of this is morally irrelevant; it doesn't matter whether she is jumping into a river or rushing into a burning building or running along the railroad tracks with the train in view. What matters from a moral point of view is that she is risking herself to save someone in danger. So the maxim of Smith's act is, "Risk yourself to save someone in danger." Kant judges acts as right or wrong by judging their maxims.

Kant's test he calls the **categorical imperative.** An imperative, in general, expresses a command or obligation:

What is an imperative?

> The conception of an objective principle, in so far as it is obligatory for a will, is called a command (of reason), and the formula of the command is called an imperative.
>
> All imperatives are expressed by the word ought [or should], and thereby indicate the relation of an objective law of reason to a will, which from its subjective constitution is not necessarily determined by it (an obligation). They say that something would be good to do or to forbear, but they say it to a will which does not always do a thing because it is conceived to be good to do it. That is practically good, however, which determines the will by means of the conceptions of reason, and consequently not from subjective causes, but objectively, that is on principles which are valid for every rational being as such. It is distinguished from the pleasant, as that which influences the will only by means of sensation from merely subjective causes, valid only for the sense of this or that one, and not as a principle of reason, which holds for every one.

Kant distinguishes *hypothetical* from *categorical* imperatives. **Hypothetical imperatives,** such as "You ought to work hard if you want to succeed," contain an 'if' and depend on circumstances or someone's goals and desires. The command "You ought to work hard" in this hypothetical imperative, for example, applies only if you want to succeed; otherwise it has no force. Categorical imperatives, in contrast, apply universally without regard to circumstances, goals, or desires.

> Now all imperatives command either hypothetically or categorically. The former represent the practical necessity of a possible action as means to something else

> that is willed (or at least which one might possibly will). The categorical imperative would be that which represented an action as necessary of itself without reference to another end, i.e., as objectively necessary.

This distinction relates interestingly to the distinction between intrinsic and instrumental goods. Hypothetical imperatives are appropriate to instrumental goods. Categorical imperatives are appropriate to intrinsic goods.

How do categorical imperatives differ from hypothetical imperatives?

> If now the action is good only as a means to something else, then the imperative is hypothetical; if it is conceived as good in itself and consequently as being necessarily the principle of a will which of itself conforms to reason, then it is categorical.
>
> Accordingly the hypothetical imperative only says that the action is good for some purpose, possible or actual. . . . The categorical imperative . . . declares an action to be objectively necessary in itself without reference to any purpose, i.e., without any other end. . . .

Hard work, for instance, is not good in itself; it is good because it brings success. So, the imperative appropriate to it is hypothetical: "You ought to work hard *if* you want to succeed." A good will is good in itself; the imperative "You ought to have a good will" is thus categorical. Indeed, it is in a sense the only possible categorical imperative, for a good will is the only intrinsic and unqualified good.

Aristotle, of course, would argue that happiness is intrinsically good, indeed the only thing always desired for its own sake and never for the sake of something else. So he might take "You ought to be happy" as a categorical imperative and take hypothetical imperatives of the form "If you want to be happy, then you should . . ." as constituting morality's primary subject matter. But that is not at all how Kant sees it. Though he agrees that a desire for happiness is universal, he sees it as having no intrinsic moral worth. The imperatives of the form "If you want to be happy, then you should. . ." constitute the subject matter not of morality but of prudence.

How does Kant's view of happiness differ from Aristotle's?

> There is one end, however, which may be assumed to be actually such to all rational beings (so far as imperatives apply to them, viz., as dependent beings), and, therefore, one purpose which they not merely may have, but which we may with certainty assume that they all actually have by a natural necessity, and this is happiness. The hypothetical imperative which expresses the practical necessity of an action as means to the advancement of happiness is assertorial. We are not to present it as necessary for an uncertain and merely possible purpose, but for a purpose which we may presuppose with certainty and a priori in every man, because it belongs to his being. Now skill in the choice of means to his own greatest well-being may be called prudence, in the narrowest sense. And thus the imperative which refers to the choice of means to one's own happiness, i.e., the precept of prudence, is still always hypothetical; the action is not commanded absolutely, but only as means to another purpose.

Happiness, then, cannot constitute the basis for a categorical imperative.

Because the only intrinsic good, for Kant, is a good will, the only categorical imperative is "You ought to have a good will." But a good will, as we've seen, is one that responds solely on the basis of universal considerations, acting out of respect for the moral law. So, we might also frame the categorical imperative as "You ought to respect the moral law"—which by itself has little content—or, more informatively, as "You ought to act on the basis of universal considerations."

> When I conceive a hypothetical imperative, in general I do not know beforehand what it will contain until I am given the condition. But when I conceive a categorical imperative, I know at once what it contains. For as the imperative contains besides the law only the necessity that the maxims shall conform to this law, while the law contains no conditions restricting it, there remains nothing but the general statement that the maxim of the action should conform to a universal law, and it is this conformity alone that the imperative properly represents as necessary.

This gives us Kant's first formulation of the categorical imperative:

> There is therefore but one categorical imperative, namely, this: Act only on that maxim whereby thou canst at the same time will that it should become a universal law.

He quickly gives a second and, he holds, equivalent formulation:

> Since the universality of the law according to which effects are produced constitutes what is properly called nature in the most general sense (as to form), that is the existence of things so far as it is determined by general laws, the imperative of duty may be expressed thus: Act as if the maxim of thy action were to become by thy will a universal law of nature.

Act, in other words, as if everyone were going to act according to your maxims. If you want other people to respect your property, you ought to respect theirs. If you would want other people to save you when you were in danger, you should save them in such circumstances. Kant sees his imperative as a more precise form of the Golden Rule: "Treat others as you would want them to treat you."

Kant maintains that the categorical imperative is the one moral axiom from which other moral imperatives can be derived as theorems: "All imperatives of duty can be deduced from this one imperative." He discusses four examples, to show how the categorical imperative works to distinguish right from wrong. The general pattern: To test whether action A would be right or wrong, (a) identify A's maxim; (b) ask whether that maxim could become a universal law; and (c) if it could, ask whether you can will it as universal law.

Kant first gives examples of **perfect duties**—duties that are specific, involving specific obligations to specific people, and giving those people rights that the duty be performed. Smith, for instance, should not kill Jones. This is specific, directed at a specific person (though it is an instance of a quite general obligation not to kill others). Jones has a correlative right not to be killed. So the obligation not to kill is perfect. Less dramatically, suppose that Smith borrows money from Jones. She has a perfect obligation to pay it back, and Jones has a right to receive it. The obligation to repay debts is thus also perfect. One may have perfect duties to oneself as well as to others.

What is the despairing man's maxim? Why can't it be universalized?

> 1. A man reduced to despair by a series of misfortunes feels wearied of life, but is still so far in possession of his reason that he can ask himself whether it would not be contrary to his duty to himself to take his own life. Now he inquires whether

the maxim of his action could become a universal law of nature. His maxim is: "From self-love I adopt it as a principle to shorten my life when its longer duration is likely to bring more evil than satisfaction." It is asked then simply whether this principle founded on self-love can become a universal law of nature. Now we see at once that a system of nature of which it should be a law to destroy life by means of the very feeling whose special nature it is to impel to the improvement of life would contradict itself and, therefore, could not exist as a system of nature; hence that maxim cannot possibly exist as a universal law of nature and, consequently, would be wholly inconsistent with the supreme principle of all duty.

What contradiction does this maxim encounter when universalized?

2. Another finds himself forced by necessity to borrow money. He knows that he will not be able to repay it, but sees also that nothing will be lent to him unless he promises stoutly to repay it in a definite time. He desires to make this promise, but he has still so much conscience as to ask himself: "Is it not unlawful and inconsistent with duty to get out of a difficulty in this way?" Suppose however that he resolves to do so: then the maxim of his action would be expressed thus: "When I think myself in want of money, I will borrow money and promise to repay it, although I know that I never can do so." Now this principle of self-love or of one's own advantage may perhaps be consistent with my whole future welfare; but the question now is, "Is it right?" I change then the suggestion of self-love into a universal law, and state the question thus: "How would it be if my maxim were a universal law?" Then I see at once that it could never hold as a universal law of nature, but would necessarily contradict itself. For supposing it to be a universal law that everyone when he thinks himself in a difficulty should be able to promise whatever he pleases, with the purpose of not keeping his promise, the promise itself would become impossible, as well as the end that one might have in view in it, since no one would consider that anything was promised to him, but would ridicule all such statements as vain pretences.

In both cases, Kant holds, the maxim fails part (b) of the test. The maxim could not hold as a universal law. Kant sees the suicidal maxim as self-contradictory, as ending life for the sake of life. Similarly, he sees the false-promising maxim as self-contradictory. If everyone went around making false promises, there would be no such thing as promising.

Imperfect duties are general, allowing an agent choice about when and how to perform them. The classic example is charity. You may be obliged to help the less fortunate without being obliged to do anything in particular for any specific person. Whom you help and how you help them is up to you. Consequently, nobody else has any right to your help. In the case of imperfect obligations, a maxim fails part (c) of Kant's test.

Why would the will contradict itself in these cases?

3. A third finds in himself a talent which with the help of some culture might make him a useful man in many respects. But he finds himself in comfortable circumstances and prefers to indulge in pleasure rather than to take pains in enlarging and improving his happy natural capacities. He asks, however, whether his maxim of neglect of his natural gifts, besides agreeing with his inclination to indulgence, agrees also with what is called duty. He sees then that a system of nature could indeed subsist with such a universal law although men (like the South Sea islanders) should let their talents rest and resolve to devote their lives merely to idleness,

> amusement, and propagation of their species—in a word, to enjoyment; but he cannot possibly will that this should be a universal law of nature, or be implanted in us as such by a natural instinct. For, as a rational being, he necessarily wills that his faculties be developed, since they serve him and have been given him, for all sorts of possible purposes.
>
> 4. A fourth, who is in prosperity, while he sees that others have to contend with great wretchedness and that he could help them, thinks: "What concern is it of mine? Let everyone be as happy as Heaven pleases, or as he can make himself; I will take nothing from him nor even envy him, only I do not wish to contribute anything to his welfare or to his assistance in distress!" Now no doubt if such a mode of thinking were a universal law, the human race might very well subsist and doubtless even better than in a state in which everyone talks of sympathy and good-will, or even takes care occasionally to put it into practice, but, on the other side, also cheats when he can, betrays the rights of men, or otherwise violates them. But although it is possible that a universal law of nature might exist in accordance with that maxim, it is impossible to will that such a principle should have the universal validity of a law of nature. For a will which resolved this would contradict itself, inasmuch as many cases might occur in which one would have need of the love and sympathy of others, and in which, by such a law of nature, sprung from his own will, he would deprive himself of all hope of the aid he desires.

In these cases, the maxim could be a universal law—there is no contradiction—but it could not be *willed* as universal law. You are a rational being; you cannot help but will not only your own survival but also your own rationality. That means that you cannot will to be ignorant, or stupid, or ineffective. Nor can you will that others fail to help you when you need their help.

Another way of putting Kant's point in the categorical imperative is this: Do not make an exception of yourself. People who do something wrong do not will that everyone should act that way; they will that other people obey the moral law. The thief does not want to be robbed; the murderer does not want to be killed. The liar does not want to be deceived; the adulterer does not want to be cuckolded. Instead, they want others to follow the rules but to make an exception for themselves. This is what gets them into trouble.

> If now we attend to ourselves on occasion of any transgression of duty, we shall find that we in fact do not will that our maxim should be a universal law, for that is impossible for us; on the contrary, we will that the opposite should remain a universal law, only we assume the liberty of making an exception in our own favour or (just for this time only) in favour of our inclination. Consequently if we considered all cases from one and the same point of view, namely, that of reason, we should find a contradiction in our own will, namely, that a certain principle should be objectively necessary as a universal law, and yet subjectively should not be universal, but admit of exceptions.

Though there is only one categorical imperative, commanding that we have a good will, Kant offers different formulations of it to bring out different aspects of having a good will. The idea that a good will acts on the basis of universal considerations rather than subjective, particular, and morally irrelevant factors generates the formulations we have seen so far. But Kant develops another formulation to stress that a good will also acts out of respect—respect for the moral law, which stems from respect for others as rational beings. Recall that a categorical imperative is appropriate only for an intrinsic good. A good will is the only intrinsic good. But a good will is nothing other than a moral agent. So, we may also think of the categorical imperative as commanding, "You ought to respect moral agents."

How does Kant argue that rational nature is an end in itself?

> Supposing, however, that there were something whose existence has in itself an absolute worth, something which, being an end in itself, could be a source of definite laws; then in this and this alone would lie the source of a possible categorical imperative, i.e., a practical law.
>
> Now I say: man and generally any rational being exists as an end in himself, not merely as a means to be arbitrarily used by this or that will, but in all his actions, whether they concern himself or other rational beings, must be always regarded at the same time as an end. All objects of the inclinations have only a conditional worth, for if the inclinations and the wants founded on them did not exist, then their object would be without value. . . . Beings whose existence depends not on our will but on nature's, have nevertheless, if they are irrational beings, only a relative value as means, and are therefore called things; rational beings, on the contrary, are called persons, because their very nature points them out as ends in themselves, that is as something which must not be used merely as means, and so far therefore restricts freedom of action (and is an object of respect). These, therefore, are not merely subjective ends whose existence has a worth for us as an effect of our action, but objective ends, that is, things whose existence is an end in itself; an end moreover for which no other can be substituted, which they should subserve merely as means, for otherwise nothing whatever would possess absolute worth; but if all worth were conditioned and therefore contingent, then there would be no supreme practical principle of reason whatever.
>
> . . . The foundation of this principle [the categorical imperative] is: rational nature exists as an end in itself. Man necessarily conceives his own existence as being so; so far then this is a subjective principle of human actions. But every other rational being regards its existence similarly, just on the same rational principle that holds for me: so that it is at the same time an objective principle, from which as a supreme practical law all laws of the will must be capable of being deduced. Accordingly the practical imperative will be as follows: So act as to treat humanity, whether in thine own person or in that of any other, in every case as an end withal, never as means only.

In this formulation, the categorical imperative is "Treat people as ends, never only as means." In other words, "Respect people; don't use them." This permits a more direct and intuitive evaluation of acts as right or wrong. Kant applies it to his previous examples:

How does the person who commits suicide use him/herself?

> Firstly, under the head of necessary duty to oneself: He who contemplates suicide should ask himself whether his action can be consistent with the idea of humanity as an end in itself. If he destroys himself in order to escape from painful circumstances, he uses a person merely as a means to maintain a tolerable condition up to the end of life. But a man is not a thing, that is to say, something which can be

> used merely as means, but must in all his actions be always considered as an end in himself. I cannot, therefore, dispose in any way of a man in my own person so as to mutilate him, to damage or kill him. (It belongs to ethics proper to define this principle more precisely, so as to avoid all misunderstanding, e.g., as to the amputation of the limbs in order to preserve myself, as to exposing my life to danger with a view to preserve it, etc. This question is therefore omitted here.)
>
> Secondly, as regards necessary duties, or those of strict obligation, towards others: He who is thinking of making a lying promise to others will see at once that he would be using another man merely as a means, without the latter containing at the same time the end in himself. For he whom I propose by such a promise to use for my own purposes cannot possibly assent to my mode of acting towards him and, therefore, cannot himself contain the end of this action. This violation of the principle of humanity in other men is more obvious if we take in examples of attacks on the freedom and property of others. For then it is clear that he who transgresses the rights of men intends to use the person of others merely as a means, without considering that as rational beings they ought always to be esteemed also as ends, that is, as beings who must be capable of containing in themselves the end of the very same action.

The person who commits suicide uses himself as a means. So, much more obviously, does the insincere promiser use the person he defrauds. The principle in this form works with imperfect duties as well:

Why must actions harmonize with humanity? What does that mean?

> Thirdly, as regards contingent (meritorious) duties to oneself: It is not enough that the action does not violate humanity in our own person as an end in itself, it must also harmonize with it. Now there are in humanity capacities of greater perfection, which belong to the end that nature has in view in regard to humanity in ourselves as the subject: to neglect these might perhaps be consistent with the maintenance of humanity as an end in itself, but not with the advancement of this end.
>
> Fourthly, as regards meritorious duties towards others: The natural end which all men have is their own happiness. Now humanity might indeed subsist, although no one should contribute anything to the happiness of others, provided he did not intentionally withdraw anything from it; but after all this would only harmonize negatively not positively with humanity as an end in itself, if every one does not also endeavour, as far as in him lies, to forward the ends of others. For the ends of any subject which is an end in himself ought as far as possible to be my ends also, if that conception is to have its full effect with me.

If I respect myself as a moral agent, I will seek to develop my talents. And if I respect others as moral agents, I will help them when they need it.

The categorical imperative differs from other, earlier principles of morality, Kant says, for it is a command we give ourselves as moral agents. Acting in accord with it, we are bound only by the rule we set for ourselves as rational beings. In living by the rule we establish for ourselves, we exhibit our **autonomy.**

What is autonomy? Why is it important?

> Looking back now on all previous attempts to discover the principle of morality, we need not wonder why they all failed. It was seen that man was bound to laws by duty, but it was not observed that the laws to which he is subject are only those of his own giving, though at the same time they are universal, and that he is only

> bound to act in conformity with his own will; a will, however, which is designed by nature to give universal laws. For when one has conceived man only as subject to a law (no matter what), then this law required some interest, either by way of attraction or constraint, since it did not originate as a law from his own will, but this will was according to a law obliged by something else to act in a certain manner. Now by this necessary consequence all the labour spent in finding a supreme principle of duty was irrevocably lost. For men never elicited duty, but only a necessity of acting from a certain interest. Whether this interest was private or otherwise, in any case the imperative must be conditional and could not by any means be capable of being a moral command. I will therefore call this the principle of autonomy of the will, in contrast with every other which I accordingly reckon as heteronomy.

The **heteronomous** person follows someone else's command; the autonomous person follows his or her own. Autonomy is what gives human beings dignity:

Why is autonomy the basis of human dignity?

> In the kingdom of ends everything has either value or dignity. Whatever has a value can be replaced by something else which is equivalent; whatever, on the other hand, is above all value, and therefore admits of no equivalent, has a dignity. Whatever has reference to the general inclinations and wants of mankind has a market value; whatever, without presupposing a want, corresponds to a certain taste, that is to a satisfaction in the mere purposeless play of our faculties, has a fancy value; but that which constitutes the condition under which alone anything can be an end in itself, this has not merely a relative worth, i.e., value, but an intrinsic worth, that is, dignity.
>
> Now morality is the condition under which alone a rational being can be an end in himself, since by this alone is it possible that he should be a legislating member in the kingdom of ends. Thus morality, and humanity as capable of it, is that which alone has dignity.
>
> . . . Autonomy then is the basis of the dignity of human and of every rational nature. . . . although the conception of duty implies subjection to the law, we yet ascribe a certain dignity and sublimity to the person who fulfils all his duties. There is not, indeed, any sublimity in him, so far as he is subject to the moral law; but inasmuch as in regard to that very law he is likewise a legislator, and on that account alone subject to it, he has sublimity. We have also shown above that neither fear nor inclination, but simply respect for the law, is the spring which can give actions a moral worth. Our own will, so far as we suppose it to act only under the condition that its maxims are potentially universal laws, this ideal will which is possible to us is the proper object of respect; and the dignity of humanity consists just in this capacity of being universally legislative, though with the condition that it is itself subject to this same legislation.

Critics

Kant's moral philosophy, while still immensely influential, has not lacked critics. Despite his emphasis on autonomy, one of Kant's central propositions is that "we are not volunteers, but conscripts in the army of the moral law." We give law to ourselves—but the law we give demands to be given; as rational beings, we can do no other.

Friedrich Nietzsche (1844–1900), a contemporary of Leo Tolstoy, Fyodor Dostoevsky, and William and Henry James, criticized Kant's conception of freedom as incoherent. Born in Saxony and educated in classics at Bonn and Leipzig, Nietzsche was appointed professor of classical philology at the University of Basel in Switzerland when he was twenty-four. Deteriorating health forced him to resign just eleven years later. During the next ten years, he wrote most of his philosophical works, finally suffering a mental and physical collapse at age forty-five.

Nietzsche sees Kantian morality as a "herd" morality, fine for the mediocre mass of people but unfit for developing true human excellence. Kantian morality is based on rules founded on purely universal considerations that admit no exceptions. A higher morality, Nietzsche thinks, would encourage exceptions and allow "subjective, particular determinations" to play a role for those capable of rising beyond the demands of herd morality. Nietzsche describes how morality must have evolved and articulates a conception of freedom very different from Kant's:

> If we place ourselves at the end of this tremendous process, where the tree at last brings forth fruit, where society and the morality of custom at last reveal *what* they have simply been the means to: then we discover that the ripest fruit is the *sovereign individual,* like only to himself, liberated again from morality of custom, autonomous and supramoral (for "autonomous" and "moral" are mutually exclusive), in short, the man who has his own independent, protracted will and the *right to make promises*—and in him a proud consciousness, quivering in every muscle, of *what* has at length been achieved and become flesh in him, a consciousness of his own power and freedom, a sensation of mankind come to completion.[4]

How is Nietzsche criticizing Kant's conception of autonomy?

For Kant, morality and autonomy are equivalent: "That action which is compatible with the autonomy of the will is permitted; that which is not compatible is forbidden." To be autonomous is to give yourself rules to live by, to lay down the law for yourself. Nietzsche views this as absurd. For him, morality and autonomy are opposites. Morality involves submission to rules; autonomy involves "liberation," an "independent, protracted will," "power and freedom." The obvious Kantian answer is that the moral and autonomous person is author of the rules to which he or she freely submits. But Nietzsche objects to Kant's idea that rationality compels such submission. The whole point, he thinks, is that we *can* do otherwise. We are volunteers, not conscripts, Nietzsche thinks; moreover, there is no army from which we can gain direction. To be autonomous is to set yourself above moral rules, to establish your own way of living when it would be perfectly rational to live differently and to take responsibility for yourself.

Contemporary critics have assailed Kant from several related points of view. British philosopher Philippa Foot, inspired by Aristotle, finds Kant's foundation for morality and its authority puzzling. She fails to see why the moral 'ought' should have any more force than the 'ought' of grammar or etiquette. 'An invitation in the third person should be answered in the third person' is an imperative of etiquette, but this doesn't, by itself, seem to give anyone reason to act on it. As Foot puts it, "Considerations of etiquette do not have any automatic reason-giving force"; you might

---

[4] Friedrich Nietzsche, *On the Genealogy of Morals,* translated by Walter Kaufmann and R. J. Hollingdale (New York: Vintage, 1967), II, 2, 59.

choose to ignore them. To use Kant's image, we are all volunteers in the army of etiquette.

From Kant's point of view, the moral law does give reasons for action. We cannot brush aside moral considerations as we can those of etiquette. But why? What is special about moral imperatives?

> Attempts have sometimes been made to show that some kind of irrationality is involved in ignoring the 'should' of morality: in saying 'Immoral—so what?' as one says 'Not *comme il faut*—so what?' . . . The fact is that the man who rejects morality because he sees no reason to obey its rules can be convicted of villainy but not of inconsistency. Nor will his action necessarily be irrational. Irrational actions are those in which a man in some way defeats his own purposes, doing what is calculated to be disadvantageous or to frustrate his ends. Immorality does not *necessarily* involve any such thing.[5]

A bit of contemporary terminology is helpful here. **Internalists** hold that moral imperatives necessarily give reasons for acting. **Externalists** deny it. Kant is an internalist, as is virtually everyone who relies on reason as the judge of right and wrong. From such a perspective, immorality is a kind of irrationality. Insofar as we have reasons to be rational, we thereby have reasons to be moral. Foot, however, is an externalist. She believes that there is at best a contingent connection between morality and reasons for acting. She sees no problem in manning the moral army with volunteers:

> We are apt to panic at the thought that we ourselves, or other people, might stop caring about the things we do care about, and we feel that the categorical imperative gives us some control over the situation. But it is interesting that the people of Leningrad were not struck by the thought that only the *contingent* fact that other citizens shared their loyalty and devotion to the city stood between them and the Germans during the terrible years of the siege. Perhaps we should be less troubled than we are by fear of defections from the moral cause; perhaps we should even have less reason to fear it if people thought of themselves as volunteers banded together to fight for liberty and justice and against inhumanity and oppression.[6]

Kant's response, clearly, would be to say that the categorical imperative gives reasons for acting in a way that hypothetical imperatives do not. They at best supply contingent reasons for acting to someone who happens to have the goal or be in the circumstances in the hypothesis. The imperatives of etiquette all fall into this category. ('Invitations in the third person should be answered in the third person' only looks categorical; it really has the form, 'If you receive an invitation in the third person, you should answer it in the third person.') The categorical imperative, however, applies to all rational beings as such. It gives every rational being a reason to act. And the immoral man, from Kant's perspective, is in some way irrational; he fails to value reason as such.

Feminist critics have dissented for other reasons. Kant, like Plato, sees morality as the triumph of reason over desire. American philosopher Genevieve Lloyd, for example, argues that this image of morality is distinctively male:

---

[5] Philippa Foot, "Morality as a System of Hypothetical Imperatives," in P. Foot, *Virtues and Vices* (Berkeley: University of California Press, 1967), 161–162.

[6] Foot, 167.

> When the Man of Reason is extolled, philosophers are not talking about idealizations of human beings. They are talking about ideals of manhood.[7]

She notes a traditional identification of reason with masculinity and passion with femininity; the model of reason controlling desire thus corresponds to a model of men controlling women. But her basic complaint is that the world takes on moral significance to us largely through the agency of desire. The passions are central to ethics, not an unfortunate distraction from it. Treating morality as the dominance of reason over desire champions

> a detachment from changeable, individual objects of concern. . . . But what remains with us as the character ideal expressed in his Man of Reason is mainly the negative detachment from all that gives warmth and compassion to human existence—his ultimate detachment from the impingement of all that is not himself.
>
> . . . the effort to transcend the distortions of a limited, individual perspective on the world remains of enduring significance. But the Man of Reason, we have seen, sheds not merely selfish, obsessive love, but also individuals as proper objects of love.

A will that acts purely on the basis of universal considerations, in other words, is a will that cannot love, for love is inherently particular, directed toward a particular person or object. Yet love seems an integral part of a good life, not an enemy of it.

HAPPINESS

How can we tell right from wrong? What *makes* right actions right and wrong actions wrong? The answer, many philosophers have held, is what makes people happy. Happiness, as Aristotle first noted, is intrinsically good. It is a small step to saying that right actions are right because they promote human happiness. Wrong actions are wrong because they detract from it. We can tell right from wrong by observing what makes people happy.

The most influential form of this answer is **utilitarianism,** a view implicit in the writings of various ancient and medieval thinkers, advocated explicitly by Francis Hutcheson (1694–1746) and William Paley (1743–1805; see Chapter 6) in the eighteenth century and brought to full development by Jeremy Bentham and John Stuart Mill. Utilitarianism can be summarized in two words: *maximize good.* Utilitarians hold that all of ethics and political philosophy reduces to that one maxim, the **principle of utility.**

As Bentham outlines the principle in politics and law:

> . . . the greatest happiness of the whole community, ought to be the end or object of pursuit, in every branch of the law—of the political rule of action, and of the constitutional branch in particular. . . . The right and proper end of government in every political community, is the greatest happiness of all the individuals of which it is composed, say, in other words, the greatest happiness of the greatest number.[8]

---

[7] Genevieve Lloyd, *The Man of Reason* (Minneapolis: University of Minnesota Press, 1984), 129.
[8] Jeremy Bentham, *Constitutional Code* (London: Simpkin, Marshall, 1841).

Generalizing to private as well as public acts:

> By the principle of utility is meant that principle which approves or disapproves of every action whatsoever, according to the tendency it appears to have to augment or diminish the happiness of the party whose interest is in question: or, what is the same thing in other words to promote or to oppose that happiness. I say of every action whatsoever, and therefore not only of every action of a private individual, but of every measure of government.[9]

Mill's version is similar:

> The creed which accepts as the foundation of morals, Utility, or the Greatest Happiness Principle, holds that actions are right in proportion as they tend to promote happiness, wrong as they tend to produce the reverse of happiness.[10]

The principle seems simple, but it has a number of far-reaching consequences. Utilitarians evaluate actions by the extent to which they maximize good. They evaluate actions, therefore, solely in terms of their consequences. To determine whether an action is right or wrong, we need only to ask, Is it for the best? What effect does it have on the total amount of good? Utilitarians are thus *consequentialists,* who hold that the moral value of an action depends entirely on its consequences.

Other moral philosophers contend that other features of actions bear on their moral value. Killing, for example, is generally a bad thing. But our judgment of a killing depends on other factors. Was it purely accidental? Was it due to negligence? Was it intentional? Was it performed in an act of rage, or was it premeditated? The history, motives, intentions, and general state of mind of the agent make a moral difference. Utilitarianism would be implausible if it were committed to denying that.

Utilitarians typically find a place for motives, intentions, and circumstances, but do so *in terms of* consequences. They define the moral value of motives, intentions, and character in terms of the moral values of actions. They say, for example,

1. An intention is good if it tends to lead to good actions.
2. A motive is good if it tends to lead to good intentions.
3. A character trait is good if it tends to lead to good motives.

They can then say—and John Stuart Mill does say—that although strictly speaking the moral value of an action depends solely on its consequences, we usually construe an action to comprise not only the physical event that constitutes it but also the agent's intentions and motives. The value of that complex still depends solely on consequences but not solely on the consequences the physical event in question actually has. We condemn an attempted murderer, for example, not on the basis of the consequences the event actually had but on the basis of the consequences such intentions and attempts *tend* to have.

Another implication of utilitarianism is **universalism:** We must consider the consequences of an action on everyone it affects. We cannot consider ourselves alone, or just our friends, or the people in our community, or our fellow citizens; we must

---

[9] Jeremy Bentham, *Introduction to the Principles of Morals and Legislation* (London: Printed for T. Payne, 1789).

[10] John Stuart Mill, *Utilitarianism* (London: Longman's, 1907; originally published 1859).

consider *everyone.* Fortunately, most decisions affect only a small number of people. Political decisions, however, may affect millions or even billions of people. Nevertheless, we must take the good of everyone affected into account. Moreover, we cannot show favoritism; we must consider everyone *equally.* As Mill puts it,

How does Bentham's dictum follow from the principle of utility?

> But this great moral duty [that society should treat all equally well who have deserved equally well of it] rests upon a still deeper foundation, being a direct emanation from the first principle of morals, and not a mere logical corollary from secondary or derivative doctrines. It is involved in the very meaning of Utility, or the Greatest Happiness Principle. That principle is a mere form of words without rational signification, unless one person's happiness, supposed equal in degree (with the proper allowance made for kind), is counted for exactly as much as another's. Those conditions being supplied, Bentham's dictum, "everybody to count for one, nobody for more than one," might be written under the principle of utility as an explanatory commentary.

To evaluate an action, we must judge its effects on the total amount of good in the universe. It makes no difference in the calculation who in particular has what amount of good; only the total matters.

Commonsense ethical reasoning does not appear to be universalist in this sense. We typically show favoritism toward our friends, our family, our neighbors, and our fellow citizens. Parents support their children, buy them gifts, pay for their educations, and so forth, not because they think that doing these things for *their* children just happens to maximize the amount of good in the universe but because they want to do good for their children. In short, parents care more about their children's welfare than they care about the welfare of others. On the face of it, at least, this violates utilitarianism, which implies that everyone's good should be considered equally.

Some utilitarians are revisionists, holding that we ought to revise commonsense moral thinking to accord with the principle of utility. More, however, hold that the principle in fact supports common sense. It is good, they maintain, that parents show favoritism toward their children, that friends show favoritism toward friends, and so on. Family relationships, friendship, and love make us all better off. There are thus good utilitarian, universalist reasons for people not to treat everyone's good as equally valuable to them in their personal lives. Utilitarianism, in short, explains why most people in most situations should not think like utilitarians. They can act in accordance with the principle of utility without consciously meaning to do so.

Finally, utilitarianism requires an independent theory of the good. The principle of utility tells us to maximize good, but it does not tell us what the good is. What should we maximize? The most common answer—the answer many take to define utilitarianism—is happiness. Jeremy Bentham and John Stuart Mill are, more specifically, **hedonists:** they believe that pleasure and pain are the only sources of value. The good, for both, is happiness, and happiness is pleasure and the absence of pain. In their view, the principle of utility tells us to maximize the balance of pleasure over pain—in short, to maximize happiness. Bentham:

> By utility is meant that property in any object, whereby it tends to produce benefit, advantage, pleasure, good, or happiness, (all this in the present case comes to the same thing) or (what comes again to the same thing) to prevent the happening of

> mischief, pain, evil, or unhappiness to the party whose interest is considered: if that party be the community in general, then the happiness of the community: if a particular individual, then the happiness of that individual.
>
> It is in vain to talk of the interest of the community, without understanding what is the interest of the individual. A thing is said to promote the interest, or to be for the interest, of an individual, when it tends to add to the sum total of his pleasures: or, what comes to the same thing, to diminish the sum total of his pains.

Mill, as usual, is more concise:

> By happiness is intended pleasure, and the absence of pain; by unhappiness, pain, and the privation of pleasure.

Other utilitarians hold other theories of the good. Some, for example, identify the good with the satisfaction of desire. That makes the good more subjective—dependent on a person's beliefs—than Bentham and Mill's hedonism, for someone may want something that is not in fact in his or her self-interest. Some utilitarians (most notably early twentieth-century British philosopher G. E. Moore, 1873–1958; see Chapter 5) maintain that the good is indefinable and cannot be identified with anything else. Some, like Maimonides, identify the good with not only happiness but virtue. And some, like Kwame Gyekye, adopt a communitarian definition of a good society, judging individual acts good or bad as they lead us closer to or farther from that ideal.

Precursors: Jainism

Various ancient philosophers both in and beyond the West anticipated features of utilitarianism. The earliest appeal to pain as a source of moral value occurs in Jainism, one of the ancient philosophies of India. Like other early Indian philosophies, Jainism proclaims a mystical, personal highest good. But Jainism is the most renowned for its ethical commitment to the value of life. Jains are vegetarians; Jain monks have been known to wear masks so that their breathing will not cause injury to microscopic insects. Noninjury, *ahimsa,* an ideal popularized in modern times by Mahatma Gandhi, was propagated in ancient and classical India foremost by Jains.

Like Buddhist scripture, the Jain canon is immense. The selection below from the *Acaranga Sutra* concerns *ahimsa* and its justification. Here the practice is justified not simply because it is conducive to one's own good or because it is the teaching of Mahavira, but because all souls are equally valuable. If I recognize that injury to me is painful for me, I must conclude that injury to others is similarly painful for them. Their souls are as valuable as my own; their pain counts as much as my pain. Therefore, I must refrain from committing injury to others at all times.

> One should not injure, subjugate, enslave, torture or kill any animal, living being, organism or sentient being.[11]

Noninjury is for everyone. But in the details of ethical precepts, monks and laypersons have different duties. The former practice not only asceticism but also pre-

[11] *Ayaro (Acaranga Sutra),* translated by Muni Mahendra Kumar (New Delhi: Today and Tomorrow's Printers and Publishers, 1981).

scribed "reflections"—for example, on the impermanence of things, human helplessness, and the difficulty of enlightenment. Lay people, "householders," desist from dishonest business practices, lying, illicit sexual relations, and so on but do not aspire to "liberation" in this lifetime. (Jainism, like Buddhism and other early Indian enlightenment theories, asserts that people are reborn or reincarnated. Jains believe that only the enlightened are liberated, that is, not reborn.)

The key to ethical living for all, however, is overcoming desire. What leads people to injure other living beings intentionally? Desire—the desire for rich food, for sensual pleasure, for wealth, for self-preservation.

> He should be dispassionate towards sensual objects.
> He should refrain from worldly desires.

Jains typically maintain that eating vegetables is permissible but eating animal flesh is not. Why? What is the difference between a carrot and a chicken? A carrot is not sentient; it has no consciousness. It cannot feel pain. A chicken, however, is aware of its surroundings and can feel pain. That is why it, unlike the carrot, merits moral consideration and why it must not be injured.

Many people draw the line between humans and other animals, not between animals and vegetables or inanimate matter, on the grounds that humans are rational. They recoil at murder but find butchery of animals morally acceptable. From a utilitarian point of view, however, that is hard to justify. As Jeremy Bentham argues,

> What else is it that should trace the insuperable line? Is it the faculty of reason, or perhaps the faculty of discourse? But a full-grown horse or dog is beyond comparison a more rational, as well as a more conversable animal, than an infant of a day or a week or even a month, old. But suppose they were otherwise, what would it avail? The question is not, Can they *reason?* nor Can they *talk?* but, Can they *suffer?*[12]

The capacity for suffering is what gives something a right to moral consideration. If something can suffer, we must take its happiness or unhappiness or, more generally, its welfare, its interests, into account. As contemporary philosopher Peter Singer has written,

> It would be nonsense to say that it was not in the interests of a stone to be kicked along the road by a schoolboy. A stone does not have interests because it cannot suffer. Nothing we could do to it could possibly make any difference to its welfare. A mouse, on the other hand, does have an interest in not being kicked along the road, because it will suffer if it is.[13]

Could a creature have interests without being able to suffer?

It follows, Jains assert, that injuring any sentient creature is morally wrong.

> All animals, living beings, organisms and sentient creatures should not be injured, governed, enslaved, tortured and killed. Know that it is non-violence which is (completely) free from sin.

[12] Jeremy Bentham, quoted in Peter Singer, *Animal Liberation* (New York Review of Books, 1975, 1990); selection reprinted in Daniel Bonevac (ed.), *Today's Moral Issues* (Mountain View: Mayfield Publishing Company, 1999), 105.

[13] Peter Singer, *Animal Liberation* (New York Review of Books, 1975, 1990); selection reprinted in Daniel Bonevac (ed.), *Today's Moral Issues* (Mountain View: Mayfield Publishing Company, 1999), 105.

The Jain argument for noninjury is straightforward. We find suffering painful; we thus have every reason to believe that other sentient creatures find it painful. What makes it wrong to injure another human being? The suffering that results, Jains answer. But then the suffering resulting from injuring any sentient being makes that wrong and for the same reason.

> O philosophers! Is suffering pleasing to you or painful? . . . just as suffering is painful to you, in the same way it is painful, disquieting and terrifying to all animals, living beings, organisms and sentient beings.
>
> . . . [Causing violence to the mobile-beings], in fact, is the knot of bondage, it, in fact, is the delusion, it, in fact, is the death, it in fact, is the hell. . . .
>
> Man (experiences pain) when forced into unconsciousness or when he is deprived of life. (So do the mobile-beings.)
>
> Having discerned this, a sage should neither use any weapon causing violence to the mobile-being, nor cause others to use it nor approve of others using it.

Jainism thus sees a creature's ability to suffer, to feel pain, as giving it the right to moral consideration. What makes an action wrong is the unhappiness it causes. This is a core idea of utilitarianism. But Jainism stops short of utilitarianism in the modern sense, for it does not similarly see us as obliged to maximize happiness. The doctrine of noninjury is negative: Do not injure any sentient creature. The doctrine of overcoming desire is also negative. There is no positive obligation to do anything to increase the happiness of one's fellow creatures.

Jainism's focus on unhappiness instead of happiness as the source of moral value leads it to differ from modern utilitarianism in another way. It permits no exceptions, no compromises; injuring sentient beings is wrong, period. Most utilitarians, however, because they consider happiness as well as unhappiness, see tradeoffs between the happiness of some and the happiness of others as inevitable. They think that we might be permitted or even obligated to injure some for the sake of the happiness of others. Thus, many utilitarians would hold that the happiness of the meat-eater could outweigh the death of the animal eaten (especially since that animal might never have been born if people did not eat meat). They would hold that, in time of war, for example, injuring or killing other human beings could be justified by an overall increase in happiness that results. Utilitarianism does not imply pacifism, though noninjury surely does.

Precursors: Moism

Another ancient precursor to utilitarianism is a Chinese school of philosophy known as **Moism.** Its founder, Mozi (Mo Tzu, 470?–391? B.C.E.), a rival of Confucius, was born in either Sung or Lu. He became the chief officer of Sung. For a time he traveled, serving as consultant to various feudal lords and public officials. He found government officials no more willing to listen, however, than Confucius or Mencius did and founded a school to train people for public service. He had around three hundred followers. Until about 200 B.C.E., Moism and Confucianism were the two most important philosophical theories in China.

Moism is a version of consequentialism. It opposes Confucianism in almost every respect. Confucius stresses the importance of rituals, ceremonies, and public respect; Mozi finds these wasteful. Confucius emphasizes tradition and continuity with the past; Mozi formulates a principle for evaluating actions that is thoroughly oriented toward the future. Confucius bases his theory of virtue on the concept of virtue or humanity (*ren*), which centers on particular human relations; Mozi founds his on righteousness or justice (*yi*), which applies universally and links directly to the will of Heaven. In this sense, Mozi opposes Confucian humanism.

More fundamentally, Mozi and Confucius have very different approaches to the moral life in general. Confucius argues that the good life is valuable in itself. In effect, he argues that virtue is its own reward. Mozi, however, advocates the good life because of its good consequences. Moism is thus strikingly similar to modern utilitarianism. Mozi believes that virtue brings many benefits to the person who has it and to the society at large. He evaluates actions by examining their effects.

Mozi uses the term 'disorder' for bad consequences and sees mutual love as the key to avoiding disorder. The problem, as Mozi sees it, is that people love themselves more than they love others and so seek advantage to themselves at the expense of others. They also love some people more than they love others, leading them to favor the former unfairly. If people loved others as they love themselves, disorder would disappear, and people would be happy.

> It is the business of the sages to effect the good government of the world. They must know, therefore, whence disorder and confusion arise, for without this knowledge their object cannot be effected. . . . They must examine therefore into the cause of disorder; and when they do so they will find it arises from the want of mutual love.[14]

Mozi is a consequentialist. The primary obligation of a good, benevolent (*ren*) person is to maximize happiness, promoting everything beneficial to the community and working against everything harmful to it:

> Our Master, the philosopher Mo, said, "That which benevolent men consider to be incumbent on them as their business, is to stimulate and promote all that will be advantageous to the nation, and to take away all that is injurious to it."

The aspect of Mozi's utilitarianism he stresses most is its universalism. Confucius holds that much moral obligation arises from specific and contingent human relations—of parent and child, for example, or sibling and sibling—whereas Mozi believes that our obligation to maximize good arises directly from the will of Heaven. Confucianism implies that our obligations to others depend on who we are, who they are, and how they relate to us. Mozi's doctrine, in contrast, implies that our obligations are universal. In keeping with Confucius's principle of reciprocity and foreshadowing Kant's categorical imperative, Mozi contends that the universal is good and the particular is bad. Immoral action involves making an exception for our friends or ourselves. Morality demands that we treat all with equal respect—indeed, in Mozi's view, with equal love—regardless of our relation to them. According to Moism, we should love everyone as we love ourselves. Only this attitude can lead to universal peace and harmony.

---

[14] Mozi, from *The Chinese Classics,* Volume II, edited and translated by James Legge (Oxford: Clarendon, 1895).

> . . . it is the principle of universal love which produces all that is most beneficial to the kingdom, and the principle of making distinctions which produces all that is injurious to it. On this account, what our Master said, "The principle of making distinctions between man and man is wrong, and the principle of universal love is right," turns out to be correct as the sides of a square.

Mozi confronts a number of objections against his doctrine of mutual love. He considers the complaint that the principle is impractical, setting an unrealistic standard for moral behavior. He counters that it supports customary, commonsense standards and that anyone contradicting it behaves in ways easily recognized as immoral and untrustworthy.

Mozi also considers the Confucian objection, often advanced against modern utilitarianism, that universalism is incompatible with family and other human relations. Parents favor their own children over the children of others; children favor their parents; husbands favor their wives, and wives favor their husbands; siblings favor siblings. Moreover, it is good that they do. What would we say of a parent who refused to pay for a child's education, saying, "There are needier and more deserving children down the street"? Or a child who said, "I don't care if you say no. Jimmy's mom said it was OK, so I'm going"? Or a husband who said, "I'm sorry, dear, but I'm going to sleep with our neighbor Jane tonight—she's lonely and needs me more than you do"?

How does this respond to the objection that utilitarianism undercuts family and other relations?

> Our Master said, "Let us bring this objection to the test:—A filial son, having the happiness of his parents at heart, considers how it is to be secured. Now, does he, so considering, wish men to love and benefit his parents? or does he wish them to hate and injure his parents?" On this view of the question, it must be evident that he wishes men to love and benefit his parents. And what must he himself do in order to gain this object? . . . It is clear that I must first address myself to love and benefit men's parents, and they will return to me love and benefit my parents. The conclusion is that a filial son has no alternative.—He must address himself in the first place to love and do good to the parents of others. . . . he who loves others will be loved, and . . . he who hates others will be hated.

Finally, Mozi argues that if only mutual love were rewarded, people would practice it more consistently. People would be happier and also more virtuous, for mutual love is a positive obligation to help others; it entails the virtues of kindness, graciousness, loyalty, obedience, and friendliness.

Precursors: Carvaka

Jainism is not the only classical Indian source of thinking about the moral significance of happiness. The most striking opposition to the religious inspiration for various Jain, Hindu, and Buddhist views comes from a school known as ***Carvaka,*** also called *lokayata,* a term meaning "those attached to the ways of the world." Carvaka philosophers are *materialists;* they believe that physical matter is the only reality. They are also *empiricists,* holding that we can know only what we perceive through our senses. According to the Carvakas, we cannot assert the validity of any inferences we make about what we perceive. Because they reject inference, the Carvakas are commonly referred to as *skeptics.*

> In this school the four elements, earth, [air, fire, and water], are the original principles; from these alone, when transformed into the body, intelligence is produced. . . . and when these are destroyed, intelligence at once perishes also. They quote the *sruti* [Vedic text] for this [*Brhadaranyaka Upanishad* ii.iv.12]: "Springing forth from these elements, itself solid knowledge, it is destroyed when they are destroyed,—after death no intelligence remains." Therefore the soul is only the body distinguished by the attribute of intelligence, since there is no evidence for any self distinct from the body, as such cannot be proved, since this school holds that perception is the only source of knowledge and does not allow inference, etc.[15]

By arguing that reasoning cannot establish anything—a position that their opponents ridicule as self-refuting!—the Carvakas attack ideas of an immortal soul, rebirth, God, and a mystical enlightenment or liberation. That is to say, by showing that inference is unreliable, whatever the topic, these skeptics seek to strip away all excesses of belief beyond the simple facts of pleasure, pain, and the body. The soul must be identified with the body. And the body exists in an inexplicable material world. The good of the soul must therefore be identified with the good of the body—that is, pleasure.

> The only end of man is enjoyment produced by sensual pleasures. . . . Hence it follows that there is no other hell than mundane pain produced by purely mundane causes, as thorns, etc.; the only Supreme is the earthly monarch whose existence is proved by all the world's eyesight; and the only liberation is the dissolution of the body.

Consequently, the only values that apply in this world are those arising from pleasure and pain. At least, those are the only values we could possibly know anything about. We can know only what we can immediately sense, and the only things we immediately sense that generate value are pleasure and pain. The Carvakas are thus hedonists: pleasure and pain in this world are the only possible sources of value.

Opponents retort that the Carvaka attack is self-defeating, for it utilizes the very processes of thinking that it aims to show invalid. The doctrine itself, that is, rests on reasoning. That our only goal is human pleasure is not itself something we perceive. The Carvaka response is that the burden of proof is on the other side and that no other goal can be justified. In any case, the Carvakas are the first philosophers to present something like utilitarianism as the only ethical system compatible with materialism (the view that everything that exists is material) and empiricism (the view that all knowledge comes from experience). Many later utilitarians, including both Bentham and Mill, have similar motivations. They are empiricists who want ethical knowledge to rest on firm foundations. Pleasure and pain establish those foundations, for we undoubtedly experience them.

The Moral Calculus

Jeremy Bentham (1748–1832), a prolific writer on law and public policy, was born in London. The most important utilitarian of the Enlightenment, Bentham was a

[15] Madhava's *Compendium of Philosophy,* from *The Sarva-Darsana-Samgraha,* translated by E. B. Cowell and A. E. Gough (London: Kegan Paul, Trench, Trubner, 1914).

contemporary of Immanuel Kant, Edmund Burke, William Paley, and Mary Wollstonecraft. Like another contemporary, Mozart, Bentham was a prodigy; he entered Oxford at twelve and graduated at fifteen. He studied law and was admitted to the bar at nineteen. But Bentham was so appalled by English law that he never practiced it, even for a day. Instead, he devoted his life to legal reform. He wrote thousands of pages and founded a group of influential thinkers, the philosophical radicals, which included James Mill, economist David Ricardo, and legal theorist John Austin. They advocated representative democracy, universal suffrage, and a scientific approach to philosophy. Bentham also founded the *Westminster Review,* a political journal, and University College, London, where his embalmed body still rests, seated, in a glass case in the library.

An Introduction to the Principles of Morals and Legislation appeared in 1789, the year of the French Revolution. Bentham objects strongly to views of morality and politics that stress individual conscience or religious conviction; both, in his view, are little more than prejudice in disguise. Bentham also rejects doctrines of natural rights, such as those invoked by the French revolutionaries, calling them "nonsense on stilts."

Bentham proposes to base ethics and politics on a single principle, the principle of utility. Roughly, Bentham's version of this principle says that a good action increases the balance of pleasure over pain in the community of people affected by it; a bad action decreases it. The principle of utility approves actions in proportion to their tendency to increase the happiness of the people affected. The best actions, then, are those that maximize happiness. From this principle, together with the facts about the effects of actions, Bentham maintains, all correct moral and political judgments follow.

The true test of an action is to evaluate its effects, not just on the agent but on the entire community. An act conforms to the principle of utility, he says, if it results in more pleasure than pain for the community at large. Bentham is an **individualist:** he holds that the good of the community is nothing but the sum of the goods of its members. We may calculate the effects on the community, therefore, by adding up the effects on its members. This holds for individual actions, for laws or other rules, and for other acts of government.

> The interest of the community is one of the most general expressions that can occur in the phraseology of morals: no wonder that the meaning of it is often lost. When it has a meaning, it is this. The community is a fictitious body, composed of the individual persons who are considered as constituting as it were its members. The interest of the community then is, what is it?—the sum of the interests of the several members who compose it.

In Bentham's view, we should evaluate actions in terms of their effects, calculating the pleasures and pains—the advantages and disadvantages, the benefits and the costs—produced by our available options. We must consider the effects, not only on ourselves but also on the entire community. Bentham outlines a method of computing the moral value of possible actions called the **moral** (or **felicific) calculus.**

> I. Pleasures then, and the avoidance of pains, are the ends that the legislator has in view; it behoves him therefore to understand their value. Pleasures and pains are the instruments he has to work with: it behoves him therefore to understand their force, which is again, in other words, their value.

II. To a person considered by himself, the value of a pleasure or pain considered by itself, will be greater or less, according to the four following circumstances:

1. Its intensity.
2. Its duration.
3. Its certainty or uncertainty.
4. Its propinquity or remoteness.

III. These are the circumstances which are to be considered in estimating a pleasure or a pain considered each of them by itself. But when the value of any pleasure or pain is considered for the purpose of estimating the tendency of any act by which it is produced, there are two other circumstances to be taken into the account; these are,

5. Its fecundity, or the chance it has of being followed by sensations of the same kind: that is, pleasures, if it be a pleasure: pains, if it be a pain.
6. Its purity, or the chance it has of not being followed by sensations of the opposite kind: that is, pains, if it be a pleasure: pleasures, if it be a pain.

These two last, however, are in strictness scarcely to be deemed properties of the pleasure or the pain itself; they are not, therefore, in strictness to be taken into the account of the value of that pleasure or that pain. They are in strictness to be deemed properties only of the act, or other event, by which such pleasure or pain has been produced; and accordingly are only to be taken into the account of the tendency of such act or such event.

IV. To a number of persons, with reference to each of whom to the value of a pleasure or a pain is considered, it will be greater or less, according to seven circumstances: to wit, the six preceding ones; viz.

1. Its intensity.
2. Its duration.
3. Its certainty or uncertainty.
4. Its propinquity or remoteness.
5. Its fecundity.
6. Its purity.

And one other; to wit:

7. Its extent; that is, the number of persons to whom it extends; or (in other words) who are affected by it.

V. To take an exact account then of the general tendency of any act, by which the interests of a community are affected, proceed as follows. Begin with any one person of those whose interests seem most immediately to be affected by it: and take an account,

1. Of the value of each distinguishable pleasure which appears to be produced by it in the first instance.
2. Of the value of each pain which appears to be produced by it in the first instance.
3. Of the value of each pleasure which appears to be produced by it after the first. This constitutes the fecundity of the first pleasure and the impurity of the first pain.
4. Of the value of each pain which appears to be produced by it after the first. This constitutes the fecundity of the first pain, and the impurity of the first pleasure.

5. Sum up all the values of all the pleasures on the one side, and those of all the pains on the other. The balance, if it be on the side of pleasure, will give the good tendency of the act upon the whole, with respect to the interests of that individual person; if on the side of pain, the bad tendency of it upon the whole.
6. Take an account of the number of persons whose interests appear to be concerned; and repeat the above process with respect to each. Sum up the numbers expressive of the degrees of good tendency, which the act has, with respect to each individual, in regard to whom the tendency of it is good upon the whole: do this again with respect to each individual, in regard to whom the tendency of it is good upon the whole: do this again with respect to each individual, in regard to whom the tendency of it is bad upon the whole. Take the balance which if on the side of pleasure, will give the general good tendency of the act, with respect to the total number or community of individuals concerned; if on the side of pain,the general evil tendency, with respect to the same community.

The calculation sounds complicated, and it is. But a table may make the idea more comprehensible:

People Affected by an Act	*Expected Pleasure*	*Expected Pain*
A	P_A	L_A
B	P_B	L_B
C	P_C	L_C
Total	P	L

Degree of goodness: P − L

List, in other words, all the people affected by the act under consideration. For each, think about the expected pleasure and expected pain the act would produce. Calculating expected pleasure or pain is already complicated, even for one person; we must take into account not only the value of the pleasure produced by a specific result of the action but the probability that the act will produce that result. Now, add up all the pleasures, and add up all the pains. Take the difference. The balance constitutes the degree of goodness of the act.

What is the link between the principle of utility and moral obligation? The more an act promotes the happiness of the community, the better it is. The best acts are those that maximize the community's happiness. It is tempting to reason as follows: We ought to perform the best acts; so, we ought to maximize happiness.

But that is not what Bentham says. When he raises the issue of obligation, he waffles:

> Of an action that is conformable to the principle of utility one may always say either that it is one that ought to be done, or at least that it is not one that ought not to be done. One may say also, that it is right it should be done; at least that it is not wrong it should be done: that it is a right action; at least that it is not a wrong action.

If an act conforms to the principle of utility—that is, if its net effect on the community's happiness is positive—then, Bentham says, we should do it, or at least we are not obliged not to do it. The act is at least permissible. So if we face a choice between several actions that conform to the principle of utility, all are ethically acceptable choices, even if some increase the happiness of the community far more than others do.

Suppose, for example, that you walk by a house and notice smoke pouring from a window. You hear shouts and suspect that someone is trapped inside. Several options quickly occur to you. You might rush into the house to try to save the person trapped there. You might rush to a telephone to call the fire department. You might shout for help. You might pass on by, muttering that life is unfair. Say that, compared to passing by without doing anything, all the other options increase the happiness of the community but that rushing into the burning house yourself increases it far more than calling the fire department or shouting for help. (Whether this is true, of course, depends on your chances of success; rushing in and sacrificing your own life without saving anyone produces a far worse outcome than doing nothing.) Bentham would say that it is *best* to rush in, in such circumstances, but that calling the fire department and shouting for help are both morally acceptable.

The person who chooses to rush into the house in these circumstances does something **supererogatory**, going above the call of duty—in a utilitarian context, doing more for the happiness of the community than morality requires. Subsequent philosophers have sometimes referred to such people as *moral saints*. The person who rushes into the burning house, the person who leaps into the ice-cold river to save accident victims from drowning, and the person who dedicates a career to helping others do more than meet the minimum demands of morality. They bring benefits to the community far greater than duty requires.

One way of interpreting Bentham's waffling, then, is this: The more an act benefits the community, the better it is. We are morally required to benefit the community. Our acts must conform to the principle of utility by producing, on balance, more pleasure than pain. We are not required to do more than that. But it is better to do more than that when we can; it is better to go above the call of duty and best of all to maximize the community's happiness.

How does Bentham argue for the principle of utility? Why think it is not only *a* but *the* fundamental principle of morality? Bentham admits that as a first principle it cannot strictly speaking be proved. Nevertheless, he advances some considerations in its favor. (1) Common sense, he contends, presupposes it; most of our ethical judgments, most of the time, correspond to the principle. (2) Arguments in favor of any other moral principle rest on the principle of utility. They all have the form, "If people didn't obey this rule, bad things would happen." And that relies on the principle of utility. (Mill later directs this argument against Kant, holding that all Kant's arguments for the categorical imperative smuggle in utility.) (3) Relying on conscience—which Bentham terms "the principle of sympathy and antipathy"—often agrees with utility but tends toward severity in some cases and lenience in others. It is capricious, as one person's conscience often disagrees with another's. Worse, it confuses a person's *motive* for acting with a *justification* of their action.

Qualities of Pleasure

John Stuart Mill (1806–1873), a contemporary of Charles Darwin, Charles Dickens, Karl Marx, and Leo Tolstoy, was the most influential philosopher of the English-speaking world in the nineteenth century. His father, James Mill (1773–1836), a friend and fellow "philosophical radical" of Jeremy Bentham, was the son of a Scottish shoemaker. He educated young John Stuart Mill at home, teaching him to read Greek by age three and Latin just a few years later. He was well read in classical literature and history by eight and studied philosophy, mathematics, and economics before reaching his teens. For thirty-five years he worked in the East India Company, which governed India under charter from the British government. In 1865 he won election to Parliament despite his refusal to campaign or defend his views.

As we have seen, Mill defends a version of utilitarianism very close to Bentham's. Mill highlights, however, several aspects of the theory. Mill stresses that pleasures (and pains) differ in quality as well as quantity. Thomas Carlyle had called Bentham's utilitarianism "pig philosophy," contending that it encouraged people to live like pigs, pursuing pleasure by any means possible. If the only good is *feeling* good, Carlyle had argued, human beings are no better than pigs. Utilitarianism is a philosophy suited to swine, not human beings. Mill answers, "It is better to be a human being dissatisfied than a pig satisfied," for human beings are capable of much better pleasures than pigs are.

How does Mill amplify the traditional Epicurean response?

> When thus attacked, the Epicureans have always answered, that it is not they, but their accusers, who represent human nature in a degrading light; since the accusation supposes human beings to be capable of no pleasures except those of which swine are capable. If this supposition were true, the charge could not be gainsaid, but would then be no longer an imputation; for if the sources of pleasure were precisely the same to human beings and to swine, the rule of life which is good enough for the one would be good enough for the other. The comparison of the Epicurean life to that of beasts is felt as degrading, precisely because a beast's pleasures do not satisfy a human being's conceptions of happiness. Human beings have faculties more elevated than the animal appetites, and when once made conscious of them, do not regard anything as happiness which does not include their gratification.
> I do not, indeed, consider the Epicureans to have been by any means faultless in drawing out their scheme of consequences from the utilitarian principle. To do this in any sufficient manner, many Stoic, as well as Christian elements require to be included. But there is no known Epicurean theory of life which does not assign to the pleasures of the intellect, of the feelings and imagination, and of the moral sentiments, a much higher value as pleasures than to those of mere sensation. It must be admitted, however, that utilitarian writers in general have placed the superiority of mental over bodily pleasures chiefly in the greater permanency, safety, uncostliness, etc., of the former—that is, in their circumstantial advantages rather than in their intrinsic nature. And on all these points utilitarians have fully proved their case; but they might have taken the other, and, as it may be called, higher ground, with entire consistency. It is quite compatible with the principle of utility to recognise the fact, that some kinds of pleasure are more desirable and more valuable than others. It would be absurd that while, in estimating all other things, quality is considered as well as quantity, the estimation of pleasures should be supposed to depend on quantity alone.[16]

[16] John Stuart Mill, *Utilitarianism* (London: Longman's, 1907; originally published 1859).

How can we rank pleasures in quality? How can we tell whether the pleasure of a cold beer on a summer's day is of higher or lower quality than the pleasure of a beautiful sunset, a good conversation with a friend, or a good book?

How do we tell whether one pleasure is more valuable than another?

> If I am asked, what I mean by difference of quality in pleasures, or what makes one pleasure more valuable than another, merely as a pleasure, except its being greater in amount, there is but one possible answer. Of two pleasures, if there be one to which all or almost all who have experience of both give a decided preference, irrespective of any feeling of moral obligation to prefer it, that is the more desirable pleasure. If one of the two is, by those who are competently acquainted with both, placed so far above the other that they prefer it, even though knowing it to be attended with a greater amount of discontent, and would not resign it for any quantity of the other pleasure which their nature is capable of, we are justified in ascribing to the preferred enjoyment a superiority in quality, so far outweighing quantity as to render it, in comparison, of small account.

Those with experience of both prefer the intellectual pleasures distinctive of human beings to the sensual pleasures we share with other animals, such as pigs.

What is dignity, for Mill? What role does it play in his argument?

> Now it is an unquestionable fact that those who are equally acquainted with, and equally capable of appreciating and enjoying, both, do give a most marked preference to the manner of existence which employs their higher faculties. Few human creatures would consent to be changed into any of the lower animals, for a promise of the fullest allowance of a beast's pleasures; no intelligent human being would consent to be a fool, no instructed person would be an ignoramus, no person of feeling and conscience would be selfish and base, even though they should be persuaded that the fool, the dunce, or the rascal is better satisfied with his lot than they are with theirs. They would not resign what they possess more than he for the most complete satisfaction of all the desires which they have in common with him. If they ever fancy they would, it is only in cases of unhappiness so extreme, that to escape from it they would exchange their lot for almost any other, however undesirable in their own eyes. A being of higher faculties requires more to make him happy, is capable probably of more acute suffering, and certainly accessible to it at more points, than one of an inferior type; but in spite of these liabilities, he can never really wish to sink into what he feels to be a lower grade of existence. We may give what explanation we please of this unwillingness; we may attribute it to pride, a name which is given indiscriminately to some of the most and to some of the least estimable feelings of which mankind are capable: we may refer it to the love of liberty and personal independence, an appeal to which was with the Stoics one of the most effective means for the inculcation of it; to the love of power, or to the love of excitement, both of which do really enter into and contribute to it: but its most appropriate appellation is a sense of dignity, which all human beings possess in one form or other, and in some, though by no means in exact, proportion to their higher faculties, and which is so essential a part of the happiness of those in whom it is strong, that nothing which conflicts with it could be, otherwise than momentarily, an object of desire to them. . . . It is better to be a human being dissatisfied than a pig satisfied; better to be Socrates dissatisfied than a fool satisfied.

> And if the fool, or the pig, are of a different opinion, it is because they only know their own side of the question. The other party to the comparison knows both sides.

Even if some pleasures were not intrinsically more valuable than others, however, utilitarianism would not be "pig philosophy"; the development and use of our higher faculties would be virtuous solely by virtue of their benefits to others.

> . . . if it may possibly be doubted whether a noble character is always the happier for its nobleness, there can be no doubt that it makes other people happier, and that the world in general is immensely a gainer by it. Utilitarianism, therefore, could only attain its end by the general cultivation of nobleness of character, even if each individual were only benefited by the nobleness of others, and his own, so far as happiness is concerned, were a sheer deduction from the benefit. But the bare enunciation of such an absurdity as this last, renders refutation superfluous.

It is worth noting that Bentham differs from Mill on one important point. He too holds that pleasures differ in quality as well as quantity:

> In regard to well-being, quality as well as quantity requires to be taken into account.
>
> Quantity depends upon *general* sensibility, sensibility to pleasure and pain in general; quality upon *particular* sensibility: upon a man's being more sensible to pleasure or pain from this or that source, than to ditto from this or that other.[17]

Each of us, Bentham says, can know the quality of our own sensibility by reflection but can only infer the qualities of the sensibilities of others from what they do and say. It follows, Bentham notes, that "every man is a better judge of what is conducive to his own well-being than any other man can be" (131). In other words, Bentham lacks Mill's confidence that those with experience of both kinds of pleasure can determine, in general, which kind of pleasure is better. Perhaps baseball is better than ballet for some, while ballet is better than baseball for others.

Rules

Mill emphasizes that the principle of utility justifies right actions. It explains what makes them right. But it does not have to be a conscious motive; it does not even have to be a practical test of what is right or wrong. Most right acts are done from other motives. And most people facing moral decisions rely on commonsense moral rules rather than utilitarian calculation.

Mill stresses the importance of **secondary principles,** commonsense rules such as "Do not murder," "Do not steal," and so on, that give us moral guidance. There is not time to do the moral calculus in the face of every decision. Nor is there any need to, for we can rely on tradition, "the whole past duration of the human species," as Mill puts it, to have determined, in general, the tendencies of certain kinds of actions to produce good or ill effects.

> . . . mankind must by this time have acquired positive beliefs as to the effects of some actions on their happiness; and the beliefs which have thus come down are the rules of morality for the multitude, and for the philosopher until he has succeeded

[17] Jeremy Bentham, *Deontology* (Oxford: Clarendon, 1983), 130.

> in finding better. That philosophers might easily do this, even now, on many subjects; that the received code of ethics is by no means of divine right; and that mankind have still much to learn as to the effects of actions on the general happiness, I admit, or rather, earnestly maintain. The corollaries from the principle of utility, like the precepts of every practical art, admit of indefinite improvement, and, in a progressive state of the human mind, their improvement is perpetually going on.

"Whatever we adopt as the fundamental principle of morality, we require subordinate principles to apply it by." These secondary, commonsense moral principles are the core of ordinary moral decision-making and moral education. They are justified by the principle of utility; following them maximizes the good. Utility thus also gives us a basis for reforming tradition, for we may find in some cases that traditional rules need to be modified or rejected outright. We need to appeal to the principle of utility directly only when secondary principles conflict.

What are moral conflicts? How does Mill propose to deal with them?

> It is not the fault of any creed, but of the complicated nature of human affairs, that rules of conduct cannot be so framed as to require no exceptions, and that hardly any kind of action can safely be laid down as either always obligatory or always condemnable. There is no ethical creed which does not temper the rigidity of its laws, by giving a certain latitude, under the moral responsibility of the agent, for accommodation to peculiarities of circumstances; and under every creed, at the opening thus made, self-deception and dishonest casuistry get in. There exists no moral system under which there do not arise unequivocal cases of conflicting obligation. These are the real difficulties, the knotty points both in the theory of ethics, and in the conscientious guidance of personal conduct. They are overcome practically, with greater or with less success, according to the intellect and virtue of the individual; but it can hardly be pretended that any one will be the less qualified for dealing with them, from possessing an ultimate standard to which conflicting rights and duties can be referred. If utility is the ultimate source of moral obligations, utility may be invoked to decide between them when their demands are incompatible. Though the application of the standard may be difficult, it is better than none at all: while in other systems, the moral laws all claiming independent authority, there is no common umpire entitled to interfere between them; their claims to precedence one over another rest on little better than sophistry, and unless determined, as they generally are, by the unacknowledged influence of considerations of utility, afford a free scope for the action of personal desires and partialities. We must remember that only in these cases of conflict between secondary principles is it requisite that first principles should be appealed to. There is no case of moral obligation in which some secondary principle is not involved; and if only one, there can seldom be any real doubt which one it is, in the mind of any person by whom the principle itself is recognised.

Plato describes a classic case of moral conflict. You've borrowed a knife from a friend, offering to return it whenever he needs it. He shows up at your door, crazed with anger, and says he needs the knife to kill a neighbor who insulted him. Do you return it? Your obligation to keep your promise conflicts with your obligation to save a life.

Plato and Confucius each discuss another sort of conflict: You learn that your father has done something criminal. Do you turn him in? Your obligation to a family member conflicts with your obligation as a citizen.

Kant describes yet another case. A child knocks on your door and says an ax-wielding madman is chasing her. You let her in and hide her in a closet. A moment later the madman bangs on the door and demands to know where the child is. Do you tell him? This time, your obligation to tell the truth conflicts with your obligation to save a life.

Normally, Mill says, we can rely on secondary principles such as "Keep your promises," "Tell the truth," "Report crimes," and "Save lives," which the principle of utility justifies as maximizing happiness. When they conflict, however, we must appeal directly to utility, looking in detail at the consequences. You should probably break your promise (in Plato's case) and tell a lie (in Kant's case), since the consequences of keeping the promise and telling the truth include an innocent person's death.

Bentham generalizes this into an argument for utilitarianism. Traditional moral rules, whether advanced by religion or common sense, have exceptions. "Thou shalt not kill"—but would the assassination of Hitler have been an immoral act? "Thou shalt not steal"—but would it be wrong to steal bread to feed your starving family? That, he thinks, is evidence that they are not fundamental principles. When we face a conflict between two or more such principles, traditional theories provide no guidance. But we still think there is a right way and a wrong way to resolve such conflicts; we think the knife should not be returned, even if it means breaking a promise, and the child should be hidden, even if it means telling a lie. There must be a fundamental principle that allows us to weigh the competing considerations in cases of moral conflict—a principle that does not have exceptions and allows us to compare different kinds of moral factors. That, of course, is the principle of utility.

Other Forms of Utilitarianism: Maimonides

Maimonides (1135–1204) offers a version of utilitarianism based on a different conception of the nonmoral good and a different conception of rules. Like Averroës, his contemporary, he was born in Córdoba, Spain. His father was a distinguished Jewish scholar. At thirteen he fled Córdoba, already under Moslem control, when an intolerant Islamic sect conquered it. Eventually he and his family settled in northern Africa. When he was thirty, Maimonides became a court physician in Egypt. He served as a leader of the Jewish community there, becoming a great authority on Jewish law, until he died at age sixty-seven.

Maimonides wrote many volumes on Jewish law, medicine, and other topics. His chief work bearing on philosophy is *The Guide of the Perplexed,* a long treatise written in Arabic on the meaning of various Hebrew words. Maimonides addresses his work to people torn between what they see as the competing claims of philosophy and religion. [Such people, called "the perplexed," are among the "weeds" of the ideal city described by al-Farabi (870–950) in his work *The Political Regime.*] Maimonides recognizes that, in the opinion of many, reason and religious belief conflict. He tries to reconcile them, showing that reason is not only compatible with but even supports religion and religious law. In his view, shallow thought challenges religion, but profound thought strengthens it.

This implies that a little learning is a dangerous thing. Maimonides wishes to encourage deep study and reflection but to discourage shallow learning. To keep the vulgar away, al-Farabi writes intentionally boring, jargon-filled treatises. To the same end, Maimonides admits that he breaks apart ideas that belong together, makes contradictory assertions, and generally tries to make his book hard to understand.

In ethics, Maimonides tries to show that the 613 commandments of God in the Torah are all consistent with reason; all that pertain to relations between humans, he contends, are actually required by reason. His argument rests on utilitarianism. All the commandments pertaining to human relations, he argues, are justified because they maximize the good.

Maimonides's utilitarianism is distinctive in two ways. First, he has a broad characterization of the good as including not only happiness but also virtue. Happiness is intrinsically good; people seek happiness for its own sake. But virtue is also intrinsically good; people seek to be honest, kind, courageous, fair, and so on, even when those virtues conflict with happiness. In maximizing good, then, we must not only promote people's *feeling* good but people's *being* good.

> The Law as a whole aims at two things: the welfare of the soul and the welfare of the body. As for the welfare of the soul, it consists in the multitude's acquiring correct opinions corresponding to their respective capacity. . . . As for the welfare of the body, it comes about by the improvement of their ways of living with one another. This is achieved through two things. One of them is the abolition of their wronging each other. This is tantamount to every individual among the people not being permitted to act according to his will and up to the limits of his power, but being forced to do that which is useful to the whole. The second thing consists in the acquisition by every human individual of moral qualities that are useful for life in society so that the affairs of the city may be ordered.[18]

The purpose of the Law is to promote both the perfection of the body and the perfection of the soul—to prevent people from harming each other and to inculcate virtue and ultimately knowledge, especially the highest knowledge, which is knowledge of God.

Second, Maimonides treats *kinds* of actions, rather than individual actions, as fundamental. He stresses the importance of rules in moral deliberation. He justifies the rules of the Torah by arguing that they maximize the good and then judges individual actions by those rules. This makes Maimonides a **rule-utilitarian.** He judges particular actions indirectly, by appeal to rules that are themselves justified as maximizing the good.

What justifies the Torah's 613 commandments, in Maimonides's view?

> . . . whenever a commandment, be it a prescription or a prohibition, requires abolishing reciprocal wrongdoing, or urging to a noble moral quality leading to a good social relationship, or communicating a correct opinion that ought to be believed either on account of itself or because it is necessary for the abolition of reciprocal wrongdoing or for the acquisition of a noble moral quality, such a commandment has a clear cause and is of manifest utility. No question concerning the end need be posed with regard to such commandments. For no one was ever so perplexed for a day as to ask why we were commanded by the Law that God is one, or why we were forbidden to kill and to steal, or why we were forbidden to exercise vengeance and retaliation, or why we were ordered to love each other.

[18] Moses Maimonides, *The Guide of the Perplexed,* translated by Schlomo Pines (Chicago: University of Chicago Press, 1963), Chapter 27.

> . . . every commandment from among these six hundred and thirteen commandments exists either with a view to communicating a correct opinion, or to putting an end to an unhealthy opinion, or to communicating a rule of justice, or to warding off an injustice, or to endowing men with a noble moral quality, or to warning them against an evil moral quality. (Chapter 28)

Many rules, Maimonides argues, aim at maximizing *being good* rather than *feeling good.* Virtue, as Aristotle says, requires moderation. That in turn requires restraint. Many rules are designed to develop the needed restraint. Those rules do not promote feeling good; often they have the opposite effect.

In most cases, **act-utilitarians**—who judge individual actions directly by their effects on the amount of good—agree with rule-utilitarians. They disagree, however, whenever it would be possible to do better by breaking the rules. "Do not murder," for example, is a good rule; following it maximizes the good. In some circumstances, however, murder might actually produce more good, or less evil, than refraining from murder. (Consider the possible assassination of Hitler.) The principle of utility, in this sort of case, conflicts with the rule it generally justifies. Which takes priority: the rule the principle of utility justifies ("Do not murder") or the principle of utility itself?

Act-utilitarians argue that the principle of utility takes priority. They find it bizarre to say that we should follow the rule rather than the underlying principle—"Maximize good"—since the rule derives its moral force solely from the justification the principle of utility provides. But rule-utilitarians hold that the rule must take priority. Maimonides, for example, argues that rules are essential to moral thinking and moral education. We cannot calculate what to do in every individual case. We simply do not know enough about what the effects of individual acts will be and what the good in particular situations amounts to. If we try to set aside the rules when we think we can do better, we will make mistakes far more often than we will get things right. (Consider, after all, what happened to those who attempted Hitler's assassination.) And our vices will tempt us to break the rules more effectively than our virtues will tempt us to transcend them. The result will be moral chaos. So, there is a utilitarian justification for following the rules even when we think we might be better off breaking them.

> . . . governance of the Law ought to be absolute and universal, including everyone, even if it is suitable only for certain individuals and not suitable for others; for if it were made to fit individuals, the whole would be corrupted and you would make out of it something that varies. (Chapter 34)

Other Forms of Utilitarianism: Gyekye

The Akan tribe lives in Ghana. They inhabit the west African coast that was home to many of the African natives brought by slave traders to North America. Contemporary African philosopher Kwame Gyekye, himself an Akan, has written about the Akan view of causality, metaphysics, religion, and ethics.

Akan ethics, as Gyekye describes it, is a version of consequentialism. Good acts are those that bring about the well-being of the society; bad actions work against the well-being of the society. The Akan thus evaluate actions by their consequences, but their view differs from that of most Western consequentialists. According to Jeremy

Bentham, John Stuart Mill, and other Western utilitarians, the good of a community is the sum of the goods of its members. Bentham and Mill add up individual pleasures and pains to obtain this sum; other utilitarians add up satisfactions and frustrations of individual desires. The Akan, in contrast, maintain that the good of the community cannot be reduced to individual goods. According to their **communitarian consequentialism,** good acts promote the well-being of society. The Akan understand social well-being in terms of social welfare, solidarity, harmony, and other features of the social order itself. The good of the community, while it does not reduce to individual well-being, nevertheless is not independent of it. Certain character traits are more conducive to social well-being than others and are therefore considered virtues: kindness, faithfulness, compassion, hospitality, and others. Akan ethics thus judges actions and character traits by appeal to their efforts on social good.

How does Akan utilitarianism differ from Bentham's?

> In Akan moral thought the sole criterion of goodness is the welfare or well-being of the community. Thus, in the course of my field research, the response I had to the question, "What do the Akan people mean by 'good' (or, goodness)?" invariably included a list of goods, that is, a list of deeds, habits, and patterns of behavior considered by the society as worthwhile because of their consequences for human well-being. The list of such goods invariably included: kindness, faithfulness, compassion, hospitality, that which brings peace, happiness, dignity, and respect, and so on. . . .
>
> On what grounds are some acts (etc.) considered good? The answer is simply that each of them is supposed (expected or known) to bring about or lead to social well-being. Within the framework of Akan social and humanistic ethics, what is morally good is generally that which promotes social welfare, solidarity, and harmony in human relationships. Moral value in the Akan system is determined in terms of its consequences for mankind and society. "Good" is thus used of actions that promote human interest. The good is identical with the welfare of the society, which is expected to include the welfare of the individual.[19]

One distinctive feature of Akan ethics is the classification of unethical actions into two categories: ordinary and extraordinary evils. Extraordinary evils bring suffering to the whole community, not just to individual members of the community. Theft, adultery, lying, and backbiting are ordinary evils; murder, rape, incest, sexual intercourse in the bush, sexual intercourse with a woman pregnant with another man's child, cursing the chief, and stealing from a deity are extraordinary evils. Performing an extraordinarily evil act, the Akan think, has religious ramifications, for it angers the gods. Still, it is the disastrous consequences for the well-being of the community that make the evil extraordinary, not the gods' disapproval.

For the Akan, people are essentially social. One can speak of the good of an individual only in terms of the good of the society he or she inhabits. People cannot achieve the good on their own; they must rely upon others. Consequently, individual good depends on the good of the community. Gyekye concludes that each must work for the good of all.

---

[19] Kwame Gyekye, *An Essay on African Philosophical Thought: The Akan Conceptual Scheme* (Cambridge: Cambridge University Press, 1987).

Gyekye seeks to reconcile communalism with a form of individualism. People have basic needs for food, shelter, health, equality of opportunity, and liberty. The common good includes these things, which are essential to human beings as human beings. He argues that the common good cannot oppose the individual good of any member of society; individual and common goods depend on each other.

Individuals, while responsible for the welfare of all, are also responsible for their own welfare. They cannot rely on the group for all their needs and desires; they must seek the good on their own.

Nevertheless, social good is something over and above individual goods. A good society contains happy people but also exhibits other specifically collective virtues: harmony, peace, mutual concern, and solidarity.

CONSCIENCE

Socrates (470–399 B.C.E.), in his defense against the charge of corrupting the youth of Athens and not believing in the Athenian gods, spoke of an "inner voice" that told him when he was about to go astray and do something wrong:

> . . . I am subject to a divine or supernatural experience. . . . It began in my early childhood—a sort of voice that comes to me, and when it comes it always dissuades me from what I am proposing to do, and never urges me on. . . .
>
> In the past the prophetic voice to which I have become accustomed has always been my constant companion, opposing me even in quite trivial things if I was going to take the wrong course. . . . my accustomed sign could not have failed to oppose me if what I was doing had not been sure to bring some good result.[20]

Socrates's inner voice warned him when he thought of doing something wrong. We still take conscience to be an excellent practical guide to what to do: "Let your conscience be your guide." We treat people without adequately developed consciences as sociopaths.

Ethical intuitionism is the view that conscience is the only reliable practical guide to what to do. Intuitionists, that is, contend that we derive our moral knowledge from our reactions to particular actions and situations. Ethical knowledge is like perceptual knowledge; we perceive things to be right or wrong just as we perceive them to be round or green. And just as we have sense organs that enable us to perceive the perceptual qualities of things, we have a **moral sense** that enables us to perceive the moral qualities of things. We react to good things with good feelings, feelings of approval, warmth, or even joy. We react to bad things with feelings of disapproval, rejection, and even horror. Our feelings are the best guide to what is right and wrong—indeed, the only guide we need.

Confucianism

Perhaps the first sophisticated version of ethical intuitionism appeared in ancient China. Mencius (372?–289? B.C.E.), originally, Mengzi (Meng Tzu, "Master Meng"),

[20] Plato, *Apology,* translated by Hugh Tredennick, from *The Last Days of Socrates* (Harmondsworth: Penguin, 1954).

was perhaps the greatest ancient disciple of Confucius. A contemporary of the great Chinese poet Chu Yuan as well as Aristotle, Euclid, and Epicurus, he lived during the turbulent Warring States period. He abides by the chief doctrines of Confucius but adds to them in some important ways.

Mencius argues that human nature is originally and essentially good. Anyone seeing a child fall into a well, he observes, would rush to help without thinking. This shows that human nature is altruistic.

How does Mencius's illustration support his conclusion?

> Mencius said, "All men have a mind which cannot bear to see the sufferings of others.
>
> "The ancient kings had this commiserating mind, and they, as a matter of course, had likewise a commiserating government. When with a commiserating mind was practised a commiserating government, to rule the kingdom was as easy a matter as to make anything go round in the palm.
>
> "When I say that all men have a mind which cannot bear to see the sufferings of others, my meaning may be illustrated thus:—even now-a-days, if men suddenly see a child about to fall into a well, they will without exception experience a feeling of alarm and distress. They will feel so, not as a ground on which they may gain the favour of the child's parents, nor as a ground on which they may seek the praise of their neighbors and friends, nor from a dislike to the reputation of having been unmoved by such a thing.
>
> "From this case we may perceive that the feeling of commiseration is essential to man, that the feeling of shame and dislike is essential to man, that the feeling of modesty and complaisance is essential to man, and that the feeling of approving and disapproving is essential to man."

Mencius holds that virtues arise from innate (that is, inborn) feelings. We innately feel compassion, which is the beginning of humanity (*ren*); shame and dislike, the beginnings of righteousness or justice (*yi*); modesty, the beginnings of propriety (*li*); and approval and disapproval, the beginnings of knowledge.

> "The feeling of commiseration is the principle of benevolence. The feeling of shame and dislike is the principle of righteousness. The feeling of modesty and complaisance is the principle of propriety. The feeling of approving and disapproving is the principle of knowledge.
>
> "Men have these four principles just as they have their four limbs. When men, having these four principles, yet say of themselves that they cannot develop them, they play the thief with themselves, and he who says of his prince that he cannot develop them plays the thief with his prince.
>
> "Since all men have these four principles in themselves, let them know to give them all their development and completion, and the issue will be like that of fire which has begun to burn, or that of a spring which has begun to find vent. Let them have their complete development, and they will suffice to love and protect all within the four seas. Let them be denied that development, and they will not suffice for a man to serve his parents with."[21]

[21] *The Works of Mencius,* edited and translated by James Legge, from *The Chinese Classics,* Volume II (Oxford: Clarendon, 1895), 2A6.

Mencius's exposition reflects two of the main motivations for intuitionism: (1) the idea that morality stems from *feelings,* not from reason alone; and (2) **pluralism,** the idea that morality rests on goods, values, principles, or feelings that differ in kind. Benevolence (*ren*), righteousness (*yi*), propriety (*li*), and knowledge are irreducibly different moral considerations, stemming from different feelings.

Mencius's picture thus at first appears to be the opposite of that painted by Plato, the Buddha, and other philosophers who stress the role of reason. We acquire virtue not by subjugating our feelings but by developing them. We are innately good; we have an innate capacity to tell right from wrong. Hence, "The path of duty lies in what is near. . . . The work of duty lies in what is easy. . . ." Being good comes naturally to us.

> Mencius said, "The ability possessed by men without having been acquired by learning is intuitive ability, and the knowledge possessed by them without the exercise of thought is their intuitive knowledge.
>
> "Children carried in the arms all know to love their parents, and when they are grown a little, they all know to love their elder brothers.
>
> "Filial affection, for parents, is the working of benevolence. Respect for elders is the working of righteousness. There is no other reason for those feelings;—they belong to all under heaven." (7A15)
>
> Mencius said, "Let a man not do what his own sense of righteousness tells him not to do, and let him not desire what his own sense of righteousness tells him not to desire;—to act thus is all he has to do." (7A17)

Because the four virtues stem from innate feelings, Mencius places great emphasis on conscience. We are born with a faculty of moral intuition, giving rise to feelings that correspond with the moral character of events. Our faculty of intuition can be developed and clarified, but it can also become beclouded by selfish desire. We all have a disposition to virtue, but we must protect and cultivate our intuition to make our feelings good guides to what is right. "The great man," Mencius says, "is he who does not lose his child's-heart" (4B12), his inborn ability to respond to the moral qualities of what happens around him. Experience, desire, and the demands of life can easily obscure our child's-heart; we can lose what we had as a child. But we can learn to find it again: "The great end of learning is nothing else but to seek for the lost mind" (6A11).

> . . . shall it be said that the mind of any man was without benevolence and righteousness? The way in which a man loses his proper goodness of mind is like the way in which the trees are denuded by axes and bills. Hewn down day after day, can it—the mind—retain its beauty? But there is a development of its life day and night, and in the calm air of the morning, just between night and day, the mind feels in a degree those desires and aversions which are proper to humanity, but the feeling is not strong, and it is fettered and destroyed by what takes place during the day. This fettering takes place again and again, the restorative influence of the night is not sufficient to preserve the proper goodness of the mind; and when this proves insufficient for that purpose, the nature becomes not much different from that of the irrational animals, and when people now see it, they think that it never had those powers which I assert. But does this condition represent the feelings proper to humanity?
>
> Therefore, if it receive its proper nourishment, there is nothing which will not grow. If it lose its proper nourishment, there is nothing which will not decay away.

> Confucius said, 'Hold it fast, and it remains with you. Let it go, and you lose it.' (6A8)

If everyone has the innate ability to tell right from wrong, then why are some people good and others evil? Some nurture and develop their innate abilities; others let them wither. Why the difference?

> The senses of hearing and seeing do not think, and are obscured by external things. When one thing comes into contact with another, as a matter of course, it leads it away. To the mind belongs the office of thinking. By thinking, it gets the right view of things; by neglecting to think, it fails to do this. (6A15)

We can now see that Mencius's picture is not so opposed to that of Plato and the Buddha as it seems. We have innate moral feelings; the origin of morality is thus in feeling, not in reason itself. But our ability to tell right and wrong fades if we do not reinforce it. The sights and sounds of the workaday world easily distract us. We must think in order to nourish our innate abilities. We must use reason, in particular, to counteract the force of desire, which beclouds the mind and obscures our natural moral feelings.

> Mencius said, "To nourish the mind there is nothing better than to make the desires few. Here is a man whose desires are few;—in some things he may not be able to keep his heart, but they will be few." (7B35)

We have seen that Mencius articulates two chief motivations for intuitionism: (1) the idea that morality stems from feelings, and (2) the idea that moral considerations differ in kind. He also articulates a third: (3) the idea that moral judgment is context-dependent. He is suspicious of universal moral principles, maintaining that all have exceptions. Because there are different moral considerations—*ren, yi, li,* and knowledge—which are independent and stem from different kinds of feelings, they can come into conflict with each other. How we should resolve these conflicts depends on the context; there is no general rule. Any rule we adopt is bound to ignore many potentially relevant considerations. Consider the conflict between self-interest and benefiting others:

> Mencius said, "The principle of the philosopher Yang was—'Each one for himself.' Though he might have benefited the whole kingdom by plucking out a single hair, he would not have done it.
>
> "The philosopher Mo loves all equally. If by rubbing smooth his whole body from the crown to the heel, he could have benefited the kingdom, he would have done it.
>
> "Zi-mo holds a medium between these. By holding that medium, he is nearer the right. But by holding it without leaving room for the exigency of circumstances, it becomes like their holding their one point.
>
> "The reason I hate that holding to one point is the injury it does to the way of right principle. It takes up one point and disregards a hundred others."

Neo-Confucianism

Mencius's most important follower was the neo-Confucian philosopher Wang Yangming (1472–1529), an influential thinker of the late Ming dynasty. He lived in a time of great turbulence and decadence characterized by incompetent, corrupt, and oppressive rulers, raids from semi-nomadic tribes, and increasing attacks on freedoms of thought and speech. He himself was hauled before the emperor of China, beaten forty times, and then banished for attacking the then-popular, highly artificial practices of recitation and flowery composition. A contemporary of Erasmus, Niccolò Macchiavelli, Thomas More, and Christopher Columbus, as well as great Italian Renaissance artists such as Michelangelo and Leonardo da Vinci, Wang developed a variant on Confucianism called **dynamic idealism.** As an idealist, he maintains that everything is mind-dependent; as he puts it, "nothing is external to the mind." (See Chapter 5.) The principles of things are to be found in the mind, not in anything outside it.

Wang's ethical theory is a form of intuitionism. Following Mencius, he holds that we have an innate intuitive knowledge of the good. Wang accepts many theses advanced by his predecessor Zhu Xi (Chu Hsi, 1130–1200); he agrees that we have a "moral mind," a conscience, an innate faculty for discerning moral truth. If so, Zhu Xi asked, why do people do wrong? He answered that the human mind strays because it also contains passions, which can overwhelm the moral mind. He held that we must depend on strength of will and rational inquiry to combat the passions and support our consciences. Wang agrees that passions threaten our ability to tell right from wrong but insists that the mind is one and emphasizes that this task is one of recovery: we must simply recover what our minds innately share, a knowledge of the highest good.

> The Teacher said, "The sages, also, have first devoted themselves to study, and thus know the truth. The common people, also, have knowledge of it from birth."
>
> Some one asked, "How can that be?"
>
> He replied: "Intuitive knowledge of good is characteristic of all men. The sage, however, guards and protects it so that nothing obscures it. His contending and anxiety do not cease, and he is indefatigable and energetic in his efforts to guard his intuitive knowledge of the good. This also involves learning. However, his native ability is greater, so that it is said of him that he is born with knowledge of the five duties and practices them with ease. There is nobody who does not in the period from his infancy to his boyhood develop this intuition of good, but it is often obscured. Nevertheless, this original knowledge of good is naturally hard to obliterate. Study and self-control should follow the lead of intuitive knowledge.[22]

Ethical living consists in fostering and extending our inborn knowledge of the good. How do we distinguish the feelings that constitute our conscience from the passions that oppose them? The latter are selfish, while the former are not.

What is the normal function of the intuitive faculty of the mind? How can we guard against its obscuration?

> Knowledge is native to the mind; the mind naturally is able to know. When it perceives the parents it naturally knows what filial piety is; when it perceives the elder brother it naturally knows what respectfulness is; when it sees a child fall into a well it naturally knows what commiseration is. His is intuitive knowledge of the good, and is not attained through external investigation. If the thing manifested emanates from the intuitive faculty, it is the more free from the obscuration of selfish purpose. This is what is meant by saying that the mind is filled with commisera-

[22] Wang Yangming, *Record of Discourses,* from *The Philosophy of Wang Yang-Ming,* translated by Frederick Goodrich Henke (Carbondale: Open Court, 1916).

> tion, and that love cannot be exhausted. However, the ordinary man is subject to the obscuration of private aims, so that it is necessary to develop the intuitive faculty to the utmost through the investigation of things in order to overcome selfishness and reinstate the rule of natural law. Then the intuitive faculty of the mind will not be subject to obscuration, but having been satiated will function normally. Thus we have a condition in which there is an extension of knowledge. Knowledge having been extended to the utmost, the purpose is sincere.[23]

In a powerful image, Wang compares the mind of the sage to a clear mirror. Just as a clear mirror reflects things as they are, the mind of the sage reflects the true moral qualities of things.

> Yueh-ren said: "The mind may be compared to a mirror. The mind of the sage is like a bright mirror, the mind of the ordinary man like a dull mirror. The saying of more recent natural philosophy may be compared to using it as a mirror to reflect things. If effort is expended in causing the mirror to reflect while the glass is still dull, how can one succeed? The natural philosophy of the Teacher is like a polished and brightened mirror. When after having been polished the mirror is bright, the power of reflecting has not been lost."

Wang thus presents a fourth fundamental idea of intuitionism: (4) the idea that moral knowledge is analogous to perceptual knowledge.

Aristotle and the Stoics

We have already examined Aristotle's moral philosophy at length in Chapter 7. Roughly, for Aristotle an act is right if it is the kind of act that a virtuous person would tend to perform and wrong if it is the kind of act a vicious person would tend to perform. Virtue is a means between extremes: one must do the right thing, to the right person, to the right extent, at the right time, with the right motive, in the right way, in the right circumstances, and for the right reasons. How do you find the intermediate in all these respects? There is no rule, Aristotle says; you must develop judgment, that is, the ability to see what to do. He takes the analogy between moral and perceptual knowledge seriously:

> But this is no doubt difficult, and especially in individual cases; for it is not easy to determine both how and with whom and on what provocation and how long one should be angry; for we too sometimes praise those who fall short and call them good-tempered, but sometimes we praise those who get angry and call them manly. The man, however, who deviates little from goodness is not blamed, whether he do so in the direction of the more or the less, but only the man who deviates more widely; for *he* does not fail to be noticed. But up to what point and to what extent a man must deviate before he becomes blameworthy it is not easy to determine by reasoning, any more than anything else that is perceived by the senses; such things depend on particular facts, and the decision rests with perception.[24]

---

[23] Wang Yangming, *Instructions for Practical Life,* from *The Philosophy of Wang Yang-Ming,* translated by Frederick Goodrich Henke (Carbondale: Open Court, 1916).

[24] Aristotle, *Nicomachean Ethics* II, 9, translated by W. D. Ross, from *The Works of Aristotle* (Oxford: Oxford University Press, 1908).

Despite the perceptual analogy, Aristotle differs sharply from Mencius and Wang Yangming on the innateness of what they call intuitive knowledge of the good and he calls practical wisdom. For Aristotle, practical wisdom is the product of experience, training, and reflection; developing it is much more than recovering "the lost mind."

Reason itself is not enough to determine what ought to be done in particular situations. It follows that precise rules for ethical behavior are impossible. The best we can do is give rules true for the most part:

> Our discussion will be adequate if it has as much clearness as the subject-matter admits of, for precision is not to be sought for alike in all discussions, any more than in all the products of the crafts. Now fine and just actions, which political science investigates, admit of much variety and fluctuation of opinion, so that they may be thought to exist only by convention, and not by nature. And goods also give rise to a similar fluctuation because they bring harm to many people; for before now men have been undone by reason of their wealth, and others by reason of their courage. We must be content, then, in speaking of such subjects and with such premisses to indicate the truth roughly and in outline, and in speaking about things which are only for the most part true and with premisses of the same kind to reach conclusions that are no better. In the same spirit, therefore, should each type of statement be received; for it is the mark of an educated man to look for precision in each class of things just so far as the nature of the subject admits; it is evidently equally foolish to accept probable reasoning from a mathematician and to demand from a rhetorician scientific proofs. (I, 3)

We have here a fifth thesis characteristic of intuitionism: (5) Ethical rules cannot be universal; they are true "only for the most part." What does this mean?

We can gain some insight by considering the ethical views of the Stoics, a group of Greek and Roman philosophers who developed a coherent set of beliefs on various philosophical topics over a period of several centuries. Zeno of Citium (334–262 B.C.E.) founded Stoicism; the school was continued by a series of Greek and, later, Roman philosophers, including Cicero (106–43 B.C.E.), Seneca (1?–65), Epictetus (55?–135?), and Roman emperor Marcus Aurelius (121–180). Seneca, a contemporary of Jesus and Paul, was born in Córdoba, Spain, but educated in Rome. The Emperor Caligula nearly condemned him to death in 39; Caligula's successor Claudius exiled him to Corsica on the charge of committing adultery with the Emperor's niece. He returned to Rome at age forty-eight to become tutor to the young Nero and became one of his principal advisers when Nero became Emperor. Accused of conspiring to dethrone Nero in 65, however, Seneca committed suicide on the Emperor's command.

Seneca saw philosophical reflection as essential to ethical development: "There is no philosophy without goodness, and no goodness without philosophy." He stressed wisdom and the elimination of desire and, like Aristotle, saw wisdom as something that could not be captured by rules. Rules are true "only for the most part" in the sense that they hold *ceteris paribus* ("other things being equal"), if no other morally relevant considerations intervene. The Sage recognizes this:

> Further, he approaches everything with reservation: "if nothing intervenes to impede." . . . I shall go to dinner even if it is freezing, since I promised; but not if it is snowing. I shall go to a wedding even if I'm still digesting, since I promised; but

> not if I'll catch a fever. I'll go bail for you, since I promised, but not if you want unlimited bail. There is silent reservation: if I can, if I ought, if things remain thus.[25]

I should keep my promises, if nothing intervenes; but if some other morally relevant consideration arises, all bets are off. In the language of twentieth-century British philosopher W. D. Ross (1877–1971), I have a ***prima facie*** obligation to keep my promises. That obligation becomes **actual**—something I really am, all things considered, obliged to do—if nothing of any moral relevance conflicts with it. If there is a conflict between *prima facie* obligations, I must judge, using practical wisdom, which obligation takes precedence. At most one can be actual; others are overridden by it. I may have promised to attend a wedding, for example. So, I have a *prima facie* obligation to go. I also have a *prima facie* obligation to look out for my health, however, and if going will make me sick with fever, my actual obligation is probably to stay home and look after my health.

David Hume

The best-known exposition of ethical intuitionism in Western thought is the philosophy of David Hume (1711–1776; see Chapters 3, 4, and 6). Hume stresses the importance of feeling as opposed to reason. There is a gulf between *is* and *ought;* factual premises can never yield a moral conclusion on their own.

> In every system of morality, which I have hitherto met with, I have always remark'd, that the author proceeds for some time in the ordinary way of reasoning, and establishes the being of a God, or makes observation concerning human affairs; when of a sudden I am surpriz'd to find, that instead of the usual copulations of propositions, *is,* and *is not,* I meet with no proposition that is not connected with an *ought,* or an *ought not.* This change is imperceptible; but is, however, of the last consequence. For as this *ought,* or *ought not,* expresses some new relation or affirmation, 'tis necessary that it shou'd be observ'd and explain'd; and at the same time that a reason should be given, for what seems altogether inconceivable, how this relation can be a deduction from others, which are entirely different from it.[26]

The fact that something is a murder, for example, does not *itself* imply that it is wrong; we need a moral principle such as 'Murder is wrong'. Moreover, purely rational motives can never provide a motive for action. Reason can lead us to conclusions, but it cannot make us *want* to do anything. In morality and in other areas where we seek to go beyond sense experience, "Reason is, and ought to be, the slave of the passions."

Hume advances a novel argument for the intuitionistic thesis that morality stems from feelings rather than reason.

How does Hume argue that morality does not stem from reason?

> If morality had naturally no influence on human passions and actions, 'twere in vain to take such pains to inculcate it; and nothing wou'd be more fruitless than that multitude of rules and precepts, with which all moralists abound. Philosophy is commonly divided into *speculative* and *practical;* and as morality is always

---

[25] Seneca, *De beneficiis* 4.34, 4.39; translated by Tad Brennan, "Reservation in Stoic Ethics," *Archiv für Geschichte der Philosophie* 2000.

[26] David Hume, *A Treatise of Human Nature,* edited by Selby-Bigge (Oxford: Clarendon, 1888), III, 1, 1.

> comprehended under the latter division, 'tis supposed to influence our passions and actions, and to go beyond the calm and indolent judgments of the understanding. And this is confirm'd by common experience, which informs us, that men are often govern'd by their duties, and are deter'd from some actions by the opinion of injustice, and impell'd to others by that of obligation.
>
> Since morals, therefore, have an influence on the actions and affections, it follows, that they cannot be deriv'd from reason; and that because reason alone, as we have already prov'd, can never have any such influence. Morals excite passions, and produce or prevent actions. Reason of itself is utterly impotent in this particular. The rules of morality, therefore, are not conclusions of our reason.

Morality is not a matter of reason. Nor is it a matter of fact:

> Take any action allow'd to be vicious: Wilful murder, for instance. Examine it in all lights, and see if you can find that matter of fact, or real existence, which you call *vice.* In which-ever way you take it, you find only certain passions, motives, volitions and thoughts. There is no other matter of fact in the case. The vice entirely escapes you, as long as you consider the object.

But if morality stems from neither reason nor facts, where does it have its root?

> You never can find it, till you turn your reflexion into your own breast, and find a sentiment of disapprobation, which arises in you, towards this action. Here is a matter of fact; but 'tis the object of feeling, not of reason. It lies in yourself, not in the object. So that when you pronounce any action or character to be vicious, you mean nothing, but that from the constitution of your nature you have a feeling or sentiment of blame from the contemplation of it. Vice and virtue, therefore, may be compar'd to sounds, colours, heat and cold, which, according to modern philosophy, are not qualities in objects, but perceptions in the mind. . . .

Morality is a matter of feeling, not of reason or fact. Moreover, its source is within us. To use a contemporary term, morality is *response-dependent:* to say that something is bad is simply to say that a normal person, all other things being equal, would disapprove of it. Moral qualities, to use terms introduced in Chapter 5, are *secondary qualities* like colors and sounds, not *primary qualities* like lengths or velocities. They pertain to the relation between the object and the perceiver or moral agent, not to the object alone.

> Thus the course of the argument leads us to conclude, that since vice and virtue are not discoverable merely by reason, or the comparison of ideas, it must be by means of some impression or sentiment they occasion, that we are able to mark the difference betwixt them. Our decisions concerning moral rectitude and depravity are evidently perceptions; and as all perceptions are either impressions or ideas, the exclusion of the one is a convincing argument for the other. Morality, therefore, is more properly felt than judg'd of; tho' this feeling or sentiment is commonly so soft and gentle, that we are apt to confound it with an idea. . . .
>
> An action, or sentiment, or character is virtuous or vicious; why? because its view causes a pleasure or uneasiness of a particular kind. In giving a reason, therefore, for the pleasure or uneasiness, we sufficiently explain the vice or virtue.

An act is right if it causes a certain kind of pleasure in a normal observer; it is wrong if it causes a certain kind of uneasiness in a normal observer.

Some philosophers have interpreted Hume as holding that morality is purely subjective, something we impose on the world. In a sense that is right; the grounds of morality are in us. But they are also in the world. Color is in a sense subjective, contributed by our perceptual faculties, but we are responding systematically to objective features of the world. So, for Hume, we give the world its "moral color," but we do so by responding systematically to objective features of the world. We cannot will murder to be right any more than we can will grass to be red.

Moreover, though Hume stresses the logical gulf dividing *ought* from *is,* his emphasis on feeling as a bridge between them allows for a view of consciousness as thoroughly moral. Twentieth-century British philosopher and novelist Iris Murdoch has developed this theme:

> . . . our morality should be fed by our whole experience and conscious awareness of our world, which is *already* filled with intimations of good and evil. Our personality and temperament, and the daily momentary quality of our consciousness, our ability to *look at particulars,* must be thought of as an organic part of our morals, and soaked in value. . . . each subject *has the object he deserves.*
>
> . . . It seems to me that one cannot 'philosophise' adequately upon the subject unless one takes it as fundamental that consciousness is a form of moral activity: what we attend to, how we attend, whether we attend. . . .
>
> Morality is and ought to be connected to the whole of our being. . . . The moral life is not intermittent or specialised, it is not a peculiar separate area of our existence. It is into ourselves that we must look: advice which may now be felt, in and out of philosophy, as out of date. The proof that every little thing matters is to be found there. Life is made up of details. . . . Happenings in the consciousness so vague as to be almost nonexistent can have moral 'colour'. All sorts of momentary sensibilities to other people, too shadowy to come under the heading of manners and communication, are still parts of moral activity. ('But are you saying that every single second has a moral tag?' Yes, roughly.) We live in the present, this strange familiar yet mysterious continuum which is so difficult to describe. This is what is nearest and it matters what kind of place it is.[27]

RELIGION

Every major world religion includes rules for living. Some are virtually universal, found in every religion. ("Do not murder" and "Do not steal," for example.) Others are advanced only by some religions. ("Do not drink alcohol" and "Do not worship graven images," for example.) **Divine command theory** holds that God distinguishes right from wrong. What God commands is obligatory; what God allows is permissible; what God forbids is wrong. We know what God commands by way of Holy Scripture (the Bible, the Koran, the Gita, the Upanishads, the Sutras, etc.), which details rules to use as a practical ethical test. And according to many divine command theorists, we know God's commands by means of our conscience, which is God's law written on the heart.

---

[27] Iris Murdoch, *Metaphysics as a Guide to Morals* (London: Penguin, 1992), 167, 495.

Hinduism

The divine command theory is first advanced in a Hindu sacred text, the *Bhagavad Gita* (Song of God), a small portion of a long epic, the *Mahabharata*. (See Chapter 6.) Underlying the *Gita*'s perspective is an ancient systematic philosophy of South Asia, *Samkhya* ("analysis of nature"), discussed in Chapter 4. Recall that Arjuna (Everyman), looking across the battle line at his friends and kin, recoils at the prospect of killing them. Krishna reveals himself as God incarnate and provides a religious and mystical answer to Arjuna's ethical crisis. He urges Arjuna to fight. In part, as we have seen, he argues that the soul is immortal and cannot be destroyed. But in part he rests his argument on religious duty.

Recall that a theme common to all varieties of *Samkhya* is an analysis of nature in terms of three *gunas,* or "strands." These are intelligence, passion, and inertia.

What should one care about, if not the fruits of action?

The Vedas have the three Strands (of matter) as their scope;
Be thou free from the three Strands, Arjuna,
Free from the pairs (of opposites), eternally fixed in goodness,
Free from acquisition and possession, self-possessed. . . .

On action alone be thy interest,
Never on its fruits;
Let not the fruits of action be thy motive,
Nor be thy attachment to inaction.

Abiding in discipline perform actions,
Abandoning attachment, Dhanamjaya,
Being indifferent to success or failure;
Discipline is defined as indifference.

For action is far inferior
To discipline of mental attitude, Dhanamjaya.
In the mental attitude seek thy (religious) refuge;
Wretched are those whose motive is the fruit (of action). . . .

For the disciplined in mental attitude, action-produced
Fruit abandoning, the intelligent ones,
Freed from the bondage of rebirth,
Go to the place that is free from illness.[28]

By practicing the yoga (discipline) of action, Krishna says, Arjuna can turn ***karma*** (habit) into *dharma* (right action) attuned to God's will. By sacrificing our superficial self-interest and natural desires to act according to God's will, we become part of God's ongoing creative activity, and our consciousness mystically widens to unite with God's. Self-sacrifice allows us to participate in God's action. And that promotes our self-interest in a deeper sense.

Perform thou action that is (religiously) required;
For action is better than inaction.

[28] The *Bhagavad Gita,* translated and interpreted by Franklin Edgerton (Cambridge: Harvard University Press, 1944).

And even the maintenance of the body for thee
Can not succeed without action.

Except action for the purpose of worship,
This world is bound by actions;
Action for that purpose, son of Kunti,
Perform thou, free from attachment (to its fruits). . . .

Therefore unattached ever
Perform action that must be done;
For performing action without attachment
Man attains the highest. . . .

Better one's own duty, (tho) imperfect,
Than another's duty well-performed;
Better death in (doing) one's own duty;
Another's duty brings danger.

We must, that is, do our religious duty; we must do what God requires. Right and wrong are distinguished not by the fruits or consequences of action but by God's command.

John Calvin

In Western philosophy, divine command theory has been a minority view. But several late medieval philosophers embraced something close to it, most notably William of Ockham (c. 1285–1347), "the More-than-Subtle Doctor," an English Scholastic philosopher famed as the father of nominalism (see Chapter 5). Divine command theory might exist today in the West primarily as a straw man were it not for its advocacy by the two leading thinkers of the Protestant Reformation, Martin Luther and John Calvin.

Calvin (1509–1564), a French theologian and contemporary of Luther, John Knox, and Erasmus, studied theology in Paris, getting a master's degree at nineteen, and then law at Orléans, receiving his doctorate at twenty-three. Two years later he devoted himself to the cause of the Reformation and at twenty-seven published his magisterial *Institutes of the Christian Religion,* which still serves as the theological foundation of Reformed traditions in Holland, Scotland, and the United States.

Calvin calls philosophy "a noble gift of God" but rejects philosophical speculation, especially of the dominant Scholastic variety deriving from Aristotle and St. Thomas Aquinas. "Nearly all the wisdom we possess consists of two parts: the knowledge of God and of ourselves." These two kinds of knowledge are intertwined. We cannot know God without some understanding of ourselves and our own limitations, but we cannot know our true nature without knowing God. Knowing God, moreover, is not merely knowing about God; it involves worshipping Him and obeying Him.

Moral knowledge, for Calvin, is knowledge of God's law; it is a kind of knowledge of God. So it too requires some degree of self-knowledge. We have some knowledge of God implanted in us by our Maker: "There is, within the human mind, and indeed by natural instinct, an awareness of divinity." So, in addition to the revelations of God's will and activity in Scripture, we have an innate faculty, conscience, that leads us to the same conclusions: "That inward law . . . written, even engraved, upon the hearts of all, in a sense asserts the very same things that are to be learned from the [Ten Commandments]" (II, viii, 1), namely, to love the Lord our God with all our heart, mind, and strength, and to love our neighbor as ourselves.

Conscience distinguishes right and wrong. But Calvin is not an intuitionist. Conscience is our usual way of knowing right from wrong. But what makes right actions right and wrong actions wrong is God's will. Conscience, in other words, is a faculty of knowledge whose object is the will of God.

Why does Calvin make God's will the root of the distinction between good and evil? One motivation is to account for Biblical passages that seem at first glance to speak of God as commanding evil. God, for example, orders Abraham to kill his son Isaac, offering him up as a burnt offering to the Lord (*Genesis* 22). He stops Abraham at the last moment, to be sure, but He nevertheless gives the command. More seriously, God orders the Hebrews to steal anything they can from Egypt as the Exodus begins (*Exodus* 12:35–36). God later orders them to kill every man, woman, child, and (in many cases) beast in such cities as Jericho, Ai, and Hebron, who did nothing to deserve this fate except live in the Promised Land (*Joshua* 6, 8, 10). Were the acts of Abraham, the fleeing Hebrews, and Joshua morally right or wrong? Morality as understood on any of the models we have considered so far implies that they are wrong. But if God commands his most illustrious servants to do evil, it would follow that God is not entirely good. Calvin rejects that alternative. So these acts must have been morally right. The only thing that differentiates them from other killings and thefts, however, is God's command. So if they are right, it must be because God has commanded them.

Plato

Plato advances the classic criticism of divine command theory in one of his earliest dialogues, the *Euthyphro*. Socrates, arriving at court to stand trial for impiety and corrupting the youth of Athens, meets Euthyphro, who is there prosecuting his own father for causing the death of a servant accused of murder. Socrates wonders at this, saying that anyone who would prosecute his own father for such a deed must have a very clear idea of what piety (or righteousness or moral uprightness) is. Euthyphro insists that he does and, after some prodding, offers a definition:

> SOCRATES. Remember that I did not ask you to give me two or three examples of piety, but to explain the general idea which makes all pious things to be pious. Do you not recollect that there was one idea which made the impious impious, and the pious pious?
>
> EUTHYPHRO. I remember.
>
> SOCRATES. Tell me what is the nature of this idea, and then I shall have a standard to which I may look, and by which I may measure actions, whether yours or those of any one else, and then I shall be able to say that such and such an action is pious, such another impious.
>
> EUTHYPHRO. I will tell you, if you like.
>
> SOCRATES. I should very much like.

EUTHYPHRO. Piety, then, is that which is dear to the gods, and impiety is that which is not dear to them.[29]

Socrates shows that this makes little sense if, as the Greeks believed, there are many gods who frequently quarrel about what to do. So, Euthyphro, with Socrates's help, revises his definition:

EUTHYPHRO. Yes, I should say that what all the gods love is pious and holy, and the opposite which they all hate, impious.

Euthyphro seems to be advocating a kind of divine command theory. Socrates recognizes, however, that his words are ambiguous. The will of the gods may be a good indicator of right and wrong—something a Kantian, utilitarian, or intuitionist could readily admit without contradiction—or it may *constitute* right and wrong. Socrates seeks to clarify:

SOCRATES. We shall know better, my good friend, in a little while. The point which I should first wish to understand is whether the pious or holy is beloved by the gods because it is holy, or holy because it is beloved of the gods.

Do the gods love pious acts because the acts are pious, however that might in turn be defined—because, for example, they satisfy the categorical imperative, are compatible with the autonomy of the will, maximize the good, cause feelings of approval in normal people, are the kind of thing virtuous people would tend to do, etc.—or are the acts pious because the gods love them? The divine command theorist advocates the latter: A pious act is pious because the gods love it. Euthyphro, confused, retreats from the divine command theory:

SOCRATES. And what do you say of piety, Euthyphro: is not piety, according to your definition, loved by all the gods?
EUTHYPHRO. Yes.
SOCRATES. Because it is pious or holy, or for some other reason?
EUTHYPHRO. No, that is the reason.
SOCRATES. It is loved because it is holy, not holy because it is loved?
EUTHYPHRO. Yes.

The divine command theorist would answer Socrates differently here, insisting that an act is holy because the gods love it and not for any other reason. Socrates continues:

SOCRATES. And that which is dear to the gods is loved by them, and is in a state to be loved of them because it is loved of them?
EUTHYPHRO. Certainly.
SOCRATES. Then that which is dear to the gods, Euthyphro, is not holy, nor is that which is holy loved of God, as you affirm; but they are two different things.
EUTHYPHRO. How do you mean, Socrates?
SOCRATES. I mean to say that the holy has been acknowledged by us to be loved of God because it is holy, not to be holy because it is loved.

---

[29] Plato, *Euthyphro,* translated by Benjamin Jowett, in *The Dialogues of Plato* (Oxford: Clarendon, 1898).

EUTHYPHRO. Yes.

SOCRATES. But that which is dear to the gods is dear to them because it is loved by them, not loved by them because it is dear to them.

An act loved by the gods is such because the gods love it, or so Socrates asserts. But a pious act is not pious because the gods love it. So, pious acts cannot be defined as those the gods love. The consistent divine command theorist must insist that good acts are good because God commands them and for no other reason.

This has made various philosophers uncomfortable, for it evidently makes the distinction between right and wrong arbitrary. Right acts are right because God wills them; wrong acts are wrong because God forbids them. Why does God will some acts and forbid others? For no reason at all, according to divine command theory. If there were any reason, then it could serve to distinguish right from wrong independently of God's will. And then God's will would play a merely epistemic role, not a constitutive one as the theory requires.

One might perhaps argue that God wills some acts and forbids others for a reason, but that we cannot know what it is. In such a view, God's command would not constitute the distinction between right and wrong but would be the only reliable indicator of it.

The Ethiopian Enlightenment

Another critique of divine command theory, which extends even to this weaker, epistemic variant, appears in African philosophy. Philosophy was practiced in Africa in medieval times, but we have virtually no texts from that period. From the early modern period, however, we have some interesting philosophical works from Ethiopia that constitute an Ethiopian enlightenment. Like the philosophers of the European Enlightenment, these seventeenth-century Ethiopian writers stress the primacy of reason and the possibility of knowledge of the world through its use.

Zera Yacob (1599–1692), the greatest of these philosophers—a contemporary of Descartes, Pascal, Hobbes, Milton, Locke, Leibniz, and Rembrandt—was born near Aksum, the religious center of Ethiopia. He was the son of a poor farmer. He attended traditional schools, studying the Psalms, sacred music, and Ethiopian literature. Such schools encouraged questions and discussions, teaching reflection, criticism, and the power of thought. Following a period of devastation brought about by foreign invasion, Ethiopia was undergoing a religious revival and suffering various religious conflicts. In 1626, in the midst of these upheavals, the King converted to Catholicism and summarily ordered obedience to Rome. A rival priest from Aksum denounced Zera Yacob as a traitor, claiming that he was inciting revolution against the Catholics and the king. Only twenty-seven years old, Zera Yacob fled for his life, taking nothing but a small amount of gold and his copy of the Psalms. On his way to Shoa, the region around Addis Ababa, he found a cave in a beautiful valley, where he stayed for two years and formulated the basic ideas of his philosophy

Returning to society, Zera Yacob acquired a literary patron, lived in his house, tutored his sons, and married his maidservant. One of his patron's sons, Walda Heywat, asked Zera Yacob to write down his philosophical views; the result (in 1667) was *The Treatise of Zera Yacob*. Fearing persecution, Zera Yacob never published it. He lived in

Enfraz happily and prosperously for twenty-five more years until his death at age ninety-three.

The book's original Geez title, *Hatata,* comes from a root meaning to question, search, investigate, or examine. The *Treatise* champions reason as a tool for understanding the world and for understanding religion. Zera Yacob argues that reason, applied to the evidence of the world, leads to the conclusion that the world, God's creation, is essentially good. His ethics rests on this foundation. Because creation is essentially good, enjoying it is appropriate and also good. Zera Yacob thus opposes traditional Ethiopian asceticism, a philosophy of denial, fasting, and monastic life, in favor of involvement with the secular world.

> I understand there is a creator, greater than all creatures; since from his overabundant greatness, he created things that are so great. He is intelligent who understands all, for he created us as intelligent from the abundance of his intelligence; and we ought to worship him, for he is the master of all things.[30]

In fact, Zera Yacob uses reason, which he calls the "light of the heart," to criticize the ethical prescriptions of various religions. He argues that Jewish law, Christian morality, and Islamic rules of conduct all go astray on basic points; they imply that the order of nature itself is wrong. Moses, for example, considers sexual intercourse impure; but this

> fails to agree with the wisdom of the creator or with the order and the laws of creation. Indeed by the will of the creator, and the law of nature, it has been ordained that man and woman would unite in a carnal embrace to generate children, so that human beings would not disappear from the earth. Now this mating, which is willed by God in his law of creation, cannot be impure since god does not stain the work of his own hands.

Similarly, Zera Yacob criticizes the Christian preference for a monastic life as unnatural and contrary to the law of God. He attacks Islam for permitting polygamy, which leaves many men without wives. He assails Judaism and Christianity for considering natural things unclean (for example, a menstruating woman or a dead body) and Islam for allowing slavery. He criticizes all three for insisting upon rituals of fasting.

Zera Yacob optimistically believes that "he who investigates with the pure intelligence set by the creator in the heart of each man and scrutinizes the order and laws of creation, will discover the truth."

> God indeed has illuminated the heart of man with understanding by which he can see the good and evil, recognize the licit and illicit, distinguish truth from error, "and by your light we see the light, oh Lord!" If we use this light of our heart properly, it cannot deceive us; the purpose of this light which our creator gave us is to be saved by it, and not to be ruined by it. Everything that the light of our intelligence shows us comes from the source of truth, but what men say comes from the source of lies and our intelligence teaches us that all that the creator established is right.

[30] *The Treatise of Zera Yacob,* from Claude Sumner, *The Source of African Philosophy: The Ethiopian Philosophy of Man* (Stuttgart: Franz Steiner Verlag, 1986).

Reason thus serves as a foundation for morality and as a test for religious beliefs. Any religion that teaches that some part of the natural order or some natural disposition is wrong cannot be correct. Sexual desire is natural, so it cannot in itself be wrong or unclean. Hunger is natural, so fasting is not obligatory. Yearning for a spouse is natural, so polygamy is wrong. Yearning for freedom is natural, so slavery is wrong.

Underlying Zera Yacob's assault on particular religious tenets is a general skepticism about deriving ethical conclusions from religious revelation. Divine command theorists take God's will as itself making some acts right and others wrong. Many other religious thinkers have believed that God reveals moral truth and that we can know that truth only because God reveals it to us. Zera Yacob argues that neither can be correct. Defenders of each religion claim that they know the only true way. Obviously, not all can be right. How can we decide who is right? How, that is, can we judge which alleged revelations really come from God? Zera Yacob argues that we cannot—we have no way to tell true revelations from pretenders—except by using reason to discover moral truth and judging the claims of those religions by the light of reason.

Soren Kierkegaard

Soren Kierkegaard (1813–1855), a Danish contemporary of Karl Marx, John Stuart Mill, and Charles Dickens, was born into an affluent but still middle-class family. He studied to become a minister but eventually abandoned his plans, spending his inheritance writing until he died at forty-two. Often considered the founder of existentialism because of his rejection of systematic philosophy and his stress on the uniqueness of the individual, Kierkegaard explores the nature of religious faith and individual choice in a strikingly personal way.

Kierkegaard is perhaps best known for his treatment of the cases that motivate the divine command theory, cases in which God appears to command evil. He writes extensively on Abraham's willingness to kill his precious son, Isaac, at God's inexplicable command. From Calvin's perspective, such a case presents us with a dilemma. We can say that God commands evil, denying God's goodness; or we can say that what God commands is for that very reason good, making His command alone constitutive of moral value. Kierkegaard sees a third option.

As traditionally understood, morality is universal. In Kant's terms, the good will acts on the basis of purely universal considerations, setting aside subjective, particular determinations—the agent's history, desires, the details of the circumstances, etc. Immorality or, in theological terms, sin is precisely asserting oneself above the universal. But this is incompatible with religious faith; it makes faith a sin. Abraham has faith, if anyone does. And yet he asserts himself above the universal (in this case, "Thou shalt not kill").

> Faith is namely this paradox that the single individual is higher than the universal—yet, please note, in such a way that the movement repeats itself, so that after having been in the universal he as the single individual isolates himself as higher than the universal. If this is not faith, then Abraham is lost. . . .[31]

[31] Søren Kierkegaard, *Fear and Trembling* (Princeton: Princeton University Press, 1941), 55.

It is not that Abraham's willingness to kill his son is morally right; nothing in morality can justify him. Rather, in his willingness to obey God's horrible command, Abraham rises above moral considerations altogether. He sets morality aside for a higher purpose of following God. This Kierkegaard calls a **teleological suspension of the ethical.**

> The story of Abraham contains just such a teleological suspension of the ethical. . . . He acts by virtue of the absurd, for it is precisely the absurd that he as the single individual is higher than the universal. . . . By his act he transgressed the ethical altogether and had a higher *telos* [end, goal, purpose] outside it, in relation to which he suspended it. (56, 59)

What is the teleological suspension of the ethical?

Notice that Abraham, unlike the tragic hero, does not offer to kill his son for any higher moral purpose—to save the nation, or to appease an angry God, or to keep a promise, or to preserve his honor. There is no moral justification.

> There is no higher expression for the ethical in Abraham's life than that the father shall love the son. The ethical in the sense of the moral is entirely beside the point. . . .
>
> Why, then, does Abraham do it? For God's sake and—the two are wholly identical—for his own sake. He does it for God's sake because God demands this proof of his faith; he does it for his own sake so that he can prove it. . . . As a rule, what tempts a person is something that will hold him back from doing his duty, but here the temptation is the ethical itself, which would hold him back from doing God's will. But what is duty? Duty is simply the expression for God's will. (59–60)

The divine command theory in effect identifies moral duty with religious duty: Moral rightness is doing God's will. But Kierkegaard's point is that the two can conflict—indeed, they conflict precisely in the most outstanding examples of religious faith. Moral acts can be justified. But true acts of faith cannot be: "faith begins precisely where thought stops" (53).

SUMMARY

We have reviewed four traditional ways of distinguishing right from wrong:

1. *Reason.* Plato, the Buddha, and Immanuel Kant hold that morality consists in bringing one's desires under control. The difference between right and wrong, in this view, amounts to the difference between rationality and irrationality.

2. *Happiness.* Many philosophers from both Western and non-Western traditions hold that we can distinguish right from wrong in terms of effects on happiness. Right actions contribute to happiness, while wrong actions detract from it.

3. *Conscience.* Aristotle, the Stoics, Mencius, Wang Yangming, and David Hume think that conscience is the best practical ethical test. They postulate a moral sense.

Ethical thinking is like perception. We see things to be right or wrong much as we see them to be green or square.

4. *God.* Every major world religion includes ethical rules. Divine command theorists (such as the author of the *Bhagavad Gita* and John Calvin) maintain that God distinguishes right from wrong. What God commands or allows is right; what God forbids is wrong. Philosophers such as Plato, Zera Yacob, and Soren Kierkegaard have criticized this view, while nevertheless seeing religion and morality as having some connection.

Review Questions

1. According to the Buddha, what does right action require? What is its goal?
2. What is the categorical imperative? How does Kant argue for it?
3. Why does Kant take his various formulations of the categorical imperative to be equivalent?
4. How might a utilitarian such as Mill criticize Kant? How might Kant criticize utilitarianism?
5. Discuss the precursors to utilitarianism. How do they differ from utilitarianism as found in the writings of Bentham and Mill?
6. How does Mill respond to Thomas Carlyle's objection that utilitarianism is "pig philosophy"? Some have charged that his response in effect abandons utilitarianism; do you agree?
7. What are moral conflicts? Contrast the treatments of them given by at least two of the following: Kant; utilitarianism; intuitionism; divine command theory.
8. What is the source of morality, according to Hume? What does that tell us about its nature?
9. What is intuitionism? How do its component theses relate to each other?
10. Explain the objections of Plato, Zera Yacob, and Kierkegaard to divine command theory. How should a divine command theorist respond, in your view?
11. A classic objection to utilitarianism: You arrive in a small village in a country torn by civil war. An army captain has lined 20 innocent villagers up against a wall and is about to order them shot. He offers a deal: If you shoot one, he will set the others free. Otherwise, all will die. The villagers and their families and friends beg you to accept. What should you do? What would utilitarianism advise you to do?

Terms for Review

actual obligation Something I really am, all things considered, obliged to do.

act-utilitarianism A moral theory that judges individual actions directly by their effects on the amount of good.

autonomy Living by the rule we establish for ourselves.

Carvaka Also called *lokayata,* a term meaning "those attached to the ways of the world," a group of ancient Indian philosophers who are materialists, empiricists, and skeptics.

categorical imperative An 'ought' statement without an 'if', applying universally, without regard to circumstances, goals, or desires. In Kant, the categorical imperative is the one moral axiom from which other moral imperatives can be derived as theorems.

communitarian consequentialism The view that good acts are those that maximize the well-being of society, where that is understood as independent of the well-being of its individual members.

communitarianism The view that the good of the community does not reduce to the good of its members.

consequentialism The view that all moral value rests ultimately on the consequences of actions.

deontological theory A moral theory holding that moral value rests at least in part on something other than the consequences of actions.

divine command theory The view that God distinguishes right from wrong. What God commands is obligatory; what God allows is permissible; what God forbids is wrong.

dukkha Pain, suffering, being out of joint.

dynamic idealism As an idealist, Wang Yangming maintains that everything is mind-dependent; as he puts it, "nothing is external to the mind."

ethical intuitionism The view that conscience is the only reliable practical guide to what to do.

externalism The view that moral imperatives do not necessarily give reasons for acting.

hedonism The view that only pain and pleasure are sources of value.

heteronomy Following someone else's command.

hypothetical imperative An 'ought' statement, such as "You ought to work hard if you want to succeed," containing an 'if' and depending on circumstances or someone's goals and desires.

imperfect duty A general obligation, allowing an agent choice about when and how to fulfill it.

individualism The view that the good of the community is nothing but the sum of the goods of its members.

internalism The view that moral imperatives necessarily give reasons for acting.

justice (*yi*) A virtue akin to piety, correctness, and justice in ancient Chinese thought, stressed especially by Mencius and Mozi.

karma Habit.

maxim "A subjective principle of action," a rule an act falls under that reflects the agent's intention but abstracts from morally irrelevant details.

Moism An ancient Chinese version of consequentialism developed by Mozi to oppose Confucianism.

moral (or **felicific) calculus** Bentham's method of computing the moral value of possible actions.

moral sense A faculty that enables us to perceive the moral qualities of things.

Noble Eightfold Path The Buddha's recommended way of living: right thought, right resolve, right speech, right conduct, right livelihood, right effort, right mindfulness, and right concentration or meditation.

perfect duty A specific obligation to specific people, giving those people rights that the duty be performed.

pluralism The thesis that morality rests on goods, values, principles, or feelings that differ in kind.

***prima facie* obligation** Something I am obliged to do, all other things being equal, if nothing intervenes.

principle of utility The thesis that we ought to maximize good; the sole axiom of morality, according to utilitarians.

righteousness (*yi*) A virtue akin to piety, correctness, and justice in ancient Chinese thought, stressed especially by Mencius and Mozi.

rule-utilitarianism A moral theory that judges particular actions indirectly by appeal to rules that are themselves justified as maximizing the good.

secondary principles In Mill, commonsense rules such as "Do not murder," "Do not steal," and so on, that give us moral guidance and follow from the principle of utility.

supererogatory act An act that goes above the call of duty—in a utilitarian context, doing more for the happiness of the community than morality requires.

tanha Selfish desire; craving; coveting; the cause of suffering.

teleological suspension of the ethical Setting morality aside for the higher purpose of following God.

universalism The view that we must consider the consequences of an action for everyone it affects.

utilitarianism The view that we ought to maximize good.

***yi* (righteousness)** A virtue akin to piety, correctness, and justice in ancient Chinese thought, stressed especially by Mencius and Mozi.

For Further Reading

An excellent overview of ethical theory is William Frankena, *Ethics* (Englewood Cliffs: Prentice-Hall, 1973). A comprehensive review of contemporary work on ethics and varieties of ethical theories is Peter Singer (ed.), *A Companion to Ethics* (Cambridge: Blackwell, 1991, 1993).

For general reading on Buddhism, see Chapter 4; on ethics specifically, see Hammalawa Saddhatissa, *Buddhist Ethics* (London: Wisdom, 1987).

On Hume, see J. L. Mackie, *Hume's Moral Theory* (London: Routledge and Kegan Paul, 1981). Recent versions of intuitionism include H. A. Pritchard, *Moral Obligation* (New York: Oxford University Press, 1949) and Jonathan Dancy, *Moral Reasons* (Oxford: Blackwell, 1993).

Recent Kantian approaches to moral theory include Stephen Darwall, *Impartial Reason* (Ithaca: Cornell University Press, 1983); Onora O'Neill, *Constructions of Reason: Explorations in Kant's Practical Philosophy* (New York: Cambridge University Press, 1989); Christine Korsgaard, *Creating the Kingdom of Ends* and *The Sources of Normativ-*

ity (Cambridge: Cambridge University Press, 1996); and David Brink, *Moral Realism and the Foundations of Ethics* (Cambridge: Cambridge University Press, 1989).

Good recent discussions of utilitarianism are J. J. C. Smart and Bernard Williams, *Utilitarianism: For and Against* (Cambridge: Cambridge University Press, 1982); Amartya Sen and Bernard Williams, *Utilitarianism and Beyond* (Cambridge: Cambridge University Press, 1982); and Samuel Scheffler (ed.), *Consequentialism and Its Critics* (Oxford: Oxford University Press, 1988). Recent defenders of utilitarian approaches are Richard Brandt, *A Theory of the Good and the Right* (New York: Oxford University Press, 1979) and Samuel Scheffler, *The Rejection of Consequentialism* (Oxford: Oxford University Press, 1982).

Sympathetic treatments of Kierkegaard are Louis Mackey, *Kierkegaard: A Kind of Poet* (Philadelphia: University of Pennsylvania Press, 1971) and Josiah Thompson, *Kierkegaard* (New York: Knopf, 1973).

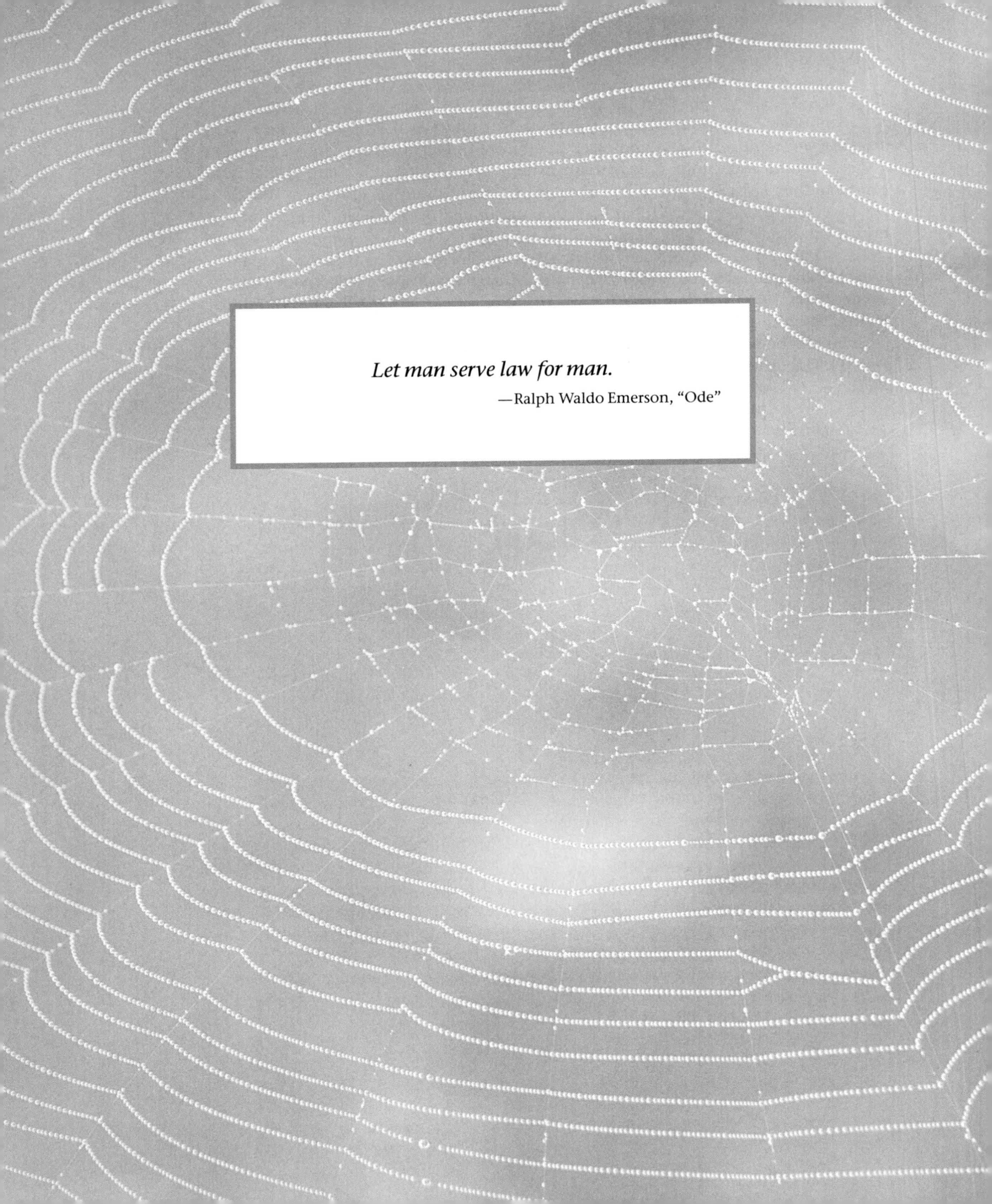

Let man serve law for man.

—Ralph Waldo Emerson, "Ode"

CHAPTER 9

Politics

Politics, Aristotle maintains, is in a sense the highest art; it is the art of the highest ends achievable by action. If How should I live? and What kind of person should I be? are the most fundamental practical questions a person can raise, How should we live together? and What kind of community should we be? are the most fundamental questions that a group of people can raise. These questions entail others, such as What is justice? How can it best be achieved? What is freedom? What are its limits? This chapter surveys some of the most important answers that political philosophers have given to these questions. As we shall see, their answers generally depend on conceptions of human nature. This is not surprising; how we should live together depends on who and what we are and what we can be.

POLITICAL VIRTUE

The question How should we live together? quickly divides into various other questions. To answer it, we need to know what rules, if any, we should live under and expect each other to follow. We need to know who has and ought to have the authority to make those rules, enforce them, and judge disagreements arising under them. We need to know what punishments may be imposed on those who violate the rules. We need to know how to construct a society that distributes both the benefits and the responsibilities of society fairly. And we need to know how to set things right again when something goes wrong.

Broadly speaking, these questions fall into two groups: questions of political authority or legitimacy and questions of justice. The first set of questions asks under what circumstances one person can have legitimate political authority over another—authority to make rules, enforce laws, judge disagreements, punish, and so on. The second set asks what it is to do these things justly. There is a connection between these questions but no consensus about exactly what the connection is. (Aristotle, for example, sees the second as the key to answering the first, for he thinks we should grant authority to those most likely to exercise it justly in order to further the ultimate end of political science, the happiness of the community. An advocate of pure democracy might hold, conversely, that justice is simply whatever the majority dictates. As we shall see, there are many intermediate and more complicated connections that have been drawn.) But the questions of political authority and justice are nonetheless separable. The right person may do the wrong thing, and the wrong person may do the right thing. That is, someone who exercises political authority legitimately may nevertheless exercise it unjustly in a particular case, and someone lacking proper political authority may nevertheless act justly in particular cases. *Who* should rule, and *how* they should rule, are different questions.

Aristotle

Aristotle (384–322 B.C.E.; see Chapter 1) bases his ethical theory, as we have seen, on the idea of virtue as human excellence. The ultimate end of human activity is happiness, understood in a broad sense of living well. To live well, we must perform our function well; our function, in turn, is rational activity, activity guided by a rational plan. Virtue is fulfilling this function well.

There are many different virtues, for humans engage in many kinds of activities and have many natural inclinations. To be virtuous is to give in to our natural inclinations at the right time, to the right extent, in the right circumstances, and for the right reason. To have a particular virtue is to do this with respect to a given natural inclination or in a given range of circumstances.

Justice, broadly understood, is virtue in relation to other people. It is, in a sense, Aristotle says, the whole of virtue, for it involves finding the mean with respect to all our natural inclinations and in all circumstances involving others.

How does justice relate to virtue as a whole, in Aristotle's view?

> . . . in one sense we call those acts just that tend to produce and preserve happiness and its components for the political society. And the law bids us do both the acts of a brave man (e.g. not to desert our post nor take to flight nor throw away our arms), and those of a temperate man (e.g. not to commit adultery nor to gratify one's lust), and those of a good-tempered man (e.g. not to strike another nor to speak evil), and similarly with regard to the other virtues and forms of wickedness, commanding some acts and forbidding others; and the rightly framed law does this rightly, and the hastily conceived one less well.
>
> This form of justice, then, is complete virtue, but not absolutely, but in relation to our neighbour. And therefore justice is often thought to be the greatest of virtues, and "neither evening star nor morning star" is so wonderful; and proverbially "in justice is every virtue comprehended." And it is complete virtue in its fullest sense, because it is the actual exercise of complete virtue. It is complete because he who possesses it can exercise his virtue not only in himself but toward his neighbour also; for many men can exercise virtue in their own affairs, but not in relations to their neighbour. This is why the saying of Bias is thought to be true, that "rule will show the man"; for a ruler is necessarily in relation to other men and a member of society. For this same reason justice, alone of the virtues, is thought to be "another's good," because it is related to our neighbour; for it does what is advantageous to another. . . . Justice in this sense, then, is not part of virtue but virtue entire, nor is the contrary injustice a part of vice but vice entire. What the difference is between virtue and justice is plain from what we have said; they are the same but their essence is not the same; what, as a relation to one's neighbor, is justice is, as a certain kind of state without qualification, virtue.[1]

The ideal ruler would of course rule justly and thus excel in justice, which is to say, in virtue in general. Slightly more specifically, the ideal ruler would excel in exer-

[1] This and subsequent quotations from Aristotle, unless otherwise noted, are from the *Nicomachean Ethics*, translated by W. D. Ross, in *The Works of Aristotle* (Oxford: Oxford University Press, 1908), Book V, Chapter 1.

cising political authority justly, promoting the happiness of the entire community. Excellence in exercising political authority is what Aristotle calls **political virtue.**

There is a simple answer, then, to the question of political authority, the question of who should rule: those with the most political virtue. A utilitarian might justify this answer by saying that the proper goal of morality and politics is to maximize the happiness of the community. Political virtue is the talent for exercising authority to maximize the community's happiness. Therefore, political authority should go to those with the most political virtue. But Aristotle is no utilitarian. His justification concerns the nature of virtue itself.

Aristotle's view that political authority should be proportional to political virtue seems plausible. Who should rule? Those who can do the best job of ruling. In a democracy, for whom should we vote? The candidates who can do the best job. It is hard to disagree. But Aristotle applied this in some unsavory ways. He thought that some people had so little political virtue that enslaving them was justifiable. He thought that men had so much more political virtue than women that politics should be strictly a male province. These views were not unusual at the time; it would be more than two thousand years before Western nations abolished slavery and granted women the right to vote and run for office. Even today, there are societies that accept slavery and deny women basic human rights. What does this tell us about the acceptability of Aristotle's theory? Slavery and patriarchy do not follow from the theory alone; they depend on the factual premises that some people lack political virtue altogether and that men have much more political virtue than women do. Today, we reject those factual assumptions. We hold that almost everyone (that is, every adult who is not seriously mentally deficient and who has not been convicted of serious crimes) has some political virtue, for example, and that the sexes are more or less equal in political virtue. In conjunction with those assumptions, Aristotle's theory implies that almost everyone should have some political power, and that men and women should have equal political rights and responsibilities.

Alhough in one sense justice comprises the whole of virtue, there are more specific senses of justice that are important in any political system. **Retributory justice** concerns punishment: What punishments may be imposed under what conditions and for what infractions? This sort of punishment is the chief business of the criminal law. **Compensatory** or **rectificatory justice** concerns compensation: How do we compensate people for injury? Once a wrong has occurred, how do we set things right again? This is the chief business of the law of torts. **Distributive** justice concerns the distribution of goods and responsibilities in society. It is the chief business of the law of property and contracts, and, very importantly, it is fundamental to the question of political authority. For we can ask about the distribution of political power and responsibilities as well as about the distribution of economic benefits and responsibilities. A full account of justice includes an account of distributive justice, which includes an account of the distribution of political powers and responsibilities. Thus, from Aristotle's point of view, the question of justice includes the question of political authority.

What, for Aristotle, is distributive justice? How should the goods and responsibilities of society be distributed among its members? Aristotle's answer is familiar to us from small-scale problems of distribution. In a given class, who deserves the best grades? The best students: those who do the best on exams, write the best papers, and so on. Who deserves to make the football team? The best players: those who do the most to help the team win. Which team deserves to win the championship? The best team: the one that wins the most games. In many contexts, we tend to think that rewards should go to people who deserve them by being the best in the relevant measure. That is exactly Aristotle's view.

> If, then, the unjust is unequal, the just is equal, as all men suppose it to be, even apart from argument. And since the equal is intermediate, the just will be an intermediate. . . . The just, therefore, involves at least four terms; for the persons for whom it is in fact just are two, and the things in which it is manifested, the objects distributed, are two. And the same equality will exist between the persons and between the things concerned; for as the latter—the things concerned—are related, so are the former; if they are not equal, they will not have what is equal, but this is the origin of quarrels and complaints—when either equals have and are awarded unequal shares, or unequals equal shares. Further, this is plain from the fact that awards should be "according to merit"; for all men agree that what is just in distribution must be according to merit in some sense. . . .
>
> This, then, is what the just is—the proportional; and unjust is what violates the proportion. Hence one term becomes too great, the other too small, as indeed happens in practice; for the man who acts unjustly has too much, and the man who is unjustly treated too little, of what is good.

Aristotle's idea is clear: a just proportion proceeds according to a ratio:

$$\frac{\text{A's share}}{\text{B's share}} = \frac{\text{A's merit}}{\text{B's merit}}$$

or, equivalently,

$$\frac{\text{A's share}}{\text{A's merit}} = \frac{\text{B's share}}{\text{B's merit}}$$

But how do we determine a person's degree of merit? Aristotle gives an example:

> All men think justice to be a sort of equality. . . . equals ought to have equality. But there still remains a question: equality or inequality of what? . . . When a number of flute players are equal in their art, there is no reason why those of them who are better born should have better flutes given to them; for they will not play any better on the flute, and the superior instrument should be reserved for him who is the superior artist.[2]

The picture is this. There are various kinds of goods, and various kinds of merit. The distribution of goods of a certain kind should take place according to merit of a corresponding kind. The best flutes, for example, should go to the best flute players. The best grades should go to the best students. The championship should go to the best team. There is no single measure of merit, for not all goods are commensurable; it is

[2] Aristotle, *Politics,* from *The Works of Aristotle,* Volume X (Oxford: Clarendon, 1921), translated by Benjamin Jowett.

not true, Aristotle says, that "any good may be compared with any other." Some people excel in flute playing; they should get the best flutes. Others excel in athletic ability; they should get to play on the team. Still others excel in political virtue; they should get the offices that give them the responsibility and power to make decisions to promote the common good.

Al-Farabi

Al-Farabi (Abu Nasr Muhammad al-Farabi, 870?–950), of Turkish descent, was born in Transoxania, now part of Uzbekistan in central Asia. He studied in Khorasan (covering parts of present-day Iran and Afghanistan) and Baghdad. Many of his teachers were from the Alexandrian School, which moved to Antioch and then Harran after the Muslim conquest of Alexandria. He combined elements from Plato, Aristotle, and neo-Platonic philosophers such as Philo into the first of what would be several great philosophical systems produced by medieval Islamic philosophers.

As we have seen in Chapter 7, Plato and Aristotle both stress the importance of virtue. But they offer different accounts of it. For the early Plato, virtue is a kind of knowledge, the knowledge of good and evil. The good person knows what to pursue and what to shun and does it. Vice is a kind of ignorance: bad people do wrong because they don't know any better. For Aristotle, this is not so. It is possible for people to exhibit weakness of will, to know what is right but not do it. Virtue requires knowledge, but it also requires action. Plato assumes that all goods and evils are comparable, but Aristotle does not. There are many different goods that constitute happiness. There is no rule for comparing them. Virtue thus requires training. A good person must develop the ability to perceive what is right and wrong in particular situations. A person with political virtue can do this in political matters involving the welfare of the entire community.

Al-Farabi combines these accounts into his own distinctive political philosophy. Aristotle distinguishes intellectual virtues, which are matters of knowledge and can be taught, from practical or moral virtues, which are matters of putting knowledge into practice and cannot strictly speaking be taught. What is the link between these virtues? What, that is, takes us from knowledge to action? Aristotle's answer is deliberation. Al-Farabi agrees, speaking of the deliberative faculty. But he gives a distinctively Platonic account of it. The deliberative faculty, he says, is "the skill and the faculty by which one discovers and discerns the variable accidents of the intelligibles whose particular instances are made to exist by the will."[3] In different language, it is the ability to recognize the properties of the results of actions. As al-Farabi elaborates the point, deliberation requires knowing what ends to pursue and what means will achieve those ends. To deliberate, in other words, you need to know what you want to accomplish and what you can do to accomplish it.

This seems reasonable enough. But al-Farabi's definition has the consequence that deliberation is a kind of knowledge. Since deliberation provides the link between

---

[3] This and subsequent passages from Al-Farabi are from *The Attainment of Happiness,* from *Alfarabi's Philosophy of Plato and Aristotle,* translated by Muhsin Mahdi (New York: Free Press, 1962).

knowledge and action, deliberative virtue—excellence at deliberation—is all you need for practical or moral virtue. Moral virtue is deliberative virtue, and deliberative virtue is knowledge. Thus, moral virtue itself becomes a kind of knowledge. Intellectual virtue, deliberative virtue, and moral virtue all go hand in hand.

> . . . the deliberative virtue cannot be separated from the theoretical virtue. It follows that the theoretical virtue, the leading deliberative virtue, the leading moral virtue, and the leading practical art are inseparable from each other. . . .

This makes sense from the perspective of Plato's view in the early dialogues. There, virtue is a kind of knowledge.

From Aristotle's perspective, however, this seems unsatisfying. We sought the link between knowledge and action and seem to have found more knowledge. Does deliberative virtue really suffice for moral virtue? How does the knowledge involved in deliberation trigger action? There must be, al-Farabi concludes, some other kind of virtue that combines with deliberative virtue to produce good action. Since reasoning about means does seem to be a matter of knowledge, this other kind of virtue comes into play in thinking about ends:

What is natural virtue, and how does it relate to other kinds of virtue?

> . . . there must be some other moral virtue—other, that is, than the one discovered by the deliberative virtue—which accompanies the deliberative virtue and enables the possessor of the deliberative virtue to wish the good and the virtuous end. *That* virtue must be *natural* and must come into being by nature, and it must be coupled with a certain deliberative virtue [that is, *cleverness*] which comes into being by nature and discovers the moral virtues formed by the will.

We are innately disposed to pursue certain ends. That natural virtue combines with deliberation to produce action. So, the ultimate link between knowledge and action is not deliberation as such but natural virtue.

What is natural virtue? To some extent, it is an inborn trait we have as humans. Just as lions tend to act courageously and foxes tend to act cunningly, humans tend to pursue certain ends. But people differ in which ends they are disposed to pursue and how strongly and persistently they tend to pursue them. Some people are thus more naturally virtuous than others. Al-Farabi concludes:

> Therefore the prince occupies his place by nature and not merely by will. . . . This being the case, the theoretical virtue, the highest deliberative virtue, the highest moral virtue, and the highest practical art are realized in those equipped for them by nature; that is, in those who possess superior natures with very great potentialities.

Great moral virtue, that is, requires excellence in knowledge—intellectual or theoretical virtue, and also deliberative virtue—as well as great natural virtue. It seems as if one could excel at one of these without the other; at any rate al-Farabi gives no argument against this possibility. But one must excel at both to have superior moral virtue.

How does all this pertain to politics? The ideal ruler would be able to make decisions that benefit the community. That requires moral and theoretical excellence. If the philosopher is one who excels in theoretical virtue, then, the ruler should be a philosopher.

> To be a truly perfect philosopher one has to possess both the theoretical sciences and the faculty for exploiting them for the benefit of all others according to their capacity. Were one to consider the case of the true philosopher, he would find no difference between him and the supreme ruler. For he who possesses the faculty for exploiting what is comprised by the theoretical matters for the benefit of all others possesses the faculty for making such matters intelligible as well as for bringing into actual existence those of them that depend on the will. The greater his power to do the latter, the more perfect is his philosophy. Therefore he who is truly perfect possesses with sure insight, first, the theoretical virtues, and subsequently the practical. Moreover, he possesses the capacity for bringing them about in nations and cities in the manner and the measure possible with reference to each. Since it is impossible for him to possess the faculty for bringing them about except by employing certain demonstrations, persuasive methods, as well as methods that represent things through images, and this either with the consent of others or by compulsion, it follows that the true philosopher is himself the supreme ruler.

How does al-Farabi argue that the true philosopher is the supreme ruler?

The true philosopher and the supreme ruler are thus the same. Moreover, persuasion requires the use of images as well as arguments, and this, al-Farabi observes, is the role of religion. The ideal ruler persuades people to do what they can do to promote the happiness of the community, and this requires an excellence at prompting the religious imagination as well as excellence at rational persuasion.

> It follows, then, that the idea of *Imam,* Philosopher, and Legislator is a single idea.

The religious leader, the *Imam,* is "one whose example is followed and who is well received." But being well received requires full use of the talents of the philosopher, religious leader, and supreme ruler. Al-Farabi's Platonic Aristotelianism thus yields a political philosophy that vests ultimate power in a single person, the person who most excels in intellectual virtues, practical virtues, and the understanding of religion and religious imagery. He provides the theoretical underpinnings of theocratic rule, which still exerts great influence in Islamic countries around the globe.

NATURAL LAW

In Western Europe, political philosophers took Aristotelian insights in a very different direction. Al-Farabi developed a theory of natural *virtue.* European philosophers developed on Aristotle's foundation a theory of natural *law.*

As we have seen, Aristotle considers happiness to be the ultimate intrinsic good, the one thing always desired for its own sake and never for the sake of something else. Happiness, in turn, is living well, fulfilling the function of a human being well. Our function stems from our nature—to act rationally. So happiness, above all, is manifested in rational activity. What we ought to do, moreover, follows from our nature as rational beings.

Thomas Aquinas

St. Thomas Aquinas (1224–1274; see Chapter 1) bases his views on ethics and political philosophy on those of Aristotle. But he adds many innovations, blending

Aristotelian insights into a Christian worldview. He develops a comprehensive theory of natural law that remains influential today. Aquinas begins with Aristotle's idea that human good depends on human nature. To live well—to excel or flourish—is to fulfill one's function well. Just as an excellent knife cuts well and an excellent eye sees well, an excellent human being displays excellence in rational activity. As these examples suggest, different things have different functions. In general, the function of a thing depends on its nature. So what something ought to do and be depends on its function, which in turn depends on its nature.

Aquinas adds God to this Aristotelian picture. God establishes the order of nature, determining the natures of things. God thus indirectly establishes not only the physical laws that constitute the order of nature but also the *natural laws* that free beings ought to obey. Since human nature is distinctively rational, law itself is essentially a matter of reason.

> It belongs to the law to command and to forbid. But it belongs to reason to command, as stated above. Therefore, law is something pertaining to reason.
>
> Law is a certain rule and measure of acts that induces people to act or refrain from acting, for *lex* [law] comes from *ligare* [to bind], because it binds one to act. Now the rule and measure of human acts is reason, the first principle of human acts . . . since it belongs to reason to direct to the end, which is the first principle in all matters of action, according to the Philosopher [Aristotle]. (Q. 90, A. 1)[4]

Aquinas distinguishes several different kinds of law. **Eternal law** is the law of nature, established by God, that governs the entire universe. Everything in the universe obeys eternal law, and does so necessarily. Science investigates eternal law and tries to describe it. **Natural law** is normative; it prescribes what things should do and be. Since a thing's nature determines its function and, thus, its virtue—what it ought to do and be—eternal law determines natural law. Natural law is the manifestation of eternal law in creatures capable of rational choice and activity.

How does natural law relate to eternal law?

> Law, being a rule and measure, can be in someone in two ways: (a) as in him that rules and measures; (b) as in what is ruled and measured; a thing is ruled and measured to the extent that it partakes of a rule or measure. So, since all things subject to divine providence are ruled and measured by the eternal law, all things partake to some extent of the eternal law—to the extent, namely, that it is imprinted on them, they derive their inclinations to their proper acts and ends. Now the rational creature is subject to divine providence in a more excellent way than anything else, for it partakes of a share of providence, by being provident both for itself and for others. So, it has a share of the eternal reason, whereby it has a natural inclination to its proper act and end. This participation in the eternal law in the rational creature is called the *natural law.* Hence the Psalmist, after saying "offer up the sacrifice of justice," as though someone asked what the works of justice are, adds: "Many

[4]This and subsequent quotations are from Thomas Aquinas, *Summa Theologica,* my translation (Rome: Ex typographica Senatus, 1886–1887; for English translations, see New York, Benziger Bros., 1947–48; Westminster: Christian Classics, 1948), I, II. Citations in the text give the question and article number (in this case, for example, 'Q. 90, A. 1' indicates question 90, article 1). Incidentally, Suárez disputes Aquinas's etymology, citing Cicero and Augustine, who contend that *lex* derives from *lectio* or *legendo,* whose root is *legere* [to read]. Modern scholarship supports Suárez, Cicero, and Augustine on this point.

> say, 'Who shows us good things?'." In answer, he says: "The light of your countenance, O Lord, is signed upon us." This implies that the light of natural reason, by which we discern what is good and what is evil, which pertains to the natural law, is nothing else than an imprint on us of the divine light. It is therefore evident that the natural law is nothing other than the rational creature's participation in the eternal law. (Q. 91, A. 2)

Natural law manifests the eternal law by way of "the light of natural reason." God imprints on us the natural ability to tell right from wrong.

Aquinas also distinguishes natural law from human law. Natural law is fully general and universal, but human law must apply to particular circumstances in specific ways. Natural law relates to human law, then, as principles relate to conclusions drawn from them:

In what sense do human laws rest on natural law?

> A law is a certain dictate of practical reason. Now evidently the same procedure takes place in practical and in speculative reason, for each goes from principles to conclusions. In speculative reason, we draw the conclusions of the various sciences from naturally known indemonstrable principles. The knowledge of them is not imparted to us by nature but acquired by the efforts of reason. So too it is from the precepts of the natural law, as from general and indemonstrable principles, that human reason needs to proceed to certain particular determinations of the laws. These particular determinations, devised by human reason, are called human laws. . . . (Q. 91, A. 3)

One can think of natural law, then, as comprising the axioms of the moral law in general.

Because natural law serves as an axiom of the moral law, it must be self-evident; it cannot be a conclusion from some other premise.

> The precepts of the natural law are to practical reason what the first principles of demonstrations are to speculative reason, because both are self-evident principles. (Q. 94, A. 2)

Precepts of natural law must be both general and obvious:

> Consequently, the first principle in practical reason is one founded on the notion of good: namely, that good is what all things seek. Hence this is the first precept of law: Good is to be done and pursued, and evil is to be avoided. All other precepts of natural law are based on this. So, whatever practical reason naturally apprehends as man's good [or evil] belongs to the precepts of natural law as something to be done or avoided. (Q. 94, A. 2)

It might seem that natural law has little content. Pursue good; avoid evil. Everyone can agree to that. But what is good? What is evil?

Here, Aquinas appeals to human nature. As Aristotle argued, human excellence depends on our characteristic function, which depends in turn on our nature. This is true in two senses. What we are determines what we ought to do and be. And what we are *tells* us what we ought to do and be. The universe is ordered so that we naturally tend to pursue good and avoid evil. Our own dispositions thus provide a test. We are naturally disposed to pursue good and avoid evil.

> Good has the nature of an end, and evil the nature of a contrary. Hence, all those things to which people have a natural inclination are naturally apprehended by reason as being good and, consequently, as objects of pursuit. Their contraries are naturally apprehended as evil and objects of avoidance. So, the order of the precepts of natural law follows the order of natural inclinations. (Q. 94, A 2)

Aquinas classifies the precepts of natural law into three groups: (1) laws of self-preservation; (2) laws of biological welfare; and (3) laws of reason.

> First, people have an inclination to good in accordance with the nature they have in common with all substances. Every substance seeks the preservation of its own being according to its nature. By reason of this inclination, whatever preserves human life and wards off its obstacles belongs to the natural law. Second, people have an inclination to things that pertain to them more specially according to that nature which they have in common with other animals. In virtue of this inclination, those things are said to belong to the natural law "which nature has taught to all animals," such as sexual intercourse, the education of offspring, and so on. Third, people have an inclination to good according to the nature of their reason, which is proper to them. Thus, people have a natural inclination to know the truth about God and to live in society. In this respect, whatever pertains to this inclination belongs to natural law: for instance, to shun ignorance, to avoid offending those among whom one has to live, and other such things. (Q. 94, A. 2)

One might crudely misread Aquinas as advocating following your own inclinations, doing whatever you feel like doing. That is not what he means. We have a natural tendency to pursue good and shun evil. But that does not mean that all inclinations reflect that tendency. We have a natural tendency not only to have certain inclinations (toward food, drink, and sex, for example), but also to control them through the exercise of reason. If lust is natural, so are rationality, shame, and self-restraint. As Aquinas says:

What distinction is Aquinas drawing? What does it explain?

> [St. John] Damascene says that "virtues are natural."[5] Therefore virtuous acts are also a subject of natural law.
>
> We may speak of virtuous acts in two ways: first, as being virtuous; secondly, as being such and such acts. If, then, we speak of acts of virtue considered as virtuous, all virtuous acts belong to natural law. For to natural law belongs everything to which people are naturally inclined. Now each thing inclines naturally to what is suitable to it according to its form. Thus, fire is inclined to give heat. So, since the rational soul is the proper form of a human being, people have a natural inclination to act according to reason. This is to act according to virtue. Consequently, considered in this way, all acts of virtue are prescribed by natural law, since each one's reason naturally dictates to him to act virtuously. But if we speak of virtuous acts considered in themselves, that is, in their proper species, not all virtuous acts are prescribed by natural law; many things are done virtuously to which nature

[5] St. John Damascene (700?–754?), *De fide orthodoxa* I, 5; in J. P. Migne (ed.), *Patrologia Latina* (Paris: Garnier fratres et J.-P. Migne successores, 1879), 32, 1228.

> does not incline us at first, but which, through the inquiry of reason, we have found conducive to living well. (Q. 94, A. 3)

Aquinas does not develop his theory of natural law into a comprehensive political philosophy. Nevertheless, several important theses follow from it.

First, human law aims at the common good.

> Law, properly speaking, regards first and foremost an ordering of the common good. (Q. 90, A. 3)
>
> Whatever is for an end should be proportioned to it. Now the end of law is the common good, because, as Isidore says, "Law should be framed, not for any private benefit, but for the common good of all the citizens."[6] Hence human laws should be proportioned to the common good. (Q. 96, A. 1)

Second, the purpose of human law is to help people follow natural law, that is, to make them virtuous. Law is essentially *paternalistic,* restricting people's freedom for their own good.

> The proper effect of law is to lead its subjects to their proper virtue. Since virtue is "what makes its subjects good," it follows that the proper effect of law is to make its subjects good, either simply or in some particular respect. (Q. 92, A. 1)

The law accomplishes this by training people to recognize right and wrong.

> People have a natural aptitude for virtue, but the perfection of virtue must be acquired by a kind of training. . . . Now, it is hard to see how a man could train himself, since the perfection of virtue consists chiefly in withdrawing him from undue pleasures, to which, above all, he is inclined. This is especially true of the young, who are more capable of being trained. Consequently, a man needs to receive this training from another to arrive at the perfection of virtue. Some young people are inclined to acts of virtue by their good natural disposition or by custom, or rather by the gift of God. For them, paternal training suffices, which is by warnings. But some are depraved, prone to vice, and not easily amenable to words. It is necessary for them to be restrained from evil by force and fear in order that they might at least desist from evil-doing and leave others in peace. They themselves, by being habituated in this way, might be brought to do willingly what they earlier did from fear and thus become virtuous. Now this kind of training, which compels through fear of punishment, is the discipline of laws. (Q. 95, A. 1)

Third, human law must be flexible. As Aristotle said, virtue is a mean; there is no strict rule for finding it. Human laws cannot take into account the full complexity of the world; they inevitably oversimplify. We must create law to regulate our behavior but also must allow for exceptions in those cases in which the law does not make sense.

---

[6] St. Isodore of Seville (560?–636), *Etymologiarum Libri* V, 21; in J. P. Migne (ed.), *Patrologia Latina* (Paris: Garnier fratres et J.-P. Migne successores, 1879), 82, 203.

> Practical reason concerns contingent matters, as do human actions. Consequently, though the general principles are necessary, the more we descend to matters of detail, the more frequently we encounter deviations. . . .
>
> Thus it is right and true for all to act according to reason. From this principle, it follows that goods entrusted to someone else should be restored to their owner. Now this is true for the majority of cases, but it may happen in a particular case that it would be harmful, and therefore unreasonable, to restore goods held in trust: for instance, if they are claimed for the purpose of fighting against one's country. (Q. 94, A. 4)

One might think that we may solve this problem by making law more specific. We might, for example, require people to return goods held in trust unless such return poses a risk to national security. But this only makes the problem worse. We are better off with general laws, flexibly applied.

> This principle will be found to fail more often as we descend further into detail: for example, if one were to say that goods held in trust should be restored with such and such a guarantee or in such and such a way. The greater the number of conditions added, the greater the number of ways in which the principle may fail, so that it is not right to restore or not to restore. (Q. 94, A. 4)

Fourth, a law that is unjust or fails to promote the common good, in general or in a particular case, has no authority as law. It should not be obeyed.

Under what circumstances should we disobey the law? Why?

> A tyrannical law, through not being according to reason, is not a law, absolutely speaking, but rather a perversion of law. . . . (Q. 92, A. 1)
>
> Every law is directed to the common welfare of people and derives the force and nature of law accordingly. But it has no power to oblige morally if it is not so directed. Hence the Jurist says: "By no reason of law or favor of equity may we interpret harshly and render burdensome those useful measures enacted for the welfare of man."[7] Now, often the observance of some point of law conduces to the common welfare in the majority of instances, and yet in some cases is very harmful. Since, then, lawgivers cannot have in view every single case, they shape the law according to what happens most frequently, by directing their attention to the common good. So, if a case arises where the observance of that law would be harmful to the general welfare, it should not be observed. For instance, suppose that, in a city under siege, there is a law that the gates of the city must be kept closed. This is good for public welfare as a general rule. But if the enemy were in pursuit of certain citizens defending the city, it would be a great loss to the city if the gates were not opened to them. So, in that case, the gates ought to be opened, contrary to the letter of the law, in order to maintain the common welfare, which the lawgivers had in view. (Q. 96, A. 6)

Aquinas's words have inspired various thinkers who have used civil disobedience as a means of social change. Reverend Martin Luther King, Jr., for example, wrote from the Birmingham Jail:

---

[7] Domitian Ulpian (170?–228), *Digest* I, 3, 25; in P. Kruger (ed.), *Corpus Juris Civilis* (Berlin: Weidmannos, 1899, 1928), 34b.

> One may well ask, "How can you advocate breaking some laws and obeying others?" The answer is found in the fact that there are two types of laws: There are just and there are unjust laws.
>
> To put it in the terms of St. Thomas Aquinas, an unjust law is a human law that is not rooted in eternal and natural law. Any law that uplifts human personality is just. Any law that degrades human personality is unjust. All segregation statutes are unjust because segregation distorts the soul and damages the personality.[8]

Finally, just as people have a natural inclination to virtue, they have a natural inclination to live in certain social structures: in families, in communities, and in a state. These social institutions are natural, not conventional; they thus have moral force. People are inherently social, as Aristotle observed. More specifically, they are naturally family members, members of communities, and citizens. Law, therefore, should serve to strengthen these natural institutions.

The idea that certain social institutions are natural and naturally conducive to human excellence marks an important divide between thinkers on the right and left of the political spectrum. Broadly speaking, conservative thinkers agree with Aquinas. They see the family and various other social institutions as natural and especially effective at promoting virtue. Liberal thinkers disagree; they see social institutions as malleable and find no reason to think that traditional arrangements are natural or especially suited to us as human beings. Indeed, they often find traditional arrangements oppressive.

Francisco Suárez

Aquinas founded a kind of philosophy known as **Scholasticism,** the Aristotelian philosophy of the Schools, that is, the universities of medieval Europe. It achieved its highest state of development in the work of Francisco Suárez (1548–1617), a contemporary of Shakespeare, Cervantes, El Greco, and St. Teresa of Avila. Suárez was born in Granada, Spain and, after a slow academic start, became a Jesuit priest and a professor of theology who taught at Segovia, Valladolid, Rome, Alcalá, and Evora. His works dominated university programs in philosophy and theology over the next two centuries, exerting substantial influence over such successors as Descartes and Leibniz.

Suárez adopts the basic outline of Aquinas's theory of natural law, which he initially defines as "that which is given all things by the inclination placed in them by the Author of nature."[9] But he finds this problematic, since sensual impulses are natural. In general, we have an inclination to sin. But "Sin!" is surely not a precept of natural law. It will not do, moreover, to treat our desire to sin as a punishment of original sin, for Adam himself must have had such an inclination, which moved him to sin in the first place. In short, Suárez thinks it is not easy to avoid the conclusion that you should do whatever you feel like doing if you begin with Aquinas's definition of natural law.

---

[8] Martin Luther King, Jr., "Letter from Birmingham City Jail" (Philadelphia: American Friends Service Committee, 1963).

[9] Francisco Suárez, *De Legibus* (Madrid: Consejo Superior de Investigaciones Cientificas, Instituto Francisco de Vitoria, 1971), I, i, 2 (my translation).

Suárez nevertheless quotes approvingly Augustine's view that natural law is "law that the Creator has written on the hearts of men" and takes seriously definitions of law as "a measure of rectitude" and "a right and honest rule" (I, i, 6). He distinguishes natural from positive law: positive law is law as it actually exists in a given society, while natural law is independent of enactments of a legislature or decrees of a Sovereign and exists in any society. Positive law varies from society to society, but natural law is universal, a "measure of moral action" that applies to anyone.

To understand natural law as universally binding without tying it to inclination, Suárez analyzes law as a mental act and treats law as essentially a matter of will rather than reason.

> Law is an act of a just and right will by which a superior wills to oblige his inferior to do this or that. (I, v, 24)

Natural law, for Suárez, is an idealized human law, human law imposed by a "just and right will." Interposing human will between eternal law and both natural and human law produces few immediate differences from Aquinas's account. But it introduces a major difference in perspective that profoundly influenced subsequent political philosophers. For Aquinas, law is essentially a matter of reason. For Suárez, it is essentially a matter of will—that is, of power. The power of law may be exercised wisely or unwisely, justly or unjustly, reasonably or oppressively. As a result, not only civil disobedience but rebellion can be justifiable in certain circumstances. Suárez foreshadows the contemporary distinction between authoritarian and totalitarian regimes when he distinguishes legitimate rulers who act tyrannically from tyrants who have usurped their power. The people may justifiably rebel against both. But they must abide by the general principles of just war in combating tyrannical but legitimate rulers. Illegitimate tyrants, in contrast, may be assassinated or removed from power by any means necessary. That had a significant impact on later political philosophers who were concerned to justify democratic revolutions. It also had an impact on Rousseau and Marx, who develop Suárez's distinction between superiors and inferiors into full-blown theories of class struggle.

AGGRESSION AND POLITICAL AUTHORITY

Aristotle, al-Farabi, Aquinas, and Suárez explicitly hold that the proper institutions, rules, and leadership of society depend on human nature. Government should promote human excellence, which depends on human nature. Most subsequent political philosophers have rejected that direct link between the goals of government and human nature. Nevertheless, there remains an indirect link. How we should live together depends on what kind of beings we are. In the rest of this chapter we shall examine three different conceptions of human nature and trace their implications for political authority and justice.

Xunzi

Xunzi (also known as Hsün Tzu; 310?–212? B.C.E.) offers a bleak portrait of human nature and politics. He was born in Zhao, one of the states that gave the Warring States period its name, in a time of intense regional conflict. Xunzi was an extremely talented student, leaving home at fifteen to study at Jixia academy, the intellectual center of ancient China. After establishing himself as the "most eminent elder scholar," he spent several years at the court of Qin, the most powerful of the warring states. Xunzi recognized that Qin, a wealthy but intellectually unsophisticated state that manifested none of the traditional Confucian virtues, nevertheless seemed both successful and well ordered. It had attracted a series of exceptionally brilliant ministers by operating as a meritocracy, granting advancement without regard to social class to those who demonstrated skill and achieved success.

Xunzi, a contemporary of Aristotle, adopts a naturalistic approach to philosophy. His ethical theory directly opposes that of Mencius (see Chapter 8). Confucius declares that all people are by nature alike but differ by training. Mencius amplifies this doctrine, claiming that everyone is by nature good. Xunzi argues, in contrast, that people are originally evil. Human nature, he insists, is entirely bad; everything good is acquired by education, training, or socialization. By nature, we are selfish, combative, envious, lecherous, and hostile. Xunzi's theory of human nature is remarkably similar to those of Western philosophers Niccolò Machiavelli (1469–1527) and Thomas Hobbes (1588–1679; see later in this section).

How is Xunzi arguing for the conclusion that human nature is evil?

> The nature of man is evil; the good which it shows is factitious. There belongs to it, even at his birth, the love of gain, and as actions are in accordance with this, contentions and robberies grow up, and self-denial and yielding to others are not to be found; there belong to it envy and dislike, and as actions are in accordance with these, violence and injuries spring up, and self-devotedness and faith are not to be found; there belong to it the desires of the ears and the eyes, leading to the love of sounds and beauty,[10] and as the actions are in accordance with these, lewdness and disorder spring up, and righteousness and propriety, with their various orderly displays, are not to be found. It thus appears, that to follow man's nature and yield obedience to his feelings will assuredly conduct to contentions and robberies, to the violation of the duties belonging to every one's lot, and the confounding of all distinctions, till the issue will be a state of savagism; and that there must be the influence of teachers and laws, and the guidance of propriety and righteousness, from which will spring self-denial, yielding to others, and an observance of the well-ordered regulations of conduct, till the issue will be a state of good government.—From all this it is plain that the nature of man is evil; the good which it shows is factitious.[11]

It is important to distinguish our natural dispositions from our natural capacities. Prior to training or education, we are disposed to evil. We nevertheless have the capacity for good. We can nurture and develop that capacity, becoming good in spite of our natures. But this requires effort.

How can we distinguish the natural from the artificial?

> Mencius said, "Man has only to learn, and his nature appears to be good;" but I reply—It is not so. To say so shows that he had not attained to a knowledge of man's

[10] Compare Plato's "lovers of sights and sounds," discussed in the *Republic*.

[11] Xunzi, "That the Nature Is Evil," edited and translated by James Legge, *The Chinese Classics*, Volume II (Oxford: Clarendon, 1895). In saying that good is factitious, Xunzi means that it is artificial, the product of effort and craft rather than nature.

> nature, nor examined into the difference between what is natural in man and what is factitious. The natural is what the constitution spontaneously moves to:—it needs not to be learned, it needs not to be followed hard after; propriety and righteousness are what the sages have given birth to:—it is by learning that men become capable of them, it is by hard practice that they achieve them. That which is in man, not needing to be learned and striven after, is what I call natural; that in man which is attained to by learning, and achieved by hard striving, is what I call factitious.

Xunzi thus opposes not only Mencius but also Taoism. For Lao Tzu, things, including people, naturally tend toward the good. This implies an ethics of noninterference; we should let things follow their natural courses. For Xunzi, in contrast, people naturally tend toward evil. This implies an ethic of active interference. People must be restrained from doing evil and taught to overcome their natural tendencies and become good.

> . . . the nature of man, being evil, must be submitted to teachers and laws, and then it becomes correct; it must be submitted to propriety and righteousness, and then it comes under government. If men were without teachers and laws, their condition would be one of deflection and insecurity, entirely incorrect; if they were without propriety and righteousness, their condition would be one of rebellious disorder, rejecting all government.

This need for restraint, according to Xunzi, justifies the existence of government. People can become good only with the help of rules of proper conduct and government to make them obey the rules. Eventually, the good person obeys the rules willingly, not from fear of being punished. But people can reach that state only through the training the rules provide.

> Let us suppose a state of things in which there shall be no majesty of rulers and governors, no influences of propriety and righteousness, no rule of laws and statutes, no restraints of punishment:—what would be the relations of men with one another, all under heaven? The strong would be injuring the weak, and spoiling them; the many would be tyrannizing over the few, and hooting them; a universal disorder and mutual destruction would speedily ensue.

Like Confucius, then, Xunzi stresses the importance of *li* (propriety), the observance of social rules. Confucius thinks of propriety as an individual virtue, an attitude or state of mind of respect for rules and traditions. Xunzi thinks of propriety much more as an external virtue akin to obedience, though, internalized, it turns one into a gentleman and ultimately a sage.

What is the function of the rules of proper conduct?

> Whence do the rules of proper conduct (*Li*) arise? Man by birth has desire. When desire is not satisfied, then he cannot be without a seeking for satisfaction. When this seeking for satisfaction is without measure or limits, then there cannot but be contention. When there is contention, there will be disorder; when there is disorder, then there will be poverty. The former Kings hated this confusion hence they established the rules of proper conduct and justice (*Yi*) in order to set limits to this confusion, to educate, and nourish men's desires, to give opportunity for this seeking of satisfaction, in order that desire should never be extinguished by things,

nor should things be used up by desire; that these two should support each other and should continue to exist. This is whence the rules of proper conduct arise.

Thus the rules of proper conduct are to educate and nourish. . . . The rules of proper conduct are the utmost of human morality (*Tao*). Moreover those who do not follow the rules of proper conduct neither are satisfied with it, are people without a direction in life; they who follow the rules of proper conduct and are satisfied with it are gentlemen who have a direction to their life.[12]

Thomas Hobbes

Thomas Hobbes (1588–1679), a contemporary of Descartes, Milton, Galileo, Rembrandt, and Anne Hutchinson, was born prematurely in Malmesbury, England, when his mother heard of the approach of the Spanish Armada. "Fear and I were born twins," he later quipped. His political philosophy shows it. Strikingly similar to Xunzi in his assessment of human nature and his justification for political authority, Hobbes offers a defense of monarchy. He tutored the future King Charles II in 1646–47 while both were in exile in Paris during Oliver Cromwell's rule. He returned to England when Charles II was restored to the throne in 1660.

Hobbes advances what has become known as **social contract theory.** What justifies political authority? What gives some the right to rule over others, establishing laws and punishing transgressors? The answer, according to social contract theory, is that people would voluntarily submit to such authority. Faced with a choice between living under government and living without it—in what Hobbes and later philosophers call the **state of nature**—we would choose government. It is rational, in short, to submit to political authority, for the alternative is anarchy and disorder, and that would be unpleasant indeed.

As we have seen, Xunzi holds that rules, government, and law are justified as ways of avoiding disorder. Hobbes agrees. But Hobbes has a somewhat subtler view of human nature. What would make the state of nature so unpleasant is not simply that human nature is evil. It is that people's desires would outstrip the resources available to satisfy them. The resulting condition of scarcity and the relative equality of people would lead inevitably to conflict.

Why does equality lead to conflict?

Nature has made men so equal in the faculties of body and mind, as that though there be found one man sometimes manifestly stronger in body, or of quicker mind than another; yet when all is reckoned together, the difference between man and man is not so considerable, as that one man can thereupon claim to himself any benefit to which another may not pretend as well as he. For as to the strength of body, the weakest has strength enough to kill the strongest, either by secret machination or by confederacy with others, that are in the same danger with himself.

And as to the faculties of the mind . . . I find yet a greater equality among men than that of strength. For prudence is but experience; which equal time equally bestows on all men in those things they equally apply themselves unto. . . .

---

[12] Xunzi, "On the Rules of Proper Conduct," in *The Works of Hsüntze,* translated by Homer H. Dubs (London: Arthur Probsthain, 1928).

> From this equality of ability, arises equality of hope in the attaining of our ends. And therefore if any two men desire the same thing, which nevertheless they cannot both enjoy, they become enemies; and in the way to their end (which is principally their own conservation, and sometimes their delectation only) endeavor to destroy or subdue one another. . . .
>
> So that in the nature of man, we find three principal causes of quarrel. First, competition; secondly, diffidence [i.e., insecurity]; thirdly, glory.
>
> The first makes men invade for gain; the second, for safety; and the third, for reputation. The first use violence to make themselves masters of other men's persons, wives, children, and cattle; the second, to defend them; the third, for trifles, as a word, a smile, a different opinion, and any other sign of undervalue. . . .[13]

The consequences of conflict are severe. The state of nature would be a war of all against all; life there, Hobbes famously says, would be "solitary, poor, nasty, brutish, and short."

What is war? What are its consequences?

> Hereby it is manifest that during the time men live without a common power to keep them all in awe, they are in that condition which is called war; and such a war as is of every man against every man. For war consists not in battle only, or the act of fighting; but in a tract of time, wherein the will to contend by battle is sufficiently known. . . . So the nature of war consists not in actual fighting, but in the known disposition thereto during all the time there is no assurance to the contrary. All other time is peace.
>
> Whatsoever therefore is consequent to a time of war, where every man is enemy to every man; the same is consequent to the time wherein men live without other security than what their own strength and their own invention shall furnish them withall. In such condition, there is no place for industry; because the fruit thereof is uncertain; and consequently no culture of the earth, no navigation, nor use of the commodities that may be imported by sea; no commodious building; no instruments of moving, and removing such things as require much force; no knowledge of the face of the earth; no account of time; no arts; no letters; no society; and which is worst of all, continual fear and danger of violent death; And the life of man, solitary, poor, nasty, brutish, and short.

Hobbes is concerned to point out that this assessment of human nature finds confirmation every time a person locks a door, hides valuables, or possesses a weapon. He also observes that it does not commit him to the view that human nature is evil:

> But neither of us accuse man's nature in it. The desires, and other passions of man, are in themselves no sin. No more are the actions, that proceed from those passions, till they know a law that forbids them: which till laws be made they cannot know: nor can any law be made, till they have agreed upon the person that shall make it.

The state of nature, therefore, rests solely on might, not right; notions of right and wrong, justice and injustice, do not yet apply.

---

[13] Thomas Hobbes, *Leviathan* (Oxford: Clarendon, 1909). Spelling has been modernized for clarity.

> To this war of every man against every man, this also is consequent; that nothing can be unjust. The notions of right and wrong, justice and injustice have no place. Where there is no common power, there is no law: where no law, no injustice. . . . It is consequent also to the same condition, that there be no propriety, no dominion, no *mine* and *thine* distinct; but only that to be every man's, that he can get; and for so long as he can keep it.

Faced with such a state of nature, we would choose to erect a government. In any contract, one must give up something to gain something else. The social contract is no different. We would be willing to sacrifice freedom in exchange for security.

Hobbes's Social Contract

We give up	*We gain*
Liberty	Security

In the state of nature, we have great liberty; we can do anything we want. Hobbes defines liberty as "the absence of external impediments"—this is the **negative conception of liberty** common to all classical liberals, as we shall see in the next section—and a right as a "liberty to do or forbear." For Hobbes, then, a right is always a right to be left alone, a right that others not interfere—an ability to do or refrain from doing something without impediment from others. A right to assemble, for example, is a right to gather without interference from others. A right to keep and bear arms entails that others not interfere with your possession of firearms. A right to exercise your religion entails that others not interfere with your worship. None of these imply any obligation on anyone else's part to help you; no one is obliged to host your meeting, buy you a gun, or build you a temple. For that reason, such rights are known as **negative** or **general rights.** For Hobbes, all rights are general rights.

Hobbes articulates several laws of nature that hold even in the state of nature. But he means by 'natural law' something more specific than the earlier natural law tradition.

> A law of nature (*lex naturalis*) is a precept, or general rule, found out by reason, by which a man is forbidden to do that which is destructive of his life or takes away the means of preserving the same and to omit that by which he thinks it may be best preserved.

This is not participation in the eternal law of God or a law written on the hearts of men; it is an obligation to self-preservation. Now Aquinas and Suárez would agree that self-preservation is a fundamental law of nature. But Hobbes understands it very broadly:

> The right of nature, which writers commonly call *jus naturale* [natural right], is the liberty each man has to use his own power, as he wills himself, for the preservation of his own nature; that is to say, of his own life; and consequently, of doing anything which in his own judgment and reasons he shall conceive to be the aptest means thereto.

In the state of nature, then, people have a right to do whatever they want to further their own interests. The result, of course, is conflict. In the face of war of all against all, the law of nature—self-preservation—implies several other laws:

How does Hobbes derive these laws of nature?

> And because the condition of man . . . is a condition of war of everyone against everyone, in which case everyone is governed by his own reason; and there is nothing he can make use of that may not be a help unto him in preserving his life against his enemies; it follows that in such a condition, every man has a right to everything, even to one another's body. And therefore, as long as this natural right of every man to every thing endures, there can be no security to any man (how strong or wise soever he be) of living out the time which nature ordinarily allows men to live. And consequently it is a precept or general rule of reason, *That every man ought to endeavor peace, as far as he has hope of obtaining it; and when he cannot obtain it, that he may seek, and use, all helps and advantages of war.* The first branch of which rule contains the first and fundamental law of nature; which is *to seek peace and follow it.* The second, the sum of the right of nature, which is *by all means we can, to defend ourselves.*

The key to Hobbes's contract is the trade of liberty for security. How much liberty should we be willing to surrender? As much as we need protection from. We retain only those liberties we are willing to grant others.

> From this fundamental law of nature, by which men are commanded to endeavor peace, is derived this second law; *That a man be willing, when others are so too, as far-forth, as for peace and defence of himself he shall think it necessary to lay down this right to all things and be contented with so much liberty against other men as he would allow other men against himself.*

We retain a right to liberty, in other words, only if we are willing to allow others that liberty against us. So we may retain a right to assembly if we are willing to grant others the right to assemble. We may retain a right to keep and bear arms if we are willing to allow others to keep and bear arms. In general, we permit ourselves to use the means to our own self-preservation that we are willing to allow others for their self-preservation.

NEGATIVE LIBERTY: CLASSICAL LIBERALISM

Hobbes, as we have seen, develops a negative conception of liberty as the absence of external impediments. According to the tradition of **classical liberalism,** that is the central goal of government. Governments exist primarily to protect liberty—that is, to protect people from external interference. As John Locke elaborates it, the central purpose of government is the preservation of property, understood broadly to include life and liberty. John Stuart Mill puts it somewhat differently: the central purpose of government is to protect people from harm at the hands of others.

Confucianism and Daoism

The earliest advocates of such a conception of government appear not in the West but in ancient China. Confucius (551–479 B.C.E.; see Chapters 6 and 7) and his contemporary Laozi advocate a minimalist view of government. They do not agree in all respects; Confucius finds a legitimate role for government, while little positive emerges from Laozi's account. Confucius's understanding of government is close to those of Aristotle and Aquinas in some ways, while Laozi's most closely approaches that of John Locke, to be discussed shortly. Nevertheless, they both hold that government should make minimal restrictions on the behavior of its citizens.

Confucius discusses government throughout the *Analects*. The core of his political philosophy, however, appears in a short work called *The Great Learning,* quoted here in its entirety:

> 1. What the Great Learning teaches is to illustrate illustrious virtue, to love the people, and to rest in the highest excellence.
> 2. Knowing where to rest, one can determine what to pursue; having determined that, one can attain peace of mind. A tranquil repose will follow that peace, and in that repose will be careful deliberation, followed by the attainment of the desired end.
> 3. Things have their roots and their branches; affairs have their ends and their beginnings. To know what is first and what is last is what the Great Learning teaches.[14]

To understand anything, one must get at the root; one must understand the fundamentals. So, to understand politics and to know how to construct a good society, one needs to understand what lies at the root of political questions. That, Confucius says, is ultimately knowledge:

Why is self-cultivation the root of everything else?

> 4. The ancients who wanted to illustrate illustrious virtue throughout the kingdom first well-ordered their states. Wanting to well-order their states, they first regulated their families. Wanting to regulate their families, they first cultivated themselves. Wanting to cultivate themselves, they first rectified their hearts. Wanting to rectify their hearts, they first sought to be sincere in their thoughts. Wanting to be sincere in their thoughts, they first extended their knowledge to the utmost. One extends knowledge by investigating things.
> 5. Things being investigated, their knowledge became complete. Their knowledge being complete, their thoughts were sincere. Their thoughts being sincere, their hearts were then rectified. Their hearts being rectified, they themselves were cultivated. They themselves being cultivated, their families were regulated. Their families being regulated, their states were well-ordered. Their states being well-ordered, the whole kingdom was made tranquil and happy.
> 6. From the Son of Heaven [that is, the Emperor] to the multitude, all considered self-cultivation to be the root of everything else.

---

[14]This and subsequent passages from Confucius, until otherwise noted, are from *The Great Learning,* from *The Sacred Books of China: The Texts of Confucianism, Part IV,* translated by James Legge (Oxford: Clarendon, 1885). I have amended the translation to improve readability.

7. When the root is neglected, what springs from it cannot be well-ordered. Never has that of great importance been slightly cared for while that of slight importance was greatly cared for.

Part of this picture is familiar from Chapter 7. Virtues of action depend on virtues of feeling, which in turn depend on virtues of thought, which in turn depend on virtues of knowledge. Here Confucius adds that the happiness of the community depends on its being well governed. The virtues of the community, in other words, depend on the virtues of government. But they in turn depend on the virtues of families, which depend on individual virtues of action. We can put these dependencies graphically:

> Virtues of the community → virtues of government → virtues of families → virtues of action → virtues of feeling → virtues of thought → virtues of knowledge

To answer the questions with which this chapter began, therefore, we must first answer questions about individual virtues. Political questions are not independent; a society will be virtuous and happy when its people are virtuous and happy. The individuals come first.

The chief task of government, in Confucius's view, is to set a proper example for the people. The virtue and happiness of the community depend on the virtue and happiness of the people within it. The leader's prime concern, therefore, should be with the virtue and happiness of the people. And that can best be promoted indirectly, not by law but by force of example.

12:17. Qi Kang asked Confucius about government. He replied, "To govern (cheng) is to rectify (cheng). If you lead correctly, who will dare to be incorrect?"

13:6. The Master said, "If a ruler acts correctly, he can govern without issuing orders. If he acts incorrectly, his orders won't be followed."

13:13. The Master said, "If a minister makes his own conduct correct, what difficulty will he have in governing? If he can't rectify himself, how can he rectify others?"[15]

The most important aspect of governing, Confucius holds, is to *rectify names:* call things by their proper appellations. In the twentieth century, British writer George Orwell exposed the misuse of language characteristic of totalitarian governments, who often called themselves "democratic republics" even though they were neither. Confucius focuses on the same issue. Knowledge is at the root of the community's welfare. For people to understand things, they must be called by what they are; names must be restored to their proper owners.

13:3. Zi-lu said, "The ruler of Wei is waiting for you to help him govern. What should be done first?" The Master replied, "Rectify names." "Really?" said Zi-lu. "You're wide of the mark. Why rectify names?" The Master said, "How uncultivated you are, Yu! A superior man shows a cautious reserve about what he doesn't know."

---

[15] This and subsequent passages from Confucius are from *The Analects,* from *The Four Books,* translated by James Legge (Oxford: Clarendon, 1893). I have amended the translation to improve readability and to conform to the Pinyin system.

It is not obvious from what Confucius says how extensive government should be. But he gives us an important clue in recommending an appropriate tax rate. A government that places too much of a burden on its people will impoverish them and so impoverish itself. Conversely, a government that encourages its people to profit will benefit the people and itself.

> 12:9. Duke Ai asked Yu Zo, "Suppose the year is one of scarcity and the government faces a deficit. What is to be done?"
>
> Yu Zo replied, "Why not demand from the people a tenth of their income?"
>
> "With two tenths there isn't enough," said the Duke. "How could I get by on one tenth?"
>
> Yu Zo answered, "If the people have plenty, their ruler will not be needy alone. If the people are needy, their ruler can't enjoy plenty alone."

In the United States, in the year 2000, the federal government takes about two-tenths of national income in taxes; state and local governments take another two-tenths. Governments in Europe, Asia, and Africa generally take more. Confucius recommends that government be only about one-fourth that size. This is not arbitrary but stems directly from Confucius's idea that government cannot itself produce prosperity or happiness. People do that. Government does best when it rectifies names, sets an example, and gets out of the way.

Laozi considers even Confucian government too intrusive. The government, according to Confucius, should try to educate its people if only by example (and by rectifying names). The first task, Confucius says, is to enrich the people; the second, to teach them. But Laozi does not see this as a proper task of government at all. His ideal is pastoral; people are at their most virtuous when they lead simple lives and have the virtues of small farmers and artisans.

> 3
>
> Do not honor the worthy, and the people will not engage in rivalry. . . .
> The sage, in governing the people, empties their minds, fills their bellies,
> Weakens their wills, and strengthens their bones.
> He keeps them in no-knowledge and no-desire,
> So they do not presume to act.
> Act by no-action, and all will be well-ordered.[16]

Interestingly, the founders of the United States also saw good government as resting on the pastoral virtues of the small farmers and artisans who formed the backbone of the new country's population: independence, self-reliance, self-control, and common sense. Laozi's conception is very much the same. Government should practice no-action, for people need to develop the virtues of self-reliance. The ideal citizen is the uncarved block (*pu*), whose straightforward simplicity keeps the community from going astray.

The ideal government, Laozi says, is one that keeps to the background, helping the people accomplish things without seeking to accomplish anything itself:

---

[16]This and subsequent selections from Laozi are from the *Dao de Jing,* in *The Texts of Taoism,* translated by James Legge (Oxford: Oxford University Press, 1891). I have altered the translation significantly to bring out the poetic quality of the original and to accord with the Pinyin system.

17

The best rulers, the people don't even know that they're there.
The next best, they love and praise.
The next best, they fear.
The worst, they despise.
When rulers lose faith in their people,
People lose faith in their rulers.

Words matter.

Work done, things accomplished,
The people say, "We did these things ourselves."

In the best state, the people accomplish things themselves. As Thomas Jefferson said, "The government that governs least governs best." Government must therefore be minimal. The more laws there are, the worse the government and the worse off the people.

What problems does government action cause? Why?

57

Govern by rectifying; fight cleverly.
Take the kingdom without trying.

How do I know?
The more prohibitions there are, the poorer the people.
The more tools there are, the greater the disorder.
The more cleverness there is, the more contrivances there are.
The more laws there are, the more criminals there are.

Therefore a sage says:
I do nothing, and the people transform themselves.
I love stillness, and the people correct themselves.
I have no business, and the people prosper themselves;
I have no ambition, and the people attain the uncarved wood themselves.

58

When the government is dull, the people are good.
When the government is meddling, the people are disappointed.

Laozi advocates minimal government because it makes the people both prosperous and virtuous. Liberty is a good thing, for it promotes living well in both material and ethical senses. And the conception of liberty is negative; government just needs to leave people alone. But in neither Confucius nor Laozi is there any conception of rights. For that, we must turn to the Western philosophers of the Enlightenment.

John Locke

John Locke (1632–1704), a contemporary of Boyle, Leibniz, and Newton, was born in Wrington, England, into a liberal Puritan family. He earned a B.A. and an M.A. from Oxford and joined the faculty there as censor in moral philosophy. When he was twenty-nine, his father died, and he received a small inheritance. He studied medicine and became personal physician to the Earl of Shaftesbury. His scientific achievements earned him appointment to the Royal Society. Political turmoil in England led Locke to spend several years in France and Holland, where he became an advisor to William of Orange. The Glorious Revolution of 1688 enabled him to return to England in the company of the future queen, Mary. Locke finally published the *Essay Concerning Human Understanding* and the *Two Treatises of Government,* the philosophical works that made him famous, and served as Commissioner of the Board of Trade and Plantations with great distinction until failing health forced him to retire.

Locke's *Second Treatise* presents a classically liberal theory of government. It had great influence on the American founders; Thomas Jefferson referred to it as a "little book on government" that is "perfect as far as it goes." Like any social contract theorist, Locke justifies government by contrasting it with a state of nature. Faced with such a choice, we would choose government. But Locke's conception of human nature and thus of the state of nature is a far cry from that of Xunzi or Hobbes.

The state of nature, "men living together according to reason, without a common superior on earth with authority to judge between them," Locke says, is a state of perfect freedom:

> To understand political power right and derive it from its original, we must consider what state all men are naturally in, and that is a state of perfect freedom to order their actions and dispose of their possessions and persons, as they think fit, within the bounds of the law of nature, without asking leave or depending upon the will of any other man.[17]

It is also a state of equality. People differ in many respects but not in authority. Apart from government, there is no basis for one person's exercising authority over another:

In what sense is everyone equal in the state of nature?

> A state also of equality, wherein all the power and jurisdiction is reciprocal, no one having more than another; there being nothing more evident than that creatures of the same species and rank, promiscuously born to all the same advantages of nature and the use of the same faculties should also be equal one amongst another without subordination or subjection. . . .

Even in the state of nature, however, we are subject to natural law.

What is the law of nature, according to Locke?

> But though this be a state of liberty, yet it is not a state of licence: though man in that state have an uncontrollable liberty to dispose of his person or possessions, yet he has not liberty to destroy himself or so much as any creature in his possession, but where some nobler use than its bare preservation calls for it. That state of nature has a law of nature to govern it, which obliges every one: and reason, which is that law, teaches all mankind who will but consult it that being all equal and independent, no one ought to harm another in his life, health, liberty, or possessions: for men being all the workmanship of one omnipotent and infinitely wise maker,

[17] This and subsequent quotations from John Locke are from *Second Treatise of Government,* from *Two Treatises of Government* (London: Printed for Awnsham Churchill, 1690). Spelling and punctuation have been modernized for clarity.

> all the servants of one sovereign master, sent into the world by his order and about his business; they are his property, whose workmanship they are, made to last during his, not one another's pleasure. . . . Every one, as he is bound to preserve himself and not to quit his station willfully, so by the like reason, when his own preservation comes not in competition, ought he as much as he can to preserve the rest of mankind and may not, unless it be to do justice to an offender, take away or impair the life or what tends to the preservation of the life, the liberty, health, limb, or goods of another.

In the state of nature, then, we have certain rights to life, health, liberty, and property. These are natural rights: we have them independently of government. These are general rights; the law of nature decrees that no one may harm another in his life, health, liberty, or possessions. It follows that, even apart from government, no one may kill, injure, enslave, imprison, or steal, except as punishment for violating that same law. That brings us to another right: each person, in the state of nature, has a right to punish those who break the law of nature.

> And that all men may be restrained from invading others' rights and from doing hurt to one another, and the law of nature be observed which wills the peace and preservation of all mankind, the execution of the law of nature is, in that state, put into every man's hands, whereby everyone has a right to punish the transgressors of that law to such a degree as may hinder its violation; for the law of nature would, as all other laws that concern men in this world, be in vain if there were no body that in the state of nature had a power to execute that law and thereby preserve the innocent and restrain offenders. And if any one in the state of nature may punish another for any evil he has done, every one may do so: for in that state of perfect equality, where naturally there is no superiority or jurisdiction of one over another, what any may do in prosecution of that law everyone must needs have a right to do.

Locke's argument here is quite clever:

> Everyone in the state of nature has equal rights.
> So, if anyone has authority to enforce the law of nature, everyone does.
> The law of nature would be in vain if no one had authority to enforce it.
> The law of nature is not in vain.
> So, everyone has authority to enforce the law of nature.

This is what keeps the state of nature from being a state of war. People's desires of course come into conflict, but rarely does that conflict erupt in violence, for everyone has the power to retaliate against anyone who attacks them or their property. There are nevertheless limits on the extent to which one can punish violators of natural law:

What are the proper justifications of and limits to punishment?

> And thus, in the state of nature, one man comes by a power over another; but yet no absolute or arbitrary power to use a criminal, when he has got him in his hands, according to the passionate heats, or boundless extravagancy of his own will; but only to retribute to him, so far as calm reason and conscience dictate, what is proportionate to his transgression, which is so much as may serve for reparation and restraint: for these two are the only reasons why one man may lawfully do harm to another, which is that we call punishment. . . . every man upon this score, by the

> right he has to preserve mankind in general, may restrain or, where it is necessary, destroy things noxious to them and so may bring such evil on anyone who has transgressed that law, as may make him repent the doing of it and thereby deter him, and by his example others, from doing the like mischief. And in the case, and upon this ground, every man has a right to punish the offender and be executioner of the law of nature.
>
> . . . each transgression may be punished to that degree and with so much severity as will suffice to make it an ill bargain to the offender, give him cause to repent, and terrify others from doing the like.

The state of nature, then, is not a war of all against all. It is a state of rational creatures living, for the most part, in accord with the law of nature, and punishing violations of it. Why, then, is it reasonable to prefer government? There is insecurity, of course; there are no police, no courts, no one whose primary responsibility is to enforce the law. Moreover, there is a danger in allowing everyone to serve as executioner of the law of nature, a danger that becomes clear whenever posses and vigilante groups become the primary means of dispensing justice. In the state of nature, each person is a judge in his or her own case. One can object

> . . . that it is unreasonable for men to be judges in their own cases, that self-love will make men partial to themselves and their friends, and, on the other side, that ill nature, passion and revenge will carry them too far in punishing others. . . . civil government is the proper remedy for the inconveniences of the state of nature, which must certainly be great where men may be judges in their own case, since it is easy to be imagined that he who was so unjust as to do his brother an injury will scarce be so just as to condemn himself for it. . . .

In short, the state of nature has its drawbacks as a protector of rights to life, liberty, and property. Locke groups all these under the general heading *property* (for it is *my* life, *my* health, *my* liberty, and *my* possessions that are at stake). We agree to submit to governmental authority to protect our property more effectively:

How does Locke justify the legislative, judicial, and executive functions of government?

> The great and chief end, therefore, of men's uniting into commonwealths, and putting themselves under government is the preservation of their property. To which in the state of nature there are many things wanting.
>
> First, there wants an established, known law, received and allowed by common consent to be the standard of right and wrong, and the common measure to decide all controversies between them; for though the law of nature be plain and intelligible to all rational creatures, yet men being biased by their interest, as well as ignorant for want of study of it, are not apt to allow of it as a law binding to them in the application of it to their particular cases.
>
> Secondly, in the state of nature there wants a known and indifferent judge with authority to determine all differences according to the established law; for everyone in that state being both judge and executioner of the law of nature, men being partial to themselves, passion and revenge is very apt to carry them too far and with too much heat in their own cases, as well as negligence and unconcernedness to make them too remiss in other men's.
>
> Thirdly, in the state of nature there often wants power to back and support the sentence when right and to give it due execution. They who by any injustice

> offended will seldom fail where they are able by force to make good their injustice; such resistance many times makes the punishment dangerous and frequently destructive to those who attempt it.

We are willing to surrender some of our natural rights in order to gain the impartial judgment of an unbiased arbitrator. But we are not willing to surrender all or even most of our rights. We enter into the social contract in order to preserve our rights to life, liberty, and property. We are willing to limit them by paying taxes to support government, carrying our share of the responsibility for maintaining it, and suffering penalties it may assess after carrying out impartial procedures (such as trials). But the only thing we are willing to give up is our right to execute the law of nature ourselves. To overcome the difficulties of each being judge in his own case, in other words, we are willing to place judgment in impartial hands and submit to its authority.

LOCKE'S SOCIAL CONTRACT

We give up	*We gain*
Right to execute the law of nature	Impartial judgment

This has an important consequence: the social contract not only justifies political authority but also limits it. The government can act only for the common good, and more specifically only to protect natural rights to life, liberty, and property. Moreover, it can act only with the consent of the people.

Locke's account of political authority entails a theory of justice. Specifically, Locke's theory is **historical:** whether a circumstance is just depends on how it came about. People have a right to property in the state of nature. Smith has a right to her own body and, Locke says, to the products of the labor of her body. If she goes into the woods and picks up some acorns, they are hers because she has worked for them (at least so long as "enough and as good is left over for others"). If she then chooses to trade them for one of Jones's wheelbarrows, she legitimately owns the wheelbarrow. If someone steals them and she gets something else as compensation for the loss, she owns that. There is no overarching scheme, rule, or pattern according to which property ought to be distributed. A situation is just if people in that situation have what they have justly. And that simply means that they worked for it, traded for it, or received it as compensation for some injury.

Adam Smith

Adam Smith (1723–1790), a contemporary of Hume, Bentham, Kant, and Mozart, was the founder of classical economics. He was born in Kirkcaldy, Scotland; his father died shortly before he was born. At fourteen he entered the University of Glasgow and three years later moved to Balliol College, Oxford. At twenty-five, he moved to Edinburgh and befriended Hume. At twenty-nine he became professor of logic at Glasgow; a year later he switched this for a professorship of moral philosophy. At thirty-six he published *A Theory of Moral Sentiments,* which made him famous and earned him appointment as tutor to the young duke of Buccleuch, who promised him a pension for life. At forty-three he retired, returned to Kirkcaldy, and spent the next ten years writing *An Inquiry into the Nature and Causes of the Wealth of Nations,* which appeared in 1776, the year of the American Revolution, to great acclaim.

Smith's argument is the economic counterpart of Locke's: governmental authority, while important for protecting people and property from harm, should be limited. A system of free exchange benefits everyone, maximizing freedom and wealth. No one needs to structure, organize, or direct the overall system; it organizes itself on the basis of the free choices of its participants. We gain great benefits, for example, from the division of labor. Each can specialize in what he or she most enjoys and does best, exchanging goods with others to fulfill his or her needs and wants. But no one made a decision to organize economic activity this way; it grew from people's free choices.

> This division of labour, from which so many advantages are derived, is not originally the effect of any human wisdom, which foresees and intends that general opulence to which it gives occasion. It is the necessary, though very slow and gradual, consequence of a certain propensity in human nature which has in view no such extensive utility; the propensity to truck, barter, and exchange one thing for another.[18]

Exchange enables us to interact with far more people than we might on the basis of friendship, kinship, or common interest. It also benefits both parties. Say that Jones buys a book from Smith for five dollars. Jones agrees to the transaction because he prefers having the book to having the five dollars; Smith agrees because she prefers the five dollars to the book. As a result of the transaction, both Smith and Jones are better off than they were before. Both benefit, even though each was interested only in benefiting him- or herself.

> But man has almost constant occasion for the help of his brethren, and it is in vain for him to expect it from their benevolence only. He will be more likely to prevail if he can interest their self-love in his favour, and show them that it is for their own advantage to do for him what he requires of them. Whoever offers to another a bargain of any kind, proposes to do this. Give me that which I want, and you shall have this which you want, is the meaning of every such offer; and it is in this manner that we obtain from one another the far greater part of those good offices which we stand in need of. It is not from the benevolence of the butcher, the brewer, or the baker, that we expect our dinner, but from their regard to their own interest. We address ourselves, not to their humanity but to their self-love, and never talk to them of our own necessities but of their advantages.

The genius of the free market is that it enables people, by pursuing their own self-interest, to develop their talents in the way most satisfying to them, while maximizing the common good.

> By nature a philosopher is not in genius and disposition half so different from a street porter, as a mastiff is from a greyhound, or a greyhound from a spaniel, or

---

[18] This and subsequent passages from Adam Smith are from *An Inquiry into the Nature and Causes of the Wealth of Nations* (London, printed for W. Strahan and T. Cadell, 1776).

> this last from a shepherd's dog. Those different tribes of animals, however, though all of the same species, are of scarce any use to one another. . . . Each animal is still obliged to support and defend itself, separately and independently, and derives no sort of advantage from that variety of talent with which nature has distinguished its fellows. Among men, on the contrary, the most dissimilar geniuses are of use to one another; the different produces of their respective talents, by the general disposition to truck, barter, and exchange, being brought, as it were, into a common stock, where every man may purchase whatever part of the produce of other men's talents he has occasion for.

Smith argues that restrictions on the freedom of the market cannot increase the welfare of society; they can only shift resources from one place to another, and they generally do that at substantial cost to the whole.

> The general industry of the society never can exceed what the capital of the society can employ. As the number of workmen that can be kept in employment by any particular person must bear a certain proportion to his capital, so the number of those that can be continually employed by all the members of a great society, must bear a certain proportion to the whole capital of that society, and can never exceed that proportion. No regulation of commerce can increase the quantity of industry in any society beyond what its capital can maintain. It can only divert a part of it into a direction into which it might not otherwise have gone; and it is by no means certain that this artificial direction is likely to be more advantageous to the society than that into which it would have gone of its own accord.

Here is Smith's argument that a system of free exchange in which each seeks his or her own self-interest maximizes the welfare of the whole society:

How does Smith move from self-interest to the advantage of society as a whole?

> Every individual is continually exerting himself to find out the most advantageous employment for whatever capital he can command. It is in his own advantage, indeed, and not that of the society which he has in view. But the study of his own advantage naturally, or rather necessarily leads him to prefer that employment which is most advantageous to the society.
>
> . . . The produce of industry is what it adds to the subject or materials upon which it is employed. In proportion as the value of this produce is great or small, so will likewise be the profits of the employer. But it is only for the sake of profit that any man employs a capital in the support of industry; and he will always, therefore, endeavor to employ it in the support of that industry of which the produce is likely to be of the greatest value, or to exchange for the greatest quantity either of money or of other goods.
>
> But the annual revenue of every society is always precisely equal to the exchangeable value of the whole annual produce of its industry, or rather is precisely the same thing with that exchangeable value. As every individual, therefore, endeavors as much as he can both to employ his capital in the support of domestic industry, and so to direct that industry that its produce may be of greatest value; every individual necessarily labours to render the annual revenue of the public interest, nor knows how much he is promoting it. . . . he intends only his own security; and by directing that industry in such a manner as its produce may be of the greatest value, he intends only his own gain, and he is in this, as in many other cases, led by

> an invisible hand to promote an end which was no part of his intention. Nor is it always the worse for the society that it was no part of it. By pursuing his own interest he frequently promotes that of the society more effectually than when he really intends to promote it. I have never known much good done by those who affected to trade for the public good.

In outline form, the argument is:

> Each person seeks to maximize his own self-interest, that is, his own profit.
> So, each person invests to maximize his own self-interest, that is, profit.
> The more a company's produce is worth, the more investors in it profit.
> So, each person invests to maximize the exchangeable value of the produce resulting from their investment.
> The wealth of society is the exchangeable value of its industry's produce.
> So, each person invests to maximize the wealth of society.

Everyone tries to work and invest to maximize the benefits to him- or herself. But the best employment of a person's time and money will consist in adding the most value to whatever is being produced. That value, moreover, is what the products are worth to other people. So each person works and invests to produce the greatest possible benefit to others in order to produce the greatest possible benefit to him- or herself.

Why do such free investment and exchange promote the welfare of society better than any regulation or central planning? Individuals with their profits on the line are closer to the situation and have more incentive to understand it accurately than any government bureaucrat. Public officials cannot know as much as private individuals working toward their own ends. Nor are they likely to care as much about the public welfare as each individual cares about his or her own welfare. Finally, centralizing these decisions creates great opportunities for stupidity and corruption.

> What is the species of domestic industry which his capital can employ, and of which the produce is likely to be of the greatest value, every individual, it is evident, can, in his local situation, judge much better than any statesman or lawgiver can do for him. The statesman, who should attempt to direct private people in what manner they ought to employ their capitals, would not only load himself with a most unnecessary attention, but assume an authority which could safely be trusted not only to no single person, but to no council or senate whatever, and which would no-where be so dangerous as in the hands of a man who had folly and presumption enough to fancy himself fit to exercise it.

Indeed, regulation can only harm the general welfare; it can never increase it.

> . . . the sum total, either of its industry, or of its revenue, can [n]ever be augmented by any such regulation. The industry of the society can augment only in proportion as its capital augments, and its capital can augment only in proportion to what can be gradually saved out of its revenue. But the immediate effects of every such regulation is to diminish its revenue, and what diminishes its revenue is certainly not very likely to augment its capital faster than it would have augmented of its own accord, had both capital and industry been left to find out their natural employments.

We cannot do better, then, than to rely on the invisible hand of the market to guide self-interest toward the common good. Regulation invariably substitutes something else for the attempts of individuals to maximize their welfare. It diminishes what people gain (their revenues) for the sake of some other good. But that slows the growth of capital—savings and investment—which in turn slows the growth of productivity. That further slows the growth of revenues, that is, people's incomes. Interfering with people's freedoms thus makes them worse off as well as less free.

John Stuart Mill

We have already discussed the ethical theory of John Stuart Mill (1806–1873; see Chapter 8), utilitarianism. Mill argues for classical liberalism from utilitarian premises. He generalizes Smith's economic arguments to the full range of human activities. No one else can know as well as you do what is likely to make you happy. No one cares as much as you do about your own happiness. Therefore, no one is in a better position than you to decide how you should live your life.

> But the strongest of all the arguments against the interference of the public with purely personal conduct is that, when it does interfere, the odds are that it interferes wrongly and in the wrong place.[19]

So long as you do not harm others, you should be free to live as you please without outside interference. Mill's *On Liberty* defends this principle, which has subsequently become known as the **harm principle:**

What can justify restricting a person's liberty, according to Mill?

> The object of this Essay is to assert one very simple principle, as entitled to govern absolutely the dealings of society with the individual in the way of compulsion and control, whether the means used be physical force in the form of legal penalties, or the moral coercion of public opinion. That principle is, that the sole end for which mankind are warranted, individually or collectively in interfering with the liberty of action of any of their number, is self-protection. That the only purpose for which power can be rightfully exercised over any member of a civilized community, against his will, is to prevent harm to others. His own good, either physical or moral, is not a sufficient warrant. He cannot rightfully be compelled to do or forbear because it will be better for him to do so, because it will make him happier, because, in the opinions of others, to do so would be wise, or even right. These are good reasons for remonstrating with him, or reasoning with him, or persuading him, or entreating him, but not for compelling him, or visiting him with any evil, in case he do otherwise. To justify that, the conduct from which it is desired to deter him must be calculated to produce evil to some one else. The only part of the conduct of any one, for which he is amenable to society, is that which concerns others. In the part which merely concerns himself, his independence is, of right, absolute. Over himself, over his own body and mind, the individual is sovereign.

There are obvious exceptions to this, of course. Mill does not mean to include children or those acting under compulsion, delusion, or misinformation. In general, however,

[19] This and subsequent quotations from John Stuart Mill are from *On Liberty* (London: Parker, 1859).

he means to say that one can restrict liberty only to prevent harm to others. This is not because we have a natural right to liberty, or because we enter or would enter into a certain kind of social contract, but because respecting liberty maximizes happiness.

> It is proper to state that I forego any advantage which could be derived to my argument from the idea of abstract right as a thing independent of utility. I regard utility as the ultimate appeal on all ethical questions; but it must be utility in the largest sense, grounded on the permanent interests of man as a progressive being. Those interests, I contend, authorize the subjection of individual spontaneity to external control, only in respect to those actions of each, which concern the interest of other people. If any one does an act hurtful to others, there is a prima facie case for punishing him, by law, or, where legal penalties are not safely applicable, by general disapprobation.

Mill's principle elaborates the bounds of proper political authority. It thus addresses the central problem of political philosophy, the relation between people and their governments—the rulers and the ruled—and specifically the basis for the rulers exercising political authority over the ruled.

When rulers acquire power through force or inheritance, they have little need to take the interests of the people into account. In a democracy, however, the rulers acquire power through elections. They must take the interests of the people into account to some degree. But even if the rulers follow the will of the majority perfectly, the possibility of conflict remains. Rule by the people, Mill points out, is really rule of each by all the rest. Nothing in the concept of democracy itself protects the minority from the majority's power. As a joke has it, sometimes democracy is like three wolves and a sheep voting on what to have for dinner. Edmund Burke therefore warned of the "oppression of the minority"; Alexis de Tocqueville similarly foresaw the "tyranny of the majority." Both generalize Aristotle's worry that "If justice is the will of the majority, . . . they will unjustly confiscate the property of the wealthy minority."[20]

The Bill of Rights—the first ten amendments to the United States Constitution—attempts to protect people from the unfettered power of undemocratic minorities and democratic majorities. By delineating people's rights, it carves out a sphere of individual liberty that government may not transgress. Mill tries to distinguish a sphere of personal liberty in a different way. He opposes Aristotle, al-Farabi, Aquinas, and other natural law theorists who hold that the aim of the law is to make citizens good. That, Mill argues, is no business of government. Its sole duty is to make people happy. The harm principle in effect says that **paternalistic laws**—laws that restrict a person's freedom for his or her own good—are illegitimate. The government may restrict liberty only to prevent harm to others. To restrict liberty to prevent people from harming themselves or to make them virtuous goes beyond the proper bounds of government authority.

One way of putting Mill's principle is that there is a sphere of liberty around each of us; we should be allowed to pursue **self-regarding actions** as we see fit. An act is self-regarding if it affects only the agent or agents of the act. It is **other-regarding** if

[20] Aristotle, *Politics,* translated by Benjamin Jowett, from *The Works of Aristotle,* Volume X (Oxford: Clarendon, 1921), VI, 3.

it affects others. An **agent,** in turn, is one who consents to and participates in an act (1) freely—without coercion; (2) voluntarily—that is, having the competence to make the decision to consent and participate; and (3) in an informed way without being deceived.

What liberties fall into the realm of self-regarding actions?

> But there is a sphere of action in which society, as distinguished from the individual, has, if any, only an indirect interest; comprehending all that portion of a person's life and conduct which affects only himself, or, if it also affects others, only with their free, voluntary, and undeceived consent and participation. When I say only himself, I mean directly, and in the first instance: for whatever affects himself, may affect others through himself; and the objection which may be grounded on this contingency, will receive consideration in the sequel. This, then, is the appropriate region of human liberty. It comprises, first, the inward domain of consciousness; demanding liberty of conscience, in the most comprehensive sense; liberty of thought and feeling; absolute freedom of opinion and sentiment on all subjects, practical or speculative, scientific, moral, or theological. The liberty of expressing and publishing opinions may seem to fall under a different principle, since it belongs to that part of the conduct of an individual which concerns other people; but, being almost of as much importance as the liberty of thought itself, and resting in great part on the same reasons, is practically inseparable from it. Secondly, the principle requires liberty of tastes and pursuits; of framing the plan of our life to suit our own character; of doing as we like, subject to such consequences as may follow; without impediment from our fellow-creatures, so long as what we do does not harm them even though they should think our conduct foolish, perverse, or wrong. Thirdly, from this liberty of each individual, follows the liberty, within the same limits, of combination among individuals; freedom to unite, for any purpose not involving harm to others: the persons combining being supposed to be of full age, and not forced or deceived.

Some self-regarding acts involve only a single agent—taking a drug or failing to wear a seat belt, for example. Others involve a group of agents. It takes at least two agents to engage in prostitution, gambling, or employment. In either case, Mill says, we can consider the act self-regarding if several conditions are satisfied. First, everyone affected by the action must be acting freely. There must be no coercion. Everyone involved must consent to the action. We can treat ordinary, consensual sexual activity as self-regarding, for example, but rape is clearly other-regarding. Second, everyone affected must be acting voluntarily. If anyone is incapable of choosing, by virtue of being a child, for example, or drugged or insane, the act is other-regarding. Finally, everyone affected must be reasonably well informed about the action. There must be no ignorance or deception about important and relevant matters. Someone who takes poison thinking it to be aspirin is not exercising freedom in any meaningful sense.

Mill defends a conception of liberty that consists not only in doing what you choose to do without others interfering with you—Hobbes's negative conception of liberty—but also in pursuing your own good as you see fit without interfering with others.

> No society in which these liberties are not, on the whole, respected, is free, whatever may be its form of government; and none is completely free in which they do

> not exist absolute and unqualified. The only freedom which deserves the name, is that of pursuing our own good in our own way, so long as we do not attempt to deprive others of theirs, or impede their efforts to obtain it. Each is the proper guardian of his own health, whether bodily, or mental or spiritual. Mankind are greater gainers by suffering each other to live as seems good to themselves, than by compelling each to live as seems good to the rest.

Mill's conception of liberty rests, as we have seen, on the distinction between self- and other-regarding actions.

> What, then, is the rightful limit to the sovereignty of the individual over himself? Where does the authority of society begin? How much of human life should be assigned to individuality, and how much to society?
>
> Each will receive its proper share if each has that which more particularly concerns it. To individuality should belong the part of life in which it is chiefly the individual that is interested; to society; the part which chiefly interests society.

But arguably there are no kinds of actions that never affect other people. Suicide, for example, affects the agent more than anyone else—it kills him or her—but still has a profound and terrible impact on the lives of others. Drinking, taking drugs, driving without a seat belt, and other putatively self-regarding actions also affect the agent more than anyone else but may have significant impact on others. If no act is purely self-regarding, then the harm principle is vacuous; it protects nothing. Mill recognizes the difficulty:

How do one person's acts affect another?

> The distinction here pointed out between the part of a person's life which concerns only himself and that which concerns others, many persons will refuse to admit. How (it may be asked) can any part of the conduct of a member of society be a matter of indifference to the other members? No person is an entirely isolated being; it is impossible for a person to do anything seriously or permanently hurtful to himself without mischief reaching at least to his near connections, and often far beyond them. If he injures his property, he does harm to those who directly or indirectly derived support from it, and usually diminishes, by a greater or less amount, the general resources of the community. If he deteriorates his bodily or mental faculties, he not only brings evil upon all who depended upon him for any portion of their happiness, but disqualifies himself for rendering the services which he owes to his fellow creatures generally, perhaps becomes a burden on their affection or benevolence; and if such conduct were very frequent hardly any offense that is committed would detract more from the general sum of good. Finally, if by his vices or follies a person does no direct harm to others, he is nevertheless (it may be said) injurious by his example, and ought to be compelled to control himself for the sake of those whom the sight or knowledge of his conduct might corrupt or mislead.

Mill answers that an act should be considered self-regarding unless it violates someone else's rights. That is, it is self-regarding unless (a) it violates an obligation to a specific person, and (b) it violates a specific obligation to people in general. Drinking is in general self-regarding, but (a) if someone spends all his time drunk, cannot hold a job, and fails to support his family, he violates their rights, and the act becomes other-regarding. He is violating an obligation to specific people, namely, his family. (b) If a police officer gets drunk on duty, she violates a specific obligation to the public, and her act becomes other-regarding.

> When, by conduct of this sort, a person is led to violate a distinct and assignable obligation to any other person or persons, the case is taken out of the self-regarding class and becomes amenable to moral disapprobation in the proper sense of the term. . . . Whenever, in short, there is a definite damage, or a definite risk of damage, either to an individual or to the public, the case is taken out of the province of liberty and placed in that of morality or law.
>
> But with regard to the merely contingent or, as it may be called, constructive injury which a person causes to society by conduct which neither violates any specific duty to the public, nor occasions perceptible hurt to any assignable individual except himself, the inconvenience is one which society can afford to bear, for the sake of the greater good of human freedom.

Near the end of *On Liberty,* Mill considers a difficult question: Should a person be permitted to sell him- or herself into slavery? Should a person be free to surrender his or her freedom? This is more than a theoretical question, for Hooker, Locke, and other earlier political philosophers had used this analogy in criticizing monarchy. How, they asked, could it ever be rational for someone to agree to submit to the authority of an absolute monarch? That would be like someone agreeing to sell him- or herself into slavery. And that, they maintained, is an absurdity. So, Mill faces a dilemma. If he does not allow voluntary slavery, he seems to contradict his own harm principle. If he does allow it, however, he becomes vulnerable to the Hobbesian argument that people have exercised their liberty by surrendering it in exchange for security or other goods and thus opens the door for monarchy or even dictatorship. In short, Mill appears to face a choice between contradicting the harm principle and undercutting its usefulness for defending freedom. Mill's answer is clear:

Why should voluntary slavery be forbidden?

> . . . it is sometimes considered a sufficient reason for releasing them from an engagement that it is injurious to themselves. In this and most other civilized countries, for example, an engagement by which a person should sell himself, or allow himself to be sold, as a slave would be null and void, neither enforced by law nor by opinion. The ground for thus limiting his power of voluntarily disposing of his own lot in life is apparent, and is very clearly seen in this extreme case. The reason for not interfering, unless for the sake of others, with a person's voluntary acts is consideration for his liberty. His voluntary choice is evidence that what he so chooses is desirable, or at least endurable, to him, and his good is on the whole best provided for by allowing him to take his own means of pursuing it. But by selling himself for a slave, he abdicates his liberty; he foregoes any future use of it beyond that single act. He therefore defeats, in his own case, the very purpose which is the justification of allowing him to dispose of himself. He is no longer free, but is thenceforth in a position which has no longer the presumption in its favor that would be afforded by his voluntarily remaining in it. The principle of freedom cannot require that he should be free not to be free. It is not freedom to be allowed to alienate his freedom.

Does this contradict the harm principle? Mill would surely say no. Suppose Smith chooses to sell herself to Jones. The question is whether their arrangement should be enforced. That issue arises if Smith subsequently decides she does not want to be Jones's slave any longer. We must decide whether to respect Smith's earlier choice (to sell herself into slavery) or her current choice (to regain her freedom). It seems that if one choice is self-regarding, the other is too. If neither is self-regarding, the harm principle is not at issue, and we can decide on the basis of effects on others. That surely would lead us to ban slavery of all kinds, voluntary or not. If both are self-regarding, then surely we should respect Smith's current choice and refuse to enforce the slavery contract. So either way, voluntary slavery should not be permitted.

This has real practical significance, as Mill recognized. What is true of a contract to sell oneself into slavery is true of other kinds of contracts as well. All contracts involve a loss of freedom. So, all contracts, in Mill's view, should be easy to escape. He applies this directly to marriage, which he thought in his day too often resembled voluntary slavery. As long as children are not involved, Mill thought, people should be able to divorce by mutual consent. More generally, in a work titled *On the Subjection of Women,* Mill argues that women are entitled to all the rights and liberties of men. Freedom may be restricted by informal social arrangements and opinions as much as by law. Mill finds that existing social arrangements and opinions limit the freedom of women more than the freedom of men. So he campaigns against those arrangements and opinions, arguing for equality for women not only in law but also in family relationships, employment, and other spheres of life.

POSITIVE LIBERTY: SOCIALISM

Classical liberals are so called because they hold liberty, in the sense of an absence of external impediments, as an extremely important value. Good societies and governments allow their members and citizens a high degree of freedom. But the term *liberalism* can easily mislead, for contemporary political liberals tend to draw on a quite different tradition in political thought. Indeed, adherents of classical liberalism on the contemporary scene tend to be known as libertarians or conservatives, depending on the specific limits they draw around the individual's sphere of liberty and the extent to which they find certain social institutions natural. In this section we will consider the tradition giving birth to contemporary liberalism, socialism, and various forms of radicalism.

This tradition centers around the notion of **positive liberty.** Hobbes defines liberty in the negative sense as the absence of external impediments. Liberty in the positive sense, in contrast, is self-determination. A person has positive liberty to the extent that he or she has control over his or her life. If Smith has positive freedom, she has control over her life, which means, among other things, that she has control over herself. She sets her own rules to follow; she is, in Kant's terms, *autonomous.* She does not merely follow the crowd, do what other people say, or give in willy-nilly to her own passing passions. Instead, she sets goals for herself and follows them.

The idea of positive freedom goes back to Plato, who, as we saw in Chapter 7, characterized virtue as a balance of the parts of the soul in the *Republic.* In particular, the rational element in the just person exerts control over the spirited and appetitive elements. Plato saw this as analogous to the control of the rational elements over other elements in the just state. Later philosophers have exploited the link between self-determination and politics in more elaborate ways.

Jean-Jacques Rousseau

Jean-Jacques Rousseau (1712–1778), a contemporary of Voltaire, Burke, Hume, Wollstonecraft, and Haydn, is one of the leading figures of the Enlightenment. His mother died a few days after he was born in Geneva. Raised by his unstable father and an aunt, he had little formal education. At sixteen he went to France. At age thirty-three, Rousseau began an affair with Thérèse Le Vasseur, with whom he had five illegitimate children—all of whom he sent to an orphanage. (Many have taken this to raise serious questions not only about his character but also about his understanding of human nature.) His intellectual career brought him into contact with many of Europe's greatest thinkers, including Diderot, Voltaire, and Hume, whom he met, befriended, and soon alienated.

Rousseau is famous for his image of noble savages in an original state of nature:

> Man's first feeling was that of his own existence, and his first care that of self-preservation. The produce of the earth furnished him with all he needed, and instinct told him how to use it. . . . nothing is more gentle than man in his primitive state, as he is placed by nature at an equal distance from the stupidity of brutes, and the fatal ingenuity of civilised man.[21]

People were like animals, having only a desire to survive and a general awareness of themselves as human.

Private property, however, changed this initial state fundamentally:

> The first man who, having enclosed a piece of ground, bethought himself of saying *This is mine,* and found people simple enough to believe him, was the real founder of civil society. From how many crimes, wars and murders, from how many horrors and misfortunes might not anyone have saved mankind, by pulling up the stakes, or filling up the ditch, and crying to his fellows, "Beware of listening to this impostor; you are undone if you once forget that the fruits of the earth belong to us all, and the earth itself to nobody."

At first, Rousseau says, the result of property was the kind of social contract described by John Locke. People had a sense of morality and enforced it themselves by punishing and taking revenge on wrongdoers. This, Rousseau admits, "must have been the happiest and most stable of epochs." But it corresponds to a primitive state of society. The development of metal tools and agriculture disrupted it utterly. Farming made property important; "men began to look forward to the future, and all had something to lose." The most important effect, however, was a change in human nature, an alteration in the balance of the soul:

---

[21] This and subsequent quotations from Jean-Jacques Rousseau, "Discourse on the Origin of Inequality," *The Social Contract and Discourses,* translated by G. D. H. Cole (London: J. M. Dent & Sons, Ltd., 1913), until otherwise noted.

> It now became the interest of men to appear what they really were not. To be and to seem became two totally different things; and from this distinction sprang insolent pomp and cheating trickery, with all the numerous vices that go in their train.

Property, in short, made people hypocrites. Why? The division of labor made people depend on interesting others in their own welfare.

What compels people to try to use others?

> . . . free and independent as men were before, they were now, in consequence of a multiplicity of new wants, brought into subjection, as it were, to all nature, and particularly to one another; and each became in some degree a slave even in becoming the master of other men; if rich, they stood in need of the services of others; if poor, of their assistance; and even a middle condition did not enable them to do without one another. Man must now, therefore, have been perpetually employed in getting others to interest themselves in his lot, and in making them, apparently, at least, if not really, find their advantage in promoting his own. Thus he must have been sly and artful in his behavior to some, and imperious and cruel to others; being under a kind of necessity to ill-use all the persons of whom he stood in need, when he could not frighten them into compliance, and did not judge it in his interest to be useful to them.

This is not merely a change of habits, but a change in human nature itself. The person who understands this change

How does civilization change human nature?

> . . . will explain how the soul and passions of men insensibly change their very nature; why our wants and pleasures in the end seek new objects; and why, the original man having vanished by degrees, society offers to us only an assembly of artificial men and factitious passions, which are the work of all these new relations, and without any real foundation in nature. . . . The savage and the civilised man differ so much in the bottom of their hearts and in their inclinations, that what constitutes the supreme happiness of one would reduce the other to despair. The former breathes only peace and liberty; he desires only to live and be free from labor. . . . Civilised man, on the other hand, is always moving, sweating, toiling and racking his brains to find still more laborious occupations. . . . He pays his court to men in power, whom he hates; and to the wealthy, whom he despises; he stops at nothing to have the honor of serving them; he is not ashamed to value himself on his own meanness and their protection; and, proud of his slavery, he speaks with disdain of those, who have not the honor of sharing it. What a sight would the perplexing and envied labors of a European minister of State present to the eyes of a Caribean? . . . In reality, the source of all those differences is, that the savage lives within himself, while social man lives constantly outside himself, and only knows how to live in the opinion of others, so that he seems to receive the consciousness of his own existence merely from the judgment of others concerning him. . . . everything being reduced to appearances, there is but art and mummery in even honor, friendship, virtue, and often vice itself . . . we have nothing to show for ourselves but a frivolous and deceitful appearance, honor without virtue, reason without wisdom, and pleasure without happiness.

The result of this change, in turn, was one of increasing inequality, in three stages:

> If we follow the progress of inequality in these various revolutions, we shall find that the establishment of laws and of the right of property was its first term, the institution of magistracy the second, and the conversion of legitimate into arbitrary power the third and last; so that the condition of rich and poor was authorized by the first period; that of powerful and weak by the second; and only by the third that of master and slave, which is the last degree of inequality, and the term at which all the rest remains, when they have got so far, till the government is either entirely dissolved by new revolutions, or brought back again to legitimacy.

In the stage of master and slave, with everyone subject to absolute and arbitrary power (for example, of a dictator or monarch), society reaches an extreme form of injustice.

> Here all private persons return to their first equality, because they are nothing; and, subjects having no law but the will of their master, and their master no restraint but his passions, all notions of good and all principles of equity again vanish. There is here a complete return to the law of the strongest, and so to a new state of nature, differing from that we set out from; for the one was a state of nature in its first purity, while this is the consequence of excessive corruption.
>
> . . . all the inequality which now prevails owes its strength and growth to the development of our faculties and the advance of the human mind, and becomes at last permanent and legitimate by the establishment of property and laws. Secondly, it follows that moral inequality, authorised by positive right alone, clashes with natural right, whenever it is not proportionate to physical inequality; a distinction which sufficiently determines what we ought to think of that species of inequality which prevails in all civilised countries; since it is plainly contrary to the law of nature, however defined, that children should command old men, fools wise men, and that the privileged few should gorge themselves with superfluities, while the starving multitude are in want of the basic necessities of life.

What we need, Rousseau insists, is a social contract that can create government anew and transform human nature, removing the artificiality that underlies gross inequality. In the stage of master and slave, government becomes a tool of arbitrary power. A social contract of the proper form, however, could make government legitimate:

> Man is born free; and everywhere he is in chains. One thinks himself the master of others, and still remains a greater slave than they. How did this change come about? I do not know. What can make it legitimate? That question I think I can answer.[22]

Rousseau, as a social contract theorist, holds that government is legitimate if people, given a choice, would choose submitting to its authority over remaining in a state of nature. For Hobbes, we have seen, people flee the state of nature to avoid the dangers of a war of all against all. For Locke, people flee the state of nature to avoid the excesses of vigilante justice. For Rousseau, people flee the state of nature because they face problems they cannot overcome without cooperation.

---

[22] This and subsequent passages from Jean-Jacques Rousseau are from *On the Social Contract,* from *The Social Contract and Discourses,* translated by G. D. H. Cole (London: J. M. Dent & Sons, Ltd., 1913).

> I suppose men to have reached the point at which the obstacles in the way of their preservation in the state of nature show their power of resistance to be greater than the resources at the disposal of each individual for his maintenance in that state. That primitive condition can then subsist no longer; and the human race would perish unless it changed its manner of existence.

But what kind of cooperation can preclude the slide into gross inequality characteristic of the stage of masters and slaves?

How does the social contract solve this problem?

> "The problem is to find a form of association which will defend and protect with the whole common force the person and goods of each associate, and in which each, while uniting himself with all, may still obey himself alone, and remain as free as before." This is the fundamental problem of which *The Social Contract* provides the solution. . . .
>
> These clauses, properly understood, may be reduced to one—the total alienation of each associate, together with all his rights, to the whole community; for, in the first place, as each gives himself absolutely, the conditions are the same for all; and, this being so, no one has any interest in making them burdensome to others.

Each person, that is, commits fully to the cooperative enterprise. Each gives everything to the group, and expects in return a full share of the fruits of cooperation.

> Finally, each man, in giving himself to all, gives himself to nobody; and as there is no associate over whom he does not acquire the same right as he yields others over himself, he gains an equivalent for everything he loses, and an increase of force for the preservation of what he has.
>
> If we discard from the social compact what is not of its essence, we shall find that it reduces itself to the following terms—
>
> *"Each of us puts his person and all his power in common under the supreme direction of the general will, and, in our corporate capacity, we receive each member as an indivisible part of the whole."*

In Rousseau's social contract, then, we surrender everything but get everything back. We give up everything to the community but gain a full share in the results of cooperation and so end up with more than we had before. The **general will** is not what the community wants but what is in its interests. The general will, that is, desires not what the community perceives as being in its interests but what is *really* in its interests. The general will, that is, is the common good. People may be ignorant or deceived; they may not know what is in their own interests. They may vote for a candidate or policy that fails to promote the common good. The vote in such a case does not reflect the general will.

What happens when people disagree? People often have different conceptions of the general will. Some think electing Smith would serve the common good; others prefer Jones. The majority may construct laws to promote the common good that others refuse to obey. In such cases, the general will must reign supreme.

> . . . whoever refuses to obey the general will shall be compelled to do so by the whole body. This means nothing less than that he will be forced to be free; for this is the condition which, by giving each citizen to his country, secures him against all personal dependence.

This is a chilling passage, which has served as a justification not only for enforcing the law but for sending political opponents to the Gulag. It not only permits but champions the tyranny of the majority. But it displays Rousseau's commitment to a positive conception of liberty. To be free, according to Rousseau, is to align one's will with the general will. It is, in other words, to want what is best for the community. The argument is something like this:

> To be free, in a positive sense, is to be rationally self-determining.
> To be rational is to seek one's own good.
> Cooperation with the community promotes one's own good.
> To cooperate with the community is to seek the common good of the community.
> To seek the common good of the community is to follow the general will.
> So, to be free, in a positive sense, is to follow the general will.

The person who disobeys the general will, then, is not being rationally self-determining. If Smith sees her own good as conflicting with the general will, she is confused, for what is rational for her is to seek the common good of the community. Her freedom consists not in doing what she wants but in doing what serves the interests of the community. Enforcing the law against her, putting her in prison, even putting her to death may in such circumstances promote her freedom. Advocates of a negative conception of liberty, of course, find this conclusion bizarre and incoherent.

As we saw above, property transforms human nature, making it artificial. The social contract, Rousseau maintains, can transform human nature into what it ought to be.

> The passage from the state of nature to the civil state produces a very remarkable change in man, by substituting justice for instinct in his conduct, and giving his actions the morality they had formerly lacked. . . . Although, in this state, he deprives himself of some advantages which he got from nature, he gains in return others so great, his faculties are so stimulated and developed, his ideas so extended, his feelings so ennobled, and his whole soul so uplifted, that, did not the abuses of this new condition often degrade him below that which he left, he would be bound to bless continually the happy moment which took him from it forever, and, instead of a stupid and unimaginative animal, made him an intelligent being and a man.
>
> Let us draw up the whole account in terms easily commensurable. What man loses by the social contract is his natural liberty and an unlimited right to everything he tries to get and succeeds in getting; what he gains is civil liberty and the proprietorship of all he possesses. . . .
>
> We might, over and above all this, add, to what man acquires in the civil state, moral liberty, which alone makes him truly master of himself; for the mere impulse of appetite is slavery, while obedience to a law which we prescribe to ourselves is liberty.

The social contract, then, gives us positive liberty, the liberty to obey "a law which we prescribe to ourselves," and frees us from the slavery of our appetites. It makes us fully human and rescues us from the artificiality engendered by the state of nature.

That artificiality, of course, was produced by property and the quest for it. What, then, does Rousseau's theory of political authority imply about property and, more generally, about justice? The simple answer is that goods should be distributed according to the general will, that is, the common good. "As nature gives each man absolute power over all his members, the social compact gives the body politic absolute power over all its members also." That does not mean that individuals have no rights and, in particular, no rights to property. But it does mean that the common good takes precedence. Each individual has only those rights that promote the common good.

> Each man alienates, I admit, by the social compact, only such part of his powers, goods and liberty as it is important for the community to control; but it must also be granted that the Sovereign [the power of the state under the direction of the general will] is sole judge of what is important.

The contrast with Locke could not be clearer. For Locke, rights are "bottom up." Each individual acquires a right to property through the labor of his or her body and yields some limitation on that right in constructing a system of law and government, but only to preserve the right. Government has legitimate power only to the extent that individuals freely consent to give it that power. For Rousseau, rights are "top down." Each individual acquires a right to property from the state, and that right is subject to the general will.

Rousseau's "top down" conception has two important consequences. The first is formal equality.

> . . . the social compact sets up among the citizens an equality of such a kind, that they all bind themselves to observe the same conditions and should therefore all enjoy the same rights. Thus, from the very nature of the compact, every act of Sovereignty, *i.e.* every authentic act of the general will, binds or favors all the citizens equally; so that the Sovereign recognizes only the body of the nation, and draws no distinctions between those of whom it is made up.

As the Fourteenth Amendment to the Constitution encodes this idea, every citizen is owed "the equal protection of the laws." Everyone has equal rights before government. Everyone must obey the same rules. The state may not distinguish some as falling under a special category of privilege or disadvantage, granting special favors to some and discriminating against others.

Second, Rousseau's account of justice implies some degree of substantive equality.

Why do rich men and beggars threaten society?

> . . . by equality, we should understand, not that the degrees of power and riches are to be absolutely identical for everybody; but that power shall never be great enough for violence, and shall always be exercised by virtue of rank and law; and that, in respect of riches, no citizen shall ever be wealthy enough to buy another, and none poor enough to be forced to sell himself: which implies, on the part of the great, moderation in goods and position, and, on the side of the common sort, moderation in avarice and covetousness. (If the object is to give the State consistency, bring the two extremes as near to each other as possible; allow neither rich men nor beggars. These two estates, which are mutually inseparable, are equally fatal to the common good; from the one come the friends of tyranny, and from the other tyrants. It is always between them that public liberty is put up for auction: the one buys, the other sells.)

Rich people and beggars must be avoided because they jeopardize the social compact and the positive liberty it creates. Circumstances of great inequality are unstable; "the social state is advantageous to men only when all have something and none too much." People with great wealth can manipulate the political process in their favor. People with nothing reasonably feel that they gain nothing through the social compact and so have no stake in its preservation. For them, the social compact produces no benefit; it is irrational for them to agree to it. But that makes government authority, applied to them, illegitimate.

Mary Wollstonecraft

Mary Wollstonecraft (1759–1797), an Enlightenment contemporary of Bentham, Burke, Kant, and Mozart, is often considered the founder of liberal feminism. She takes seriously both formal and substantive equality, applying them specifically to the condition of women. At age thirty-one she published *A Vindication of the Rights of Men,* which, like Thomas Paine's *The Rights of Man,* articulated a theory of rights in reaction to Edmund Burke's *Reflections on the Revolution in France,* which criticized the French Revolution and the concept of rights underlying it. Burke specifically attacked the idea of substantive equality, writing that "Men have equal rights, but not to equal *things.*"

In responding to Burke, Wollstonecraft seems to be defending Rousseau. Two years later, however, she published *A Vindication of the Rights of Woman,* which attacked him for taking equality as an equality of *men* and insisting that boys and girls ought to be educated differently. Rousseau held that boys should be educated as future citizens while women should be taught to keep house. Boys should be taught to follow rules while women should be taught delicacy of feeling. Virtues, in this conception, are sex-relative; what it is to be a virtuous man is not the same as what it is to be a virtuous woman. Wollstonecraft finds this absurd.

One of her central arguments is that women, as mothers, play a crucial part in transmitting culture and specifically virtue to the young of both sexes. If women lack a virtue, how can the young attain it?

> Contending for the rights of woman, my main argument is built on this simple principle, that if she not be prepared by education to become the companion of man, she will stop the progress of knowledge and virtue; for truth must be common to all, or it will be inefficacious with respect to its influence on general practice. And how can woman be expected to cooperate unless she know why she ought to be virtuous? unless freedom strengthen her reason till she comprehend her duty, and see in what manner it is connected with her real good? If children are to be educated to understand the true principle of patriotism, their mother must be a patriot; and the love of mankind, from which an orderly train of virtues spring, can only be produced by considering the moral and civil interest of mankind; but the education and situation of woman, at present, shuts her out from such investigations.[23]

---

[23] This and subsequent quotations from Mary Wollstonecraft are from *A Vindication of the Rights of Woman* (London: J. Johnson, 1792), 4.

Another argument rests on formal equality. The state, Locke and Rousseau affirm, must treat all citizens equally. What does this mean? Surely the state can distinguish murderers from law-abiding citizens and punish only the former. But the state cannot have one set of laws for the rich and another for the poor, or one set of laws for people of one race and another set for those of another race. The state, in short, can draw distinctions, but only those that are morally relevant. A distinction must be rationally related to some legitimate purpose of government to be legitimate itself. Distinguishing murderers does have a rational relation to a legitimate purpose of government, namely, protecting the citizens and their rights. Distinguishing rich from poor or people of different races typically does not.

Wollstonecraft argues that sex is not a morally relevant distinction. The law can legitimately give men and women different rights only if the distinction between men and women relates rationally to some legitimate government purpose—the protection of rights, for example, or the promotion of the common good. There must in short be some rationale for drawing the distinction. The only possible rationale for the distinctions Rousseau and traditional society draw, Wollstonecraft argues, would be that women are incapable of rationality.

> . . . surely, Sir, you will not assert, that a duty can be binding which is not founded on reason? If indeed this be their destination, arguments may be drawn from reason: and thus augustly supported, the more understanding women acquire, the more they will be attached to their duty—comprehending it—for unless they comprehend it, unless their morals be fixed on the same immutable principle as those of man, no authority can make them discharge it in a virtuous manner. They may be convenient slaves, but slavery will have its constant effect, degrading the master and the abject dependent.
>
> But, if women are to be excluded, without having a voice, from a participation of the natural rights of mankind, prove first, to ward off the charge of injustice and inconsistency, that they want reason—else this flaw in your NEW CONSTITUTION will ever shew that man must, in some shape, act like a tyrant, and tyranny, in whatever part of society it rears its brazen front, will ever undermine morality. . . . if women are not permitted to enjoy legitimate rights, they will render both men and themselves vicious, to obtain illicit privileges.

Wollstonecraft makes a straightforward argument:

> In what does man's pre-eminence over the brute creation consist? The answer is as clear as that a half is less than a whole; in Reason.
>
> What acquirement exalts one being above another? Virtue; we spontaneously reply.
>
> For what purpose were the passions implanted? That man by struggling with them might attain a degree of knowledge denied to the brutes; whispers Experience.
>
> Consequently, the perfection of our nature and capability of happiness, must be estimated by the degree of reason, virtue, and knowledge, that distinguish the individual, and direct the laws which bind society; and that from the exercise of reason, knowledge and virtue naturally flow, is equally undeniable, if mankind be viewed collectively.

We might summarize this as

Reason distinguishes humans from other animals (brutes).
One person becomes better than another by developing virtues.
Passions are means to knowledge.
So, the only morally relevant distinctions to be drawn among people are those based on reason, virtue, and knowledge.
Knowledge and virtue stem from the exercise of reason.
So, the only morally relevant distinctions to be drawn among people are those based on reason.

But notice that reason distinguishes humans—both male and female—from brutes. Both men and women, then, possess reason. Since men and women do not differ in any way based on reason, therefore, no morally relevant distinction is to be drawn between men and women. Moreover, because

> . . . the society is formed in the wisest manner, whose constitution is founded on the nature of man. . . .

the best society will treat men and women equally. Perhaps no society has ever done so. But Wollstonecraft finds no objection in that:

> Rousseau exerts himself to prove that all *was* right originally; a crowd of authors that all *is* now right; and I, that all will *be* right.

Since men and women are equally endowed with reason, formal equality under the law and in custom, she maintains, will produce substantive equality. Mill, in *On the Subjection of Women,* agrees. This is one issue dividing liberal from radical feminists. Liberal feminists such as Wollstonecraft and Mill hold that formal equality leads to substantive equality. Radical feminists doubt it. Some fear that social institutions and practices may favor men in subtle ways. Formal equality with respect to those institutions will still deny women substantive equality. They thus see formal equality as insufficient. Some see formal equality as undesirable; they hold that men and women differ in fundamental ways that have to be recognized in social arrangements. In this, they agree with traditionalists such as Aristotle. But they have a very different concept of how the sexes differ.

Some, finally, see liberalism as self-contradictory. Wollstonecraft and Mill campaign against social arrangements that treat men and women differently. But what of the freedom of people to maintain those arrangements? People may freely choose to harbor opinions or live in arrangements that strike Wollstonecraft and Mill as unjust. If they enter into such arrangements freely, voluntarily, and knowing what they are doing, their acts are self-regarding and may not be restricted. Men's clubs are an obvious example of this kind of conflict. The liberty of those who seek to associate solely with other men in the club conflicts with the liberty of women who would like to join. If men's clubs should be required to admit women, moreover, shouldn't women's clubs be required to admit men? The liberal feminist thus faces a dilemma: Either she leaves in place social arrangements that keep women from achieving substantive equality, or she violates the sphere of freedom that liberalism generally defends even for women themselves.

Karl Marx and Friedrich Engels

Karl Marx (1818–1883) and Friedrich Engels (1820–1895) see formal equality as, in many cases, a cover for substantive inequality. Marx, a contemporary of John Stuart Mill, Charles Darwin, Charles Dickens, George Eliot, and the Brontë sisters, was born in Treves, in the German Rhineland, to a Jewish family that had converted to Lutheranism. After studying law in Bonn and philosophy and history in Berlin, he earned his doctorate at Jena at age twenty-three. He became editor of a liberal Cologne newspaper, which was suppressed two years later. There he met Engels, also from the Rhineland, who was the son of a wealthy textile manufacturer. Engels worked for his father in Manchester, England, as a clerk, manager, and part owner. Expelled from Germany, Marx fled to Paris, where he again ran into Engels. Two years after that he was expelled and fled to Brussels. In 1848, a year that brought revolution to Paris as well as to Berlin, Vienna, Venice, Milan, and Parma, Marx and Engels collaborated to write *The Communist Manifesto*. That got Marx expelled from Belgium. He went to England and lived in London, supported by Engels, for the rest of his life.

Much of Marx's work concerns economics, political science, and sociology and has exerted enormous influence in these fields. But philosophical ideas underlie his work even when they are not evident on its surface. One way to understand them is to begin with Rousseau's account of the devolution of the state of nature from an idyllic state in which all our needs are satisfied to a desperate circumstance in which a few gorge themselves on luxuries while the multitude lack necessities. Marx endorses this picture. Rousseau's idea that society would naturally evolve into a split between masters and slaves echoes in Marx's distinction between the **bourgeoisie**, the owners of the means of production, and the **proletariat**, the workers:

> The history of all hitherto existing society is the history of class struggles.
>
> Freeman and slave, patrician and plebian, lord and serf, guild-master and journeyman, in a word, oppressor and oppressed, stood in constant opposition to one another, carried on an uninterrupted, now hidden, now open fight, a fight that each time ended, either in a revolutionary re-constitution of society at large, or in the common ruin of the contending classes. . . .
>
> Our epoch, the epoch of the bourgeoisie, possesses, however, this distinctive feature: it has simplified the class antagonisms: Society as a whole is more and more splitting up into two great hostile camps, into two great classes directly facing each other: Bourgeoisie and Proletariat.[24]

Marx's economic analyses predict that society splits into two large camps, for, in his view, capitalism by definition makes some people owners and others workers. (In his day, there were no public corporations; all enterprises were privately held.) The owners earn the profits and get greater profits the less they pay their workers. Hence, the owners get richer while the workers get poorer.

> In proportion as the bourgeoisie, *i.e.,* capital, is developed, in the same proportion is the proletariat, the modern working class, developed—a class of labourers, who

[24] Karl Marx and Friedrich Engels, *The Manifesto of the Communist Party* (New York: International Publishers, 1932).

> live only so long as they find work, and who find work only so long as their labour increases capital. These labourers, who must sell themselves piece-meal, are a commodity, like every other article of commerce, and are consequently exposed to all the vicissitudes of competition, to all the fluctuations of the market. . . . But the price of a commodity, and therefore also of labour, is equal to its cost of production. In proportion, therefore, as the repulsiveness of the work increases, the wage decreases.[25]

There are four distinctively philosophical ideas underlying this picture. First is the Kantian idea that everyone should be treated with respect. (See Chapter 8.) We should treat all people as ends-in-themselves, not merely as means. This means that everyone has a right to be treated with respect. Capitalism, in Marx's view, inevitably violates the categorical imperative, for it treats workers merely as means to production, as commodities, as objects.

Second is German philosopher G. W. F. Hegel's (1770–1831) idea that the workers inevitably internalize this treatment; they see themselves and their labour as nothing more than objects.

Why is labor alienating, according to Marx?

> The worker becomes all the poorer the more wealth he produces, the more his production increases in power and range. The worker becomes an ever cheaper commodity the more commodities he creates. With the *increasing value* of the world of things proceeds in direct proportion the *devaluation* of the world of men. Labour produces not only commodities; it produces itself and the worker as a *commodity*—and does so in the proportion in which it produces commodities generally.
>
> This fact expresses merely that the object which labour produces—labour's product—confronts it as *something alien,* as a *power independent* of the producer. The product of labour is labour which has been congealed into an object, which has become material: it is the *objectification* of labour. Labour's realization is its objectification. In the conditions dealt with by political economy this realization of labour appears as a *loss of reality* for the workers; objectification as *loss of the object* and *object bondage;* appropriation as *estrangement,* as *alienation.*[26]

Capitalism uses workers, and, moreover, the workers know that their survival depends on their being used. So workers see the product of their labor not as an expression of their creativity and power but as a symbol of their dependence and powerlessness. They see their work and its products as separate from and in fact hostile to their own goals and desires. In a sense, then, workers are estranged from themselves. As Locke says, we own our bodies and the work they do if we own anything at all. But in a capitalist society workers come to view their labour as alien to themselves, as external, as belonging to someone else. The result is that workers feel estranged from a part of themselves.

> What, then, constitutes the alienation of labour?
>
> First, the fact that labour is *external* to the worker, i.e., it does not belong to his essential being; that in his work, therefore, he does not affirm himself but de-

[25] Karl Marx and Friedrich Engels, *The Manifesto of the Communist Party* (Chicago: C. H. Kerr & Company, 1888).

[26] This and subsequent passages from Karl Marx, until otherwise noted, are from "Estranged Labour," from *The Marx-Engels Reader,* edited by Robert C. Tucker, translated by Martin Milligan (New York: Norton, 1978).

> nies himself, does not feel content but unhappy, does not develop freely his physical and mental energy but mortifies his body and ruins his mind. The worker therefore only feels himself outside his work, and in his work feels outside himself. He is at home when he is not working, and when he is working he is not at home. His labour is therefore not voluntary, but coerced; it is *forced labour.* It is therefore not the satisfaction of a need; it is merely a *means* to satisfy needs external to it. Its alien character emerges clearly in the fact that as soon as no physical or other compulsion exists, labour is shunned like the plague. External labour, labour in which man alienates himself, is a labour of self-sacrifice, or mortification. Lastly, the external character of labour for the worker appears in the fact that it is not his own, but someone else's, that it does not belong to him, that in it he belongs, not to himself, but to another.

Recall Mill's view that we exercise liberty only when we act freely, voluntarily, and with adequate information. The worker, Marx argues, cannot exercise liberty through labour, for the worker labours under the coercion of economic necessity. The products of his or her labour belong to the employer, not to the worker; they are alien in the direct sense that they belong to someone else. Since workers cannot exercise liberty through their labour, they cannot be self-determining. They are not free in any positive sense of freedom.

Third is the centrality of private property to alienation. Rousseau saw the turning point in the devolution of society as the introduction of private property, "the first man who, having enclosed a piece of ground, bethought himself of saying *This is mine,* and found people simple enough to believe him." For Marx, the relationship between private property and alienation is more complicated. Private property "is the *product* of alienated labour, and . . . is the *means* by which labour alienates itself, the *realization of this alienation.*" The worker's alienation from the products of labour in part stems from, but in part creates the social institutions of private property, for it makes the worker feel that labour and its products belong to someone else.

> The relationship of the worker to labour engenders the relation to it of the capitalist, or whatever one chooses to call the master of labour. *Private property* is thus the product, the result, the necessary consequence, of *alienated labour,* of the external relation of the worker to nature and to himself.

The social institution of private property is also a condition of the continued estrangement of labour. As the means by which labour alienates itself, it is crucial to the worker's self-estrangement. To overcome estrangement, then, one must get rid of private property.

> In this sense, the theory of the Communists may be summed up in the single sentence: Abolition of private property. . . .[27]

The bourgeoisie are the owners of the means of production. They are the holders of private property. Abolishing private property thus abolishes the bourgeoisie,

---

[27] Karl Marx and Friedrich Engels, *The Manifesto of the Communist Party* (Chicago: C. H. Kerr & Company, 1888).

overcoming the divide between the bourgeoisie and the proletariat and at last ending the class struggle. Abolishing private property also ends the workers' estrangement from themselves, enabling them to be truly self-determining. "In a higher phase of communist society," Marx writes,

> . . . the enslaving subordination of the individual to the division of labour, and therewith also the antithesis between mental and physical labour, has vanished; . . . labour has become not only a means of life but life's prime want; . . . the productive forces have also increased with the all-round development of the individual, and all the springs of co-operative wealth flow more abundantly. . . .[28]

Abolishing private property thus brings about positive freedom, a freedom to be self-determining, acting autonomously on the basis of a fully integrated self.

Finally, so long as the workers must work to meet their needs, their work cannot be an exercise of liberty; it must be external and thus alienated. Workers can only express themselves through their work, and come to feel that their work and its products are truly theirs, when they work freely, not under the threat of external or economic compulsion. So, overcoming estrangement requires meeting people's needs. Marx summarizes his theory of justice in a slogan:

> From each according to his ability, to each according to his needs!

The just society is one that meets people's needs. Moreover, it distributes goods quite generally according to need, and responsibilities quite generally according to abilities to fulfill them. The person with few abilities and many needs gets much in exchange for little, while the person with many abilities and few needs gets little in exchange for much.

This may seem to make Marx's theory of justice grossly unfair. People commonly think those who contribute much should receive much of the rewards. Marx denies it. That, he says, is a conception of formal equality that perpetuates inequality. It is equality in name only:

> This *equal* right is an unequal right for unequal labour. It recognizes no class differences, because everyone is only a worker like everyone else; but it tacitly recognizes unequal individual endowment and thus productive capacity as natural privileges. *It is, therefore, a right of inequality, in its content, like every right.* Right by its very nature can consist only in the application of an equal standard; but unequal individuals (and they would not be different individuals if they were not unequal) are measurable only by an equal standard in so far as they are brought under an equal point of view. . . . Further, one worker is married, another not; one has more children than another, and so on and so forth. Thus, with an equal performance of labour, and hence an equal share in the social consumption fund, one will in fact receive more than another, one will be richer than another, and so on. To avoid all these defects, right instead of being equal would have to be unequal.

People, in short, have different natural talents. Some grew up with many advantages; others, with few. Some are lucky; some aren't. None of these things make one person

[28] This and further passages from Karl Marx, unless otherwise noted, are from *Critique of the Gotha Program* (New York: International Publishers, 1933).

deserve more than another, for none are under anyone's control. You cannot be held responsible for the circumstances of your upbringing, your natural talents, or your luck. So why should you be rewarded or penalized for them? Moreover, the married worker with many children and the single worker with no dependents, paid the same wage, will in fact have very different standards of living. Is that fair? Marx argues that formal equality in such cases, far from promoting substantive equality, as Wollstonecraft argues, is incompatible with it.

Hannah Arendt

Hannah Arendt (1906–1975) was born in Germany and studied with Martin Heidegger and Karl Jaspers. In 1933, when Hitler took power, she fled to France. Eight years later she came to the United States, where she spent the rest of her life teaching at various universities.

Arendt finds much to admire in Marx. But she located a contradiction at the heart of Marx's thought about labor. Marx defines man not as a rational animal but as an animal who labors. Animals work to gather food, find shelter, find mates, rear young, and so on, but only humans have *jobs*. This, however, is what produces estrangement. Humans are essentially social, and societies past a certain early stage of development involve a division of labor. In what Marx calls "the realm of necessity," people must labor, must do their jobs, in order to survive. And this divides the worker from himself.

The "realm of freedom," in contrast, involves liberation from this necessity:

> The realm of freedom begins only where labor determined through want and external utility ceases. . . .[29]

People can be positively free—autonomous and self-determining—only when they can labor to express their individuality. Only then can estrangement cease. Marx describes the ideal, communist society as one in which the state "withers away" (or, better perhaps, "is transcended") and people

> do this today and that tomorrow, who hunt in the morning, go fishing in the afternoon, raise cattle in the evening, are critics after dinner, as they see fit, without for that matter ever becoming hunters, fishermen, shepherds, or critics.[30]

As Arendt writes,

> In communist or socialist society, all professions would, as it were, become hobbies: there would be no painters but people who among other things spend their time also on painting. . . .[31]

But now the contradiction is evident:

> People distinguish themselves from other animals through their labor.
> In the ideal society, however, there would be no labor.

[29] Karl Marx, *Capital* (Chicago: C. H. Kerr & Company, 1906–09), III.
[30] Karl Marx and Friedrich Engels, *The German Ideology* (New York: International Publishers, 1939).
[31] Hannah Arendt, *The Human Condition* (Chicago: University of Chicago Press, 1958), 118n.

It seems to follow that

> In the ideal society there would be no people.

Perhaps this is too harsh. At the very least, however, we seem to face a dilemma:

> The fact remains that in all stages of his work he [Marx] defines man as an *animal laborans* [laboring animal] and then leads him into a society in which this greatest and most human power is no longer necessary. We are left with the rather distressing alternative between productive slavery and unproductive freedom. (105)

We might, of course, embrace Marx's pastoral ideal in which all activity has the character of a hobby rather than an occupation. That has always been true of the wealthy elite who do not have to work to survive. Increasing affluence has made it true for larger segments of the population than ever before. But it is hard to see how such a society could be affluent enough to free everyone, or even most people, from the physical necessity of laboring to survive. In any case, such a situation, if possible at all, remains distant.

To avoid the dilemma Arendt notes, stemming from the simple two-premise argument above, there are only three other options:

1. We might reject Marx's definition of man as the animal who labors. Most philosophers, East and West, have defined humanity very differently, seeing man as the animal who is rational, who draws distinctions, who is capable of self-consciousness, or who worships. Then, the move to a society in which hobbies replace labor does nothing to threaten humanity itself.

2. We might reject Marx's view that the ideal society would replace labor with hobbies. Perhaps, in the ideal society, people would be affluent enough to choose their occupations, not from necessity, but as expressions of who they are. They would still be hunters, or fishermen, or shepherds, or critics, but their choice to be so would be fully free. For that reason, they would not find the choice alienating.

3. We might contend that the argument trades on an ambiguity. This, in essence, is Arendt's position. She distinguishes labor from work, and both from action:

How does work differ from labor?

> Labor is the activity which corresponds to the biological process of the human body, whose spontaneous growth, metabolism, and eventual decay are bound to the vital necessities produced and fed into the life process itself by labor. The human condition of labor is life itself.
>
> Work is the activity which corresponds to the unnaturalness of human existence, which is not embedded in, and whose mortality is not compensated by, the species' ever-recurring life cycle. Work provides an "artificial" world of things, distinctly different from all natural surroundings. Within its borders each individual life is housed, while this world itself is meant to outlast and transcend them all. The human condition of work is worldliness.
>
> Action, the only activity that goes on directly between men without the intermediary of things or matter, corresponds to the human condition of plurality, to the fact that men, not Man, live on the earth and inhabit the world. (7)

Arendt defines human beings as the creatures who *labor, work, and act.* While her definition thus expands Marx's, she agrees with him that labor is essential to humanity. She thus does not escape the dilemma through route 1; labor is indeed part of what distinguishes humanity from the rest of the animal kingdom. We can see the ambiguity she alleges by looking at route 2: In the ideal society, there would be no *mere* labor, no struggle for survival brought about solely by physical necessity. Certainly there would be no estranged labor. In another sense, however, there would *of course* be labor. Humans must labor to survive, by definition. If we define labor as meeting one's physical needs as a biological organism, as Arendt does, then in the ideal society people will labor, because they will still have to meet their biological needs. Even in the ideal society, people have to eat! Perhaps Marx means to say that, to put his point in Arendt's terms, the ideal society would contain no work. The hunter, fisherman, shepherd, and critic all engage in labor; they labor to meet biological needs. They do not produce any objects that outlive them. The toolmaker can produce hammers, plows, or microchips that outlast her, but that is not true of the hunter, fisherman, etc. But this would be a world, Arendt observes, in which there is no permanence, no durability, even, perhaps, no objectivity, for there would be no objects that last more than a very short time.

In Arendt's conception, the ideal society would not be a society without labor or without work. It would be a society in which activity became central and labor and work were in its service. She approvingly quotes Dante:

> For in every action what is primarily intended by the doer, whether he acts from natural necessity or out of free will, is the disclosure of his own image. Hence it comes about that every doer, in so far as he does, takes delight in doing; since everything that is desires its own being, and since in action the being of the doer is somehow intensified, delight necessarily follows. . . . Thus, nothing acts unless [by acting] it makes patent its latent self.[32]

Action is not estranged; it discloses the image of the agent, "makes patent its latent self," expresses its personality. By acting we "insert ourselves into the human world," Arendt proclaims.

> In acting and speaking, men show who they are, reveal actively their unique personal identities and thus make their appearance in the human world. . . . (179)

Action is thus the foundation of human dignity. It is more than mere making; it essentially involves interaction with other people, since our acts can reveal us and thereby give us delight only if they reveal us to others.

John Rawls

Contemporary American philosopher John Rawls singlehandedly revived interest in political philosophy in American philosophical circles with his influential book, *A*

---

[32] Dante, quoted in Arendt, *The Human Condition,* 175.

Theory of Justice. Rawls takes his inspiration from social contract theory and especially Rousseau. But he develops Rousseau's insights in a distinctly democratic direction.

Rawls begins with the question of justification and the insight of social contract theorists such as Hobbes, Locke, and Rousseau that a theory of justice, political authority, or set of social institutions is justified if people would voluntarily agree to it. Government is justified if people would prefer it to the state of nature. A particular theory of justice is justified if people would choose to live under it.

We must, however, think carefully about the circumstances of the choice. To mean anything, it must be a knowledgeable choice. Imagine designing a society in which you would want to live. Setting up the institutions of that society wisely would require a great deal of knowledge about how society works. You would have to know vast amounts of economics, sociology, political science, psychology, and so on, to know what effects the institutions you design would have in practice. The same knowledge would be needed to choose intelligently among competing sets of social institutions.

But is that all you would need? Is it enough, in other words, that the choice be knowledgeable? Rawls thinks not. Jones, for example, might love baseball and choose a set of institutions that would maximize the spread of baseball. Smith might be a Buddhist who chooses institutions that would spread the ideal of the *bodhisattva.* Jones might be a risk-taker, choosing institutions that would reward risk, while Smith might be risk averse and choose institutions that reward playing it safe. Jones may be poor, choosing institutions that would redistribute wealth from the rich to those less well off, while Smith may be wealthy and choose institutions that make no effort to redistribute wealth. In short, people may have all sorts of preferences that would affect their choice of social institutions in ways that seem morally irrelevant.

So, Rawls says, we must consider the choices that people would make from behind a **veil of ignorance.** Imagine that you do not know where you will fit into the social order that you create. Imagine that you do not even know anything about your own character, preferences, or conception of the good. You do not know anything about your own level of intelligence, abilities, strength, social status, education, race, origin, age, sex, and so on. You do not know, in other words, whether you are going to be rich or poor, whether you are risk-taking or risk averse, or whether you are a fan of baseball or Buddhism.

> This ensures that no one is advantaged or disadvantaged in the choice of principles by the outcome of natural chance or the contingency of social circumstances. Since all are similarly situated and no one is able to design principles to favor his particular condition, the principles of justice are the result of a fair agreement or bargain.[33]

Now, Rawls asks, what rules and social institutions would people choose from behind the veil of ignorance, in what he calls the **original position**? Whatever they would be—and Rawls thinks he knows what we would choose under such circumstances—they are the rules and social institutions that can be justified. They are legitimate, for people would choose them under fair conditions of choice. People would

[33] This and subsequent quotations from John Rawls are from *A Theory of Justice* (Cambridge: Harvard University Press, 1970).

choose them not because they are fair, just, or right, but because they are advantageous. People would expect to be better off as a result of living under them. Putting irrelevancies aside, it would be rational to choose to live under them.

> This explains the propriety of the name "justice as fairness": it conveys the idea that the principles of justice are agreed to in an initial situation that is fair.

The original position thus corresponds to the state of nature in Hobbes, Locke, and Rousseau. It is the hypothetical circumstance under which you would have to choose the authority, if any, under which you are willing to live. Rawls's innovation is to say that it must be a *fair* circumstance for the outcome of your choice to count as a justification.

What would you choose from behind the veil of ignorance? Some philosophers fear that there is no definite answer. Perhaps you would know so little about yourself, having abstracted away from your abilities, preferences, etc., that you would have no basis for choice. Others fear that we could come to no agreement, that different people would choose different institutions and principles of justice. But Rawls thinks we would settle on two principles of justice:

> First: each person is to have an equal right to the most extensive basic liberty compatible with a similar liberty for others.
>
> Second: social and economic inequalities are to be arranged that they are both (a) reasonably expected to be to everyone's advantage and (b) attached to positions and offices open to all. . . .

The first principle depends on the idea of a basic liberty, that is, a liberty central to citizenship. Basic liberties includes freedoms of speech, association, movement, voting, eligibility for political office, and so on. These are fundamental to making political decisions. So before settling anything else, we would agree that people should have equal rights to such liberties, and as much of them as is compatible with people having equal rights. The inspiration for Rawls's first principle is Hobbes's law of nature that we should maintain as much liberty for ourselves as we are willing to allow others against ourselves.

Rawls's second principle has two parts. The second requires that the positions to which inequalities attach be open to all. It is a principle of equal opportunity. People earn money by performing certain jobs and holding certain offices—by teaching at a university, keeping the books at a plumbing supply firm, fixing cars, or being mayor. Some jobs pay more than others. Rawls finds that acceptable as long as two conditions are satisfied. The jobs (professor, bookkeeper, mechanic, mayor) must be open to all; everyone must have an equal chance to compete for them. That does not mean that everyone must have an equal to chance to *get* them; people have different talents, abilities, and interests. Most mechanics would make bad professors, and most professors would make bad mechanics. But everyone has the right to equal consideration, to have a chance to compete with others on an equal footing.

So far, we have been considering the parts of Rawls's principles that concern formal equality. They are relatively uncontroversial, although there are arguments over details. The real debate begins when we move to the issue of substantive equality.

That brings us to the first part of the second principle, stating that inequalities are justified only if they can reasonably be expected to be to everyone's advantage.

This requirement, called the **difference principle,** is very strong. It implies that jobs may pay differently, for example, only if *everyone* can reasonably expect to benefit from that difference. Suppose that Smith has a better-paying job than Jones. Obviously she benefits from the difference in pay. But what about Jones? The difference is justifiable only if he also can reasonably expect to benefit.

But how might Jones benefit from Smith's higher salary? Perhaps Smith pays more in taxes, which benefits Jones in various ways. Perhaps Smith earns enough to hire Jones, or at least do business with whoever employs Jones. Perhaps the higher salary attached to Smith's job is needed to attract people to a position that is demanding, intense, time-consuming, highly skilled, and so on; if people with such jobs did not earn more, no one would agree to do them. Or perhaps Jones values having highly skilled people in Smith's profession and thinks he is better off if such jobs pay more to attract top talent. In short, Smith may deserve her higher salary, but only if it benefits Jones and others less well off.

In a free-market economy, that will often be the case. But not always. Sometimes, one person earns more than another because of personal qualities, connections, biases, personal preferences, and countless random factors. Inequalities that result are unjust. So Rawls's principles are meant to justify something like a democratic welfare state. The first principle is essentially democratic; it says that political liberties should be as widely and equally dispersed as possible. The second, as we have seen, permits many of the inequalities that result from a free-market economy. But it does not justify all. The government must play a role in redistributing income in order to guarantee that inequalities actually benefit everyone, even those on the bottom of the income scale. Justice demands government intervention to temper inequality.

> All social values—liberty and opportunity, income and wealth, and the bases of self-respect—are to be distributed equally unless an unequal distribution of any, or all, of these values is to everyone's advantage.
>
> Injustice, then, is simply inequalities that are not to the benefit of all.

Why does Rawls think we would agree to these principles? It is easy to understand the liberty and equal opportunity principles. In the original position, you know nothing about the position you will have in society, your own abilities, talents, preferences, and so on. Naturally, you want to participate in the goods of the society you are constructing as much as you can. So you want rights to participate in decision making and to compete for positions and goods. You will not agree to any provision that advantages some over others in political participation or economic competition because you do not know anything about yourself that would let you know what provisions might advantage you. You can expect something to benefit you only if you can expect it to benefit everyone. So you agree to have as much political freedom as everyone can have, and you agree that positions and offices to which goods attach should be open to all.

The same holds of the difference principle. You know nothing about yourself that would let you know whether a given inequality would help or harm you. So just as with liberties and opportunities, you can expect something to benefit you only if you can expect it to benefit everyone. You will therefore permit only those inequalities that benefit everyone.

Rawls's principles, while promoting democracy and an economy that is market based though also regulated and accompanied by redistribution, give people positive rights. You have the right to your share of basic liberties; you have the general rights to free speech and association but also the positive right to vote and run for office. You have the positive right to compete with others on an equal footing. And you have the positive right to a certain amount of welfare. You do not have the right to substantive equality, but you do have the right to enough goods that further inequalities work to your advantage.

One inspiration for the difference principle is Rousseau's dictum that "the social state is advantageous only when everyone has something and none too much." It is crucial that everyone have reason to consent to the social contract. If anyone does not reasonably expect to benefit from the contract, he or she has no reason to agree to it; government authority is then illegitimate with respect to him or her, and social institutions are similarly unjustified. There are practical reasons as well; anyone who has no reason to expect to benefit from the social order has reason to rebel against it. Injustice is thus quite directly a source of social instability. But the basic problem is that any attempt to justify social and political institutions on the basis of the (hypothetical or real) consent of the people fails if some people have no reason to consent.

SUMMARY

What kind of community should we be? How should we govern ourselves? How can we best promote liberty and justice? Many philosophers see the answers to these fundamental questions of politics as stemming from a theory of human nature. Aristotle and al-Farabi construct answers depending on a theory of virtue. For Aristotle, there are different kinds of goods, so there are different kinds of merit that determine a just distribution of goods and responsibilities in society. For al-Farabi, practical, deliberative, and intellectual virtues are ultimately one. The ideal ruler, the ideal philosopher, and the ideal religious leader thus end up being the same person.

Aquinas and Suárez develop a theory of natural law on the base that Aristotle's theory provides. A thing's virtue or excellence depends on its nature and function. God assigns things their natures and functions. God thus determines the excellence of each thing. There are certain natural institutions that best promote the excellence of individual human beings living in groups.

Hobbes and Xunzi justify government in a different way. Human nature is essentially competitive and selfish; life without government would be "solitary, poor, nasty, brutish, and short." So people would choose to live under the rule of government, surrendering their own liberty to a considerable degree to be protected from their fellow creatures. Hobbes initiates an influential approach known as social contract theory: government is justified because people would rationally choose to submit to its authority.

Legitimate government authority stops at the boundaries of individual liberty. Two conceptions of liberty have been important in political philosophy: (1) the negative conception of liberty as "the absence of external impediments," that is, freedom from interference; and (2) the positive conception of liberty as autonomy, that is, self-governance. Confucius and Laozi rely on the negative conception of liberty to argue for a minimally intrusive state. Locke does the same in the context of social contract theory, developing in the process a theory of rights. Everyone has natural rights to life, liberty, and property; they agree to submit to government to protect those rights. John Stuart Mill, relying on a negative conception of liberty, advocates the harm principle, postulating that the government (or private citizens, for that matter) may interfere with individual liberty only to prevent harm to others.

Rousseau, like Hobbes and Locke, rests his theory on the idea of a social contract. But his conception of liberty is positive. Each person commits all to the community in entering into the social contract and earns in return a full share of the benefits of communal cooperation. In doing so, a person becomes free; freedom consists in willing the good of all. Wollstonecraft, while pursuing her quest for women's equality in the context of classical liberalism, nevertheless bases her view on Rousseau's conception of rights and holds that people have a right to equal consideration regardless of sex or other morally irrelevant considerations. Marx and Engels take seriously Rousseau's claim that the founder of civil society was the first person to claim land and find people fool enough to believe him. That, they contend, was the root of all social injustice. Urging that private property be abolished, they press for a positive conception of liberty, encoded in their slogan, "From each according to his abilities, to each according to his needs!" Finally, Rawls pursues Rousseau's positive conception of liberty, developing a democratic theory of justice that provides for political freedom and participation, equal opportunity, and some degree of substantive equality.

In Chapter 1, I said that philosophy, the pursuit of good judgment, is in a sense the most practical of all disciplines. It is often abstract, and philosophical reflection frequently leads one far from practical concerns. But in the end, good judgment is of immense practical importance. The goal of philosophy is to live wisely, and few things can produce more practical benefit than that.

Nowhere is this more obvious than in politics. The philosophers we have considered in this chapter answer the central questions of political philosophy by constructing theories that might seem far removed from everyday life, even in legislatures and government agencies. Lives, however, hang in the balance—even when philosophical theories seem distant and abstruse. As Iris Murdoch remarks,

> Metaphysical systems have consequences. Those who think that the individual has reality only through the system do not only sit in studies, they sit in places of political power. Political systems break against individuals, but may also break individuals, which it is easier to do now than in the days of Hobbes.[34]

Review Questions

1. What role should the law play in developing character? Contrast the views of Aristotle, al-Farabi, Aquinas, and Mill.

[34] Iris Murdoch, *Metaphysics as Guide to Morals* (London: Penguin, 1992), 197.

2. Mill insists that voluntary slavery ought to be prohibited, although it might appear to fall into the realm of individual liberty. Why? Is his view consistent with the harm principle?
3. What is a law of nature? Compare the views of Aquinas, Hobbes, and Locke.
4. How does one's view of human nature shape one's conception of the proper role of government? Consider in your answer the views of Xunzi, Hobbes, Confucius, and Laozi.
5. How does Locke's conception of the state of nature differ from that of Hobbes? What difference does this make for their conceptions of government?
6. Contrast the views of economic activity and, in particular, work found in Locke, Smith, Rousseau, Marx, and Arendt.
7. Why do people enter into the social contract? What do they give up? What do they hope to gain? Compare the answers of Hobbes, Locke, and Rousseau.
8. What is the chief purpose of government, according to Hobbes? Locke? Rousseau? Marx?
9. Compare Rawls's account of distributive justice with that of Rousseau. How are they similar? How do they differ?
10. Thomas Jefferson, in the Declaration of Independence, proclaimed that all men are created equal. Contrast the likely reactions of at least two of Aristotle, al-Farabi, Hobbes, Locke, Rousseau, and Wollstonecraft to this statement. What implications do they take their views of equality to have for politics?

Terms for Review

agent One who consents to and participates in an act (1) freely, without coercion; (2) voluntarily, that is, having the competence to make the decision to consent and participate; and (3) in an informed way, without being deceived.

bourgeoisie In Marx, the owners of the means of production.

classical liberalism The view that governments exist primarily to protect liberty—that is, to protect people from external interference.

compensatory (or **rectificatory**) **justice** The kind of justice that concerns compensation: How do we compensate people for injury? Once a wrong has occurred, how do we set things right again?

difference principle Rawls's principle that inequalities are justified only if everyone may reasonably expect to benefit from them. It implies that jobs may pay differently, for example, only if everyone can reasonably expect to benefit from that difference.

distributive justice The kind of justice that concerns the distribution of goods and responsibilities in society.

eternal law The law of nature, established by God, that governs the entire universe. Everything in the universe obeys eternal law and does so necessarily. Science investigates eternal law and tries to describe it.

general (or **negative**) **right** A right to be left alone; a right that others not interfere; an ability to do or refrain from doing something without impediment from others.

general will What is in the community's interests; the common good. The general will desires not what the community perceives as being in its interests but what is *really* in its interests.

harm principle Mill's thesis that one may restrict liberty only to prevent harm to others.

historical theory of justice The view that whether a circumstance is just depends on how it came about.

natural law The law, ordained by God, that prescribes what things should do and be.

negative (or **general) right** A right to be left alone; a right that others not interfere; an ability to do or refrain from doing something without impediment from others.

negative conception of liberty Hobbes's conception of liberty as "the absence of external impediments," common to all classical liberals.

original position In Rawls, the situation in which you choose principles of justice from behind the veil of ignorance.

other-regarding act An act that affects people other than the agents of the act.

paternalistic law A law that restricts a person's freedom for his or her own good.

political virtue In Aristotle and Aquinas, the virtue of being able to benefit other people and society as a whole by exercising political power.

positive conception of liberty Self-determination, autonomy. A person has positive liberty to the extent that he or she has control over his or her life.

proletariat In Marx, the workers.

rectificatory (or **compensatory) justice** The kind of justice that concerns compensation: How do we compensate people for injury? Once a wrong has occurred, how do we set things right again?

retributory justice The kind of justice that concerns punishment: What punishments may be imposed, under what conditions, and for what infractions?

Scholasticism The philosophy of European medieval universities, especially that of Aquinas and his followers.

self-regarding act An act that affects only the agent or agents of the act.

social contract theory The view that government is legitimate to the extent that people would voluntarily submit to its authority.

state of nature In social contract theory, a hypothetical situation without government or other political authority.

veil of ignorance Rawls's imaginary circumstance in which you do not know where you will fit into the social order that you create: You do not know anything about your own character, preferences, conception of the good, level of intelligence, abilities, strength, social status, education, race, origin, age, sex, and so on.

For Further Reading

The classic exposition of the distinction between negative and positive conceptions of liberty is Sir Isaiah Berlin's brilliant but difficult "Two Concepts of Liberty," in his *Four Essays on Liberty* (London: Oxford University Press, 1969). On Aristotle's *Politics,* see Richard Kraut, *Aristotle and the Human Good* (Princeton: Princeton University Press, 1989); David Keyt and Fred D. Miller, Jr. (eds.), *A Companion to Aristotle's Politics* (Cambridge: Blackwell, 1991); Fred Miller, *Nature, Justice, and Rights in Aristotle's Politics*

(Oxford: Clarendon, 1995). On medieval political philosophy in the West and Middle East, see Ralph Lerner and Muhsin Mahdi (eds.), *Medieval Political Philosophy: a Sourcebook* (New York: Free Press of Glencoe, 1963).

On Hobbes and Locke, see C. B. Macpherson, *The Political Theory of Possessive Individualism: Hobbes to Locke* (Oxford: Clarendon Press, 1962); Vere Chappell (ed.), *John Locke: Political Philosophy* (New York: Garland, 1992).

There is a vast literature on Marx and Marxism. A classic study is Schlomo Avinieri, *The Social and Political Thought of Karl Marx* (London: Cambridge University Press, 1968). See also Robert Paul Wolff, *Understanding Marx* (Princeton: Princeton University Press, 1984).

Rawls's work has sparked a vast literature on justice and related issues. Some important contributions are Robert Nozick, *Anarchy, State, and Utopia* (New York: Basic Books, 1974), which defends a Lockean conception of rights and justice; and R. M. Dworkin, *A Matter of Principle* (Cambridge: Harvard University Press, 1985), which defends a conception closer to that of Rawls.

An outstanding overview of contemporary work on political philosophy is Robert E. Goodin and Philip Pettit (eds.), *A Companion to Contemporary Political Philosophy* (Cambridge: Blackwell, 1993).

APPENDIX

Writing Philosophical Essays

Reading philosophy is not quite like reading anything else. Philosophers don't tell many stories. They don't present many facts. They don't tell many jokes. What do philosophers do? They reflect. They ponder. Frequently, they argue; you have to learn to follow them as they do. So learning to read philosophy requires a new set of skills.

The same is true of writing philosophy. Writing a philosophical essay differs from writing a story, report, or essay on most other topics. To do it well, you must learn to reflect, ponder, and argue well. The needed skills take years to develop. But there are tips that can help you get started.

UNDERSTANDING THE ASSIGNMENT

The first step to writing a good philosophical essay is knowing what kind of essay you want to write. For most readers of this book, that means knowing what kind of essay your teacher wants you to write.

First, you should *understand the topic.* Are you writing about an issue, a position, a principle, a theory, or an argument? The assignment might concern a philosophical issue:

Is it possible to justify a belief and thus defend it from skeptical attacks?
Do we have any knowledge of the world independently of experience?
Is God's existence compatible with the existence of evil?
Is '7 + 5 = 12' an analytic or synthetic truth?
Could murder ever be morally justified?

Or it might concern a position on such an issue: skepticism, judgment rationalism, the view that the existence of evil demonstrates that there is no God, or the view that murder could never be morally justified.

The assignment might concern a general principle:

Discuss the medieval principle that nothing can be in the understanding without first being in the senses.
What is the principle of utility?
Discuss the Buddha's Third Noble Truth, that one can eliminate suffering by eliminating selfish desire.

Or it might concern a philosophical theory that comprises a number of definitions, principles, positions, and so on.

Explain the primary elements of Confucius's theory of virtue.
Discuss the Hindu theory of the self.

The assignment might also concern one or more arguments:

How does Russell argue against the coherence theory of truth?
Explain Nagarjuna's infinite regress argument. Do you find it convincing?
Discuss and evaluate the ontological argument for God's existence.

Finally, an assignment may involve more than one of these. It may ask about the role of a principle in a philosophical theory, for example. It may ask you to say what a theory implies about a particular issue. It may ask how one might argue for a certain position. Finally, it may ask you to compare and contrast two positions, principles, theories, or arguments.

Discuss the role the categorical imperative plays in Kant's moral theory.
What does utilitarianism imply about the ethics of keeping and breaking promises?
How might one argue against the correspondence theory of truth?
Compare the Hindu and Buddhist conceptions of the self. What do they have in common? How do they differ?

Second, you should *understand what you are expected to do.* Educational psychologists think of tasks that teachers expect students to perform as falling into five groups, arranged in order from the most complex to the simplest:

Synthesis
Analysis
Application
Understanding
Recall

The simplest assignments are matters of recall: Who studied under Plato and taught Alexander the Great? What does Kant call his fundamental principle of morality? What is *henotheism*? Many short-answer and multiple choice exam questions demand recall. Writing an essay generally requires much more. But recall is important, even in essay writing. Writing a good essay requires seeing connections, thinking of possible objections, envisioning possible responses, and so on. Recall—a thorough knowledge of philosophers' ideas and theories—gives you the bank of knowledge you need to do more advanced thinking. As Confucius says, "Thought without learning is perilous."

The other half of his saying, however, is that "Learning without thought is labor lost." Recall is enough for only the simplest tasks. Most philosophical assignments involve one or more of the other four cognitive levels. Let's proceed through them, from simplest to most complex, surveying the kinds of assignments you may encounter.

UNDERSTANDING

The first step beyond recall is understanding. It's good to remember that Kant's fundamental principle of morality is the categorical imperative; better to remember what the categorical imperative is, and better still to understand it. You may be able to recite the words "Act only on that maxim you can will to be universal law" without understanding what they mean. Beginners in philosophy should take time to make sure they understand basic concepts and principles. A good test is to see whether you can define the concept or state the principle in your own words. If you can't, you don't really understand it.

Many introductory philosophy assignments or exam questions ask you to demonstrate understanding. Here, for example, are possible essay questions or short (one- to three-page) paper topics:

Issue

Explain the issue dividing internalists and externalists in the theory of knowledge.

Position

What is concept empiricism? Judgment empiricism? How do they differ?

Principle

What is the "one simple principle" Mill argues for in *On Liberty*?

Theory

What is Peirce's pragmatic theory of truth?

Argument

What is the ontological argument for God's existence?

These are partly matters of recall. And a well-placed quotation from Peirce, Locke, Hume, Anselm, or Mill could be very effective. But a good answer goes beyond recall. It shows that you know what you're talking about—that you not only remember what someone says or the definition of a key term but that you can also *use* it. Consider the difference between these two answers to the fourth question on the list:

I. Peirce says that a statement is true if we are fated to agree on it. No matter what, we're bound to think it's true. So we might as well call it true.
II. Peirce says that a statement is true if we would agree to it in the ideal limit of scientific inquiry. Imagine a community of scientists trying to discover things about the world. They are bound to make mistakes along the way. If they use scientific method in a consistent, fair-minded way, however, they will discover and eliminate those mistakes. Eventually, given enough time, they will converge on a set of beliefs that survive all the tests that scientific method can provide. Those beliefs, Peirce stipulates, are true.

Answer I states Peirce's theory correctly—"a statement is true if we are fated to agree on it"—but doesn't display much understanding. In fact, the "no matter what" makes it sound as if Peirce is talking primarily about fate rather than scientific method. And the "we might as well call it true" suggests an attitude that seems foreign to Peirce. Answer II is longer, as an answer in which you take time to state things in your own words often will be. But it shows that the author can *explain* as well as state the theory.

To help yourself explain rather than merely state a principle, argument, or theory, imagine talking to a friend who says, "I don't understand. What does that mean?" Write as if writing to that friend.

Assignments based on understanding may take the form of questions or quotations. You may be asked to explain passages such as the following. The assignment in each case might be to explain the meaning and significance of the quotation in context. This requires that you state who said it, explain what it means, and explain why it is important to the overall position or argument.

> "But what then am I? A thing which thinks."
>
> "So act as to treat humanity, whether in your own person or in that of any other, in every case as an end in itself, never as means only."
>
> "If you seek after anything, you will always suffer. It is better not to do anything."
>
> "To say of what is that it is not, or of what is not that it is, is false, while to say of what is that it is, and of what is not that it is not, is true."
>
> "Let us weigh the gain and the loss in wagering that God is. Let us estimate these two chances. If you gain, you gain all; if you lose, you lose nothing. Wager, then, without hesitation that He is."

There is an art to explaining such passages. It extends to answering questions as well, since often the answer to an understanding-type question could be embodied in a brief passage from a philosopher.

First, restate the quotation in your own words. Sometimes, as with the second and fourth quotations above, that takes some doing. Sometimes, as with the others, it is straightforward. But in either case it is important to show that you understand what the quotation itself says.

Second, explain the significance of the quotation in its immediate context. Is it a definition? A fundamental principle? An argument? The conclusion of an argument? The fourth quotation above, for example, is Aristotle's definition of truth. Part of understanding it is recognizing that it is a definition. Similarly, the fifth passage is Pascal's argument for believing in God. Part of understanding it is recognizing that it is an argument.

Third, explain the significance of the quotation in the context of that philosopher's thought as a whole. Part of understanding the second quotation, Kant's categorical imperative, for example, is understanding that it is the fundamental principle on which he bases all of morality. Part of understanding Descartes's characterization of a human being as a thing that thinks is seeing how it follows from the *cogito,* the 'I think', as a solution to skeptical doubts, and also as a premise from which Descartes draws the conclusion that I can know nothing better than my own mind. Similarly, understanding the third quotation, Yixuan's advice not to do anything, requires seeing its relation to the Buddha's Four Noble Truths.

Finally, explain the importance of the quotation in relation to the issue it concerns. Why is a definition of truth important? Why does it matter whether I am first and foremost a thing that thinks? Understanding the passages above requires understanding their overall importance as well as what they say.

Whether you are answering a question or commenting on a quotation, writing a short paper faces you with many of the same issues. Here are some tips that I have given my students over the years:

1. *Be direct.* Answer the question. Explain the quotation. Don't waste time writing an introductory paragraph giving the philosopher's biography, etc., unless it relates directly to your answer.

2. *Focus on key elements;* don't waste time on details. Make it clear that you understand what's important.
3. *Tie your explanation* to the question or quotation itself as clearly as possible. Make the relevance of your points clear.
4. *Organize your explanation.* Make it easy for your reader to follow.
5. *Be cautious with your emotions.* The reader wants rational explanations, not emotional outpourings.
6. *Use conversational language* as much as possible. Imagine that you are writing to a friend in the class. It sometimes helps to imagine that you are writing a letter rather than a paper.
7. *Use quotations sparingly,* carefully, with explanations. But a well-placed quotation can be very effective.
8. *Explain things in your own words.* Think about what the philosopher means. Many philosophical statements are hard to understand. They may be abstract or even obscure; they may be complicated or deceptively simple. They may involve unfamiliar terms and ideas. Don't shy away from using them—but be sure to explain them.
9. *Talk about examples.* Philosophers often write abstractly. But what motivate them are examples: down-to-earth instances of general principles. Be specific by using examples, from your own life, from books or movies, or from your imagination to illustrate your point.
10. *Don't get too personal.* It's good to relate ideas to your own life. But keep the focus on the ideas. This is not Dear Abby, and it's not the Mental Health Hotline. Nor is it a newspaper editorial.
11. *Don't just give your opinions; give reasons.* Philosophy isn't just a matter of taste. If you like or don't like some idea or system of thought, it's fine to say so. But also say why. Does the philosopher get things wrong? Leave things out? Give only one side of the story? If called upon to give your own opinion, say as specifically as you can why you have that opinion. Explain what is wrong or left out and illustrate with an example.

Sample

Here is an actual (and excellent but imperfect) student paper that aims to demonstrate understanding by explaining the second quotation listed above. ("So act as to treat humanity, whether in your own person or in that of any other, in every case as an end in itself, never as means only.") Notice how the author is direct, immediately identifying the source of the quotation and explaining it in her own words.

> The quotation is from Immanuel Kant's *Grounding of the Metaphysics of Morals.* It is a practical rule proposed by Kant that we should respect others and ourselves and not try to take advantage of (or use) them.

She then proceeds to explain the role of the quotation in context. Let's consider what she says step by step.

> Kant is making an argument for the basis of moral principles, and he says that it all comes down to one categorical imperative.

The author wisely tries to locate the quotation in the context of Kant's overall argument. Calling it an "argument for the basis of moral principles" is a bit vague; it would be better to say that Kant is arguing that all of morality rests on a single principle.

> So this quotation serves as the practical imperative of Kant's principle of the categorical imperative of morality.

Here, unfortunately, the author becomes confused. What does 'the practical imperative of Kant's principle of the categorical imperative' mean? There is no need to speak of an imperative of a principle of an imperative here; the imperative *is* the principle, and Kant is giving us a *version* of the imperative. So, it would have been better to say, "This quotation states a version of Kant's fundamental principle, the categorical imperative." But the author helps to clarify her point with the next sentence:

> In other words, Kant has provided a principle of the basis of morality and now, with the quotation, he provides a conclusion as to how we should apply that principle to our actions.

The quotation, that is, states a version of the categorical imperative that is (a) the conclusion of an argument and (b) of more direct practical use than the original version, applying more readily to actions.

In the next paragraph, the paper locates the quotation in the structure of Kant's overall argument. Notice how nicely the author expresses the categorical imperative in her own words.

> Kant claims that there is only one categorical imperative and it provides that we act on principle and not make exceptions for ourselves. It also provides that we respect people and not use them. Kant argues that a first principle of morality must be categorical in that it is independent of particular goals and circumstances and that it is imperative, focusing on what *ought* to occur. Kant discusses why we need a first principle of morality. He states that, when considering morality, the only thing good within itself is a good will and good will acts on principle; therefore we must determine a first principle of morality.

This paragraph is direct and clear. The author is using her own words and explaining things in conversational language. The only gap is the final "therefore"; it would be better to explain further the link between a good will acting on principle and the need for one first principle of morality. It would also be good to explain Kant's argument for this specific version of the principle, that is, why he thinks we must treat all rational beings as ends in themselves.

In the next paragraph, the author takes us through some of Kant's examples, explaining the quotation by applying it to particular cases. This is a fine way of demonstrating understanding. So the general strategy is excellent. The author loses focus here, however, appealing to the first version of the categorical imperative rather than the one under discussion. That would not only have been more straightforward but would have done far more to clarify the quotation itself.

> Kant discusses how the notion of "act[ing] as if the maxims of your action were to become through your will a universal law of nature" becomes the imperative of duty. Kant's meaning of this universality law can be seen in his example of a man contemplating suicide. The man's maxim is that he will end his life because contin-

> uing to live results in more harm than good. This maxim cannot be a universal law of nature because it violates the man's claim of self-love as his reason for ending his life, when self-love should actually promote life.

This explanation leaves out something important even just in connection with Kant's "universality" version of the categorical imperative. Where does universality come in? It sounds as if the man is simply contradicting himself; he wants to end his life to promote it. In any case, the quotation speaks of treating people as ends rather than means; it would have been far more direct to speak in those terms and say that, from Kant's perspective, the man is using himself.

The author now goes on to explain where Kant's argument goes from here, thus filling out the context of the quotation and explaining its significance. The second half of the paragraph becomes somewhat redundant, indicating that the author does not have Kant's argument clearly in mind. Still, given the difficulty of Kant's argument, this is an impressive performance.

> Kant also calls his principle of morality the principle of the autonomy of the will. By this he means that every rational individual will judge *himself* according to *his* will's maxims that are in accordance with the universal laws of nature and independent of other goals and circumstances. Kant says that everything that is an end in itself has intrinsic worth, which is dignity. Kant proposes that because morality is a condition under which man can be an end in himself, morality has dignity. He then concludes that the universal laws to which a man should hold his maxims also have dignity, which man should respect. For this reason, Kant says that autonomy is the basis of the dignity of human nature.

Finally, the author tries to explain the significance of the point in the context of the issue in general. She does so by contrasting Kant with Aristotle.

> Kant provides a different basis of morality from that of Aristotle. Aristotle argues that the only intrinsic good is happiness and that moral virtue results from habit. Kant says that a first principle of morality must be something we can know independently of experience and because it is categorical (independent of particular goals), it must not depend on goals that we have for ourselves, such as happiness. So, Kant disagrees with Aristotle's view that intrinsic good comes from a desire for happiness and practice or habit.

Again, the author does the right thing but could have done it better. She has already said that Kant thinks the only thing good purely for its own sake is a good will; she could have contrasted that with Aristotle's view that happiness is the only purely intrinsic good. She also could have tied the contrast back to the quotation itself. Kant's central point is that rational beings must be treated as ends in themselves. How does that specifically mark a contrast with Aristotle or other philosophers? How does it fit into moral philosophy as a whole?

APPLICATION

Many writing assignments involve application. And indeed one of the best ways to show that you understand a principle or theory is to explain it by applying it to an example. Someone might, for example, answer the question about Peirce's theory of truth by writing,

> III. Peirce says that a belief is true if we are bound to agree to it in the ideal limit of inquiry. Consider, for example, the scientific claim that all electrons have the same mass. We can never prove that; we can never look at every electron, at every time and place, and measure its mass. But we can subject the claim to various tests. Perhaps, someday, the results of an experiment will lead scientists to give it up. Perhaps they will decide that electrons differ in mass among themselves. But suppose that never happens. Suppose, in fact, it never would happen, even if ideally competent and dedicated scientists were to study the question until the end of time. Then, Peirce would say, the claim is true. Indeed, that's what it means for it to be true: No matter how long one might study the question, one would have reason to believe it rather than the opposite.

The example helps to illustrate the point. It also helps to demonstrate that the author understands Peirce. So applying a principle or theory can be an excellent way of displaying understanding even when the assignment doesn't require it.

Many assignments, however, do require application. Consider these exam questions or short (three- to six-page) paper topics:

Issue

Discuss a particular case on which utilitarians and Kant would disagree.

Position

Give an example of an allegedly synthetic a priori truth. How would Hume account for our supposed knowledge of this truth?

Principle

Apply Kant's categorical imperative to the question of whether someone drafted into an army is obliged to fight.

Theory

Apply Aristotle's theory of virtue to Bart Simpson. Which virtues and vices does Bart exhibit?

Argument

How would Nagarjuna try to undermine your knowledge that there is a book in front of you?

The first asks you to think of and discuss a case in which Kant and utilitarians would disagree. The second asks you to apply Hume's account to a particular truth. Questions such as this, which allow you to choose the example to which you apply the principle or theory, may vary considerably in difficulty depending on the example you choose. So choose carefully; think through your example carefully before you commit to writing about it. The third and fourth questions pose a different difficulty: Bart exhibits virtues *and* vices, and the categorical imperative might generate some arguments on both sides. So you must see that the application of the theory in these cases is many-sided. Apply it in one way, and think carefully about whether it could be applied on the other side. The fifth question asks you not simply to state Nagarjuna's arguments but to apply them to a particular case, your knowledge that there is a book in front of you. This may require adapting and selecting from among the arguments as well as directing them at a specific instance.

I recommend application, whether or not the assignment explicitly calls for it, and, indeed, whether or not you have any assignment. Philosophical positions are often abstract and difficult to understand. There is no better way to see whether you understand a position than to think about how it would apply to a particular case. You find Kant's model of the mind (Chapter 3) confusing? Think about a particular case—someone's seeing a bright red ball, for instance—and see how Kant's model would apply. You aren't sure whether you understand the principle of utility? Think about a particular decision—whether or not to travel to see a friend for the weekend, say—and see how to calculate what you ought to do. In doing this, it's helpful to think about both easy and hard cases. In moral matters, for example, some cases are easy—Should I kill my roommate? for example—while others are hard (for instance, Should I consent to an operation on my mother, who is no longer able to decide for herself, that might save her life but might also kill her?). Easy cases are good for testing understanding; hard cases are good for testing the theory.

ANALYSIS

Many philosophical assignments require analysis: breaking down a thesis, argument, or position into its parts and explaining their relations to each other. This is more difficult than understanding or application and usually takes longer. It is the main task expected in many five- to ten-page papers. But even shorter papers or questions may require some analysis, and longer papers almost always require it even if they also require more.

Here are some questions or paper topics that center on analysis:

Issue

Rationalists and empiricists disagree about whether there are any innate concepts and about whether there are any synthetic a priori truths. How do these two issues relate to each other?

Position

What is "dogmatic empiricism"? How might a proponent respond to the charge—which a traditional rationalist might make—that such a position is ultimately incoherent?

Principle

What are Kant's main formulations of the categorical imperative? Why does he take them to be equivalent?

Theory

Discuss the epistemological problem that faces Plato's theory of forms.

Argument

Outline Hume's criticisms of the argument from design.

To analyze an issue, position, principle, theory, or argument effectively, one must (a) break it down into its parts and (b) explain how those parts relate to each other. This takes on a slightly different character depending on what you are analyzing.

Analyzing Issues

Think of an issue as a question or combination of questions—for example, Are there innate concepts? Are there synthetic a priori truths? How do those questions relate? To break the issue down into parts, you must first understand it. Then you must think about the different parts or aspects of the issue. To do that, think about what is at stake. In this case, the question concerns two ways of distinguishing rationalists from empiricists. We can ask whether there are innate concepts, distinguishing concept rationalists from concept empiricists. And we can ask whether there are synthetic a priori truths, distinguishing judgment rationalists from judgment empiricists. The issue concerns the relation between those two distinctions. The question itself identifies the main parts we must be concerned about: the issue of whether there are innate concepts and the issue of whether there are synthetic a priori truths.

Once you have identified the parts, think about how they might relate. Often, in philosophy, the most important relations to ask about are logical. Does a certain answer to one question imply an answer to another? If there are innate concepts, for example, does it follow that there are synthetic a priori truths? If there are no innate concepts, does it follow that there are no synthetic a priori truths? But not all relations are ones of logical implication. One issue may presuppose another, in the sense that it cannot even arise unless the other is resolved in a certain way.

Analyzing Theories

Philosophical theories generally consist of various theses. The central task in analyzing them is to break them down into those theses. Then you can ask what each thesis means and how the various theses relate to each other. In Chapter 3, for example, I analyze rationalism as consisting of two theses: (a) concept rationalism, the thesis that there are innate concepts, and (b) judgment rationalism, the thesis that we can know something about the world independently of experience. In Chapter 4, I analyze theories of the self in Plato, Hinduism, and Buddhism. Each theory postulates various components of the self (for example, senses, mind, desire, reason, soul, and so on) and says something about how they relate to each other. Each theory thus postulates the existence of certain things and says something about their relation. Analyzing theories is important not only to understanding them but to understanding where they succeed and where they fail. Often a theory contains certain insights but also makes mistakes. It's important to be able to distinguish what is true from what is false in such a theory, and analysis helps you do that.

Analyzing Arguments

If an argument is at stake, the first task, breaking it down into its parts, becomes a matter of identifying premises and conclusions. Once those are identified—and that can be a tricky task—three important questions remain.

First, is the argument, as reconstructed, valid? If not, is it inductively reliable?
Second, if it is not valid, it can always be made valid by adding one or more assumptions to the list of premises. What assumptions would be required?
Third, is the argument sound? That is, are the premises (and any additional assumptions needed) all true?

In Chapter 6, for example, I reconstruct several arguments for and against God's existence. Descartes's ontological argument, for example, is simply

God has all perfections.
Existence is a perfection.
Therefore, God exists.

This is valid; if the premises are true, the conclusion must be true. (From the premises, it follows that God has existence, and that implies that God exists.) We can still ask whether the premises are true. Descartes claims that the first is simply the definition of God. So the question becomes, is the second premise true? Is existence a perfection? That is exactly where Kant attacks the argument.

The argument from evil, which purports to show that there is no God, might be reconstructed:

If there is a God, God is all-good and all-powerful.
If God is all-good, God is willing to prevent evil.
If God is all-powerful, God is able to prevent evil.
If God is able and willing to prevent evil, then evil does not exist.
But evil does exist.
Therefore, there is no God.

This argument is valid. If the premises are all true, the conclusion must be true as well. But is the argument sound? Are the premises all true? Most theists attack the fourth premise, pointing out, for example, that eliminating some evil might require either the toleration of some other evil or the prevention of some greater good.

To see the importance of underlying assumptions, consider the Indian philosopher Udayana's version of the cosmological argument:

Things like the earth must have a cause.
Because they are effects.
Like a pot.

This argument is highly compressed. It does not even state its intended conclusion, namely, that God exists. And it contains another argument. So let's reconstruct it with premises and conclusion:

Things like the earth are effects.
Therefore, things like the earth must have a cause.
Therefore, God exists.

Plainly this is not valid as stated. But consider the first argument, that things like the earth are effects and so must have a cause. We can make that valid by adding a hidden assumption:

Things like the earth are effects.
[Every effect has a cause.]
Therefore, things like the earth must have a cause.

The assumption that every effect has a cause seems safe; it seems true by definition. Now, how do we get from there to the conclusion that God exists? We might first think of reaching a conclusion about the earth (which Udayana seems to take as meaning "the universe"):

> Things like the earth must have a cause.
> [The earth is a thing like the earth.]
> Therefore, the earth has a cause.

Again, the added assumption seems obviously true. Now, to reach the conclusion, we need to identify the cause of the earth as God:

> The earth has a cause.
> [The earth's cause is God.]
> Therefore, God exists.

That argument, too, is now valid. So, we have constructed a valid inference to the conclusion that God exists from the premise:

> Things like the earth are effects.

with the help of the additional assumptions

> Every effect has a cause.
> The earth is a thing like the earth.
> The earth's cause is God.

We then need to ask whether the argument is sound. So, we must consider whether the premise and the added assumptions are true. The first two assumptions are surely true, and the third, Udayana would presumably say, is his definition of God. So, the question becomes, Is it true that things like the earth are effects?

Analyzing Positions and Principles

Perhaps the most difficult task is analyzing positions and principles. On their face they appear unified as answers to a certain philosophical question or as single philosophical claims. Prominent philosophical positions and principles, for example, include the following (one from each chapter of this book):

> Truth is correspondence with reality.
> Knowledge is justified true belief.
> All knowledge comes from experience.
> There is no soul.
> Every substance consists of matter and form.
> God exists.
> Virtue is a mean between extremes.
> You should treat other people as ends, not merely as means.
> Everyone has a right to life.

But these positions and principles only *seem* simple. Each relates concepts in a certain way. We can ask what concepts are involved and how they relate, just as we can ask about the relations of theses within a theory or premises and conclusions within an argument. The position that truth is correspondence with reality, for example, we can see as involving the concepts of reality and correspondence. What is reality? To what, that is, are truths supposed to correspond? And exactly what is the relation of correspondence? Similarly, the principle that every substance consists of matter and form involves concepts of matter, form, and constitution. We can ask what matter is, what form is, how they relate to each other, and how they constitute substance. Even the simplest theses on the list—'There is no soul' and 'God exists'—involve the concepts of soul and God. What is a soul? What is God? To analyze a position or principle, then, ask what concepts it involves. Try to understand each, and try to understand how they relate.

EVALUATION

Many philosophy questions and paper topics require more than analysis. They require you to take a position of your own. The topics above, for example, with just slight additions, require you to say what you think about an issue:

Issue

Rationalists and empiricists disagree about whether there are any innate concepts and about whether there are any synthetic a priori truths. How do these two issues relate to each other? Can one coherently combine concept rationalism with judgment empiricism or vice versa?

Position

What is "dogmatic empiricism"? How might a proponent respond to the charge—which a traditional rationalist might make—that such a position is ultimately incoherent? Do you consider that response successful?

Principle

What are Kant's main formulations of the categorical imperative? Why does he take them to be equivalent? Do you consider them equivalent? Why or why not?

Theory

Discuss the epistemological problem that faces Plato's theory of forms. Does Plato succeed in solving it, in your view?

Argument

Outline Hume's criticisms of the argument from design. Do you find his criticisms persuasive? Why or why not?

All these assignments ask you to develop, state, and defend a stance of your own.

The first step to synthesizing a position of your own is to evaluate someone else's position. This is one reason why philosophers often begin by criticizing the work of previous philosophers. It is also one reason why philosophy teachers usually ask students to critique a philosophical position or argument. Criticizing something requires understanding it. Usually it requires being able to apply it; showing that the theory has absurd implications is a favorite technique of the critic. Often it requires analyzing it. To know what is wrong with an argument or theory, one must break it down into its parts to see which are plausible and which might be mistaken. It may also be necessary to tease out hidden assumptions that underlie the position or argument. But it requires something more: taking a point of view on the position or argument, saying what is wrong with it or, for independent reasons, why it is correct.

That suggests that evaluating a position or argument can be broken down into several steps:

1. *Understanding:* Make sure you understand it. State it in your own words.
2. *Application:* Make sure you see how it applies. Pick an example and think through what the principle, theory, or argument says about that particular case.
3. *Analysis:* Break it down into its parts. If you are criticizing a principle, think about whether it can be broken down into several principles. If you are criticizing a theory, think about the various assertions of the theory and how they relate to each other. If you are criticizing an argument, identify the premises and conclusions. Ask whether the conclusion really follows from those premises—see the appendix to Chapter 1, "Logic in a Nutshell"—and whether the premises are true.
4. *Evaluation:* Take a point of view. Do you agree with the principle? Are you persuaded by the argument? If so, explain why. (Not all evaluation is negative; sometimes you may want to argue that the philosopher gets it right!) If not, say why. Be as specific as you can in identifying what goes wrong. That is why the analysis step is so important. To criticize something effectively, you must be able to point out the mistake. And you can do that only by analyzing the position or argument into its parts.
5. *Synthesis:* Give *reasons* for your point of view. It is not enough to say, "Yixuan's view implies that you shouldn't try to do anything at all beyond your daily bodily functions. That's not true." Explain *why* you don't think it's true. In short, you must construct an argument of your own to justify your criticism. If you think the philosopher is right, you must give an independent argument backing up that conclusion. If you think the philosopher is wrong, you must give an argument for your stance. Taking a point of view, in other words, is not just taking a stand, staking out a bit of "logical space." It is *defending* that space, justifying what you think, giving reasons.

The most common shortcoming of student papers of this kind is precisely that they don't give reasons. It is not enough to say that you agree or disagree with a position. It is not enough to say that you find an argument persuasive or unpersuasive. *You must explain why.*

SYNTHESIS

The highest level assignment you can be given asks you to synthesize a view of your own. The first step in this is criticizing someone else's view. To do that, you must develop and defend a point of view of your own. But it is one thing to take a stand about what someone else has said; it is quite another to stake out a position of your own and defend it independently. But most long assignments and many shorter ones ask you to do just that.

How do you go about developing, articulating, and defending your own point of view? That is not an easy question. In many ways, it is simply the question, How do you do philosophy? Still, there are tips that can help you. Let's consider the three steps independently: developing, articulating, and defending a point of view.

Developing a Point of View

Begin with the issue you are addressing and the questions that define it. Ask yourself those questions. Think about how various philosophers answer them. What is your own view? Perhaps you agree with some philosopher you have studied. Perhaps you want to defend an opposing view. Perhaps you see a way to combine insights from various thinkers. In any case, you must decide how you want to answer the philosophical questions that you are addressing. Sometimes you may find that you can think this out in advance of writing. Often you may find that you don't know what you think until you write it out. Both methods can be effective. But it is important to keep the central questions in mind and return to them frequently, whether or not you have an answer worked out when you begin writing. Even the person who has thought out an answer in advance may find that writing changes his or her view of the matter.

It is also important to keep in mind *all* the relevant questions. It is easy to focus on one question while neglecting other, closely related questions. Someone trying to answer the question of whether there are any innate concepts, for example, should consider what concepts are, what it is for a concept to be innate, what kinds of concepts might be innate, whether innate concepts would give us a priori knowledge, and so on. A good philosophical essay recognizes the depth of the issue it addresses partly by seeing the various questions involved.

Articulating a Point of View

To articulate a point of view, you need to find a way to put your perspective into words, making it intelligible to someone else. That can be difficult. If you cannot explain your point of view, you probably have not thought it through clearly and carefully. So if you find yourself having trouble writing, ask first whether you have defined what you want to say.

There are other reasons, of course, why articulating your view may be difficult. There may be several different questions it addresses; you may not be sure where to begin. You may not know whether to start by explaining your view or by criticizing someone else's view. There is no set answer to these questions; which approach works best depends on the details. There are two general models: the paper that starts with the thesis to be defended and then considers opposing views, and the paper that begins with opposing views and develops its own thesis by examining their shortcomings. Let's call these the *positive* and the *critical* approaches.

Whichever approach you take, think through the general structure of your paper. Write a general outline that has the major topics you will cover. Any paper that is more than a few pages long should have an introductory paragraph that introduces the topic, says what you are going to say about it and generally how you will argue for your position. It need not be long, but it should catch the reader's attention and make clear the general approach of your paper. If you are going to figure out what you want to say as you write, then write the introduction last. But do not neglect it. Students often think that a paper is more effective if it keeps the reader in suspense, saving the conclusion of the argument for the end for dramatic effect. But a philosophical essay is not a mystery story. A reader who does not understand what a paper is trying to do or where it is going typically finds it hard to follow.

Then, what you do depends on which approach you are taking. Say that you are taking a positive approach, starting by laying out your own ideas. Then do that. Outline your view for the reader. There may be details, qualifications, and so on that can wait until later, when you consider other views, possible objections to your view, possible revisions or alternatives, and so on. You need not include those at the beginning (though you may want to warn the reader that some are coming later). But you want to explain your point of view. In doing this, imagine that you are engaged in an understanding-type assignment—except that what you are trying to understand, in this case, is your own view. Make sure you can explain it in your own words, ideally in several different ways. Give an example or two to show what your view means in practice.

Then argue for your view. Outline your reasons for believing it. Show how your view differs from other possible (or actual) views. Show what makes it distinctive. Where do you agree with other thinkers? Where do you disagree? What advantages does your view have over those alternatives? In this part of the paper, you should be arguing that your view is better than the other options: it solves or avoids problems they encounter; it explains things they fail to explain; it explains several things all at once; it gives a simpler explanation; etc.

If you take a critical approach, then begin by outlining one or more alternative views and criticizing them. Why are they inadequate? What makes you think that we need a new perspective on the issue? Then, once you have explained the problems with current approaches, outline your own view as the solution to those problems. Do not forget to go back and explain how your view accounts for the things that motivated those alternative views. It is no good, after all, if you explain some things they don't only to leave unexplained things they handle very well. Also, argue for your view; explain why it is a good solution to the problems you have sketched.

Defending a Point of View

Once you have articulated your point of view, then defend it. Explain why it is better than the alternatives. Imagine someone holding another view criticizing your account. What objection might an opponent advance? How would you respond? It is important to think through various possible objections in order to be sure that your position makes sense and forms a plausible answer.

To think of possible objections, return to the alternative positions you have considered in formulating your own view. What motivates those positions? What do advocates of those positions see as their greatest strengths? How do they argue for their positions? They are likely to object that your view does not capture the insights that their perspectives embody and does not take adequate account of their arguments. So, think about how you might respond to their arguments.

Suppose, for example, that you are arguing that no knowledge is absolutely certain (a position known as *fallibilism*). To think of possible objections to your view, think about things that various philosophers have taken to be certain: Descartes's 'I think, therefore I am'; G. E. Moore's 'I have two hands'; and other philosophers' 'It appears to me that I have two hands.' Each forms the basis of a possible objection to your view. So to make your case effectively, you need to say something about those examples. It can be helpful to think about what they have in common. (They are all, for example, first-person.) Responding to that may take care of a number of objections at once.

Finally, you should write a conclusion to your paper, summarizing your position, your basic reasons for holding it, and perhaps further issues that it raises. Remind the reader, in other words, what your main points have been and why they matter. On the debate team in high school, I received the advice, "Tell 'em what you're going to tell 'em; tell 'em; and then tell 'em what you told 'em." It is good advice in philosophy as well.

OUTLINES

Here are two paper outlines: one for a positive paper, laying out a view and then arguing for it; the other for a critical paper, beginning by discussing and then criticizing a view.

A Positive Paper Outline

Introduction

- Topic: Introduce the topic.
- Point of View: Say what you are going to say about it.
- Argument: Say how you will argue for your position.

Exposition

- Outline: State your point of view.
- Explanation: Explain your point of view in your own words.
- Examples: Give an example or two to show what your view means in practice.

Argument

- Rationale: Outline your reasons for holding your view.
- Contrast: Show how your view differs from other possible (or actual) views.
  - Agreements: Where do you agree with other thinkers?
  - Disagreements: Where do you disagree?
  - Advantages: What advantages does your view have over those alternatives?

Defense

- Possible objection(s): What objection might an opponent advance?
- Response(s): How would you respond?

Conclusion

- Position: Restate your view.
- Argument: Remind the reader of your main arguments.

A Critical Paper Outline

Introduction
- Topic: Introduce the topic.
- Point of View: Say what you are going to say about it.
- Argument: Say how you will argue for your position.

Exposition of an Opposing View
- Outline: State the point of view.
- Explanation: Explain the point of view in your own words.
- Examples: Give an example or two to show what it means in practice.

Critique of the Opposing View
- Objection: Explain why the opposing view is wrong.
- Analysis: Analyze the opposing view to understand why it is wrong.

[Exposition of Another Opposing View] (optional)

[Critique of That Opposing View] (optional)

Exposition of Your View
- Outline: State your point of view.
- Explanation: Explain your point of view in your own words.
- Examples: Give an example or two to show what your view means in practice.

Argument for Your View
- Rationale: Show how your view solves the problems afflicting other views.
- Analysis: Show why it solves them.
- Contrast: What is the crucial difference between your view and its competitors?

Defense
- Possible objection(s): What objection might an opponent advance?
- Response(s): How would you respond?

Conclusion
- Position: Restate your view.
- Argument: Remind the reader of your main arguments.

It is ideal to be able to fill in such an outline before you begin writing your paper. But even if you find that you need to develop your ideas as you write, an outline can be useful. Fill in the outline as you go. It will help you to structure your paper in a clear, understandable way; remind you to argue for your view, consider objections, and so on; and help you to understand what your view is and why you hold it. Your paper will be better as a result.

Credits

P. xviii Reprinted by permission of the publishers and the Trustees of Amherst College from *The Poems of Emily Dickinson,* Thomas H. Johnson, ed., Cambridge, Mass.: The Belknap Press of Harvard University Press. Copyright © 1951, 1955, 1979 by the President and Fellows of Harvard College. Excerpts from Bertrand Russell, *The Problems of Philosophy,* London: Williams and Norgate, 1912, 121. With permission from Oxford University Press. Excerpts from *The Collected Works of Charles Sanders Peirce,* Volume 5, edited by Paul Weiss and Charles Hartshorne, Cambridge, Mass.: Harvard University Press. Copyright © 1934 by the President and Fellows of Harvard College. Reprinted by permission of the publisher. Excerpts from Jose Ortega y Gasset, *The Modern Theme,* translated by James Cleugh, Harper and Row, 1961. Originally published by C. W. Daniel Company Ltd., 1931.

Chapter 2 Excerpts from the *Nyaya-sutra,* translated by Mrinalkanti Gangopadhyay, Calcutta: Indian Studies, 1982. Excerpts from *Chung Tzu, Taoist Philosopher and Chinese Mystic,* translated by Herbert A. Giles, London: Allen and Unwin, 1926. Excerpts from *Philo,* Volume I and Volume III, translated by F. H. Colson and G. H. Whitaker and Volume VII, translated by F. H. Colson, Cambridge, Mass.: Harvard University Press, 1929, 1930, and 1937. The Loeb Classical Library® is a registered trademark of the President and Fellows of Harvard College. Reprinted by permission of the publisher and Trustees of the Loeb Classical Library. Excerpts from *Sextus Empiricus,* Volume I, *Outlines of Pyrrhonism* Loeb Classical Library Volume #273, translated by R. G. Bury, Cambridge, Mass.: Harvard University Press, 1933. The Loeb Classical Library® is a registered trademark of the President and Fellows of Harvard College. Reprinted by permission of the publisher and Trustees of the Loeb Classical Library. Excerpts from Ludwig Wittgenstein, *On Certainty,* Harper and Row, 1969. Reprinted with permission of the publisher.

Chapter 3 Excerpts from the *Yogasutra,* translated by Stephen Phillips. Copyright © Stephen Phillips. Reprinted with permission. Excerpts from St. Teresa of Avila, *Interior Castle,* translated by E. Allison Peers, in *Collected Works of St. Teresa of Avila,* Sheed & Ward, 1946. Reprinted by permission of Sheed & Ward, an Apostolate of the Priests of the Sacred Heart, 7373 South Lover's Lane Road, Franklin, Wisconsin 53132.

Chapter 4 p. 160 Reprinted by permission of the publishers and the Trustees of Amherst College from *The Poems of Emily Dickinson,* Thomas H. Johnson, ed., Cambridge, Mass.: The Belknap Press of Harvard University Press. Copyright © 1951, 1955, 1979 by the President and Fellows of Harvard College. Excerpts from *The Recorded Conversations of Zen Master I-Hsuan,* in Wing-tsit Chan, ed., *A Source Book in Chinese Philosophy,* Princeton University Press, 1963. Copyright © 1963 Princeton University Press. Reprinted with permission from the publisher. Excerpts from *The Lankavatara Sutra,* translated by Sri Aurobindo.

Chapter 5 p. 208 John Burt, *Work without Hope: Poetry by John Burt,* p. 82, Johns Hopkins University Press, 1996. Reprinted with permission from Johns Hopkins University Press. Excerpts from *Philo,* Volume I and Volume III, translated by F. H. Colson and G. H. Whitaker and Volume VII, translated by F. H. Colson, Cambridge, Mass.: Harvard University Press, 1929, 1930, and 1937. The Loeb Classical Library® is a registered trademark of the President and Fellows of Harvard College. Reprinted by permission of the publisher and Trustees of the Loeb Classical Library. Excerpts from *The Surviving Works of Wang Fu-Chih,* in Wing-tsit Chan, ed., *A Source Book in Chinese Philosophy,* Princeton University Press, 1963. Copyright © 1963 by Princeton University Press. Reprinted with permission from the publisher.

Chapter 6 p. 264 Reprinted by permission of the publishers and the Trustees of Amherst College from *The Poems of Emily Dickinson,* Thomas H. Johnson, ed., Cambridge, Mass.: The Belknap Press of Harvard University Press. Copyright © 1951, 1955, 1979 by the President and Fellows of Harvard College. Excerpts from *Averroes' Tahafut al Tahafut (The Incoherence of the Incoherence),* translated by Simon van den Bergh, Luzac & Co., 1954.

Chapter 7 p. 312 John Burt, *Work without Hope: Poetry by John Burt,* p. 82, Johns Hopkins University Press, 1996. Reprinted with permission from Johns Hopkins University Press. Excerpts from *The Large Sutra on Perfect Wisdom,* edited and translated by Edward Conze, University of California Press, 1975. Copyright © 1975 The Regents of the University of California. Reprinted with permission from the publisher. Excerpts from Moses Maimonides, *The Guide of the Perplexed,* translated by Schlomo Pines, The University of Chicago Press, 1963. Reprinted with permission from the publisher.

Chapter 9 Excerpts from *The Attainment of Happiness* in *Alfarabi's Philosophy of Plato and Aristotle,* translated by Muhsin Mahdi, Free Press, 1962. With permission from the translator. Excerpts from Jean-Jacques Rousseau, *The Social Contract and Discourses,* translated by G. D. H. Cole, J. M. Dent & Sons, Ltd., 1913. Excerpts from "Estranged Labor" by Karl Marx, translated by Martin Milligan, from *The Marx-Engels Reader, Second Edition* by Robert C. Tucker. Copyright © 1978, 1972 by W. W. Norton & Company, Inc. Used by permission of W. W. Norton & Company, Inc.

Glossary/Index

a posteriori proposition A proposition whose truth value can be known only through experience, 109–114, 123, 129, 144, 146, 285, 295, 308
a priori proposition A proposition whose truth value can be known independently of experience, 109–114, 119–123, 125, 129–130, 133, 136–144, 147, 183, 251, 281, 284–285, 308
Abraham, 402, 406–407
absence, 224–225
absolutism (or objectivism) The thesis that we can speak of sentences, assertions, or beliefs—in a given language and given context—as objectively true or false, period, without reference to a speaker, society, or interpretive community, 29–35
abstraction, 115, 129, 222
Acaranga Sutra, 372–374
accent The fallacy of trying to justify a conclusion by relying on presuppositions arising from a change in stress in a premise, 56
accident An argument that tries to justify its conclusion by treating an accidental feature of something as essential, 53
accidental quality, 229
action, 300, 427, 430
  Arendt on, 464–465
  category, 224, 227
  ethics and, 313, 326, 328, 334, 336
  human excellence and, 414, 418–420
  pragmatism, knowledge and, 16, 147–148
  religious, 265–267
  right and wrong, 256, 353–408
actual object (*alambana*) The cause of a perception; in Dignaga, atoms, 233, 240, 249–250, 253, 258
actual obligation Something I am, all things considered, obliged to do, 397
act-utilitarianism A moral theory that judges individual actions directly by their effects on the amount of good, 388
***ad hominem* (or *ad personam*) argument** An argument that attempts to refute a position by attacking those who hold or argue for it, 50–51
adequacy, 8
***advaita* (or non-dualism)** The view that the self (*atman*) is in reality nothing other than Brahman, 161–162, 166, 241–242, 273–274
affirming the consequent An informal fallacy having the form "If p, then q; q; therefore, p", 40
African philosophy, 1, 20, 38, 42, 94, 388–390, 404–406
African religion, 265–267, 271–272
African Religions from a Philosophical Point of View (Wiredu), 272
agent One who consents to and participates in an act (1) freely—without coercion; (2) voluntarily—that is, having the competence to make the decision to consent and participate; and (3) in an informed way, without being deceived, 446–449
***ahimsa* (noninjury)** The thesis that one should not injure or kill any sentient being, 24, 150, 372–374
Akan, 388–390
al-'Adawiyya, Rabi'a, 153, 299
***alambana* (actual object)** The cause of a perception; in Dignaga, atoms, 233, 240, 249–250, 253, 258
Alambanapariksa (Dignaga), 233, 240
Alexander the Great, 36, 80, 323
Alexandria, 80, 82, 216, 218, 303, 417
Al-Farabi, 288–289, 386, 417–419, 426, 445, 469
Al-Ghazali, 289–291
alienation, 460–463
aloneness (*kaivalya*) The goal of mystical insight and bliss in yoga, 150, 162
ambiguity, 55–56
amphiboly An ambiguity in sentence structure; also, an argument relying on such an ambiguity, 55–56
Analects, The, (Confucius), 5–7, 266, 275, 330–336, 433–435
analogy A similarity, in certain respects, between distinct things, 46–48, 68, 73, 86, 89, 105, 147, 203, 272, 296, 300
analytic method A philosophical method of seeking to understand complex wholes by breaking them down into their parts, 12–13
analytic philosophy The style of philosophy that has dominated the philosophical community in Britain and the United States throughout the twentieth century but extends back to Plato and Aristotle, centering on breaking down complex problems into simple parts, 12–13
analytic statement One that is true or false by virtue of the meanings of its words, 72, 107–110, 120–121, 142, 283–284
***anatman* (no-soul)** The Buddhist view that there is no self, 85, 172–175, 256, 357
Animal Liberation (Singer), 373
Anselm, St., of Canterbury, 271, 282–285
antifoundationalism (or coherentism) The thesis that justification does not require a foundation or level of ultimate justifiers, 70–71, 88–89
Apelles, 84
Apology (Plato), 2–4, 314, 390
appeal to authority An argument that tries to justify its conclusion by citing the opinions of authorities, 52–53
appeal to common practice An argument that tries to justify a kind of action by appealing to the common practice of the community, 51
appeal to force An argument that tries to justify a kind of action by threatening the audience, 52
appeal to ignorance An argument that tries to justify its conclusion by appealing to what is not known, 52
appeal to pity An argument that tries to justify a kind of action by arousing sympathy or pity in the audience over the consequences of the action, 52

and ethics, 354–358
no-soul doctrine, 168–176, 256
on objects, 222, 241
on reincarnation, 229, 373
and skepticism, 84–87
and virtue, 341–344
Zen, 188–201, 204
Buddhist idealism The thesis that there is no self but everything is mind-dependent, 147, 174–176
Burke, Edmund, 378, 445, 450, 456
butterfly, 79–80

Calvin, John, 401–402, 406
Capital (Marx), 463
care, 344–346
Carlyle, Thomas, 382
Carneades, 94
Cartesian circle, 282–283
carvaka Also called *lokayata,* a term meaning "those attached to the ways of the world," a group of ancient Indian philosophers who were materialists, empiricists, and skeptics, 376–377
categorical imperative An 'ought' statement without an 'if', applying universally without regard to circumstances, goals, or desires; in Kant, the one moral axiom from which other moral imperatives can be derived as theorems, 359–369, 375, 381, 460
Categories (Aristotle), 223, 227–230
category In Aristotle, a general kind of thing to which linguistic expressions refer; in Kant, a pure concept of the understanding, an innate cognitive ability of a very general kind; a possible logical form of an object, 138–146, 223–230, 252
causal-role functionalism The view that types of mental entities and events correspond to causal roles that physical entities and events can play, 203–204
cause Aristotle distinguishes four kinds of causes or explanations: *formal,* relying on essence or definition; *material,* relying on matter; *efficient,* relying on a causal chain of events; and *final,* relying on some goal, purpose, or function, 174–176, 179–180, 198
a priori concept, 138–140, 251
a priori principles, 121, 144
and the argument from thought, 278–282
causal fallacies, 54–55
causal inferences, 74, 90–91, 109
causal power, 115
and the cosmological argument, 286–293
empiricism, 128, 130, 132–135
and existence, 148–149
four kinds of, 230
mental, 201, 203–204
of perception, 233, 236, 240, 249, 253–260
cave, 118, 212–214, 218–220
ceteris paribus clause, 396–397
chariot, 162–168, 171–174, 256, 306, 357
Charles I, 11, 17, 18
***chi* (material force)** In neo-Confucianism, something akin to matter but with the dynamic character of force or energy; or, material objects, that is, concrete, tangible things, 254–256
chiliagon, 181
Christianity, 94, 151, 217–222, 265–267, 269–272, 286, 302, 332, 344, 382, 405, 420
Cicero, 49, 94, 396, 420n
circumstantiality, 26–27, 30–31
City of God, The, (Augustine), 304
class struggle, 426, 459–463
classical liberalism The view that governments exist primarily to protect liberty—to protect people from external interference, 432–449
classical theism The view that there exists an almighty (omnipotent), all-knowing (omniscient), eternal, omnipresent, transcendent, and compassionate God, 270–272, 276, 308
classical Western concept of God The concept of a being who is almighty (omnipotent), all-knowing (omniscient), eternal, omnipresent, transcendent, and compassionate, 270–272, 276, 308
clear and distinct ideas, 235, 281–282
clear mind, 195, 199
cogent argument An inductively strong argument with true premises, 44
cogito 'I think'; the foundation of all knowledge, according to Descartes, 98–100, 119–120, 129, 181, 184, 195, 281
cognitio (knowledge), 100
coherence theory of truth The theory holding that a sentence or belief is true if it coheres with a comprehensive theory of the world, 13–16, 18–19, 34
coherentism (or antifoundationalism) The thesis that justification does not require a foundation or level of ultimate justifiers, 70–71, 88–89
commensurability, 416–417
Commentar zu Kant's Kritik der Reinen Vernunft (Vaihinger), 119n, 136n
Commentary on Kant's Critique of Pure Reason (Smith), 135
common good, 417, 423–424, 427–429, 440–444, 453–457
common sense, 35, 91–92, 241, 243, 260, 376, 381, 385–386
communication, 34–35, 92–93, 399
Communist Manifesto (Marx and Engels), 459–463
communitarian consequentialism The view that good acts are those that maximize the well-being of society, where that is understood as independent of the well-being of its individual members, 388–390
communitarianism The view that the good of the community does not reduce to the good of its members, 388–390
Compendium of Philosophy (Madhava), 377
compensatory (or rectificatory) justice The kind of justice that concerns compensation: How do we compensate people for injury? Once a wrong has occurred, how do we set things right again? 415
complex ideas Compounds of other ideas, 127, 139
complex question A question that presupposes a conclusion; also, an argument relying on such a premise, 49
composition The fallacy of attributing something to a whole or group because it can be attributed to the parts or members, 56
concept, 14, 106–108, 112–114, 123–125, 127, 136–141, 148, 155, 175, 183, 222, 252, 277–278, 283–285
concept empiricism The view that all concepts come from experience, 113, 124–125, 278
concept rationalism The view that there are innate concepts—that we have concepts that we do not derive from experience, 112–113, 144
conceptualism The view that universals are mind-dependent, 210–222
Concerning Noah's Work as a Planter (Philo), 217

conclusion The thesis an argument tries to justify, 37
concordance In Peirce, coherence; the agreement with the ideal limit of inquiry that defines truth, 18
Confessions (Augustine), 304–305
conflict, 161, 168, 173, 321–323, 334, 345–349, 385–387, 393, 396–397, 407, 429–432, 438, 445, 458
conformity, 10–11
Confucianism, 123, 196, 265–267, 275, 336, 346, 374–376, 390–395, 427, 432–435
Confucius
  contemporaries, 24, 169, 209
  on family, 385
  on God, 275
  Mencius and, 390–391
  Mozi's criticism of, 374–376
  on philosophy, 2, 4–7
  on politics, 432–436, 470
  on virtue, 329–336, 338, 342, 344–346, 349
conscience, 353, 390–399, 402, 446
consciousness, 233, 399, 464
  Buddhism on, 162, 168–169, 171, 174–177, 240–242
  contemporary theories of, 200–204
  Hume on, 176–177
  Kant on, 142–144, 168, 177, 249–252
  Locke on, 184–188
  mystical, 149–150
  realists on, 257
  Zen on, 192, 194, 198
consciousness-only, 174–176, 192, 202
consequences, 16–17, 358–359, 370, 374–376, 388–390, 400, 470
consequentialism The view that all moral value rests ultimately on the consequences of actions, 358, 370, 374–376, 388–390
conservatism, 35, 425
consistency, 15
Constitution, United States, 445, 455
Constitutional Code, The, (Bentham), 369
context, 15, 20, 30–31, 33, 89, 393
contextualism A method that stresses understanding things in the contexts in which they occur, 15, 26–27, 30–31
contingent proposition A proposition that is neither necessary nor impossible—that is, that could be true and could be false, 13, 111–112, 114, 129, 146, 288
contradictory (or impossible) proposition A proposition that cannot be true, 13, 111, 284–285
Copernican revolution in philosophy Kant's view that the laws governing the realm of experience are not in the objects themselves but in us: "... we can know in things a priori only what we ourselves place in them," 82, 136–137, 148
Copi, Irving, 53
correlation, 54–55
correspondence theory of truth The theory holding that a sentence (or statement or belief) is true if it corresponds with reality—if, that is, it corresponds to some fact, 9–14, 16–17, 29, 34–35
cosmological argument The argument that God exists as a first cause of the universe or necessary being on which all other beings depend, 285–294
counterexample To an argument: An argument of the same form with true premises but a false conclusion. To a principle: A particular case in which the principle gives the wrong result, 40–42
counterfactual, 13, 123
Cratylus (Plato), 22–24
craving, 173, 307–308, 354–357
Crest-Jewel of Discrimination (Sankara), 241–242
Critique of Pure Reason (Kant), 55, 107–108, 121–122, 135–146, 249–253, 283–285, 300–301
Critique of the Gotha Program (Marx), 462

Damascene, St. John, 422
Dao In Confucius, the Way or Path; the proper way to live. In Laozi, the way the universe works; the One, which underlies everything but admits no description, 5–7, 76–79, 256, 267, 275–277, 331, 333, 336–341, 429
Dao de Jing (Tao te ching) (Laozi), 266, 275–277, 336–341, 435–436
Daoism One of the world's great religions, stemming from the thought of Laozi, stressing the underlying unity of the world and championing the virtues of noninterference and tranquility, 75–80, 189, 256, 265–267, 275–277, 308, 336–341, 346, 349, 428, 435–436
Darshana, 161
Darwin, Charles, 201, 295–296, 381, 459
day aspect The world as revealed to consciousness; the world as it seems to us prereflectively. The world consists of things that have shape, color, and texture. Things have goals and purposes. We ruminate, make decisions, and act on the basis of reasons. In this consists our freedom. Life is at the center of our concerns. We see things as being meaningful; the world is full of value. There are good and evil, right and wrong, virtue and vice, 200–204
de A thing's power, force, nature, character, or virtue; Dao embodied in a particular thing, 77, 336–341
De Benificiis (Seneca), 396–397
De Fide Orthodoxa (Damascene), 422
De Interpretatione (Aristotle), 37
De Legibus (Suárez), 425–426
De Principiis (Origen), 218–220
De Trinitate (Augustine), 220–222
De Veritate (Aquinas), 10–11
death, 166, 170, 187, 194, 198, 201, 204, 267–268, 275, 306, 386, 430, 454
Declaration of Independence, 71
deconstruction A method of uncovering inconsistencies in theories, literary or philosophical works, or intellectual traditions, that focuses on binary oppositions—good/bad, right/wrong, true/false, for example—that reveal the structure of the thought being analyzed and proceeds to show how the theory, work, or tradition under consideration undermines those very oppositions, 28–34
deductively valid argument An argument in which the truth of the premises guarantees the truth of the conclusion, 39–44, 294
defeasibility, 148
Defense of Common Sense (Moore), 92
definition, 2, 129, 214, 225, 230–231, 283, 314–321, 465
deism The view that God exists and created the world but has had no further interaction with it, 272
deliberative virtue, 417–419, 433, 469
democracy, 413, 415, 426, 445, 468–470
Democritus, 94, 209, 233
demonstrative premise A premise advanced as true, 38
denying the antecedent An informal fallacy having the form "If p, then q; not p; therefore, not q", 40
deontological theory A moral theory holding that moral value rests at least in part on something other

than the consequences of actions, 358–359
Deontology (Bentham), 384
Derrida, Jacques, 28–34
Descartes, René, 12–13, 41, 71, 195, 200, 202, 204, 404, 425, 429
on doubt, 96–100
on innate concepts and a priori knowledge, 119–121, 128, 135, 137–138, 146
on the mind/body problem, 181–184
on primary and secondary qualities, 234–236, 240, 243, 251, 254, 260
on proofs of God's existence, 278–285, 292, 298
designated matter A specific bit of matter, for example, "this flesh and that blood," 232
desire 10, 203, 280, 359, 374, 465
Buddhism on, 149, 173, 193, 197, 199, 307–308, 342–344, 354–357
Confucius on, 330
consciousness and, 177, 180
Hobbes on, 430
Locke on, 438
Mencius and Wang on, 256, 392–396
Plato on, 167–169, 322
Xunzi on, 427–428
Dewey, John, 36
Dhammapada, 354–357
dharma Duty; the aggregate of qualities or states of consciousness; appearances, 85, 175, 192, 194, 198–199, 400
Dharmakirti, 71, 147–149
Dharmapala, 175
Dharmottara, 147–149
dialectic (also called the Socratic method) Socrates's process of questioning and showing that proposed definitions cannot be correct, 2, 211
dialectical premise A premise advanced as a hypothesis or as an assumption reduced to absurdity, 38
dialogue, 2, 6
Dialogues Concerning Natural Religion (Hume), 295–299
difference principle Rawls's principle that inequalities are justified only if everyone may reasonably expect to benefit from them, 468
differences, 29
Dignaga, 233, 236, 238, 240–241, 249–250, 253, 258, 260
dignity, 366, 383, 465
dilemma, 49–50, 54
direct realism The view that sensations can justify knowledge without themselves constituting knowledge, 71
Discourse on the Origin of Inequality (Rousseau), 450–452
disjunctive syllogism, 39
distributive justice The kind of justice that concerns the distribution of goods and responsibilities in society, 415–417, 469
divine command theory The view that God distinguishes right from wrong: What God commands is obligatory; what God allows is permissible; what God forbids is wrong, 399–408
division The fallacy of arguing from the properties of a group or whole to the properties of members or parts, 56
dog-faced baboon, 23
dogmatic empiricism The view that we can know something about the world as it really is, beyond the reach of the senses, even if all knowledge depends on experience, 146–156
dogmatism The view that it is possible to attain knowledge of the world as it is, 75, 83, 90, 137, 147
Domitian Ulpian, 424n
doubt, 88–99, 181, 280
dreams, 22, 79–81, 95, 97, 259
Dropping Ashes on the Buddha, 197–199
dualism The view that there are two kinds of thing: form and matter, or mind and body, or, in Hinduism, individual and God, 162, 166, 183–184, 194, 202, 204, 241
dukkha Pain, suffering, being out of joint, 307, 354–357
Duration of Life, The, (Buddhaghosa), 171
dynamic idealism Wang Yangming's view that everything is mind-dependent, 394–395
Dynamics of Faith (Tillich), 269–270

effect, 16, 46, 74, 130, 132–135, 148–149, 175, 255, 278–279, 286, 359, 378
Elements of Logic (Whately), 49
eliminativism The view that in principle we can and should give up speaking of ordinary objects and mental states and replace this talk with the language of science, 203–204
Elizabeth, Princess of Bohemia, 183–184, 200
emanation, 118
empirical consciousness, 168, 177, 250–252
empiricism The view that all knowledge of the world comes from experience, 106, 109–110, 113–115, 123–135, 146–147, 155, 376–377
emptiness, 174, 189, 192, 198–200, 204, 276
Enchiridion (Augustine), 302–305
Engels, Friedrich, 459–463, 470
Enlightenment, 135, 149, 162, 169, 188–201, 241, 303, 342–344, 354–357, 373, 376, 377, 436
Enquiry Concerning Human Understanding (Hume), 110, 124–134, 136, 246, 249
enumeration, 43–45, 49–50
Epictetus, 396
Epicurus, 94, 301, 306, 382, 391
epistemology The theory of knowledge, studying what we know, how we know it, and what, if anything, lies beyond the bounds of knowledge, 1, 6, 65–100, 145–146, 249–252
equality, 390, 416, 437–438, 449, 451–470
equilibrium, 19–20
equivocation An ambiguity in a word or phrase; also, an argument relying on such an ambiguity, 55
Erasmus, 75, 394, 401
error, 21–23, 81–82, 258
error theory The view that ordinary, commonsense views are literally false, even if we cannot do without them, 203–204
Essay Concerning Human Understanding (Locke), 106–107, 111, 113, 124–127, 129, 132, 136, 184–188, 437
Essay on African Philosophical Thought: The Akan Conceptual Scheme (Gyekye), 389
Essay on Classical Indian Theories of Knowledge (Matilal), 86–87
Essays on Truth and Reality (Bradley), 13–15
esse est percipi To be is to be perceived; a primary thesis of Berkeley, 21, 145, 249, 252, 254, 256
esse est posse percipi To be is to be perceivable; a consequence of Kant's transcendental idealism, 145, 252, 256
essence The properties necessary to a thing, without which it would not be what it is, 53, 181, 199, 229–233, 238–240, 414

Derrida on, 28
enlightenment as highest, 162
and evil, 197, 201, 302–305, 320, 399, 402, 405, 417
form of, 118, 213–217
God as, 128, 281–282
stoics on, 396
utilitarianism on, 369–371, 377, 387–389, 447
Wang Fuzhi on, 256
gravity, 183–184
great chain of being, 216
Great Learning (Confucius), 433–434
Greece, 1–4, 75, 80, 344
Grosz, Elizabeth, 30–31, 34–35
Groundwork of the Metaphysics of Morals (Kant), 357–369
Guide of the Perplexed (Maimonides), 386–388
gunas In Samkhya, "strands": *sattva* (light, clarity, intelligence); *rajas* (passion, dynamism); and *tamas* (darkness, inertia, stupidity), 150, 162, 164, 168, 400
Gyekye, Kwame, 372, 388–390

Haack, Susan, 35
habit, 131, 133, 193–194, 327, 330, 335–336, 348, 451
haecceity Individual essence; "thisness," 230
happiness 353, 413
a priori principles, 122
al-Farabi on, 417, 419
Aristotle on, 324–326, 415, 417
Confucius on, 434
Kant on, 300, 357–358, 360
Locke on, 187–188, 451
Plato on, 167–168
utilitarianism on, 56, 369–390, 444–445
Wollstonecraft on, 457
harm principle Mill's thesis that one may restrict liberty only to prevent harm to others, 444–449, 470
Hartshorne, Charles, 285
hasty generalization An argument that draws a conclusion about a kind or large class of things on the basis of a small or biased sample, 45, 54
Hatata (Zera Yacob), 405
Heart Sutra, 198
hedonism The view that only pain and pleasure are sources of value, 371, 377
Hegel, Georg Wilhelm Friedrich, 253, 256, 450
Heidegger, Martin, 200, 463
Heliogabalus, 185
henotheism The view that there is one God who takes many forms, 273–274
Heraclitus, 2, 177, 222
heteronomy Following someone else's command, 366
Hinduism, 150, 161–166, 174, 189, 229, 241, 265–267, 273–274, 357, 400–401
historical theory of justice The view that whether a circumstance is just depends on how it came about, 440
historicism The thesis that truth is relative to a culture or historical epoch, 26–28, 33
Hobbes, Thomas
as analytic philosopher, 12
contemporaries, 96, 183, 254, 404
on infinity, 38, 41
on the state of nature, 427, 429–432, 437, 446, 448–449, 452, 466–467, 469–470
hogs, 185
holism The thesis that we must ultimately evaluate beliefs by evaluating their coherence with a comprehensive system of beliefs, 13–15
Holmes, Sherlock, 52
Holt, Edwin, 257, 260
home schooling, 11, 91, 382
Hongren, 196
How to Make Our Ideas Clear (Peirce), 16
Huang-Po, 190–191
Huineng, 196
Human Condition, The, (Arendt), 463
human nature, 275, 419–421, 426–430, 437, 441–444, 450–458, 469
humanism The view that value is to be defined in purely human terms, 275
Hume, David, 12, 176–181, 204, 280, 440, 450
on arguments for God's existence, 295–302, 306
on empiricism, 110, 121, 124–140, 142, 146, 148–149
on ethics, 397–399
on idealism, 242, 249–250, 253, 256, 260
Hutcheson, Francis, 369
hypocrisy, 51, 91
hypothetical imperative An 'ought' statement, such as "You ought to work hard if you want to succeed," containing an 'if' and depending on circumstances or someone's goals and desires, 359–360

Ibn-Rushd (Averroës), 271
Idea of the Holy, The, (Otto), 268–269
ideal limit In Peirce's thought, the state of knowledge we approach more and more closely as we engage in scientific inquiry under perfect conditions, 17–19
idealism The thesis that reality is mind-dependent, 13, 145–148, 202–204, 233, 240–253, 256–260, 394–395
Idealist View of Life, The, (Radhakrishnan), 150
identity, 178–180, 184–188, 465
ignoratio elenchi An argument ignorant of its own goal or purpose that misses the point, in effect slipping one conclusion in place of another, 50
illumination In Augustine, what enables us to know the forms; God illumines the intelligible world, making it intelligible to us, 119, 121, 219–222
imagination, 144, 181–182, 251
Imam, 419
immanence, 144
immortality, 105, 122, 144, 306, 400
imperfect duty A general obligation, allowing an agent choice about when and how to fulfill it, 362
impossible (or contradictory) proposition A proposition that cannot be true, 13
impression In Hume, sensation or reflection, 125–128, 134–135, 138–139, 148, 176–180, 243, 248
inaction (*wuwei*) In Laozi, the policy of letting nature take its course, 337, 339
Incoherence of the Incoherence (Averroës), 289–292
Incoherence of the Philosophers (al-Ghazali), 289–292
incomplete enumeration An argument presupposing a disjunction that does not include all available possibilities, 49–50
individualism The view that the good of the community is nothing but the sum of the goods of its members, 378, 390
individualizer, 224–225
induction Reasoning from the known to the unknown, in John Stuart Mill's phrase; the truth of the premises does not guarantee the truth of the conclusion, but if the argument is reliable, does make it probable, 39, 43–48, 52–55, 130–135

inductively strong (or reliable) argument An argument in which the truth of the premises does not guarantee the truth of its conclusion but does make the truth of the conclusion probable, 39, 43–48, 52–55
inference, 73–75, 105, 130, 147, 294, 376–377
infinite regress In Aristotle, the answering of a question of justification with an instrumental good rather than an intrinsic good—which merely invites further question, 83, 85–86, 89, 225, 289–292
informal fallacy An argument that violates rules of evidence, relevance, or clarity in particular contexts, 48–56
inherence, 140, 224–225, 247
innate concepts Inborn cognitive abilities not acquired or derived from experience, 106, 112–114, 123–125, 128–129, 137, 155, 252, 278–282, 391–395, 402
Inquiry into the Nature and Causes of the Wealth of Nations, An, (Smith), 441–444
Institutes of the Christian Religion (Calvin), 401–402
institutions, 425, 449, 466–470
Instructions for Practical Life (Wang Yang-ming), 394–395
instrumental goods Things desired for the sake of something else, 323, 360
intellect, 10–11, 108–109, 120–121, 162–163, 168, 216, 282, 400
intellectual virtue, 327, 417–419, 469
intelligible world The realm of Platonic forms, 115, 118, 211–219
intentional object An object of thought, 279
intentionality, 176
Interior Castle (Teresa of Avila), 151–152
internal object (*artha*) What a perception is or appears to be a perception of, 233, 249–250, 253, 258
internalism The thesis that knowledge is true belief for which the knower can provide a justification, 66–71, 74–75, 94–100; also, the view that moral imperatives necessarily give reasons for acting, 368
intrinsic goods Things desired for their own sake, 323, 330, 360, 419
introspection, 142–143, 168, 177–178
intuition In Kant, sensation or reflection, 109, 112, 129, 136–144
Investigation of the Object of Awareness (Dignaga), 233, 240
Islam, 151–153, 265–267, 269–272, 286–293, 386, 405, 417–419
Isidore, St., of Seville, 423
Isvarakrsna, 162

Jainism, 24–26, 372–374
James, William, 18–20, 22, 151n, 269, 299–300, 367
Jaspers, Karl, 463
Jefferson, Thomas, 436–437
Jesus, 7, 396
John (gospel of), 7
Johnson, Samuel, 50–51
Judaism, 151, 265–267, 269–272, 286, 288, 386, 405
judgment, 7, 112, 139–141, 249, 313, 470
judgment empiricism The view that there are no synthetic a priori truths; anything that really yields content about the world can be known only through experience, 113, 125, 129
judgment rationalism The view that some of our knowledge of the world is innate—that we can know some synthetic truths a priori, 113
junzi Superior person; literally, "child of a ruler"; in Confucius, one of noble character, 4–7, 329–336
Just Caring (Manning), 344–346
justice, 214, 320–321, 328, 332–333, 338, 375, 414–417, 424–426, 430–431, 439–440, 451, 455, 462, 465–470
justice (*yi*) A virtue akin to piety, correctness, and justice in ancient Chinese thought, stressed especially by Mencius and Mozi, 6, 47–48, 330, 336, 338–339, 375, 391–393, 428
justification, 66–71, 86–87, 93–94, 130–131, 323–325, 381, 467–470

Kant, Immanuel, 55, 82, 105, 165, 168, 177, 184, 222, 265, 296, 375, 378, 381, 386, 403, 406, 440, 449, 456, 460
  on analytic truth, 107–108
  on a priori truth, 110, 119, 121–122
  on the Copernican revolution, 129, 135–146, 148, 155
  on ethics, 357–369
  on a moral argument for God's existence, 300–301
  on the ontological argument, 283–285
  on transcendental idealism, 249–253, 256, 258–260
Kaozi, 47–48, 214
karma: Habit, 193–194, 198, 400
Kennedy, John Fitzgerald, 27
Kepler, Johannes, 12
Kierkegaard, Søren, 406–407
King, Martin Luther, Jr., 424–425
knowledge 65–100, 105–156, 272, 466
  Aquinas on, 10–11, 230, 232
  Augustine on, 94–96, 118–119
  Bradley on, 14–15
  Confucius on, 5–6
  Descartes on, 96–99, 119
  Dharmakirti on, 147–149
  externalist theories of, 71–75
  of good and evil, 305, 320, 323, 401–402
  Hume on, 124–135
  internalist theories of, 66–71
  Jainism on, 24
  Kant on, 135–146, 250–252
  Leibniz on, 122–123
  Locke on, 124–135
  mystical, 149–156
  Nyaya on, 71–75, 88–91
  Plato on, 66–71, 114–118, 214
  realists on, 259
  and skepticism, 75–100, 289, 377
  sources of, 105–156
  and testimony, 52–53
  and virtue, 330, 333–336, 339–340, 391–395, 417–419, 433–434, 456–458
  Wang Chung on, 123–124
  Wittgenstein on, 91–94
koan Zen paradoxes, puzzling questions (sometimes with responses), meant to break down rational thought and force the mind to recognize its true nature, 189–190, 195
Kripke, Saul, 146
Kwei Zhi (K'uei-chi), 175
Kyoto school, 194, 200

labor, 440–444, 451, 455, 460–465
Laches (Plato), 265, 314–321
Lame Deer, John, 154–155
language, 20, 30, 32–35, 180, 191, 192–194, 272, 276, 325
language-game A practice or form of life that involves using language according to certain rules, 92–94
Lankavatara Sutra, 192–196
Laozi (Lao Tzu), 4, 24, 75–77, 169, 275–277, 336–341, 344, 346, 428, 433, 435–436, 470
Large Sutra on Perfect Wisdom, 342–343
Lavoisier, 12

law, 413, 420–426, 429–432, 436, 452, 454–455
legitimacy, 413, 469–470
Leibniz, Gottfried Wilhelm von, 55–56, 106, 111–114, 119–123, 242, 292–293, 303, 404, 425, 436
Leviathan (Hobbes), 38, 429–432
***li* (principle)** In neo-Confucianism, something (akin to form) prior to and independent of material force, 254–256
***li* (propriety)** The observance of proper rites, ceremonies, and principles, 5–7, 335–336, 338–339, 391–393, 427–428
liar paradox, 8–9
liar sentence A sentence that asserts its own falsehood (for example, 'This sentence is false'), 8–9
liberalism, 449, 458
liberation (*mukti*) In Hinduism, freedom from consciousness and desire, 149, 373, 376
liberty, 390, 431–432, 436–449, 451, 461–462, 467–470
Linji school, 190
Lloyd, Genevieve, 368–369
Locke, John, 12–13, 55–56, 168, 181, 292, 404
  on empiricism, 106–108, 111, 113, 120–121, 124–129, 132, 135–136, 139, 148
  on personal identity, 184–188, 204
  on politics, 432, 436–441, 450, 452, 455, 457, 460, 466–467, 470
  on primary and secondary qualities, 236–240, 243, 246–247, 255, 258, 260
logic, 11–13, 15, 72, 95, 97–98, 119, 121, 129, 181, 254, 257–260, 284
Logic, or, the Art of Thinking (Arnauld), 48, 53
logical atomism The view advocated by Bertrand Russell that the world consists of items that are logically simple (that is, indefinable but capable together of defining everything else), 11–13
lost mind, 392, 396
luck, 325, 347–349, 463
Luther, Martin, 401

Macchiavelli, Niccolò, 394, 427
Madhava, 377
Madhyamika Buddhism A school of Buddhist idealism, founded by Nagarjuna, known for its skepticism, 85–87
Mahabharata, 162, 400
Mahavira, 24, 372
Mahayana Buddhism The Northern branch of Buddhism popular in China, Korea, and Japan, taking the *bodhisattva* as its ideal, 84–85, 169, 189, 341–344, 349
Maimonides, Moses, 24, 271, 372, 386–388
Majjhima-Nikaya, 307
Malcolm, Norman, 285
Man and People (Ortega y Gasset), 26
Man of Reason (Lloyd), 368–369
manifest image The world as revealed to consciousness; the world as it seems to us prereflectively, 200–204
manifold of intuition In Kant, the collection of sensations and reflections—sights, sounds, tastes, smells, feels, and introspections—that someone experiences at a given time, 140–144
Manning, Rita, 344–346
Marcus Aurelius, 396
market, 441–444, 468
Marvin, Walter, 257
Marx, Karl, 229, 325, 381, 406, 426, 459–465, 470
material force (*chi*) In neo-Confucianism, something akin to matter but with the dynamic character of force or energy, 254–256
materialism (or physicalism) The view that there is only one kind of stuff, and it is material or physical, 202–204, 242, 254–256, 376–377
mathematics
  as a priori, 110, 129
  as deductive, 43, 396
  knowledge of, 95, 97–98, 119–123, 181
  mathematical properties, 232, 235–236
  Plato on, 210, 213, 215
  realists on, 257
  and scientific image, 201
Matilal, B. K., 86–87, 89–90
matter of fact, 110, 130, 398
maxim "A subjective principle of action," a rule an act falls under that reflects the agent's intention but abstracts from morally irrelevant details, 359–363
maybeism The Jain thesis that every view should be regarded as right *maybe* (*'syat'*, 'in some respects'); there is at least a grain of truth in every position, 24–26
Mazeroski, Bill, 65–67, 87
mean, 256, 327, 334–335, 345, 347, 395, 414
meaning, 16–17, 28–35, 150, 200–204
meditation, 150–151, 162, 169, 188–189, 234, 307
Meditations (Descartes), 181–184, 234–236, 278–285
Mencius, 38, 47–48, 214–215, 256, 390–396, 427–428
Meno (Plato), 115–118, 215
merit, 416, 427, 469
metalanguage A language expanded to include a truth predicate for another language, 9
metaphysics The study of what there is and how those things relate to each other, 1, 6, 30, 122–123, 135–136, 144–146, 161, 169, 209–260
Metaphysics (Aristotle), 9, 21, 32, 226–230
Metaphysics as a Guide to Morals (Murdoch), 33–35, 399, 470
Middle Way, 169, 354
Milindapanha (Questions to King Milinda), 171–172, 256
Mill, James, 378, 381
Mill, John Stuart, 11, 43, 56
  on ethics, 369–373, 381–386, 406
  on politics, 432, 444–449, 458–459, 461, 470
mind, 99, 134–135, 141–146, 148, 152, 161–207, 255, 394–395
mind/body problem If mind and body exist and are separable, how can they interact? 99, 170, 183–184, 200–204
mirror, 195, 199, 256, 395
misapplication An argument that tries to justify its conclusion about a particular case by appealing to a rule that is generally sound but inapplicable or outweighed by other considerations in that case, 53–54
modality, 285
modeling, 46–47
Modern Theme (Ortega y Gasset), 26–27
modus ponens, 39
modus tollens, 39
Moism An ancient Chinese version of consequentialism developed by Mozi to oppose Confucianism, 374–376
Monadology (Leibniz), 111, 121, 292
monism The view that there is only one fundamental kind of stuff, 202–204, 242
monkeys, 78–79

monotheism The view that there is exactly one God, 273
Montague, William Pepperel, 257–258, 260
Moore, George Edward, 91–92, 259, 372
moral argument The argument that morality compels belief in God; recognizing injustice, we must think God exists and will right these injustices in the afterlife, 300–301
moral (or felicific) calculus Bentham's method of computing the moral value of possible actions, 377–381
Moral Realism and Moral Dilemmas (Foot), 346–347
moral saints, 381
moral sense A faculty that enables us to perceive the moral qualities of things, 390
moral virtues, 327, 417–419
Morality as a System of Hypothetical Imperatives (Foot), 368
More, Thomas, 394
Mozi (Mo Tzu), 333, 374–376, 393
mukti In Hinduism, liberation—freedom from consciousness and desire, 149, 373, 376
Murdoch, Iris, 33–35, 399, 470
mysticism The view that there are ways of gaining access to reality that do not involve sense perception or rational, conscious thought, 149–156, 162, 241, 272, 289, 306, 372

Nagarjuna, 84–87, 90, 93, 192
naive realism, 257
naked philosophers, 80
names, 434–435
Naming and Necessity (Kripke), 146
Native American philosophy, 153–155
Native American religion, 265–267
natural kinds, 239, 291
natural law The law, ordained by God, that prescribes what things should do and be; or, moral principles that would hold in the state of nature, 293, 302–303, 419–426, 431–432, 437–440, 445, 467, 469
natural right, 431–432, 438–440, 445
Natural Theology (Paley), 294–295
natural virtue, 418–419
naturalism, 123–124, 427
nature What makes a thing what it is; that by virtue of which a thing is what it is, 77, 78, 144, 150, 162, 199, 214, 229–231, 235, 238–240, 255, 420, 469
Nature of Thought, The, (Blanshard), 14
naya In Jainism, a perspective; a way of seeing and understanding the world, 24–26
necessary proposition A proposition that cannot be false, 13, 111–112, 114, 122–123, 128, 130, 132–135, 139–143, 146, 179, 251, 285, 287–292
negative conception of liberty Hobbes's conception of liberty as "the absence of external impediments," common to all classical liberals, 431, 446, 454, 469–470
negative (or general) right A right to be left alone; a right that others not interfere; an ability to do or refrain from doing something without impediment from others, 431–432
neo-Confucianism, 254–256, 393–395
neoplatonism, 118
New Essays on Human Understanding (Leibniz), 112–114, 122–123
Newton, Isaac, 12, 106, 111, 123, 254, 436
Nicomachean Ethics (Aristotle), 323–329, 395–396, 414–417
Nietzsche, Friedrich, 25, 29, 50, 201, 367
night aspect The scientific image; the world as portrayed by science, 200–204
nihilism The view that there is no ultimate meaning to life, 200
nihsvabhava In Nagarjuna, "without a reality of its own," 85
Nineveh, 73
nirvana A universal, impersonal, unconceptualizable bliss and awareness that somehow underlies appearance, 84, 169–170, 175, 189, 307, 354
Nishida, Kitaro, 194
Nishitani, Keiji, 200–201, 204
Noble Eightfold Path The Buddha's recommended way of living: right thought, right resolve, right speech, right conduct, right livelihood, right effort, right mindfulness, and right concentration or meditation, 307, 343, 354–357
Noddings, Nel, 344
nominal essence In Locke, the quiddity of a thing or kind of thing, that is, what a definition of it would express, 238–240, 258–259
nominalism The view that universals do not exist at all—that everything is particular, 210–222, 401
nonabsolutism The Jain view that no metaphysical claim should be taken as absolutely true, 24–26
non-dualism (or *advaita*) The view that the self (*atman*) is in reality nothing other than Brahman, 161–162, 166, 241–242, 273–274
noninjury (*ahimsa*) The thesis that one should not injure or kill any sentient being, popularized in modern times by Mahatma Gandhi and propagated in ancient and classical India foremost by Jains, 24, 150, 372–374
nonreductive materialism The view that a translation of ordinary talk of objects and mental states to scientific terms is impossible, even in principle, but that microparticles and their properties nevertheless determine what is true of ordinary objects and mental states, 203–204
normative term A term such as 'ought', 'should', 'good', 'bad', 'may', duty', 'responsible', and 'obligation', that speaks of how things should be or what ought to be done, 313
no-soul (in Sanskrit, *anatman;* in Pali, *anatta*) The Buddhist thesis that there is no self, 172–175, 256, 357
noumenon A thing-in-itself; a thing as it really is, independently of our faculties of knowledge, 137–138, 144–145, 147, 250–253, 258
numinous The holy, 268–269
Nussbaum, Martha, 347–349
Nyaya, 46, 53, 71–74, 85, 87–90, 147, 161, 242, 286
Nyayakusumanjali (Udayana), 286
Nyaya-sutra (Gautama, with commentary by Vatsyayana), 53, 71–74, 82, 87–90, 147

object language A language without the predicate 'true', 9
objectification, 460–463
objective reality The world as it is; in Descartes, the reality of the contents of our ideas—their objects, what our ideas are about, 119, 138, 235, 278–279
objectivism (or absolutism) The thesis that we can speak of sentences, assertions, or beliefs—in a given language and given context—as objectively true or false, period, without reference to a speaker, society, or interpretive community, 20–35
objectivity, 20, 25, 30–31, 76–77, 119, 145, 164, 249, 399, 465
Occam (Ockham), William of, 90, 401

possible world, 146
post hoc, ergo propter hoc "After this, therefore because of this"; an argument drawing a causal conclusion simply from the temporal ordering of events, 54
power, 128, 155
Daoism on, 336–341
of God, 221, 272
as a good, 305, 357, 367
political, 30–31, 417, 426, 430–431, 437, 445, 452, 455, 459–463
and qualities, 237
practical argument An argument with a practical conclusion about what ought to be done; or, in the philosophy of religion, an argument that belief in God is inevitable or at least rational, 298–301
practical reason, 424
practical wisdom (*phronesis*) The ability to find the mean between extremes and thus act virtuously, 313, 326, 328, 347, 396–397
pragmatism, 15–20, 22, 34–36, 90–91, 257
Pragmatism: A New Name for Some Old Ways of Thinking (James), 18
pragmatist theory of truth The theory holding that truth is "the opinion which is fated to be agreed to by all who investigate," 15–20, 93
prakrti Nature; in Samkhya, one of two irreducible elements, 162
pramana A source of knowledge, such as perception, testimony, etc., 72–75, 85–90
prameya An object of knowledge, 88–90
pratyekbuddha An *arhat*, a saint who achieves enlightenment, 341–344
prayer, 266–267, 272
prediction, 65, 87, 300
premise One of the initial assertions of an argument, used to justify the conclusion, 37
prereflective experience "Clear mind": experience without thought or self-awareness. The clear mind is like a mirror, reflecting the world just as it is, 195, 199
prescriptive term A term such as 'ought', 'should', 'good', 'bad', 'may', duty', 'responsible', and 'obligation', that speaks of how things should be or what ought to be done, 313
pre-Socratics Ancient Greek philosophers such as Thales, Heraclitus, and Parmenides, who preceded Socrates, 2, 177
presupposition, 49
prima facie obligation Something I am obliged to do, all other things being equal, if nothing intervenes, 345, 397, 445
primary quality A property inseparable from body; the qualities matter has according to the atomic theory of matter, 233–240, 243–244, 247, 255, 260, 398
primary substance, 227
prime mover The first cause, 287
Princess Elizabeth of Bohemia, 183–184, 200
Principia Mathematica (Russell and Whitehead), 11
principle (*li*) In neo-Confucianism, something (akin to form) prior to and independent of material force, 254–256
principle of individuation What makes one object differ from another; in Aquinas, designated matter, 232
principle of utility The thesis that we ought to maximize good; the sole axiom of morality, according to utilitarians, 56, 369–372, 378–382, 384–386, 388, 391
Principles of Human Knowledge (Berkeley), 245–249
Principles of Morals and Legislation, Introduction to the (Bentham), 370–373, 378–382
Principles of Philosophy (Descartes), 120–121
Prior Analytics (Aristotle), 37, 48, 49
problem of evil The problem posed by the argument from evil: How can God let bad things happen to good people? 301–309
problem of the criterion The skeptical argument based on variability and undecidability: There are many ways of seeing things and no way to decide which way of seeing things is the right way; where could we get a criterion for deciding which is right? 78–81, 83, 85, 89–90
Problems of Philosophy (Russell), 11–13, 15, 67, 259–260
profession, 38, 355, 463
Program and First Platform of Six Realists (Holt, Marvin, Montague, Perry, Pitkin, and Spaulding), 257–259
proletariat In Marx, the workers, 459–463
promise, 54, 362, 365, 386, 407
Proof of an External World (Moore), 92
property (private), 432, 439–440, 450–456, 461, 470
propriety (*li*) The observance of proper rites, ceremonies, and principles, 5–7, 335–336, 338–339, 391–393, 427–428, 431
Proslogion (Anselm), 282–283
Protagoras, 20–23, 26, 28, 34, 36, 146, 232
providence, 302–303
***pu* (uncarved block)** In Laozi, something that is what it is and does not try to be anything else, 339–340, 435–436
purusa The conscious being; in Samkhya, one of two irreducible elements, 162
Purva Mimamsa, 161
Putnam, Hilary, 22
Pyrrho, 75, 80, 84, 93

quality, 223–230, 236–240, 247, 251, 353, 390, 398–399
quality of pleasures, 382–384
Questions to King Milinda, 171–172, 256
quiddity From the Latin *quidditas,* literally, "whatness," which in turn is meant to capture the Greek phrase meaning "what it is," 231–232, 238–240
Quine, Willard van Orman, 223

Rabi'a al-'Adawiyya, 153, 299
Radhakrishnan, Sarvepalli, 150
rationalism The view that we can attain some knowledge independently of experience, 106, 109, 113–114, 119–123, 137, 144–146, 155
rationalist Someone who thinks that some concepts are innate and that we can attain some real knowledge of the world independently of experience; in Ortega, someone who believes that objective truth can be captured in a single perspective, 26–28, 106, 109, 113–114
Rawls, John, 465–470
real essence In Locke, the nature of a thing; that which makes it what it is, stemming from the real internal constitution of the object or kind, 238–240, 255, 258
real internal constitution In Locke, the internal structure of a thing or kind according to the atomic theory of matter, 238–240, 255, 258
realism (or platonism) The view that universals are real and mind-

independent, 210–222; also, the thesis that human thought can discover the nature of objective reality, 119–123, 138, 144, 147, 241; or, the view that something exists independently of mind, 35, 241–243, 253–260
reality, 10–11, 17, 21, 26–30, 138–146, 148, 161, 173, 175, 189, 203, 209–260, 278–285
reason, 186, 249, 348
  Kant on, 135–146
  and natural law, 431–432, 437–438
  Ortega on, 26
  as a part of the soul, 166–168, 175, 210–215, 322
  and religion, 298, 386, 392–398, 405–406
  skeptical attacks on, 234–235, 289
  as source of ethical knowledge, 353–369
  versus custom or habit, 131, 133
  and virtue, 326, 420–421, 423–424, 426, 456–458
reciprocity (*zhong*), 332, 336, 375
recollection, 115–118
Record of Discourses (Wang Yangming), 394
rectificatory (or compensatory) justice The kind of justice that concerns compensation: How do we compensate people for injury? Once a wrong has occurred, how do we set things right again? 415
rectifying names, 434–436
red herring An argument that tries to undermine an opponent's argument by introducing a point irrelevant to the issue at hand, 51
reductionism The view that our ordinary ways of speaking are true because such talk is reducible to scientific language, 203–204
reflection
  introspection, 125–126, 128–129, 140, 152, 155, 168, 177–178, 186, 199, 251, 384
  philosophical, 184, 213, 386, 396
reflective experience Experience that involves thought and self-awareness, 195
reincarnation, 25, 163, 174, 186–187, 229, 267, 306, 373
relations of ideas, 110, 180
relativism The thesis that there are no universally valid truths about the world, 20–35, 42–43
relevance, 50
reliability, 32, 39, 43–48, 50–51, 72–75, 86, 100, 148
religion, 150–156, 215–222, 253, 265–308, 386, 399–408, 419, 431
ren In Confucius, virtue, humanity, or benevolence; it involves both being true to the principles of our nature and acting benevolently toward others, 47–48, 276, 329–336, 338–339, 375, 391
representative sample A sample that mirrors the total population in its relevant characteristics, 45, 54
Republic (Plato), 54, 114–115, 118, 166, 210–215, 266, 314, 321–323, 427n, 449
reservation, 396–397
respect, 166, 334, 364, 375, 460
response-dependent quality A quality that consists in generating a certain kind of response in a perceiver, 238, 240, 260, 398
responsibility, 34–35, 187–188, 304, 413, 415, 417, 463
retributory justice The kind of justice that concerns punishment: What punishments may be imposed, under what conditions, and for what infractions? 415
Rg Veda, 273
Ricardo, David, 378
right and wrong, 28, 201, 256, 313, 328, 330, 353–408, 413, 423, 430–431
righteousness (*yi*) A virtue akin to piety, correctness, and justice in ancient Chinese thought, stressed especially by Mencius and Mozi, 5–7, 47–48, 330, 336, 338–339, 375, 391–393, 402–404, 427–428
rights, 378, 415, 431–432, 438, 448–449, 455–458, 462, 467–470
Rights of Man, The, (Paine), 456
Rinzai (Linji) The most radical of the ninth-century Zen schools, founded by Yixuan, which stresses the "lightning" method of shouting and beating to prepare the mind for enlightenment, 190, 195
Roosevelt, Franklin Delano, 25
root, 5, 276, 433–434
Rorty, Richard, 22, 29, 135
Ross, W. D., 397
Rousseau, Jean-Jacques, 29, 110, 426, 450–459, 461, 466–467, 469–470
Ruhula, Walpola, 173–174
rule 440, 449, 455–456
  concept as, 138, 141–142
  ethical, 326, 358, 384–388, 393, 395–397, 423–424
  law as, 420, 426, 429, 431–432
  political, 413
rule-utilitarianism A moral theory that judges particular actions indirectly by appeal to rules that are themselves justified as maximizing the good, 387–388
Russell, Bertrand, 11–13, 15, 45, 67, 91, 259–260

S5, 285
Samkhya Analysis of nature; the view that reality consists of two irreducible elements: nature (*prakrti*) and the conscious being (*purusa*), 161–162, 400
samkhya-karika, 162
sample, 45, 54
Sankara, 241–242, 260
sanzen Consultation; person-to-person transmission of Zen, 189
satori Enlightenment; the goal of Zen, 189
Schleiermacher, Friedrich, 268
Scholasticism The philosophy of European medieval universities, especially that of Aquinas and his followers, 114, 401, 425
science 135, 215, 299, 378, 396
  atomic theory, 233, 239
  method, 12–13
  pragmatism and, 17–20
  realism and, 254, 257–260
  relativism and, 32–35
  scientific image, 200–204
  scientific law, 122–123, 128–130
  skepticism and, 97
Science and Zen (Nishitani), 200–204
Science, Perception, and Reality (Sellars), 200–202
scientia (knowledge), 100
scientific image The world as portrayed by science, 200–204
secondary principles In Mill, commonsense rules such as "Do not murder," "Do not steal," and so on, that give us moral guidance and follow from the principle of utility, 384–386
secondary quality Effects of primary qualities on our sense organs and nervous systems, 233–240, 243–244, 247, 255, 260, 398
secondary substance, 227
self, 143, 150, 161–207, 306, 331, 462
self-control, 167–168, 314, 320–323, 344, 357, 434

self-evident belief A belief that provides its own justification, 66, 71, 100, 421
self-knowledge, 5–7, 96, 151–152, 161, 195, 334, 401
self-preservation, 422, 431–432, 438
self-regarding act An act that affects only the agent or agents of the act, 445–449, 458
Sellars, Wilfrid, 200–202, 209
semantic theory of truth A theory that gives an account of the meaning of the word 'true' by accounting for inferences we make involving that word, 7–9
Seneca, 396–397
sensation
  empiricists on, 125–126, 128, 134
  idealists on, 152, 172, 174–176, 248
  Kant on, 138–143, 250–253
  and qualities, 234, 236–237
  realists on, 258–260
  as source of knowledge, 86, 109, 222
Seung Sahn, 196–199
Sextus Empiricus, 80, 82–85, 94
Shakespeare, William, 53, 266, 327, 425
Shinto, 265
ship of Theseus, 179
silver rule, 332
simple ideas Ideas that are not compounds of other ideas, 127, 148
Singer, Peter, 373
skeptical rationalism The view that we can know something about the world independently of experience but not beyond the bounds of experience and not about things-in-themselves, 146
skepticism The view that beliefs of certain kinds are unreliable or unjustified, 25, 28, 75–100, 123, 137–138, 145–147, 181, 183, 243, 246, 289, 296–300, 376–377
slavery, 405, 415, 448–449, 451–453, 457, 464
Smith, Adam, 110, 440–444
Smith, Huston, 166
Smith, Norman Kemp, 135
snow, 7–9, 29
Social Contract, The, (Rousseau), 452–456
social contract theory The view that government is legitimate to the extent that people would voluntarily submit to its authority, 429–432, 436–440, 445, 450–456, 465–470
socialism, 449–470
Socrates 169
  on conscience, 390
  on divine command theory, 402–404
  in examples, 185, 187, 224–225, 228–232
  on the forms, 116–118
  on knowledge, 66–70, 116–118
  method, 214–215, 265
  on philosophy, 2–4
  on relativism, 21–24
  on self-knowledge, 161
  on virtue, 314–323
Socratic method (also called *dialectic*) Socrates's process of questioning and showing that proposed definitions cannot be correct, 2, 211
Sosa, Ernest, 100
soul
  absent, 170, 172–177
  and body, 232, 372, 376, 387
  Descartes and Elizabeth on, 183–184
  immortality, 144, 188, 306, 400
  parts of, 163–168, 314–323, 357, 449–451
  Plato on, 166–168, 214, 314–323, 357, 449–451
  St. Teresa on, 151–152
sound argument A valid argument with true premises, 41
Spaulding, E. G., 257–258
Special Laws (Philo), 217–218
Sriharsa, 242
stability, 19–20, 22–24, 28
state of nature In social contract theory, a hypothetical situation without government or other political authority, 429–432, 437–438, 450–453, 459, 466–470
statement A sentence that can be true or false, 37
stoicism, 382, 395–397
strands (*gunas*) In Samkhya, *sattva* (light, clarity, intelligence); *rajas* (passion, dynamism); and *tamas* (darkness, inertia, stupidity), 150, 162, 164, 168, 400
straw man An argument that tries to justify rejecting a position by attacking a different and usually weaker position, 51
Striker, Gisela, 77
structure, 28–30
Structure, Sign, and Play in the Discourse of the Human Sciences (Derrida), 29–30
Suárez, Francisco, 420n, 425–426, 431, 469
subjectivism, 30, 78, 399
subjectivity, 76–78, 168, 279, 399, 406
substance 260
  a priori principles, 120, 122
  Aristotle on, 222–230, 233
  attack on, 171, 174, 180, 198, 246–247, 255
  Avicenna on, 288
  innate idea of, 128, 139–140, 280
  Kant on, 251
  Locke on, 184, 188, 255
substantive equality, 455–470
suffering, 173, 189, 197, 199, 302–308, 355–357, 373–374, 383
sufficient reason, 121, 292–293
Sufism A mystical movement within Islam that stresses the possibility of experiencing Allah directly, 152–153, 289
Summa Theologica (Aquinas), 285–288, 420–424
supererogatory act An act that goes beyond the call of duty, doing more for the happiness of the community than morality requires, 381
superimposition In Sankara, "The apparent presentation, in the form of remembrance, to consciousness of something previously observed, in some other things. . . . [in other words,] the apparent presentation of the attributes of one thing in another thing," 242
superior person (*junzi*) In Confucius, one of noble character, 4–7, 329–336
Survey of Pragmaticism (Peirce), 18
Suzuki, D. T., 192n, 194–196
syat 'Maybe', 'in some respects', 'from some perspective', 24–26
syllogism In Aristotle's original usage, a valid argument; now, usually, an argument consisting of two premises and a conclusion, together containing three general terms, 37, 39
synthesis, 139–141
synthetic statement One not true or false by virtue of the meanings of its words, 72, 107–110, 113–114, 119–123, 125, 129, 137, 143–144, 147, 252, 283–284
System of Logic, A, (Mill), 43

tabula rasa, 113
tanha Selfish desire; craving; coveting; the cause of suffering, 173, 307–308, 354–357
target sentences (or (T)-sentences) Sentences of the form "'Snow is white' is true if and only if snow is white," 7–9, 11
Tarski, Alfred, 7–9, 11
taxes, 435
Teacher, The, (Augustine), 220